Lecture Notes in Computer Science 6015

Commenced Publication in 1973
Founding and Former Series Editors:
Gerhard Goos, Juris Hartmanis, and Jan van Leeuwen

Advanced Research in Computing and Software Science
Subline of Lectures Notes in Computer Science

Javier Esparza   Rupak Majumdar (Eds.)

Tools and Algorithms for the Construction and Analysis of Systems

16th International Conference, TACAS 2010
Held as Part of the Joint European Conferences
on Theory and Practice of Software, ETAPS 2010
Paphos, Cyprus, March 20-28, 2010. Proceedings

 Springer

Volume Editors

Javier Esparza
Technische Universität München
Institut für Informatik
85748 Garching, Germany
E-mail: esparza@in.tum.de

Rupak Majumdar
University of California
Department of Computer Science
Los Angeles, CA 90095, USA
E-mail: rupak@cs.ucla.edu

Library of Congress Control Number: 2010921913

CR Subject Classification (1998): F.3, D.2, C.2, D.3, D.2.4, C.3

LNCS Sublibrary: SL 1 – Theoretical Computer Science and General Issues

ISSN   0302-9743
ISBN-10   3-642-12001-6 Springer Berlin Heidelberg New York
ISBN-13   978-3-642-12001-5 Springer Berlin Heidelberg New York

springer.com

© Springer-Verlag Berlin Heidelberg 2010
Printed in Germany

Typesetting: Camera-ready by author, data conversion by Scientific Publishing Services, Chennai, India
Printed on acid-free paper   06/3180   5 4 3 2 1 0

Foreword

ETAPS 2010 was the 13th instance of the European Joint Conferences on Theory and Practice of Software. ETAPS is an annual federated conference that was established in 1998 by combining a number of existing and new conferences. This year it comprised the usual five sister conferences (CC, ESOP, FASE, FOSSACS, TACAS), 19 satellite workshops (ACCAT, ARSPA-WITS, Bytecode, CMCS, COCV, DCC, DICE, FBTC, FESCA, FOSS-AMA, GaLoP, GT-VMT, LDTA, MBT, PLACES, QAPL, SafeCert, WGT, and WRLA) and seven invited lectures (excluding those that were specific to the satellite events). The five main conferences this year received 497 submissions (including 31 tool demonstration papers), 130 of which were accepted (10 tool demos), giving an overall acceptance rate of 26%, with most of the conferences at around 24%. Congratulations therefore to all the authors who made it to the final programme! I hope that most of the other authors will still have found a way of participating in this exciting event, and that you will all continue submitting to ETAPS and contributing to make of it the best conference on software science and engineering.

The events that comprise ETAPS address various aspects of the system development process, including specification, design, implementation, analysis and improvement. The languages, methodologies and tools which support these activities are all well within its scope. Different blends of theory and practice are represented, with an inclination toward theory with a practical motivation on the one hand and soundly based practice on the other. Many of the issues involved in software design apply to systems in general, including hardware systems, and the emphasis on software is not intended to be exclusive.

ETAPS is a confederation in which each event retains its own identity, with a separate Programme Committee and proceedings. Its format is open-ended, allowing it to grow and evolve as time goes by. Contributed talks and system demonstrations are in synchronised parallel sessions, with invited lectures in plenary sessions. Two of the invited lectures are reserved for 'unifying' talks on topics of interest to the whole range of ETAPS attendees. The aim of cramming all this activity into a single one-week meeting is to create a strong magnet for academic and industrial researchers working on topics within its scope, giving them the opportunity to learn about research in related areas, and thereby to foster new and existing links between work in areas that were formerly addressed in separate meetings.

ETAPS 2010 was organised by the University of Cyprus in cooperation with:

▷ European Association for Theoretical Computer Science (EATCS)
▷ European Association for Programming Languages and Systems (EAPLS)
▷ European Association of Software Science and Technology (EASST)

and with support from the Cyprus Tourism Organisation.

The organising team comprised:

General Chairs: Tiziana Margaria and Anna Philippou
Local Chair: George Papadopoulos
Secretariat: Maria Kittira
Administration: Petros Stratis
Satellite Events: Anna Philippou
Website: Konstantinos Kakousis.

Overall planning for ETAPS conferences is the responsibility of its Steering Committee, whose current membership is:

Vladimiro Sassone (Southampton, Chair), Parosh Abdulla (Uppsala), Luca de Alfaro (Santa Cruz), Gilles Barthe (IMDEA-Software), Giuseppe Castagna (CNRS Paris), Marsha Chechik (Toronto), Sophia Drossopoulou (Imperial College London), Javier Esparza (TU Munich), Dimitra Giannakopoulou (CMU/NASA Ames), Andrew D. Gordon (MSR Cambridge), Rajiv Gupta (UC Riverside), Chris Hankin (Imperial College London), Holger Hermanns (Saarbrücken), Mike Hinchey (Lero, the Irish Software Engineering Research Centre), Martin Hofmann (LM Munich), Joost-Pieter Katoen (Aachen), Paul Klint (Amsterdam), Jens Knoop (Vienna), Shriram Krishnamurthi (Brown), Kim Larsen (Aalborg), Rustan Leino (MSR Redmond), Gerald Luettgen (Bamberg), Rupak Majumdar (Los Angeles), Tiziana Margaria (Potsdam), Ugo Montanari (Pisa), Oege de Moor (Oxford), Luke Ong (Oxford), Fernando Orejas (Barcelona) Catuscia Palamidessi (INRIA Paris), George Papadopoulos (Cyprus), David Rosenblum (UCL), Don Sannella (Edinburgh), João Saraiva (Minho), Michael Schwartzbach (Aarhus), Perdita Stevens (Edinburgh), Gabriele Taentzer (Marburg), and Martin Wirsing (LM Munich).

I would like to express my sincere gratitude to all of these people and organisations, the Programme Committee Chairs and members of the ETAPS conferences, the organisers of the satellite events, the speakers themselves, the many reviewers, all the participants, and Springer for agreeing to publish the ETAPS proceedings in the ARCoSS subline.

Finally, I would like to thank the organising Chair of ETAPS 2010, George Papadopoulos, for arranging for us to have ETAPS in the most beautiful surroundings of Paphos.

January 2010   Vladimiro Sassone

Preface

This volume contains the proceedings of the 16th International Conference on Tools and Algorithms for the Construction and Analysis of Systems (TACAS 2010). TACAS 2010 took place in Paphos, Cyprus, March 22–25, 2010, as part of the 13th European Joint Conferences on Theory and Practice of Software (ETAPS 2010), whose aims, organization, and history are presented in the foreword of this volume by the ETAPS Steering Committee Chair, Vladimiro Sassone.

TACAS is a forum for researchers, developers, and users interested in rigorously based tools and algorithms for the construction and analysis of systems. The conference serves to bridge the gaps between different communities that share common interests in tool development and its algorithmic foundations. The research areas covered by such communities include, but are not limited to, formal methods, software and hardware verification, static analysis, programming languages, software engineering, real-time systems, and communications protocols. The TACAS forum provides a venue for such communities at which common problems, heuristics, algorithms, data structures, and methodologies can be discussed and explored. TACAS aims to support researchers in their quest to improve the usability, utility, flexibility, and efficiency of tools and algorithms for building systems. Tool descriptions and case studies with a conceptual message, as well as theoretical papers with clear relevance for tool construction, are all encouraged. The specific topics covered by the conference include, but are not limited to, the following: specification and verification techniques for finite and infinite-state systems, software and hardware verification, theorem-proving and model-checking, system construction and transformation techniques, static and run-time analysis, abstraction techniques for modeling and validation, compositional and refinement-based methodologies, testing and test-case generation, analytical techniques for safety, security, or dependability, analytical techniques for real-time, hybrid, or stochastic systems, integration of formal methods and static analysis in high-level hardware design or software environments, tool environments and tool architectures, SAT and SMT solvers, and applications and case studies.

TACAS traditionally considers two types of papers: research papers and tool demonstration papers. Research papers are full-length papers that contain novel research on topics within the scope of the TACAS conference and have a clear relevance for tool construction. Tool demonstration papers are shorter papers that give an overview of a particular tool and its applications or evaluation. TACAS 2010 received a total of 134 submissions including 24 tool demonstration papers and accepted 35 papers of which 9 papers were tool demonstration papers. Each submission was evaluated by at least three reviewers. After a six-week reviewing process, the program selection was carried out in a two-week electronic Program

Committee meeting. We believe that the committee deliberations resulted in a strong technical program.

Joseph Sifakis from Verimag, France, gave the unifying ETAPS 2010 invited talk on "Embedded Systems Design — Scientific Challenges and Work Directions." The abstract of his talk is included in this volume. Jean-François Raskin from the Université Libre de Bruxelles, Belgium gave the TACAS 2010 invited talk on "Antichain Algorithms for Finite Automata."

As TACAS 2010 Program Committee Co-chairs we would like to thank the authors of all submitted papers, the Program Committee members, and all the referees for their invaluable contribution in guaranteeing such a strong technical program. We also thank the EasyChair system for hosting the conference submission and program selection process and automating much of the proceedings generation process. We would like to express our appreciation to the ETAPS Steering Committee and especially its Chair, Vladimiro Sassone, as well as the Organizing Committee for their efforts in making ETAPS 2010 such a successful event.

Finally, we remember with sadness the sudden passing of Amir Pnueli in 2009. His intellectual leadership and his patronage will be missed by the entire ETAPS community.

January 2010   Javier Esparza
                                                              Rupak Majumdar

Organization

Steering Committee

Ed Brinksma	ESI and University of Twente, The Netherlands
Rance Cleaveland	University of Maryland, College Park and Fraunhofer USA Inc., USA
Kim G. Larsen	Aalborg University, Denmark
Bernhard Steffen	University of Dortmund, Germany
Lenore Zuck	University of Illinois at Chicago, USA

Program Committee

Parosh Abdulla	Uppsala University, Sweden
Josh Berdine	Microsoft Research Cambridge, UK
Armin Biere	Johannes Kepler University, Linz, Austria
Bruno Blanchet	École Normal Supérieure de Paris, France
Bernard Boigelot	University of Liège, Belgium
Rance Cleaveland	University of Maryland, College Park and Fraunhofer USA Inc., USA
Giorgio Delzanno	University of Genova, Italy
Leonardo de Moura	Microsoft Research Redmond, USA
Javier Esparza	Technische Universität München, Munich, Germany
Susanne Graf	VERIMAG, Grenoble-Gières, France
Vineet Kahlon	NEC Labs, Princeton, USA
Joost-Pieter Katoen	RWTH Aachen, Germany
Stefan Kowalewski	RWTH Aachen, Germany
Daniel Kroening	Oxford University, UK
Orna Kupferman	Hebrew University, Jerusalem, Israel
Kim G. Larsen	Aalborg University, Denmark
Rupak Majumdar	University of California, Los Angeles, USA
Ken McMillan	Cadence Berkeley Labs, USA
Madhavan Mukund	Chennai Mathematical Institute, India
Anca Muscholl	LABRI, Bordeaux, France
Doron Peled	Bar-Ilan University, Israel
C.R. Ramakrishnan	SUNY, Stony Brook, USA
S. Ramesh	GM India Science Laboratory, Bangalore, India
Sanjit Seshia	University of California, Berkeley, USA
Oleg Sokolsky	University of Pennsylvania, USA
Bernhard Steffen	University of Dortmund, Germany
Tayssir Touili	LIAFA, University of Paris 7, France
Lenore Zuck	University of Illinois, Chicago, USA

Referees

David Arney
Mohamed Faouzi Atig

Domagoj Babic
Shoham Ben-David
Jesper Bengtsson
Nikolaj Bjørner
Nicolas Blanc
Henrik Bohnenkamp
Marius Bozga
Bryan Brady
Jörg Brauer
Angelo Brillout
Robert Brummayer
Supratik Chakraborty
Satrajit Chatterjee
Taolue Chen
Yu-Fang Chen
Adam Chlipala

Hana Chockler
Rebecca Collins
Pierre Corbineau
Pepijn Crouzen
Vijay D'silva
Deepak D'Souza
Alexandre David
Manoj Dixit
Markus Doedt
Alastair Donaldson
Cezara Dragoi
Constantin Enea
Lars-Henrik Eriksson
Bernd Finkbeiner
Dana Fisman
Blaise Genest
Hugo Gimbert
Patrice Godefroid
Valentin Goranko
Dominique Gückel
Leopold Haller
Youssef Hamadi
Tingting Han
Arild M. M. Haugstad

Daniel Holcomb
Falk Howar

Radu Iosif
Himanshu Jain
David N. Jansen
Susmit Jha
Barbara Jobstmann
Kenneth Yrke Joergensen
Matti Järvisalo
Alexander Kaiser
Volker Kamin
Carsten Kern
Daniel Klink
Alexander Krauss
Jan Křetínský
Christian Kubczak
Viktor Kuncak
Anna-Lena Lamprecht

Jérôme Leroux
Shuhao Li
Wenchao Li
Rhishikesh Limaye
Kamal Lodaya
Gavin Lowe
Roman Manevich
Nicolas Markey
Matthieu Martel
Sean McLaughlin
Daniel Merschen
Roland Meyer
Marius Mikučionis
Jean-Vivien Millo
Todd Millstein
Alan Mishchenko
Swarup Mohalik
Laurent Mounier
Anders Møller
K. Narayan Kumar
Johannes Neubauer
Viet Yen Nguyen
Dejan Nickovic
Thomas Noll

David Parker
Madhusudan
  Parthasarathy
Mikkel Larsen Pedersen
Michael Perin
Linh Thi Xuan Phan
Andreas Podelski
Mitra Purandare
Shaz Qadeer
R. Ramanujam
Jacob Illum Rasmussen
Pascal Raymond
Ahmed Rezine
Partha Roop
Philipp Rümmer
Michal Rutkowski
Oliver Rüthing
Yaniv Sa'ar
Prahladavaradan
  Sampath
Sriram Sankaranarayanan
Manoranjan Satpathy
Sven Schewe
Bastian Schlich
Sylvain Schmitz
Stefan Schwoon
Cristina Seceleanu
Koushik Sen
Axel Simon
Steve Simon
Mariëlle I. A. Stoelinga
Scott Stoller
S.P. Suresh
Mark Timmer
Sinha Umeno
Frits Vaandrager
Peter van Rossum
Shobha Vasudevan
Berthold Vöcking
Tomáš Vojnar
Thomas Wahl
Igor Walukiewicz
Shaohui Wang
Andrzej Wąsowski

Nannan He   Aditya Nori   Carsten Weise
Jonathan Heinen   Gethin Norman   Georg Weissenbacher
Keijo Heljanko   Ulrik Nyman   Christoph M. Wintersteiger
Marijn Heule   Petur Olsen   Verena Wolf
Alexander Heußner   Ghassan Oreiby

Table of Contents

Tools I

Automata Theory

Liveness

Tools II

Software Verification

Tools III

Real Time and Information Flow

Testing

Embedded Systems Design – Scientific Challenges and Work Directions

Joseph Sifakis

Verimag

The development of a satisfactory Embedded Systems Design Science provides a timely challenge and opportunity for reinvigorating Computer Science.

Embedded systems are components integrating software and hardware jointly and specifically designed to provide given functionalities, which are often critical. They are used in many applications areas including transport, consumer electronics and electrical appliances, energy distribution, manufacturing systems, etc.

Embedded systems design requires techniques taking into account extra-functional requirements regarding optimal use of resources such as time, memory and energy while ensuring autonomy, reactivity and robustness.

Jointly taking into account these requirements raises a grand scientific and technical challenge: extending Computer Science with paradigms and methods from Control Theory and Electrical Engineering. Computer Science is based on discrete computation models not encompassing physical time and resources which are by their nature very different from analytic models used by other engineering disciplines.

We summarize some current trends in embedded systems design and point out some of their characteristics, such as the chasm between analytical and computational models, and the gap between safety critical and best-effort engineering practices. We call for a coherent scientific foundation for embedded systems design, and we discuss a few key demands on such a foundation: the need for encompassing several manifestations of heterogeneity, and the need for design paradigms ensuring constructivity and adaptivity.

We discuss main aspects of this challenge and associated research directions for different areas such as modelling, programming, compilers, operating systems and networks.

J. Esparza and R. Majumdar (Eds.): TACAS 2010, LNCS 6015, p. 1, 2010.
© Springer-Verlag Berlin Heidelberg 2010

Antichain Algorithms for Finite Automata[*]

Laurent Doyen[1] and Jean-François Raskin[2]

[1] LSV, ENS Cachan & CNRS, France
[2] U.L.B., Université Libre de Bruxelles, Belgium

Abstract. We present a general theory that exploits simulation relations on transition systems to obtain antichain algorithms for solving the reachability and repeated reachability problems. Antichains are more succinct than the sets of states manipulated by the traditional fixpoint algorithms. The theory justifies the correctness of the antichain algorithms, and applications such as the universality problem for finite automata illustrate efficiency improvements. Finally, we show that new and provably better antichain algorithms can be obtained for the emptiness problem of alternating automata over finite and infinite words.

1 Introduction

Finite state-transition systems are useful for the design and verification of program models. One of the essential model-checking questions is the *reachability problem* which asks, given an initial state s and a final state s', if there exists a (finite) path from s to s'. For reactive (non-terminating) programs, the *repeated reachability problem* asks, given an initial state s and a final state s', if there exists an infinite path from s that visits s' infinitely often.

The (repeated) reachability problem underlies important verification questions. For example, in the automata-based approach to model-checking [26,27], the correctness of a program A with respect to a specification B (where A and B are finite automata) is defined by the language inclusion $L(A) \subseteq L(B)$, that is all traces of the program (executions) should be traces of the specification. The language inclusion problem is equivalent to the *emptiness problem* "is $L(A) \cap L^c(B)$ empty ?" where $L^c(B)$ is the complement of $L(B)$. If G is a transition system (or an automaton) defined as the product of A with an automaton B^c obtained by complementation of B, then the emptiness problem can be viewed as a reachability question on G for automata on finite words, and as a repeated reachability question for Büchi automata on infinite words. Note that complementation procedures resort to exponential subset constructions [18,21,17,22]. Therefore,

[*] This research was supported by the projects: (*i*) Quasimodo: "Quantitative System Properties in Model-Driven-Design of Embedded Systems", http://www.quasimodo.aau.dk, (*ii*) Gasics: "Games for Analysis and Synthesis of Interactive Computational Systems", http://www.ulb.ac.be/di/gasics/, and (*iii*) Moves: "Fundamental Issues in Modelling, Verification and Evolution of Software", http://moves.ulb.ac.be, a PAI program funded by the Federal Belgian Government.

J. Esparza and R. Majumdar (Eds.): TACAS 2010, LNCS 6015, pp. 2–22, 2010.
© Springer-Verlag Berlin Heidelberg 2010

while the (repeated) reachability problem, which is NLogSpace-complete, can be solved in linear time in the size of G, the language inclusion problem, which is PSpace-complete, requires exponential time (in the size of B). In practice, implementations for finite words give reasonably good results (see e.g. [24]), while the complementation constructions for infinite words are difficult to implement and automata with more than around ten states are intractable [15,25].

Recently, dramatic performance improvements have been obtained by so-called *antichain algorithms* for the reachability and repeated reachability problems on the subset construction and its variants for infinite words [8,5,11]. The idea is always to exploit the special structure of the subset constructions. As an example, consider the classical subset construction for the complementation of automata on finite words. States of the complement automaton are sets of states of the original automaton, that we call *cells* and denote by s_i. Set inclusion between cells is a partial order that turns out to be a simulation relation for the complement automaton: if $s_2 \subseteq s_1$ and there is a transition from s_1 to s_3, then there exists a transition from s_2 to some $s_4 \subseteq s_3$. This structural property carries over to the sets of cells manipulated by reachability algorithms: if $s_2 \subseteq s_1$ and a final cell can be reached from s_1, then a final cell can be reached from s_2. Therefore, in a breadth-first search algorithm with backward state traversal, if s_1 is visited by the algorithm, then s_2 is visited simultaneously; the algorithm manipulates $\subseteq$-downward closed sets of cells that can be canonically and compactly represented by the *antichain* of their $\subseteq$-maximal elements. Antichains serve as a symbolic data-structure on which efficient symbolic operations can be defined. Antichain algorithms have been implemented for automata on finite words [8], on finite trees [5], on infinite words [11,14], and for other applications where exponential constructions are involved such as model-checking of linear-time logic [10], games of imperfect information [7,4], and synthesis of linear-time specifications [12]. They outperform explicit and BDD-based algorithms by orders of magnitude [9,3,12].

In Section 3, we present an abstract theory to justify the correctness of antichain algorithms. For backward state traversal algorithms, we first show that forward simulation relations (such as set inclusion in the above example) are required to maintain closed sets in the algorithms. This corresponds to view antichains as a suitable symbolic data-structure to represent closed sets. Then, we develop a new approach in which antichains are sets of *promising states* in the (repeated) reachability analysis. This view is justified by mean of backward simulation relations. In our example, it turns out that set inclusion is also a backward simulation which implies that if $s_2 \subseteq s_1$ and s_2 is reachable, then s_1 is reachable. Therefore, an algorithm which traverses the state space in a backward fashion need not to explore the predecessors of s_2 if s_1 has been visited previously by the algorithm. We say that s_1 is more promising[1] than s_2. As a consequence, the algorithms can safely drop non-$\subseteq$-maximal cells, hence keeping

---

[1] Note that this is not a heuristic: if s_1 is more promising that s_2, then the exploration of the predecessors of s_2 can be omitted without spoiling the correctness of the analysis.

$\subseteq$-maximal cells only. While the two views coincide when set inclusion is used for finite automata, we argue that the promising state view provides better algorithms in general. This is illustrated on finite automata where algorithms in the symbolic view remain unchanged when coarser (hence improved) simulation relations are used, while in the promising state view, we obtain new antichain algorithms that are provably better: fixed points can be reached in fewer iterations, and the antichains that are manipulated are smaller. Dual results are obtained for forward state traversal algorithms.

In Section 4, we revisit classical problems of automata theory: the universality problem for nondeterministic automata, the emptiness problem for alternating automata on finite and infinite words, and the emptiness of a product of automata. In such applications, the transition systems are of exponential size and thus they are not constructed prior to the reachability analysis, but explored on-the-fly. And consequently, simulation relations needed by the antichain algorithms should be given without any computation on the transition system itself (which is the case of set inclusion for the subset construction). However, we show that by computing a simulation relation on the original automaton, coarser simulation relations can be induced on the exponential constructions. On the way, we introduce a new notion of backward simulation for alternating automata.

2   Preliminaries

Relations. A *pre-order* over a finite set V is a binary relation $\preceq \subseteq V \times V$ which is reflexive and transitive. If $v_1 \preceq v_2$, we say that v_1 is smaller than v_2 (or v_2 is greater than v_1). A pre-order $\preceq'$ is *coarser* than $\preceq$ if for all $v_1, v_2 \in V$, if $v_1 \preceq v_2$, then $v_1 \preceq' v_2$. The $\preceq$-*upward closure* of a set $S \subseteq V$ is the set $\mathsf{Up}(\preceq, S) = \{v_1 \in V \mid \exists v_2 \in S : v_2 \preceq v_1\}$ of elements that are greater than some element in S. A set S is $\preceq$-*upward-closed* if it is equal to its $\preceq$-upward closure, and $\mathsf{Min}(\preceq, S) = \{v_1 \in S \mid \forall v_2 \in S : v_2 \preceq v_1 \rightarrow v_1 \preceq v_2\}$ denotes the minimal elements of S. Note that $\mathsf{Min}(\preceq, S) \subseteq S \subseteq \mathsf{Up}(\preceq, S)$. Analogously, define the $\preceq$-*downward closure* $\mathsf{Down}(\preceq, S) = \{v_1 \in V \mid \exists v_2 \in S : v_1 \preceq v_2\}$ of a set S, say that S is $\preceq$-*downward-closed* if $S = \mathsf{Down}(\preceq, S)$, and let $\mathsf{Max}(\preceq, S) = \{v_1 \in S \mid \forall v_2 \in S : v_1 \preceq v_2 \rightarrow v_2 \preceq v_1\}$ be the set of maximal elements[2] of S.

A set $S \subseteq V$ is a *quasi-antichain* if for all $v_1, v_2 \in S$, either v_1 and v_2 are $\preceq$-incomparable, or $v_1 \preceq v_2$ and $v_2 \preceq v_1$. The sets $\mathsf{Min}(\preceq, S)$ and $\mathsf{Max}(\preceq, S)$ are quasi-antichains. A *partial order* is a pre-order which is antisymmetric. For partial orders, the sets $\mathsf{Min}(\preceq, S)$ and $\mathsf{Max}(\preceq, S)$ are *antichains*, i.e., sets of pairwise $\preceq$-incomparable elements. By abuse of language, we call antichains the sets of minimal (or maximal) elements even if the pre-order is not a partial order, and denote by $\mathcal{A}$ the set of antichains over 2^V.

Antichains can be used as a symbolic data-structure to represent $\preceq$-upward-closed sets. Note that the union and intersection of $\preceq$-upward-closed sets is $\preceq$-upward-closed. The symbolic representation of an $\preceq$-upward-closed set S is the

---

[2] We also denote this set by $\mathsf{Max}(\succeq, S)$, and we equally say that a set is $\preceq$-downward-closed or $\succeq$-downward-closed, etc.

antichain $\widetilde{S} = \mathrm{Min}(\preceq, S)$. Operations on antichains are defined as follows. The membership question "given v and S, is $v \in S$?" becomes "given v and $\widetilde{S}$, is there $\tilde{v} \in \widetilde{S}$ such that $\tilde{v} \preceq v$?"; the emptiness question is unchanged as $S = \varnothing$ if and only if $\widetilde{S} = \varnothing$; the relation of set inclusion $S_1 \subseteq S_2$ becomes $\widetilde{S}_1 \sqsubseteq \widetilde{S}_2$ defined by $\forall v_1 \in \widetilde{S}_1 \cdot \exists v_2 \in \widetilde{S}_2 : v_2 \preceq v_1$. If $\langle V, \preceq \rangle$ is a semi-lattice with least upper bound lub, then $\langle \mathcal{A}, \sqsubseteq \rangle$ is a complete lattice (the *lattice of antichains*) where the intersection $S_1 \cap S_2$ is represented by $\widetilde{S}_1 \sqcap \widetilde{S}_2 = \mathrm{Min}(\preceq, \{\mathsf{lub}(v_1, v_2) \mid v_1 \in \widetilde{S}_1 \wedge v_2 \in \widetilde{S}_2\})$, and the union $S_1 \cup S_2$ by $\widetilde{S}_1 \sqcup \widetilde{S}_2 = \mathrm{Min}(\preceq, \widetilde{S}_1 \cup \widetilde{S}_2)$. Analogous definitions exist for antichains of $\preceq$-downward-closed sets if $\langle V, \preceq \rangle$ is a semi-lattice with greatest lower bound. Other operations mixing $\preceq$-upward-closed sets and $\preceq$-downward-closed sets can be defined over antichains (such as mixed set inclusion, or emptiness of mixed intersection).

Simulation relations. Let $G = (V, E, \mathsf{Init}, \mathsf{Final})$ be a transition system with finite set of states V, transition relation $E \subseteq V \times V$, initial states $\mathsf{Init} \subseteq V$, and final states $\mathsf{Final} \subseteq V$. We define two notions of *simulation* [19]:

- a pre-order $\preceq_f$ over V is a *forward simulation* for G ("$v_2 \preceq_f v_1$" reads v_2 forward simulates v_1) if for all $v_1, v_2, v_3 \in V$, if $v_2 \preceq_f v_1$ and $E(v_1, v_3)$, then there exists $v_4 \in V$ such that $v_4 \preceq_f v_3$ and $E(v_2, v_4)$;
- a pre-order $\succeq_b$ over V is a *backward simulation* for G, ("$v_2 \succeq_b v_1$" reads v_2 backward simulates v_1), if for all $v_1, v_2, v_3 \in V$, if $v_2 \succeq_b v_1$ and $E(v_3, v_1)$, then there exists $v_4 \in V$ such that $v_4 \succeq_b v_3$ and $E(v_4, v_2)$.

The notations $\preceq_f$ and $\succeq_b$ are inspired by the fact that in the subset construction for finite automata, $\subseteq$ is a forward simulation and $\supseteq$ is a backward simulation (see also Section 4.1). Note that a forward simulation for G is a backward simulation for the transition system with transition relation $E^{-1} = \{(v_1, v_2) \mid (v_2, v_1) \in E\}$.

We say that a simulation over V is *compatible* with a set $S \subseteq V$ if for all $v_1, v_2 \in V$, if $v_1 \in S$ and v_2 (forward or backward) simulates v_1, then $v_2 \in S$. Note that a forward simulation $\preceq_f$ is compatible with S if and only if S is $\preceq_f$-downward-closed, and a backward simulation $\succeq_b$ is compatible with S if and only if S is $\succeq_b$-upward-closed. In the sequel, we will be interested in simulation relations that are compatible with Init, or Final, or with both.

Fixpoint algorithms. Let $G = (V, E, \mathsf{Init}, \mathsf{Final})$ be a transition system and let $S, S' \subseteq V$ be sets of states. The sets of *predecessors* and *successors* of S in one step are denoted $\mathsf{pre}(S) = \{v_1 \mid \exists v_2 \in S : E(v_1, v_2)\}$ and $\mathsf{post}(S) = \{v_1 \mid \exists v_2 \in S : E(v_2, v_1)\}$ respectively. We denote by $\mathsf{pre}^*(S)$ the set $\bigcup_{i \geq 0} \mathsf{pre}^i(S)$ where $\mathsf{pre}^0(S) = S$ and $\mathsf{pre}^i(S) = \mathsf{pre}(\mathsf{pre}^{i-1}(S))$ for all $i \geq 1$, and by $\mathsf{pre}^+(S)$ the set $\bigcup_{i \geq 1} \mathsf{pre}^i(S)$. The operators post^* and post^+ are defined analogously. A finite *path* in G is a sequence $v_0 v_1 \ldots v_n$ of states such that $E(v_i, v_{i+1})$ for all $0 \leq i < n$. Infinite paths are defined analogously. We say that S' is *reachable* from S if there exists a finite path $v_0 v_1 \ldots v_n$ with $v_0 \in S$ and $v_n \in S'$.

The *reachability problem* for G asks if Final is reachable from Init, and the *repeated reachability problem* for G asks if there exists an infinite path starting from Init and passing through Final infinitely many times. To solve these problems, we can use the following classical fixpoint algorithms:

1. The *backward reachability algorithm* computes the sequence of sets:

   $B(0) = $ Final and $B(i) = B(i-1) \cup \mathsf{pre}(B(i-1))$ for all $i \geq 1$.

2. The *backward repeated reachability algorithm* computes the sequence of sets:

   $BB(0) = $ Final and $BB(i) = \mathsf{pre}^+(BB(i-1)) \cap$ Final for all $i \geq 1$.

3. The *forward reachability algorithm* computes the sequence of sets:

   $F(0) = $ Init and $F(i) = F(i-1) \cup \mathsf{post}(F(i-1))$ for all $i \geq 1$.

4. The *forward repeated reachability algorithm* computes the sequence of sets:

   $FF(0) = $ Final $\cap \mathsf{post}^*($Init$)$ and $FF(i) = \mathsf{post}^+(FF(i-1)) \cap$ Final for all $i \geq 1$.

The above sequences converge to a fixpoint because the operations involved are monotone. We denote by B^*, BB^*, F^*, and FF^* the respective fixpoints. Note that $B^* = \mathsf{pre}^*($Final$)$ and $F^* = \mathsf{post}^*($Init$)$. Call *recurrent* the states that have a cycle through them. The set BB^* contains the final states that can reach a recurrent final state, and FF^* contains the final states that are reachable from a reachable recurrent final state.

Theorem 1. *Let $G = (V, E, $ Init$, $ Final$)$ be a transition system. Then,*

(a) the answer to the reachability problem for G is YES if and only if $B^* \cap$ Init is nonempty if and only if $F^* \cap$ Final is nonempty;

(b) the answer to the repeated reachability problem for G is YES if and only if BB^* is reachable from Init if and only if FF^* is nonempty.

3   Antichain Fixpoint Algorithms

In this section, we show that the sets in the sequences B, BB, F, and FF can be replaced by antichains for well chosen pre-orders. Two views can be developed: when backward algorithms are combined with forward simulation pre-orders (or forward algorithms with backward simulations), antichains are *symbolic representations* of closed sets; when backward algorithms are combined with backward simulation pre-orders (or forward algorithms with forward simulations), antichains are sets of *promising states*. It may be surprising to consider algorithms for the reachability problem (which can be solved in linear time), based on simulation relations (which can be computed in quadratic time). However, such algorithms are useful for applications where the transition systems have a special structure for which simulation relations *need not to be computed*. For example, the relation of set inclusion is always a forward simulation in the subset construction for finite automata (see Section 4 for details and other applications). We develop these two views below.

3.1   Antichains as a Symbolic Representation

Backward reachability. First, we show that the sets computed by the backward algorithm B are $\preceq_f$-downward-closed for *all* forward simulations $\preceq_f$ of the transition system G compatible with Final.

Lemma 2. *Let* $G = (V, E, \mathsf{Init}, \mathsf{Final})$ *be a transition system. A pre-order* $\preceq_f$ *over V is a forward simulation in G if and only if* $\mathsf{pre}(S)$ *is* $\preceq_f$*-downward-closed for all* $\preceq_f$*-downward-closed sets* $S \subseteq V$.

Proof. First, assume that $\preceq_f$ is a forward simulation in G, and let $S \subseteq V$ be a $\preceq_f$-downward-closed set. We show that $\mathsf{pre}(S)$ is $\preceq_f$-downward-closed, i.e. that if $v_1 \in \mathsf{pre}(S)$ and $v_2 \preceq_f v_1$, then $v_2 \in \mathsf{pre}(S)$. As $v_1 \in \mathsf{pre}(S)$, there exists $v_3 \in S$ such that $E(v_1, v_3)$. By definition of forward simulation, there exists v_4 such that $E(v_2, v_4)$ and $v_4 \preceq_f v_3$. Since S is $\preceq_f$-downward-closed and $v_3 \in S$, we conclude that $v_4 \in S$, and thus $v_2 \in \mathsf{pre}(S)$.

    Second, assume that $\mathsf{pre}(S)$ is $\preceq_f$-downward-closed when S is $\preceq_f$-downward-closed. We show that $\preceq_f$ is a forward simulation in G. Let $v_1, v_2, v_3 \in V$ such that $v_2 \preceq_f v_1$ and $E(v_1, v_3)$. Let $S = \mathsf{Down}(\preceq_f, \{v_3\})$ so that $\mathsf{pre}(S)$ is $\preceq_f$-downward-closed. Since $v_1 \in \mathsf{pre}(S)$ and $v_2 \preceq_f v_1$, we have $v_2 \in \mathsf{pre}(S)$ and thus there exists $v_4 \in S$ (i.e., $v_4 \preceq_f v_3$) such that $E(v_2, v_4)$. This shows that $\preceq_f$ is a forward simulation in G.   □

Assume that we have a forward simulation $\preceq_f$ in G compatible with Final, and call this hypothesis **H1**.

Lemma 3. *Under* **H1***, the sets* $\mathsf{B}(i)$ *and* $\mathsf{BB}(i)$ *are* $\preceq_f$*-downward-closed for all* $i \geq 0$.

Proof. By induction, using Lemma 2 and the fact that $\mathsf{B}(0) = \mathsf{BB}(0) = \mathsf{Final}$ is $\preceq_f$-downward-closed since $\preceq_f$ is compatible with Final.   □

Since the sets in the backward algorithms B and BB are $\preceq_f$-downward-closed, we can use the antichain of their maximal elements as a symbolic representation, and adapt the fixpoint algorithms accordingly. Given a forward simulation $\preceq_f$ in G compatible with Final, the antichain algorithm for backward reachability is as follows:

- $\widetilde{\mathsf{B}}(0) = \mathsf{Max}(\preceq_f, \mathsf{Final})$;
- $\widetilde{\mathsf{B}}(i) = \mathsf{Max}(\preceq_f, \widetilde{\mathsf{B}}(i-1) \cup \mathsf{pre}(\mathsf{Down}(\preceq_f, \widetilde{\mathsf{B}}(i-1))))$, for all $i \geq 1$.

Lemma 4. *Under* **H1***,* $\widetilde{\mathsf{B}}(i) = \mathsf{Max}(\preceq_f, \mathsf{B}(i))$ *and* $\mathsf{B}(i) = \mathsf{Down}(\preceq_f, \widetilde{\mathsf{B}}(i))$ *for all* $i \geq 0$.

Corollary 5. *Under* **H1***, for all* $i \geq 0$, $\mathsf{B}(i+1) = \mathsf{B}(i)$ *if and only if* $\widetilde{\mathsf{B}}(i+1) = \widetilde{\mathsf{B}}(i)$.

Theorem 6. *Under* **H1***,* $\mathsf{B}^* \cap \mathsf{Init} \neq \varnothing$ *if and only if* $\mathsf{Down}(\preceq_f, \widetilde{\mathsf{B}}^*) \cap \mathsf{Init} \neq \varnothing$.

So the antichain algorithm for backward reachability computes exactly the same information as the classical algorithm and the two algorithms reach their fixpoint after exactly the same number of iterations. However, the antichain algorithm can be more efficient in practice if the symbolic representation by antichains is significantly more succinct and if the computations on the antichains can be done efficiently. In particular, the predecessors of $\mathsf{Down}(\preceq_f, \widetilde{\mathsf{B}}(i-1))$ needed to obtain $\widetilde{\mathsf{B}}(i)$ should be computed in a way that avoids constructing $\mathsf{Down}(\preceq_f, \widetilde{\mathsf{B}}(i-1))$. For applications of the antichain algorithm in automata theory (see also Section 4), it can be shown that this operation can be computed efficiently (see e.g. [8,11]).

Remark 1. Antichains as a data-structure have been used previously for representing the sets of backward reachable states in *well-structured transition systems* [1,13]. So, the sequence $\widetilde{\mathsf{B}}$ converges also when the underlying state space is infinite and $\preceq_f$ is a well-quasi order.

Backward repeated reachability. Let $\preceq_f$ be a forward simulation for G compatible with Final (**H1**). The antichain algorithm for repeated backward reachability is defined as follows:

- $\widetilde{\mathsf{BB}}(0) = \mathsf{Max}(\preceq_f, \mathsf{Final})$;
- $\widetilde{\mathsf{BB}}(i) = \mathsf{Max}(\preceq_f, \mathsf{pre}^+(\mathsf{Down}(\preceq_f, \widetilde{\mathsf{BB}}(i-1)))) \cap \mathsf{Final}$, for all $i \geq 1$.

Note that a symbolic representation of $\mathsf{pre}^+(\mathsf{Down}(\preceq_f, \widetilde{\mathsf{BB}}(i-1)))$ is computed by the antichain algorithm $\widetilde{\mathsf{B}}$ with $\widetilde{\mathsf{B}}(0) = \mathsf{Max}(\preceq_f, \mathsf{pre}(\mathsf{Down}(\preceq_f, \widetilde{\mathsf{BB}}(i-1))))$. Using Lemma 3, we get the following result and corollary.

Lemma 7. *Under* **H1**, $\widetilde{\mathsf{BB}}(i) = \mathsf{Max}(\preceq_f, \mathsf{BB}(i))$ *and* $\mathsf{BB}(i) = \mathsf{Down}(\preceq_f, \widetilde{\mathsf{BB}}(i))$ *for all* $i \geq 0$.

Corollary 8. *Under* **H1**, *for all* $i \geq 0$, $\mathsf{BB}(i+1) = \mathsf{BB}(i)$ *if and only if* $\widetilde{\mathsf{BB}}(i+1) = \widetilde{\mathsf{BB}}(i)$.

Theorem 9. *Under* **H1**, BB^* *is reachable from* Init *if and only if* $\mathsf{Down}(\preceq_f, \widetilde{\mathsf{BB}}^*)$ *is reachable from* Init.

Forward algorithms. We state the dual of Lemma 2 and Lemma 3 for the forward algorithms F and FF, and obtain antichain algorithms $\widetilde{\mathsf{F}}$ and $\widetilde{\mathsf{FF}}$ using backward simulations. The proofs and details are omitted as they are analogous to the backward algorithms.

Lemma 10. *Let* $G = (V, E, \mathsf{Init}, \mathsf{Final})$ *be a transition system. A pre-order* $\succeq_b$ *over* V *is a backward simulation in* G *if and only if* $\mathsf{post}(S)$ *is* $\succeq_b$-*upward-closed for all* $\succeq_b$-*upward-closed sets* $S \subseteq V$.

Lemma 11. *Let* $G = (V, E, \mathsf{Init}, \mathsf{Final})$ *be a transition system and let* $\succeq_b$ *be a backward simulation in* G. *If* $\succeq_b$ *is compatible with* Init, *then* $\mathsf{F}(i)$ *is* $\succeq_b$-*upward-closed for all* $i \geq 0$. *If* $\succeq_b$ *is compatible with* Init *and* Final, *then* $\mathsf{FF}(i)$ *is* $\succeq_b$-*upward-closed for all* $i \geq 0$.

3.2   Antichains of Promising States

Traditionally, the antichain approaches have been presented as symbolic algorithms using forward simulations to justify backward algorithms, and vice versa (see above and e.g., [8,10,11]). In this section, we develop an original theory called *antichains of promising states* that uses backward simulations to justify backward algorithms, and forward simulations to justify forward algorithms. We obtain new antichain algorithms that do not compute the same information as the classical algorithms. In particular, we show that convergence is reached at least as soon as in the original algorithms, but it may be reached sooner. On this basis, we define in Section 4 new antichain algorithms that are provably better than the antichain algorithms of [8,11].

Backward reachability. Let $\succeq_b$ be a backward simulation relation compatible with Init (**H2**). The *sequence of antichains of backward promising states* is defined as follows:

- $\widehat{B}(0) = \mathsf{Max}(\succeq_b, \mathsf{Final})$;
- $\widehat{B}(i) = \mathsf{Max}(\succeq_b, \widehat{B}(i-1) \cup \mathsf{pre}(\widehat{B}(i-1)))$, for all $i \geq 1$.

Note that while in the sequence $\widetilde{B}$ we took the $\preceq_f$-downward-closure of $\widetilde{B}(i-1)$ before computing pre, this is not necessary here. And note that the original sets $B(i)$ are $\preceq_f$-downward-closed (and represented symbolically by $\widetilde{B}(i)$), while they are not necessarily $\succeq_b$-downward-closed (here, $\widehat{B}(i) \subseteq B(i)$ is a set of most promising states in $B(i)$). The correctness of this algorithm is justified by monotonicity properties. Define the pre-order $\sqsubseteq_b \subseteq 2^V \times 2^V$ as follows: $S_1 \sqsubseteq_b S_2$ if $\forall v_1 \in S_1 \cdot \exists v_2 \in S_2 : v_2 \succeq_b v_1$. We write $S_1 \approx_b S_2$ if $S_1 \sqsubseteq_b S_2$ and $S_2 \sqsubseteq_b S_1$.

Lemma 12. *Under* **H2**, *the operators* pre, $\mathsf{Max}(\succeq_b, \cdot)$, *and* $\cup$ *(and their compositions) are* $\sqsubseteq_b$-*monotone.*

Proof. First, assume that $S_1 \sqsubseteq_b S_2$ and show that $\mathsf{pre}(S_1) \sqsubseteq_b \mathsf{pre}(S_2)$. For all $v_3 \in \mathsf{pre}(S_1)$, there exists $v_1 \in S_1$ such that $E(v_3, v_1)$ (by definition of pre). Since $S_1 \sqsubseteq_b S_2$ and $v_1 \in S_1$, there exists $v_2 \in S_2$ with $v_2 \succeq_b v_1$. By definition of $\succeq_b$, there exists $v_4 \succeq_b v_3$ with $E(v_4, v_2)$ hence $v_4 \in \mathsf{pre}(S_2)$.

Second, assume that $S_1 \sqsubseteq_b S_2$ and show that $\mathsf{Max}(\succeq_b, S_1) \sqsubseteq_b \mathsf{Max}(\succeq_b, S_2)$. For all $v_1 \in \mathsf{Max}(\succeq_b, S_1)$, we have $v_1 \in S_1$ and thus there exists $v_2 \in S_2$ such that $v_2 \succeq_b v_1$. Hence there exists $v_2' \in \mathsf{Max}(\succeq_b, S_2)$ such that $v_2' \succeq_b v_2 \succeq_b v_1$.

Third, assume that $S_1 \sqsubseteq_b S_2$ and $S_3 \sqsubseteq_b S_4$, and show that $S_1 \cup S_3 \sqsubseteq_b S_2 \cup S_4$. For all $v_{13} \in S_1 \cup S_3$, either $v_{13} \in S_1$ and then there exists $v_{24} \in S_2$ such that $v_{24} \succeq_b v_{13}$, or $v_{13} \in S_3$ and then there exists $v_{24} \in S_4$ such that $v_{24} \succeq_b v_{13}$. In all cases, $v_{24} \in S_2 \cup S_4$.   □

Lemma 13. *Under* **H2**, $\widehat{B}(i) \approx_b B(i)$ *for all* $i \geq 0$.

Proof. By induction, using the fact that $B(0) = \mathsf{Final} \approx_b \mathsf{Max}(\succeq_b, \mathsf{Final}) = \widehat{B}(0)$ (which holds trivially since $S \approx_b \mathsf{Max}(\succeq_b, S)$ for all sets S) and Lemma 12.   □

	B(0) = {1}	$\widehat{B}(0) = \{1\} = \widehat{B}^\natural$
	B(1) = {1, 2}	$\widehat{B}(1) = \{1, 2\}$
	B(2) = {1, 2, 3}	$\widehat{B}(2) = \{1, 2\}$
	...	...

Fig. 1. Backward reachability with Final = {1}

Corollary 14 (Early convergence). *Under* **H2**, *for all* $i \geq 0$, *(a) if* $B(i+1) = B(i)$, *then* $\widehat{B}(i+1) \approx_b \widehat{B}(i)$, *and (b)* $B(i) \cap \mathsf{Init} \neq \varnothing$ *if and only if* $\widehat{B}(i) \cap \mathsf{Init} \neq \varnothing$.

Denote by $\widehat{B}^\natural$ the value $\widehat{B}(i)$ for the smallest $i \geq 0$ such that $\widehat{B}(i) \approx_b \widehat{B}(i+1)$. Corollary 14 ensures that convergence (modulo $\approx_b$) on the sequence $\widehat{B}$ occurs at the latest when B converges. Also, as $\succeq_b$ is compatible with Init, if $B(i)$ intersects Init then we know that $\widehat{B}(i)$ also intersects Init. So, for both positive and negative instances of the reachability problem, we never need to compute more iterations in the sequence $\widehat{B}$ than in the sequence B. We establish the correctness of the sequence $\widehat{B}$ to decide the reachability problem.

Theorem 15 (Correctness). *Under* **H2**, $B^* \cap \mathsf{Init} \neq \varnothing$ *if and only if* $\widehat{B}^\natural \cap \mathsf{Init} \neq \varnothing$.

Proof. Assume that $v \in B^* = B(i)$ and $v \in \mathsf{Init}$. Since $\widehat{B}(i) \approx_b B(i)$ by Lemma 13, there exists $v' \in \widehat{B}(i) \cap \mathsf{Init}$ by Corollary 14(b). By Corollary 14(a), we have $\widehat{B}^\natural \approx_b \widehat{B}(j)$ for some $j \leq i$, and by Lemma 12 all sets $\widehat{B}(k)$ for $k \geq j$ are $\approx_b$-equivalent. In particular (for $k = i$), $B(i) \approx_b \widehat{B}(i) \approx_b \widehat{B}^\natural$, and thus there exists $v'' \in \widehat{B}^\natural$ such that $v'' \succeq_b v'$, yielding $v'' \in \mathsf{Init}$ since $\succeq_b$ is compatible with Init. Hence $\widehat{B}^\natural \cap \mathsf{Init} \neq \varnothing$. For the other direction, we use the fact that $\widehat{B}(i) \subseteq B(i)$ for all $i \geq 0$.   □

Example 1. Consider the transition system in Fig. 1 where Final = {1} and Init = {0}. The classical backward reachability algorithm computes the sequence $B(0) = \{1\}, B(1) = \{1, 2\}, \ldots, B(i) = \{1, 2, \ldots, i+1\}$ and converges to $\{1, \ldots, n\}$ after $O(n)$ iterations. Consider the backward simulation $\succeq_b$ as depicted on Fig. 1. States 1 and 2 are mutually simulated by each other, and $i \succeq_b i + 1$ for all $1 \leq i < n$. The antichain algorithm for backward reachability based on $\succeq_b$ computes the sequence $\widehat{B}(0) = \{1\}, \widehat{B}(1) = \{1, 2\}$ and the algorithm halts since $\widehat{B}(0) \approx_b \widehat{B}(1)$, i.e. $\widehat{B}^\natural = \widehat{B}(0)$. We get early convergence because state 1 is more promising than all other states, yet is not reachable from Init.

Backward repeated reachability. Let $\succeq_b$ be a backward simulation relation compatible with both Final and Init (**H3**). Using such a relation, we define the *sequence of antichains of backward repeated promising states* as follows:

- $\widehat{BB}(0) = \mathsf{Max}(\succeq_b, \mathsf{Final})$;
- $\widehat{BB}(i) = \mathsf{Max}(\succeq_b, \mathsf{pre}^+(\widehat{BB}(i-1)) \cap \mathsf{Final})$, for all $i \geq 1$.

Note that the computation of $S_i = \mathsf{pre}^+(\widehat{\mathsf{BB}}(i-1))$ can be replaced by algorithm $\widehat{\mathsf{B}}$ with $\widehat{\mathsf{B}}(0) = \mathsf{Max}(\succeq_\mathsf{b}, \mathsf{pre}(\widehat{\mathsf{BB}}(i-1)))$. This yields $\widehat{\mathsf{B}}^\natural \approx_\mathsf{b} S_i$ which is sufficient to ensure correctness of the algorithm. We have required that $\succeq_\mathsf{b}$ is compatible with Final to have the following property.

Lemma 16. *Under* **H3**, *the operator* $\lambda S \cdot S \cap \mathsf{Final}$ *is* $\sqsubseteq_\mathsf{b}$*-monotone.*

Proof. Assume that $S_1 \sqsubseteq_\mathsf{b} S_2$ and show that $S_1 \cap \mathsf{Final} \sqsubseteq_\mathsf{b} S_2 \cap \mathsf{Final}$. For all $v_1 \in S_1$, there exists $v_2 \in S_2$ such that $v_2 \succeq_\mathsf{b} v_1$. In particular, for $v_1 \in S_1 \cap \mathsf{Final}$ there exists $v_2 \in S_2$ such that $v_2 \succeq_\mathsf{b} v_1$, and $v_2 \in \mathsf{Final}$ since $\succeq_\mathsf{b}$ is compatible with Final, hence $v_2 \in S_2 \cap \mathsf{Final}$.   □

Lemma 17. *Under* **H3**, *for all* $i \geq 0$, $\widehat{\mathsf{BB}}(i) \approx_\mathsf{b} \mathsf{BB}(i)$.

Proof. By induction, using Lemma 16, Lemma 12 (since **H3** implies **H2**), and the fact that $\mathsf{BB}(0) = \mathsf{Final} \approx_\mathsf{b} \mathsf{Max}(\succeq_\mathsf{b}, \mathsf{Final}) = \widehat{\mathsf{BB}}(0)$.   □

Corollary 18 (Early convergence). *Under* **H3**, *for all* $i \geq 0$, *if* $\mathsf{BB}(i+1) = \mathsf{BB}(i)$ *then* $\widehat{\mathsf{BB}}(i+1) \approx_\mathsf{b} \widehat{\mathsf{BB}}(i)$.

Denote by $\widehat{\mathsf{BB}}^\natural$ the value $\widehat{\mathsf{BB}}(i)$ for the smallest $i \geq 0$ such that $\widehat{\mathsf{BB}}(i) \approx_\mathsf{b} \widehat{\mathsf{BB}}(i+1)$.

Theorem 19 (Correctness). *Under* **H3**, BB^* *is reachable from* Init *if and only if* $\widehat{\mathsf{BB}}^\natural$ *is reachable from* Init.

Proof. We know that $\mathsf{BB}^* \approx_\mathsf{b} \widehat{\mathsf{BB}}^\natural$. This is a consequence of Lemma 17 and the fact that pre^+, $\lambda S \cdot S \cap \mathsf{Final}$, and $\mathsf{Max}(\succeq_\mathsf{b}, \cdot)$ are $\sqsubseteq_\mathsf{b}$-monotone operators (by Lemma 12 and Lemma 16). Assume that BB^* is reachable from Init and let $v_0 v_1 \ldots v_n$ be a path in G such that $v_0 \in \mathsf{Init}$, $v_n \in \mathsf{BB}^*$. We show by induction that there exists a path $v'_0 v'_1 \ldots v'_n$ in G such that $v'_i \succeq_\mathsf{b} v_i$ for all i, $0 \leq i \leq n$.
Base case: $i = n$. By lemma 17, as $v_n \in \mathsf{BB}^*$, there exists $v'_n \in \widehat{\mathsf{BB}}^\natural$ such that $v'_n \succeq_\mathsf{b} v_n$. Inductive case $0 \leq i < n$. By induction hypothesis, we know that there exists a path $v'_{i+1} \ldots v'_n$ in G such that $v'_j \succeq_\mathsf{b} v_j$ for all j such that $i+1 \leq j \leq n$. As $v'_{i+1} \succeq_\mathsf{b} v_{i+1}$, by properties of $\succeq_\mathsf{b}$, we know that there exists v' such that $v' \succeq_\mathsf{b} v_i$ and $E(v', v'_{i+1})$, so we take $v'_i = v'$. As $\succeq_\mathsf{b}$ is compatible with Init, we conclude that as $v_0 \in \mathsf{Init}$, we have $v'_0 \in \mathsf{Init}$ as well, and we are done. For the other direction, we use the fact that $\widehat{\mathsf{BB}}(i) \subseteq \mathsf{BB}(i)$ for all $i \geq 0$.   □

Forward reachability algorithm. Let $\preceq_\mathsf{f}$ be a forward simulation relation compatible with Final (**H4**). Using such a relation, we define the sequence of *antichains of forward reachable promising states* as follows:

- $\widehat{\mathsf{F}}(0) = \mathsf{Min}(\preceq_\mathsf{f}, \mathsf{Init})$;
- $\widehat{\mathsf{F}}(i) = \mathsf{Min}(\preceq_\mathsf{f}, \widehat{\mathsf{F}}(i-1) \cup \mathsf{post}(\widehat{\mathsf{F}}(i-1)))$, for all $i \geq 1$.

The following results are proved in an analogous way as the ones for the backward algorithms in the previous paragraphs. Let $S_1, S_2 \subseteq V$, we define the pre-order $\sqsubseteq_f \subseteq 2^V \times 2^V$ as follows: $S_1 \sqsubseteq_f S_2$ if $\forall v_1 \in S_1 \cdot \exists v_2 \in S_2 : v_2 \preceq_f v_1$. We write $S_1 \approx_f S_2$ if $S_1 \sqsubseteq_f S_2$ and $S_2 \sqsubseteq_f S_1$.

Lemma 20. *Under* **H4**, *the operators* post, $\mathsf{Min}(\preceq_f, \cdot)$, $\lambda S \cdot S \cap \mathsf{Final}$, *and* $\cup$ *(and their compositions) are* $\sqsubseteq_f$-*monotone.*

Lemma 21. *Under* **H4**, $\widehat{\mathsf{F}}(i) \approx_f \mathsf{F}(i)$ *for all* $i \geq 0$.

Corollary 22 (Early convergence). *Under* **H4**, *for all* $i \geq 0$, *(a) if* $\mathsf{F}(i+1) = \mathsf{F}(i)$, *then* $\widehat{\mathsf{F}}(i+1) \approx_f \widehat{\mathsf{F}}(i)$, *and (b)* $\mathsf{F}(i) \cap \mathsf{Final} \neq \varnothing$ *if and only if* $\widehat{\mathsf{F}}(i) \cap \mathsf{Final} \neq \varnothing$.

Denote by $\widehat{\mathsf{F}}^\natural$ the set $\widehat{\mathsf{F}}(i)$ for the smallest $i \geq 0$ such that $\widehat{\mathsf{F}}(i) \approx_b \widehat{\mathsf{F}}(i+1)$.

Theorem 23 (Correctness). *Under* **H4**, $\mathsf{F}^* \cap \mathsf{Final} \neq \varnothing$ *if and only if* $\widehat{\mathsf{F}}^\natural \cap \mathsf{Final} \neq \varnothing$.

Forward repeated reachability algorithm. Let $\preceq_f$ be a forward simulation relation which is compatible with Final. The *forward repeated reachability sequence of promising states* is defined as follows:

- $\widehat{\mathsf{FF}}(0) = \mathsf{Final} \cap \widehat{\mathsf{F}}^\natural$;
- $\widehat{\mathsf{FF}}(i) = \mathsf{Min}(\preceq_f, \mathsf{post}^+(\widehat{\mathsf{FF}}(i-1)) \cap \mathsf{Final}$, for all $i \geq 1$.

Lemma 24. *Under* **H4**, $\widehat{\mathsf{FF}}(i) \approx_f \mathsf{FF}(i)$ *for all* $i \geq 0$,

Proof. By induction, using the fact that $\mathsf{FF}(0) = \mathsf{Final} \cap \mathsf{F}^* \approx_f \mathsf{Final} \cap \mathsf{F}^\natural = \widehat{\mathsf{FF}}(0)$ because $\mathsf{F}^* \approx_f \mathsf{F}^\natural$ (using Lemma 21 and monotonicity of $\lambda S \cdot S \cap \mathsf{Final}$) and Lemma 20. □

We denote by $\widehat{\mathsf{FF}}^\natural$ the set $\widehat{\mathsf{FF}}(i)$ for the smallest $i \geq 0$ such that $\widehat{\mathsf{FF}}(i) \approx_f \widehat{\mathsf{FF}}(i+1)$.

Corollary 25 (Early convergence). *Under* **H4**, *for all* $i \geq 0$, *if* $\mathsf{FF}(i+1) = \mathsf{FF}(i)$ *then* $\widehat{\mathsf{FF}}(i+1) \approx_f \widehat{\mathsf{FF}}(i)$.

Theorem 26 (Correctness). *Under* **H4**, FF^* *is nonempty if and only if* $\widehat{\mathsf{FF}}^\natural$ *is nonempty.*

Remark 2. Note that here the relation $\preceq_f$ needs only to be compatible with Final (and not with Init). This is in contrast with the relation $\succeq_b$ that needs to be both compatible with Init and Final to ensure correctness of the sequence of backward repeated promising states.

Remark 3. In antichain algorithms of promising states, if $\preceq^1$ is coarser than $\preceq^2$, then the induced relation $\approx^1$ on sets of states is coarser than $\approx^2$ which entails that convergence modulo $\approx^1$ occurs at the latest when convergence modulo $\approx^2$ occurs, and possibly earlier. This is illustrated in the next section.

4   Applications

In this section, we present applications of the antichain algorithms to solve classical (and computationally hard) problems in automata theory. We consider automata running on finite and infinite words.

An *alternating automaton* [6] is a tuple $A = (Q, q_\iota, \Sigma, \delta, \alpha)$ where:

- Q is a finite set of states;
- $q_\iota \in Q$ is the initial state;
- Σ is a finite alphabet;
- $\delta : Q \times \Sigma \to 2^{2^Q}$ is the transition relation that maps each state q and letter σ to a set $\{C_1, \ldots, C_n\}$ where each $C_i \subseteq Q$ is a *choice*;
- $\alpha \subseteq Q$ is the set of accepting states.

In an alternating automaton, the (finite or infinite) input word $w = \sigma_0 \sigma_1 \ldots$ over Σ is processed by two players in a turn-based game played in rounds. Each round starts in a state of the automaton, and the first round starts in q_ι. In round i, the first player makes a choice $C \in \delta(q_i, \sigma_i)$ where q_i is the state in round i and σ_i is the ith letter of the input word. Then, the second player chooses a state $q_{i+1} \in C$, and the next round starts in q_{i+1}. A finite input word is accepted by A if the first player has a strategy to force an accepting state of A in the last round; an infinite input word is accepted by A if the first player has a strategy to force infinitely many rounds to be in an accepting state of A. A run of an alternating automaton corresponds to a fixed strategy of the first player.

Formally, a *run* of A over a (finite or infinite) word $w = \sigma_0 \sigma_1 \ldots$ is a tree $\langle T_w, r \rangle$ where $T_w \subseteq \mathbb{N}^*$ is a prefix-closed subset of $\mathbb{N}$, and $r : T_w \to Q$ is a labelling function such that $r(\epsilon) = q_\iota$ and for all $x \in T_w$, there exists $C = \{q_1, \ldots, q_c\} \in \delta(r(x), \sigma_{|x|})$ such that $x \cdot i \in T_w$ and $r(x \cdot i) = q_i$ for each $i = 1, \ldots, k$.

A run $\langle T_w, r \rangle$ of A on an a finite word w is *accepting* if $r(x) \in \alpha$ for all nodes $x \in T_w$ of length $|w|$ reachable from ϵ; and a run $\langle T_w, r \rangle$ of A on an infinite word w is *accepting* if all paths from ϵ visit nodes labeled by accepting states infinitely often (i.e., all paths satisfy a Büchi condition). A (finite or infinite) word w is *accepted* by A if there exists an accepting run on w. Alternating automata on finite words are called AFA, and alternating automata on infinite words are called ABW. The *language* of an AFA (resp., ABW) A is the set $L(A)$ of finite (resp., infinite) words accepted by A.

The *emptiness problem* for alternating automata is to decide if the language of a given alternating automaton (AFA or ABW) is empty. This problem is PSpace-complete for both AFA and ABW [18,23]. For finite words, we also consider the *universality problem* which is to decide if the language of a given AFA with alphabet Σ is equal to Σ^*, which is PSpace-complete even for the special case of nondeterministic automata. A *nondeterministic automaton* (NFA) is an AFA such that $\delta(q, \sigma)$ is a set of singletons for all states q and letters σ.

We use antichain algorithms to solve the emptiness problem of AFA and ABW, as well as the universality problem for NFA, and the emptiness problem for NFA specified by a product of automata. In the case of NFA, it is more convenient to represent the transition relation as a function $\delta : Q \times \Sigma \to 2^Q$ where $\delta(q, \sigma) = \{q_1, \ldots, q_n\}$ represents the set of singletons $\{\{q_1\}, \ldots, \{q_n\}\}$.

4.1   Universality Problem for NFA

Let $A = (Q, q_\iota, \Sigma, \delta, \alpha)$ be an NFA, and define the subset construction $G(A) = (V, E, \mathsf{Init}, \mathsf{Final})$ as follows: $V = 2^Q$, $\mathsf{Init} = \{v \in V \mid q_\iota \in v\}$, $\mathsf{Final} = \{v \in V \mid v \subseteq Q \setminus \alpha\}$, and $E(v_1, v_2)$ if there exists $\sigma \in \Sigma$ such that $\delta(q, \sigma) \subseteq v_2$ for all $q \in v_1$. A classical result shows that $L(A) \neq \Sigma^*$ if and only if Final is reachable from Init in $G(A)$, and thus we can solve the universality problem for A using antichain algorithms for the reachability problem on $G(A)$.

Antichains as symbolic representation. Consider the relation $\preceq_\mathsf{F}$ on the states of $G(A)$ defined by $v_2 \preceq_\mathsf{F} v_1$ if and only if $v_2 \subseteq v_1$. Note that $\preceq_\mathsf{F}$ is a partial order.

Lemma 27. $\preceq_\mathsf{F}$ *is a forward simulation in* $G(A)$ *compatible with* Final.

Proof. First, if $v_1 \in \mathsf{Final}$ and $v_2 \preceq_\mathsf{F} v_1$, then $v_2 \subseteq v_1 \subseteq Q \setminus \alpha$ i.e., $v_2 \in \mathsf{Final}$. Second, if $v_2 \preceq_\mathsf{F} v_1$ and $E(v_1, v_3)$, then for some $\sigma \in \Sigma$, we have $\delta(q, \sigma) \subseteq v_3$ for all $q \in v_1$, and thus also for all $q \in v_2$ i.e., $E(v_2, v_4)$ for $v_4 = v_3$, and trivially $v_4 \preceq_\mathsf{F} v_3$. □

The antichain algorithm for backward reachability is instantiated as follows:

- $\widetilde{\mathsf{B}}(0) = \mathsf{Max}(\subseteq, \mathsf{Final}) = \{Q \setminus \alpha\}$;
- $\widetilde{\mathsf{B}}(i) = \mathsf{Max}(\subseteq, \widetilde{\mathsf{B}}(i-1) \cup \mathsf{pre}(\mathsf{Down}(\subseteq, \widetilde{\mathsf{B}}(i-1))))$, for all $i \geq 1$.

Details about efficient computation of this sequence as well as experimental comparison with the classical algorithm based on determinization can be found in [8].

Antichains of promising states. Consider the relation $\succeq_\mathsf{B}$ such that $v_2 \succeq_\mathsf{B} v_1$ if $v_2 \supseteq v_1$. Note that $v_2 \succeq_\mathsf{B} v_1$ if and only if $v_1 \preceq_\mathsf{F} v_2$.

Lemma 28. $\succeq_\mathsf{B}$ *is a backward simulation in* $G(A)$ *compatible with* Init.

Proof. First, if $v_1 \in \mathsf{Init}$ and $v_2 \succeq_\mathsf{B} v_1$, then $q_\iota \in v_1 \subseteq v_2$ i.e., $v_2 \in \mathsf{Init}$. Second, if $v_2 \succeq_\mathsf{B} v_1$ and $E(v_3, v_1)$, then for some $\sigma \in \Sigma$, we have $\delta(q, \sigma) \subseteq v_1 \subseteq v_2$ for all $q \in v_3$, and thus $E(v_4, v_2)$ for $v_4 = v_3$, and trivially $v_4 \succeq_\mathsf{B} v_3$. □

The corresponding antichain algorithm for backward reachability is instantiated as follows:

- $\widehat{\mathsf{B}}(0) = \mathsf{Max}(\supseteq, \mathsf{Final}) = \{Q \setminus \alpha\}$;
- $\widehat{\mathsf{B}}(i) = \mathsf{Max}(\supseteq, \widehat{\mathsf{B}}(i-1) \cup \mathsf{pre}(\widehat{\mathsf{B}}(i-1)))$, for all $i \geq 1$.

It should be noted that $\widetilde{\mathsf{B}}(i) = \widehat{\mathsf{B}}(i)$, for all $i \geq 0$. In this particular case, the two views coincide due to the special structure of the transition system $G(A)$ (namely $\subseteq$ is a forward simulation and its inverse $\supseteq$ is a backward simulation).

In the rest of the paper, we establish the existence of simulation relations for various constructions in automata theory, and we omit the instantiation of the corresponding antichain algorithms in the promising state view.

Coarser simulations. We show that the algorithms based on antichains of promising states can be improved using coarser simulations (obtained by exploiting the structure of the NFA before subset construction). We illustrate this below for backward algorithms and coarser backward simulations. Then we show that coarser forward simulations do not improve the backward antichain algorithms (in the symbolic view).

We construct a backward simulation coarser than $\succeq_B$, using a pre-order $\gg_b \subseteq Q \times Q$ on the state space of A such that for all $\sigma \in \Sigma$, for all $q_1, q_2, q_3 \in Q$, if $q_2 \gg_b q_1$, then

(i) if $q_1 = q_\iota$, then $q_2 = q_\iota$, and
(ii) if $q_1 \in \delta(q_3, \sigma)$, then there exists $q_4 \in Q$ such that $q_2 \in \delta(q_4, \sigma)$ and $q_4 \gg_b q_3$.

Such a relation $\gg_b$ is usually called a *backward simulation relation* for the NFA A, and a maximal backward simulation relation (which is unique) can be computed in polynomial time (see e.g. [16]). Given $\gg_b$, define the relation $\succeq_{B+}$ on $G(A)$ as follows: $v_2 \succeq_{B+} v_1$ if $\forall q_2 \notin v_2 \cdot \exists q_1 \notin v_1 : q_1 \gg_b q_2$.

Lemma 29. $\succeq_{B+}$ *is a backward simulation for $G(A)$ compatible with* Init.

Proof. Let $v_2 \succeq_{B+} v_1$. First, if $v_2 \notin$ Init, then $q_\iota \notin v_2$ and by definition of $\succeq_{B+}$, there exists $q \notin v_1$ such that $q \gg_b q_\iota$, thus $q = q_\iota$. Therefore $q_\iota \notin v_1$ and thus $v_1 \notin$ Init. Second, if $E(v_3, v_1)$, then for some $\sigma \in \Sigma$, we have $\delta(q, \sigma) \subseteq v_1$ for all $q \in v_3$. Let $v_4 = \{q \in Q \mid \delta(q, \sigma) \subseteq v_2\}$. We have $E(v_4, v_2)$ and we show that $v_4 \succeq_{B+} v_3$ i.e., for all $q_4 \notin v_4$, there exists $q_3 \notin v_3$ such that $q_3 \gg_b q_4$. If $q_4 \notin v_4$, then there exists $q_2 \in \delta(q_4, \sigma)$ with $q_2 \notin v_2$. Since $v_2 \succeq_{B+} v_1$, there exists $q_1 \notin v_1$ such that $q_1 \gg_b q_2$. Then, by definition of $\gg_b$ there exists $q_3 \in Q$ such that $q_1 \in \delta(q_3, \sigma)$ and $q_3 \gg_b q_4$. Since $q_1 \notin v_1$, we have $q_3 \notin v_3$.   □

Note that $\succeq_{B+}$ is coarser than $\succeq_B$ because $v_2 \supseteq v_1$ is equivalent to say that for all $q_2 \notin v_2$, there exists $q_1 \notin v_1$ such that $q_1 = q_2$ (which implies that $q_1 \gg_b q_2$ since $\gg_b$ is a pre-order). Therefore, the antichains in the antichain algorithm based on $\succeq_{B+}$ are subsets of those based on $\succeq_B$. By Corollary 14, the number of iterations of the algorithms based on $\succeq_{B+}$ and $\succeq_B$ is the same when $L(A) \neq \Sigma^*$, and Example 2 below shows that the algorithm based on $\succeq_{B+}$ may converge faster when $L(A) = \Sigma^*$.

Example 2. Consider the nondeterministic finite automaton A with alphabet $\Sigma = \{a, b\}$ in Fig. 2. Note that every word is accepted by A i.e., $L(A) = \Sigma^*$ (it suffices to always go to state 3 from state 4). The backward antichain algorithm applied to the subset construction $G(A)$ (using $\succeq_B$) converges after 3 iterations, and the intersection of $\widehat{B}^\natural = \{\{1,2\}\}$ with the initial states of $G(A)$ is empty. Now, let $\gg_b$ be the maximal backward simulation relation for A. We have $3 \gg_b 2$, $3 \gg_b 1$, and $q \gg_b q$ for all $q \in \{1, 2, 3, 4\}$. The induced relation $\succeq_{B+}$ is such that $\{1\} \succeq_{B+} \{1, 2\}$ and $\{1, 2\} \succeq_{B+} \{1\}$. Therefore, using the relation $\succeq_{B+}$, we get $\widehat{B}(0) \approx_b \widehat{B}(1)$ and the backward antichain algorithm based on $\succeq_{B+}$ converges faster, namely after 2 iterations.

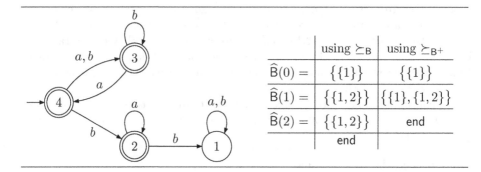

Fig. 2. Improved antichain algorithm for the universality problem of NFA (Example 2)

Now, we consider coarser forward simulations (induced by pre-orders on the original NFA as above) and we show that they do not improve the algorithm based on antichains as symbolic data-structure. We prove this surprising result as follows. A *forward simulation relation* $\ll_f \subseteq Q \times Q$ for A is a pre-order such that for all $\sigma \in \Sigma$, for all $q_1, q_2, q_3 \in Q$, if $q_2 \ll_f q_1$, then

(i) if $q_1 \in \alpha$, then $q_2 \in \alpha$, and
(ii) if $q_3 \in \delta(q_1, \sigma)$, then there exists $q_4 \in \delta(q_2, \sigma)$ such that $q_4 \ll_f q_3$.

Given a forward simulation relation $\ll_f$ for A, define the relation $\preceq_{F+}$ on $G(A)$ as follows: $v_2 \preceq_{F+} v_1$ if $\forall q_2 \in v_2 \cdot \exists q_1 \in v_1 : q_1 \ll_f q_2$.

Lemma 30. $\preceq_{F+}$ *is a forward simulation for* $G(A)$ *compatible with* Final.

Proof. Let $v_2 \preceq_{F+} v_1$. First, if $v_2 \notin$ Final, then $v_2 \cap \alpha \neq \varnothing$ and let $q_2 \in v_2 \cap \alpha$. By definition of $\preceq_{F+}$, there exists $q_1 \in v_1$ such that $q_1 \ll_f q_2$, thus $q_1 \in \alpha$. Therefore $v_1 \cap \alpha \neq \varnothing$ and $v_1 \notin$ Final. Second, if $E(v_1, v_3)$, then for some $\sigma \in \Sigma$, we have $\delta(q, \sigma) \subseteq v_3$ for all $q \in v_1$. Let $v_4 = \bigcup_{q \in v_2} \delta(q, \sigma)$. We have $E(v_2, v_4)$ and we show that $v_4 \preceq_{F+} v_3$ i.e., for all $q_4 \in v_4$, there exists $q_3 \in v_3$ such that $q_3 \ll_f q_4$. If $q_4 \in v_4$, then there exists $q_2 \in \delta(q_4, \sigma)$ with $q_2 \in v_2$. Since $v_2 \preceq_{F+} v_1$, there exists $q_1 \in v_1$ such that $q_1 \ll_f q_2$. Then, by definition of $\ll_f$ there exists $q_3 \in \delta(q_1, \sigma)$ (such that $q_3 \ll_f q_4$). Since $q_1 \in v_1$, we have $q_3 \in v_3$.   □

Lemma 31. *For all* $i \geq 0$, *all sets* $v \in \widetilde{\mathsf{B}}(i)$ *are* $\ll_f$-*upward-closed (where* $\widetilde{\mathsf{B}}$ *is computed using* $\preceq_{F+}$*).*

Proof. First, for $\widetilde{\mathsf{B}}(0) = \{Q \setminus \alpha\}$ we show that $Q \setminus \alpha$ is $\ll_f$-upward-closed. Let $q_1 \in Q \setminus \alpha$ and $q_1 \ll_f q_2$. Then $q_2 \notin \alpha$ (as if $q_2 \in \alpha$, then we would have $q_1 \in \alpha$) and thus $q_2 \in Q \setminus \alpha$. Second, by induction assume that all sets $v \in \widetilde{\mathsf{B}}(i)$ are $\ll_f$-upward-closed, and let $v \in \widetilde{\mathsf{B}}(i+1)$. Either $v \in \widetilde{\mathsf{B}}(i)$ and then v is $\ll_f$-upward-closed, or $v \in \mathsf{pre}(\mathsf{Down}(\subseteq, \widetilde{\mathsf{B}}(i)))$ and for some $\sigma \in \Sigma$ and $v' \in \mathsf{Down}(\subseteq, \widetilde{\mathsf{B}}(i))$, we have $\delta(q, \sigma) \subseteq v'$ for all $q \in v$. Without loss of generality, we can assume that $v' \in \widetilde{\mathsf{B}}(i)$ and thus v' is $\ll_f$-upward-closed (by induction hypothesis). In this case, assume towards contradiction that v is not $\ll_f$-upward-closed i.e., there exist $q_2 \in v$ and $q_1 \notin v$ such that $q_2 \ll_f q_1$. We consider two cases: (i) if $\delta(q_1, \sigma) \subseteq v'$, then $v \cup \{q_1\} \in \mathsf{pre}(\mathsf{Down}(\subseteq, \tilde{\mathsf{B}}(i-1)))$ and v is a strict subset of $v \cup \{q_1\}$ showing that v is not $\subseteq$-maximal in $\tilde{\mathsf{B}}(i)$, a contradiction; (ii) if there exists $q_3 \in \delta(q_1, \sigma)$ with $q_3 \notin v'$, then since $q_2 \ll_f q_1$ there exists $q_4 \in \delta(q_2, \sigma)$ such that $q_4 \ll_f q_3$. Since $q_2 \in v$, we have $\delta(q_2, \sigma) \subseteq v'$ and $q_4 \in v'$. Hence $q_4 \in v'$, $q_3 \notin v'$ and $q_4 \ll_f q_3$ i.e., v' is not $\ll_f$-upward-closed, a contradiction. □

Lemma 32. *For all $\ll_f$-upward-closed sets v_1, v_2, we have $v_2 \preceq_{F+} v_1$ if and only if $v_2 \preceq_F v_1$.*

Proof. Let v_1, v_2 be $\ll_f$-upward-closed sets. First, if $v_2 \preceq_F v_1$, then $v_2 \subseteq v_1$ and for all $q_2 \in v_2$ there exists $q_1 \in v_1$ such that $q_2 = q_1$, and thus $q_1 \ll_f q_2$. Hence $v_2 \preceq_{F+} v_1$. Second, if $v_2 \preceq_{F+} v_1$, then for all $q_2 \in v_2$ there exists $q_1 \in v_1$ such that $q_1 \ll_f q_2$. Since v_1 is $\ll_f$-upward-closed, $q_1 \in v_1$ implies $q_2 \in v_1$. Hence, for all $q_2 \in v_2$ we have $q_2 \in v_1$ i.e., $v_2 \subseteq v_1$ and $v_2 \preceq_F v_1$. □

Corollary 33. *The antichain algorithms for backward reachability $\tilde{\mathsf{B}}$ based on $\preceq_{F+}$ and $\preceq_F$ compute exactly the same sequences of sets.*

4.2   Emptiness Problem for AFA

In this section, we use a new definition of backward simulation for alternating automata on finite words to construct an induced backward simulation on the subset construction for AFA.

Let $A = (Q, q_\iota, \Sigma, \delta, \alpha)$ be an AFA. Define the subset construction $G(A) = (V, E, \mathsf{Init}, \mathsf{Final})$ where $V = 2^Q$, $E = \{(v_1, v_2) \in V \times V \mid \exists \sigma \in \Sigma \cdot \forall q \in v_1 \cdot \exists C \in \delta(q, \sigma) : C \subseteq v_2\}$, $\mathsf{Init} = \{v \in V \mid q_\iota \in v\}$, and $\mathsf{Final} = \{v \in V \mid q \subseteq \alpha\}$.

As before, it is easy to see that $L(A) \neq \varnothing$ if and only if Final is reachable from Init in $G(A)$, and the emptiness problem for A can be solved using antichain algorithms for the reachability problem in $G(A)$ e.g., using the relation $\succeq_B$ such that $v_2 \succeq_B v_1$ if $v_2 \supseteq v_1$ which is a backward simulation in $G(A)$ compatible with Init.

As in the case of the universality problem for NFA, the relation $\succeq_B$ can be improved using an appropriate notion of backward simulation relation defined on the AFA A. We introduce such a new notion as follows. An *backward alternating simulation relation* for an alternating automaton $A = (Q, q_\iota, \Sigma, \delta, \alpha)$ is a preorder $\gg_b$ which is the reflexive closure of a relation $>_b$ such that for all $\sigma \in \Sigma$, for all $q_1, q_2, q_3 \in Q$, if $q_2 >_b q_1$, then

(i) if $q_1 = q_\iota$, then $q_2 = q_\iota$, and
(ii) if there exists $C \in \delta(q_3, \sigma)$ such that $q_1 \in C$, then there exists $q_4 \in Q$ such that (a) $q_2 \in C'$ for all $C' \in \delta(q_4, \sigma)$, and (b) $q_4 >_b q_3$.

It can be shown that a unique maximal backward simulation relation exists for AFA (because the union of two backward simulation relations is again a backward simulation relation), and it can be computed in polynomial time using analogous fixpoint algorithms for computing standard simulation relations [16], e.g. the fixpoint iterations defined by $R_0 = \{(q_1, q_2) \in Q \times Q \mid q_1 = q_\iota \to q_2 = q_\iota\}$ and $R_i = \{(q_1, q_2) \in R_{i-1} \mid \forall q_3 \in Q : (\exists C \in \delta(q_3, \sigma) : q_1 \in C) \to \exists q_4 \in Q : (\forall C' \in \delta(q_4, \sigma) : q_2 \in C') \wedge (q_3, q_4) \in R_{i-1}\}$ for all $i \geq 1$. Note that for so-called *universal finite automata* (UFA) which are AFA where $\delta(q, \sigma)$ is a singleton for all $q \in Q$ and $\sigma \in \Sigma$, our definition of backward alternating simulation coincides with ordinary backward simulation for the dual of the UFA (which is an NFA with transition relation $\delta'(q, \sigma) = \{q \in C \mid \delta(q, \sigma) = \{C\}\}$).

As before, given a backward alternating simulation relation $\gg_b$ for A, we define the relation $\succeq_{B+}$ on $G(A)$ as follows: $v_2 \succeq_{B+} v_1$ if $\forall q_2 \notin v_2 \cdot \exists q_1 \notin v_1 : q_1 \gg_b q_2$.

Lemma 34. $\succeq_{B+}$ *is a backward simulation in* $G(A)$ *compatible with* Init.

Proof. Let $v_1 \succeq_{B+} v_2$. First, if $v_2 \notin$ Init, then $q_\iota \notin v_2$ and there exists $q_1 \notin v_1$ such that $q_1 \gg_b q_\iota$, hence either $q_1 = q_\iota$, or $q_1 >_b q_\iota$ implying $q_1 = q_\iota$. In both cases $q_\iota = q_1 \notin v_1$ i.e., $v_1 \notin$ Init. Second, assume $E(v_3, v_1)$ and $\sigma \in \Sigma$ is such that for all $q \in v_3$, there exists $C \in \delta(q, \sigma)$ such that $C \subseteq v_1$. Let $v_4 = \{q \mid \exists C' \in \delta(q, \sigma) : C' \subseteq v_2\}$. By definition of $G(A)$, we have $E(v_4, v_2)$. We show that $v_4 \succeq_{B+} v_3$. To do this, pick an arbitrary $q_4 \notin v_4$ and show that there exists $q_3 \notin v_3$ such that $q_3 \gg_b q_4$. Note that if $q_4 \notin v_3$, then we take $q_3 = q_4$ and we are done. So, we can assume that $q_4 \in v_3$. Hence there exists $C \in \delta(q_4, \sigma)$ such that $C \subseteq v_1$. And since $q_4 \notin v_4$, there exist $q_2 \in C$ and $q_2 \notin v_2$. As $v_2 \succeq_{B+} v_1$, we know that there exists $q_1 \notin v_1$ such that $q_1 \gg_b q_2$. Since $q_2 \in C$ and $C \subseteq v_1$, we have $q_2 \in v_1$ and therefore we cannot have $q_2 = q_1$, thus we have $q_1 >_b q_2$. Since $q_2 \in C \in \delta(q_4, \sigma)$, and by definition of $>_b$, there exists q_3 such that $q_3 >_b q_4$ (and thus $q_3 \gg_b q_4$) and $q_1 \in C'$ for all $C' \in \delta(q_3, \sigma)$. Since $q_1 \notin v_1$, this implies that $q_3 \notin v_3$. $\square$

4.3   Emptiness Problem for ABW

The emptiness problem for ABW can be solved using a subset construction due to Miyano and Hayashi [20,10,11].

Given an ABW $A = (Q, q_\iota, \Sigma, \delta, \alpha)$, define the Miyano-Hayashi transition system $\mathsf{MH}(A) = (V, E, \mathsf{Init}, \mathsf{Final})$ where $V = 2^Q \times 2^Q$, and

- Init $= \{\langle s, \varnothing \rangle \mid q_\iota \in s \subseteq V\}$,
- Final $= 2^Q \times \{\varnothing\}$, and
- for all $v_1 = \langle s_1, o_1 \rangle$, and $v_2 = \langle s_2, o_2 \rangle$, we have $E(v_1, v_2)$ if there exists $\sigma \in \Sigma$ such that $\forall q \in s_1 \cdot \exists C \in \delta(q, \sigma) : C \subseteq s_2$, and either (i) $o_1 \neq \varnothing$ and $\forall q \in o_1 \cdot \exists C \in \delta(q, \sigma) : C \subseteq o_2 \cup (s_2 \cap \alpha)$, or (ii) $o_1 = \varnothing$ and $o_2 = s_2 \setminus \alpha$.

A classical result shows that $L(A) \neq \varnothing$ if and only if there exists an infinite path from Init in $\mathsf{MH}(A)$ that visits Final infinitely many times. Therefore, the emptiness problem for ABW can be reduced to the repeated reachability problem, and we can use an antichain algorithm (e.g., based on forward simulation) for repeated reachability to solve it. We construct a forward simulation for $\mathsf{MH}(A)$ using a classical notion of alternating simulation.

A pre-order $\ll_f \subseteq Q \times Q$ is an *alternating forward simulation relation* [2] for an alternating automaton A if for all $\sigma \in \Sigma$, for all $q_1, q_2, q_3 \in Q$, if $q_2 \ll_f q_1$, then

(i) if $q_1 \in \alpha$, then $q_2 \in \alpha$, and
(ii) for all $C_1 \in \delta(q_1, \sigma)$, there exists $C_2 \in \delta(q_2, \sigma)$ such that for all $q_4 \in C_2$, there exists $q_3 \in C_1$ such that $q_4 \ll_f q_3$.

Given a forward alternating simulation relation $\ll_f$ for A, define the relation $\preceq_{F+}$ on $\mathsf{MH}(A)$ such that $\langle s_2, o_2 \rangle \preceq_{F+} \langle s_1, o_1 \rangle$ if the following conditions hold: (a) $\forall q_2 \in s_2 \cdot \exists q_1 \in s_1 : q_2 \ll_f q_1$, (b) $\forall q_2 \in o_2 \cdot \exists q_1 \in o_1 : q_2 \ll_f q_1$, and (c) $o_1 = \varnothing$ if and only if $o_2 = \varnothing$.

Lemma 35. $\preceq_{F+}$ *is a forward simulation in* $\mathsf{MH}(A)$ *compatible with* Final.

Proof. Let $\langle s_2, o_2 \rangle \preceq_{F+} \langle s_1, o_1 \rangle$. First, if $\langle s_1, o_1 \rangle \in$ Final, then $o_1 = \varnothing$ and thus $o_2 = \varnothing$ by definition of $\preceq_{F+}$. Hence $\langle s_2, o_2 \rangle \in$ Final. Second, assume $E(\langle s_1, o_1 \rangle, \langle s_3, o_3 \rangle)$ and $\sigma \in \Sigma$ is such that for all $q \in s_1$, there exists $C \in \delta(q, \sigma)$ such that $C \subseteq s_3$, and either (i) $o_1 \neq \varnothing$ and $\forall q \in o_1 \cdot \exists C \in \delta(q, \sigma) : C \subseteq o_3 \cup (s_3 \cap \alpha)$, or (ii) $o_1 = \varnothing$ and $o_3 = s_3 \setminus \alpha$.

In the first case (i), we construct $\langle s_4, o_4 \rangle$ such that $E(\langle s_2, o_2 \rangle, \langle s_4, o_4 \rangle)$ and $\langle s_4, o_4 \rangle \preceq_{F+} \langle s_3, o_3 \rangle$, using the following intermediate constructions.

(1) For each $q_2 \in s_2$, we construct a set $\mathsf{succ}(q_2)$ as follows. By definition of $\preceq_{F+}$, for $q_2 \in s_2$, there exists $q_1 \in s_1$ such that $q_2 \ll_f q_1$. Since $q_1 \in s_1$, there exists $C_1 \in \delta(q_1, \sigma)$ with $C_1 \subseteq s_3$, and since $q_2 \ll_f q_1$, there exists $C_2 \in \delta(q_2, \sigma)$ such that for all $q_4 \in C_2$, there exists $q_3 \in C_1$ such that $q_4 \ll_f q_1$. We take $\mathsf{succ}(q_2) = C_2$.

(2) For each $q_2 \in o_2$, we construct two sets $\mathsf{succ}^\alpha(q_2)$ and $\mathsf{succ}^{\neg\alpha}(q_2)$ as follows. By definition of $\preceq_{F+}$, for $q_2 \in o_2$, there exists $q_1 \in o_1$ such that $q_2 \ll_f q_1$. Since $q_1 \in o_1$, there exists $C_1 \in \delta(q_1, \sigma)$ with $C_1 \subseteq o_3 \cup (s_3 \cap \alpha)$, and since $q_2 \ll_f q_1$, there exists $C_2 \in \delta(q_2, \sigma)$ such that for all $q_4 \in C_2$, there exists $q_3 \in C_1$ such that $q_4 \ll_f q_3$. We take $\mathsf{succ}^\alpha(q_2) = \{q \in C_2 \cap \alpha \mid \exists q' \in s_3 : q \ll_f q'\}$ and $\mathsf{succ}^{\neg\alpha}(q_2) = C_2 \setminus \mathsf{succ}^\alpha(q_2)$.

Let $s_4 = \bigcup_{q_2 \in s_2} \mathsf{succ}(q_2) \cup \bigcup_{q_2 \in o_2} \mathsf{succ}^\alpha(q_2)$, and $o_4 = o_3 \cup \bigcup_{q_2 \in o_2} \mathsf{succ}^{\neg\alpha}(q_2)$. To prove that $E(\langle s_2, o_2 \rangle, \langle s_4, o_4 \rangle)$, we can check that for all $q_2 \in s_2$ there exists $C_2 \in \delta(q_2, \sigma)$ such that $C_2 = \mathsf{succ}(q_2) \subseteq s_4$, and that $o_2 \neq \varnothing$ (because $o_1 \neq \varnothing$ and $\langle s_2, o_2 \rangle \preceq_{F+} \langle s_1, o_1 \rangle$) and for all $q_2 \in o_2$ there exists $C_2 \in \delta(q_2, \sigma)$ such that $C_2 \subseteq o_4 \cup (s_4 \cap \alpha)$ (because $\mathsf{succ}^{\neg\alpha}(q_2) \subseteq o_4$ and $\mathsf{succ}^\alpha(q_2) \subseteq s_4 \cap \alpha$). To prove that $\langle s_4, o_4 \rangle \preceq_{F+} \langle s_3, o_3 \rangle$, we can check that

(a) for all $q_4 \in s_4$, there exists $q_3 \in s_3$ such that $q_4 \ll_f q_3$. This holds since either $q_4 \in \mathsf{succ}(q_2)$ for some $q_2 \in s_2$ and by part (1) of the construction, there exists $q_3 \in s_3$ such that $q_4 \ll_f q_3$, or $q_4 \in \mathsf{succ}^\alpha(q_2)$ for some $q_2 \in o_2$ and by definition of succ^α there exists $q' \in s_3$ such that $q_4 \ll_f q'$;
(b) for all $q_4 \in o_4$, there exists $q_3 \in o_3$ such that $q_4 \ll_f q_3$. This holds since either $q_4 \in o_3$ and we can take $q_3 = q_4$, or $q_4 \in \mathsf{succ}^{\neg\alpha}(q_2)$ for some $q_2 \in o_2$

and by part (2) of the construction, there exists $q_3 \in o_3 \cup (s_3 \cap \alpha)$ such that $q_4 \ll_f q_3$. Now, either $q_4 \in \alpha$ and then $q_3 \notin s_3$ by definition of $\mathsf{succ}^{\neg \alpha}$, thus $q_3 \in o_3$; or $q_4 \notin \alpha$ and then $q_3 \notin \alpha$ by definition of $\ll_f$, thus again $q_3 \in o_3$;

(c) if $o_3 \neq \varnothing$, then $o_4 \neq \varnothing$ since $o_3 \subseteq o_4$. And by (ii), if $o_4 \neq \varnothing$, then $o_3 \neq \varnothing$. Hence $o_3 = \varnothing$ if and only if $o_4 = \varnothing$.

In the second case (ii), we construct the sets $\mathsf{succ}(q_2)$ for each $q_2 \in s_2$ as in part (1) of the construction above, and define $s_4 = s_3 \cup \bigcup_{q_2 \in s_2} \mathsf{succ}(q_2)$ and $o_4 = s_4 \setminus \alpha$. We can check that $E(\langle s_2, o_2 \rangle, \langle s_4, o_4 \rangle)$ since for all $q_2 \in s_2$ there exists $C_2 \in \delta(q_2, \sigma)$ such that $C_2 = \mathsf{succ}(q_2) \subseteq s_4$, and that $o_2 = \varnothing$ (since $o_1 = \varnothing$ and $\langle s_2, o_2 \rangle \preceq_{\mathsf{F}+} \langle s_1, o_1 \rangle$) and $o_4 = s_4 \setminus \alpha$. We prove that $\langle s_4, o_4 \rangle \preceq_{\mathsf{F}+} \langle s_3, o_3 \rangle$ as follows: first, as in (i) above, we have for all $q_4 \in s_4$, there exists $q_3 \in s_3$ such that $q_4 \ll_f q_3$; second, by definition of $\ll_f$ if $q_4 \notin \alpha$, then $q_3 \notin \alpha$ thus for all $q_4 \in o_4$, there exists $q_3 \in o_3$ such that $q_4 \ll_f q_3$; third, this implies that if $o_4 \neq \varnothing$, then $o_3 \neq \varnothing$. And since $o_3 \subseteq o_4$, if $o_3 \neq \varnothing$, then $o_4 \neq \varnothing$. Hence $o_3 = \varnothing$ if and only if $o_4 = \varnothing$. $\qquad \square$

4.4   Emptiness Problem for a Product of NFA

Consider NFAs $A_i = (Q_i, q^i_\iota, \Sigma \cup \{\tau_i\}, \delta_i, \alpha_i)$ for $1 \leq i \leq n$ where $\tau_1, \dots, \tau_n$ are internal actions, and Σ is a shared alphabet. The *synchronized product* $A_1 \otimes A_2 \otimes \cdots \otimes A_n$ is the transition system $(V, E, \mathsf{Init}, \mathsf{Final})$ where

- $V = Q_1 \times Q_2 \times \cdots \times Q_n$;
- $E(v_1, v_2)$ if $v_1 = (q^1_1, q^2_1, \dots, q^n_1)$, $v_2 = (q^1_2, q^2_2, \dots, q^n_2)$ and either $q^i_2 \in \delta_i(q^i_1, \tau_i)$ for all $1 \leq i \leq n$, or there exists $\sigma \in \Sigma$ such that $q^i_2 \in \delta_i(q^i_1, \sigma)$ for all $1 \leq i \leq n$;
- $\mathsf{Init} = \{(q^1_\iota, q^2_\iota, \dots, q^n_\iota)\}$;
- $\mathsf{Final} = \alpha_1 \times \alpha_2 \times \cdots \times \alpha_n$.

For each $i = 1 \dots n$, let $\ll^i_f \subseteq Q_i \times Q_i$ be a forward simulation relation for A_i. Define the relation $\preceq_{\mathsf{F}+}$ such that $(q^1_2, q^2_2, \dots, q^n_2) \preceq_{\mathsf{F}+} (q^1_1, q^2_1, \dots, q^n_1)$ if $q^i_2 \ll^i_f q^i_1$ for all $1 \leq i \leq n$.

Lemma 36. $\preceq_{\mathsf{F}+}$ *is a forward simulation in* $A_1 \otimes \cdots \otimes A_n$ *compatible with* Final.

Acknowledgements. We would like to warmly thank T. Brihaye, V. Bruyère, and M. Ducobu for giving helpful comments on a draft of this paper.

References

1. Abdulla, P.A., Cerans, K., Jonsson, B., Tsay, Y.-K.: General decidability theorems for infinite-state systems. In: LICS, pp. 313–321. IEEE Comp. Soc., Los Alamitos (1996)
2. Alur, R., Henzinger, T.A., Kupferman, O., Vardi, M.Y.: Alternating refinement relations. In: Sangiorgi, D., de Simone, R. (eds.) CONCUR 1998. LNCS, vol. 1466, pp. 163–178. Springer, Heidelberg (1998)

3. Berwanger, D., Chatterjee, K., De Wulf, M., Doyen, L., Henzinger, T.A.: Alpaga: A tool for solving parity games with imperfect information. In: Kowalewski, S., Philippou, A. (eds.) TACAS 2009. LNCS, vol. 5505, pp. 58–61. Springer, Heidelberg (2009)
4. Berwanger, D., Chatterjee, K., Doyen, L., Henzinger, T.A., Raje, S.: Strategy construction for parity games with imperfect information. In: van Breugel, F., Chechik, M. (eds.) CONCUR 2008. LNCS, vol. 5201, pp. 325–339. Springer, Heidelberg (2008)
5. Bouajjani, A., Habermehl, P., Holík, L., Touili, T., Vojnar, T.: Antichain-based universality and inclusion testing over nondeterministic finite tree automata. In: Ibarra, O.H., Ravikumar, B. (eds.) CIAA 2008. LNCS, vol. 5148, pp. 57–67. Springer, Heidelberg (2008)
6. Chandra, A.K., Kozen, D., Stockmeyer, L.J.: Alternation. J. ACM 28(1), 114–133 (1981)
7. Chatterjee, K., Doyen, L., Henzinger, T.A., Raskin, J.-F.: Algorithms for omega-regular games of incomplete information. Logical Meth. in Comp. Sc. 3(3,4) (2007)
8. De Wulf, M., Doyen, L., Henzinger, T.A., Raskin, J.-F.: Antichains: A new algorithm for checking universality of finite automata. In: Ball, T., Jones, R.B. (eds.) CAV 2006. LNCS, vol. 4144, pp. 17–30. Springer, Heidelberg (2006)
9. De Wulf, M., Doyen, L., Maquet, N., Raskin, J.-F.: Alaska: Antichains for logic, automata and symbolic kripke structures analysis. In: Cha, S(S.), Choi, J.-Y., Kim, M., Lee, I., Viswanathan, M. (eds.) ATVA 2008. LNCS, vol. 5311, pp. 240–245. Springer, Heidelberg (2008)
10. De Wulf, M., Doyen, L., Maquet, N., Raskin, J.-F.: Antichains: Alternative algorithms for LTL satisfiability and model-checking. In: Ramakrishnan, C.R., Rehof, J. (eds.) TACAS 2008. LNCS, vol. 4963, pp. 63–77. Springer, Heidelberg (2008)
11. Doyen, L., Raskin, J.-F.: Antichains for the automata-based approach to model-checking. Logical Methods in Computer Science 5(1,5) (2009)
12. Filiot, E., Jin, N., Raskin, J.-F.: An antichain algorithm for LTL realizability. In: Bouajjani, A., Maler, O. (eds.) Computer Aided Verification. LNCS, vol. 5643, pp. 263–277. Springer, Heidelberg (2009)
13. Finkel, A., Schnoebelen, P.: Well-structured transition systems everywhere! Theor. Comput. Sci. 256(1-2), 63–92 (2001)
14. Fogarty, S., Vardi, M.Y.: Büchi complementation and size-change termination. In: Kowalewski, S., Philippou, A. (eds.) TACAS 2009. LNCS, vol. 5505, pp. 16–30. Springer, Heidelberg (2009)
15. Gurumurthy, S., Kupferman, O., Somenzi, F., Y. Vardi, M.: On complementing nondeterministic Büchi automata. In: Geist, D., Tronci, E. (eds.) CHARME 2003. LNCS, vol. 2860, pp. 96–110. Springer, Heidelberg (2003)
16. Henzinger, M.R., Henzinger, T.A., Kopke, P.W.: Computing simulations on finite and infinite graphs. In: Proc. of FOCS, pp. 453–462. IEEE, Los Alamitos (1995)
17. Kupferman, O., Vardi, M.Y.: Weak alternating automata are not that weak. ACM Trans. Comput. Log. 2(3), 408–429 (2001)
18. Meyer, A.R., Stockmeyer, L.J.: The equivalence problem for regular expressions with squaring requires exponential space. In: FOCS, pp. 125–129. IEEE, Los Alamitos (1972)
19. Milner, R.: An algebraic definition of simulation between programs. In: Proc. of IJCAI, pp. 481–489. British Computer Society (1971)
20. Miyano, S., Hayashi, T.: Alternating finite automata on omega-words. In: Proc. of CAAP, pp. 195–210. Cambridge University Press, Cambridge (1984)

21. Safra, S.: On the complexity of ω-automata. In: Proc. of FOCS: Foundations of Computer Science, pp. 319–327. IEEE, Los Alamitos (1988)
22. Schewe, S.: Tighter bounds for the determinisation of Büchi automata. In: de Alfaro, L. (ed.) FOSSACS 2009. LNCS, vol. 5504, pp. 167–181. Springer, Heidelberg (2009)
23. Sistla, A.P., Vardi, M.Y., Wolper, P.: The complementation problem for Büchi automata with applications to temporal logic. Th. Comp. Sci. 49, 217–237 (1987)
24. Tabakov, D., Vardi, M.Y.: Experimental evaluation of classical automata constructions. In: Sutcliffe, G., Voronkov, A. (eds.) LPAR 2005. LNCS (LNAI), vol. 3835, pp. 396–411. Springer, Heidelberg (2005)
25. Tabakov, D., Vardi, M.Y.: Model-checking Büchi specifications. In: Pre-proceedings of LATA: Language and Automata Theory and Applications (2007)
26. Vardi, M.Y., Wolper, P.: An automata-theoretic approach to automatic program verification (preliminary report). In: LICS, pp. 332–344. IEEE, Los Alamitos (1986)
27. Vardi, M.Y., Wolper, P.: Reasoning about infinite computations. Inf. Comput. 115(1), 1–37 (1994)

Assume-Guarantee Verification
for Probabilistic Systems

Marta Kwiatkowska[1], Gethin Norman[2], David Parker[1], and Hongyang Qu[1]

[1] Oxford University Computing Laboratory, Parks Road, Oxford, OX1 3QD, UK
[2] Department of Computing Science, University of Glasgow, Glasgow, G12 8RZ, UK

Abstract. We present a compositional verification technique for systems that exhibit both probabilistic and nondeterministic behaviour. We adopt an assume-guarantee approach to verification, where both the assumptions made about system components and the guarantees that they provide are regular safety properties, represented by finite automata. Unlike previous proposals for assume-guarantee reasoning about probabilistic systems, our approach does not require that components interact in a fully synchronous fashion. In addition, the compositional verification method is efficient and fully automated, based on a reduction to the problem of multi-objective probabilistic model checking. We present asymmetric and circular assume-guarantee rules, and show how they can be adapted to form quantitative queries, yielding lower and upper bounds on the actual probabilities that a property is satisfied. Our techniques have been implemented and applied to several large case studies, including instances where conventional probabilistic verification is infeasible.

1 Introduction

Many computerised systems exhibit probabilistic behaviour, for example due to the use of randomisation (e.g. in distributed communication or security protocols), or the presence of failures (e.g. in faulty devices or unreliable communication media). The prevalence of such systems in today's society makes techniques for their formal verification a necessity. This requires models and formalisms that incorporate both *probability* and *nondeterminism*. Although efficient algorithms for verifying such models are known [3,8] and mature tool support [11,7] exists, applying these techniques to large, real-life systems remains challenging, and hence techniques to improve scalability are essential.

In this paper, we focus on *compositional* verification techniques for probabilistic and nondeterministic systems, in which a system comprising multiple interacting components can be verified by analysing each component in isolation, rather than verifying the much larger model of the whole system. In the case of *non-probabilistic* models, a successful approach is the use of *assume-guarantee* reasoning. This is based on checking queries of the form $\langle A \rangle M \langle G \rangle$, with the meaning "whenever component M is part of a system satisfying the *assumption* A, then the system is *guaranteed* to satisfy property G". Proof rules can then

J. Esparza and R. Majumdar (Eds.): TACAS 2010, LNCS 6015, pp. 23–37, 2010.
© Springer-Verlag Berlin Heidelberg 2010

be established that show, for example, that if $\langle true \rangle\, M_1\, \langle A \rangle$ (process M_1 satisfies assumption A in any environment) and $\langle A \rangle\, M_2\, \langle G \rangle$ hold, then the combined system $M_1 \| M_2$ satisfies G. For *probabilistic* systems, compositional approaches have also been studied, but a distinct lack of practical progress has been made. In this paper, we address this limitation, presenting the first fully-automated technique for compositional verification of systems exhibiting both probabilistic and nondeterministic behaviour, and illustrating its applicability and efficiency on several large case studies.

We use *probabilistic automata* [20,21], a well-studied formalism that is naturally suited to modelling multi-component probabilistic systems. Indeed, elegant proof techniques have been developed and used to manually prove correctness of large, complex randomised algorithms [18]. Several branching-time preorders (simulation and bisimulation) have been proposed for probabilistic automata and have been shown to be compositional (i.e. preserved under parallel composition) [21], but such branching-time equivalences are often too fine to give significant practical advantages for compositional verification.

A coarser linear-time preorder can be obtained through *trace distribution* (probability distributions over sequences of observable actions) inclusion [20]; however, it is well known that this relation is not preserved under parallel composition [19]. Various attempts have been made to characterise refinement relations that *are* preserved, e.g. [20,15]. An alternative direction is to restrict the forms of parallel composition that are allowed. One example is the formalism of switched probabilistic I/O automata [6], which places restrictions on the scheduling between parallel components. Another is [1] which uses a probabilistic extension of Reactive Modules, restricted to synchronous parallel composition. A limitation of all these approaches is that the relations used, such as trace distribution inclusion and weak probabilistic simulation, are not efficiently computable.

We propose an assume-guarantee verification technique for probabilistic automata, that has no restrictions on the parallel composition permitted between components, allowing greater flexibility to model complex systems. To achieve this, we represent both the assumptions made about system components and the guarantees that they provide as *safety properties*. In the context of probabilistic systems, safety properties capture a wide range of useful properties, e.g. "the maximum probability of an error occurring is at most 0.01" or "the minimum probability of terminating within k time-units is at least 0.75".

We represent safety properties using finite automata and show that verifying assume-guarantee queries reduces to the problem of *multi-objective model checking* for probabilistic automata [10], which can be implemented efficiently using linear programming. Another key benefit of using finite automata in this way is illustrated by the (non-probabilistic) assume-guarantee verification framework of [16]. There, not only is the verification of queries fully automated, but the assumptions themselves (represented as finite automata) are generated automatically using learning techniques. This opens the way for applying learning techniques to compositional verification in the probabilistic case.

We use our definitions of probabilistic assume guarantee reasoning to formulate and prove several assume-guarantee proof rules, representing commonly occurring patterns of processes. We also discuss how to employ *quantitative* reasoning, in particular obtaining lower and upper bounds on the actual probability that a system satisfies a safety property. The techniques have been implemented in a prototype tool and applied to several large case studies. We demonstrate significant speed-ups over traditional, non-compositional verification, and successfully verify models that cannot be analysed without compositional techniques.

A full version of this paper, including additional proofs, is available as [12].

Related work. In addition to the compositional techniques for probabilistic systems surveyed above [6,1,15,18,19,20,21], we mention several other related pieces of work. In particular, our approach was inspired by the large body of work by Giannakopoulou, Pasareanu et al. (see e.g. [16]) on *non-probabilistic* assume guarantee techniques. We also build upon ideas put forward in [10], which suggests using multi-objective verification to check probabilistic assume-guarantee queries. Also relevant are: [9], which presents an assume/guarantee framework using probabilistic contracts for non-probabilistic models; [4], which presents a theoretical framework for compositional verification of quantitative (but not probabilistic) properties; and [17], which uses probabilistic automata to model the environment of non-probabilistic components.

2   Background

We begin by briefly reviewing probabilistic automata and techniques for their verification. We also introduce safety properties, in the context of probabilistic systems, and discuss multi-objective model checking.

In the following, we use $Dist(S)$ to denote the set of all discrete probability distributions over a set S, η_s for the point distribution on $s \in S$, and $\mu_1 \times \mu_2 \in Dist(S_1 \times S_2)$ for the product distribution of $\mu_1 \in Dist(S_1)$ and $\mu_2 \in Dist(S_2)$.

2.1   Probabilistic Automata

Probabilistic automata [20,21] are a modelling formalism for systems that exhibit both probabilistic and nondeterministic behaviour.

Definition 1. *A probabilistic automaton (PA) is a tuple $M = (S, \overline{s}, \alpha_M, \delta_M, L)$ where S is a set of states, $\overline{s} \in S$ is an initial state, α_M is an alphabet, $\delta_M \subseteq S \times (\alpha_M \cup \{\tau\}) \times Dist(S)$ is a probabilistic transition relation and $L : S \to 2^{AP}$ is a labelling function, assigning atomic propositions from a set AP to each state.*

In any state s of a PA M, a *transition*, denoted $s \xrightarrow{a} \mu$, where a is an *action* label and μ is a discrete probability distribution over states, is available[1] if $(s, a, \mu) \in \delta_M$. In an execution of the model, the choice between the available

---

[1] Markov decision processes, another commonly used model, are PAs with the restriction that action labels are unique amongst the available transitions for each state.

transitions in each state is nondeterministic; the choice of successor state is then made randomly according to the distribution μ. A *path* through M is a (finite or infinite) sequence $s_0 \xrightarrow{a_0,\mu_0} s_1 \xrightarrow{a_1,\mu_1} \cdots$ where $s_0 = \bar{s}$ and, for each $i \geqslant 0$, $s_i \xrightarrow{a_i} \mu_i$ is a transition and $\mu_i(s_{i+1}) > 0$. The sequence of actions $a_0, a_1, \ldots$, after removal of any "internal actions" τ, from a path π is called a *trace* and is denoted $tr(\pi)$.

To reason about PAs, we use the notion of *adversaries* (also called schedulers or strategies), which resolve the nondeterministic choices in a model, based on its execution history. Formally an adversary σ maps any finite path to a sub-distribution over the available transitions in the last state of the path. Adversaries are defined in terms of sub-distributions because they can opt to (with some probability) take none of the available choices and remain in the current state. For this reason, they are are sometimes called *partial* adversaries. Occasionally, we will distinguish between these and *complete* adversaries, in which all the distributions are total.

We denote by $Path_M^\sigma$ the set of all paths through M when controlled by adversary σ, and by Adv_M the set of all possible adversaries for M. Under an adversary σ, we define a probability space Pr_M^σ over the set of paths $Path_M^\sigma$, which captures the (purely probabilistic) behaviour of M under σ.

To reason about probabilistic systems comprising multiple components, we will need the notions of *parallel composition* and *alphabet extension*:

Definition 2 (Parallel composition of PAs). *If $M_1 = (S_1, \bar{s}_1, \alpha_{M_1}, \delta_{M_1}, L_1)$ and $M_2 = (S_2, \bar{s}_2, \alpha_{M_2}, \delta_{M_2}, L_2)$ are PAs, then their parallel composition, denoted $M_1 \| M_2$, is given by the PA $(S_1 \times S_2, (\bar{s}_1, \bar{s}_2), \alpha_{M_1} \cup \alpha_{M_2}, \delta_{M_1 \| M_2}, L)$ where $\delta_{M_1 \| M_2}$ is defined such that $(s_1, s_2) \xrightarrow{a} \mu_1 \times \mu_2$ if and only if one of the following holds:*

- $s_1 \xrightarrow{a} \mu_1$, $s_2 \xrightarrow{a} \mu_2$ *and* $a \in \alpha_{M_1} \cap \alpha_{M_2}$
- $s_1 \xrightarrow{a} \mu_1$, $\mu_2 = \eta_{s_2}$ *and* $a \in (\alpha_{M_1} \backslash \alpha_{M_2}) \cup \{\tau\}$
- $s_2 \xrightarrow{a} \mu_2$, $\mu_1 = \eta_{s_1}$ *and* $a \in (\alpha_{M_2} \backslash \alpha_{M_1}) \cup \{\tau\}$

and $L(s_1, s_2) = L_1(s_1) \cup L_2(s_2)$.

Definition 3 (Alphabet extension). *For any PA $M = (S, \bar{s}, \alpha_M, \delta_M, L)$ and set of actions Σ, we extend the alphabet of M to Σ, denoted $M[\Sigma]$, as follows: $M[\Sigma] = (S, \bar{s}, \alpha_M \cup \Sigma, \delta_{M[\Sigma]}, L)$ where $\delta_{M[\Sigma]} = \delta_M \cup \{(s, a, \eta_s) \mid s \in S \wedge a \in \Sigma \backslash \alpha_M\}$.*

We also require the notion of *projections*. First, for any state $s = (s_1, s_2)$ of $M_1 \| M_2$, the projection of s onto M_i, denoted by $s\!\restriction_{M_i}$, is s_i. We extend this notation to distributions over the state space $S_1 \times S_2$ of $M_1 \| M_2$ in the standard manner. Next, for any path π of $M_1 \| M_2$, the projection of π onto M_i, denoted $\pi\!\restriction_{M_i}$, is the path obtained from π by projecting each state of π onto M_i and removing all the actions not in α_{M_i} together with the subsequent states.

Definition 4 (Projections of adversaries). *Let M_1 and M_2 be PAs and σ an adversary of $M_1 \| M_2$. The projection of σ onto M_i, denoted $\sigma\!\restriction_{M_i}$, is the adversary on M_i where, for any finite path π of M_i:*

$$\sigma\!\restriction_{M_i}(\dot{\pi})(a, \mu) = \sum \{ Pr(\pi') \cdot \sigma(\pi')(a, \mu') \mid \pi' \in Path_{M_1 \| M_2}^\sigma \wedge \pi'\!\restriction_{M_i} = \pi \wedge \mu'\!\restriction_{M_i} = \mu \}.$$

Compositional reasoning about PAs, and in particular adversary projections, necessitates the use of partial, rather than complete, adversaries. In particular, even if an adversary σ of $M_1 \| M_2$ is complete, the projection $\sigma\lceil_{M_i}$ onto one component may be partial.

2.2   Model Checking for PAs

The verification of PAs against properties specified either in temporal logic or as automata has been well studied. In this paper, both the states and transitions of PAs are labelled (with sets of atomic propositions and actions, respectively) and we formulate properties that refer to both types of labels. For the former, we will express properties in linear temporal logic (LTL), and for the latter, we will use safety properties represented by deterministic finite automata.

LTL Verification. For an LTL formula ψ, PA M and adversary $\sigma \in Adv_M$:

$$Pr_M^\sigma(\psi) \overset{\text{def}}{=} Pr_M^\sigma\{\pi \in Path_M^\sigma \mid \pi \models \psi\}$$

where $\pi \models \psi$ denotes satisfaction according to the standard semantics of LTL. Verifying an LTL specification ψ against M typically involves checking that the probability of satisfying ψ meets a probability bound for all adversaries. This reduces to computing the minimum or maximum probability of satisfying ψ:

$$Pr_M^{\min}(\psi) \overset{\text{def}}{=} \inf_{\sigma \in Adv_M} Pr_M^\sigma(\psi) \quad \text{and} \quad Pr_M^{\max}(\psi) \overset{\text{def}}{=} \sup_{\sigma \in Adv_M} Pr_M^\sigma(\psi).$$

The complexity of this computation is polynomial in the size of M and doubly exponential in the size of ψ [8]. In practice, the LTL formula ψ is small and, for simple, commonly used cases such as $\Diamond ap$ ("eventually ap") or $\Box ap$ ("globally ap"), model checking is polynomial [3]. Furthermore, efficient implementations of LTL verification exist in tools such as PRISM [11] and LiQuor [7].

Safety Properties. A *regular safety property* A represents a set of infinite words, denoted $\mathcal{L}(A)$, that is characterised by a regular language of *bad prefixes*, finite words of which any extension is not in $\mathcal{L}(A)$. More precisely, we will define a regular safety property A by a (complete) deterministic finite automaton (DFA) $A^{err} = (Q, \bar{q}, \alpha_A, \delta_A, F)$, comprising states Q, initial state $\bar{q} \in Q$, alphabet α_A, transition function $\delta_A : Q \times \alpha_A \to Q$ and accepting states $F \subseteq Q$. The DFA A^{err} defines, in standard fashion, a regular language $\mathcal{L}(A^{err}) \subseteq (\alpha_A)^*$. The language $\mathcal{L}(A)$ is then defined as $\mathcal{L}(A) = \{w \in (\alpha_A)^\omega \mid$ no prefix of w is in $\mathcal{L}(A^{err})\}$.

Given a PA M, adversary $\sigma \in Adv_M$ and regular safety property A with $\alpha_A \subseteq \alpha_M$, we define the probability of M under σ satisfying A as:

$$Pr_M^\sigma(A) \overset{\text{def}}{=} Pr_M^\sigma\{\pi \in Path_M^\sigma \mid tr(\pi)\lceil_{\alpha_A} \in \mathcal{L}(A)\}$$

where $w\lceil_\alpha$ is the projection of word w onto a subset α of its alphabet. We then define $Pr_M^{\min}(A)$ and $Pr_M^{\max}(A)$ as for LTL above.

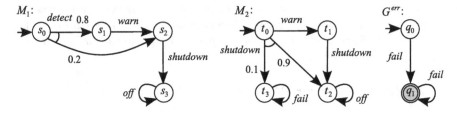

Fig. 1. Two probabilistic automata M_1, M_2 and the DFA for a safety property G

Definition 5 (Probabilistic safety properties). *A probabilistic safety property $\langle A \rangle_{\geqslant p}$ comprises a regular safety property A and a rational probability bound p. We say that a PA M satisfies the property, denoted $M \models \langle A \rangle_{\geqslant p}$, if the probability of satisfying A is at least p for any adversary:*

$$M \models \langle A \rangle_{\geqslant p} \quad \Leftrightarrow \quad \forall \sigma \in Adv_M \,.\, Pr_M^\sigma(A) \geqslant p \quad \Leftrightarrow \quad Pr_M^{\min}(A) \geqslant p.$$

Safety properties can be used to represent a wide range of useful properties of probabilistic automata. Examples include:

- "the probability of an error occurring is at most 0.01"
- "event A always occurs before event B with probability at least 0.98"
- "the probability of terminating within k time-units is at least 0.75"

The last of these represents a very useful class of properties for *timed* probabilistic systems, perhaps not typically considered as safety properties. Using the *digital clocks* approach of [13], verifying real-time probabilistic systems can often be reduced to analysis of a PA with time steps encoded as a special action type. Such requirements are then naturally encoded as safety properties.

Example 1. Figure 1 shows two PAs M_1 and M_2. Component M_1 represents a controller that powers down devices. Upon receipt of the *detect* signal, it first issues the *warn* signal followed by *shutdown*; however, with probability 0.2 it will fail to issue the *warn* signal. M_2 represents a device which, given the *shutdown* signal, powers down correctly if it first receives the *warn* signal and otherwise will only power down correctly 90% of the time. We consider a simple safety property G "action *fail* never occurs", represented by the DFA G^{err} also shown in Figure 1. Composing the two PAs in parallel and applying model checking, we have that $Pr_{M_1 \| M_2}^{\min}(G) = 0.98$. Thus, $M_1 \| M_2 \models \langle G \rangle_{\geqslant 0.98}$.

Safety Verification. Using standard automata-based techniques for model checking PAs [8], verifying correctness of probabilistic safety properties reduces to model checking the product of a PA and a DFA:

Definition 6 (PA-DFA product). *The product of a PA $M = (S, \overline{s}, \alpha_M, \delta_M, L)$ and DFA $A^{err} = (Q, \overline{q}, \alpha_A, \delta_A, F)$ with $\alpha_A \subseteq \alpha_M$ is given by the PA $M \otimes A^{err} = (S \times Q, (\overline{s}, \overline{q}), \alpha_M, \delta', L')$ where:*

- $(s, q) \xrightarrow{a} \mu \times \eta_{q'}$ *if $s \xrightarrow{a} \mu$ and $q' = \delta_A(q, a)$ if $a \in \alpha_A$ and $q' = q$ otherwise;*
- $L'(s, q) = L(s) \cup \{err_A\}$ *if $q \in F$ and $L'(s, q) = L(s)$ otherwise.*

Proposition 1. *For PA M and regular safety property A, we have:*

$$Pr_M^{\min}(A) = 1 - Pr_{M \otimes A^{err}}^{\max}(\Diamond err_A).$$

Thus, using [3], satisfaction of the probabilistic safety property $\langle A \rangle_{\geqslant p}$ can be checked in time polynomial in the size of $M \otimes A^{err}$. Note that maximum reachability probabilities, and therefore satisfaction of probabilistic safety properties, are independent of whether complete or partial adversaries are considered.

Multi-objective Model Checking. In addition to traditional probabilistic model checking techniques, the approach presented in this paper requires the use of *multi-objective* model checking [10]. The conventional approach described above allows us to check whether, for all adversaries (or, dually, for at least one adversary), the probability of some property is above (or below) a given bound. Multi-objective queries allow us to check the existence of an adversary satisfying *multiple* properties of this form. In particular, consider k predicates of the form $Pr_M^{\sigma}(\psi_i) \sim_i p_i$ where ψ_i is an LTL formula, $p_i \in [0,1]$ is a rational probability bound and $\sim_i \in \{\geqslant, >\}$. Using the techniques in [10], we can verify whether:

$$\exists \sigma \in Adv_M \cdot \wedge_{i=1}^{k} (Pr_M^{\sigma}(\psi_i) \sim_i p_i)$$

by a reduction to a linear programming (LP) problem. Like for (single-objective) LTL verification, this can be done in time polynomial in the size of M (and doubly exponential in the sizes of ψ_i). In fact, [10] also shows that this technique generalises to checking existential or universal queries over a Boolean combination of predicates for which $\sim_i \in \{\geqslant, >, \leqslant, <\}$. In all cases, if an adversary which satisfies the predicates exists, then it can also easily be obtained.

Finally, through a trivial extension of this approach (and without increasing the complexity), we can formulate *quantitative* multi-objective queries. For example, given a conjunction of the above predicates $\Psi = \wedge_{i=1}^{k} Pr_M^{\sigma}(\psi_i) \sim_i p_i$, and an additional LTL formula ψ_0, we can compute the maximum probability of ψ_0 that is achievable whilst also satisfying Ψ:

$$Pr_M^{\max}(\psi_0 \,|\, \Psi) \stackrel{\text{def}}{=} \sup\{Pr_M^{\sigma}(\psi_0) \,|\, \sigma \in Adv_M \wedge \Psi)\}.$$

3 Compositional Verification for PAs

We now describe our approach for compositional verification of probabilistic automata. We first define the basic underlying ideas and then present several different proof rules. For clarity, we present the simplest of these rules in some detail and then discuss some generalisations and extensions.

We extend the notion of *assume-guarantee* reasoning to PAs using *probabilistic assume-guarantee triples* of the form $\langle A \rangle_{\geqslant p_A} M \langle G \rangle_{\geqslant p_G}$, where $\langle A \rangle_{\geqslant p_A}$ and $\langle G \rangle_{\geqslant p_G}$ are probabilistic safety properties and M is a PA. Informally, the meaning of this is "whenever M is part of a system satisfying A with probability at least p_A, then the system will satisfy G with probability at least p_G". Formally:

Definition 7 (Assume-guarantee semantics). *If $\langle A \rangle_{\geqslant p_A}$ and $\langle G \rangle_{\geqslant p_G}$ are probabilistic safety properties, M is a PA and $\alpha_G \subseteq \alpha_A \cup \alpha_M$, then*

$$\langle A \rangle_{\geqslant p_A} M \langle G \rangle_{\geqslant p_G} \Leftrightarrow \forall \sigma \in Adv_{M[\alpha_A]} \cdot \left(Pr^\sigma_{M[\alpha_A]}(A) \geqslant p_A \rightarrow Pr^\sigma_{M[\alpha_A]}(G) \geqslant p_G \right).$$

The use of $M[\alpha_A]$, i.e. M extended to the alphabet of A, in this definition is required for the case where the property G includes actions that are not in M.

We write $\langle true \rangle M \langle G \rangle_{\geqslant p_G}$ to denote the absence of any assumption, i.e. the query $\langle true \rangle M \langle G \rangle_{\geqslant p_G}$ is equivalent to $M \models \langle G \rangle_{\geqslant p_G}$ which, as described above, is standard model checking [3]. In the general case, we check the satisfaction of a probabilistic assume-guarantee triple using multi-objective PA model checking:

Proposition 2 (Assume-guarantee model checking). *Let M be a PA, $\langle A \rangle_{\geqslant p_A}$, $\langle G \rangle_{\geqslant p_G}$ be probabilistic safety properties and $M' = M[\alpha_A] \otimes A^{err} \otimes G^{err}$. The probabilistic assume-guarantee triple $\langle A \rangle_{\geqslant p_A} M \langle G \rangle_{\geqslant p_G}$ holds if and only if:*

$$\neg \exists \sigma' \in Adv_{M'} \cdot \left(Pr^{\sigma'}_{M'}(\Box \neg err_A) \geqslant p_A \wedge Pr^{\sigma'}_{M'}(\Diamond err_G) > 1 - p_G \right)$$

which can be checked in time polynomial in $|M'|$ by solving an LP problem [10].

We now present, using the definitions above, several assume-guarantee proof rules to allow compositional verification.

An asymmetric proof rule. The first rule we consider is *asymmetric*, in the sense that we require only a single assumption about one component. Experience in the non-probabilistic setting [16] indicates that, despite its simplicity, rules of this form are widely applicable.

Theorem 1. *If M_1, M_2 are probabilistic automata and $\langle A \rangle_{\geqslant p_A}, \langle G \rangle_{\geqslant p_G}$ probabilistic safety properties such that $\alpha_A \subseteq \alpha_{M_1}$ and $\alpha_G \subseteq \alpha_{M_2} \cup \alpha_A$, then the following proof rule holds:*

$$\frac{\langle true \rangle M_1 \langle A \rangle_{\geqslant p_A}}{\langle A \rangle_{\geqslant p_A} M_2 \langle G \rangle_{\geqslant p_G}} \quad (\text{ASYM})$$
$$\overline{\langle true \rangle M_1 \| M_2 \langle G \rangle_{\geqslant p_G}}$$

Theorem 1 means that, given an appropriate assumption $\langle A \rangle_{\geqslant p_A}$, we can check the correctness of a probabilistic safety property $\langle G \rangle_{\geqslant p_G}$ on $M_1 \| M_2$, without constructing and model checking the full model. Instead, we perform one instance of (standard) model checking on M_1 (to check the first condition of rule (ASYM)) and one instance of multi-objective model checking on $M_2[\alpha_A] \otimes A^{err}$ (to check the second). If A^{err} is much smaller than M_1, we can expect significant gains in terms of the verification performance.

Example 2. We illustrate the rule (ASYM) on the PAs M_1, M_2 and property $\langle G \rangle_{\geqslant 0.98}$ from Example 1. Figure 2 (left) shows a DFA A^{err} representing the

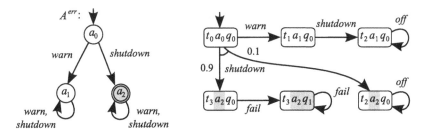

Fig. 2. DFA for safety property A and the product PA $M_2 \otimes A^{err} \otimes G^{err}$ (see Figure 1)

safety property A *"warn occurs before shutdown"*. We will use the probabilistic safety property $\langle A \rangle_{\geqslant 0.8}$ as the assumption about M_1 in (ASYM).

Checking the first condition of (ASYM) amounts to verifying $M_1 \models \langle A \rangle_{\geqslant 0.8}$, which can be done with standard probabilistic model checking. To complete the verification, we need to check the second condition $\langle A \rangle_{\geqslant 0.8} M_2 \langle G \rangle_{\geqslant 0.98}$, which, from Proposition 2, is achieved though multi-objective model checking on the product[2] $M_2 \otimes A^{err} \otimes G^{err}$. More precisely, we check there is no adversary under which the probability of remaining within states not satisfying err_A is at least 0.8 *and* the probability of reaching an err_G state is above $1 - 0.98 = 0.02$. The product is shown in Figure 2 (right), where we indicate states satisfying err_A and err_G by highlighting the accepting states a_2 and q_1 of DFAs A^{err} and G^{err}.

By inspection, we see that no such adversary exists, so we can conclude that $M_1 \| M_2 \models \langle G \rangle_{\geqslant 0.98}$. Consider, however, the adversary σ which, in the initial state, chooses *warn* with probability 0.8 and *shutdown* with probability 0.2. This satisfies $\square \neg err_A$ with probability 0.8 and $\Diamond err_G$ with probability 0.02. Hence, $\langle A \rangle_{\geqslant 0.8} M_2 \langle G \rangle_{\geqslant p_G}$ does *not* hold for any value of $p_G > 1 - 0.02 = 0.98$.

Proof of Theorem 1. We give below the proof of Theorem 1. This requires the following lemma, which is a simple extension of [20, Lemma 7.2.6, page 141].

Lemma 1. *Let* M_1, M_2 *be PAs,* $\sigma \in Adv_{M_1 \| M_2}$, $\Sigma \subseteq \alpha_{M_1 \| M_2}$ *and* $i = 1, 2$*. If* A *and* B *are regular safety properties such that* $\alpha_A \subseteq \alpha_{M_i}$ *and* $\alpha_B \subseteq \alpha_{M_i[\Sigma]}$*, then*

$$\text{(a) } Pr^{\sigma}_{M_1 \| M_2}(A) = Pr^{\sigma \restriction M_i}_{M_i}(A) \quad \text{and} \quad \text{(b) } Pr^{\sigma}_{M_1 \| M_2}(B) = Pr^{\sigma \restriction M_i[\Sigma]}_{M_i[\Sigma]}(B).$$

Note that the projections onto $M_i[\Sigma]$ in the above are well defined since the condition $\Sigma \subseteq \alpha_{M_1 \| M_2}$ implies that $M_1 \| M_2 = M_1[\Sigma] \| M_2 = M_1 \| M_2[\Sigma]$.

Proof (of Theorem 1). The proof is by contradiction. Assume that there exist PAs M_1 and M_2 and probabilistic safety properties $\langle A \rangle_{\geqslant p_A}$ and $\langle G \rangle_{\geqslant p_G}$ such that $\langle true \rangle M_1 \langle A \rangle_{\geqslant p_A}$ and $\langle A \rangle_{\geqslant p_A} M_2 \langle G \rangle_{\geqslant p_G}$ hold, while $\langle true \rangle M_1 \| M_2 \langle G \rangle_{\geqslant p_G}$ does not. From the latter, it follows that there exists an adversary $\sigma \in Adv_{M_1 \| M_2}$

---

[2] In this example, $\alpha_A = \{warn, shutdown\} \subseteq \alpha_{M_2}$ so $M_2[\alpha_A] = M_2$.

such that $Pr^\sigma_{M_1 \| M_2}(G) < p_G$. Now, since $\langle true \rangle \, M_1 \, \langle A \rangle_{\geqslant p_A}$ and $\sigma{\restriction}_{M_1} \in Adv_{M_1}$, it follows that:

$$Pr^{\sigma{\restriction}_{M_1}}_{M_1}(A) \geqslant p_A \Rightarrow Pr^\sigma_{M_1 \| M_2}(A) \geqslant p_A \qquad \text{by Lemma 1(a) since } \alpha_A \subseteq \alpha_{M_1}$$

$$\Rightarrow Pr^{\sigma{\restriction}_{M_2[\alpha_A]}}_{M_2[\alpha_A]}(A) \geqslant p_A \quad \text{by Lemma 1(b) since } \alpha_A \subseteq \alpha_{M_2[\alpha_A]}$$

$$\Rightarrow Pr^{\sigma{\restriction}_{M_2[\alpha_A]}}_{M_2[\alpha_A]}(G) \geqslant p_G \qquad \text{since } \langle A \rangle_{\geqslant p_A} \, M_2 \, \langle G \rangle_{\geqslant p_G}$$

$$\Rightarrow Pr^\sigma_{M_1 \| M_2}(G) \geqslant p_G \quad \text{by Lemma 1(b) since } \alpha_G \subseteq \alpha_{M_2[\alpha_A]}$$

which contradicts the assumption that $Pr^\sigma_{M_1 \| M_2}(G) < p_G$. $\qquad\square$

Generalising the proof rule. Next, we state two useful generalisations of the above proof rule. First, using $\langle A_1, \ldots, A_k \rangle_{\geqslant p_1, \ldots, p_k}$ to denote the conjunction of probabilistic safety properties $\langle A_i \rangle_{\geqslant p_i}$ for $i = 1, \ldots, k$, we have:

$$\frac{\begin{array}{c} \langle true \rangle \, M_1 \, \langle A_1, \ldots, A_k \rangle_{\geqslant p_1, \ldots, p_k} \\ \langle A_1, \ldots, A_k \rangle_{\geqslant p_1, \ldots, p_k} \, M_2 \, \langle G \rangle_{\geqslant p_G} \end{array}}{\langle true \rangle \, M_1 \, \| \, M_2 \, \langle G \rangle_{\geqslant p_G}} \quad (\textsc{Asym-Mult})$$

Definition 7 extends naturally to k assumptions, replacing α_A with $\cup_{i=1}^k \alpha_{A_i}$ and the single probabilistic safety property on the left-hand side of the implication with the conjunction. In similar fashion, by adapting Proposition 2, model checking of the query $\langle A_1, \ldots, A_k \rangle_{\geqslant p_1, \ldots, p_k} \, M \, \langle G \rangle_{\geqslant p_G}$ reduces to multi-objective model checking on the product $M[\cup_{i=1}^k \alpha_{A_i}] \otimes A_1^{err} \otimes \cdots \otimes A_k^{err} \otimes G^{err}$.

Secondly, we observe that, through repeated application of (\textsc{Asym}), we obtain a rule of the following form for n components:

$$\frac{\begin{array}{c} \langle true \rangle \, M_1 \, \langle A_1 \rangle_{\geqslant p_1} \\ \langle A_1 \rangle_{\geqslant p_1} \, M_2 \, \langle A_2 \rangle_{\geqslant p_2} \\ \cdots \\ \langle A_{n-1} \rangle_{\geqslant p_{n-1}} \, M_n \, \langle G \rangle_{\geqslant p_G} \end{array}}{\langle true \rangle \, M_1 \, \| \cdots \| M_n \, \langle G \rangle_{\geqslant p_G}} \quad (\textsc{Asym-N})$$

A circular proof rule. One potential limitation of the rule (\textsc{Asym}) is that we may not be able to show that the assumption A_1 about M_1 holds without making additional assumptions about M_2. This can be overcome by using the following *circular* proof rule:

Theorem 2. *If M_1, M_2 are PAs and $\langle A_1 \rangle_{\geqslant p_1}$, $\langle A_2 \rangle_{\geqslant p_2}$ and $\langle G \rangle_{\geqslant p_G}$ probabilistic safety properties such that $\alpha_{A_2} \subseteq \alpha_{M_2}$, $\alpha_{A_1} \subseteq \alpha_{M_1} \cup \alpha_{A_2}$ and $\alpha_G \subseteq \alpha_{M_2} \cup \alpha_{A_1}$, then the following circular assume-guarantee proof rule holds:*

$$\frac{\begin{array}{c} \langle true \rangle \, M_2 \, \langle A_2 \rangle_{\geqslant p_2} \\ \langle A_2 \rangle_{\geqslant p_2} \, M_1 \, \langle A_1 \rangle_{\geqslant p_1} \\ \langle A_1 \rangle_{\geqslant p_1} \, M_2 \, \langle G \rangle_{\geqslant p_G} \end{array}}{\langle true \rangle \, M_1 \, \| \, M_2 \, \langle G \rangle_{\geqslant p_G}} \quad (\textsc{Circ})$$

An asynchronous proof rule. This rule is motivated by the fact that, often, part of a system comprises several *asynchronous* components, that is, components with disjoint alphabets. In such cases, it can be difficult to establish useful probability bounds on the combined system if the fact that the components act *independently* is ignored. For example, consider the case of n independent coin flips; in isolation, we have that the probability of any coin not returning a tail is $1/2$. Now, ignoring the independence of the coins, all we can say is that the probability of any of them not returning a tail is at least $1/2$. However, using their independence, we have that this probability is at least $1-1/2^n$.

Theorem 3. *For any PAs M_1, M_2 and probabilistic safety properties $\langle A_1 \rangle_{\geqslant p_{A_2}}$, $\langle A_2 \rangle_{\geqslant p_{A_1}}$, $\langle G_1 \rangle_{\geqslant p_{G_1}}$ and $\langle G_2 \rangle_{\geqslant p_{G_2}}$ such that $\alpha_{M_1} \cap \alpha_{M_2} = \emptyset$, $\alpha_{G_1} \subseteq \alpha_{M_1} \cup \alpha_{A_1}$ and $\alpha_{G_2} \subseteq \alpha_{M_2} \cup \alpha_{A_2}$, we have the following asynchronous assume-guarantee proof rule:*

$$\frac{\begin{array}{c} \langle A_1 \rangle_{\geqslant p_{A_1}} \, M_1 \, \langle G_1 \rangle_{\geqslant p_{G_1}} \\ \langle A_2 \rangle_{\geqslant p_{A_2}} \, M_2 \, \langle G_2 \rangle_{\geqslant p_{G_2}} \end{array}}{\langle A_1, A_2 \rangle_{\geqslant p_{A_1}, p_{A_2}} \, M_1 \| M_2 \, \langle G_1 \vee G_2 \rangle_{\geqslant p_{G_1} + p_{G_2} - p_{G_1} \cdot p_{G_2}}} \qquad (\text{ASYNC})$$

where the disjunction of safety properties G_1 and G_2 is obtained by taking the intersection of the DFAs G_1^{err} and G_2^{err}.

4   Quantitative Assume-Guarantee Queries

Practical experience with probabilistic verification suggests that it is often more useful to adopt a *quantitative* approach. For example, rather than checking the correctness of a probabilistic safety property $\langle G \rangle_{\geqslant p_G}$, it may be preferable to just compute the actual worst-case (minimum) probability $Pr_M^{\min}(G)$ that G is satisfied. In this section we consider how to formulate such quantitative queries in the context of assume-guarantee reasoning. For simplicity, we restrict our attention here to the rule (ASYM) for fixed PAs M_1 and M_2, and property G. Similar reasoning applies to the other rules presented above.

Maximal lower bounds. Rule (ASYM) allows us to establish *lower bounds* for the probability $Pr_{M_1 \| M_2}^{\min}(G)$, i.e. it can be used to prove, for certain values of p_G, that $Pr_{M_1 \| M_2}^{\min}(G) \geqslant p_G$. We consider now how to obtain the highest such lower bound, say $p_G^\star$. First, we note that, from Definition 7, it is clear that the highest value of p_G for which $\langle A \rangle_{\geqslant p_A} \, M_2 \, \langle G \rangle_{\geqslant p_G}$ holds will be obtained by using the maximum possible value of p_A. For rule (ASYM) to be applicable, this is equal to $Pr_{M_1}^{\min}(A)$, since for any higher value of p_A the first condition will fail to hold. Now, by Proposition 2, and letting $M' = M_2[\alpha_A] \otimes A^{err} \otimes G^{err}$, the value $p_G^\star$ can be obtained through multi-objective model checking as follows:

$$p_G^\star = 1 - Pr_{M'}^{\max}(\lozenge \, err_G \mid \Psi) \text{ where } \Psi = Pr_{M'}^{\sigma}(\square \neg err_A) \geqslant p_A.$$

Parameterised queries. Let us assume that component M_1 is parameterised by a variable x in such a way that varying x changes the probability of M_1 satisfying the assumption A. For example, increasing the value of x might increase the probability $Pr_{M_1}(A)$, but simultaneously worsen some other performance measure or cost associated with M_1. In this situation, it is desirable to establish a trade-off between the probability of $M_1 \| M_2$ satisfying G and the secondary 'cost' of M_1. Our use of multi-objective model checking for compositional verification offers two choices here. Firstly, we can pick a suitable threshold for $Pr_{M_1 \| M_2}(G)$ and then compute the lowest value of $Pr_{M_1}(A)$ which guarantees this, allowing an appropriate value of x to be chosen. Alternatively, we can consider the so-called *Pareto curve*: the set of achievable combinations of $Pr_{M_1 \| M_2}(G)$ and $Pr_{M_1}(A)$, which will present a clear view of the trade-off. For the latter, we can use the techniques of [10] for approximate exploration of the Pareto curve.

Upper bounds. Since application of (ASYM) gives lower bounds on $Pr_{M_1 \| M_2}^{\min}$ (G), it is desirable to also generate *upper* bounds on this probability. This can be done as follows. When checking condition 2 of (ASYM), using multi-objective model checking, we also obtain an adversary $\sigma \in Adv_{M_2[\alpha_A] \otimes A^{err}}$ that satisfies $\langle A \rangle_{\geqslant p_A}$ and gives the minimum (i.e. worst-case) probability of satisfying G. This can then be projected onto M_2, giving an adversary σ_2 which achieves the worst-case behaviour of the single component M_2 with respect to G satisfying $\langle A \rangle_{\geqslant p_A}$. Furthermore, from σ_2, we can easily construct a PA $M_2^{\sigma_2}$ that represents the behaviour of M_2 under σ_2.

Finally, we compute the probability of satisfying G on $M_1 \| M_2^{\sigma_2}$. Because $M_2^{\sigma_2}$ is likely to be much smaller than M_2, there is scope for this to be efficient, even if model checking $M_1 \| M_2$ in full is not feasible. Since $M_1 \| M_2^{\sigma_2}$ represents only a subset of the behaviour of $M_1 \| M_2$, the probability computed is guaranteed to give an upper bound on $Pr_{M_1 \| M_2}^{\min}(G)$. We use σ_2 (which achieves the worst-case behaviour with respect to G), rather than an arbitrary adversary of M_2, in order to obtain a tighter upper bound.

5 Implementation and Case Studies

We have implemented our compositional verification approach in a prototype tool. Recall that, using the rules given in Section 3, verification requires both standard (automata-based) model checking and multi-objective model checking. Our tool is based on the probabilistic model checker PRISM [11], which already supports LTL model checking of probabilistic automata. Model checking of probabilistic safety properties, represented by DFAs, can be achieved with existing versions of PRISM, since DFAs can easily be encoded in PRISM's modelling language. For multi-objective model checking, we have extended PRISM with an implementation of the techniques in [10]. This requires the solution of Linear Programming (LP) problems, for which we use the ECLiPSe Constraint Logic Programming system with the COIN-OR CBC solver, implementing a branch-and-cut algorithm. All experiments were run on a 2GHz PC with 2GB RAM. Any run exceeding a time-limit of 24 hours was disregarded.

We demonstrate the application of our tool to two large case studies. The first is the randomised consensus algorithm of Aspnes & Herlihy [2]. The algorithm allows N processes in a distributed network to reach a consensus and employs, in each round, a shared coin protocol parameterised by K. The PA model is based on [14] and consists of an automaton for each process and for the shared coin protocol of each round. We analyse the minimum probability that the processes decide by round R. The compositional verification employs $R-2$ uses of the ASYNC rule to return a probabilistic safety property satisfied by the (asynchronous) composition of the shared coin protocols for the first $R-2$ rounds. This is then used as the assumption of an ASYM rule for the subsystem representing the processes.

The second case study is the Zeroconf network configuration protocol [5]. We use the PA model from [13] consisting of two components, one representing a new host joining the network (parameterised by K, the number of probes it sends before using an IP address), and the second representing the environment, i.e. the existing network. We consider two properties: the minimum probability that a host employs a fresh IP address and that a host is configured by time T. In each case the compositional verification uses one application of the CIRC rule.

Table 1 shows experimental results for these case studies. We present the total time required for both compositional verification, as described in this paper, and

Table 1. Experimental results, comparing with non-compositional verification

Case study [parameters]		Non-compositional			Compositional		
		States	Time (s)	Result[†]	LP size	Time (s)	Result[†]
consensus (2 processes) [R K]	3 2	5,158	1.6	0.108333	1,064	**0.9**	0.108333
	3 20	40,294	108.1	0.012500	1,064	**7.4**	0.012500
	4 2	20,886	3.6	0.011736	2,372	**1.2**	0.011736
	4 20	166,614	343.1	0.000156	2,372	**7.8**	0.000156
	5 2	83,798	7.7	0.001271	4,988	**2.2**	0.001271
	5 20	671,894	1,347	0.000002	4,988	**8.8**	0.000002
consensus (3 processes) [R K]	3 2	1,418,545	18,971	0.229092	40,542	**29.6**	0.229092
	3 12	16,674,145*	time-out	-	40,542	**49.7**	0.041643
	3 20	39,827,233*	time-out	-	40,542	**125.3**	0.024960
	4 2	150,487,585	78,955	0.052483	141,168	**376.1**	0.052483
	4 12	1,053,762,385*	mem-out	-	141,168	**396.3**	0.001734
	4 20	2,028,200,209*	mem-out	-	141,168	**471.9**	0.000623
zeroconf [K]	2	91,041	39.0	2.0e-5	6,910	**9.3**	3.1e-4
	4	313,541	103.9	7.3e-7	20,927	**21.9**	3.1e-4
	6	811,290	275.2	2.6e-8	40,258	**54.8**	2.5e-4
	8	1,892,952	592.2	9.5e-10	66,436	**107.6**	9.0e-6
zeroconf (time bounded) [K T]	2 10	665,567	**46.3**	5.9e-5	62,188	89.0	2.1e-4
	2 14	106,177	**63.1**	2.0e-8	101,313	170.8	8.1e-8
	4 10	976,247	**88.2**	3.3e+0	74,484	170.8	3.3e+0
	4 14	2,288,771	**128.3**	7.0e-5	166,203	430.6	3.1e-4

* These models can be constructed, but not model checked, in PRISM.

[†] Results are maximum probabilities of error so actual values are these subtracted from 1.

non-compositional verification using PRISM (with the fastest available engine). Note that, in each case, we use the quantitative approach described in Section 4 and give actual (bounds on) probabilities computed. To give an indication of the size of the models considered, we give the number of states for the full (non-compositional) models and the number of variables in the LP problems used for multi-objective model checking in the compositional case.

In summary, we see that the compositional approach is faster in the majority of cases. Furthermore, it allows verification of several models for which it is infeasible with conventional techniques. For the cases where compositional verification is slower, this is due to the cost of solving a large LP problem, which is known to be more expensive than the highly optimised techniques used in PRISM. Furthermore, LP solution represents the limiting factor with respect to the scalability of the compositional approach. We expect that improvements to our technique can be made that will reduce LP problem sizes and improve performance. Finally, we note that the numerical values produced using compositional verification are generally good; in fact, for the consensus case study, the bounds obtained are precise.

6   Conclusions

We have presented a compositional verification technique, based on assume-guarantee rules, for probabilistic automata. Properties of these models are represented as probabilistic safety properties, and we show how verifying the resulting assume-guarantee queries reduces to the problem of multi-objective model checking. We also show how this can be leveraged to provide a *quantitative* approach to compositional verification. In contrast to existing work in this area, our techniques can be implemented efficiently and we demonstrate successful results on several large case studies.

There are several interesting directions for future work. In particular, we plan to experiment with the use of learning techniques to automatically produce the assumptions required for compositional reasoning. We also intend to further develop our compositional proof rules and investigate to what extent they are complete. Finally, we plan to expand the range of properties that can be verified, including for example reward-based specifications.

Acknowledgments. The authors are supported in part by EPSRC grants EP/D07956X and EP/D076625 and European Commission FP 7 project CONNECT (IST Project Number 231167). We also gratefully acknowledge several useful discussions with Kousha Etessami.

References

1. de Alfaro, L., Henzinger, T., Jhala, R.: Compositional methods for probabilistic systems. In: Larsen, K.G., Nielsen, M. (eds.) CONCUR 2001. LNCS, vol. 2154, pp. 351–365. Springer, Heidelberg (2001)
2. Aspnes, J., Herlihy, M.: Fast randomized consensus using shared memory. Journal of Algorithms 15(1) (1990)

3. Bianco, A., de Alfaro, L.: Model checking of probabilistic and nondeterministic systems. In: Thiagarajan, P.S. (ed.) FSTTCS 1995. LNCS, vol. 1026. Springer, Heidelberg (1995)
4. Chatterjee, K., de Alfaro, L., Faella, M., Henzinger, T., Majumdar, R., Stoelinga, M.: Compositional quantitative reasoning. In: Proc. QEST 2006 (2006)
5. Cheshire, S., Adoba, B., Gutterman, E.: Dynamic configuration of IPv4 link local addresses, http://www.ietf.org/rfc/rfc3927.txt
6. Cheung, L., Lynch, N., Segala, R., Vaandrager, F.: Switched probabilistic I/O automata. In: Liu, Z., Araki, K. (eds.) ICTAC 2004. LNCS, vol. 3407, pp. 494–510. Springer, Heidelberg (2005)
7. Ciesinski, F., Baier, C.: Liquor: A tool for qualitative and quantitative linear time analysis of reactive systems. In: Proc. QEST 2006 (2006)
8. Courcoubetis, C., Yannakakis, M.: Markov decision processes and regular events. In: Paterson, M. (ed.) ICALP 1990. LNCS, vol. 443. Springer, Heidelberg (1990)
9. Delahaye, B., Caillaud, B.: A model for probabilistic reasoning on assume/guarantee contracts. Tech. Rep. 6719, INRIA (2008)
10. Etessami, K., Kwiatkowska, M., Vardi, M.Y., Yannakakis, M.: Multi-objective Model Checking of Markov Decision Processes. In: Grumberg, O., Huth, M. (eds.) TACAS 2007. LNCS, vol. 4424, pp. 50–65. Springer, Heidelberg (2007)
11. Hinton, A., Kwiatkowska, M., Norman, G., Parker, D.: PRISM: A tool for automatic verification of probabilistic systems. In: Hermanns, H., Palsberg, J. (eds.) TACAS 2006. LNCS, vol. 3920, pp. 441–444. Springer, Heidelberg (2006)
12. Kwiatkowska, M., Norman, G., Parker, D., Qu, H.: Assume-guarantee verification for probabilistic systems. Tech. Rep. RR-09-17, Oxford University Computing Laboratory (December 2009)
13. Kwiatkowska, M., Norman, G., Parker, D., Sproston, J.: Performance analysis of probabilistic timed automata using digital clocks. Formal Methods in System Design 29 (2006)
14. Kwiatkowska, M., Norman, G., Segala, R.: Automated verification of a randomized distributed consensus protocol using Cadence SMV and PRISM. In: Berry, G., Comon, H., Finkel, A. (eds.) CAV 2001. LNCS, vol. 2102, pp. 194–206. Springer, Heidelberg (2001)
15. Lynch, N., Segala, R., Vaandrager, F.: Observing branching structure through probabilistic contexts. SIAM Journal on Computing 37(4), 977–1013 (2007)
16. Pasareanu, C., Giannakopoulou, D., Bobaru, M., Cobleigh, J., Barringer, H.: Learning to divide and conquer: Applying the L* algorithm to automate assume-guarantee reasoning. Formal Methods in System Design 32(3) (2008)
17. Pavese, E., Braberman, V., Uchitel, S.: Probabilistic environments in the quantitative analysis of (non-probabilistic) behaviour models. In: Proc. ESEC/FSE 2009 (2009)
18. Pogosyants, A., Segala, R., Lynch, N.: Verification of the randomized consensus algorithm of Aspnes and Herlihy: A case study. Dist. Comp. 13(4) (2000)
19. Segala, R.: A compositional trace-based semantics for probabilistic automata. In: Lee, I., Smolka, S.A. (eds.) CONCUR 1995. LNCS, vol. 962, pp. 234–248. Springer, Heidelberg (1995)
20. Segala, R.: Modelling and Verification of Randomized Distributed Real Time Systems. Ph.D. thesis, Massachusetts Institute of Technology (1995)
21. Segala, R., Lynch, N.: Probabilistic simulations for probabilistic processes. Nordic Journal of Computing 2(2) (1995)

Simple $O(m \log n)$ Time Markov Chain Lumping

Antti Valmari[1] and Giuliana Franceschinis[2]

[1] Tampere University of Technology, Department of Software Systems
P.O. Box 553, FI-33101 Tampere, Finland
`Antti.Valmari@tut.fi`
[2] Dip. di Informatica, Univ. del Piemonte Orientale
viale Teresa Michel 11, 15121 Alessandria, Italy
`Giuliana.Franceschinis@mfn.unipmn.it`

Abstract. In 2003, Derisavi, Hermanns, and Sanders presented a complicated $O(m \log n)$ time algorithm for the Markov chain lumping problem, where n is the number of states and m the number of transitions in the Markov chain. They speculated on the possibility of a simple algorithm and wrote that it would probably need a new way of sorting weights. In this article we present an algorithm of that kind. In it, the weights are sorted with a combination of the so-called possible majority candidate algorithm with any $O(k \log k)$ sorting algorithm. This works because, as we prove in the article, the weights consist of two groups, one of which is sufficiently small and all weights in the other group have the same value. We also point out an essential problem in the description of the earlier algorithm, prove the correctness of our algorithm in detail, and report some running time measurements.

1 Introduction

Markov chains are widely used to analyze the behaviour of dynamic systems and to evaluate their performance or dependability indices. One of the problems that limit the applicability of Markov chains to realistic systems is state space explosion. Among the methods that can be used to keep this problem under control, *lumping* consists of aggregating states of the Markov chain into "macrostates", hence obtaining a smaller Markov chain while preserving the ability to check desired properties on it.

We refer to [4,8] for different lumpability concepts and their use in the analysis of systems. For the purpose of this article it suffices that in the heart of their use is the problem of constructing the coarsest lumping quotient of a Markov chain. We define this problem formally in Section 2, and call it "the lumping problem" for brevity.

Let n denote the number of states and m the number of transitions in the Markov chain. An $O(n + m \log n)$ time algorithm for the lumping problem was given in [6,5]. It is (loosely) based on the Paige–Tarjan relational coarsest partition algorithm [10] of similar complexity. Unless the input is pathological with many isolated states, we have $n = O(m)$ implying $O(n + m \log n) = O(m \log n)$. Therefore, it is common practice to call these algorithms $O(m \log n)$.

J. Esparza and R. Majumdar (Eds.): TACAS 2010, LNCS 6015, pp. 38–52, 2010.
© Springer-Verlag Berlin Heidelberg 2010

The Paige–Tarjan algorithm starts with an initial partition of the set of states and refines it until a certain condition is met. Sets of the partition are traditionally called *blocks*. A basic operation in the Paige–Tarjan algorithm is the splitting of a block to at most three subblocks. We call one of the subblocks the *middle group*, and another one the *left block*. Their precise definitions will be presented in Section 6.

When applying the Paige–Tarjan algorithm to the lumping problem, the block splitting operation has to be modified. The middle group may have to be split further to one or more *middle blocks*. On the other hand, the rather complicated mechanism used by the Paige–Tarjan algorithm for separating the left block from the middle group is not needed any more, because the refined splitting operation can do that, too.

The authors of [6] first discussed a general balanced binary tree approach to implementing the refined splitting operation. They proved that it yields $O(m \log^2 n)$ time complexity to the algorithm as a whole. Then they proved $O(m \log n)$ time complexity for the special case where the trees are splay trees.

The authors of [6] speculated whether $O(m \log n)$ time complexity could be obtained with a simpler solution than splay trees. In this article we show that this is the case. Instead of always processing the left block and middle group together with a binary search tree, our algorithm processes them separately when necessary. Separation is obtained with the so-called possible majority candidate algorithm. The left block need not be split further. The splitting of the middle group is based on sorting it with just any $O(k \log k)$ time algorithm, where k is the number of items to be sorted. To show that this yields the desired complexity, we take advantage of a special property of middle blocks that sets an upper bound to the number of times each state can be in a middle block. The left block lacks this property. Our algorithm sometimes separates some middle block instead of the left block, but when this happens, the left block is so small that it does not matter.

The articles [6,5] do not show a correctness proof of their algorithm. Indeed, the description and pseudocode in them ignore an essential issue. This makes direct implementations produce wrong results every now and then, as we show in Section 4 with an example. The splitting operation uses one block, called *splitter*, as input. If block B has been used as a splitter and is then itself split to $B_1, B_2, \ldots, B_k$, then it suffices that all but one of them are used as splitters later on. The good performance arises from not using a biggest one among the B_i in the future. However, if B has not been used as a splitter, then every B_i must be used in the future. The articles [6,5] fail to say that. Because of this, we felt it appropriate to discuss the correctness issue in great detail in this article.

In Section 2 we describe the lumping problem rigorously. Section 3 introduces the less well known old algorithms and data structures that our new algorithm uses. Our new algorithm is presented in Section 4 and proven correct in Section 5. That it runs in $O(n + m \log n)$ (or $O(m \log n)$) time is shown in Section 6. Section 7 presents some measurements made with a test implementation, and Section 8 presents our conclusions.

2   The Lumping Problem

The input of the lumping problem consists of a weighted directed graph (S, Δ, W) together with an initial partition $\mathcal{I}$. In the definition, $\Delta \subseteq S \times S$, and W is a function from Δ to real numbers. The elements of S, Δ, and W are called *states*, *transitions*, and *weights*, respectively. We let n denote the number of states and m the number of transitions. For convenience, we extend W to $S \times S$ by letting $W(s, s') = 0$ whenever $(s, s') \notin \Delta$. We also extend W to the situation where the second argument is a subset of S by $W(s, B) = \sum_{s' \in B} W(s, s')$. By $s \to s'$ we mean that $(s, s') \in \Delta$. If $B \subseteq S$, then $s \to B$ denotes that there is some $s' \in B$ such that $s \to s'$.

In many applications, the values $W(s, s')$ are non-negative. We do not make that assumption, however, because there are also applications where $W(s, s)$ is deliberately chosen as $-W(s, S \setminus \{s\})$, making it usually negative. It is also common that $W(s, S)$ is the same for every $s \in S$, but we do not make that assumption either.

A *partition* of a set A is a collection $\{A_1, A_2, \ldots, A_k\}$ of pairwise disjoint nonempty sets such that their union is A. The initial partition $\mathcal{I}$ is a partition of S. The elements of a partition of S are traditionally called *blocks*. A partition $\mathcal{B}'$ is a *refinement* of a partition $\mathcal{B}$ if and only if each element of $\mathcal{B}'$ is a subset of some element in $\mathcal{B}$.

A partition $\mathcal{B}$ of S is *compatible* with W if and only if for every $B \in \mathcal{B}$, $B' \in \mathcal{B}$, $s_1 \in B$, and $s_2 \in B$ we have $W(s_1, B') = W(s_2, B')$. Let *croip* be an abbreviation for "compatible refinement of initial partition", that is, a partition of S that is a refinement of $\mathcal{I}$ and compatible with W. The objective of the lumping problem is to find the coarsest possible croip, that is, the croip whose blocks are as big as possible. Our new algorithm solves it.

Sometimes a variant problem is of interest where compatibility is defined in a different way. In it, compatibility holds if and only if for every $B \in \mathcal{B}$, $B' \in \mathcal{B} \setminus \{B\}$, $s_1 \in B$, and $s_2 \in B$ we have $W(s_1, B') = W(s_2, B')$. The variant problem can be solved by, for each state s, replacing $W(s, s)$ by $-W(s, S \setminus \{s\})$, and then using the algorithm for the lumping problem [5]. This is an instance of a more general fact, given by the next proposition.

Proposition 1. *For every $I \in \mathcal{I}$, let w_I be an arbitrary real number and $U_I = I \cup \bigcup \mathcal{I}_I$, where $\mathcal{I}_I$ is an arbitrary subset of $\mathcal{I}$. Let W' be defined by*

$$W'(s, s') := W(s, s') \text{ when } s' \neq s, \text{ and}$$
$$W'(s, s) := w_I - W(s, U_I \setminus \{s\}), \text{ where } I \text{ is the } I \in \mathcal{I} \text{ that contains } s.$$

Then the coarsest lumping-croip with W' is the coarsest variant-croip with W.

Proof. The value of $W(s, B)$ has no role in the definition of variant-compatibility whenever $s \in B$. This implies that the value of $W(s, s)$ has never any role. So W and W' yield the same variant-croips. The claim follows, if we now show that with W', every lumping-croip is a variant-croip and vice versa.

It is immediate from the definitions that every lumping-croip is a variant-croip. To prove the opposite direction with W', let $\mathcal{B}$ be a variant-croip, $B \in \mathcal{B}$,

$s_1 \in B$, and $s_2 \in B$. We have to prove that $W'(s_1, B') = W'(s_2, B')$ for every $B' \in \mathcal{B}$. This is immediate when $B' \neq B$ by the definition of variant-croips. We prove next that $W'(s_1, B) = W'(s_2, B)$, completing the proof.

Let I be the initial block that contains s_1, and let B_1, B_2, ..., B_k be the blocks to which the blocks in $\{I\} \cup \mathcal{I}_I$ have been split in $\mathcal{B}$. Clearly $s_2 \in I$, B is one of the B_i, $B_1 \cup \cdots \cup B_k = U_I$, and $\sum_{i=1}^{k} W'(s, B_i) = W'(s, U_I) = w_I$ when $s \in I$. Without loss of generality we may index the B_i so that $B = B_1$. Then $W'(s_1, B) = w_I - \sum_{i=2}^{k} W'(s_1, B_i) = w_I - \sum_{i=2}^{k} W'(s_2, B_i) = W'(s_2, B)$, because $W'(s_1, B') = W'(s_2, B')$ when $B' \neq B$. □

3 Background Data Structures and Algorithms

In this section we introduce those algorithms and data structures that are needed in the rest of the article, not new, but not presented in typical algorithm textbooks either.

Refinable Partition. Our lumping algorithm needs a data structure for maintaining the blocks. We present two suitable data structures that provide the following services.

They make it possible in constant time to find the size of a block, find the block that a given state belongs to, mark a state for subsequent splitting of a block, and tell whether a block contains marked states. They also facilitate scanning the states of a block in constant time per scanned element, assuming that states are not marked while scanning. Finally, there is a block splitting operation that runs in time proportional to the number of marked states in the block. It makes one subblock of the marked states and another of the remaining states, provided that both subblocks will be nonempty. If either subblock will be empty, it does not split the block. In both cases, it unmarks the marked states of the block. It is important to the efficiency of the lumping algorithm that the running time of splitting is only proportional to the number of marked, and not all, states in the block.

A traditional refinable partition data structure represents each block with two doubly linked lists: one for the marked states and another for the remaining states [1, Sect. 4.13]. The record for the block contains links to the lists, together with an integer that stores the size of the block. It is needed, because the size must be found fast. The record for a state contains a link to the block that the state belongs to, and forward and backward links.

Marking of an unmarked state consists of unlinking it from its current list and adding it to the list of the marked states of its block. In the splitting, the new block is made of the marked states, and unmarked states stay in the old block. This is because all states of the new block must be scanned, to update the link to the block that the state belongs to. The promised running time does not necessarily suffice for scanning the unmarked states. (For simplicity, we ignore the other alternative where the smaller subblock is made the new block.)

A more recent refinable partition data structure was inspired by [9] and presented in [12]. In it, states and blocks are represented by numbers. All states

```
count := 0
for i := 1 to k do
    if count = 0 then
        pmc := A[i] ;  count := 1
    else if A[i] = pmc then
        count := count + 1
    else
        count := count − 1
```

Fig. 1. Finding a possible majority candidate

(that is, their numbers) are in an array *elems* so that states that belong to the same block are next to each other. The segment for a block is further divided to a first part that contains the marked states and second part that contains the rest. There is another array that, given the number of a state, returns its location in *elems*. A third array denotes the block that each state belongs to.

Three arrays are indexed by block numbers. They tell where the segment for the block in *elems* starts and ends, and where is the borderline between the marked and other states. An unmarked state is marked by swapping it with the first unmarked state of the same block, and moving the borderline one step.

Possible Majority Candidate. A possible majority candidate *pmc* of an array $A[1 \ldots k]$ is any value that has the following properties. If some value occupies more than half of the positions of A, then *pmc* is that value. Otherwise *pmc* is just any value that occurs in A.

The algorithm in Figure 1 finds a possible majority candidate in linear time [3, Sect. 4.3.3]. To see that it works, let $f(x) = count$ when $pmc = x$ and $f(x) = -count$ when $pmc \neq x$. When $A[i] = x$, then $f(x)$ increases by one independently of the value of *pmc*, and when $A[i] \neq x$, then $f(x)$ increases or decreases by one. If x occurs in more than half of the positions, then $f(x)$ increases more times than decreases, implying that at the end of the algorithm $f(x) > 0$. This guarantees that $pmc = x$, because otherwise *count* would have to be negative, and the tests in the code prevent it from becoming negative.

4   The Lumping Algorithm

Our new lumping algorithm is shown in Figure 2. The grey commands on lines 1 and 3 are not part of it. They are added because of the needs of the proofs of the correctness and performance of the algorithm. They will be discussed in Sections 5 and 6. We will prove that their presence or absence does not affect the output of the algorithm.

The input to the algorithm consists of S, Δ, W, and $\mathcal{I}$. We assume that Δ is available as the possibility to scan the input transitions of each state in constant time per scanned transition, and define $\bullet s' = \{s \mid s \to s'\}$.

The algorithm maintains a refinable partition of states. The initial value of the partition is $\mathcal{I}$. Each block has an identity (number or address) with which it

```
1   U_B := I ;  B_T := ∅ ;  w[s] := unused for every s ∈ S :  C := {S ∪ {s_⊥}}
2   while U_B ≠ ∅ do
3       let B' be any block in U_B ;  U_B := U_B \ {B'} :  C := C \ {C_{B'}} ∪ {B'. C_{B'} \ B'}
4       S_T := ∅
5       for s' ∈ B' do for s ∈ •s' do
6           if w[s] = unused then S_T := S_T ∪ {s} ;  w[s] := W(s, s')
7           else w[s] := w[s] + W(s, s')
8       for s ∈ S_T do if w[s] ≠ 0 then
9           B := the block that contains s
10          if B contains no marked states then B_T := B_T ∪ {B}
11          mark s in B
12      while B_T ≠ ∅ do
13          let B be any block in B_T ;  B_T := B_T \ {B}
14          B_1 := marked states in B ;  B := remaining states in B
15          if B = ∅ then give the identity of B to B_1 else make B_1 a new block
16          pmc := possible majority candidate of the w[s] for s ∈ B_1
17          B_2 := {s ∈ B_1 | w[s] ≠ pmc} ;  B_1 := B_1 \ B_2
18          if B_2 = ∅ then ℓ := 1 else
19              sort and partition B_2 according to w[s], yielding B_2, ..., B_ℓ
20              make each of B_2, ..., B_ℓ a new block
21          if B ∈ U_B then add B_1, ..., B_ℓ except B to U_B
22          else add [B,]^? B_1, ..., B_ℓ except a largest to U_B
23      for s ∈ S_T do w[s] := unused
```

Fig. 2. The coarsest lumping algorithm

can be found via an index or pointer. We saw in Section 3 that when a block is split, the splitting operation decides which subblock inherits the identity of the original block.

The array w has one slot for each $s \in S$. It stores numbers. One value that could not otherwise occur is reserved for a special purpose and denoted with "unused" in the pseudocode. In our implementation, unused = DBL_MAX, that is, the maximal double precision floating point value of the computer.

The algorithm maintains a set U_B of "unprocessed" blocks, that is, blocks that have to be used later for splitting. Similarly, S_T maintains a set of "touched" states and B_T a set of "touched" blocks that will be processed later. The algorithm has been designed so that only very simple operations are needed on them. In particular, when something is being added, it is certain that it is not already there. It is thus easy to implement these sets efficiently as stacks or other data structures. The sets contain indices of or pointers to blocks and states, not copies of the block and state data structures. Therefore, when a block that is in U_B is split, the subblock that inherits its identity also inherits the presence in U_B.

Initially U_B contains all blocks. The body of the main loop of the algorithm (lines 3 to 23) takes and removes an arbitrary block B' from U_B and splits all blocks using it. The splitting operation may add new blocks to U_B. This is repeated until U_B becomes empty. A block that is used in the role of B' is called a *splitter*.

Let $\bullet B'$ denote the set of states which have transitions to B', that is, $\bullet B' = \{s \mid \exists s' \in B' : s \to s'\}$. Lines 4 to 7 find those states, collect them into S_T, and compute $W(s, B')$ for them. Each $W(s, B')$ is stored in $w[s]$. The if test ensures that each state is added to S_T only once. The used $w[s]$ are reset back to "unused" on line 23. This is a tiny bit more efficient than resetting the $w[s]$ before use via $\bullet s'$, as was done in [6].

Lines 8 to 11 mark those states in $\bullet B'$ that have $W(s, B') \neq 0$, and collect into B_T the blocks that contain such states. We saw in Section 3 that the marking operation moves the state to a new place in the refinable partition data structure (to another linked list or to another part of an array). As a consequence, the marking operation interferes with the scanning of states. It would confuse the scanning of B' on line 5, if it were done in that loop. This is the main reason for the seemingly clumsy operation of collecting $\bullet B'$ into S_T and scanning it anew from there. Another reason is that it makes it easy to get rid of states that have $W(s, B') = 0$.

Lines 12 to 22 scan each block that has at least one s such that $W(s, B') \neq 0$, and split it so that the resulting subblocks are compatible with B'. Lines 14 and 15 are the same as the splitting operation in Section 3. They split B to those states that have and those that do not have $W(s, B') \neq 0$. The former are stored in B_1 and the latter remain in B. The latter include those that do not have transitions to B'. If B would become empty, then B_1 will not be a new block but inherits the identity (number or address) of B. It must be kept in mind in the sequel that B_1 may be different from B or the same block as B.

Line 16 finds a possible majority candidate among the $w[s]$ of the states in B_1. Lines 17 to 20 split B_1 to $B_1, B_2, \ldots, B_\ell$ so that s_1 and s_2 are in the same B_i if and only if $W(s_1, B') = W(s_2, B')$. After the sorting on line 19, the s with the same $W(s, B')$ are next to each other and can easily be converted to a new block. The sorting operation is new compared to Section 3. However, it is well known how a doubly linked list or an array segment can be sorted in $O(k \log k)$ time, where k is the number of elements to be sorted.

The subblock whose $W(s, B')$ is the possible majority candidate is processed separately because of efficiency reasons. As was mentioned above, the sorting operation costs $O(k \log k)$. As was pointed out in [6], paying $O(k \log k)$ where $k = |B_1 \cup \cdots \cup B_\ell|$ would invalidate the proof of the $O(n + m \log n)$ performance of the algorithm as a whole. The solution of [6] to this problem was to split B_1 to $B_1, \ldots, B_\ell$ with the aid of splay trees. However, we will prove in Section 6 that $O(k \log k)$ is not too costly, if those states whose $W(s, B')$ is the possible majority candidate are not present in the sorting.

The set of blocks that will have to be used as splitters in the future is updated on lines 21 and 22. There are two cases. If B is in U_B, then all subblocks of the original B must be in U_B after the operation. Because B is already there, it suffices to put the B_i into U_B. However, B_1 may have inherited the identity of B on line 15 and must not be put into U_B for a second time.

If $B \notin U_B$, then it suffices that all but one of the subblocks is put into U_B. The good performance of the algorithm relies on putting only such subblocks into U_B

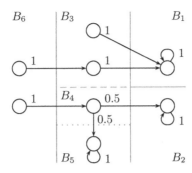

Fig. 3. A counter-example to never putting all subblocks into $\mathsf{U_B}$

whose sizes are at most half of the size of the original B. This is implemented by finding the largest, or one of the largest if there are many of maximal size, and not putting that subblock into $\mathsf{U_B}$. This works, because there can be at most one subblock whose size is more than half of the original size. The notation $[B,]^?$ reminds that if B and B_1 refer to the same block, then only one of them should be considered.

Testing whether $B \in \mathsf{U_B}$ can be made fast, if each block has a bit that is set when the block is put into $\mathsf{U_B}$ and reset when the block is removed from $\mathsf{U_B}$.

The articles [6,5] do not discuss the distinction represented by lines 21 and 22. They seem to always work according to line 22, even if $B \in \mathsf{U_B}$. The example in Figure 3 demonstrates that this is incorrect. The initial partition is $\{B_1, B_2, B_3 \cup B_4 \cup B_5, B_6\}$. If B_1 is used as the first splitter, it splits $B_3 \cup B_4 \cup B_5$ to B_3 and $B_4 \cup B_5$. Assume that B_3 is not and $B_4 \cup B_5$ is put into $\mathsf{U_B}$. If B_2 is used as the next splitter, it splits $B_4 \cup B_5$ to B_4 and B_5. It may be that then B_5 is put into $\mathsf{U_B}$ and B_4 is not. At this stage, B_3 and B_4 are not in $\mathsf{U_B}$, and none of the other blocks induces any splitting. Thus B_6 is never split, although it should be. This problem makes implementations based directly on [6,5] yield wrong results.

5   Correctness

In this section we prove the correctness of the algorithm presented in the previous section. In the proof, we will keep track of some information on blocks that have been used as splitters and then have been split themselves. For this purpose we introduce *compound blocks*. A compound block is always a union of ordinary blocks. The idea is that always on line 2, the splitting that any compound block C_1 would cause has already been done, either by having used C_1 as a splitter, or by having used $C, C_2, \ldots, C_k$ as splitters, where $C = C_1 \cup \cdots \cup C_k$ and the C_i are pairwise disjoint. This will be made precise later.

The grey statements in Figure 2 maintain the compound blocks. The compound blocks constitute a partition $\mathcal{C}$ of $S \cup \{s_\perp\}$, where $s_\perp$ will be explained soon. Initially $\mathcal{C}$ consists of one compound block that contains all states, including $s_\perp$. On line 3, the compound block $C_{B'}$ that covers the ordinary block B' is split to two compound blocks B' and $C_{B'} \setminus B'$. (The invariant after the proof of Lemma 2 will imply that $C_{B'} \setminus B' \neq \emptyset$.)

The purpose of $s_\perp$ is to make it easier to formulate two invariants that will be used in the last part of the correctness proof. Without $s_\perp$, the last part would be very difficult to follow. The easy formulation needs initially such a compound block C_i that $S \subseteq C_i$ and $W(s, C_i)$ is the same for every $s \in C_i$. Unfortunately, $W(s, S)$ is not necessarily the same for every $s \in S$. Fortunately, we can fix this without affecting the operation of the algorithm by adding a new imaginary state $s_\perp$. Its adjacent transitions are chosen such that $W(s, s_\perp) = -W(s, S)$ when $s \in S$, and $s_\perp$ has no output transitions. Thus $W(s, S \cup \{s_\perp\}) = 0$ for every $s \in S \cup \{s_\perp\}$, and we can let $C_i = S \cup \{s_\perp\}$. The grey statement on line 1 makes C_i the only compound block.

We now show that the addition of $s_\perp$ changes the correct answer only by adding $\{s_\perp\}$ as an extra block to it. Clearly $\mathcal{B}$ is a refinement of $\mathcal{I}$ if and only if $\mathcal{B} \cup \{\{s_\perp\}\}$ is a refinement of $\mathcal{I} \cup \{\{s_\perp\}\}$. Furthermore, $W(s_1, B) = W(s_2, B)$ holds trivially when $\{s_1, s_2\} \subseteq \{s_\perp\}$. If $W(s_1, B) = W(s_2, B)$ for every $B \in \mathcal{B}$, then $W(s_1, \{s_\perp\}) = -\sum_{B \in \mathcal{B}} W(s_1, B) = -\sum_{B \in \mathcal{B}} W(s_2, B) = W(s_2, \{s_\perp\})$. From these it can be seen that $\mathcal{B}$ is compatible with the original W if and only if $\mathcal{B} \cup \{\{s_\perp\}\}$ is compatible with W extended with the transitions adjacent to $s_\perp$. So the two systems have the same croips, except for the addition of $\{s_\perp\}$.

The next important fact is that not implementing $s_\perp$ and the grey statements changes the output of the algorithm only by removing $\{s_\perp\}$ from it. The statement $\mathsf{U_B} := \mathcal{I}$ does not put $\{s_\perp\}$ into $\mathsf{U_B}$. (This is similar to line 22, where all except one subblocks of B are put into $\mathsf{U_B}$.) Therefore, $s_\perp$ never occurs as the s' on line 5. Because $s_\perp$ has no output transitions, it cannot occur as the s on line 5 either. Its only effect on the execution of the algorithm is thus that $\{s_\perp\}$ is an extra block that is never accessed. The set $\mathcal{C}$ of compound blocks has no effect on the output, because its content is not used for anything except for the computation of new values of $\mathcal{C}$ on line 3.

We have shown the following.

Lemma 1. *Without the grey statements the algorithm in Figure 2 computes the correct result for S, Δ, W, and $\mathcal{I}$ if and only if with the grey statements it computes the correct result when $s_\perp$ and its adjacent transitions have been added.*

We now prove that the algorithm computes the correct result in the presence of $s_\perp$ and the grey statements. The next lemma states that it does not split blocks unnecessarily.

Lemma 2. *Let $s_1 \in S \cup \{s_\perp\}$ and $s_2 \in S \cup \{s_\perp\}$. If the algorithm ever puts s_1 and s_2 into different blocks, then there is no croip where s_1 and s_2 are in the same block.*

Proof. We show that it is an invariant property of the main loop of the algorithm (that is, always valid on line 2) that if two states are in different blocks of the algorithm, then they are in different blocks in every croip.

If s_1 and s_2 are in different blocks initially, then they are in different blocks in $\mathcal{I} \cup \{\{s_\perp\}\}$ and thus in every croip.

The case remains where lines 14 to 20 separate s_1 and s_2 to different blocks. This happens only if $W(s_1, B') \neq W(s_2, B')$. Let $\mathcal{B} \cup \{\{s_\perp\}\}$ be an arbitrary croip. It follows from the invariant that each block of $\mathcal{B} \cup \{\{s_\perp\}\}$ is either disjoint with B' or a subset of B', because otherwise the algorithm would have separated two states that belong to the same block of a croip. Therefore, there are blocks $B'_1, \ldots, B'_k$ in $\mathcal{B} \cup \{\{s_\perp\}\}$ such that $B'_1 \cup \cdots \cup B'_k = B'$. The fact $W(s_1, B') \neq W(s_2, B')$ implies that there is $1 \leq i \leq k$ such that $W(s_1, B'_i) \neq W(s_2, B'_i)$. So s_1 and s_2 belong to different blocks in $\mathcal{B} \cup \{\{s_\perp\}\}$. □

Proving that the algorithm does all the splittings that it should is more difficult. We first show that the following is an invariant of the main loop.

For each C in $\mathcal{C}$, $\mathsf{U_B}$ contains all but one blocks B that are subsets of C.

This is initially true because $\mathsf{U_B}$ contains all blocks except $\{s_\perp\}$, and $\mathcal{C} = \{C_i\}$ where $C_i = S \cup \{s_\perp\}$. On line 3, B' is removed from $\mathsf{U_B}$ but also subtracted from $C_{B'}$, so the invariant becomes valid for $C_{B'} \setminus B'$. It becomes valid for the new compound block B', because it consists of one block that is not any more in $\mathsf{U_B}$. Lines 21 and 22 update $\mathsf{U_B}$ so that either B was in $\mathsf{U_B}$ before the splitting operation and all of its subblocks are in $\mathsf{U_B}$ after the operation, or B was not in $\mathsf{U_B}$ beforehand and precisely one of its subblocks is not in $\mathsf{U_B}$ afterwards. Thus they do not change the number of blocks that are subsets of C and not in $\mathsf{U_B}$.

The invariant implies that each compound block contains at least one ordinary block, namely the one that is not in $\mathsf{U_B}$.

At this point it is easy to prove that the algorithm terminates. Termination of all loops other than the main loop is obvious. Each iteration of the main loop splits one compound block to two non-empty parts. There can be at most $|S|$ splittings, because after them each compound block would consist of a single state, and thus of precisely one block. By the previous invariant, that block is not in $\mathsf{U_B}$, and hence $\mathsf{U_B}$ is empty.

Another important invariant property of the main loop is

For every block B, $s_1 \in B$, $s_2 \in B$, and $C \in \mathcal{C}$ we have $W(s_1, C) = W(s_2, C)$.

This is initially true because initially $\mathcal{C} = \{S \cup \{s_\perp\}\}$, and $W(s, S \cup \{s_\perp\}) = 0$ for every $s \in S \cup \{s_\perp\}$. Assume that the invariant holds for $C = C_{B'}$. The splitting of $C_{B'}$ to B' and $C_{B'} \setminus B'$ on line 3 violates the invariant, but the rest of the main loop re-establishes it for $C = B'$. Regarding $C = C_{B'} \setminus B'$, if s_1 and s_2 are in the same block, then $W(s_1, C_{B'} \setminus B') = W(s_1, C_{B'}) - W(s_1, B') = W(s_2, C_{B'}) - W(s_2, B') = W(s_2, C_{B'} \setminus B')$. So the invariant remains valid.

Lines 1 and 3 imply that each ordinary block is a subset of a compound block. When the algorithm terminates, $\mathsf{U_B} = \emptyset$. Then, by the first invariant, each compound block consists of a single ordinary block. Therefore, ordinary and compound blocks are then the same thing. In this situation, the second invariant reduces to the claim that the partition is compatible. We have proven the following lemma.

Lemma 3. *The algorithm terminates, and when it does that, the partition is compatible.*

So the algorithm terminates with a croip. By Lemma 2, all other croips are refinements of the one produced by the algorithm. This means that the output is the coarsest croip. Now Lemma 1 yields Theorem 1.

Theorem 1. *The algorithm in Figure 2 (without $s_\perp$ and the grey statements) finds the coarsest refinement of $\mathcal{I}$ that is compatible with W.*

We did not assume in the correctness proof of the algorithm that the coarsest croip exists. Therefore, our proof also proves that it exists.

It can be reasoned from the proof that if for every initial block B and every $s_1 \in B$ and $s_2 \in B$ we have $W(s_1, S) = W(s_2, S)$, then it is correct to put initially all but one of the initial blocks into $\mathsf{U_B}$.

6 Performance

In this section we show that the algorithm in Figure 2 runs in $O(n + m \log n)$ time, where n is the number of states and m is the number of transitions.

Line 1 runs clearly in $O(n)$ time.

Let us now consider one iteration of the main loop. Lines 3 to 7 run in $O(|B'|) + O(\sum_{s' \in B'} |\bullet s'|)$ time. They find $|\bullet B'| \leq \sum_{s' \in B'} |\bullet s'|$ states and store them into $\mathsf{S_T}$. Lines 8 to 11 and 23 scan the same states and thus run in $O(|\bullet B'|)$ time. Lines 12 to 22 scan a subset of the blocks that contain these states. By Section 3, the running time of lines 14 and 15 is only proportional to the number of these states. Therefore, excluding the sorting operation on line 19, lines 12 to 22 run in $O(|\bullet B'|)$ time. To summarize, excluding the sorting operation, lines 3 to 23 run in $O(|B'|) + O(\sum_{s' \in B'} |\bullet s'|)$ time. The $O(|B'|)$ term can be charged in advance, when B' is put into $\mathsf{U_B}$. This leaves $O(|\bullet s'|)$ time for each $s' \in B'$.

Assume that B' is used as a splitter and later on some $B'' \subseteq B'$ is used as a splitter. There has been a sequence $B'_0, \ldots, B'_k$ of blocks such that $k \geq 1$, $B' = B'_0$, $B'_k = B''$, and B'_i has been created by splitting B'_{i-1} when $1 \leq i \leq k$. When B'_1 was created, B'_0 was not in $\mathsf{U_B}$ because it had been used as a splitter. When B'_k was created, it was put into $\mathsf{U_B}$ or inherited a position in $\mathsf{U_B}$, because it was later used as a splitter. There is thus at least one i between 1 and k such that B'_{i-1} was not in $\mathsf{U_B}$ and B'_i was put into $\mathsf{U_B}$ when B'_i was created. We see that B'_i was put into $\mathsf{U_B}$ by line 22. As a consequence, $|B'_i| \leq \frac{1}{2}|B'_{i-1}|$. Clearly $|B'_0| \geq |B'_1| \geq \ldots \geq |B'_k|$. So $|B''| \leq \frac{1}{2}|B'|$.

This implies that each time when a state s' is used for splitting, it belongs to a splitter whose size is at most half of the size in the previous time. Therefore, the state can occur in a splitter at most $\log_2 n + 1$ times. The contribution of s' to the execution time of the algorithm as a whole is thus $O((\log n)|\bullet s'|)$ plus the share of s' of the time needed for sorting. When this is summed over every $s' \in S$ and added to the $O(n)$ from line 1, it yields $O(n + m \log n)$, because then $\bullet s'$ goes through all transitions.

We have proven the following lemma.

Lemma 4. *Excluding the sorting operations on line 19, the algorithm in Figure 2 runs in $O(n + m \log n)$ time.*

We still have to analyse the time consumption of the sorting operations. For that purpose, consider the B' and $C_{B'} \setminus B'$ of line 3. We say that a subblock B_i of block B on lines 13 to 22 is

- the *left block*, if $W(s, B') \neq 0$ and $W(s, C_{B'} \setminus B') = 0$ for every $s \in B_i$,
- a *middle block*, if $W(s, B') \neq 0$ and $W(s, C_{B'} \setminus B') \neq 0$ for every $s \in B_i$, and
- the *right block*, if $W(s, B') = 0$ for every $s \in B_i$.

This definition covers all subblocks of B, because $W(s, C_{B'})$ is the same for every $s \in B$ by the second invariant of Section 5. In particular, every state in the left block has the same $W(s, B')$, because it is $W(s, C_{B'})$. The union of the middle blocks of B is called the *middle group*. The following lemma says an important fact about the middle groups.

Lemma 5. *If the middle groups are sorted with an $O(k \log k)$ sorting algorithm (such as heapsort or mergesort), then the total amount of time spent in sorting is $O(m \log n)$. This remains true even if each sorting operation processes also at most as many additional states as is the size of the middle group.*

Proof. Let $\#_c(s)$ denote the number of compound blocks C such that $s \to C$. Let $s\bullet = \{s' \mid s \to s'\}$. Clearly $\#_c(s) \leq |s\bullet|$ and $\sum_{s \in S} \#_c(s) \leq \sum_{s \in S} |s\bullet| = m$. Each time when s is in a middle block, we have both $s \to B'$ and $s \to C_{B'} \setminus B'$, so $\#_c(s)$ increases by one. As a consequence, if $\#_m(s)$ denotes the number of times that s has been in a middle block, then $\#_m(s) \leq \#_c(s)$. Therefore, $\sum_{s \in S} \#_m(s) \leq \sum_{s \in S} \#_c(s) \leq m$.

Let K denote the total number of middle groups processed during the execution of the algorithm, and let k_i be the size of the ith middle group. Thus $k_i \leq n$ and $\sum_{i=1}^{K} k_i = \sum_{s \in S} \#_m(s) \leq m$. We have $\sum_{i=1}^{K} 2k_i \log(2k_i) \leq 2 \sum_{i=1}^{K} k_i \log(2n) = 2\left(\sum_{i=1}^{K} k_i\right) \log(2n) \leq 2m \log(2n) = 2m \log n + 2m \log 2$. Therefore, the total amount of time spent in sorting the middle groups and at most an equal number of additional states with any $O(k \log k)$ sorting algorithm is $\sum_{i=1}^{K} O(2k_i \log(2k_i)) = O(m \log n)$. $\square$

The B_1 on line 16 is the union of the left block and the middle group. Every state in the left block has the same $W(s, B')$. If the left block contains more states than the middle group, then line 16 assigns its $W(s, B')$ to pmc, line 17 separates it from the middle group, and line 19 only sorts the middle group. In the opposite case, B_1, and thus its subset B_2, contains at most twice as many states as the middle group. Both cases satisfy the assumptions of Lemma 5. This implies that the sorting operations take altogether $O(m \log n)$ time.

The memory consumption of every data structure is clearly $O(m)$ or $O(n)$, and the data structures for the blocks and $\bullet s'$ are $\Omega(n)$ and $\Omega(m)$. Heapsort and mergesort use $O(n)$ additional memory. We have proven the following theorem.

Theorem 2. *If the details are implemented as described above, then the algorithm in Figure 2 runs in $O(n + m \log n)$ time and $\Theta(n + m)$ memory.*

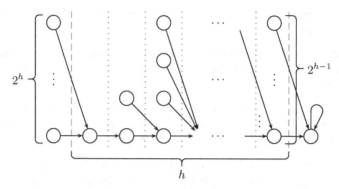

Fig. 4. An example where sorting the union of the middle and left blocks with a $\Theta(k \log k)$ algorithm costs too much. Each transition has weight 1.

Processing the possible majority candidate's block separately from B_2 is not necessary for correctness. We show now that it is necessary for guaranteeing the performance. Assume that a $\Theta(k \log k)$ sorting algorithm is applied to the union of the middle and left blocks. Consider the family of systems in Figure 4. In the figure, the initial partition is shown by dashed lines.

Assume that the initial block in the center is used as the first splitter. It splits itself into two halves along the rightmost dotted line. The leftmost half is used for further splitting, because it has $2^{h-1} - 1$ states, while the other half has 2^{h-1} states. When it is used as a splitter, it splits itself to two halves of sizes 2^{h-2} and $2^{h-2} - 1$ states. Again, the leftmost half is smaller. This repeats $h - 1$ times, plus one time which does not cause any splitting. Each time the leftmost initial block is processed as a left block. We have h sorting operations on at least 2^h elements each, taking altogether $\Omega(h(2^h \log 2^h)) = \Omega(n \log^2 n) = \Omega(m \log^2 n)$ time, because $m = n = 2^{h+1}$. This is not $O(m \log n)$.

7   Testing and Measurements

Our lumping algorithm was implemented in C++ and tested in two different ways.

The first series of tests used as inputs more than 250 randomly generated graphs of various sizes, densities, numbers of initial blocks, and numbers of different transition weights. Unfortunately, there is no straightforward way of fully checking the correctness of the output. Therefore, each graph was given to the program in four different versions, and it was checked that the four outputs had the same number of states and the same number of transitions. Two of the versions were obtained by randomly permuting the numbering of states in the original version, and the first output was used as the fourth input. This is similar to the testing described in [11]. Indeed, the programs written for [11] were used as a starting point when implementing both the lumping program and the testing environment.

Table 1. Some timing measurements. The times are in seconds.

	input		output		reading	lumping
source	states	transitions	states	transitions	input	algorithm
random	30 000	1 000 000	29 982	995 044	7.3	0.7
random	30 000	1 000 000	29 973	952 395	6.9	1.0
random	30 000	1 000 000	1	0	6.3	0.3
random	30 000	10 000 000	29 974	9 950 439	71.4	7.5
random	30 000	10 000 000	29 931	9 522 725	68.9	7.6
random	30 000	10 000 000	1	0	63.9	3.6
GreatSPN	184 756	2 032 316	139	707	5.2	2.0
GreatSPN	646 646	7 700 966	139	707	21.2	32.8
GreatSPN	1 352 078	16 871 582	195	1 041	49.5	126.6
GreatSPN	2 704 156	35 154 028	272	1 508	111.3	825.4

The ability of the testing environment to reveal errors was tested by modifying the lumping program so that it initially puts one too few blocks into U_B. The testing environment detected the error quickly.

The upper part of Table 1 shows some running times on a laptop with 2 GiB of RAM and 1.6 GHz clock rate. The bottleneck in the tests was the capacity of the testing environment and the time spent in input and output, not the time spent by the lumping algorithm.

The Markov chains used in the second set of experiments were made with the GreatSPN tool [2,7] from a family of stochastic Petri net models. The nets exhibit symmetries, making it possible for GreatSPN to also compute the lumped Markov chains directly. The sizes of the results obtained by running our program on unlumped Markov chains produced by GreatSPN were compared to the sizes of lumped Markov chains produced directly by GreatSPN, and found identical. Correctness was also checked by computing some performance indices.

These experiments were made on a laptop with 2 GiB of RAM and 2.2 GHz clock rate. Their results are reported in the lower part of Table 1. They suggest that our program has good performance even with more than 10^6 states and 10^7 transitions.

8   Conclusions

We presented an $O(m \log n)$ time algorithm for the lumping problem, where n is the number of states and m is the number of transitions. It is not the first algorithm for this problem with this complexity. However, it is much simpler than its predecessor [6], because the use of splay trees was replaced by an application of just any $O(k \log k)$ sorting algorithm together with a simple possible majority algorithm. We also believe that our presentation is the first that is sufficiently detailed and non-misleading from the point of view of programmers. Thus we hope that this article is of value to solving the lumping problem in practice.

Our simplification is based on the observation that the sum of the sizes of the so-called middle blocks during the execution of the Paige–Tarjan algorithm is at most m. Therefore, the extra time taken by sorting them is so small that it does not add to the overall time complexity of $O(m \log n)$ of the Paige–Tarjan algorithm. We demonstrated with an example that this does not extend to so-called left blocks. As a consequence, the left blocks must often be processed separately. Fortunately, this was easy to do with the possible majority candidate algorithm.

Our algorithm does not implement the compound blocks of [10]. However, we used compound blocks extensively in the proofs. They are a handy way of keeping track of splitting that has already been done. Without referring to them it would be impossible to define the middle blocks and justify the correctness of the technique that underlies the good performance, that is, sometimes not putting some block into U_B. Compound blocks are thus essential for understanding the algorithm, although they are not explicitly present in it.

Acknowledgments. We thank the reviewers of this article for exceptionally many good comments.

References

1. Aho, A.V., Hopcroft, J.E., Ullman, J.D.: The Design and Analysis of Computer Algorithms. Addison-Wesley, Reading (1974)
2. Baarir, S., Beccuti, M., Cerotti, D., De Pierro, M., Donatelli, S., Franceschinis, G.: The GreatSPN tool: recent enhancements. SIGMETRICS Performance Evaluation Review, Special Issue on Tools for Performance Evaluation 36(4), 4–9 (2009)
3. Backhouse, R.C.: Program Construction and Verification. Prentice-Hall International Series in Computer Science, UK (1986)
4. Buchholz, P.: Exact and ordinary lumpability in finite Markov chains. Journal of Appl. Prob. 31, 309–315 (1994)
5. Derisavi, S.: Solution of Large Markov Models Using Lumping Techniques and Symbolic Data Structures. Dissertation, University of Illinois at Urbana-Champaign (2005)
6. Derisavi, S., Hermanns, H., Sanders, W.H.: Optimal state-space lumping in Markov chains. Information Processing Letters 87(6), 309–315 (2003)
7. GRaphical Editor and Analyzer for Timed and Stochastic Petri Nets, http://www.di.unito.it/%7egreatspn/ (last update September 25, 2008)
8. Kemeny, J.G., Snell, J.L.: Finite Markov Chains. Springer, Heidelberg (1960)
9. Knuutila, T.: Re-describing an algorithm by Hopcroft. Theoret. Comput. Sci. 250, 333–363 (2001)
10. Paige, R., Tarjan, R.: Three partition refinement algorithms. SIAM J. Comput. 16(6), 973–989 (1987)
11. Valmari, A.: Bisimilarity minimization in $O(m \log n)$ time. In: Franceschinis, G., Wolf, K. (eds.) PETRI NETS 2009. LNCS, vol. 5606, pp. 123–142. Springer, Heidelberg (2009)
12. Valmari, A., Lehtinen, P.: Efficient minimization of DFAs with partial transition functions. In: Albers, S., Weil, P. (eds.) STACS 2008, Symposium on Theoretical Aspects of Computer Science, Bordeaux, France, pp. 645–656 (2008), http://drops.dagstuhl.de/volltexte/2008/1328/

Model Checking Interactive Markov Chains[*]

Lijun Zhang[1] and Martin R. Neuhäußer[2,3]

[1] Oxford University Computing Laboratory, UK
[2] Software Modeling and Verification Group, RWTH Aachen University, Germany
[3] Formal Methods and Tools Group, University of Twente, The Netherlands

Abstract. Hermanns has introduced interactive Markov chains (IMCs) which arise as an orthogonal extension of labelled transition systems and continuous-time Markov chains (CTMCs). IMCs enjoy nice compositional aggregation properties which help to minimize the state space incrementally. However, the model checking problem for IMCs remains unsolved apart from those instances, where the IMC can be converted into a CTMC. This paper tackles this problem: We interpret the continuous stochastic logic (CSL) over IMCs and define the semantics of probabilistic CSL formulas with respect to the class of fully time and history dependent schedulers. Our main contribution is an efficient model checking algorithm for verifying CSL formulas on IMCs. Moreover, we show the applicability of our approach and provide some experimental results.

1 Introduction

The success of Markovian models for quantitative performance and dependability evaluation is based on the availability of efficient and quantifiably precise solution methods for continuous-time Markov chains (CTMCs) [3]. On the specification side, the continuous stochastic logic (CSL) [2,3] allows to specify a wide variety of performance and dependability measures of interest. A CTMC can be conceived as a labelled transition system (LTS) whose transitions are delayed according to an exponential distribution. Opposed to classical concurrency theory, CTMCs neither support compositional modelling [19] nor do they allow nondeterminism in the model. Several efforts have been undertaken to overcome this limitation, including formalism like the stochastic Petri box calculus [22], statecharts [7] and process algebras [20,17].

Interactive Markov chains (IMCs) [18] conservatively extend process algebras with exponentially distributed delays and comprise most of the other approaches' benefits [10]: As they strictly separate *interactive* from *Markovian* transitions, IMCs extend LTSs with exponential delays in a fully orthogonal way. This enables compositional modelling with intermittent weak bisimulation minimization [17] and allows to augment existing untimed process algebra specifications with random timing [7]. Moreover, the IMC formalism is not restricted to exponential delays but allows to encode arbitrary phase-type distributions such as hyper- and hypoexponentials [26].

Since IMCs smoothly extend classical LTSs, the model has received attention in academic as well as in industrial settings [8,14,15]. In practice however, the theoretical

---
[*] Supported by the NWO projects QUPES (612.000.420), by the EU grant FP7-ICT-2007-1 (QUASIMODO) and the DFG as part of SFB/TR 14 AVACS.

J. Esparza and R. Majumdar (Eds.): TACAS 2010, LNCS 6015, pp. 53–68, 2010.

benefits have partly been foiled by the fact that the analysis of IMCs is restricted to those instances, where the composed IMC could be transformed into a CTMC. However, IMCs support nondeterminism which arises both implicitly from parallel composition and explicitly by the deliberate use of underspecification in the model [18]. Therefore IMCs are strictly more expressive than CTMCs. As a result, model checking IMCs is an unexplored topic thus far.

In this paper, we overcome this limitation and propose an efficient model checking algorithm to verify CSL formulas on arbitrary IMCs. In our analysis, we use fully time and history dependent schedulers to resolve all of the IMC's nondeterministic choices.

The crucial point in model checking CSL is to compute the maximum (and minimum) probability to visit a set of goal states in some time interval I. We characterize this probability as the least fixed point of a higher-order operator which involves integration over the time domain. Then we use *interactive probabilistic chains* (IPCs) [15] to define a discretization which reduces the time interval bounded reachability problem in IMCs to the problem of computing step-interval bounded reachability probabilities in IPCs. More precisely, we approximate the quantitative behaviour of the IMC up to an a priori specified error bound $\varepsilon > 0$ by its induced IPC and prove that its maximum step-interval bounded reachability coincides (up to ε) with the achievable time-interval bounded reachability probability in the underlying IMC. The resulting IPC is then subject to a modified value iteration algorithm [5], which maximizes the step-interval bounded reachability probability. The time complexity of our approach is in $\mathcal{O}\big(|\Phi| \cdot \big(n^{2.376} + \big(m + n^2\big) \cdot (\lambda b)^2/\varepsilon\big)\big)$, where $|\Phi|$ is the size of the formula, and n, m are the number of states and transitions of the IMC, respectively. Further, $b = \sup I$ is the upper time interval bound and λ is the maximal exit rate in the IMC.

Although we present all results only for maximum time-bounded reachability probabilities, all proofs can easily be adapted to the dual problem of determining the minimum time-bounded reachability probability.

Most of the technical details have been omitted from the paper. However, all proofs and the technicalities that are necessary to establish the error bounds that are stated within the paper can be found in [23, Chapter 6].

Organisation of the paper. The paper proceeds by first giving necessary definitions and background in Section 2. Section 3 presents algorithms for computing the time-interval bounded reachability for IMCs. Section 4 focuses on model checking algorithms for CSL, followed by experimental results in Sec. 5. Section 6 discusses related work and concludes the paper.

2 Preliminaries

Let $\mathcal{X}$ be a finite set. Probability distributions over $\mathcal{X}$ are functions $\mu : \mathcal{X} \to [0, 1]$ with $\sum_{x \in \mathcal{X}} \mu(x) = 1$. If $\mu(x) = 1$ for some $x \in \mathcal{X}$, μ is *degenerate*, denoted $\mu = \{x \mapsto 1\}$; in this case, we identify μ and x. The set of all probability distributions over $\mathcal{X}$ is denoted $Distr(\mathcal{X})$. Accordingly, $\mu(X) = \sum_{x \in X} \mu(x)$ for all $X \subseteq \mathcal{X}$.

2.1 Interactive Markov Chains

We recall the definition of interactive Markov chains (IMCs) given in [17]:

Definition 1 (Interactive Markov chain). *An interactive Markov chain is a tuple* $\mathcal{M} = (\mathcal{S}, Act, IT, MT, \nu)$ *where* $\mathcal{S}$ *and* Act *are nonempty sets of states and actions,* $IT \subseteq \mathcal{S} \times Act \times \mathcal{S}$ *is a set of interactive transitions and* $MT \subseteq \mathcal{S} \times \mathbb{R}_{>0} \times \mathcal{S}$ *is a set of Markovian transitions. Further,* $\nu \in Distr(\mathcal{S})$ *is the initial distribution.*

We distinguish *external* actions in Act_e from *internal* actions in Act_i and set $Act = Act_e \cup Act_i$. Several IMCs may be composed via synchronisation over the set Act_e of external actions, yielding again an IMC. For details, we refer to [17]. In this paper, we consider *closed* IMCs [21], that is, we focus on the IMC $\mathcal{M}$ that is obtained after composition. Accordingly, $\mathcal{M}$ is not subject to any further synchronisation and all remaining external actions can safely be hidden. Therefore, we assume that $Act_e = \emptyset$ and identify the sets Act and Act_i.

For Markovian transitions, $\lambda, \mu \in \mathbb{R}_{>0}$ denote rates of exponential distributions. $IT(s) = \{(s, \alpha, s') \in IT\}$ is the set of interactive transitions that leave state s; similarly, for Markovian transitions we set $MT(s) = \{(s, \lambda, s') \in MT\}$. A state $s \in \mathcal{S}$ is *Markovian* iff $MT(s) \neq \emptyset$ and $IT(s) = \emptyset$; it is *interactive* iff $MT(s) = \emptyset$ and $IT(s) \neq \emptyset$. Further, s is a *hybrid state* iff $MT(s) \neq \emptyset$ and $IT(s) \neq \emptyset$; finally, s is a *deadlock state* iff $MT(s) = IT(s) = \emptyset$. $MS \subseteq \mathcal{S}$ and $IS \subseteq \mathcal{S}$ denote the sets of Markovian and interactive states in $\mathcal{M}$. We define $post^M(s) = \{s \in \mathcal{S} \mid \mathbf{R}(s, s') > 0\}$.

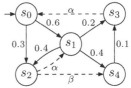

Fig. 1. Example IMC

Example 1. Let $\mathcal{M}$ be the IMC depicted in Fig. 1. Then s_0 is a Markovian state with a transition $(s_0, 0.3, s_2) \in MT(s)$ (depicted by a solid line) to state s_2 with rate $\lambda = 0.3$. The transition's delay is exponentially distributed with rate λ; hence, it executes in the next $z \in \mathbb{R}_{\geq 0}$ time units with probability $\int_0^z \lambda e^{-\lambda t} dt = \left(1 - e^{-0.3z}\right)$. As state s_0 has two Markovian transitions, they compete for execution and the IMC moves along the transition whose delay expires first. Clearly, in such a *race*, the *sojourn time* in s_0 is determined by the first transition that executes. As the minimum of exponential distributions is exponentially distributed with the sum of their rates, the sojourn time in a state s is determined by the *exit rate* $E(s) = \sum_{s' \in \mathcal{S}} \mathbf{R}(s, s')$ of state s, where $\mathbf{R}(s, s') = \sum \{\lambda \mid (s, \lambda, s') \in MT(s)\}$. In general, the probability to move from a state $s \in MS$ to a successor state $s' \in \mathcal{S}$ equals the probability that (one of) the Markovian transitions that lead from s to s' wins the race. Therefore, the *discrete branching probability* to move to s' is given by $\mathbf{P}(s, s') = \frac{\mathbf{R}(s, s')}{E(s)}$. Accordingly, for state s_0 of our example, we have $\mathbf{R}(s_0, s_2) = 0.3$, $E(s_0) = 0.3 + 0.6 = 0.9$ and $\mathbf{P}(s_0, s_2) = \frac{1}{3}$.

For interactive transitions, we adopt the *maximal progress assumption* [17, p. 71] which states that internal transitions (i.e. interactive transitions labelled with internal actions) trigger instantaneously. This implies that they take precedence over all Markovian transitions whose probability to execute immediately is 0. Therefore all Markovian transitions that emanate a hybrid state can be removed without altering the IMC's semantics. We do so and assume that $MT(s) \cap IT(s) = \emptyset$ for all $s \in \mathcal{S}$.

To ease the development of the theory, we assume w.l.o.g. that each internal action $\alpha \in Act_i$ has a unique successor state, denoted $succ(\alpha)$; note that this is no restriction, for if $(s, \alpha, u), (s, \alpha, v) \in IT(s)$ are internal transitions with $u \neq v$, we may replace them by new transitions (s, α_u, u) and (s, α_v, v) with fresh internal actions α_u and α_v.

We assume that entering a deadlock state results in a time lock. Therefore, we equip deadlock states $s \in S$ with internal self-loop (s, α, s). However, our approach also allows for a different deadlock state semantics, where time continues; in this case, we would add a Markovian instead of an internal self-loop. The *internal successor relation* $\leadsto_i \subseteq S \times S$ is given by $s \leadsto_i s'$ iff $(s, \alpha, s') \in IT$; further, the *internal reachability relation* $\leadsto_i^*$ is the reflexive and transitive closure of $\leadsto_i$. Accordingly, we define $post^i(s) = \{s' \in S \mid s \leadsto_i s'\}$ and $Reach^i(s) = \{s' \in S \mid s \leadsto_i^* s'\}$.

2.2   Paths and Events in IMCs

We use a special action $\bot \notin Act$ and let σ range over $Act_\bot = Act \cup \{\bot\}$. A finite *path* is a sequence $\pi = s_0 \xrightarrow{t_0, \sigma_0} s_1 \xrightarrow{t_1, \sigma_1} \cdots \xrightarrow{t_{n-1}, \sigma_{n-1}} s_n$ where $s_i \in S$, $t_i \in \mathbb{R}_{\geq 0}$ and $\sigma_i \in Act_\bot$ for $i \leq n$; n is the length of π, denoted $|\pi|$. We use $\pi[k] = s_k$ and $\delta(\pi, k) = t_k$ to refer to the $(k+1)$-th state on π and its associated sojourn time. Accordingly, $\Delta(\pi, i) = \sum_{k=0}^{i} t_k$ is the total time spent on π until (including) state $\pi[i]$. If π is finite with $|\pi| = n$, then $\Delta(\pi) = \Delta(\pi, n-1)$ is the total time spent on π; similarly, $\pi\downarrow = s_n$ is the last state on π.

Internal transitions occur immediately. Thus an IMC can traverse several states at one point in time. We use $\pi@t \in (S^* \cup S^\omega)$ for the sequence of states traversed on π at time $t \in \mathbb{R}_{\geq 0}$: Formally, let i be the smallest index s.t. $t \leq \Delta(\pi, i)$; if no such i exists, we set $\pi@t = \langle \rangle$. Otherwise, if $t < \Delta(\pi, i)$ we define $\pi@t = \langle s_i \rangle$; if $t = \Delta(\pi, i)$, let j be the largest index (or $+\infty$, if no such finite index exists) such that $t = \Delta(\pi, j)$. Then $\pi@t = \langle s_i \ldots s_j \rangle$. We write $s \in \langle s_i \ldots s_j \rangle$ if $s \in \{s_i, \ldots, s_j\}$; further, if $s \in \langle s_i \ldots s_j \rangle$ we define $Pref(\langle s_i \ldots s_j \rangle, s) = \langle s_i, \ldots s_k \rangle$, where $s = s_k$ and k minimal. If $s \notin \langle s_i \ldots s_j \rangle$, we set $Pref(\langle s_i \ldots s_j \rangle, s) = \langle \rangle$. The definitions for *time-abstract* paths are similar.

A path π (time-abstract path π') is a concatenation of a state and a sequence of *combined transitions* (*time-abstract combined transitions*) from the set $\Omega = \mathbb{R}_{\geq 0} \times Act_\bot \times S$ ($\Omega_{abs} = Act_\bot \times S$); hence, $\pi = s_0 \circ m_0 \circ m_1 \circ \ldots \circ m_{n-1}$ with $m_i = (t_i, \sigma_i, s_{i+1}) \in \Omega$ ($m_i = (\sigma_i, s_{i+1}) \in \Omega_{abs}$). Thus $Paths^n(\mathcal{M}) = S \times \Omega^n$ is the set of paths of length n in $\mathcal{M}$; further, $Paths^*(\mathcal{M})$, $Paths^\omega(\mathcal{M})$ and $Paths(\mathcal{M})$ are the sets of finite, infinite and all paths in $\mathcal{M}$. To refer to time-abstract paths, we add the subscript abs; further the reference to $\mathcal{M}$ is omitted wherever possible.

The measure-theoretic concepts are mentioned only briefly; we refer to [21] for an in-depth discussion. Events in $\mathcal{M}$ are measurable sets of paths; as paths are Cartesian products of combined transitions, we define the σ-field $\mathfrak{F} = \sigma\left(\mathfrak{B}(\mathbb{R}_{\geq 0}) \times \mathfrak{F}_{Act_\bot} \times \mathfrak{F}_S\right)$ on subsets of Ω where $\mathfrak{F}_S = 2^S$ and $\mathfrak{F}_{Act_\bot} = 2^{Act_\bot}$. Then we derive the product σ-field $\mathfrak{F}_{Paths^n} = \sigma\left(\{S_0 \times M_0 \times \cdots \times M_{n-1} \mid S_0 \in \mathfrak{F}_S, M_i \in \mathfrak{F}\}\right)$ of measurable subsets of $Paths^n$. The cylinder-set construction [1] extends this to infinite paths in the usual way.

2.3   Resolving Nondeterminism by Schedulers

An IMC $\mathcal{M}$ is *nondeterministic* iff there exists $(s, \alpha, u), (s, \beta, v) \in IT(s)$ with $u \neq v$: If both internal transitions (to states s_1 and s_4) in state s_2 of Fig. 1 execute instantaneously, the successor state is not uniquely determined. To resolve this nondeterminism, we use *schedulers*: If $\mathcal{M}$ reaches state s_2 along a *history* $\pi \in Paths^\star$, a scheduler yields a probability distribution over the set $Act_i(\pi\downarrow) = \{\alpha, \beta\}$ of *enabled actions* in s_2.

Definition 2 (Generic measurable scheduler). *A* generic scheduler *on an IMC* $\mathcal{M} = (\mathcal{S}, Act, IT, MT, \nu)$ *is a* partial *mapping* $D : Paths^\star \times \mathfrak{F}_{Act_i} \to [0, 1]$ *with* $D(\pi, \cdot) \in Distr(Act_i(\pi\downarrow))$ *for all* $\pi \in Paths^\star$ *with* $\pi\downarrow \in IS$. *A generic scheduler* D *is* measurable *(GM scheduler) iff for all* $A \in \mathfrak{F}_{Act}$, $D^{-1}(A) : Paths^\star \to [0, 1]$ *is measurable.*

Measurability states that $\{\pi \mid D(\pi, A) \in B\} \in \mathfrak{F}_{Paths^\star}$ holds for all $A \in \mathfrak{F}_{Act}$ and $B \in \mathfrak{B}([0, 1])$; intuitively, it excludes schedulers which resolve the nondeterminism in a way that induces non-measurable sets. Recall that no nondeterminism occurs if $\pi\downarrow \in MS$. However, we slightly abuse notation and assume that $D(\pi, \cdot) = \{\bot \mapsto 1\}$ if $\pi\downarrow \in MS$ so that D yields a distribution over $Act_\bot$. A GM scheduler D is *deterministic* iff $D(\pi, \cdot)$ is degenerate for all $\pi \in Paths^\star$. We use *GM* (and *GMD*) to denote the class of generic measurable (deterministic) schedulers. Further, a *GM* scheduler D_{abs} is *time-abstract* (*GM*$_{abs}$) iff $abs(\pi) = abs(\pi')$ implies $D_{abs}(\pi, \cdot) = D_{abs}(\pi', \cdot)$.

Example 2. If state s_2 in Fig. 1 is reached along path $\pi = s_0 \xrightarrow{0.4, \bot} s_2$, then $D(\pi)$ might yield the distribution $\{\alpha \mapsto \frac{1}{2}, \beta \mapsto \frac{1}{2}\}$, whereas for history $\pi' = s_0 \xrightarrow{1.5, \bot} s_2$, it might return a different distribution, say $D(\pi) = \{\alpha \mapsto 1\}$.

2.4 Probability Measures for IMCs

In this section, we define the probability measure [21] induced by D on the measurable space $(Paths^\omega, \mathfrak{F}_{Paths^\omega})$. We first derive the probability of measurable sets of combined transitions, i.e. of subsets of Ω:

Definition 3. *Let* $\mathcal{M} = (\mathcal{S}, Act, IT, MT, \nu)$ *be an IMC and* $D \in GM$. *For all* $\pi \in Paths^\star$, *we define the probability measure* $\mu_D(\pi, \cdot) : \mathfrak{F} \to [0, 1]$ *by:*

$$\mu_D(\pi, M) = \begin{cases} \sum_{\alpha \in Act_i(\pi\downarrow)} \mathbf{1}_M(\alpha, 0, succ(\alpha)) \cdot D(\pi, \{\alpha\}) & \text{if } s \in IS \\ \int_{\mathbb{R}_{\geq 0}} E(s) e^{-E(s)t} \cdot \sum_{s' \in \mathcal{S}} \mathbf{1}_M(\bot, t, s') \cdot \mathbf{P}(s, s') \ dt & \text{if } s \in MS. \end{cases}$$
(1)

Here, $\mathbf{1}_M$ denotes an indicator, i.e. $\mathbf{1}_M(\sigma, t, s') = 1$ if $(\sigma, t, s') \in M$ and 0, otherwise. Intuitively, $\mu_D(\pi, M)$ is the probability to continue along one of the combined transition in the set M. For an interactive state $s \in IS$, it is the probability of choosing $\alpha \in Act_i(\pi\downarrow)$ such that $(\alpha, 0, succ(\alpha))$ is a transition in M; if $s \in MS$, $\mu_D(\pi, M)$ is given by the density for the Markovian transition to trigger at time t and the probability that a successor state is chosen respecting M. As paths are inductively defined using combined transitions, we can lift the probability measure $\mu_D(\pi, \cdot)$ to $\mathfrak{F}_{Paths^n}$:

Definition 4 (Probability measure). *Let* $\mathcal{M} = (\mathcal{S}, Act, IT, MT, \nu)$ *be an IMC and* $D \in GM$. *For* $n \geq 0$, *we define the probability measures* $Pr^n_{\nu, D}$ *inductively on the measurable space* $(Paths^n, \mathfrak{F}_{Paths^n})$:

$$Pr^0_{\nu, D} : \mathfrak{F}_{Paths^0} \to [0, 1] \ : \ \Pi \mapsto \sum_{s \in \Pi} \nu(s) \quad \text{and for } n > 0$$

$$Pr^n_{\nu, D} : \mathfrak{F}_{Paths^n} \to [0, 1] \ : \ \Pi \mapsto \int_{Paths^{n-1}} Pr^{n-1}_{\nu, D}(d\pi) \int_{\Omega} \mathbf{1}_\Pi(\pi \circ m) \ \mu_D(\pi, dm).$$

Observe that $Pr^n_{\nu,D}$ measures a set of paths Π of length n by multiplying the probabilities $Pr^{n-1}_{\nu,D}(d\pi)$ of path prefixes π (of length $n-1$) with the probability $\mu_D(\pi, dm)$ of a combined transition $m \in M$ which extends π to a path in Π. Together, the measures $Pr^n_{\nu,D}$ extend to a unique measure on $\mathfrak{F}_{Paths^\omega}$: if $B \in \mathfrak{F}_{Paths^n}$ is a measurable base and $C = Cyl(B)$, we define $Pr^\omega_{\nu,D}(C) = Pr^n_{\nu,D}(B)$. Due to the inductive definition of $Pr^n_{\nu,D}$, the Ionescu–Tulcea extension theorem [1] applies, which yields a unique extension of $Pr^\omega_{\nu,D}$ to arbitrary sets in $\mathfrak{F}_{Paths^\omega}$.

2.5 Interactive Probabilistic Chains

Interactive probabilistic chains (IPCs) [15] are the discrete-time analogon of IMCs:

Definition 5 (Interactive probabilistic chain). *An* interactive probabilistic chain *(IPC) is a tuple* $\mathcal{P} = (\mathcal{S}, Act, IT, PT, \nu)$, *where* $\mathcal{S}, Act, IT$ *and* ν *are as in Def. 1 and* $PT : \mathcal{S} \times \mathcal{S} \to [0,1]$ *is a transition probability function s.t.* $\forall s \in \mathcal{S}. \ PT(s, \mathcal{S}) \in \{0,1\}$.

A state s in an IPC $\mathcal{P}$ is *probabilistic* iff $\sum_{s' \in \mathcal{S}} PT(s, s') = 1$ and $IT(s) = \emptyset$; PS denotes the set of all probabilistic states. The sets of interactive, hybrid and deadlock states are defined as for IMCs, with the same assumption imposed on deadlock states. Further, we assume any IPC to be closed, that is $(s, \alpha, s') \in IT$ implies $\alpha \in Act_i$. As for IMCs, we adopt the *maximal progress assumption* [17, p. 71]; hence, internal transitions take precedence over probabilistic transitions.

Definition 6 (IPC scheduler). *Let* $\mathcal{P} = (\mathcal{S}, Act, IT, PT, \nu)$ *be an IPC. A function* $D : Paths^\star_{abs} \to Distr(Act_i)$ *with* $D(\pi) \in Distr(Act_i(\pi\downarrow))$ *is a time abstract history dependent randomized (GM$_{abs}$) scheduler.*

Note that in the discrete-time setting, measurability issues do not arise. To define a probability measure on sets of paths in $\mathcal{P}$, we define the probability of a single transition:

Definition 7 (Combined transitions in IPCs). *Let* $\mathcal{P} = (\mathcal{S}, Act, IT, PT, \nu)$ *be an IPC,* $s \in \mathcal{S}$, $\sigma \in Act_\perp$, $\pi \in Paths^\star_{abs}$ *and* $(\sigma, s) \in \Omega_{abs}$ *a time abstract combined transition. For scheduler* $D \in GM_{abs}$, *we define*

$$\mu^{abs}_D\big(\pi, \{(\sigma, s)\}\big) = \begin{cases} \mathbf{P}(\pi\downarrow, s) & \text{if } \pi\downarrow \in PS \wedge \sigma = \perp \\ D(\pi, \{\sigma\}) & \text{if } \pi\downarrow \in IS \wedge succ(\sigma) = s \\ 0 & \text{otherwise.} \end{cases}$$

is the probability of the combined transition (σ, s). *For a set of combined transitions* $M \subseteq \Omega_{abs}$, *we set* $\mu^{abs}_D\big(\pi, M\big) = \sum_{(\sigma, s) \in M} \mu^{abs}_D\big(s, \{(\sigma, s)\}\big)$.

The measures μ^{abs}_D extend to a unique measure on sets of paths in $\mathcal{P}$ in the same way as it was shown for the IMC case in Sec. 2.4.

3 Interval Bounded Reachability Probability

We discuss how to compute the maximum probability to visit a given set of *goal states* during a given time interval. Therefore, let $\mathcal{I}$ be the set of nonempty intervals over the nonnegative reals and let $\mathcal{Q}$ be the set of nonempty intervals with nonnegative rational bounds. For $t \in \mathbb{R}_{\geq 0}$ and $I \in \mathcal{I}$, we define $I \ominus t = \{x - t \mid x \in I \wedge x \geq t\}$ and $I \oplus t = \{x + t \mid x \in I\}$. Obviously, if $I \in \mathcal{Q}$ and $t \in \mathbb{Q}_{\geq 0}$, this implies $I \ominus t \in \mathcal{Q}$ and $I \oplus t \in \mathcal{Q}$.

3.1   A Fixed Point Characterization for IMCs

Let $\mathcal{M}$ be an IMC. For a time interval $I \in \mathcal{I}$ and a set of goal states $G \subseteq \mathcal{S}$, we define the event $\Diamond^I G = \{\pi \in Paths^\omega \mid \exists t \in I. \exists s' \in \pi @ t.\ s' \in G\}$ as the set of all paths that are in a state in G during time interval I. The maximum probability induced by $\Diamond^I G$ in $\mathcal{M}$ is denoted $p_{max}^{\mathcal{M}}(s, I)$. Formally, it is obtained by the supremum under all GM schedulers:

$$p_{max}^{\mathcal{M}}(s, I) = \sup_{D \in GM} Pr_{\nu_s, D}^\omega(\Diamond^I G).$$

Theorem 1 (Fixed point characterization for IMCs). *Let $\mathcal{M}$ be an IMC as before, $G \subseteq \mathcal{S}$ a set of goal states and $I \in \mathcal{I}$ such that $\inf I = a$ and $\sup I = b$. The function $p_{max}^{\mathcal{M}} : \mathcal{S} \times \mathcal{I} \to [0, 1]$ is the least fixed point of the higher-order operator $\Omega : (\mathcal{S} \times \mathcal{I} \to [0, 1]) \to (\mathcal{S} \times \mathcal{I} \to [0, 1])$ which is defined as follows:*

1. For Markovian states $s \in MS$: $\Omega(F)(s, I)$ equals

$$\begin{cases} \int_0^b E(s) e^{-E(s)t} \cdot \sum_{s' \in \mathcal{S}} \mathbf{P}(s, s') \cdot F(s', I \ominus t)\, dt & \text{if } s \notin G \\ e^{-E(s)a} + \int_0^a E(s) e^{-E(s)t} \cdot \sum_{s' \in \mathcal{S}} \mathbf{P}(s, s') \cdot F(s', I \ominus t)\, dt & \text{if } s \in G. \end{cases}$$

2. For interactive states $s \in IS$: $\Omega(F)(s, I)$ equals 1 if $s \in G$ and $0 \in I$, and otherwise, $\Omega(F)(s, I) = max\{F(s', I) \mid s' \in post(s)\}$.

Example 3. The fixed point characterization suggests to compute $p_{max}^{\mathcal{M}}(s, I)$ analytically: Consider the IMC $\mathcal{M}$ depicted in Fig. 1 and assume that $G = \{s_3\}$. For $I = [0, b]$, $b > 0$ we have $p_{max}^{\mathcal{M}}(s_3, I) = 1$, $p_{max}^{\mathcal{M}}(s_4, I) = 1 - e^{-0.1b}$ and $p_{max}^{\mathcal{M}}(s_1, I) = \int_0^b e^{-t} \left(\frac{2}{5} \cdot p_{max}^{\mathcal{M}}(s_2, I \ominus t) + \frac{1}{5} \cdot p_{max}^{\mathcal{M}}(s_3, I \ominus t) + \frac{2}{5} \cdot p_{max}^{\mathcal{M}}(s_4, I \ominus t) \right) dt$. For interactive state s_2, we derive $p_{max}^{\mathcal{M}}(s_2, I) = max \left\{ p_{max}^{\mathcal{M}}(s_4, I), p_{max}^{\mathcal{M}}(s_1, I) \right\}$, which yields $p_{max}^{\mathcal{M}}(s_0, I) = \int_0^b 0.9 e^{-0.9t} \cdot \left(\frac{2}{3} \cdot p_{max}^{\mathcal{M}}(s_1, I \ominus t) + \frac{1}{3} \cdot p_{max}^{\mathcal{M}}(s_2, I \ominus t) \right) dt$. Hence, an IMC generally induces an integral equation system over the maximum over functions, which is not tractable. Moreover, the iterated integration is numerically unstable [3].

Therefore, we resort to a discretization approach: Informally, we divide the time horizon into small time slices. Then we consider a discrete-time model whose steps correspond to the IMC's behaviour during a single time slice. First, we develop a fixed-point characterization for step bounded reachability on interactive probabilistic chains (IPCs); then we reduce the maximum time interval bounded reachability problem in IMCs to the step interval bounded reachability problem in the discretized IPC. Finally, we show how to solve the latter by a modified value iteration algorithm.

3.2   A Fixed Point Characterization for IPCs

Similar to the timed paths in IMCs, we define $\pi@n \in \mathcal{S}^* \cup \mathcal{S}^\omega$ for the time abstract paths in IPCs: Let $\#^{PS}(\pi, k) = \big|\{i \in \mathbb{N} \mid 0 \le i \le k \wedge \pi[i] \in MS\}\big|$; then $\#^{PS}(\pi, k)$ is the number of probabilistic transitions that occur up to the $(k+1)$-th state on π. For fixed $n \in \mathbb{N}$, let i be the smallest index such that $n = \#^{PS}(\pi, i)$. If no such i exists, we set $\pi@n = \langle\rangle$; otherwise i is the index of the n-th probabilistic state that is hit on path π. Similarly, let $j \in \mathbb{N}$ be the largest index (or $+\infty$ if no such finite index exists) such that $n = \#^{PS}(\pi, j)$. Then j denotes the position on π directly before its $(n+1)$-th probabilistic state. With these preliminaries, we define $\pi@n = \langle s_i, s_{i+1}, \ldots, s_{j-1}, s_j \rangle$ to denote the state sequence between the n-th and the $(n+1)$-th probabilistic state of π. To define step-interval bounded reachability for IPCs, let $k, k' \in \mathbb{N}$ and $k \le k'$: Then

$$\Diamond^{[k,k']} G = \{\pi \in Paths_{abs}^\omega \mid \exists n \in \{k, k+1, \ldots, k'\} . \exists s' \in \pi@n. \, s' \in G\}$$

is the set of paths that visit G between discrete time-step k and k' in an IPC $\mathcal{P}$.

Accordingly, we define the maximum probability for the event $\Diamond^{[k,k']} G$:

$$p_{max}^{\mathcal{P}}(s, [k, k']) = \sup_{D \in GM_{abs}} Pr_{\nu_s, D}^\omega (\Diamond^{[k,k']} G).$$

Theorem 2 (Fixed point characterisation for IPCs). *Let $\mathcal{P} = (\mathcal{S}, Act, IT, PT, \nu)$ be an IPC, $G \subseteq \mathcal{S}$ a set of goal states and $I = [k, k']$ a step interval. The function $p_{max}^{\mathcal{P}}$ is the least fixed point of the higher-order operator $\Omega : (\mathcal{S} \times \mathbb{N} \times \mathbb{N} \to [0, 1]) \to (\mathcal{S} \times \mathbb{N} \times \mathbb{N} \to [0, 1])$ where*

1. for probabilistic states $s \in PS$:

$$\Omega(F)\big(s, [k, k']\big) = \begin{cases} 1 & \text{if } s \in G \wedge k = 0 \\ 0 & \text{if } s \notin G \wedge k = k' = 0 \\ \sum_{s' \in \mathcal{S}} PT(s, s') \cdot F\big(s', [k, k'] \ominus 1\big) & \text{otherwise;} \end{cases}$$

2. for interactive states $s \in IS$: $\Omega(F)\big(s, [k, k']\big) = 1$ if $s \in G$ and $k = 0$. Otherwise, $\Omega(F)\big(s, [k, k']\big) = max_{s' \in post(s)} F\big(s', [k, k']\big)$.

Observe that for IMCs, the recursive expression of the probabilistic reachability does not decrease the time interval I for interactive states, whereas for IPCs, the recursive expression does not decrease the corresponding step interval $[k, k']$.

3.3   A Discretization That Reduces IMCs to IPCs

For an IMC $\mathcal{M}$ and a *step duration* $\tau > 0$, we define the discretized IPC $\mathcal{M}_\tau$ of $\mathcal{M}$:

Definition 8 (Discretization). *An IMC $\mathcal{M} = (\mathcal{S}, Act, IT, MT, \nu)$ and a step duration $\tau > 0$ induce the discretized IPC $\mathcal{M}_\tau = (\mathcal{S}, Act, IT, PT, \nu)$, where*

$$PT(s, s') = \begin{cases} \big(1 - e^{-E(s)\tau}\big) \cdot \mathbf{P}(s, s') & \text{if } s \neq s' \\ \big(1 - e^{-E(s)\tau}\big) \cdot \mathbf{P}(s, s') + e^{-E(s)\tau} & \text{if } s = s'. \end{cases} \tag{2}$$

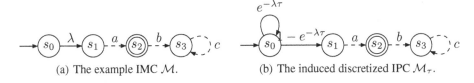

(a) The example IMC $\mathcal{M}$.   (b) The induced discretized IPC $\mathcal{M}_\tau$.

Fig. 2. Interval bounded reachability in IMCs with lower interval bounds

In $\mathcal{M}_\tau$, each probabilistic transition $PT(s, s') > 0$ corresponds to one *time step* of length τ in the underlying IMC $\mathcal{M}$: More precisely, $PT(s, s')$ is the probability that a transition to state s' occurs within τ time units. In case that $s' = s$, the first summand in $PT(s, s')$ is the probability to take a self-loop back to s, i.e. a transition that leads from s back to s executes; the second summand denotes the probability that no transition occurs within the next τ time units and thus, the systems stays in state $s = s'$.

Now we state the correctness of the discretization: To compute the probability $p_{max}^{\mathcal{M}}(s, [a, b])$, we analyze step-interval bounded reachability in the discretized IPC $\mathcal{M}_\tau$, where each step *approximately* corresponds to τ time units. First we show that $p_{max}^{\mathcal{M}_\tau}(s, [0, \lceil \frac{b}{\tau} \rceil])$ converges from below to $p_{max}^{\mathcal{M}}(s, [0, b])$ if $\tau \to 0$:

Theorem 3. *Let* $\mathcal{M} = (\mathcal{S}, Act, IT, MT, \nu)$ *be an IMC,* $G \subseteq \mathcal{S}$ *a set of goal states,* $I = [0, b] \in \mathcal{Q}$ *a time interval with* $b > 0$ *and* $\lambda = max_{s \in MS} E(s)$. *Further, let* $\tau > 0$ *be such that* $b = k_b \tau$ *for some* $k_b \in \mathbb{N}_{>0}$. *For all* $s \in \mathcal{S}$ *it holds:*

$$p_{max}^{\mathcal{M}_\tau}(s, [0, k_b]) \leq p_{max}^{\mathcal{M}}(s, I) \leq p_{max}^{\mathcal{M}_\tau}(s, [0, k_b]) + k_b \cdot \frac{(\lambda \tau)^2}{2}.$$

Example 4. Consider the IMC $\mathcal{M}$ and its discretized IPC $\mathcal{M}_\tau$ in Fig. 2(a) and Fig. 2(b), resp. Assume that $G = \{s_2\}$ and fix some $\tau > 0$, $k \in \mathbb{N}_{>0}$. Further, let $I = [0, k\tau]$. In the IMC $\mathcal{M}$, it holds that $p_{max}^{\mathcal{M}}(s_0, I) = \int_0^{k\tau} \lambda e^{-\lambda t} \cdot p_{max}^{\mathcal{M}}(s_1, I \ominus t) dt = 1 - e^{-\lambda k\tau}$. In $\mathcal{M}_\tau$, we obtain $p_{max}^{\mathcal{M}}(s_0, [0, k]) = \sum_{i=1}^{k} (e^{-\lambda \tau})^{i-1} (1 - e^{-\lambda \tau}) = 1 - e^{-\lambda k\tau}$, which is the geometric distribution function for parameter $p = 1 - e^{-\lambda \tau}$.

So far, we only considered intervals of the form $I = [0, b]$, $b > 0$. In what follows, we extend our results to arbitrary intervals. However, this is slightly involved:

If $s \in MS$ is a Markovian state and $b > 0$, then $p_{max}^{\mathcal{M}}(s, (0, b]) = p_{max}^{\mathcal{M}}(s, [0, b])$. However this is not true for interactive states: If s_1 (instead of s_0) is made the only initial state in $\mathcal{M}$ and $\mathcal{M}_\tau$ of Fig. 2, the probability to reach s_2 within interval $[0, b]$ is 1 whereas it is 0 for the right-semiclosed interval $(0, b]$. Further, the discretization is imprecise for point intervals: To see this, note that if $I = [\tau, \tau]$, then $p_{max}^{\mathcal{M}}(s_0, I) = 0$, whereas $p_{max}^{\mathcal{M}_\tau}(s_0, [1, 1]) = 1 - e^{-\lambda \tau}$.

Now, let $I = [k_a \tau, k_b \tau]$ be a *closed* interval with $k_a, k_b \in \mathbb{N}$ and $0 < k_a < k_b$. In the IMC $\mathcal{M}$ in Fig. 2(a), we obtain $p_{max}^{\mathcal{M}}(s_0, I) = \int_{k_a \tau}^{k_b \tau} \lambda e^{-\lambda t} \cdot p_{max}^{\mathcal{M}}(s_1, I \ominus t) dt = e^{-\lambda k_a \tau} - e^{-\lambda k_b \tau}$, whereas for its discretized IPC $\mathcal{M}_\tau$ (see Fig. 2(b)), we derive

$$p_{max}^{\mathcal{M}_\tau}(s_0, [k_a, k_b]) = \sum_{i=k_a}^{k_b} (e^{-\lambda \tau})^{i-1} \cdot (1 - e^{-\lambda \tau}) = e^{-\lambda(k_a-1)\tau} - e^{-\lambda k_b \tau}.$$

Clearly, the two probabilities differ in the first term by a factor of $e^{\lambda\tau}$. To see the reason, let $k_a = 2$ and $k_b = 3$: We have $p_{max}^{\mathcal{M}}(s, [2\tau, 3\tau]) = e^{-2\lambda\tau} - e^{-3\lambda\tau}$; however, in $\mathcal{M}_\tau$ it holds $p_{max}^{\mathcal{M}_\tau}(s, [2, 3]) = e^{-\lambda\tau} \cdot (1 - e^{-\lambda\tau}) + e^{-2\lambda\tau} \cdot (1 - e^{-\lambda\tau}) = e^{-\lambda\tau} - e^{-3\lambda\tau}$. As each step in $\mathcal{M}_\tau$ corresponds to a time interval of length τ (cf. Fig. 3), the interval bounds 2τ and 3τ fall in different discretization steps. Hence in the discretization, we add two steps which leads to an error. If instead we compute $p_{max}^{\mathcal{M}}(s, (2\tau, 3\tau])$, we obtain $p_{max}^{\mathcal{M}_\tau}(s, (2, 3]) = p_{max}^{\mathcal{M}_\tau}(s, [3, 3]) = e^{-2\lambda\tau} - e^{-3\lambda\tau}$, as desired.

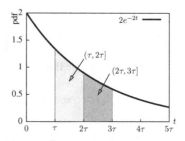

Fig. 3. Discretization steps

Based on these observations, we extend Thm. 3 to intervals with positive lower bounds. To avoid some technicalities, we first restrict to right-semiclosed intervals:

Theorem 4. *Let* $\mathcal{M} = (\mathcal{S}, Act, IT, MT, \nu)$ *be an IMC,* $G \subseteq \mathcal{S}$ *a set of goal states,* $I = (a, b] \in \mathcal{Q}$ *a time interval with* $a < b$ *and* $\lambda = max_{s \in MS} E(s)$. *If* $\tau > 0$ *is such that* $a = k_a\tau$ *and* $b = k_b\tau$ *for some* $k_a, k_b \in \mathbb{N}$, *then it holds for all* $s \in \mathcal{S}$:

$$p_{max}^{\mathcal{M}_\tau}\left(s, (k_a, k_b]\right) - k_a \cdot \frac{(\lambda\tau)^2}{2} \leq p_{max}^{\mathcal{M}}(s, I) \leq p_{max}^{\mathcal{M}_\tau}\left(s, (k_a, k_b]\right) + k_b \cdot \frac{(\lambda\tau)^2}{2} + \lambda\tau.$$

The error bounds for the case of lower interval bounds that are stated in Thm. 4 are derived using double induction over k_a and k_b, respectively.

Theorem 5. *If* $\mathcal{M}$, G *and* τ *are as in Thm. 4 and* $I \in \mathcal{Q}$ *is a time interval with* $\inf I = a$ *and* $\sup I = b$ *such that* $a < b$ *and* $a = k_a\tau$, $b = k_b\tau$ *for* $k_a, k_b \in \mathbb{N}$ *and* $0 \notin I$, *then*

$$p_{max}^{\mathcal{M}_\tau}\left(s, (k_a, k_b]\right) - k_a \cdot \frac{(\lambda\tau)^2}{2} \leq p_{max}^{\mathcal{M}}(s, I) \leq p_{max}^{\mathcal{M}_\tau}\left(s, (k_a, k_b]\right) + k_b \cdot \frac{(\lambda\tau)^2}{2} + \lambda\tau.$$

For the remaining cases, note that for all states $s \in \mathcal{S}$ and intervals $I = \emptyset$ or $I = [a, a]$ with $a > 0$ it holds that $p_{max}^{\mathcal{M}}(s, I) = 0$. Finally, for the case that $I = [0, 0]$, an interactive reachability analysis suffices to compute $p_{max}^{\mathcal{M}}(s, I)$, which is either 1 or 0.

3.4 Solving the Problem on the Reduced IPC

Let $\mathcal{P} = (\mathcal{S}, Act, IT, PT, \nu)$ be an IPC, $G \subseteq \mathcal{S}$ a set of goal states and $[k_a, k_b]$ a step interval. In this section, we discuss how to compute $p_{max}^{\mathcal{P}}(s, [k_a, k_b])$ via a modification of the well known *value iteration* algorithm [5]. The adaptation is non-trivial, as we consider step intervals that correspond to the number of *probabilistic steps* that are taken. This is reflected in our algorithm which only decreases the step counter for probabilistic, but not for internal transitions. We discuss step bounded reachability first:

Step Bounded Reachability: We aim at computing $p_{max}^{\mathcal{P}}(s, [0, k])$ for $0 \leq k$. This works as follows: In each step $i = 0, 1, \ldots, k$ of the iteration, we use two vectors $\vec{v}_i \in [0, 1]^{\mathcal{S}}$ and $\vec{u}_i \in [0, 1]^{\mathcal{S}}$, where $\vec{v}_i$ is the probability vector obtained from $\vec{u}_{i-1}$ by one step in the classical value iteration algorithm and $\vec{u}_i$ is obtained by computing the backwards closure along interactive transitions w.r.t. $\vec{v}_{i-1}$.

Each of the k value iteration steps consists of two phases: First, $\vec{v}_i$ is computed: If $s \in PS \cap G$, then $\vec{v}_i(s) = 1$. If $s \in PS \setminus G$, then $\vec{v}_i(s)$ is the weighted sum of the probabilistic successor states s' of s, multiplied by the result $\vec{u}_{i-1}(s')$ of the previous step. In the second phase, $\vec{u}_i$ is obtained by the backward closure of $\vec{v}_i$ along internal transitions. Initially, we set $\vec{v}_0(s) = 1$ if $s \in G$, and $\vec{v}_0(s) = 0$, otherwise. Then: $\forall i \in \{0, \ldots, k\} . \; \vec{u}_i(s) = max \{\vec{v}_i(s') \mid s \leadsto_i^* s'\}$ and for $\vec{v}_i$:

$$\forall i \in \{1, \ldots, k\} . \; \vec{v}_i(s) = \begin{cases} \sum_{s' \in \mathcal{S}} PT(s, s') \cdot \vec{u}_{i-1}(s') & \text{if } s \in PS \setminus G \\ 1 & \text{if } s \in PS \cap G \\ \vec{u}_{i-1}(s) & \text{if } s \in IS. \end{cases}$$

For efficiency reasons the set $\{s' \in \mathcal{S} \mid s \leadsto_i^* s'\}$ can be precomputed by a backwards search in the interactive reachability graph of $\mathcal{P}$.

After k value iteration steps $p_{max}^{\mathcal{P}}(s, [0, k])$ is obtained as the probability in $\vec{u}_k(s)$.

Step-Interval Bounded Reachability: In this part, we compute $p_{max}^{\mathcal{P}}(s, [k_a, k_b])$, for interval bounds $0 < k_a < k_b$. Again, we compute a sequence $\vec{v}_0, \vec{u}_0, \ldots, \vec{v}_{k_b}, \vec{u}_{k_b}$. As $k_a > 0$, we split the value iteration in two parts: In the first $k_b - k_a$ value iteration steps, we proceed as before and compute the probability vectors $\vec{v}_0, \vec{u}_0, \ldots, \vec{v}_{k_b - k_a}, \vec{u}_{k_b - k_a}$. Thus, we compute the probabilities $p_{max}^{\mathcal{P}}(s, [0, k_b - k_a])$ for all $s \in \mathcal{S}$.

The vector $\vec{v}_{k_b - k_a}$ provides the initial probabilities of the second part: In the remaining $i \in \{k_b - k_a + 1, \ldots, k_b\}$ value iteration steps, we set $\vec{v}_i(s) = 0$ if $s \in IS$ and $\vec{v}_i(s) = \sum_{s' \in \mathcal{S}} PT(s, s') \cdot \vec{u}_{i-1}(s')$ if $s \in PS$. The vectors $\vec{u}_i$ are as before. To see why, note that the value iteration algorithm proceeds in a backward manner, starting from the goal states. We do not set $\vec{v}_i(s) = 1$ if $s \in G$ in the last k_a iteration steps, as in the first k_a transitions, reaching a goal state does not satisfy our reachability objective. To avoid that the probabilities of interactive states $s \in IS$ erroneously propagate in the vectors $\vec{u}_i(s)$ from the first to the second part, in the second part we define $\vec{v}_i(s) = 0$ for all $s \in IS$ (instead of $\vec{v}_i(s) = \vec{u}_{i-1}(s)$ as in the first part). Let us illustrate this:

Example 5. We compute $p_{max}^{\mathcal{P}}(s, [1, 2])$ in the IPC $\mathcal{P}$ in Fig. 4 for initial state s_0 and goal state s_3: In the first part, apply the value iteration to compute $\vec{u}_1$: $\vec{v}_0(s) = 1$ if $s = s_3$ and 0, otherwise. By the backwards closure, $\vec{u}_0 = (1, 0, 0, 1)$. Thus $p_{max}^{\mathcal{P}}(s_0, [0, 0]) = 1$, as s_0 can reach G by the interactive α-transition. For $\vec{v}_1$, we have $\vec{v}_1(s_0) = \vec{u}_0(s_0) = 1$ and $\vec{v}_1(s_1) = \frac{1}{2}\vec{u}_0(s_3) + \frac{1}{2}\vec{u}_0(s_2) = \frac{1}{2}$. In this way, we obtain $\vec{v}_1 = (1, \frac{1}{2}, \frac{1}{4}, 1)$ and $\vec{u}_1 = (1, \frac{1}{2}, \frac{1}{4}, 1)$. With the probabilities $\vec{u}_1$, the first part ends after $k_b - k_a = 1$ value iteration steps. As $k_a = 1$, one iteration for the lower step bound follows. Here $\vec{v}_2(s_0) = \vec{v}_2(s_3) = 0$ as $s_0, s_3 \in IS$; further $\vec{v}_2(s_1) = \frac{1}{2}\vec{u}_1(s_3) + \frac{1}{2}\vec{u}_1(s_2) = \frac{5}{8}$ and $\vec{v}_2(s_2) = \frac{1}{2}\vec{u}_1(s_2) + \frac{1}{4}\vec{u}_1(s_3) + \frac{1}{4}\vec{u}_1(s_1) = \frac{1}{2}$. Finally, $\vec{u}_2 = (\frac{5}{8}, \frac{5}{8}, \frac{1}{2}, \frac{1}{2})$. Therefore, we obtain that $p_{max}^{\mathcal{P}}(s_0, [1, 2]) = \vec{u}_2(s_0) = \frac{5}{8}$.

3.5 Algorithm and Complexity

Let $\mathcal{M}, G, \varepsilon$ and I as before, with $b = \sup I$. For $\varepsilon > 0$, choose k_b such that $k_b \cdot \frac{(\lambda\tau)^2}{2} + \lambda\tau \leq \varepsilon$. With $\tau = \frac{b}{k_b}$, the smallest such k_b is $k_b = \lceil \frac{\lambda^2 b^2 + 2\lambda b}{2\varepsilon} \rceil$. Then the step duration τ induces the discretized IPC $\mathcal{M}_\tau$. By Thm. 5, $p_{max}^{\mathcal{M}}(s_0, I)$ can be approximated (up to ε) by $p_{max}^{\mathcal{M}_\tau}(s_0, (k_a, k_b])$. Let $n = |S|$ and $m = |IT| + |MT|$ be the number of states and transitions of $\mathcal{M}$, respectively. In the worst case, $\mathcal{M}_\tau$ has n states, and $m + n$ transitions. In each value iteration step, the update of the vector $\vec{v}_i$ takes at most time $m + n$; for $\vec{u}_i$, the sets $Reach^i(s)$ are precomputed. In the general case, the best theoretical complexity for computing the reflexive transitive closure is in $\mathcal{O}\left(n^{2.376}\right)$, as given by [13]. As $m^* \subseteq \mathcal{S} \times \mathcal{S}$, the number of transitions in the closure m^* is bounded by n^2.

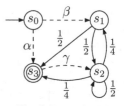

Fig. 4. Example IPC

Hence, with an appropriate precomputation of m^*, updating $\vec{u}_i$ takes time $\mathcal{O}(n^2)$. Therefore, with k_b value iteration steps, the worst case time complexity of our approach is in $n^{2.376} + (m + n + n^2) \cdot (\lambda b) \cdot (\lambda b + 2)/(2\varepsilon) \in \mathcal{O}\left(n^{2.376} + (m + n^2) \cdot (\lambda b)^2/\varepsilon\right)$.

4   Model Checking the Continuous Stochastic Logic

For model checking, we consider a finite set $AP = \{a, b, c, \ldots\}$ of *atomic propositions* and *state labelled* IMCs: A *state labelling function* $L : \mathcal{S} \to 2^{AP}$ assigns to each state the set of atomic propositions that hold in that state. To specify quantitative properties, we extend the continuous stochastic logic (CSL) [3,12], which reasons about qualitative and quantitative properties of CTMCs to the nondeterministic setting:

Definition 9 (CSL syntax). *For $a \in AP$, $p \in [0,1]$, $I \subseteq \mathcal{Q}$ an interval and $\trianglelefteq \in \{<, \leq, \geq, >\}$, CSL state and CSL path formulas are defined by*

$$\Phi ::= a \mid \neg\Phi \mid \Phi \wedge \Phi \mid \mathcal{P}_{\trianglelefteq p}(\varphi) \qquad and \qquad \varphi ::= \mathcal{X}^I \Phi \mid \Phi \mathcal{U}^I \Phi.$$

Intuitively, a path $\pi \in Paths^\omega$ satisfies the formula $\mathcal{X}^I \Phi$ ($\pi \models \mathcal{X}^I \Phi$) if the first transition on π occurs in time-interval I and leads to a successor state in $Sat(\Phi)$. Similarly, π satisfies the until formula $\Phi \mathcal{U}^I \Psi$ if a state in $Sat(\Psi)$ is reached at some time point $t \in I$ and before that, all states satisfy state formula Φ.

Definition 10 (CSL semantics). *Let $\mathcal{M} = (\mathcal{S}, Act, IT, MT, AP, L, \nu)$ be a state labelled IMC, $s \in \mathcal{S}$, $a \in AP$, $I \in \mathcal{Q}$, $\trianglelefteq \in \{<, \leq, \geq, >\}$ and $\pi \in Paths^\omega$. For state formulas, we define $s \models a$ iff $a \in L(s)$, $s \models \neg\Phi$ iff $s \not\models \Phi$ and $s \models \Phi \wedge \Psi$ iff $s \models \Phi$ and $s \models \Psi$. Further, $s \models \mathcal{P}_{\trianglelefteq p}(\varphi)$ iff for all $D \in GM$ it holds that $Pr^\omega_{\nu_s, D}\{\pi \in Paths^\omega \mid \pi \models \varphi\} \trianglelefteq p$. For path formulas, we define*

$$\pi \models \mathcal{X}^I \Phi \iff \pi[1] \models \Phi \wedge \delta(\pi, 0) \in I$$
$$\pi \models \Phi \mathcal{U}^I \Psi \iff \exists t \in I. \exists s \in \pi@t. \, s \models \Psi \wedge \forall s' \in Pref(\pi@t, s). \, s' \models \Phi$$
$$\wedge \forall t' \in [0, t). \, \forall s'' \in \pi@t'. \, s'' \models \Phi.$$

To model check an IMC w.r.t. a CSL state formula Φ, we successively consider the state subformulas Ψ of Φ and calculate the sets $Sat(\Psi) = \{s \in \mathcal{S} \mid s \models \Psi\}$. For atomic propositions, conjunction and negation, this is easy as $Sat(a) = \{s \in \mathcal{S} \mid a \in L(s)\}$, $Sat(\neg\Psi) = \mathcal{S} \setminus Sat(\Psi)$ and $Sat(\Psi_1 \wedge \Psi_2) = Sat(\Psi_1) \cap Sat(\Psi_2)$. Therefore we only discuss the probabilistic operator $\mathcal{P}_{\trianglelefteq p}(\varphi)$ for next and bounded until formulas. To decide $Sat(\mathcal{P}_{\trianglelefteq p}(\varphi))$, it suffices to maximize (or minimize, which can be done similarly) $Pr^{\omega}_{\nu_s,D}(\{\pi \in Paths^{\omega} \mid \pi \models \varphi\})$ w.r.t. all schedulers $D \in GM$. We define $p^{\mathcal{M}}_{max}(s,\varphi) = \sup_{D \in GM} Pr^{\omega}_{\nu_s,D}(\{\pi \in Paths^{\omega} \mid \pi \models \varphi\})$ and consider both types of path formulas:

The Next Formula. Computing $p^{\mathcal{M}}_{max}(s, \mathcal{X}^I \Phi)$ is easy: We proceed inductively on the structure of the formula and assume that $Sat(\Phi)$ is already computed. Let $a = \inf I$, $b = \sup I$ and $s \in MS$. Then $p^{\mathcal{M}}_{max}(s, \mathcal{X}^I \Phi) = \int_a^b E(s)e^{-E(s)t} \cdot \sum_{s' \in Sat(\Phi)} \mathbf{P}(s,s')\, dt = \mathbf{P}(s, Sat(\Phi)) \cdot (e^{-E(s)a} - e^{-E(s)b})$, where $\mathbf{P}(s, Sat(\Phi)) = \sum_{s' \in Sat(\Phi)} \mathbf{P}(s, s')$ is the probability to move to a successor state $s' \in Sat(\Phi)$. If $s \in IS, 0 \in I$ and $post(s) \cap Sat(\Phi) \neq \emptyset$, then $p^{\mathcal{M}}_{max}(s, \mathcal{X}^I \Phi) = 1$; otherwise $p^{\mathcal{M}}_{max}(s, \mathcal{X}^I \Phi) = 0$.

The Until Formula. Let $\varphi = \Phi \mathcal{U}^I \Psi$ with $I \in \mathcal{Q}$ and assume that $Sat(\Phi)$ and $Sat(\Psi)$ are already computed. We reduce the problem to compute $p^{\mathcal{M}}_{max}(s,\varphi)$ to the maximum interval-bounded reachability problem: Therefore, define $\mathcal{S}^{\varphi}_{=0} = \{s \in \mathcal{S} \mid s \models \neg\Phi\}$. In the next step, we turn all states $s \in \mathcal{S}^{\varphi}_{=0}$ into absorbing states by replacing all its outgoing transitions by a single interactive self loop. This is similar to the approach taken in [3,6] for model checking CTMCs and MDPs. Formally, a state $s \in IS$ is *absorbing* iff $post^i(s) = \{s\}$. Hence, as soon as a path enters an absorbing state, it cannot reach a different state anymore. Moreover, due to the maximal progress assumption, time does not progress any further in absorbing states. Intuitively, making $\mathcal{S}^{\varphi}_{=0}$-states absorbing is justified as follows. If a path π enters a state $s \in \mathcal{S}^{\varphi}_{=0}$, it can be decided immediately whether $\pi \models \Phi \mathcal{U}^I \Psi$, or not: If $s \models \Psi$ holds and if state s is entered at some time in the interval I, then $\pi \models \Phi \mathcal{U}^I \Psi$. Otherwise $\pi \not\models \Phi \mathcal{U}^I \Psi$ holds.

Theorem 6 (Time-bounded until). *Let* $\mathcal{M} = (\mathcal{S}, Act, IT, MT, AP, L, \nu)$ *be a state labelled IMC,* $\varphi = \Phi \mathcal{U}^I \Psi$ *a CSL path formula with* $I \in \mathcal{Q}$ *and* $G = Sat(\Psi)$ *the set of goal states. Further, assume that all states* $s \in \mathcal{S}^{\varphi}_{=0}$ *are made absorbing. Then*

$$p^{\mathcal{M}}_{max}(s, \Phi \mathcal{U}^I \Psi) = p^{\mathcal{M}}_{max}(s, I) \qquad \text{for all } s \in \mathcal{S}.$$

Theorem 6 reduces the problem to compute $p^{\mathcal{M}}_{max}(s, \Phi \mathcal{U}^I \Psi)$ of the until formula to the problem of computing the interval bounded reachability probability $p^{\mathcal{M}}_{max}(s, I)$ with

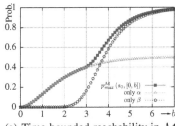

(a) Time-bounded reachability in $\mathcal{M}$

problem	states	ε	λ	b	prob.	time
$Erl(30, 10)$	35	10^{-3}	10	4	0.672	50s
$Erl(30, 10)$	35	10^{-3}	10	7	0.983	70s
$Erl(30, 10)$	35	10^{-4}	10	4	0.6718	268s
ws-cl, $N=4$	820	10^{-6}	2	10^1	$3.3 \cdot 10^{-5}$	2d
ws-cl, $N=4$	820	10^{-4}	2	10^2	$4 \cdot 10^{-4}$	15h
ws-cl, $N=4$	820	10^{-3}	2	10^3	$5 \cdot 10^{-3}$	6d

(b) Computation time for different parameters

Fig. 5. Experimental results for $Erl(30, 10)$ and the workstation cluster from [16]

respect to the set of goal states $G = Sat(\Psi)$. The latter can be computed efficiently by the discretization approach introduced in Sec. 3.3.

For CSL state-formula Φ, let $|\Phi|$ be the number of state subformulas of Φ. In the worst case, the interval bounded reachability probability is computed $|\Phi|$ times. Hence the model checking problem has time complexity $\mathcal{O}\big(|\Phi| \cdot \big(n^{2.376} + \big(m + n^2\big) \cdot (\lambda b)^2/\varepsilon\big)\big)$.

5   Experimental Results

We consider the IMC in Fig. 6, where $Erl(30, 10)$ denotes a transition with an Erlang (k, λ) distributed delay: This corresponds to $k = 30$ consecutive Markovian transitions each of which has rate λ. The mean time to move from s_2 to the goal s_4 is $\frac{k}{\lambda} = 3$ with a variance of $\frac{k}{\lambda^2} = \frac{3}{10}$. Hence, with very high probability we move from s_2 to s_4 after approximately 3 time units. The decision that maximizes the probability to reach s_4 in time interval $[0, b]$ in state s_1 depends on the sojourn in state s_0. Fig. 5(a) depicts the computed maxima for time dependent schedulers and the upper part of Tab. 5(b) lists some performance measurements.

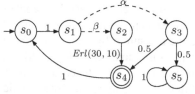

Fig. 6. The $Erl(30, 10)$ model $\mathcal{M}$

If $AP = \{g\}$ and s_4 is the only state labelled with g, we can verify the CSL formula $\Phi = \mathcal{P}_{\geq 0.5}\big(\Diamond^{[3,4]}g\big)$ by computing $p_{max}^{\mathcal{M}}(s_0, [3, 4])$ with the modified value iteration. The result $p_{max}^{\mathcal{M}}(s_0, [3, 4]) = 0.6057$ meets the bound ≥ 0.5 in Φ, implying that $s_0 \models \Phi$.

Finally, the lower part of Tab. 5(b) lists the performance of our approach for a large scale example [16], where we conduct a dependability analysis of a cluster of $2N$ workstations to estimate its failure probability over a finite time horizon. This rather stiff model has a high computational complexity in our prototypical implementation, as the failure events are very rare which leads to a large time horizon.

All measurements were carried out on a $2.2\,GHz$ Xeon CPU with $16\,GB$ RAM.

6   Related Work and Conclusions

In the setting of stochastic games, the time-bounded reachability problem has been studied extensively in [11], with extensions to timed automata in [9]. Closely related to ours is the work in [7], where globally uniform IMCs — which require the sojourn times in all Markovian states to be equally distributed — are transformed into continuous-time Markov decision processes (CTMDPs). Subsequently, the algorithm in [4] is used to compute the maximum time-bounded reachability probability in the resulting globally uniform CTMDP. However, the applicability of this approach is severely restricted, as global uniformity is hard (and often impossible) to achieve.

Further, the above approaches rely on time-abstract schedulers which are proved to be strictly less powerful than the time-dependent ones that we consider here [4,24].

In [25], we relax the restriction to global uniformity and consider locally uniform CTMDPs for which we propose a discretization that computes maximum time-bounded reachability probabilities under *late schedulers*: In locally uniform CTMDPs, late schedulers outperform *early schedulers* [24], which are the largest class of history and time dependent schedulers definable on general CTMDPs [21].

The discretization approach in this paper resembles that of [25]. However, the results are complementary: In general, transforming IMCs to CTMDPs as done in [21] does not yield locally uniform CTMDPs. Hence, the approach in [25] is inapplicable for the analysis of IMCs. However, we expect to solve the problem of computing time-interval bounded reachability in CTMDPs by analysing the CTMDP's induced IMC.

By providing an efficient and quantifiably precise approximation algorithm to compute interval bounded reachability probabilities, this paper solves a long standing open problem in the area of performance and dependability evaluation. Moreover, we solve the CSL model checking problem on arbitrary IMCs.

Acknowledgement. We thank Holger Hermanns and Joost-Pieter Katoen for their comments and for many fruitful discussions about earlier versions of this work.

References

1. Ash, R., Doléans-Dade, C.: Probability & Measure Theory, 2nd edn. Academic Press, London (2000)
2. Aziz, A., Sanwal, K., Singhal, V., Brayton, R.K.: Verifying continuous time Markov chains. In: Alur, R., Henzinger, T.A. (eds.) CAV 1996. LNCS, vol. 1102, pp. 269–276. Springer, Heidelberg (1996)
3. Baier, C., Haverkort, B.R., Hermanns, H., Katoen, J.-P.: Model-checking algorithms for continuous-time Markov chains. IEEE TSE 29, 524–541 (2003)
4. Baier, C., Hermanns, H., Katoen, J.-P., Haverkort, B.R.: Efficient computation of time-bounded reachability probabilities in uniform continuous-time Markov decision processes. Theor. Comp. Sci. 345, 2–26 (2005)
5. Bertsekas, D.: Dynamic Programming and Optimal Control, vol. II. Athena Scientific, Belmont (1995)
6. Bianco, A., de Alfaro, L.: Model checking of probabilistic and nondeterministic systems. In: Thiagarajan, P.S. (ed.) FSTTCS 1995. LNCS, vol. 1026, pp. 499–513. Springer, Heidelberg (1995)
7. Böde, E., Herbstritt, M., Hermanns, H., Johr, S., Peikenkamp, T., Pulungan, R., Rakow, J., Wimmer, R., Becker, B.: Compositional dependability evaluation for STATEMATE. IEEE Trans. Software Eng. 35, 274–292 (2009)
8. Boudali, H., Crouzen, P., Haverkort, B.R., Kuntz, M., Stoelinga, M.: Architectural dependability evaluation with Arcade. In: DSN, pp. 512–521. IEEE, Los Alamitos (2008)
9. Bouyer, P., Forejt, V.: Reachability in stochastic timed games. In: Albers, S., Marchetti-Spaccamela, A., Matias, Y., Nikoletseas, S., Thomas, W. (eds.) ICALP 2009. LNCS, vol. 5556, pp. 103–114. Springer, Heidelberg (2009)
10. Bravetti, M., Hermanns, H., Katoen, J.-P.: YMCA: Why Markov chain algebra? In: Essays on Algebraic Process Calculi. Electronic Notes in Theoretical Computer Science, vol. 162, pp. 107–112. Elsevier, Amsterdam (2006)
11. Brazdil, T., Forejt, V., Krcal, J., Kretinsky, J., Kucera, A.: Continuous-time stochastic games with time-bounded reachability. In: FSTTCS. LIPIcs (2009) (to appear)
12. Cerotti, D., Donatelli, S., Horváth, A., Sproston, J.: CSL model checking for generalized stochastic Petri nets. In: QEST, pp. 199–210. IEEE, Los Alamitos (2006)

13. Coppersmith, D., Winograd, S.: Matrix multiplication via arithmetic progressions. In: ACM Symposium on Theory of Computing. ACM, New York (1987)
14. Coste, N., Garavel, H., Hermanns, H., Hersemeule, R., Thonnart, Y., Zidouni, M.: Quantitative evaluation in embedded system design: Validation of multiprocessor multithreaded architectures. In: DATE, pp. 88–89. IEEE, Los Alamitos (2008)
15. Coste, N., Hermanns, H., Lantreibecq, E., Serwe, W.: Towards performance prediction of compositional models in industrial GALS designs. In: Bouajjani, A., Maler, O. (eds.) Computer Aided Verification. LNCS, vol. 5643, pp. 204–218. Springer, Heidelberg (2009)
16. Haverkort, B.R., Hermanns, H., Katoen, J.-P.: On the use of model checking techniques for dependability evaluation. In: Reliable Distributed Systems, pp. 228–239. IEEE, Los Alamitos (2000)
17. Hermanns, H. (ed.): Interactive Markov Chains: The Quest for Quantified Quality. LNCS, vol. 2428. Springer, Heidelberg (2002)
18. Hermanns, H., Herzog, U., Katoen, J.-P.: Process algebra for performance evaluation. Theor. Comp. Sci. 274, 43–87 (2002)
19. Hermanns, H., Katoen, J.-P.: Automated compositional Markov chain generation for a plain-old telephone system. Sci. Comput. Program. 36, 97–127 (2000)
20. Hillston, J.: A Compositional Approach to Performance Modelling. Cambridge University Press, Cambridge (1996)
21. Johr, S.: Model Checking Compositional Markov Systems. PhD thesis, Saarland University, Saarbrücken, Germany (2007)
22. Maciá, H., Valero, V., Cuartero, F., Ruiz, M.C.: sPBC: A Markovian extension of Petri box calculus with immediate multiactions. Fundamenta Informaticae 87, 367–406 (2008)
23. Neuhäußer, M.R.: Model Checking Nondeterministic and Randomly Timed Systems. PhD thesis, RWTH Aachen University, Aachen, Germany (2010)
24. Neuhäußer, M.R., Stoelinga, M., Katoen, J.-P.: Delayed nondeterminism in continuous-time Markov decision processes. In: de Alfaro, L. (ed.) FOSSACS 2009. LNCS, vol. 5504, pp. 364–379. Springer, Heidelberg (2009)
25. Neuhäußer, M.R., Zhang, L.: Time-bounded reachability in continuous-time Markov decision processes. Technical report, RWTH Aachen University (2009)
26. Pulungan, R.: Reduction of Acyclic Phase-Type Representations. PhD thesis, Universität des Saarlandes, Saarbrücken, Germany (2009)

Approximating the Pareto Front of Multi-criteria Optimization Problems*

Julien Legriel[1,2], Colas Le Guernic[1], Scott Cotton[1], and Oded Maler[1]

[1] CNRS-VERIMAG, 2, av. de Vignate, 38610 Gieres, France
@imag.fr
[2] STMICROELECTRONICS
12, rue Jules Horowitz, 38019 Grenoble, France

Abstract. We propose a general methodology for approximating the Pareto front of multi-criteria optimization problems. Our search-based methodology consists of submitting queries to a constraint solver. Hence, in addition to a set of solutions, we can guarantee bounds on the distance to the actual Pareto front and use this distance to guide the search. Our implementation, which computes and updates the distance efficiently, has been tested on numerous examples.

1 Introduction

Many problems in the design of complex systems are formulated as *optimization* problems, where design choices are encoded as valuations of decision variables and the relative merits of each choice are expressed via a utility/cost function over the decision variables. In most real-life optimization situations, however, the cost function is *multi-dimensional*. For example, a cellular phone that we want to develop or purchase can be evaluated according to its cost, size, power autonomy and performance, and a configuration s which is better than s' according to one criterium, can be worse according to another. Consequently, there is no *unique* optimal solution but rather a set of *efficient* solutions, also known as Pareto[1] solutions, characterized by the fact that their cost cannot be improved in one dimension without being worsened in another. The set of all Pareto solutions, the *Pareto front*, represents the problem trade-offs, and being able to sample this set in a representative manner is a very useful aid in decision making.

Multiple-criteria or multi-objective optimization problems have been studied since the dawn of modern optimization using diverse techniques, depending on the nature of the underlying optimization problems (linear, nonlinear, combinatorial) [10,4,5,3]. One approach consists of defining an aggregate one-dimensional cost/utility function by taking a weighted sum of the various costs. Each choice of a set of coefficients for this sum will lead to an optimal solution for the one-dimensional problem which is also a Pareto solution for the original problem. Another popular class of techniques is

---

* This work was partially supported by the French MINALOGIC project ATHOLE.

[1] In honor of V. Pareto who introduced them in the context of economic theory [9] to express the fact that different members of society may have different goals and hence social choices cannot be optimal in the one-dimensional sense, a fact consistently ignored in most public debates.

J. Esparza and R. Majumdar (Eds.): TACAS 2010, LNCS 6015, pp. 69–83, 2010.

based on heuristic search, most notably genetic/evolutionary algorithms [1,11], which are used to solve problems related to design-space exploration of embedded systems, the same problems that motivate our work. A major issue in these heuristic techniques is finding meaningful measures of quality for the sets of solutions they provide [12].

In this paper we explore an alternative approach to solve the problem based on *satisfiability/constraint solvers* that can answer whether there is an assignment of values to the decision variables which satisfies a set of constraints. It is well known, in the single-criterium case, that such solvers can be used for optimization by searching the space of feasible costs and asking queries of the form: *is there a solution which satisfies the problem constraints* **and** *its cost is not larger than some constant?* Asking such questions with different constants we obtain both positive (*sat*) and negative (*unsat*) answers. Taking the minimal cost x among the *sat* points and the maximal cost y among the *unsat* points we obtain *both* an approximate solution x and an upper bound $x - y$ on its distance from the optimum, that is, on the quality of the approximation.

In this work we extend the idea to multi-criteria optimization problems. Our goal is to use the *sat* points as an *approximation* of the Pareto front of the problem, use the *unsat* points to guarantee *computable bounds* on the distance between these points and the actual Pareto front and to *direct* the search toward parts of the cost space so as to *reduce* this distance. To this end we define an appropriate metric on the cost space as well as efficient ways to recompute it incrementally as more *sat* and *unsat* points accumulate. A prototype implementation of our algorithm demonstrates the quality and efficiency of our approach on numerous Pareto fronts.

The rest of the paper is organized as follows. Section 2 defines the problem setting including the notions of distance between the *sat* and *unsat* points which guides our search algorithm. In Section 3 we describe some fundamental properties of special points on the boundary of the *unsat* set (*knee points*) which play a special role in computing the distance to the *sat* points, and show how they admit a natural tree structure. In Section 4 we describe our exploration algorithm and the way it updates the distance after each query. Section 5 reports our implementation and experimental results on some purely-synthetic benchmarks of varying dimension and accuracy as well as some scheduling problems where we show the trade-offs between execution time and power consumption. Conclusions and suggestions for future work close the paper.

2   Preliminary Definition

Constrained optimization (we use *minimization* henceforth) problems are often specified as

$$\min c(x) \text{ s.t. } \varphi(x)$$

where x is a vector of decision variables, φ is a set of constraints on the variables that define which solution is considered feasible and c is a cost function defined over the decision variables. We prefer to reformulate the problem by moving costs to the constraint side, that is, letting $\varphi(x, c)$ denote the fact that x is a feasible solution whose cost is c. Hence the optimum is

$$\min\{c : \exists x \; \varphi(x, c)\}.$$

Moving to multi-criteria optimization, c becomes a d-dimensional vector $(c_1, \ldots c_d)$ that we assume, without loss of generality,[2] to range over the bounded hypercube $C = [0, 1]^d$, that we call the *cost space*. We use notation $\mathbf{r}$ for $(r, \ldots, r)$.

We assume that the maximal cost $\mathbf{1}$ is feasible and that any cost with some $c_i = 0$ is infeasible. This is expressed as an initial set of *unsat* points $\{\mathbf{0}_i\}_{i=1..d}$ where $\mathbf{0}_i$ is a point with $c_i = 0$ and $c_j = 1$ for every $j \neq i$. The set C is a lattice with a partial-order relation defined as:

$$s \leq s' \equiv \forall i \; s_i \leq s'_i \tag{1}$$

Pairs of points such that $s \not\leq s'$ and $s' \not\leq s$ are said to be *incomparable*, denoted by $s \| s'$. The strict version of $\leq$ is

$$s < s' \equiv s \leq s' \wedge \exists j \; s_j < s'_j \tag{2}$$

meaning that s strictly improves upon s' in at least one dimension without being worse on the others. In this case we say that s *dominates* s'. We will make an assumption that if cost s is feasible so is any cost $s' > s$ (one can add a slack variable to the cost). The *meet* and *join* on C are defined as

$$s \sqcap s' = (\min\{s_1, s'_1\}, \ldots, \min\{s_d, s'_d\})$$
$$s \sqcup s' = (\max\{s_1, s'_1\}, \ldots, \max\{s_d, s'_d\})$$

We say that a point in the cost space s' is an *i-extension* of a point s if $s'_i > s_i$ and $s'_j = s_j$ for every $i \neq j$.

A point s in a subset $S \subseteq C$ is *minimal* if it is not dominated by any other point in S, and is *maximal* if it does not dominate any point in S. We denote the sets of minimal and maximal elements of S by $\underline{S}$ and $\overline{S}$, respectively. We say that a set S of points is domination-free if all pairs of elements $s, s' \in S$ are incomparable, which is true by definition for $\underline{S}$ and $\overline{S}$. The domination relation associates with a point s two *rectangular cones* $B^+(s)$ and $B^-(s)$ consisting of points dominated by (resp. dominating) s:

$$B^-(s) = \{s' \in C, s' < s\} \text{ and } B^+(s) = \{s' \in C, s < s'\}.$$

These notions are illustrated in Figure 1. Note that both $B^-(s) \cup \{s\}$ and $B^+(s) \cup \{s\}$ are closed sets. If cost s is feasible it is of no use to look for solutions with costs in $B^+(s)$ because they are not Pareto solutions. Likewise, if s is infeasible, we will not find solutions in $B^-(s)$.[3] We let $B^-(S)$ and $B^+(S)$ denote the union of the respective cones of the elements of S and observe that $B^+(S) = B^+(\underline{S})$ and $B^-(S) = B^-(\overline{S})$.

Suppose that we have performed several queries and the solver has provided us with the sets S_0, and S_1 of *unsat* and *sat* points, respectively. Our state of knowledge is summarized by the two sets $K_1 = B^+(S_1)$ and $K_0 = B^-(S_0)$. We know that K_1 contains no Pareto points and K_0 contains no solutions. The domain for which S_0 and S_1 give us *no information* is $\tilde{K} = (C - K_0) \cap (C - K_1)$. We use $bd(K_0)$ and $bd(K_1)$ to

---

[2] One can normalize the cost functions accordingly.

[3] Note that the query is formulated as $c \leq s$ and if the problem is discrete and there is no solution whose cost is exactly s, the solver would provide a solution with $c = s' < s$ if such a solution exists.

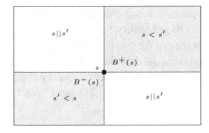

Fig. 1. A point s and its backward and forward cones

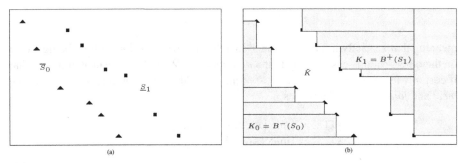

Fig. 2. (a) Sets S_0 and S_1 represented by their extremal points $\overline{S}_0$ and $\underline{S}_1$; (b) The gaps in our knowledge at this point as captured by K_0, K_1 and $\tilde{K}$. The actual Pareto front is contained in the closure of $\tilde{K}$.

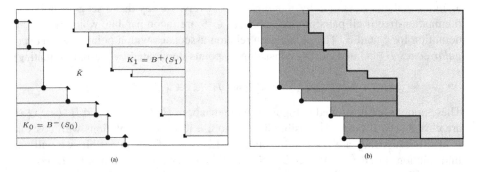

Fig. 3. (a) Knee points, denoted by circles; (b) Knee points viewed as the minimal points of $C - K_0$

denote the boundaries between $\tilde{K}$ and K_0 and K_1, respectively. It is the "size" of $\tilde{K}$ or the *distance* between the boundaries $bd(K_0)$ and $bd(K_1)$ which determines the quality of our current approximation, see Figure 2. Put another way, if S_1 is our approximation of the Pareto surface, the boundary of K_0 defines the limits of potential improvement of the approximation, because no solutions can be found beyond it. This can be formalized as an appropriate (directed) distance between S_1 and K_0. Note that no point in S_1 can dominate a point in K_0.

Definition 1 (Directed Distance between Points and Sets). *The directed distance* $\rho(s, s')$ *between two points is defined as*

$$\rho(s, s') = \max\{s'_i \dot{-} s_i : i = 1..d\},$$

where $x \dot{-} y = x - y$ *when* $x > y$ *and* 0 *otherwise. The distance between a point s and a set* S' *is the distance between s to the closest point in* S':

$$\rho(s, S') = \min\{\rho(s, s') : s' \in S'\}.$$

The Hausdorff directed distance between two sets S *and* S'

$$\rho(S, S') = \max\{\rho(s, S') : s \in S\}.$$

In all these definitions we assume $s' \not< s$ *for any* $s \in S$ *and* $s' \in S'$.

In other words

$$\rho(S, S') = \max_{s \in S} \min_{s' \in S'} \max_{i=1..d} s'_i \dot{-} s_i.$$

Definition 2 (ε-Approximation). *A set of points* S *is an ε-approximation[4] of a Pareto front* P *if* $\rho(P, S) \leq \epsilon$.

Since the Pareto surface is bounded from below by $bd(K_0)$ we have:

Observation 1. *Consider an optimization problem such that* S_0 *is included in the set of infeasible solutions, with* $K_0 = B^-(S_0)$. *Then any set* S_1 *of solutions which satisfies* $\rho(bd(K_0), S_1) \leq \epsilon$ *is an ε-approximation of the Pareto set* P.

Our goal is to obtain an ε-approximation of P by submitting as few queries as possible to the solver. To this end we will study the structure of the involved sets and their distances. We are not going to prove new complexity results because the upper and lower bounds on the number of required queries are almost tight:

Observation 2 (Bounds)

1. *One can find an ε-approximation of any Pareto front* $P \subseteq C$ *using* $(1/\epsilon)^d$ *queries;*
2. *Some Pareto fronts cannot be approximated by less than* $(1/\epsilon)^{d-1}$ *points.*

Proof. For (1), similarly to [8], define an ε-grid over C, ask queries for each grid point and put them in S_0 and S_1 according to the answer. Then take S_1 as the approximation whose distance from $bd(S_0)$ is at most $1/\epsilon$ by construction. For (2), consider a "diagonal" surface

$$P = \{(s_1, \ldots, s_d) : \sum_{i=1}^{d} s_i = 1\}$$

which has dimension $d - 1$.   ⌐

---

[4] This definition is similar to that of [8] except for the fact that their definition requires that for every $p \in P$ there exists $s \in S$ such that $s \leq p + \epsilon p$ and ours requires that $s \leq p + \epsilon$.

Remark: The lower bound holds for continuous Pareto surfaces. In discrete problems where the solutions are sparse in the cost space one may hope to approximate P with less than $(1/\epsilon)^d$ points, maybe with a measure related to the actual *number* of Pareto solutions. However since we do not work directly with P but rather with S_0, it is not clear whether this fact can be exploited. Of course, even for continuous surfaces the lower bound is rarely obtained: as the orientation of the surface deviates from the diagonal, the number of needed points decreases. A surface which is almost axes-parallel can be approximated by few points.

Updating the distance $\rho(bd(K_0), S_1)$ as more *sat* and *unsat* points accumulate is the major activity of our algorithm hence we pay a special attention to its efficient implementation. It turns out that it is sufficient to compute the distance $\rho(G, S_1)$ where G is a finite set of special points associated with any set of the from $B^-(S)$.

3   Knee Points

Definition 3 (Knee Points). *A point s in $bd(K_0)$ is called a knee point if by subtracting a positive number from any of its coordinates we obtain a point in the interior of K_0. The set of all such points is denoted by G.*

In other words the knee points, illustrated in Figure 3-(a), represent the most *unexplored corners* of the cost space where the maximal potential improvement resides. This is perhaps best viewed if we consider an alternative definition of G as the minimal set such that $C - K_0 = B^+(G)$, see Figure 3-(b). Since $\rho(s, s')$ can only increase as s moves *down* along the boundary we have:

Observation 3 (Distance and Knee Points). $\rho(bd(K_0), S_1)) = \rho(G, S_1)$.

Our algorithm keeps track of the evolution of the knee points as additional *unsat* points accumulate. Before giving formal definitions, let us illustrate their evolution using an example in dimension 2. Figure 4-(a) shows a knee point g generated by two *unsat* points s^1 and s^2. The effect of a new *unsat* point s on g depends, of course, on the relative position of s. Figure 4-(b) shows the case where $s \not\succ g$: here knee g is not affected at all and the new knees generated are extensions of other knees. Figure 4-(c) shows two *unsat* points dominated by g: point s^5 induces two extensions of g and point s^6 which does not. The general rule is illustrated in Figure 4-(d): s will create an extension of g in direction i iff $s_i < h_i$ where h_i is the extent to which the hyperplane perpendicular to i can be translated forward without eliminating the knee, that is, without taking the intersection of the d hyperplanes outside K_0.

Let S be a set of incomparable points and let $\{s^1, \ldots, s^d\} \subseteq S$ be a set of d points such that for every i and every $j \neq i$ $s_i^i \leq s_i^j$. The *ordered meet* of $s^1, \ldots, s^d$ is

$$[s^1, \ldots, s^d] = (s_1^1, s_2^2, \ldots, s_d^d). \tag{3}$$

Note that this definition coincides with the usual meet operation on partially-ordered sets, but our notation is ordered, insisting that s^i attains the minimum in dimension i. The knee points of S are maximal elements of the set of points thus obtained. With every knee $g \in G$ we associate a vector h defined as $h = \langle s^1, s^2, \ldots, s^d \rangle = (h_1, \ldots, h_d)$ with $h_i = \min_{j \neq i} s_i^j$ for every i, characterizing the extendability of s in direction i.

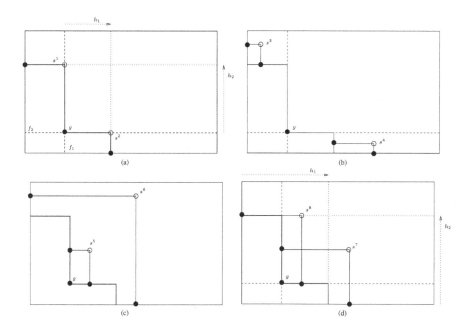

Fig. 4. (a) A knee g generated by s^1 and s^2. It is the intersection of the two hyperplanes f_1 and f_2 (dashed lines); (b) new *unsat* points s^3 and s^4 which are not dominated by g and have no influence on it; (c) new *unsat* points s^5 and s^6 which are dominated by g and hence eliminate it as a knee point. Point s^5 generates new knees as "extensions" of g while the knees generated by s^6 are not related to g; (d) point s^7 generates an extension of g in direction 2 and point s^8 generates an extension in direction 1. These are the directions i where the coordinates of the *unsat* points are strictly smaller than h_i (dotted lines).

Proposition 1 (Knee Generation). *Let S be a set of* unsat *points with a set of knees G, let s be a new* unsat *point and let G' be the new set of knees associated with $S \cup \{s\}$. Then the following holds for every $g \in G$ such that $g = [s^1, \ldots, s^d]$ and $h = \langle s^1, s^2, \ldots, s^d \rangle$*

1. *Knee g is kept in G' iff $g \not< s$*
2. *If $g \in G - G'$, then for every i such that $s_i < h_i$, G' contains a new knee g', the i-descendant of g, defined as $g' = [s^1, \ldots, s, \ldots, s^d]$, extending g in direction i.*

Before describing the tree data structure we use to represent the knee points let us make another observation concerning the potential contribution of a new *sat* point in improving the minimal distance to a knee or a set of knees.

Observation 4 (Distance Relevance). *Let g, g^1 and g^2 be knee points with $\rho(g, S) = r$, $\rho(g^1, S) = r^1$ and $\rho(g^2, S) = r^2$ and let s be a new* sat *point. Then*

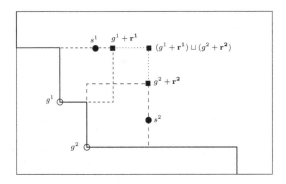

Fig. 5. Two knees g^1 and g^2 and their respective nearest points s^1 and s^2. Points outside the upper dashed square will not improve the distance to g^1 and those outside the lower square will not improve the distance to g^2. Points outside the enclosing dotted rectangle can improve neither of the distances.

1. *The distance* $\rho(g, s) \leq r$ *iff* $s \in B^-(g + \mathbf{r})$;
2. *Point s cannot improve the distance to any of $\{g^1, g^2\}$ if it is outside the cone* $B^-((g^1 + \mathbf{r^1}) \sqcup (g^2 + \mathbf{r^2}))$.

Note that for the second condition, being in that cone is necessary but not sufficient. The sufficient condition for improving the distance of at least one of the knees is $s \in B^-((g^1 + \mathbf{r^1}) \cup (g^2 + \mathbf{r^2}))$ as illustrated in Figure 5.

We represent G as a tree whose nodes are either leaf nodes that stand for current knee points, or other nodes which represent points which were knees in the past and currently have descendant knees that extend them. A node is a tuple

$$N = (g, [s^1, \ldots, s^k], h, (\mu^1, \ldots, \mu^k), r, b)$$

where g is the point, $[s^1, \ldots, s^k]$ are its *unsat* generators and h is the vector of its extension bounds. For each dimension i, μ^i points to the i-descendant of N (if such exists) and the set of all direct descendants of N is denoted by μ. For leaf nodes $N.r = \rho(N.g, S_1)$ is just the distance from the knee to S_1 while for a non-leaf node $N.r = \max_{N' \in N.\mu} N'.r$, the maximal distance to S_1 over all its descendants. Likewise $N.b$ for a leaf node is the maximal point such that any *sat* point in the interior of its back cone improves the distance to $N.g$. For a non leaf node $N.b = \bigsqcup_{N' \in N.\mu} N'.b$, the join of the bounds associated with its descendants.

4   The Algorithm

The following iterative algorithm submits queries to the solver in order to decrease the distance between S_1 and G.

Algorithm 1 (Approximate Pareto Surface)

initialize
repeat
  select(s)
  query(s)   %   *ask whether there is a solution with cost $\leq s$*
  if sat
    update-sat(s)
  else
    update-unsat(s)
until $\rho(G, S_1) < \epsilon$

The initialization procedure lets $S_0 = \{\mathbf{0}_1, \ldots, \mathbf{0}_d\}$, $S_1 = \{(1, \ldots, 1)\}$ and hence initially $G = \{g^0\}$ with $g^0 = [\mathbf{0}_1, \ldots, \mathbf{0}_d] = (0, \ldots, 0)$ and $h = \langle \mathbf{0}_1, \ldots, \mathbf{0}_d \rangle = (1, \ldots, 1)$. The initial distance is $\rho(G, S_1) = 1$. The *update-sat* and *update-unsat* procedures recompute distances according to the newly observed point by propagating s through the knee tree. In the case of a *sat* point, the goal is to track the knee points g such that $\rho(g, s) < \rho(g, S_1)$, namely points whose distance has decreased due to s. When s is an *unsat* point, we have to update G (removing dominated knees, adding new ones), compute the distance from the new knees to S_1 as well as the new maximal distance. The algorithm stops when the distance is reduced beyond ϵ. Note that since $\rho(G, S_1)$ is maintained throughout the algorithm, even an impatient user who aborts the program before termination will have an approximation guarantee for the obtained solution.

The propagation of a new *sat* point s is done via a call to the recursive procedure *prop-sat*(N_0, s) where N_0 is the root of the tree.

Algorithm 2 (Prop-Sat)

proc *prop-sat*(N, s)

if $s < N.b$ %   *s may reduce the distance to $N.g$ or its descendants*
  $r := 0$ %   *temporary distance over all descendants*
  $b := 0$ % *temporary bound on relevant sat points*
  if $N.\mu \neq \emptyset$ % *a non-leaf node*
    for *every i s.t. $N' = N.\mu^i \neq \emptyset$* **do**   % *for every descendant*
      prop-sat(N', s)
      $r := \max\{r, N'.r\}$
      $b := b \sqcap N'.b$
  else   % *leaf node*
    $r := \min\{N.r, \rho(N.g, s)\}$ % *improve if s is closer*
    $b := N.g + \mathbf{r}$
  $N.r := r$
  $N.b := b$

The propagation of a new *unsat* point s, which is more involved, is done by invoking the recursive procedure *prop-unsat*(N_0, s). The procedure returns a bit ex indicating whether the node still exists after the update (is a knee or has descendants).

Algorithm 3 (Prop-Unsat)
proc *prop-unsat*(N, s)

$ex := 1$
if $N.g < s$ % *knee is influenced*
  $ex := 0$ % *temporary existence bit*
  $r := 0$ % *temporary distance over all descendants*
  $b := \mathbf{0}$ % *temporary relevance bound*
  if $N.\mu \neq \emptyset$ % *a non-leaf node*
    for *every i s.t.* $N' = N.\mu^i \neq \emptyset$ **do**   % *for every descendant*
      $ex' :=$*prop-unsat*(N', s)
      if $ex' = 0$
        $N.\mu^i := \emptyset$ % *node N' is removed*
      else
        $ex := 1$
        $r := \max\{r, N'.r\}$
        $b := b \sqcup N'.b$
  else   % *leaf node*
    for $i = 1..d$ **do**
      if $s_i < N.h_i$ % *knee can extend in direction i*
        $ex := 1$
        create a new node $N' = N.\mu^i$ *with*
          $N'.g = [N.s^1, \ldots, s, \ldots, N.s^k]$
          $N'.h = \langle N.s^1, \ldots, s, \ldots, N.s^k \rangle$
          $N'.r = \rho(N'.g, S_1)$
          $N'.b = N'.g + N'.r$
          $N'.\mu^i = \emptyset$ *for every i*
        $r := \max\{r, N'.r\}$
        $b := b \sqcup N'.b$
  $N.r := r$
  $N.b := b$
return(ex)

The *prop-unsat* procedure has to routinely solve the following sub problem: given a knee point g and a set of non-dominating *sat* points S, find a point $s \in S$ nearest to g and hence compute $\rho(g, S)$. The distance has to be non negative so there is at least one dimension i such that $g_i \leq s_i$. Hence a lower bound on the distance is

$$\rho(g, S) \geq \min\{s_i - g_i : (i = 1..d) \wedge (s \in S) \wedge (s_i \geq g_i)\},$$

and an upper bound is:

$$\rho(g, S) \leq \max\{s_i - g_i : (i = 1..d) \wedge (s \in S)\}.$$

We now present an algorithm and a supporting data structure for computing this distance. Let $(L_i, <_i)$ be the linearly-ordered set obtained by projecting $S \cup \{g\}$ on dimension i. For every $v \in L_i$ let $\Theta_i(v)$ denote all the points in S whose i^{th} coordinate is v. Let $\sigma^i(s)$ be the successor of s_i according to $<_i$, that is, the smallest s_i' such that $s_i < s_i'$. Our goal is to find the minimal value v in some L_i such that for every $s \in \Theta_i(v)$, s_i defines the maximal distance to g, that is, $s_i - g_i > s_j - g_j$ for every $j \neq i$.

The algorithm keeps a frontier $F = \{f_1, \ldots, f_d\}$ of candidates for this role. Initially, for every i, $f_i = \sigma^i(g_i)$, the value next to g_i and the candidate distances are kept in $\Delta = \{\delta_1, \ldots, \delta_d\}$ with $\delta_i = f_i - g_i$. The algorithm is simple: each time we pick the minimal $\delta_i \in \Delta$. If for some $s \in \Theta_i(f_i)$ and for every $j \neq i$ we have $s_j - g_j < s_i - g_i$ then we are done and found a nearest point s with distance δ_i. Otherwise, if every $s \in \Theta(f_i)$ admits some j such that $s_j - g_j > s_i - g_i$ we conclude that the distance should be greater than δ_i. We then let $f_i = \sigma^i(f_i)$, update δ_i accordingly, take the next minimal element of Δ and so on. This procedure is illustrated in Figure 6. The projected order relations are realized using an auxiliary structure consisting of d linked lists.

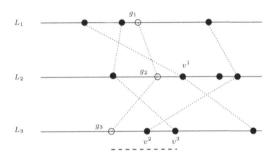

Fig. 6. Finding the nearest neighbor of g: the first candidate for the minimal distance is v^1, the nearest projection which is on dimension 2, but the point associated with it has a larger distance on dimension 3; The next candidate is v^2, the closest in dimension 3 but the corresponding point also has larger coordinates. Finally, the point associated with v^3, the next value on L_3, has all its distances in other dimensions smaller and hence it is the closest point which defines the distance (dashed line)

Selecting the next query to ask is an important ingredient in any heuristic search algorithm, including ours. We currently employ the following simple rule. Let g and s be a knee and a *sat* point whose distance $\rho(g, s)$ is maximal and equal to $r = s_i - g_i$ for some i. The next point for which we ask a query is $s' = s + \mathbf{r}/2$. If s' turns out to be a *sat* point, then the distance from g to S_1 is reduced by half. If s' is an *unsat* point then g is eliminated and is replaced by zero or more new knees, each of which is r-closer to S_1 in one dimension. For the moment we do not know to compute an upper bound on the worst-case number of queries needed to reach distance ϵ except for some hand-waving arguments based on a discretized version of the algorithm where queries are restricted to the ϵ-grid. Empirically, as reported below, the number of queries was significantly smaller than the upper bound.

5   Experimentation

We have implemented Algorithm 1 and tested it on numerous Pareto fronts produced as follows. We generated artificial Pareto surfaces by properly intersecting several convex and concave halfspaces generated randomly. Then we sampled $10,000$ points in this surface, defined the Pareto front as the boundary of the forward cone of these points and run our algorithm for different values of ϵ. Figure 7 shows how the approximate solutions and the set of queries vary with ϵ on a 2-dimensional example. One can see that indeed, our algorithm concentrates its efforts on the neighborhood of the front. Table 1 shows some preliminary results obtained as follows. For every dimension d we generate several fronts, run the algorithm with several values of ϵ, compute the average number of queries and compare it with the upper bound $(1/\epsilon)^d$. As one can see the number of queries is only a small fraction of the upper bound. Note that in this class of experiments we do not use a constraint solver, only an oracle for the feasibility of points in the cost space based on the generated surface.

We also have some preliminary results on the following problem which triggered this research: given an application expressed as a task-data graph (a partially-ordered set of tasks with task duration and inter-task communication volume) and a heterogenous multi-processor architecture (a set of processors with varying speeds and energy consumptions, and a communication topology), find a mapping of tasks to processors

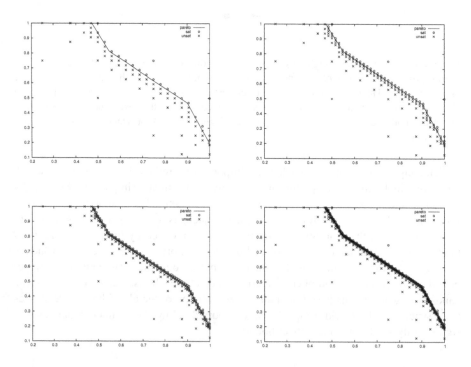

Fig. 7. The results of our algorithm for the same front for $\epsilon = 0.05, 0.125, 0.001, 0.0005$

Table 1. The average number of queries for surfaces of various dimensions and values of ϵ

d	no tests	ϵ	$(1/\epsilon)^d$	min no queries	avg no queries	max no queries
2	40	0.050	400	5	11	27
		0.025	1600	6	36	111
		0.001	1000000	21	788	2494
3	40	0.050	8000	5	124	607
		0.025	64000	6	813	3811
	20	0.002	125000000	9	30554	208078
4	40	0.050	160000	5	1091	5970
		0.025	2560000	10	11560	46906

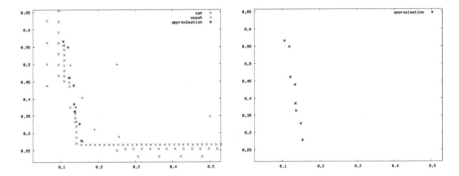

Fig. 8. Scheduling a task-data graph of 20 tasks on an architecture with 8 processors with 3 different levels of speed/consumption: (a) the queries asked; (b) the final front approximation (makespan is horizontal and energy cost is vertical)

and a schedule so as to optimize some performance criteria. In [6] we have used the SMT solver Yices [2] to solve the single-criterium problem of finding the cheapest (in terms of energy) configuration on which such a task graph can be scheduled while meeting a *given* deadline. We applied our algorithm to solve a multi-criteria version of the problem, namely to show trade offs between energy cost and execution time. We were able to find 0.05-approximations of the Pareto front for problem with up to 30 tasks on an architecture with 8 processors of 3 different speeds and costs. The behavior of our algorithm is illustrated in Figure 8 where both execution time and energy are normalized to $[0, 1]$. For reasons discussed in the sequel, it is premature to report the computational cost of the algorithm on these examples.

6 Conclusions

We have presented a novel approach for approximating the Pareto front. The difficulty of the problem decomposes into two parts which can, at least to some extent, be decoupled. The first is related to the hardness of the underlying constraint satisfaction problem, which can be as easy as linear programming or as hard as combinatorial or nonlinear optimization. The second part is less domain specific: approximate the boundary between two mutually-exclusive subsets of the cost space which are not known a priori, based on adaptive sampling of these sets, using the constraint solver as an oracle. We have proposed an algorithm, based on a careful study of the geometry of the cost space, which unlike some other approaches, provides *objective* guarantees for the quality of the solutions in terms of a bound on the approximation error. Our algorithm has been shown to behave well on numerous examples.

The knee tree data structure represents effectively the state of the algorithm and reduces significantly the number of distance calculations per query. We speculate that this structure and further geometrical insights can be useful as well to other approaches for solving this problem. We have investigated additional efficiency enhancing tricks, most notably, *lazy* updates of the knee tree: if it can be deduced that a knee g does not maximize the distance $\rho(S_0, S_1)$, then its distance to it $\rho(g, S_1)$ need not be updated in every step. Many other such improvement are on our agenda.

In the future we intend to investigate specializations and adaptations of our general methodology to different classes of problems. For example, in convex linear problems the Pareto front resides on the surface of the feasible set and its approximation may benefit from convexity and admit some symbolic representation via inequalities. More urgently, for hard combinatorial and mixed problems, such as mapping and scheduling, where computation time grows drastically as one approaches the Pareto front, we have to cope with computations that practically do not terminate. We are developing a variant of our algorithm with a limited time budget per query where in addition to *sat* and *unsat*, the solver may respond with a *time-out*. Such an algorithm will produce an ϵ-approximation of the best approximation obtainable with that time budget per query. Adding this feature will increase the size of mapping and scheduling problems that can be robustly handled by our algorithm. To conclude, we believe that the enormous progress made during the last decade in SAT and SMT solvers will have a strong impact on the optimization domain [7] and we hope that this work can be seen as an important step in this direction.

References

1. Deb, K.: Multi-objective optimization using evolutionary algorithms. Wiley, Chichester (2001)
2. Dutertre, B., de Moura, L.M.: A fast linear-arithmetic solver for DPLL(T). In: Ball, T., Jones, R.B. (eds.) CAV 2006. LNCS, vol. 4144, pp. 81–94. Springer, Heidelberg (2006)
3. Ehrgott, M.: Multicriteria optimization. Springer, Heidelberg (2005)
4. Ehrgott, M., Gandibleux, X.: A survey and annotated bibliography of multiobjective combinatorial optimization. OR Spectrum 22(4), 425–460 (2000)
5. Figueira, J., Greco, S., Ehrgott, M.: Multiple criteria decision analysis: state of the art surveys. Springer, Heidelberg (2005)
6. Legriel, J., Maler, O.: Meeting deadlines cheaply. Technical Report 2010-1, VERIMAG (January 2010)
7. Nieuwenhuis, R., Oliveras, A.: On SAT Modulo Theories and Optimization Problems. In: Biere, A., Gomes, C.P. (eds.) SAT 2006. LNCS, vol. 4121, pp. 156–169. Springer, Heidelberg (2006)

8. Papadimitriou, C.H., Yannakakis, M.: On the approximability of trade-offs and optimal access of web sources. In: FOCS, pp. 86–92 (2000)
9. Pareto, V.: Manuel d'économie politique. Bull. Amer. Math. Soc. 18, 462–474 (1912)
10. Steuer, R.E.: Multiple criteria optimization: Theory, computation, and application. John Wiley & Sons, Chichester (1986)
11. Zitzler, E., Thiele, L.: Multiobjective evolutionary algorithms: A comparative case study and the strength pareto approach. IEEE transactions on Evolutionary Computation 3(4), 257–271 (1999)
12. Zitzler, E., Thiele, L., Laumanns, M., Fonseca, C.M., da Fonseca, V.G.: Performance assessment of multiobjective optimizers: An analysis and review. IEEE Transactions on Evolutionary Computation 7(2), 117–132 (2003)

An Alternative to SAT-Based Approaches for Bit-Vectors*

Sébastien Bardin, Philippe Herrmann, and Florian Perroud

CEA LIST, Software Safety Laboratory,
Point Courrier 94, Gif-sur-Yvette, F-91191 France
first.name@cea.fr

Abstract. The theory BV of bit-vectors, i.e. fixed-size arrays of bits equipped with standard low-level machine instructions, is becoming very popular in formal verification. Standard solvers for this theory are based on a bit-level encoding into propositional logic and SAT-based resolution techniques. In this paper, we investigate an alternative approach based on a word-level encoding into bounded arithmetic and Constraint Logic Programming (CLP) resolution techniques. We define an original CLP framework (domains and propagators) dedicated to bit-vector constraints. This framework is implemented in a prototype and thorough experimental studies have been conducted. The new approach is shown to perform much better than standard CLP-based approaches, and to considerably reduce the gap with the best SAT-based BV solvers.

1 Introduction

The first order theory of bit-vectors allows reasoning about variables interpreted over fixed-size arrays of bits equipped with standard low-level machine instructions such as machine arithmetic, bitwise logical instructions, shifts or extraction. An overview of this theory can be found in Chapter 6 of [17]. The bit-vector theory, and especially its quantifier-free fragment (denoted QFBV, or simply BV), is becoming increasingly popular in automatic verification of both hardware [3,5] and software [6,8,9]. Most successful BV solvers (e.g. [2,15,26]) rely on encoding the BV formula into an equi-satisfiable propositional logic formula, which is then submitted to a SAT solver. The encoding relies on *bit-blasting*: each bit of a bit-vector is represented as a propositional variable and BV operators are modelled as logical circuits. The main advantage of the method is to ultimately rely on the great efficiency of modern DPLL-based SAT solvers [21]. However, this approach has a few shortcomings. First, bit-blasting may result in very large SAT formulas, difficult to solve for the best current SAT solvers. This phenomenon happens especially on "arithmetic-oriented" formulas. Second, the SAT-solving process cannot rely on any information about the word-level structure of the problem, typically missing simplifications such as arithmetic identities. State-of-the-art approaches complement optimised bit-blasting [22] with word-level preprocessing [15] and dedicated SAT-solving heuristics [26].

---

* Work partially funded by Agence Nationale de la Recherche (grant ANR-08-SEGI-006).

J. Esparza and R. Majumdar (Eds.): TACAS 2010, LNCS 6015, pp. 84–98, 2010.

Constraint Logic Programming. Constraint Logic Programming (CLP) over finite domains can be seen as a natural extension of the basic DPLL procedure to the case of finite but non boolean domains, with an interleaving of propagation and search steps [11]. Intuitively, the search procedure explores exhaustively the tree of all partial valuations of variables to find a solution. Before each labelling step, a propagation mechanism narrows each variable domain by removing some inconsistent values. In the following, constraints over bounded arithmetic are denoted by $\mathbb{N}^{\leq M}$. Given a theory T, CLP(T) denotes CLP techniques designed to deal with constraints over T.

Alternative word-level (CLP-based) approach for BV. In order to keep advantage of the high-level structure of the problem, a BV constraint can be encoded into a $\mathbb{N}^{\leq M}$ constraint using the standard (one-to-one) encoding between bit-vectors of size k and unsigned integers less than or equal to $2^k - 1$. A full encoding of BV requires non-linear operators and case-splits [12,25,27]. At first sight, CLP($\mathbb{N}^{\leq M}$) offers an interesting framework for word-level solving of BV constraints, since non-linear operations and case-splits are supported. However, there are two major drawbacks leading to poor performance. Firstly, bitwise BV operators cannot be encoded directly and require a form of bit-blasting. Secondly the encoding introduces too many case-splits and non-linear constraints. Recent experiments show that the naive word-level approach is largely outperformed by SAT-based approaches [23]. In the following, we denote by $\mathbb{N}^{\leq M}_{BV}$ bounded integer constraints coming from an encoding of BV constraints.

The problem. Our longstanding goal is to design an efficient word-level CLP-based solver for BV constraints. In our opinion, such a solver could outperform SAT-based approaches on arithmetic-oriented BV problems typically arising in software verification. This paper presents a first step toward this goal. We design new efficient domains and propagators in order to develop a true CLP($\mathbb{N}^{\leq M}_{BV}$) solver, while related works rely on standard CLP($\mathbb{N}^{\leq M}$) techniques [12,25,27]. We also deliberately restrict our attention to the conjunctive fragment of BV in order to focus only on BV propagation issues, without having to consider the orthogonal issue of handling formulas with arbitrary boolean skeletons. Note that the conjunctive fragment does have practical interests of its own, for example in symbolic execution [6,8].

Contribution. We rely on the CLP($\mathbb{N}^{\leq M}$) framework developed in COLIBRI, the solver integrated in the model-based testing tool GaTeL [20].

The main results of this paper are twofold. First, we set up the basic ingredients of a dedicated CLP($\mathbb{N}^{\leq M}_{BV}$) framework, avoiding both bit-blasting and non-linear encoding into $\mathbb{N}^{\leq M}$. The paper introduces two main features: (1) $\mathbb{N}^{\leq M}_{BV}$-propagators for existing domains (union of intervals with congruence [18], denoted Is/C), and (2) a new domain bit-list $\mathcal{BL}$ designed to work in combination with Is/C and $\mathcal{BL}$-propagators. While Is/C comes with efficient propagators on linear arithmetic constraints, $\mathcal{BL}$ is equipped with efficient propagators on "linear" bitwise constraints, i.e. bitwise operations with one constant operand. Second, these ideas have been implemented in a prototype on top of COLIBRI and thorough empirical evaluations have been performed. Experimental results prove that dedicated Is/C-propagators and $\mathcal{BL}$ allow a significant increase of performance compared to a direct CLP($\mathbb{N}^{\leq M}$) approach, as well as considerably lowering the gap with state-of-the-art SAT-based approaches. Moreover, the CLP($\mathbb{N}_{BV}^{\leq M}$)-based approach scales better than the SAT-based approach with the size of bit-vector variables, and is superior on non-linear arithmetic problems.

Outline. The rest of the paper is structured as follows. Section 2 describes the relevant background on BV and CLP, Sections 4 and 5 presents dedicated propagators and domains, Section 6 presents experimental results and benchmarks. Section 7 discusses related work and Section 8 provides a conclusion.

2   Background

2.1   Bit-Vector Theory

Variables in BV are interpreted over bit-vectors, i.e. fixed-size arrays of bits. Given a bit-vector a, its size is denoted by S_a and its i-th bit is denoted by a_i, a_1 being the least significant bit of a. A bit-vector a represents (and is represented by) a unique non-negative integer between 0 and $2^{S_a} - 1$ (power-two encoding) and also a unique integer between -2^{S_a-1} and $2^{S_a-1} - 1$ (two's complement encoding). The unsigned encoding of a is denoted by $[\![a]\!]_u$. Common operators consist of: bitwise operators "and" (&), "or" (|), "xor" (xor) and "not" ($\sim$); bit-array manipulations such as left shift ($\ll$), unsigned right shift ($\gg_u$), signed right shift ($\gg_s$), concatenation (::), extraction ($a[i..j]$), unsigned and signed extensions ($ext_u(a, i)$ and $ext_s(a, i)$); arithmetic operators ($\oplus$, $\ominus$, $\otimes$, $\oslash_u$, modulo $\%_u$, $<_u$, $\leq_u$, $\geq_u$, $>_u$) with additional constructs for signed arithmetic ($\oslash_s$, $\%_s$, $<_s$, $\leq_s$, $\geq_s$, $>_s$); and a case-split operator $ite(cond, term_1, term_2)$. The exact semantics of all operators can be found in [17]. The following provides only a brief overview. Most operators have their intuitive meaning. Signed extension and signed shift propagate the sign-bit of the operand to the result. Arithmetic operations are performed modulo 2^N, with N the size of both operands. Unsigned (resp. signed) operations consider the unsigned (resp. signed) integer encoding.

Conjunctive fragment. This paper focuses on the conjunctive fragment of BV, i.e. no other logical connector than $\wedge$ is allowed.

2.2   Constraint Logic Programming

Let $\mathcal{U}$ be a set of values. A constraint satisfaction problem (CSP) over $\mathcal{U}$ is a triplet $\mathcal{R} = \langle \mathcal{X}, \mathcal{D}, \mathcal{C} \rangle$ where the domain $\mathcal{D} \subseteq \mathcal{U}$ is a finite cartesian product $\mathcal{D} = d_1 \times \ldots \times d_n$, $\mathcal{X}$ is a finite set of variables $x_1, \ldots, x_n$ such that each variable x_i ranges over d_i and $\mathcal{C}$ is a finite set of constraints $c_1, \ldots, c_m$ such that each constraint c_i is associated with a set of solutions $L_{c_i} \subseteq \mathcal{U}$. In the following, we consider only the case of finite domains, i.e. $\mathcal{U}$ is finite. The set $L_{\mathcal{R}}$ of solutions of $\mathcal{R}$ is equal to $\mathcal{D} \cap \bigcap_i L_{c_i}$. A value of x_i participating in a solution of $\mathcal{R}$ is called a legal value, otherwise it is said to be spurious. In other words, the set $L_{\mathcal{R}}(x_i)$ of legal values of x_i in $\mathcal{R}$ is defined as the i-th projection of $L_{\mathcal{R}}$. Let us also define $L_c(x_i)$ as the i-th projection of L_c, and $L_{c,\mathcal{D}}(x_i) = L_c(x_i) \cap d_i$. The CLP approach follows a search-propagate scheme. Intuitively, propagation narrows the CSP domains, keeping all legal values of each variable but removing some of the spurious values. Formally, a propagator P refines a CSP $\mathcal{R} = \langle \mathcal{X}, \mathcal{D}, \mathcal{C} \rangle$ into another CSP $\mathcal{R}' = \langle \mathcal{X}, \mathcal{D}', \mathcal{C} \rangle$ with $\mathcal{D}' \subseteq \mathcal{D}$. Only the current domain $\mathcal{D}$ is actually refined, hence we write $P(\mathcal{D})$ for $\mathcal{D}'$. A propagator P is correct (or ensures correct propagation) if $L_{\mathcal{R}}(x_1) \times \ldots \times L_{\mathcal{R}}(x_n) \subseteq P(\mathcal{D}) \subseteq \mathcal{D}$. The use of correct propagators ensures that no legal value is lost during propagation, which in turn ensures that no solution is lost, i.e. $L_{\mathcal{R}'} = L_{\mathcal{R}}$. Usually, propagators are defined locally to each constraint c. Such a propagator P_c is said to be locally correct over domain $\mathcal{D}$ if $L_{c,\mathcal{D}}(x_1) \times \ldots \times L_{c,\mathcal{D}}(x_n) \subseteq P_c(\mathcal{D}) \subseteq \mathcal{D}$. Local correctness implies correctness. A constraint c over domain $\mathcal{D}$ is locally arc-consistent if for all i, $L_{c,\mathcal{D}}(x_i) = \mathcal{D}_i$. This means that from the point of view of constraint c only, there is no spurious value in any d_i. A CSP $\mathcal{R}$ is globally arc-consistent if all its constraints are locally arc-consistent. A propagator is said to ensure local (global) arc-consistency if the resulting CSP is locally (globally) arc-consistent. Such propagators are considered as an interesting trade-off between large pruning and fast propagation.

2.3   Efficient CLP over Bounded Arithmetic

An interesting class of finite CSPs is the class of CSPs defined over bounded integers ($\mathbb{N}^{\leq M}$). $\mathbb{N}^{\leq M}$ problems coming from verification issues have the particularity to exhibit finite but huge domains. Specific CLP($\mathbb{N}^{\leq M}$) techniques have recently been developed for such problems.

Abstract domains. Domains are not represented concretely by enumeration, they are rather compactly encoded by a symbolic representation allowing efficient (but usually approximated) basic manipulations such as intersection and union of domains or emptiness testing. Even though primarily designed for static analysis, abstract interpretation [7] provides a convenient framework for abstract domains in CLP. An abstract domain $d^{\#}_x$ belonging to some complete lattice $(\mathcal{A}, \sqcap, \sqcup, \sqsubseteq, \bot, \top)$ is attached to each variable x. This abstract domain defines a set of integers $[\![d^{\#}_x]\!]$ that must over-approximate the set of legal values of x, i.e. $L_{\mathcal{R}}(x) \subseteq [\![d^{\#}_x]\!]$. The concretisation function $[\![\cdot]\!]$ must satisfy: $a \sqsubseteq b \implies [\![a]\!] \subseteq [\![b]\!]$ and $[\![\bot]\!] = \emptyset$. Given an arbitrary set of integers d, the minimal $\mathcal{A}$-abstraction of d, denoted $\langle d \rangle$, is defined as the least element $d^{\#} \in \mathcal{A}$ such that $d \subseteq [\![d^{\#}]\!]$. The existence of such an element follows from the lattice completeness property. Several abstract domains can be combined with (finite) cartesian product, providing that the concretisation of the cartesian product is defined as the intersection of concretisations of each abstract domain, and that abstract operations are performed in component-wise fashion. Intervals I are a standard abstract domain for $\mathbb{N}^{\leq M}$. The congruence domain C has been recently proposed [18].

In the context of CLP over abstract domains, it is interesting to consider new kinds of consistency. Given a certain class of abstract domains $\mathcal{A}$ and a CSP $\mathcal{R}$ over abstract domains $d^{\#}_1, \ldots, d^{\#}_n \in \mathcal{A}$, a constraint $c \in \mathcal{R}$ over domain $\mathcal{D}$ is locally $\mathcal{A}$-arc-consistent if for all i, $[\![d^{\#}_i]\!] = L_{c,\mathcal{D}}(x_i)$. Intuitively, a propagator ensuring local $\mathcal{A}$-arc-consistency ensures local arc-consistency only for domains representable in $\mathcal{A}$. The constraint c is locally abstract $\mathcal{A}$-arc-consistent if for all i, $[\![d^{\#}_i]\!] = [\![\langle L_{c,\mathcal{D}}(x_i) \rangle]\!]$. Intuitively, no more local propagation can be performed for c because of the limited expressiveness of $\mathcal{A}$.

Other features for solving large CLP($\mathbb{N}^{\leq M}$) problems. Other techniques for solving large $\mathbb{N}^{\leq M}$ problems include global constraints to quickly detect unsatisfiability (e.g. global difference constraint [14]) and restricted forms of rewriting rules *(simplification rules)* to dynamically perform syntactic simplifications of the CSP [13]. Note that in that case, the formal framework for propagation presented so far must be modified to allow propagators to add and delete constraints.

3   Encoding BV into Non-linear Arithmetic

This section describes how to encode BV constraints into non-linear arithmetic problems. First, each bit-vector variable a is encoded as $[\![a]\!]_u$. Then BV constraints over bit-vectors a, b, etc. are encoded as $\mathbb{N}^{\leq M}$ constraints over integer variables $[\![a]\!]_u$, $[\![b]\!]_u$, etc. Unsigned relational operators correspond exactly to those of integer arithmetic, e.g. $a \leq_u b$ is equivalent to $[\![a]\!]_u \leq [\![b]\!]_u$. Unsigned arithmetic operators can be encoded into non-linear arithmetic using the corresponding integer operator and a modulo operation. For example, $[\![a \oplus b]\!]_u = ([\![a]\!]_u + [\![b]\!]_u) \bmod 2^N$, with $N = S_a = S_b$. Concatenation of a and b is encoded as $[\![a]\!]_u \times 2^{S_b} + [\![b]\!]_u$. Extraction can be viewed as a concatenation of three variables. Unsigned extension just becomes an equality between (integer) variables. Unsigned left and right shifts with a constant shift argument b are handled respectively like multiplications and divisions by $2^{[\![b]\!]_u}$. Signed operators can be encoded into unsigned operators, using case-splits (ite) based on operand signs (recall that $a \geq_s 0$ iff $a <_u 2^{S_a-1}$). For example, the signed extension $r = ext_s(a, k)$ is encoded as $ite([\![a]\!]_u < 2^{S_a-1}, [\![a]\!]_u, [\![a]\!]_u + 2^k - 2^{S_a})$. Except for the bitwise "not" operation $\sim$ which is efficiently encoded as $[\![\sim x]\!]_u = 2^{S_x} - 1 - [\![x]\!]_u$, encoding other bitwise operations requires a bit-blasting like method. For each BV variable a, this encoding introduces a new boolean variable per bit of a (denoted a_i for bit i), a N-ary consistency constraint relating the a_i to $[\![a]\!]_u$: $\sum_{i=1}^{N} a_i \times 2^{i-1} = [\![a]\!]_u$ and $3N$ ternary constraints over bits of operands and results modelling the bit operation. For example, the "and" operator on a single bit can be encoded with a $\times$ or a min operator.

This direct encoding suffers from at least two drawbacks. First, the size of the encoding of bitwise constraints depends on the number of bits, adding both a linear number of new variables, a linear number of ternary constraints and three N-ary constraints. Second, the encoding introduces many constructs which are not well handled by current CLP($\mathbb{N}^{\leq M}$) solvers, such as case-splits and non-linear operations. Actually, only a very small fragment of BV is encoded in an efficient manner for CLP($\mathbb{N}^{\leq M}$): concatenation, extraction, bitwise not, unsigned shifts and unsigned relational operators. Current state-of-the-art CLP domains and propagators for $\mathbb{N}^{\leq M}$ do not perform well for problems typically coming from BV. For example, considering the constraint $a \oplus 3 = b$ with a and b on 8 bits, domains $d_a = [251..255]$ and $d_b = [0..255]$, a perfect propagation would reduce d_b to $d_b' = [0..2] \cup [254..255]$, thus a perfect interval propagation cannot do better than $d_b'' = [0..255]$, i.e. no spurious value is removed, keeping 250 spurious values out of 256 possible values. The same problem occurs with signed operations. It is thus not surprising that common CLP($\mathbb{N}^{\leq M}$) solvers perform very badly on $\mathbb{N}_{BV}^{\leq M}$ problems, as experimentally shown in [23] and confirmed in Section 6.

Our approach. Considering these different issues, we propose the following directions to design an efficient CLP($\mathbb{N}_{BV}^{\leq M}$) framework. First, it seems mandatory to rely on unions of intervals plus congruence (Is/C) rather than single intervals (plus congruence). This is an original point of view in CLP, since COLIBRI [20] is the only CLP solver based on unions of intervals. Second, we propose the two following improvements: (1) the use of original Is/C-propagators designed for BV-constraints instead of relying on combination of existing $\mathbb{N}^{\leq M}$ propagators; and (2) a new domain $\mathcal{BL}$ to efficiently propagate information of bitwise operations without relying on bit-blasting in order to complement Is/C, which is well suited for linear arithmetic. This CLP($\mathbb{N}_{BV}^{\leq M}$) framework works as follows: each variable x has a numerical domain Is/C and a $\mathcal{BL}$ domain, legal values for x being restricted to the intersection of the concretisations of the two domains; each constraint has two associated finite sets of propagators: one for Is/C and one for $\mathcal{BL}$; domains can be synchronised together, i.e. specific propagators are designed to propagate information from one domain to another.

4   Dedicated $\mathbb{N}_{BV}^{\leq M}$-Propagators for Is/C Domains

This section describes dedicated propagators for a CLP($\mathbb{N}_{BV}^{\leq M}$) framework over Is/C domains. The goal is to completely avoid bit-blasting and the introduction of additional case-splits and non-linear constraints at the CLP level.

4.1   Propagators for Union of Intervals

Propagators for unsigned BV constraints are based on performing modular arithmetic or integer arithmetic operations directly on single intervals, with forward and backward propagation steps. These operations are extended to unions of intervals by distribution over all pairs of intervals. Then, local propagators are defined by interleaving these propagation steps until a local fixpoint is reached. For example, for constraint $A \oplus B = R$ over N bits, the forward propagation step over single interval, denoted $\oplus_I$, is defined by ($\sqcup$ denotes union of intervals with normalisation, without any approximation):

$$[m_1..M_1] \oplus_I [m_2..M_2] = \begin{array}{ll} [m_1 + m_2..M_1 + M_2] & \text{if } M_1 + M_2 < 2^N \\ [m_1 + m_2 - 2^N..M_1 + M_2 - 2^N] & \text{if } m_1 + m_2 \geq 2^N \\ [m_1 + m_2..2^N - 1] \sqcup [0..M_1 + M_2 - 2^N] & \text{otherwise} \end{array}$$

This definition is extended to unions of intervals $\oplus_{Is}$ by distribution and $\ominus_{Is}$ is defined similarly. Forward and backward propagation steps are defined as follows:

$$\rho_r : (d^{\#}{}_A, d^{\#}{}_B, d^{\#}{}_R) \mapsto (d^{\#}{}_A, d^{\#}{}_B, d^{\#}{}_A \oplus_{Is} d^{\#}{}_B)$$
$$\rho_a : (d^{\#}{}_A, d^{\#}{}_B, d^{\#}{}_R) \mapsto (d^{\#}{}_R \ominus_{Is} d^{\#}{}_B, d^{\#}{}_B, d^{\#}{}_R)$$
$$\rho_b : (d^{\#}{}_A, d^{\#}{}_B, d^{\#}{}_R) \mapsto (d^{\#}{}_A, d^{\#}{}_R \ominus_{Is} d^{\#}{}_A, d^{\#}{}_R)$$

The propagator for $\oplus$ is then defined as a greatest fixpoint of all propagation steps: $\nu X.(\rho_a(X) \sqcap \rho_b(X) \sqcap \rho_r(X) \sqcap X)(X_0)$. Existence follows from the Knaster-Tarski theorem, effective computability comes from Kleene fixed-point theorem and domain finiteness. It can be computed using the procedure presented in Figure 1.

Such propagators and domains are very well-suited to $\oplus$, $\ominus$, unsigned comparisons, unsigned extension and bitwise negation: they ensure local Is-arc consistency for these

---

procedure propagate-add-is(Is_A, Is_B, Is_R)
1: $(d^\#{}_A, d^\#{}_B, d^\#{}_R) := (Is_A, Is_B, Is_R)$
2: $d^\#{}_R := (d^\#{}_A \oplus_{Is} d^\#{}_B) \sqcap d^\#{}_R$;
3: $d^\#{}_A := (d^\#{}_R \ominus_{Is} d^\#{}_B) \sqcap d^\#{}_A$;
4: $d^\#{}_B := (d^\#{}_R \ominus_{Is} d^\#{}_A) \sqcap d^\#{}_B$;
5: if $(d^\#{}_A, d^\#{}_B, d^\#{}_R) \neq (Is_A, Is_B, Is_R)$ then
6:      propagate-add-is($d^\#{}_A, d^\#{}_B, d^\#{}_R$)
7: else return $(d^\#{}_A, d^\#{}_B, d^\#{}_R)$

Fig. 1. Is-propagator for constraint A $\oplus$ B = R

constraints. For signed operations, the main idea is to perform inside each propagation step a case-split based on sign, compute interval propagation for each case and then join all the results. Note that all these computations are performed locally to the propagators, such that no extra variables nor constraints are added at the CLP level. Propagation steps for signed extension are depicted in Figure 2.

---

procedure Propagator for exts (A, N$'$) = R
  A: bit-vector of size N, R: bit-vector of size $N' > N$
  Propagation steps
  $\rho_r : (d^\#{}_A, d^\#{}_R) \mapsto ((d^\#{}_A \sqcap [0..2^{N-1} - 1]) \sqcup (d^\#{}_A \sqcap [2^{N-1}..2^N - 1]) +_{I_s} (2^{N'} - 2^N), d^\#{}_R)$
  $\rho_a : (d^\#{}_A, d^\#{}_R) \mapsto (d^\#{}_A, (d^\#{}_R \sqcap [0..2^{N-1} - 1]) \sqcup$
  $\qquad\qquad\qquad (d^\#{}_R \sqcap [2^{N-1} + 2^{N'} - 2^N..2^{N'} - 1]) -_{I_s} (2^{N'} - 2^N))$
  propagator: $\nu X.(\rho_a(X) \sqcap \rho_r(X) \sqcap X)(Is_A, Is_R)$.

Fig. 2. Is-propagator for constraint exts (A, N$'$) = R

Non-linear arithmetic, concatenation, extraction and shifts can be dealt with in the same way. However only correct propagation is ensured. Propagators for &, | and xor are tricky to implement without bit-blasting. Since $\mathcal{BL}$-propagators (see Section 5) are very efficient for linear bitwise constraints, only coarse but cheap Is-propagators are considered here and the exact computation is delayed until both operands are instantiated. Approximated propagation for & relies on the fact that $r = a$ & b implies both $[\![r]\!]_u \leq [\![a]\!]_u$ and $[\![r]\!]_u \leq [\![b]\!]_u$. The same holds for | by replacing $\geq$ with $\leq$. No approximate Is-propagator for xor is defined, relying only on $\mathcal{BL}$, simplification rules (see Section 4.2) and delayed exact computation.

Property 1. *Is-propagators ensure local Is-arc-consistency for $\oplus$, $\ominus$, comparisons, extensions and bitwise not. Moreover, correct propagation is ensured for non-linear BV arithmetic operators, shifts, concatenation and extraction.*

Efficiency. While unions of intervals are more precise than single intervals, they can in principle induce efficiency issues since the number of intervals could grow up to half of the domain sizes. Note that it is always possible to bound the number of intervals in a domain, adding an approximation step inside the propagators. Moreover, we did not observe any interval blow-up during our experiments (see Section 6).

4.2   Other Issues

Simplification rules. These rules perform syntactic simplifications of the CSP [13]. It is different from preprocessing in that the rules can be fired at any propagation step. Rules can be local to a constraint (e.g. rewriting $A \otimes 1 = C$ into $A = C$) or global (syntactic equivalence of constraints, functional consistency, etc.). Moreover, simplification rules may rewrite signed constraints into unsigned ones (when signs are known) and $\mathbb{N}_{\overline{BV}}^{\leq M}$-constraints into $\mathbb{N}^{\leq M}$-constraints (when presence or absence of overflow is known). The goal of this last transformation is to benefit both from the integer global difference constraint and better congruence propagation on integer constraints.

Congruence domain. Since the new $\mathcal{BL}$ domain can already propagate certain forms of congruence via the consistency propagators (see Section 5), only very restricted C-propagators are considered for BV-constraints, based on parity propagation. However, efficient C-propagation is performed when a BV-constraint is rewritten into a standard integer constraint via simplification. Consistency between congruence domains and interval domains (i.e. all bounds of intervals respect the congruence) is enforced in a standard way with an additional consistency propagator [18].

5   New Domain: BitList $\mathcal{BL}$

This section introduces the BitList domain $\mathcal{BL}$, a new abstract domain designed to work in synergy with intervals and congruences. Indeed, Is/C models well linear integer arithmetic while $\mathcal{BL}$ is well-suited to linear bitwise operations (except for *xor*), i.e. bitwise operations with one constant operand.

A $\mathcal{BL}$ is a fixed-size array of values ranging over $\{\bot, 0, 1, \star\}$: these values are denoted $\star$-bit in the following. Intuitively, given a $\mathcal{BL}$ $bl = (bl_1, \ldots, bl_N)$, $bl_i = 0$ forces bit i to be equal to 0, $bl_i = 1$ forces bit i to be equal to 1, $bl_i = \star$ does not impose anything on bit i and $bl_i = \bot$ denotes an unsatisfiable constraint. The set $\{\bot, 0, 1, \star\}$ is equipped with a partial order $\sqsubseteq$ defined by $\bot \sqsubseteq 0 \sqsubseteq \star$ and $\bot \sqsubseteq 1 \sqsubseteq \star$. This order is extended to $\mathcal{BL}$ in a bitwise manner. A non-negative integer k is in accordance with bl (of size N), denoted $k \sqsubseteq bl$, if its unsigned encoding on N bits, denoted $[\![k]\!]_{BV}^N$, satisfies $[\![k]\!]_{BV}^N \sqsubseteq bl$. The concretisation of bl, denoted $[\![bl]\!]$, is defined as the set of all (non-negative) integers k such that $k \sqsubseteq bl$. As such, the concretisation of a $\mathcal{BL}$ containing $\bot$ is the empty set. Join (resp. meet) operator $\sqcup$ (resp. $\sqcap$) are defined on $\star$-bits as min and max operations over the complete lattice $(\bot, 0, 1, \star, \sqsubseteq)$, and are extended in a component-wise fashion to $\mathcal{BL}$.

$\mathcal{BL}$-**propagators.** Precise and cheap propagators can be obtained for all constraints involving only local (bitwise) reasoning, i.e. bitwise operations, unsigned shifts, concatenation, extraction and unsigned extension. They can be solved with N independent fixpoint computation on $\star$-bit variables. $\mathcal{BL}$-propagator for constraint A & B = R is presented in Figure 3, where $\wedge_\star$ extends naturally $\wedge$ over $\star$-bits.

Signed shift and signed extension involve mostly local reasoning, however, non-local propagation steps must be added to ensure that all $\star$-bits of the result representing the sign take the same value, and that signs of operands and results are consistent. As $\mathcal{BL}$

---

procedure Propagator for   A & B = R
A, B, R bit-vectors of size N
At the $\star$-bit level (a_i, b_i, r_i being $\star$-bit values)
    $\rho_r : (a_i, b_i, r_i) \mapsto (a_i, b_i, a_i \wedge_\star b_i)$
    $\rho_a : (a_i, b_i, r_i) \mapsto (ite(r_i = 1, 1, ite(b_i = 1, r_i, a_i)), b_i, r_i)$
    ρ_b : similar to ρ_a
propagator $\rho_\star$ for $\star$-bit: $\nu X.(\rho_a(X) \sqcap \rho_b(X) \sqcap \rho_r(X) \sqcap X)(X_0)$.
propagator for the constraint: perform $\rho_\star$ in a component-wise manner

---

Fig. 3. $\mathcal{BL}$-propagator for constraint A & B = R

cannot model equality constraints between unknown $\star$-bit values, these propagators ensure only local abstract $\mathcal{BL}$-arc-consistency. The same idea holds for comparisons. Propagators are simple and cheap: for A $\leq_u$ B, propagate the longest consecutive sequence of 1s (resp. 0s) starting from the most significant $\star$-bit from A to B (resp. B to A). Again, these propagators ensure only local abstract $\mathcal{BL}$-arc-consistency.

Arithmetic constraints involve many non-local reasoning and intermediate results. Moreover backward propagation steps are difficult to define. Thus, this work focuses only on obtaining cheap and correct propagation. Propagators for non-linear arithmetic use a simple forward propagation step (no fixpoint) based on a circuit encoding of the operations interpreted on $\star$-bit values. Propagators for $\oplus$ and $\ominus$ are more precise since they use a complete forward propagation and some limited backward propagation. The $\mathcal{BL}$-propagator for $\oplus$ is depicted in Figure 4. An auxiliary $\mathcal{BL}$ representing the carry is introduced locally to the propagator and the approach relies on the standard circuit encoding for $\oplus$: N local equations $r_i = a_i$ xor b_i xor c_i to compute the result, and N non-local equations for carries $c_{i+1} = (a_i \wedge b_i) \vee (a_i \wedge c_i) \vee (b_i \wedge c_i)$. Note that the local equations are easy to invert thanks to properties of xor. Information in the $\mathcal{BL}$ is propagated from least significant bit to most significant bit (via the carry). A maximal propagation would require also a propagation in the opposite way. However, experiments show that this alternative is expensive without any clear positive impact. All these operations may appear to be a form of bit-blasting, but the encoding is used only locally to the propagator and no new variables are added.

Property 2. *$\mathcal{BL}$-propagators ensure local $\mathcal{BL}$-arc-consistency for bitwise constraints, unsigned shifts, unsigned extension, concatenation and restriction. $\mathcal{BL}$-propagators ensure local abstract $\mathcal{BL}$-arc-consistency for signed shift, signed extension and all comparisons. Finally, $\mathcal{BL}$-propagators are correct for all arithmetic constraints.*

Ensuring consistency between Is/C and $\mathcal{BL}$. Specific propagators are dedicated to enforce consistency between the numerical domain Is/C and the $\mathcal{BL}$ domain. Let us consider a variable x with domains bl, $I_s = \cup_j[m_j..M_j]$ and congruence (c, M) indicating that $x \equiv c \bmod M$. Information can be propagated from $\mathcal{BL}$ to Is/C in two ways, one for intervals and one for congruence. First, it is easy to compute an interval $I_b = [m_b..M_b]$ such that $[\![bl]\!]_u \subseteq I_b$, $m_b \sqsubseteq bl$ and $M_b \sqsubseteq bl$: to compute m (resp. M), just replace all $\star$ values in bl with a 0 (resp. 1). The domain I_s can then be refined to $I_s \sqcap I_b$. Second, if seq is the longest sequence of well-defined (i.e. 0

```
A, B, R: bitlist
let N be the size of A, B and B
 1: (A', B', R') := (A, B, R)
 2: C := * * * ... * 0        /* bit-vector of size N+1 */
 3: for i = 1 to N do
 4:    R'_i := (A'_i xor_* B'_i xor_* C'_i) ⊓ R'_i
 5:    A'_i := (R'_i xor_* B'_i xor_* C'_i) ⊓ A'_i
 6:    B'_i := (A'_i xor_* R'_i xor_* C'_i) ⊓ B'_i
 7:    C'_i := (A'_i xor_* B'_i xor_* R'_i) ⊓ C'_i
 8:    C'_{i+1} := ((A'_i ∧_* B'_i) ∨_* (A'_i ∧_* C'_i) ∨_* (B'_i ∧_* C'_i)) ⊓ C'_{i+1}.
 9: end for
10: return (A', B', R')
```

Fig. 4. $\mathcal{BL}$-propagator for constraint A ⊕ B = R

or 1) least significant $\star$-bits of bl, one can infer a congruence constraint on x such that $x \equiv [\![seq]\!]_u \bmod 2^{size(seq)}$. For example, if $bl = \star 1 \star 101$ (on 6 bits), then $x \equiv 5 \bmod 8$, and $x \in [21..61]$. Information can also be propagated from intervals and congruences to $\mathcal{BL}$: if (c, M) is such that M is equal to some 2^k then the k least bits of bl can be replaced by the encoding of c on k bits. Moreover, let k' be the smallest integer such that the maximal bound I_M of I satisfies $I_M \leq 2^{k'}$. Then the most significant bits of rank greater than k' of bl must be replaced by 0s. These consistency propagators do not impose that all interval bounds in Is satisfy the $\mathcal{BL}$ constraint. This situation can be detected and it is always possible to increment/decrement the min/max-bound values until a value suiting both Is/C and $\mathcal{BL}$ is reached. However, experiments (not reported in this paper) suggest that it is too expensive to be worthwhile.

6 Experiments

This section presents an empirical evaluation of the techniques developed so far. These experiments have two goals. The first goal (Goal 1) is to assess the practical benefit of the new CLP($\mathbb{N}_{BV}^{\leq M}$) framework, if any, compared to off-the-shelf CLP solvers and straightforward non-linear encoding. To this end, a comparison is performed between non-linear integer encoding for some well-known CLP solvers and a prototype implementing our results. All tools are compared on a common set of search heuristics to evaluate the stability of the results w.r.t. the search heuristic. The second goal (Goal 2) is to compare the current best SAT-based approaches and the best CLP-based approach identified above. We focus on quantifying the gap between the two approaches, comparing the benefits of each approach on different classes of constraints and evaluating scalability issues w.r.t. domain sizes (i.e. bit-width).

CLP($\mathbb{N}_{BV}^{\leq M}$) implementation. COLIBRI is a CLP($\mathbb{N}^{\leq M}$) solver integrated in the model-based testing tool GaTeL [20]. It provides abstract numerical domains (unions of intervals, congruence), propagators and simplification rules for all common arithmetic constraints and advanced optimisations like global difference constraint [14]. COLIBRI is written in Eclipse [1], however it does not rely on the CLP($\mathbb{N}^{\leq M}$) library Eclipse/IC. Our own prototype is written on top of COLIBRI (version v2007), adding the $\mathcal{BL}$ domain and all $\mathcal{BL}$- and Is/C-propagators described in sections 4 and 5. The following implementation choices have been made: (1) for Is domains the number of intervals is limited to 500; (2) the consistency propagator between Is/C and $\mathcal{BL}$ is approximated: only inconsistent singleton are removed from Is. Four different searches have been implemented (min, rand, split, smart). The three first searches are basic dfs with value selection based on the minimal value of the domain (min), a random value (rand) or splitting the domain in half (split). The smart search is an enhancement of min: the search selects at each step the most constrained variable for labelling ; after one unsuccessful labelling, the variable is put in *quarantine*: its domain is split and it cannot be labelled anymore until all non labelled variables are in quarantine.

Experimental setting. All problems are conjunctive QFBV formulas (including *ite* operators). There are two different test benches. The first one (T1) is a set of 164 problems coming from the standard SMT benchmark repository [24] or automatically generated by the test generation tool OSMOSE [6]. (T1) is intended to compare tool performance on a large set of medium-sized examples. Problems involve mostly 8-bit and 32-bit width bit-vectors and range from small puzzles of a few dozen operators to real-life problems with 20,000 operators and 1,700 variables. (T1) is partitioned into a roughly equal number of bitwise problems, linear arithmetic problems and non-linear arithmetic problems. There are also roughly as many SAT instances as UNSAT instances. The second test bench (T2) is a set of 87 linear and non-linear problems taken from (T1) and automatically extended to bit-width of 64, 128, 256 and 512 (difficulty of the problem may be altered). (T2) is intended to compare scalability on arithmetic constraints w.r.t. the domain size.

Competing tools are described hereafter. Our own prototype comes in 3 versions, depending on domains and propagators used: COL (COLIBRI version v2007 with non-linear encoding), COL-D (COLIBRI v2007 with dedicated Is/C-propagators) and COL-D-BL (COL-D with $\mathcal{BL}$). A new version of COLIBRI (v2009) with better support for non-linear arithmetic is also considered (COL-2009). The other CLP solvers are the standard tools GNU Prolog [10], Eclipse/IC [1], Choco [16] and Abscon [19]. GNU Prolog and Eclipse/IC use single interval domains while Choco and Abscon represent domains by enumeration. GNU Prolog and Eclipse/IC are used with built-in dfs-min, dfs-random and dfs-split heuristics. Choco and Abscon are used with settings of the CLP competition. Selected SAT-based solvers are STP [15] (winner of the 2006 SMT-BV competition [24]), Boolector [2] (winner 2008) and MathSat [4] (winner 2009). We take the last version of each tool.

All experiments were performed on a PC Intel 2Ghz equipped with 2GBytes of RAM. Time out is set up to 20s for (T1) and 50s for (T2).

Results. A problem with all the CLP solvers we have tried except COLIBRI is that they may report overflow exception when domain values are too large: integer values are limited to 2^{24} in GNU Prolog, between 2^{24} and 2^{32} in Choco and Abscon and 2^{53} in Eclipse/IC. In particular, GNU Prolog and ABSCON report many bugs due to overflows in internal computations. Moreover, Choco and Abscon are clearly not designed for large domains and perform very poorly on our examples, confirming previous experimental results [23]. Thus, we report in the following only results of Eclipse/IC. Results are presented in Table 1 (a) (T1) and (c) (T2). A detailed comparison of COLIBRI-D-BL-smart, STP, Boolector and MathSat can be found in Table 1 (b).

A few remarks about the results. First, Eclipse/IC performs surprisingly better than the standard version of COLIBRI. Actually, the non-linear encoding of BV problems prevents most of the optimisations of COLIBRI to succeed, since they target linear integer arithmetic. However, COLIBRI v2009 with optimised propagators for non-linear arithmetic performs much better than Eclipse/IC. Second, MathSat appears to be less efficient than Boolector and STP, which is rather surprising since it won the 2009 SMT competition. Recall that we consider only conjunctive problems and that our test bench exhibits a large proportion of (non-linear) arithmetic problems.

A few remarks about our implementation. (1) We did not observe any interval blowup during computation, even when setting up a larger limit (2000 intervals per domain). (2) We have implemented a full consistency propagation between domains Is/C and $\mathcal{BL}$ as described in Section 5: it appears to be less efficient than the restricted consistency propagation described earlier in this section.

Comments. *Goal 1.* It is clear from Table 1 that the CLP($\mathbb{N}_{BV}^{\leq M}$) framework developed so far allows a significant improvement compared to the standard CLP($\mathbb{N}^{\leq M}$) approach with non-linear encoding. Actually, our complete CLP($\mathbb{N}_{BV}^{\leq M}$) solver with smart search is able to solve 1.7x more examples in 2.4x less time than Eclipse/IC, and 3x more examples in 3.5x less time than standard COLIBRI. Additional interesting facts must be highlighted:

– Each new feature allows an additional improvement: COL-D-BL performs better than COL-D which performs better than COL. Moreover, this improvement is observed for each of the four heuristics considered here.
– The smart search permits an additional gain only when dedicated propagators are used. It does not add anything to the standard version of COLIBRI.
– Every enhanced version of COLIBRI (v2007) performs better than Eclipse/IC and COLIBRI v2009.

Goal 2. According to (T1), global performance of our prototype lies within those of MathSat and STP in both number of successes and computation time, Boolector being a step ahead of the other three tools. Surprisingly, our prototype performs better than the BV-winner 2009, but worse than the BV-winner 2006. We can then conclude that, at least for medium-sized conjunctive problems, CLP can compete with current SAT-based approaches. Considering results by category (Table 1 (b)), our prototype is the best on non-linear UNSAT problems and very efficient on non-linear SAT problems (Boolector solves one more example, but takes 1.5x more time). Finally, considering results from T2 and Table 1 (c), CLP($\mathbb{N}_{BV}^{\leq M}$) scales much better than SAT-based approaches on arithmetic problems: the number of time outs and computation time is almost stable between 64-bit and 512-bit. STP reports very poor scalability. Here, MathSat both performs and scales much better than the other SAT-based tools. Note that due to the automatic scaling of examples, many LA SAT problems are turned into LA UNSAT problems where MathSat is much better.

Table 1. Experimental results

Tool	Category	Time	# success
Eclipse/IC-min	$N^{\leq M}$	1760	78/164
Eclipse/IC-rand	$N^{\leq M}$	2040	72/164
Eclipse/IC-split	$N^{\leq M}$	1750	79/164
COL-min	$N^{\leq M}$	2436	43/164
COL-rand	$N^{\leq M}$	2560	36/164
COL-split	$N^{\leq M}$	2550	40 /164
COL-smart	$N^{\leq M}$	2475	40/164
COL-2009-min	$N^{\leq M}$	1520	89/164
COL-2009-rand	$N^{\leq M}$	1513	89/164
COL-2009-split	$N^{\leq M}$	1682	85/164
COL-2009-smart	$N^{\leq M}$	1410	95/164
COL-D-min	$N_{BV}^{\leq M}$	1453	94/164
COL-D-rand	$N_{BV}^{\leq M}$	1392	96/164
COL-D-split	$N_{BV}^{\leq M}$	1593	89/164
COL-D-smart	$N_{BV}^{\leq M}$	893	125 /164
COL-D-BL-min	$N_{BV}^{\leq M}$	1174	108/164
COL-D-BL-rand	$N_{BV}^{\leq M}$	1116	111/164
COL-D-BL-split	$N_{BV}^{\leq M}$	1349	103/164
COL-D-BL-smart	$N_{BV}^{\leq M}$	712	138/164
MathSat	SAT	794	128/164
STP	SAT	618	144/164
Boolector	SAT	291	157/164

(a) T1: Time and #successes
Time out = 20s

category	COL-D-BL smart	STP	Boolect	MathSat
BW SAT	30 (30/30)	2 (30/30)	0 (30/30)	2 (30/30)
BW UNSAT	3 (30/30)	12 (30/30)	0 (30/30)	4 (30/30)
LA SAT	164 (28/30)	88 (30/30)	9 (30/30)	303 (15/30)
LA UNSAT	360 (7/25)	68 (25/25)	42 (23/25)	223 (16/25)
NLA SAT	148 (23/29)	357 (13/29)	220 (24/29)	221 (18/29)
NLA UNSAT	7 (20/20)	82 (16/20)	20 (20/20)	41 (19/20)
Total	712 (138/164)	589 (145/164)	291 (157/164)	794 (128/164)

(b) T1: Time and # successes for Time out=20s
(BW: bitwise LA: linear arith. NLA: non-linear arith.)

bit-width	64	128	256	512
COL-D-BL-smart	8 TO, 443s	10 TO, 500s	10 TO, 503s	10 TO, 510s
STP	10 TO, 1093s	17 TO, 2054s	27 TO, 3500s	35 TO, 3686s
Boolector	2 TO, 213s	6 TO, 385s	8 TO, 656s	16 TO, 1056s
MathSat	2 TO, 180s	2 TO, 308s	2 TO, 379s	2 TO, 545s

(c) T2: #TO and time, Time out = 50s

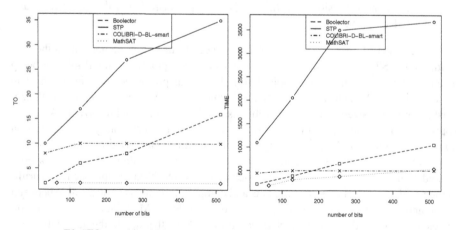

T2: #TO w.r.t. bit-width

T2: Total time w.r.t. bit-width

7   Related Work

Word-level BV solving has already been investigated through translations into non-linear arithmetic [12,25,27]. On the one hand, none of these works consider specific resolution techniques: they all rely on standard approaches for integer arithmetic. On the other hand, these encodings require bit-blasting at least for bitwise operations which leads to large formulas. Experiments are performed only with very low bit-width (4 or 8) and no experimental comparison with SAT-based solvers is conducted. The work reported in [5] presents many similarities with this paper. In particular, the authors describe a dedicated domain similar to $\mathcal{BL}$ and they advocate the use of dedicated propagators for domain I (single interval). There are several significant differences with our own work. First, our experiments demonstrate that more elaborated domains are necessary to gain performance. Second, their dedicated domains and propagators are not described, they do not seem to handle signed operations and it is not clear whether or not they rely on bit-blasting for bitwise operations. Moreover, issues such as consistency or efficiency are not discussed. Third, there is no empiric evaluation against other approaches. Finally, experimental results reported in [23] confirm our own experiments concerning SAT-based approaches and traditional CLP($\mathbb{N}^{\leq M}$)-based approaches.

8   Conclusion

Ideas presented in this paper allow a very significant improvement of word-level CLP-based BV solving, considerably lowering the gap with SAT-based approaches and even competing with them on some particular aspects (non-linear BV arithmetic, scalability). There is still room for improvement on both the search aspect and the propagation aspect. And there remain many challenging issues: the best SAT-based approaches are still ahead on arbitrary conjunctive QFBV formulas, and formulas with arbitrary boolean skeletons and array operations should be investigated as well.

Acknowledgements. We are very grateful to Bruno Marre and Benjamin Blanc for developing COLIBRI, as well as for many insightful comments and advices.

References

1. Apt, K.R., Wallace, M.: Constraint Logic Programming using Eclipse. Cambridge University Press, New York (2007)
2. Brummayer, R., Biere, A.: Boolector: An Efficient SMT Solver for Bit-Vectors and Arrays. In: Kowalewski, S., Philippou, A. (eds.) TACAS 2009. LNCS, vol. 5505, pp. 174–177. Springer, Heidelberg (2009)
3. Biere, A., Cimatti, A., Clarke, E.M., Zhu, Y.: Symbolic model checking without BDDs. In: Cleaveland, W.R. (ed.) TACAS 1999. LNCS, vol. 1579, pp. 193–207. Springer, Heidelberg (1999)
4. Bruttomesso, R., Cimatti, A., Franzén, A., Griggio, A., Sebastiani, R.: The MathSAT 4 SMT Solver. In: Gupta, A., Malik, S. (eds.) CAV 2008. LNCS, vol. 5123, pp. 299–303. Springer, Heidelberg (2008)
5. Barray, F., Codognet, P., Diaz, D., Michel, H.: Code-based test generation for validation of functional processor descriptions. In: Garavel, H., Hatcliff, J. (eds.) TACAS 2003. LNCS, vol. 2619, pp. 569–584. Springer, Heidelberg (2003)

6. Bardin, S., Herrmann, P.: Structural Testing of Executables. In: 1st Int. Conf. on Software Testing, Verification, and Validation, pp. 22–31. IEEE Computer Society, Los Alamitos (2008)

7. Cousot, P., Cousot, R.: Abstract Interpretation: A Unified Lattice Model for Static Analysis of Programs by Construction or Approximation of Fixpoints. In: 4th ACM Symposium on Principles of Programming Languages, pp. 238–252. ACM, New York (1977)

8. Cadar, C., Ganesh, V., Pawlowski, P.M., Dill, D.L., Engler, D.R.: EXE: automatically generating inputs of death. In: 13th ACM Conf. on Computer and Communications Security, pp. 322–335. ACM, New York (2006)

9. Clarke, E.M., Kroening, D., Lerda, F.: A tool for checking ANSI-C programs. In: Jensen, K., Podelski, A. (eds.) TACAS 2004. LNCS, vol. 2988, pp. 168–176. Springer, Heidelberg (2004)

10. Diaz, D., Codognet, P.: Design and Implementation of the GNU Prolog System. J. Functional and Logic Programming, 2001. EAPLS (2001)

11. Dechter, R.: Constraint Processing. Morgan Kaufmann, San Francisco (2003)

12. Ferrandi, F., Rendine, M., Sciuto, D.: Functional verification for SystemC descriptions using constraint solving. In: 5th Conf. on Design, Automation and Test in Europe, pp. 744–751. IEEE Computer Society, Los Alamitos (2002)

13. Frühwirth, T.: Theory and Practice of Constraint Handling Rules. J. Logic Programming 37(1-3), 95–138 (1998)

14. Feydy, T., Schutt, A., Stuckey, P.J.: Global difference constraint propagation for finite domain solvers. In: 10th Int. ACM SIGPLAN Conf. on Principles and Practice of Declarative Programming, pp. 226–236. ACM, New York (2008)

15. Ganesh, V., Dill, D.L.: A Decision Procedure for Bit-Vectors and Arrays. In: Damm, W., Hermanns, H. (eds.) CAV 2007. LNCS, vol. 4590, pp. 519–531. Springer, Heidelberg (2007)

16. Jussien, N., Rochart, G., Lorca, X.: The CHOCO constraint programming solver. In: CPAIOR 2008 Workshop on Open-Source Software for Integer and Contraint Programming (2008)

17. Kroening, D., Strichman, O.: Decision Procedures: An Algorithmic Point of View. Springer, Heidelberg (2008)

18. Leconte, M., Berstel, B.: Extending a CP Solver With Congruences as Domains for Software Verification. In: CP 2006 Workshop on Constraints in Software Testing, Verification and Analysis (2006)

19. Lecoutre, C., Tabary, S.: Abscon 112: Toward more Robustness. In CSP Solver Competition, held with CP 2008 (2008)

20. Marre, B., Blanc, B.: Test selection strategies for Lustre descriptions in GATeL. Electr. Notes Theor. Comput. Sci. 111, 93–111 (2005)

21. Moskewicz, M., Madigan, C., Zhao, Y., Zhang, L., Malik, S.: Chaff: engineering an efficient SAT solver. In: 38th Design Automation Conf., pp. 530–535. ACM, New York (2001)

22. Manolios, P., Vroon, D.: Efficient circuit to CNF conversion. In: Marques-Silva, J., Sakallah, K.A. (eds.) SAT 2007. LNCS, vol. 4501, pp. 4–9. Springer, Heidelberg (2007)

23. Sülflow, A., Kühne, U., Wille, R., Große, D., Drechsler, R.: Evaluation of SAT like proof techniques for formal verification of word level circuits. In: 8th IEEE Workshop on RTL and High Level Testing, pp. 31–36. IEEE Computer Society, Los Alamitos (2007)

24. SMT competition, http://www.smtcomp.org/

25. Vemuri, R., Kalyanaraman, R.: Generation of design verification tests from behavioral VHDL programs using path enumeration and constraint programming. IEEE Transactions on VLSI Systems 3(2), 201–214 (1995)

26. Wille, R., Fey, G., Große, D., Eggersglüß, S., Drechsler, R.: SWORD: A SAT like prover using word level information. In: 18th Int. Conf. on Very Large Scale Integration of Systems-on-Chip, pp. 88–93. IEEE, Los Alamitos (2007)

27. Zeng, Z., Ciesielski, M., Rouzeyre, B.: Functional test generation using Constraint Logic Programming. In: 11th Int. Conf. on Very Large Scale Integration of Systems-on-Chip, pp. 375–387. Kluwer, Dordrecht (2001)

Satisfiability Modulo the Theory of Costs: Foundations and Applications[*]

Alessandro Cimatti[1], Anders Franzén[1], Alberto Griggio[2],
Roberto Sebastiani[2], and Cristian Stenico[2]

[1] FBK-Irst, Trento, Italy
[2] DISI, University of Trento, Italy

Abstract. We extend the setting of Satisfiability Modulo Theories (SMT) by introducing a theory of costs $\mathcal{C}$, where it is possible to model and reason about resource consumption and multiple cost functions, e.g., battery, time, and space. We define a decision procedure that has all the features required for the integration withint the lazy SMT schema: incrementality, backtrackability, construction of conflict sets, and deduction. This naturally results in an SMT solver for the disjoint union of $\mathcal{C}$ and any other theory $\mathcal{T}$.

This framework has two important applications. First, we tackle the problem of *Optimization Modulo Theories*: rather than checking the existence of a satisfying assignment, as in SMT, we require a satisfying assignment that minimizes a given cost function. We build on the decision problem for SMT with costs, i.e., finding a satisfying assignment with cost within an admissibility range, and propose two algorithms for optimization. Second, we use multiple cost functions to deal with *PseudoBoolean constraints*. Within the SMT($\mathcal{C}$) framework, the effectively PseudoBoolean constraints are dealt with by the cost solver, while the other constraints are reduced to pure boolean reasoning.

We implemented the proposed approach within the MathSAT SMT solver, and we experimentally evaluated it on a large set of benchmarks, also from industrial applications. The results clearly demonstrate the potential of the approach.

1 Motivations and Goals

Important verification problems are naturally encoded as Satisfiability Modulo Theory (SMT) problems, i.e. as satisfiability problems for decidable fragments of first order logic. Efficient SMT solvers have been developed, that combine the power of SAT solvers with dedicated decision procedures for several theories of practical interest.

In many practical domains, problems require modeling and reasoning about resource consumption and multiple cost functions, e.g., battery, time, and space. In this paper, we extend SMT by introducing a *theory of costs* $\mathcal{C}$. The language of the theory of costs is very expressive: it allows for multiple cost functions and, for each of these, arbitrary Boolean conditions may be stated to result in a given cost increase; costs may be be both lower- and upper-bounded, also depending on Boolean conditions. In the current

---

[*] A. Cimatti is supported in part by the European Commission FP7-2007-IST-1-217069 CO-CONUT. A. Franzén, A. Griggio and R. Sebastiani are supported in part by SRC under GRC Custom Research Project 2009-TJ-1880 WOLFLING, and by MIUR under PRIN project 20079E5KM8_002.

J. Esparza and R. Majumdar (Eds.): TACAS 2010, LNCS 6015, pp. 99–113, 2010.

paper, we concentrate on the case of Boolean cost functions, where costs are bound by and function of Boolean atoms (including relations over individual variables). For the theory of costs, it is possible to define a decision procedure that has all the features required for the integration within the lazy SMT schema: incrementality, backtracka-bility, construction of conflict sets, and deduction. This naturally results in a solver for SMT($\mathcal{C}$), and, given the assumption of Boolean cost functions, also in a solver for the disjoint union of $\mathcal{C}$ and any other theory $\mathcal{T}$.

Based on the theory of costs, we propose two additional contributions. First, we extend SMT by tackling the problem of *Optimization Modulo Theories*: rather than checking the existence of a satisfying assignment, as in SMT, we require a satisfying assignment that minimizes a given cost function. We build on the decision problem for SMT with costs, i.e. finding a satisfying assignment with cost within an admissibility range. The optimization problem is then tackled as a sequence of decision problems, where the admissibility range is adapted from one problem to the next. We propose two algorithms: one is based on branch-and-bound, where the admissibility range is increasingly tightened, based on the best valued solution so far. The other one, based on binary search, proceeds by bisecting the admissible interval, and leveraging under-approximations as well as over-approximations.

Second, we show how to exploit the feature of multiple cost functions to deal with the well known problem of *PseudoBoolean (PB) constraints*. The approach can be seen as dealing with PB problems as in an SMT paradigm. The PB constraints are dealt with by the cost solver (as if it were a solver for the theory of PB constraints), while the other constraints are reduced to pure Boolean reasoning. The approach is enabled by the ability of the cost theory to deal with multiple cost functions. The resulting solution is very elegant and extremely simple to implement.

We implemented the proposed approach within the MathSAT SMT solver. We ex-perimentally evaluate it on a wide set of benchmarks, including artificial benchmarks (obtained by adding cost functions to the problems in SMT-LIB), real-world (from two different industrial domains) benchmarks, and benchmarks from the PB solver compe-tition. The results show that the approach, despite its simplicity, is very effective: it is able to solve complex case studies in SMT($\mathcal{T} \cup \mathcal{C}$) and, despite its simplicity, it shows surprising efficiency in some Boolean and PB optimization problems, outperforming the winners of the most recent comptetition.

This paper is structured as follows. In §2 we present some background. The theory of costs and the decision procedure are presented in §3. In §4 we show how to tackle optimization problems. In §5 we show how to encode PseudoBoolean constraints as SMT($\mathcal{C}$). In §6 we experimentally evaluate our approach. In §7 we discuss some related approaches. In §8 we draw some conclusions and outline directions for future research. The proofs and some possibly-useful material are reported in [8].

2   Background on SMT and SMT Solving

Satisfiability Modulo (the) Theory $\mathcal{T}$, SMT($\mathcal{T}$), is the problem of deciding the satisfia-bility of (typically) ground formulas under a background theory $\mathcal{T}$. (Notice that $\mathcal{T}$ can also be a combination of simpler theories: $\mathcal{T} \stackrel{\text{def}}{=} \bigcup_i \mathcal{T}_i$.) We call an *SMT($\mathcal{T}$) solver* any tool able to decide SMT($\mathcal{T}$). We call a *theory solver for* $\mathcal{T}$, $\mathcal{T}$-*solver*, any tool able to decide the satisfiability in $\mathcal{T}$ of sets/conjunctions of ground atomic formulas and their negations ($\mathcal{T}$-*literals*). If the input set of $\mathcal{T}$-literals μ is $\mathcal{T}$-unsatisfiable, then $\mathcal{T}$-*solver* returns unsat and the subset η of $\mathcal{T}$-literals in μ which was found $\mathcal{T}$-unsatisfiable; (η is hereafter called a $\mathcal{T}$-*conflict set*, and $\neg\eta$ a $\mathcal{T}$-*conflict clause*.) if μ is $\mathcal{T}$-satisfiable, then $\mathcal{T}$-*solver* returns sat; it may also be able to return some unassigned $\mathcal{T}$-literal l s.t. $\{l_1, ..., l_n\} \models_{\mathcal{T}} l$, where $\{l_1, ..., l_n\} \subseteq \mu$. We call this process $\mathcal{T}$-deduction and ($\bigvee_{i=1}^{n} \neg l_i \vee l$) a $\mathcal{T}$-*deduction clause*. Notice that both $\mathcal{T}$- and $\mathcal{C}$-conflict and $\mathcal{T}$-deduction clauses are valid in $\mathcal{T}$. We call them $\mathcal{T}$-*lemmas*.

We adopt the following terminology and notation. The bijective function $\mathcal{T}2\mathcal{B}$ ("$\mathcal{T}$-to-Boolean"), called *Boolean abstraction*, maps propositional variables into themselves, ground $\mathcal{T}$-atoms into fresh propositional variables, and is homomorphic w.r.t. Boolean operators and set inclusion. The symbols φ, ψ, ϕ denote $\mathcal{T}$-formulas, and μ, η denote sets of $\mathcal{T}$-literals. If $\mathcal{T}2\mathcal{B}(\mu) \models \mathcal{T}2\mathcal{B}(\varphi)$, then we say that μ *propositionally satisfies* φ written $\mu \models_p \varphi$. With a little abuse of terminology, we will often omit specifying "the Boolean abstraction of" when referring to propositional reasoning steps, as if these steps were referred to the ground $\mathcal{T}$-formula/assignment/clause rather than to their Boolean abstraction. (E.g., we say "φ is given in input to DPLL" rather "$\mathcal{T}2\mathcal{B}(\varphi)$ is..." or "μ is a truth assignment for φ" rather than "$\mathcal{T}2\mathcal{B}(\mu)$ is a truth assignment for $\mathcal{T}2\mathcal{B}(\varphi)$".) This is done w.l.o.g. since $\mathcal{T}2\mathcal{B}$ is bijective.

In a lazy SMT($\mathcal{T}$) solver the truth assignments for φ are enumerated and checked for $\mathcal{T}$-satisfiability, returning either sat if one $\mathcal{T}$-satisfiable truth assignment is found, unsat otherwise. In practical implementations, φ is given as input to a modified version of DPLL, and when an assignment μ is found s.t. $\mu \models_p \varphi$ μ is fed to the $\mathcal{T}$-*solver*; if μ is $\mathcal{T}$-consistent, then φ is $\mathcal{T}$-consistent; otherwise, $\mathcal{T}$-*solver* returns the conflict set η causing the inconsistency. Then the $\mathcal{T}$-conflict clause $\neg\eta$ is fed to the backjumping and learning mechanism of DPLL ($\mathcal{T}$-*backjumping* and $\mathcal{T}$-*learning*).

Important optimizations are *early pruning* and $\mathcal{T}$-*propagation*: the $\mathcal{T}$-solver is invoked also on an intermediate assignment μ: if it is $\mathcal{T}$-unsatisfiable, then the procedure can backtrack; if not, and if the $\mathcal{T}$-*solver* performs a $\mathcal{T}$-deduction $\{l_1, ..., l_n\} \models_{\mathcal{T}} l$, then l can be unit-propagated, and the $\mathcal{T}$-deduction clause ($\bigvee_{i=1}^{n} \neg l_i \vee l$) can be used in backjumping and learning. The above schema is a coarse abstraction of the procedures underlying all the state-of-the-art lazy SMT tools. The interested reader is pointed to, e.g., [6], for details and further references.

3   Satisfiability Modulo the Theory of Costs

3.1   Modeling Cost Functions

We extend the SMT framework by adding *cost functions*. Let $\mathcal{T}$ be a first-order theory. We consider a pair $\langle\varphi, \underline{costs}\rangle$, s.t. $\underline{costs} \stackrel{\text{def}}{=} \{cost^i\}_{i=1}^{M}$ is an array of M integer cost functions over $\mathcal{T}$ and φ is a Boolean combination on ground $\mathcal{T}$-atoms and atoms in the form $(cost^i \leq c)$ s.t. c is some integer value.[1] We focus on problems in which each $cost^i$ is a *Boolean cost function* in the form

---

[1] Notice that every atom in the form $(cost^i \bowtie c)$ s.t. $\bowtie \in \{=, \neq, <, \leq, >, \geq\}$ can be expressed as a Boolean combination of constraints in the form $(cost^i \leq c)$.

$$cost^i = \sum_{j=1}^{N_i} ite(\psi_j^i, c_{j1}^i, c_{j2}^i), \tag{1}$$

s.t., for every i, ψ_j^i is a formula in $\mathcal{T}$ and c_{j1}^i, c_{j2}^i are integer constants values and ite (term if-then-else) is a function s.t. $ite(A_j^i, c_{j1}^i, c_{j2}^i)$ returns c_{j1}^i if A_j^i holds, c_{j2}^i otherwise. We notice that the problem is very general, and it can express a wide amount of different interesting problems, as it will be made clear in the next sections.

Hereafter w.l.o.g. we can restrict our attention to problems $\langle \varphi, \underline{costs} \rangle$ in which:

$$cost^i = \sum_{j=1}^{N_i} ite(A_j^i, c_j^i, 0), \tag{2}$$

for every i, s.t. for every j, A_j^i is a Boolean literal and $0 < c_j^i \leq c_{j+1}^i$. (Passing from (1) to (2) is straighforward [8].) We denote by $bound_{max}^i$ the value $\sum_{j=1}^{N_i} c_j^i$, for every i.

We notice that we can easily encode (2) into subformulas in the theory of linear arithmetic over the integers ($\mathcal{LA}(\mathbb{Z})$) and hence the whole problem $\langle \varphi, \underline{costs} \rangle$ into a ground $\mathcal{T} \cup \mathcal{LA}(\mathbb{Z})$-formula, where $\mathcal{T}$ and $\mathcal{LA}(\mathbb{Z})$ are completely-disjoint theories, and have it solved by an SMT solver. Unfortunately this technique is inefficient in practice. (An explanation of this fact is reported in [8].) Instead, we cope with this problem by defining an ad-hoc theory of costs.

3.2   A Theory of Costs $\mathcal{C}$

We address the problem by introducing a "theory of costs" $\mathcal{C}$ consisting in:

- a collection of M fresh variables $c^1, \ldots, c^M$, denoting the output of the functions $cost^1, \ldots, cost^M$;
- a fresh binary predicate BC ("bound cost"), s.t. $BC(c^i, c)$ mean "$(c^i \leq c)$", c^i and c are one of the cost variables and an integer value respectively;
- a fresh ternary predicate IC ("incur cost"), s.t. $IC(c^i, j, c_j^i)$ means "c_j^i is added to c^i as jth element in the sum (2)", c^i, j, and c_j^i being one of the cost variables, an integer value denoting the index in the sum (2), and the corresponding integer value respectively.[2] We introduce exactly $\sum_{i=1}^{M} N_i$ distinct atoms $IC(c^i, j, c_j^i)$, one for each c_j^i in (2).

We call $\mathcal{C}$-atoms all atoms in the form $BC(c^i, c)$, $IC(c^i, j, c_j^i)$, and $\mathcal{C}$-literals all $\mathcal{C}$-atoms and their negations. We call a $\mathcal{T} \cup \mathcal{C}$-formula any Boolean combination of ground $\mathcal{T}$- and $\mathcal{C}$-atoms (simply $\mathcal{C}$-formula if $\mathcal{T}$ is pure Boolean logic).

Intuitively, the theory of costs allows for modeling domains with multiple costs c^i by means of $\mathcal{C}$- or $\mathcal{T} \cup \mathcal{C}$-formulas. For instance, in the domain of planning for an autonomous rover, different costs may be battery consumption, and elapsed time. In the theory of costs, IC statements can be used to state the cost associated to specific partial configurations. For instance, a specific drilling action may require 5 seconds and 20mAh of battery energy, $Drill \rightarrow (IC(battery, 1, 5) \wedge IC(time, 1, 20))$, while moving can have different impact on the available resources: $Move \rightarrow (IC(battery, 2, 20) \wedge$

---

[2] Notice that the index j in $IC(c^i, j, c_j^i)$ is necessary to avoid using the same predicate for two constants c_j^i and $c_{j'}^i$ with the same value but different indexes j, j'.

$\mathsf{IC}(time, 2, 10))$. The BC predicates can be used to state for instance that the achievement of a certain goal G_1 should not require more than a certain amount of energy, while another goal should always be completed within a certain time bound and with a certain energy consumption: $G_1 \rightarrow \mathsf{BC}(battery, 20)$ and $G_2 \rightarrow \mathsf{BC}(battery, 20) \wedge \mathsf{BC}(time, 10)$. Notice that it is also possible to state lower bounds, e.g. the overall plan should never take less than a certain amount of time.

We consider a generic set $\mu \overset{\text{def}}{=} \mu_B \cup \mu_T \cup \mu_C$ s.t. μ_B is a set of Boolean literals, μ_T is a set of $\mathcal{T}$-literals, and $\mu_C \overset{\text{def}}{=} \bigcup_{i=1}^{M} \mu_C^i$ is a set of $\mathcal{C}$-literals s.t., for every i, μ_C^i is:

$$\mu_C^i \overset{\text{def}}{=} \{\mathsf{BC}(c^i, \mathsf{ub}^i_{(k)}) \mid k \in [1, ...K_i]\} \cup \{\neg \mathsf{BC}(c^i, \mathsf{lb}^i_{(m)} - 1) \mid m \in [1, ..., M_i]\} \quad (3)$$

$$\cup \, \{\mathsf{IC}(c^i, j, c^i_j) \mid j \in J^{i+}\} \cup \{\neg \mathsf{IC}(c^i, j, c^i_j) \mid j \in J^{i-}\}, \quad (4)$$

where $\mathsf{ub}^i_{(1)}, \ldots, \mathsf{ub}^i_{(K_i)}, \mathsf{lb}^i_{(1)}, \ldots, \mathsf{lb}^i_{(M_i)}$ are positive integer values, J^{i+} and J^{i-} are two sets of indices s.t. $J^{i+} \cap J^{i-} = \emptyset$ and $J^{i+} \cup J^{i-} \subseteq \{1, \ldots, N_i\}$, and no literal occurs both positively and negatively in μ. We say μ_C^i is *total* if $J^{i+} \cup J^{i-} = \{1, \ldots, N_i\}$, *partial* otherwise. Notice that every truth assignment μ for a SMT$(\mathcal{T} \cup \mathcal{C})$ formula φ is in the form $\mu_B \cup \mu_T \cup \mu_C$ described above, s.t. μ_B, μ_T and μ_C are the restriction of μ to its Boolean, $\mathcal{T}$- and $\mathcal{C}$-literals respectively.

Let $\mathsf{lb}^i_{max} \overset{\text{def}}{=} max(\{\mathsf{lb}^i_{(1)}, \ldots, \mathsf{lb}^i_{(M_i)}\})$ and $\mathsf{ub}^i_{min} \overset{\text{def}}{=} min(\{\mathsf{ub}^i_{(1)}, \ldots, \mathsf{lb}^i_{(K_i)}\})$.

Definition 1. *If μ_C^i is total, we say that μ_C^i is $\mathcal{C}$-consistent if and only if*

$$\mathsf{lb}^i_{max} \leq \textstyle\sum_{j \in J^{i+}} c^i_j \leq \mathsf{ub}^i_{min}. \quad (5)$$

If μ_C^i is partial, we say that μ_C^i is $\mathcal{C}$-consistent if and only if there exists a total $\mathcal{C}$-consistent superset of μ_C^i, that is, a $\mathcal{C}$-consistent set μ_C^{i*} in the form

$$\mu_C^i \cup \{\mathsf{IC}(c^i, j, c^i_j) \mid j \in K^{i+}\} \cup \{\neg \mathsf{IC}(c^i, j, c^i_j) \mid j \in K^{i-}\} \quad (6)$$

s.t. $(J^{i+} \cup K^{i+}) \cap (J^{i-} \cup K^{i-}) = \emptyset$ and $(J^{i+} \cup K^{i+} \cup J^{i-} \cup K^{i-}) = \{1, \ldots, N_i\}$.

Proposition 1. *If $\mathsf{lb}^i_{max} > \mathsf{ub}^i_{min}$, then μ_C^i is $\mathcal{C}$-inconsistent.*

Proposition 2. *A partial set μ_C^i (3)-(4) is $\mathcal{C}$-consistent if and only if the following two conditions hold:*

$$\textstyle\sum_{j \in J^{i+}} c^i_j \leq \mathsf{ub}^i_{min} \quad (7)$$

$$(\mathsf{bound}^i_{max} - \textstyle\sum_{j \in J^{i-}} c^i_j) \overset{\text{def}}{=} \textstyle\sum_{j \in \{1, ..., N_i\} \setminus J^{i-}} c^i_j \geq \mathsf{lb}^i_{max}. \quad (8)$$

Intuitively, if μ_C^i violates (8), it cannot be expanded into a $\mathcal{C}$-consistent set by adding positive or negative $\mathcal{C}$-literals. Notice that if μ_C^i is total, then $\{1, \ldots, N_i\} \setminus J^{i-}$ is J^{i+}, so that (7) and (8) collapse into the right and left part of (5) respectively. Hereafter we call $\sum_{j \in J^{i+}} c^i_j$ the *i-th cost* of μ, denoted as $\mathsf{CostOf}_i(\mu)$ or $\mathsf{CostOf}_i(\mu_C^i)$, and we call $(\mathsf{bound}^i_{max} - \sum_{j \in J^{i-}} c^i_j)$ the *maximum possible i-th cost* of μ, denoted as $\mathsf{MCostOf}_i(\mu)$ or $\mathsf{MCostOf}_i(\mu_C^i)$.

The notion of C-consistency is extended to the general assignment μ above as follows. We say that $\mu_C \overset{\text{def}}{=} \bigcup_{i=1}^{M} \mu_C^i$ is C-consistent if and only if μ_C^i is C-consistent for every i. We say that $\mu \overset{\text{def}}{=} \mu_B \cup \mu_T \cup \mu_C$ is $T \cup C$-consistent if and only if μ_T is T-consistent and μ_C is C-consistent. (Notice that μ_B is consistent by definition.) A $T \cup C$-formula is $T \cup C$-satisfiable if and only if there exists a $T \cup C$-satisfiable assignment μ defined as above which propositionally satisfies it.

3.3 A Decision Procedure for the Theory of Costs: C-Solver

We add to the SMT(T) solver one theory solver for the theory of costs C (C-solver hereafter). C-solver takes as input a truth assignment $\mu \overset{\text{def}}{=} \mu_B \cup \mu_T \cup \mu_C$ selecting only the C-relevant part $\mu_C \overset{\text{def}}{=} \bigcup_{i=1}^{M} \mu_C^i$, and for every i, it checks whether μ_C^i is C-satisfiable according to Propositions 1 and 2. This works as follows:

1. if $\mathsf{lb}_{max}^i > \mathsf{ub}_{min}^i$, then C-solver returns unsat and the C-conflict clause

$$\mathsf{BC}(c^i, \mathsf{lb}_{max}^i - 1) \vee \neg \mathsf{BC}(c^i, \mathsf{ub}_{min}^i); \tag{9}$$

2. if $\mathsf{CostOf}_i(\mu_C^i) > \mathsf{ub}_{min}^i$, then C-solver returns unsat and the C-conflict clause

$$\neg \mathsf{BC}(c^i, \mathsf{ub}_{min}^i) \vee \bigvee_{j \in K^{i+}} \neg \mathsf{IC}(c^i, j, c_j^i) \tag{10}$$

where K^{i+} is a minimal subset of J^{i+} s.t. $\sum_{j \in K^{i+}} c_j^i > \mathsf{ub}_{min}^i$;

3. if $\mathsf{MCostOf}_i(\mu_C^i) < \mathsf{lb}_{max}^i$, then C-solver returns unsat and the C-conflict clause

$$\mathsf{BC}(c^i, \mathsf{lb}_{max}^i - 1) \vee \bigvee_{j \in K^{i-}} \mathsf{IC}(c^i, j, c_j^i) \tag{11}$$

where K^{i-} is a minimal subset of J^{i-} s.t. $\sum_{j \in K^{i-}} c_j^i < \mathsf{lb}_{max}^i$;

If neither condition above is verified for every i, then C-solver returns sat, and the current values of c^i (i.e., $\mathsf{CostOf}_i(\mu)$) for every i. In the latter case, theory propagation for C (C-propagation hereafter) can be performed as follows:

4. every unassigned literal $\mathsf{BC}(c^i, \mathsf{ub}_{(r)}^i)$ s.t. $\mathsf{ub}_{(r)}^i \geq \mathsf{ub}_{min}^i$ and every unassigned literal $\neg \mathsf{BC}(c^i, \mathsf{lb}_{(s)}^i - 1)$ s.t. $\mathsf{ub}_{(s)}^i \leq \mathsf{lb}_{max}^i$ can be returned ("C-deduced"). It is possible to build the corresponding C-deduction clause by applying step 1. to $\mu_C^i \cup \{\mathsf{BC}(c^i, \mathsf{ub}_{(r)}^i)\}$ and $\mu_C^i \cup \{\neg \mathsf{BC}(c^i, \mathsf{lb}_{(s)}^i - 1)\}$ respectively;

5. if $\mathsf{CostOf}_i(\mu_C^i) \leq \mathsf{ub}_{min}^i$ but $\mathsf{CostOf}_i(\mu_C^i \cup \{\mathsf{IC}(c^i, j, c_j^i)\}) > \mathsf{ub}_{min}^i$ for some $j \notin (J^{i+} \cup J^{i-})$, then $\neg \mathsf{IC}(c^i, j, c_j^i)$ is C-deduced. It is possible to build the corresponding C-deduction clause by applying step 2. to $\mu_C^i \cup \{\mathsf{IC}(c^i, j, c_j^i)\}$;

6. if $\mathsf{MCostOf}_i(\mu_C^i) \geq \mathsf{lb}_{max}^i$ but $\mathsf{MCostOf}_i(\mu_C^i \cup \{\neg \mathsf{IC}(c^i, j, c_j^i)\}) < \mathsf{lb}_{max}^i$ for some $j \notin (J^{i+} \cup J^{i-})$, then $\mathsf{IC}(c^i, j, c_j^i)$ is C-deduced. It is possible to build the corresponding C-deduction clause by applying step 3. to $\mu_C^i \cup \{\neg \mathsf{IC}(c^i, j, c_j^i)\}$.

C-solver can be easily implemented in order to meet all the standard requirements for integration within the lazy SMT schema. In particular, it can work incrementally, by updating $\mathsf{CostOf}_i(\mu)$ and $\mathsf{MCostOf}_i(\mu)$ each time a literal in the form $\mathsf{IC}(c^i, j, c^i_j)$ or $\neg\mathsf{IC}(c^i, j, c^i_j)$ is added to μ. Detecting the $\mathcal{C}$-inconsistency inside $\mathcal{C}$-*solver* is computationally very cheap, since it consists in performing only one sum and one comparison each time a $\mathcal{C}$-literals is incrementally added to $\mu_\mathcal{C}$. (Thus, is O(1) for every incremental call.) The cost of performing $\mathcal{C}$-propagation is linear in the number of literals propagated (in fact, it suffices to scan the $\mathsf{IC}(c^i, j, c^i_j)$ literals in decreasing order, until none is $\mathcal{C}$-propagated anymore).

3.4   A SMT($\mathcal{T} \cup \mathcal{C}$)-Solver

A SMT($\mathcal{T} \cup \mathcal{C}$)-solver can be implemented according to the standard lazy SMT architecture. Since the theories $\mathcal{T}$ and $\mathcal{C}$ have no logic symbol in common ($\mathcal{C}$ does not have equality) so that they do not interfere to each other, $\mathcal{T}$-*solver* and $\mathcal{C}$-*solver* can be run independently. In its basic version, a SMT($\mathcal{T} \cup \mathcal{C}$) solver works as follows: an internal DPLL solver enumerates truth assignments propositionally satisfying $\varphi_\mathcal{C}$ and both $\mathcal{C}$-*solver* and $\mathcal{T}$-*solver* are invoked on on each of them. If both return sat, then the problem is satisfiable. If one of the two solvers returns unsat and a conflict clause C, then C is used as a theory conflict clause by the rest of the SMT($\mathcal{T} \cup \mathcal{C}$) solver for theory-driven backjumping and learning. The correctness an completeness of this process is a direct consequence of that of the standard lazy SMT paradigm, of Proposition 3 and of the definitions of $\mathcal{C}$- and $\mathcal{T} \cup \mathcal{C}$-consistency. As with plain SMT($\mathcal{T}$), the SMT($\mathcal{T} \cup \mathcal{C}$) solver can be enhanced by means of early-pruning calls to $\mathcal{C}$-*solver* and $\mathcal{C}$-propagation.

4   Optimization Modulo Theories via SMT($\mathcal{T} \cup \mathcal{C}$)

In what follows, we consider the problem of finding a satisfying assignment to an SMT($\mathcal{T}$) formula which is subject to some bound constraints to some Boolean cost functions and such that one Boolean cost function is minimized. We refer to this problem as *Boolean Optimization Modulo Theory (BOMT)*. We first address the decision problem (§4.1) and then the minimization problem (§4.2).

4.1   Addressing the SMT($\mathcal{T}$) Cost Decision Problem

An SMT($\mathcal{T}$) cost decision problem is a triple $\langle \varphi, \underline{costs}, \underline{bounds} \rangle$ s.t. φ is a $\mathcal{T}$-formula, *costs* are in the form (2), and $\underline{bounds} \stackrel{\text{def}}{=} \{\langle \mathsf{lb}^i, \mathsf{ub}^i \rangle\}_{i=1}^M$, where $\mathsf{lb}^i, \mathsf{ub}^i$ are integer values s.t. $0 \le \mathsf{lb}^i \le \mathsf{ub}^i \le \mathsf{bound}^i_{max}$. We call $\mathsf{lb}^i, \mathsf{ub}^i$ and $[\mathsf{lb}^i, ..., \mathsf{ub}^i]$ the *lower bound*, the *upper bound* and the *range* of *cost*^{i} respectively. (If some of the lb^i's and ub^i's are not given, we set w.l.o.g. $\mathsf{lb}^i = 0$ and $\mathsf{ub}^i = \mathsf{bound}^i_{max}$.)

We encode the decision problem $\langle \varphi, \underline{costs}, \underline{bounds} \rangle$ into the SMT($\mathcal{T} \cup \mathcal{C}$)-satisfiability problem of the following formula:

$$\varphi_\mathcal{C} \stackrel{\text{def}}{=} \varphi \wedge \bigwedge_{i=1}^M \left(\mathsf{BC}(c^i, \mathsf{ub}^i) \wedge \neg\mathsf{BC}(c^i, \mathsf{lb}^i - 1) \wedge \bigwedge_{j=1}^{N_i}(A^i_j \leftrightarrow \mathsf{IC}(c^i, j, c^i_j)) \right) \quad (12)$$

Proposition 3. *A decision problem $\langle \varphi, \underline{costs}, \underline{bounds} \rangle$ has a solution if and only if $\varphi_\mathcal{C}$ is $\mathcal{T} \cup \mathcal{C}$-satisfiable. In such a solution, for every i, the value of c^i is $\mathsf{CostOf}_i(\mu)$, μ being the $\mathcal{T} \cup \mathcal{C}$-satisfiable truth assignment satisfying $\varphi_\mathcal{C}$.*

```
1.  int IncLinearBOMT(φ_C, c^1)
2.      mincost = +∞; bound = ub^1;
3.      do
4.          ⟨status, cost⟩ = IncrementalSMT_{T∪C}(φ_C, BC(c^1, bound));
5.          if (status==sat)
6.          then {
7.              φ_C = φ_C ∧ BC(c^1, bound); //activates learned C-lemmas
8.              mincost = cost;
9.              bound = cost-1; }
10.     while (status==sat);
11.     return mincost;
```

Fig. 1. A BOMT(T) algorithm based on linear search and incremental SMT($T \cup C$)

4.2   Addressing the SMT(T) Cost Minimization Problem

A SMT(T) cost minimization problem is a triple $\langle \varphi, \underline{costs}, \underline{bounds} \rangle$ s.t. φ, $\underline{costs}$ and $\underline{bounds}$ are as in §4.1; the problem consists in finding one of the T-models for φ whose value of $cost^1$ is minimum. We call $cost^1$ the *goal cost function.* (That is, we adopt the convention of considering the goal function the first function.) Using SMT($T \cup C$), we addressing BOMT(T) with two approaches, one based on linear-search/branch&bound, and the other based on binary-search.

A Linear search/branch&bound approach. Consider the $T \cup C$-formula φ_C in (12). In linear search, if φ_C is found $T \cup C$-satisfiable with a certain cost $cost$ for the cost variable c^1, we know that the minimum value of c^1 is at most $cost$. We can then conjunct $BC(c^1, cost - 1)$ to φ_C and try again. We repeat this step until the formula is unsatisfiable, and then the last solution found is optimal.

The pseudo-code of the algorithm can be seen in Fig. 1. The procedure receives as input the formula φ_C as in (12) and the cost variable c^1 to minimize. Initially, $bound$ is set to the value ub^1 in (12). Each call IncrementalSMT$_{T∪C}(\varphi_C, BC(c^1, bound))$ is a call to an incremental SMT($T \cup C$)-solver, which asserts $BC(c^1, bound)$ before starting the search, returning unsat if $\varphi_C \wedge BC(c^1, bound)$ is $T \cup C$-inconsistent, sat plus the value $cost \stackrel{\text{def}}{=} \text{CostOf}_1(\mu)$, μ being the $T \cup C$-consistent satisfying assignment, otherwise. The fact of having an *incremental* SMT($T \cup C$) solver is crucial for efficiency, since it can reuse the Boolean, T- and C-lemmas learned in the previous iterations to prune the search. To this extent, the fact of explicitly conjoining $BC(c^1, bound)$ to φ_C (7.) is not necessary for correctness, but it allows for reusing the C-lemmas (10) from one call to the other to prune the search.

Termination is straightforward, since $mincost$ is a suitable ranking function. The correctness and completeness of the algorithm is also straightforward: in the last iteration we prove that there exist no solution better than the current value of $mincost$, so $mincost$ is optimal. (If no solution exists, then the procedure returns $+∞$.)

A binary-search approach. A possibly faster way of converging on the optimal solution is binary search over the possible solutions. Instead of tightening the upper bound

```
1. int IncBinaryBOMT(φc,c¹)
2.      lower = lb¹;  upper = ub¹;
3.      mincost = +∞;  guess = ub¹;
4.      do
5.          ⟨status,cost⟩ = IncrementalSMT_{T∪C}(φc,BC(c¹,guess));
6.          if (status==sat)
7.          then {
8.              φc = φc ∧ BC(c¹,guess);  // activates learned C-lemmas
9.              mincost = cost;
10.             upper = cost-1; }            // more efficient than guess-1
11.         else {
12.             φc = φc ∧ ¬BC(c¹,guess);  // activates learned C-lemmas
13.             lower = guess +1; }
14.         guess = ⌊(lower + upper)/2⌋;
15.     while (lower ≤ upper);
16.     return mincost;
```

Fig. 2. A BOMT($\mathcal{T}$) algorithm based on binary search and incremental SMT($\mathcal{T} \cup \mathcal{C}$)

with the last solution found, we keep track of the interval of all possible solutions $[lower, upper]$, and we proceed bisecting such interval, each time picking a guess as $\lfloor (lower + upper)/2 \rfloor$.

The pseudo-code of this algorithm can be seen in Fig. 2. As before, the procedure receives as input φ_C and c^1. $[lower, upper]$ is initialized to $[lb^1, ub^1]$, $mincost$ to $+\infty$ and $guess$ to ub^1; each call IncrementalSMT$_{\mathcal{T} \cup \mathcal{C}}(\varphi_C, BC(c^1, bound))$ either returns sat plus the value $cost \overset{\text{def}}{=} CostOf_1(\mu)$, or it returns unsat. In the first case, the range is restricted to $[lower, cost - 1]$ (10.), in the latter to $[guess + 1, upper]$ (13.). (Notice that, unlike with standard binary search, restricting to $[lower, cost - 1]$ rather than to $[lower, guess - 1]$ allows for exploiting the $cost$ information to further restrict the search.) Moreover, in the first case $BC(c^1, bound)$ is conjoined to φ_C (8.), $\neg BC(c^1, bound)$ in the latter (12.), which allows for reusing the previously-learned $\mathcal{C}$-lemmas (10) end (11) respectively to prune the search.

Termination is straightforward, since $upper - lower$ is a suitable a ranking function. Correctness and completeness are similarly obvious, since the interval of possible solutions will always contain the optimal solution.

5   PseudoBoolean and MAX-SAT/SMT as SMT($\mathcal{C}$)/SMT($\mathcal{T} \cup \mathcal{C}$)

The PseudoBoolean (PB) problem can be defined as the problem:

$$\text{minimize} \sum_{j=1}^{N_1} c_j^1 A_j^1 \text{ under the constraints } \{\sum_{j=1}^{N_i} c_j^i A_j^i \geq lb^i \mid i \in [2, ..., M]\} \quad (13)$$

where A_j^1 are Boolean atoms, A_j^i Boolean literals, and c_j, c_j^i, lb^i positive integer values. This is an extension of the SAT problem which can efficiently express many problems of practical interest.

The $SMT(\mathcal{C})$ problem is closely related to the PB problem, in fact they are equally expressive. First, we notice that $\sum_j c_j^i A_j^i$ can be rewritten as $\sum_j ite(A_j^i, c_j^i, 0)$, s.t. we immediately see that the PB problem (13) is a subcase of the BOMT$(\mathcal{T})$ problem of §4.2 where $\mathcal{T}$ is plain Boolean logic, and as such it can be solved using the SMT$(\mathcal{T} \cup \mathcal{C})$ encoding in (12) and the SMT$(\mathcal{T} \cup \mathcal{C})$-based procedures in §4.2.

For solving PB problems by translation into $SMT(\mathcal{C})$ in practice, the above translation can be improved. As an example, PB constraints of the form $\sum_j A_j^i \geq 1$ can be translated into the single propositional clause $\bigvee_j A_j^i$. In general, it may be advantageous to translate PB constraints into propositional clauses when the number of resulting clauses is low. See for instance [10] for some possibilities.

Proposition 4. *For every* $SMT(\mathcal{C})$ *instance, there exists a polynomial-time translation into an equivalent instance of the PB problem*

In the *Weighted Partial Max-SMT(T)* problem, in a CNF $\mathcal{T}$-formula $\phi \stackrel{\text{def}}{=} \phi_h \wedge \phi_s$ each clause C_j in ϕ_s is tagged with a positive cost value c_j, and the problem consists in finding a $\mathcal{T}$-consistent assignment μ which propositionally satisfies ϕ_h and maximizes the sum $\sum_{j \ s.t. \mu \models_p C_j} c_j$ (that is, minimizes $\sum_{j \ s.t. \mu \not\models_p C_j} c_j$). The problem is not "Weighted" iff $c_j^i = 1$ for every j, and it is not "Partial" iff ϕ_h is the empty set of clauses; the [Weighted] [Partial] Max-SAT problem is the [Weighted] [Partial] Max-SMT$(\mathcal{T})$ problem where $\mathcal{T}$ is plain Boolean logic.

A Weighted Partial Max-SMT$(\mathcal{T})$ problem (and hence all its subcases described above) can be encoded into a SMT$(\mathcal{T})$ cost minimization problem $\langle \varphi, \underline{costs}, \underline{bounds} \rangle$ s.t. $\varphi \stackrel{\text{def}}{=} \phi_h \wedge \bigwedge_j (C_j \vee A_j^i)$, $\underline{costs} \stackrel{\text{def}}{=} \{cost^1\} = \{\sum_j ite(A_j^i, c_j^i, 0)\}$ and $\underline{bounds} \stackrel{\text{def}}{=} \{\langle 0, \sum_j c_j^i \rangle\}$, which can be addressed as described in §4.2.

Vice versa, a SMT$(\mathcal{T})$ cost minimization problem $\langle \varphi, \underline{costs}, \underline{bounds} \rangle$ s.t. $\underline{costs} \stackrel{\text{def}}{=} \{cost^1\} = \{\sum_j ite(A_j^1, c_j^1, 0)\}$ and $\underline{bounds} \stackrel{\text{def}}{=} \{\}$, can be encoded into a Weighted Partial Max-SMT$(\mathcal{T})$ problem $\phi \stackrel{\text{def}}{=} \phi_h \wedge \phi_s$ where $\phi_h \stackrel{\text{def}}{=} \varphi$ and $\phi_s \stackrel{\text{def}}{=} \bigwedge_j (\neg A_j^1)$ s.t. each unit-clause $(\neg A_j^1)$ is tagged with the cost c_j^i.

6   Empirical Evaluation

The algorithms described in the previous sections have been implemented within the MATHSAT SMT solver. In order to demonstrate the versatility and the efficiency of our approach, we have tested MATHSAT in several different scenarios: BOMT$(\mathcal{T})$, Max-SMT, Max-SAT, and PseudoBoolean optimization.

6.1   Results on Max-SMT

In the first part of our experiments, we evaluate the behaviour of MATHSAT on problems requiring the use of a combination of $\mathcal{C}$ and another theory $\mathcal{T}$. For this evaluation, we have collected two kinds of benchmarks. First, we have randomly-generated some Max-SMT problems,[3] starting from standard SMT problems taken from the SMT-LIB.

---

[3] As observed in §5 BOMT$(\mathcal{T})$ with a single cost function is equivalent to weighted partial Max-SMT, and therefore we only refer to Max-SMT here.

The second group of benchmarks comes from two real-world industrial case studies. These are the case studies that actually prompted us towards this research, because a plain encoding in SMT without costs resulted in unacceptable performance. Interestingly, although the application domains are very different, all the problems can be thought of as trying to find optimal displacement for some components in space. Unfortunately, we can not disclose any further details.

As regards the comparison with other systems, to the best of our knowledge there are two other SMT solvers that support Max-SMT, namely YICES [9] and BARCELOGIC [13], which were therefore the natural candidates for comparison. Unfortunately however, it was not possible to obtain from the authors a version of BARCELOGIC with support for optimization, so we had to exclude it from our analysis.

We have performed experiments on weigthed Max-SMT and partial weighted Max-SMT problems. For weighted Max-SMT, we have generated benchmarks by combining n independent unsatisfiable CNF formulas in the SMT-LIB (for $n = 2$ and $n = 3$) and assigning random weights to each clause. In order to obtain partial weighted Max-SMT instances, instead, we have first generated random $\text{BOMT}(\mathcal{T})$ problems by assigning random costs to a subset of the atoms (both Boolean and $\mathcal{T}$-atoms) of some satisfiable formulas in the SMT-LIB, and then encoded the $\text{BOMT}(\mathcal{T})$ problems into partial weighted Max-SMT ones, as descrbed in §5. The same encoding into partial weighted Max-SMT was used also to convert the $\text{BOMT}(\mathcal{T})$ instances coming from the industrial case studies.

We ran MATHSAT using both binary and linear search for optimization, and compared it with YICES. All the experiments have been performed on 2.66Ghz Intel Xeon machines with 6Mb of cache, running Linux. The time limit was set to 300 seconds, and the memory limit to 2Gb.

The results for problems generated from SMT-LIB instances are reported in Table 1. For each solver, the table lists the number of instances for which the optimal solution was found (the total number of instances was 200), the number of instances for which the given solver was the only one to find the optimal solution, and the total and average execution times on the solved instances. From the results, we can see that binary search outperforms linear search for this kind of problems. This is true in particular on the first group of benchmarks, where binary search can find the optimum for more than twice as many instances as linear search. In both cases, moreover, MATHSAT outperforms also YICES, both in number of optimal solutions found and in execution time.

We also measured the overhead of performing optimization on these instances compared to solving the decision problem given the known optimal bound. For partial Max-SMT and binary search the mean was 9.5, the median 4.1 and the maximal ratio 49.6, meaning that solving the optimization problem took on average 9.5 times as long as determining that the optimal solution is indeed a solution. Similarly, for partial Max-SMT and linear search the mean of the ratio was 45.8, the median 24.3 and the maximal 222.3 showing that the overhead in linear search can be considerable. In the weighted partial Max-SMT problem the overhead was slightly lower. Using binary search the mean was 2.6, the median 3.4 and the maximal 22.1. Using linear search we get a mean of 4.4, a median of 5.9 and a maximal of 54.

Table 1. Performance on Max-SMT and BOMT(T) problems. For each category, the solvers are sorted from "best" to "worst". Optimum is the number of instances where the optimum was found, and Unique is the number of optimal solutions found by a the given solver only. Time is the total execution time in seconds for all instances where an optimum was found. Mean and median is the mean and median of those times.

Category	Solver	Optimum	Unique	Time	Mean	Median
Weighted	MATHSAT-binary	56	6	4886.59	87.26	68.38
Max-SMT	YICES	47	3	5260.67	111.92	86.21
	MATHSAT-linear	23	0	4777.45	207.71	251.00
Weighted partial	MATHSAT-binary	206	1	1462.98	7.10	2.45
Max-SMT	MATHSAT-linear	206	1	2228.39	10.81	4.02
(BOMT(T))	YICES	195	0	3559.53	18.25	3.19

Finally, we compared MATHSAT-linear, MATHSAT-binary and YICES on the two industrial case studies we had. In the first one, all three solvers could find the optimum on all the 7 instances of the set. YICES turned out to be the fastest, with a median run time of 0.5 seconds. The median time for MATHSAT-binary was of 1.54 seconds, and that of MATHSAT-linear of 64.84 seconds. In the second case study, composed of two instances, however, the outcome was the opposite: MATHSAT-linear and MATHSAT-binary could compute the optimum for both instances in approximately the same time, with the former being slightly faster (about 35 seconds for the easiest problem for both solvers, about 370 and 405 seconds respectively for the hardest). Yices, instead, could not compute the optimum for the hardest problem even with a timeout of 30 minutes (taking about 11 seconds on the easiest instead).

6.2   Results on Max-SAT

We have also performed comparisons with several Max-SAT solvers from the 2009 Max-SAT Evaluation [1]. For each of the three industrial categories containing pure Max-SAT, partial Max-SAT and partial weighted Max-SAT respectively we have chosen 100 instances randomly (in the case of partial weigted Max-SAT, we chose all 80 instances). We chose 3 solvers (MsUncore [11], SAT4J [4], and Clone [14]) participating in the 2009 competition that were readily available together with the YICES SMT solver [9], and ran each of them on all instances supported by that particular solver. We run MATHSAT using both binary and linear search. All solvers were run with a timeout of 300 seconds, and a memory limit of 2 GB. The results are summarized in table 2. We count both the number of optimal solutions found and the number of non-optimal solutions found. We report also the total execution time taken to find all optimal solutions and unsatisfiable answers as well as the mean and median of these times.

We can see that for pure Max-SAT, MATHSAT is not competitive in finding optimal solutions, although it can find many solutions. This can be attributed to the encoding; All clauses are marked with one IC predicate, and any cost theory conflict is very likely to be extremely large, and not helping prune search effectively. For partial Max-SAT most of the clauses are hard constraints, so the number of IC predicates is more

Table 2. Performance on Max-SAT problems. For each category, the solvers are sorted from "best" to "worst". Optimum is the number of instances where the optimum was found, and Sat is the number of instances where some non-optimal solution was found. Time is the total execution time in seconds for all instances where either an optimum or unsat was found. Mean and median is the mean and median of those times.

Category	Solver	Optimum	Sat	Time	Mean	Median
Max-SAT	MsUncore	83	0	2191.17	26.40	6.94
	Yices	56	0	1919.79	34.28	8.16
	SAT4J	30	50	1039.07	34.64	12.54
	MATHSAT-binary	16	71	1017.87	63.62	20.41
	Clone	15	0	2561.06	170.74	129.06
	MATHSAT-linear	5	82	466.91	93.38	72.05
Partial Max-SAT	Yices	71	0	1643.60	23.15	0.23
	SAT4J	67	31	1943.81	29.01	1.48
	MATHSAT-binary	55	43	248.00	4.51	0.07
	MATHSAT-linear	53	45	611.52	11.54	0.10
	MsUncore	46	0	353.84	7.69	0.20
	Clone	44	29	1743.54	39.63	6.59
Weighted partial Max-SAT	MATHSAT-binary	80	0	110.49	1.38	1.23
	SAT4J	80	0	271.86	3.40	3.26
	MsUncore	80	0	579.20	7.24	7.09
	MATHSAT-linear	79	1	1104.10	13.97	8.95
	Clone	0	0	0.00	N/A	N/A

moderate, and performance is noticeably better. This is also true for weighted partial Max-SAT, where MATHSAT using binary search outperforms the winner of the 2009 Max-SAT Evaluation, SAT4J.

Overall, we can notice that binary search seems to outperform linear search in the number of optimal solutions found, although both binary and linear search can find some solution for the same number of instances as expected given that the first iteration in both algorithms are identical.

6.3 Results on PseudoBoolean Solving

Finally, we tested the performance of MATHSAT on PseudoBoolean (PB) optimization problems. We compared MATHSAT, using both linear and binary search, with several PB solvers from the 2009 PB Evaluation [3], namely SCIP [7] (the winner in the OPT-SMALLINT category), BSOLO [12], PBCLASP [2] and SAT4J [4] (the winner in the OPT-BIGINT category). We selected a subset of the instances used in the 2009 PB Evaluation in the categories OPT-SMALLINT (optimization with small coefficients) and OPT-BIGINT (optimization with large coefficients, requiring multi-precision arithmetic), and ran all the solvers in the categories they supported.

The results are summarized in table 3. They show that, although MATHSAT is not competitive with the two best PB solvers currently available in the SMALLINT

Table 3. Performance on PB problems. For each category, the solvers are sorted from "best" to "worst". Optimum is the number of instances where the optimum was found, Sat is the number of instances where some non-optimal solution was found and Unsat is the number of instances that were found unsatisfiable. Time is the total execution time in seconds for all instances where either an optimum or unsat was found. Mean and median is the mean and median of those times.

Category	Solver	Optimum	Unsat	Sat	Time	Mean	Median
SMALLINT	SCIP	98	8	62	3078.88	29.04	3.49
	BSOLO	88	7	110	1754.31	18.46	0.43
	PBCLASP	67	7	127	869.66	11.75	0.05
	MATHSAT-linear	63	7	132	1699.69	24.28	0.21
	MATHSAT-binary	63	7	132	2119.07	30.27	0.22
	SAT4J	59	6	127	1149.96	17.69	1.34
BIGINT	MATHSAT-binary	52	13	45	2373.35	36.51	15.54
	MATHSAT-linear	48	13	49	1610.04	26.39	13.40
	SAT4J	19	18	51	759.15	20.51	3.55

category, its performace is comparable to that of PBCLASP, which got the third place in the 2009 PB Evaluation. Moreover, MATHSAT (with both binary and linear search) outperforms the winner of the BIGINT category, solving more than twice as many problems as SAT4J within the timeout. It is worth observing that these results were obtained without using any specific heuristic for improving performance of MATHSAT.

Finally, we observe that also in this case binary search seems to be better than linear search. For PB problems it has been reported [5] that linear search is more effective than binary search. In our case, the opposite appears to be the case. A possible explanation is that, since our solver is still very basic, it does not find a very good initial solution. For linear search we often need a large number of iterations to locate the optimum, and this search appears to be short-circuited by the binary search algorithm. This happens not only on PB problems, but also on Max-SAT and Max-SMT problems.

7   Related Work

The closest work to ours is the work presented in [13], where the idea of optimization in SMT was introduced, in particular wrt the Max-SMT problem, in the setting of SMT with increasingly- strong theories. There are however several differences wrt [13]. The first one is that our approach is more general, since we allow for multiple cost functions. Consequently, we can handle more expressive problems (e.g. the rover domain) with multiple cost functions, and PB constraints. The second one is that there is no need to change the framework to deal with increments in the theory. In fact, this has also the advantage that the extension of a theory is not "permanent". Thus, differently from the approach in [13], our framework can also deal with binary search, while theirs can not (once inconsistency is reached, the framewrok does not support changes in the theory).

Optimization problems are also supported by Yices, but we could obtain no information about the algorithm being used.

8 Conclusions and Future Work

In this paper we have addressed the problem of Satisfiability Modulo the Theory of Costs. We have shown that dealing with costs in a dedicated manner allows to tackle significant SMT problems. Furthermore, the SMT($\mathcal{C}$) solver provides a very effective framework to deal with optimization problems. Our solver shows decent performance even in Boolean and PseudoBoolean optimization problems, providing an answer (albeit suboptimal) more often than other solvers. In a couple of categories, our MathSAT outperforms the highly tuned solvers winners of the most recent competitions.

In the future, we expect to experiment in several application domains that require reasoning about resources (e.g. planning, scheduling, WCET). We also plan to investigate applications to minimization in bounded model checking, for instance to provide more user-friendly counter-examples, and in error localization and debugging. From the technological point of view, we will investigate whether it is possible to borrow effective techniques from PseudoBoolean solvers, given the similarities with the theory of costs. Finally, we will address the problem of minimization in the case costs are a function of individual (rather than Boolean) variables.

References

1. Max-SAT 2009 Evaluation (2009), http://www.maxsat.udl.cat/09/
2. PBclasp, http://potassco.sourceforge.net/labs.html
3. Pseudo-Boolean Competition 2009 (2009),
   http://www.cril.univ-artois.fr/PB09/
4. SAT4J, http://www.sat4j.org/
5. Aloul, F.A., Ramani, A., Sakallah, K.A., Markov, I.L.: Solution and optimization of systems of pseudo-boolean constraints. IEEE Transactions on Computers 56(10) (2007)
6. Barrett, C.W., Sebastiani, R., Seshia, S.A., Tinelli, C.: Satisfiability Modulo Theories. In: Handbook of Satisfiability. IOS Press, Amsterdam (2009)
7. Berthold, T., Heinz, S., Pfetsch, M.E.: Solving Pseudo-Boolean Problems with SCIP. Technical Report ZIB-Report 08-12, K. Zuse Zentrum für Informationdtechnik Berlin (2009)
8. Cimatti, A., Franzén, A., Griggio, A., Sebastiani, R., Stenico, C.: Satisfiability Modulo the Theory of Costs: Foundations and Applications (Extended version). Technical Report DISI-10-001 (2010), http://disi.unitn.it/~rseba/tacas10_extended.pdf
9. Dutertre, B., de Moura, L.: A Fast Linear-Arithmetic Solver for DPLL(T). In: Ball, T., Jones, R.B. (eds.) CAV 2006. LNCS, vol. 4144, pp. 81–94. Springer, Heidelberg (2006)
10. Eén, N., Sörensson, N.: Translating Pseudo-Boolean Constraints into SAT. JSAT 2(1-4) (2006)
11. Manquinho, V., Marques-Silva, J., Planes, J.: Algorithms for Weighted Boolean Optimization. In: Kullmann, O. (ed.) SAT 2009. LNCS, vol. 5584, pp. 495–508. Springer, Heidelberg (2009)
12. Manquinho, V.M., Marques-Silva, J.: Effective Lower Bounding Techniques for Pseudo-Boolean Optimization. In: Proc. DATE. IEEE Computer Society, Los Alamitos (2005)
13. Nieuwenhuis, R., Oliveras, A.: On SAT Modulo Theories and Optimization Problems. In: Biere, A., Gomes, C.P. (eds.) SAT 2006. LNCS, vol. 4121, pp. 156–169. Springer, Heidelberg (2006)
14. Pipatsrisawat, K., Palyan, A., Chavira, M., Choi, A., Darwiche, A.: Solving Weighted Max-SAT Problems in a Reduced Search Space: A Performance Analysis. JSAT, 4 (2008)

Optimal Tableau Algorithms for Coalgebraic Logics

Rajeev Goré[1], Clemens Kupke[2], and Dirk Pattinson[2]

[1] Computer Science Laboratory, The Australian National University
[2] Department of Computing, Imperial College London

Abstract. Deciding whether a modal formula is satisfiable with respect to a given set of (global) assumptions is a question of fundamental importance in applications of logic in computer science. Tableau methods have proved extremely versatile for solving this problem for many different individual logics but they typically do not meet the known complexity bounds for the logics in question. Recently, it has been shown that optimality can be obtained for some logics while retaining practicality by using a technique called "global caching". Here, we show that global caching is applicable to all logics that can be equipped with coalgebraic semantics, for example, classical modal logic, graded modal logic, probabilistic modal logic and coalition logic. In particular, the coalgebraic approach also covers logics that combine these various features. We thus show that global caching is a widely applicable technique and also provide foundations for optimal tableau algorithms that uniformly apply to a large class of modal logics.

1 Introduction

Modal logics have many applications in computer science, and e.g. provide a rigorous foundation for reasoning about programs [15] and knowledge [7]. Typically, we are given a set formulas Δ that represents our assumptions (e.g. knowledge about a particular domain) and are faced with the task of deciding whether a formula A (that we may think of as a hypothesis) is logically consistent with Δ. From a model theoretic perspective, this means that there exists at least one model that validates Δ everywhere, but also makes A true in at least one point. The elements of Δ are usually referred to as global assumptions in modal logic, or as a TBox in description logic. Various automated theorem proving techniques have been developed to handle this task but it is fair to say that tableau methods have proved particularly versatile for solving this problem [1,9,26].

Tableau algorithms, however, often do not meet the known complexity bounds for the logics in question. For example, the traditional tableau algorithm for the modal logic K requires double exponential time in the worst case, even though the global satisfiability problem for this logic is known to be EXPTIME-complete [1]. The success of suboptimal tableau algorithms in practice, implemented in reasoners like Racer [14] and Fact++[27], lies in the vast array of optimisations that

J. Esparza and R. Majumdar (Eds.): TACAS 2010, LNCS 6015, pp. 114–128, 2010.

have been developed for the underlying tableau methods [17]. In contrast, the (optimal) algorithms that underly typical complexity proofs either perform rather wholesale fixpoint computations or employ semantical means, which is infeasible in practice. Clearly the ideal situation is to have optimal tableau algorithms that remain amenable to proven optimisation techniques.

The main reason for the suboptimal behaviour of tableau algorithms is that they proceed by searching one branch at a time, using backtracking, and the same node can appear on multiple branches. The second occurrence of the node in a different branch will repeat the computations already performed by its previous incarnation, since the previous branch will have been reclaimed via backtracking. Although optimal tableau algorithms that avoid this behaviour are known [6], they are rarely used by practitioners because they are difficult to implement [1]. Recently, it has been shown that both optimality and ease of implementation can be reconciled while keeping the feasibility of tableau-based algorithms for the description logics $\mathcal{ALC}$ and $\mathcal{ALCI}$ [10,13] by employing so-called "global caching". The resulting tableau algorithms explore a graph of nodes, rather than a tree with distinct branches, since subsequent incarnations of a node lead to a "cache hit" to the first incarnation on a previous branch. It has been experimentally demonstrated that global caching compares very favourably with other caching techniques known in the literature [12].

Here, we show that global caching can be applied not only to logics with an underlying relational semantics, but also to a large class of logics that is amenable to coalgebraic semantics. This class contains many different logics such as classical modal logic, graded modal logic, probabilistic modal logic and coalition logic, as well as their various combinations. We first construct a complete tableau calculus for coalgebraic logics with global assumptions where all closed tableaux are finite trees, and show that global caching is applicable to this type of calculus. Both results are self-contained, and completeness of global caching readily applies to any tableau calculus that can be encoded as reachability game. In summary, we derive a concrete algorithm to decide satisfiability of modal formulas in presence of global assumptions that uniformly applies to a large class of logics. We illustrate the technical development by instantiating the coalgebraic framework to three different logics: probabilistic modal logic, coalition logic, and coalition logic with probabilistic outcomes that arises as a combination of both. In summary, we not only extend the applicability of global caching by a large margin, but also obtain new and optimal tableau algorithms for a large class of logics, including e.g. probabilistic modal logic, for which no tableau-based decision procedure is so far known to exist.

Related Work. Global caching has so far been used for logics with relational semantics in [10,11]. The extension of global caching, given in this paper, to logics that do not have an underlying relational semantics is new. The complexity of coalgebraic logics has been studied previously in [24] without global assumptions, and [25] establishes an EXPTIME complexity bound in the presence of global assumptions. The tableau calculus given here is new, and unlike the algorithm in *op.cit.* which is based on Hintikka sets, the resulting algorithm is easily implementable.

2 Preliminaries and Notation

To keep our treatment parametric in the underlying modal logic, we fix a *modal simlarity type* Λ consisting of modal operators with arities, and a denumerable set V of *propositional variables*. In the sequel, we will only consider formulas in negation normal form and abbreviate $\overline{V} = \{\overline{p} \mid p \in V\}$ and similary $\overline{\Lambda} = \{\overline{\heartsuit} \mid \heartsuit \in \Lambda\}$ where we consider $\overline{\heartsuit}$ as a modal operator with the same arity as $\heartsuit$. The set $\mathcal{F}(\Lambda)$ of Λ-*formulas* is given by the grammar below

$$\mathcal{F}(\Lambda) \ni A_1, \ldots, A_n ::= p \mid \overline{p} \mid A_1 \wedge A_2 \mid A_1 \vee A_2 \mid \heartsuit(A_1, \ldots, A_n) \mid \overline{\heartsuit}(A_1, \ldots, A_n)$$

where $\heartsuit \in \Lambda$ is an n-ary operator. The *rank* of a formula $A \in \mathcal{F}(\Lambda)$ is the maximal nesting depth of modal operators in A and is denoted by $\mathsf{rank}(A)$, and $\mathsf{subf}(A)$ denotes the set of subformulas of A. The *closure* $\mathsf{cl}(A)$ of A contains all subformulas of A and their negations, i.e. $\mathsf{cl}(A) = \mathsf{subf}(A) \cup \overline{\mathsf{subf}(A)}$. We write

$$(\Lambda \cup \overline{\Lambda})(F) = \{\heartsuit(A_1, \ldots, A_n) \mid \heartsuit \in \Lambda \cup \overline{\Lambda} \; n\text{-ary}, A_1, \ldots, A_n \in F\}$$

for the set of all formulas that can be constructed by applying a (possibly negated) modal operator to elements of a set F of formulas.

A Λ-*tableau-sequent*, short Λ-*sequent* or just *sequent*, is a finite set of Λ-formulas that we read conjunctively, and we write $\mathcal{S}(\Lambda)$ for the set of Λ-sequents. The rank of a sequent Γ is the maximum of the ranks of the elements of Γ and we put $\mathsf{rank}(\emptyset) = 0$. The closure of a sequent is given by $\mathsf{cl}(\Gamma) = \bigcup\{\mathsf{cl}(A) \mid A \in \Gamma\}$. As usual, we identify a formula $A \in \mathcal{F}(\Lambda)$ with the singleton sequent $\{A\} \in \mathcal{S}(\Lambda)$ and write Γ, Δ for the union of Γ and Δ. We write $\mathsf{State}(\Lambda)$ for the set of Λ-sequents that neither contain a top-level propositional connective nor a pair $p, \overline{p}$ of complementary propositional variables. As we only deal with formulas in negation normal form, negation becomes a derived operation, and we write $\overline{A}$ for the negation of a formula $A \in \mathcal{F}(\Lambda)$ given by $\overline{\overline{p}} = p$, $\overline{(A \wedge B)} = \overline{A} \vee \overline{B}$, $\overline{A \vee B} = \overline{A} \wedge \overline{B}$, $\overline{\heartsuit(A_1, \ldots A_n)} = \overline{\heartsuit}(\overline{A}_1, \ldots, \overline{A}_n)$ and $\overline{\overline{\heartsuit}(A_1, \ldots, A_n)} = \heartsuit(\overline{A}_1, \ldots, \overline{A}_n)$. This notation extends to sequents so that $\overline{\Gamma} = \{\overline{A} \mid A \in \Gamma\}$. A *substitution* is a mapping $\sigma : V \to \mathcal{F}(\Lambda)$, and the result of replacing every occurrence of $p \in V$ in a formula $A \in \mathcal{F}(\Lambda)$ is denoted by $A\sigma$. Again, this extends to sequents, and $\Gamma\sigma = \{A\sigma \mid A \in \Gamma\}$ if $\Gamma \in \mathcal{S}(\Lambda)$.

On the semantical side, parametricity is achieved by adopting coalgebraic semantics [19]: formulas are interpreted over T-coalgebras, where T is an endofunctor on sets, and we recover the semantics of a large number of logics by specific choices for T (Example 1). To interpret the modal operators $\heartsuit \in \Lambda$, we require that T extends to a Λ-*structure*, i.e. T comes equipped with a predicate lifting (natural transformation) of type $[\![\heartsuit]\!] : 2^n \to 2 \circ T^{\mathrm{op}}$ for every n-ary modality $\heartsuit \in \Lambda$, where $2 : \mathsf{Set} \to \mathsf{Set}^{\mathrm{op}}$ is the contravariant powerset functor. In elementary terms, this amounts to assigning a set-indexed family of functions $(\llbracket\heartsuit\rrbracket_X : \mathcal{P}(X)^n \to \mathcal{P}(TX))_{X\in\mathsf{Set}}$ to every n-ary modal operator $\heartsuit \in \Lambda$ such that $(Tf)^{-1} \circ \llbracket\heartsuit\rrbracket_X(A_1,\ldots,A_n) = \llbracket\heartsuit\rrbracket_Y(f^{-1}(A_1),\ldots,f^{-1}(A_n))$ for all sets X,Y and all functions $f : Y \to X$. If $\heartsuit \in \Lambda$ is n-ary, we put $\llbracket\overline{\heartsuit}\rrbracket_X(A_1,\ldots,A_n) = (TX)\setminus\llbracket\heartsuit\rrbracket_X(X\setminus A_1,\ldots,X\setminus A_n)$. We often leave the predicate liftings implicit and refer to a Λ-structure just in terms of the underlying endofunctor T.

In the coalgebraic approach, the role of frames is played by T-*coalgebras*, i.e. pairs (C,γ) where C is a (state) set and $\gamma : C \to TC$ is a (transition) function. A T-*model* is a triple (C,γ,π) where (C,γ) is a T-coalgebra and $\pi : V \to \mathcal{P}(C)$ is a valuation of the propositional variables. For a Λ-structure T and a T-model $M = (C,\gamma,\pi)$, the *truth set* $\llbracket A\rrbracket_M$ of a formula $A \in \mathcal{F}(\Lambda)$ w.r.t. M is given inductively by the following, where $\heartsuit \in \Lambda\cup\overline{\Lambda}$ is n-ary: $\llbracket p\rrbracket_M = \pi(p)$, $\llbracket\overline{p}\rrbracket_M = C\setminus\pi(p)$ and

$$\llbracket\heartsuit(A_1,\ldots,A_n)\rrbracket_M = \gamma^{-1}\circ\llbracket\heartsuit\rrbracket_C(\llbracket A_1\rrbracket_M,\ldots,\llbracket A_n\rrbracket_M).$$

We write $M,c \models A$ if $c \in \llbracket A\rrbracket_M$ and $M \models A$ if $M,c \models A$ for all $c \in C$. Again, this extends to sequents under a conjunctive reading, and we put $\llbracket\Gamma\rrbracket_M = \bigcap\{\llbracket A\rrbracket_M \mid A \in \Gamma\}$ and write $M \models \Gamma$ if $M \models A$ for all $A \in \Gamma$. We denote the model class of a sequent $\Delta \in \mathcal{S}(\Lambda)$ by $\mathsf{Mod}(\Delta)$, which comprises the class of all T-models M with $M \models \Delta$, that is, M globally validates Δ. If $\Gamma,\Delta \in \mathcal{S}(\Lambda)$ are sequents, we say that Γ is *satisfiable in* $\mathsf{Mod}(\Delta)$ if there exists $M \in \mathsf{Mod}(\Delta)$ such that $\llbracket\Gamma\rrbracket_M \neq \emptyset$.

Our main interest in this paper is the *global satisfiability problem*, that is, to determine whether a sequent Γ is satisfiable in $\mathsf{Mod}(\Delta)$, for a set Δ of global assumptions. The generality of the coalgebraic approach allows us to treat this problem uniformly for a large class of structurally different modal logics that is moreover closed under composition, as the following example demonstrates.

Example 1. The generic approach of coalgebraic semantics specialises to a large class of different logics by instantiating the signature functor T appropriately. The class of these logics comprises classical and monotone modal logic in the sense of [2], the modal logic K, graded modal logic [8], probabilistic modal logic [16], coalition logic [21] and conditional logic [2]. We refer to [20,24] for details on their coalgebraic treatment. Here, we concentrate on probabilistic modal logic, coalition logic and a combination of both.

1. Coalition logic over a finite set N of agents has similarity type $\Lambda_{\mathsf{G}} = \{[C] \mid C \subseteq N\}$, and is interpreted over game frames, i.e. coalgebras for the functor

$$\mathsf{G}(X) = \{(f,(S_i)_{i\in N}) \mid \emptyset \neq S_i \subseteq \mathbb{N} \text{ finite for all } i \in \mathbb{N}, f : \prod_{i\in N} S_i \to X\}.$$

The S_i are the strategies of agent i and f is an outcome function. We read $[C]A$ as "coalition C can achieve A in the next round of the game", captured by

$$\llbracket[C]\rrbracket_X(A) = \{(f,(S_i)_{i\in N}) \in \mathsf{G}(X) \mid$$
$$\exists(s_i)_{i\in C} \in (S_i)_{i\in C}.\forall(s_i)_{i\in N\setminus C} \in (S_i)_{i\in N\setminus C}.f((s_i)_{i\in N}) \in A\}$$

that induces – up to the move to finite sets of strategies – the standard semantics of coalition logic [21].

2. The syntax of probabilistic modal logic is induced by the similarity type $\Lambda_\mathsf{D} = \{\langle p\rangle \mid p \in [0,1] \cap \mathbb{Q}\}$ and we put $[p] = \overline{\langle p\rangle}$. The formula $\langle p\rangle A$ reads as "A holds with probability at least p in the next state". The semantics of the probabilistic modal logic is given by the structure

$$\mathsf{D}(X) = \{\mu\colon X \to_f [0,1] \mid \mu(X) = 1\} \quad [\![\langle p\rangle]\!]_X(A) = \{\mu \in \mathsf{D}(X) \mid \mu(A) \geq p\}$$

where $X \to_f [0,1]$ is the set of all functions $f : X \to [0,1]$ with finite support, i.e. $f(x) \neq 0$ for only finitely many $x \in X$, and $\mu(A) = \sum_{x\in A}\mu(x)$. Coalgebras for D are precisely image-finite Markov chains.

3. A combination of probabilistic modal logic and coalition logic over a set N of agents arises by considering the (combined) similarity type

$$\Lambda_{\mathsf{D}\circ\mathsf{G}} = \{\langle p\rangle[C] \mid p \in [0,1] \cap \mathbb{Q}, C \subseteq N\}$$

and we read the formula $\langle p\rangle[C]A$ as "with probability p coalition C has a collaborative strategy to achieve A in the next round of the game". Formulas are interpreted over coalgebras for the (combined) endofunctor $\mathsf{D} \circ \mathsf{G}$ by the (combined) predicate lifting

$$[\![\langle p\rangle[C]]\!]_X = [\![\langle p\rangle]\!]_{\mathsf{G}X} \circ [\![[C]]\!]_X : \mathcal{P}(X) \to \mathcal{P}(\mathsf{D} \circ \mathsf{G}(X))$$

where the interpretation of the individual modalities $[\![\langle p\rangle]\!]$ and $[\![[C]]\!]$ is as above. In a $\mathsf{D}\circ\mathsf{G}$-coalgebra (C, γ), the transition function γ delivers a probability distribution over possible outcomes of a strategic game. The predicate lifting $[\![\langle p\rangle[C]]\!]$ singles out all those distributions that assign probability $\geq p$ to the set of those outcomes for which coalition C can achieve A.

Note that this is just one possible combination that naturally finds its place in the coalgebraic framework and refer the reader to [3,5,23] for details.

3   Tableaux and Games for Global Consequence

The first goal of this paper is to set up a sound and complete tableau system for global satisfiability in coalgebraic modal logics. Completeness is established via winning strategies in the associated reachability games. We begin by introducing a generic version of both that we later specialise to coalgebraic logics.

Definition 2. A *tableau system* is a pair (S, R) where S is a set (of sequents) and R is a set of rules of the form Γ/Ψ where $\Gamma \in S$ and $\Psi \subseteq S$ is finite.

A sequent $\Gamma \in S$ has a *closed tableau* in the system (S, R) if Γ is an element of the least set closed under the rules in R, that is, an element of the least fixpoint of the (evidently monotone) operator

$$M : \mathcal{P}(S) \to \mathcal{P}(S), M(X) = \{\Gamma \in S \mid \exists \Psi \subseteq X.(\Gamma, \Psi) \in R\}.$$

We say that (S, R) is *finite*, if both S and R are finite.

We understand axioms as rules $\Gamma/\emptyset$ with no conclusions so that the least fixpoint of M will contain all sequents Γ for which we can construct a closed tableau, i.e. a tree with root Γ constructed according to the rules in R whose leaves are all axioms. Tableau systems can be described in terms of reachability games:

Definition 3. A *reachability game* played by the two players $\exists$ (Éloise) and $\forall$ (Abelard) is a tuple $G = (B_\exists, B_\forall, E)$ with $B_\exists \cap B_\forall = \emptyset$, where

  - $B_\exists$ and $B_\forall$ are the *positions* owned by the players $\exists$ and $\forall$, respectively
  - $E \subseteq (B_\exists \cup B_\forall)^2$ is a binary relation that indicates the allowed moves.

The *board* B of a reachability game $(B_\exists, B_\forall, E)$ is the disjoint union of positions, i.e. $B = B_\exists \cup B_\forall$. A *play* in G is a finite or infinite sequence of positions $(b_0, b_1, \dots)$ with the property that $(b_i, b_{i+1}) \in E$ for all i, i.e. all moves are legal, and b_0 is the *initial position* of the play. A *full play* is either infinite, or a finite play ending in a position b_n where $E[b_n] = \{b \in B \mid (b_n, b) \in E\} = \emptyset$, i.e. no more moves are possible. A finite play is lost by the player who cannot move, and infinite plays are lost by $\forall$. A *history-free strategy* for a player $P \in \{\exists, \forall\}$ is a partial function $f : B_P \to B$ such that $f(b)$ is defined whenever $E[b] \neq \emptyset$ and $(b, f(b)) \in E$ in this case. A play $(b_0, b_1, \dots)$ is *played according to f* if $b_{i+1} = f(b_i)$ for all i with $b_i \in B_P$, and f is a *history-free winning strategy* from position $b \in B$ if P wins all plays with initial position b that are played according to f. A position $b' \in B$ is called *f-reachable* from $b \in B$ if there is a play $(b_0, b_1, \dots, b_k)$ that is played according to f and such that $b_0 = b$ and $b_k = b'$.

Reachability games are history-free determined, i.e. from every position b of the game board, one of the players has a history-free winning strategy (this holds for the more general class of parity games [18]). To every tableau system we associate the following reachability game.

Definition 4. The *tableau game* induced by a tableau system (S, R) is reachability game $(B_\exists, B_\forall, E)$ where

  - $B_\exists = \{\Psi \subseteq S \mid \Psi \text{ finite}\}$ and $B_\forall = S$
  - $E = \{(\Psi, \Gamma) \in B_\exists \times B_\forall \mid \Gamma \in \Psi\} \cup \{(\Gamma, \Psi) \in B_\forall \times B_\exists \mid \Gamma/\Psi \in R\}$.

In other words, $\forall$ plays a tableau rule, and $\exists$ selects one of its conclusions. Note that $\exists$ wins all infinite plays, which correspond to infinite paths in a tableau. As a consequence, $\forall$ has a winning strategy from position Γ in a tableau game, if he can select a tableau rule applicable to Γ so that every conclusion that $\exists$ can possibly choose eventually leads to a tableau axiom, at which point $\forall$ wins.

Proposition 5. *Suppose (S, R) is a tableau system. Then $\Gamma \in S$ has a closed tableau if and only if $\forall$ has a winning strategy in the associated tableau game starting from position Γ.*

We will come back to this general formulation of tableaux in Section 5 and now introduce tableau systems for coalgebraic logics with global assumptions. These are most conveniently formulated in terms of *one-step rules*.

Definition 6. A *one-step tableau rule* over Λ is a tuple $(\Gamma_0, \Gamma_1, \ldots, \Gamma_n)$, written as $\Gamma_0/\Gamma_1 \ldots \Gamma_n$, where $\Gamma_0 \subseteq (\Lambda \cup \overline{\Lambda})(\mathsf{V} \cup \overline{\mathsf{V}})$ and $\Gamma_i \subseteq \mathsf{V} \cup \overline{\mathsf{V}}$ so that every variable that occurs in the conclusion $\Gamma_1 \ldots \Gamma_n$ also occurs in the premise Γ_0, and every propositional variable occurs at most once in the premise Γ_0.

We can think of one-step rules as a syntactic representation of the inverse image $\gamma^{-1} : \mathcal{P}(TC) \to \mathcal{P}(C)$ of a generic coalgebra map $\gamma : C \to TC$ in that the premise describes a property of successors, whereas the conclusion describes states. The requirement that propositional variables do not occur twice in the premise is for technical convenience, as it later allows us to speak of injective substitutions, rather than substitutions that do not identify elements of the premise. While this rigid format of one-step rules suffices to completely axiomatise all coalgebraic logics [22], they do not accommodate frame conditions like transitivity ($\Box p \to \Box\Box p$) which require separate consideration.

Example 7. One-step rules that axiomatise the logics in Example 1 can be found (in the form of proof rules) in [20,24]. Continuing Example 1, we single out coalition logic, probabilistic modal logic and their combination.

1. A tableau system for coalition logic is induced by the set $\mathsf{R_G}$ that comprises

$$(C_1)\frac{[C_1]p_1, \ldots, [C_n]p_n}{p_1, \ldots, p_n} \qquad (C_2)\frac{[C_1]p_1, \ldots, [C_n]p_n, \overline{[D]}q, \overline{[N]}r_1, \ldots, \overline{[N]}r_m}{p_1, \ldots, p_n, q, r_1, \ldots, r_m}$$

for $n, m \geq 0$ provided that the $C_i \subseteq N$ are pairwise disjoint sets of coalitions, and additionally $C_i \subseteq D$ in (C_2) for all $i = 1, \ldots, n$.

2. The rules $\mathsf{R_D}$ for probabilistic modal logic contain

$$(P)\frac{\langle a_1\rangle p_1, \ldots, \langle a_n\rangle p_n, [b_1]q_1, \ldots, [b_m]q_m}{\sum_{j=1}^{m} s_j \overline{q}_j - \sum_{i=1}^{n} r_i p_i < k}$$

where $n, m \in \mathbb{N}$ and $r_i, s_j \in \mathbb{N} \setminus \{0\}$ satisfy the side condition $\sum_{i=1}^{n} r_i a_i - \sum_{j=1}^{m} s_j b_j \leq k$ if $n > 0$ and $-\sum_{j=1}^{m} s_j b_j < k$ if $n = 0$. The conclusion of (P) contains all clauses in the disjunctive normal form of the associated $\{0, 1\}$-valued predicate.

3. Games with quantitative uncertainty are described by the rule set $\mathsf{R_{DoG}}$

$$\frac{\Gamma_0 \sigma}{\Sigma_1^1 \sigma_1 \quad \ldots \quad \Sigma_{k_1}^1 \sigma_1 \quad \ldots \quad \Sigma_1^n \sigma_n \quad \ldots \quad \Sigma_{k_n}^n \sigma_n}$$

that can be constructed from rules $\Gamma_0/\Gamma_1 \ldots \Gamma_n \in \mathsf{R_D}$ and $\Sigma_0^i/\Sigma_1^i \ldots \Sigma_{k_i}^i \in \mathsf{R_G}$ ($1 \leq i \leq n$) by injective substitutions $\sigma : \mathsf{V} \to (\Lambda_\mathsf{G} \cup \overline{\Lambda}_\mathsf{G})(\mathsf{V} \cup \overline{\mathsf{V}})$ and $\sigma_1, \ldots, \sigma_n : \mathsf{V} \to \mathsf{V}$ satisfying $\Gamma_i \sigma = \Sigma_0^i \sigma_i$. That is, rules for the combined logic first de-construct the top-level probabilistic modal operators by means of a probabilistic rule in $\mathsf{R_D}$, and then apply a rule of coalition logic ($\mathsf{R_G}$) to each conclusion.

Given a sequent Δ that represents the global assumptions, every set of one-step rules induces a tableau system that arises by adding Δ to each of the conclusions of modal rules. To reduce the bureaucracy of dealing with propositional rules, we use *skeletal tableaux* where they are subsumed into a single rule schema.

Definition 8. Suppose $\Delta \in \mathcal{S}(\Lambda)$ is a set of global assumptions and R is a set of one-step tableau rules over Λ. The *skeletal system* over R with global assumptions Δ is the tableau system $(\mathcal{S}(\Lambda), \mathsf{S}(\mathsf{R}))$ where $\mathsf{S}(\mathsf{R})$ contains $\Gamma/\mathsf{sat}(\Gamma)$ for all $\Gamma \in \mathcal{S}(\Lambda)$ and all rules $\Gamma_0\sigma, \Gamma'/\Gamma_1\sigma, \Delta \quad \ldots \quad \Gamma_n\sigma, \Delta$ where $\Gamma_0/\Gamma_1 \ldots \Gamma_n \in \mathsf{R}$, $\sigma : \mathsf{V} \to \mathcal{F}(\Lambda)$ is an injective substitution and $\Gamma' \in \mathcal{S}(\Lambda)$ is arbitrary. The operation $\mathsf{sat} : \mathcal{S}(\Gamma) \to \mathcal{S}(\Gamma)$ is called *saturation* and is inductively given by

$$\mathsf{sat}(\Delta') = \{\Delta'\} \qquad \mathsf{sat}(A \vee B, \Gamma) = \mathsf{sat}(A, \Gamma) \cup \mathsf{sat}(B, \Gamma)$$
$$\mathsf{sat}(p, \overline{p}, \Gamma) = \emptyset \qquad \mathsf{sat}(A \wedge B, \Gamma) = \mathsf{sat}(A, B, \Gamma)$$

where $A, B \in \mathcal{F}(\Lambda)$ are formulas, $\Gamma \in \mathcal{S}(\Lambda)$ is a sequent, $p \in \mathsf{V}$ is a propositional variable and $\Delta' \in \mathsf{State}(\Lambda)$ is a state, i.e. contains neither complementary propositional variables nor top-level propositional connectives.

We often leave the underlying set of one-step rules implicit and say that Γ has a closed skeletal tableau with global assumptions Δ, and refer to the induced tableau game as the skeletal game with global assumptions Δ. An easy confluence argument shows that sat is well-defined, i.e. the sequence of steps when computing $\mathsf{sat}(\Gamma)$ is immaterial. Given $\Gamma \in \mathcal{S}(\Lambda)$, the restriction to injective substitutions avoids a possible source of infinity when computing rules that can be applied to Γ. Conclusions are always contained in the closure of its premise and the global assumptions:

Lemma 9. *Suppose* $\Gamma, \Delta \in \mathcal{S}(\Lambda)$ *and* $\Sigma \subseteq \mathsf{cl}(\Gamma, \Delta)$. *Then* $\Sigma_i \subseteq \mathsf{cl}(\Gamma, \Delta)$ *for all* $i = 1, \ldots, n$ *if* $\Sigma/\Sigma_1 \ldots \Sigma_n \in \mathsf{S}(\mathsf{R})$. *Moreover,* $\mathsf{cl}(\Gamma, \Delta)$ *is finite.*

4   Soundness and Completeness

It is evidently impossible to prove even as much as soundness of skeletal tableaux unless the underlying set of one-step rules is suitably linked to the intended (coalgebraic) semantics. This is achieved by imposing coherence conditions that relate premise and conclusions of one-step rules to the underlying (coalgebraic) semantics that can be checked locally, i.e. without reference to models.

Definition 10. Suppose that T is a Λ-structure, X is a set and $\tau : \mathsf{V} \to \mathcal{P}(X)$ is a valuation. The interpretation of a propositional sequent $\Gamma \subseteq \mathsf{V} \cup \overline{\mathsf{V}}$ over X, τ is given by $[\![\Gamma]\!]_{X,\tau} = \bigcap\{\tau(p) \mid p \in \cdot \Gamma\} \cap \bigcap\{X \setminus \tau(p) \mid \overline{p} \in \Gamma\} \subseteq X$. Modalised sequents $\Gamma \subseteq (\Lambda \cup \overline{\Lambda})(\mathsf{V} \cup \overline{\mathsf{V}})$ are interpreted as subsets of TX by

$$[\![\Gamma]\!]_{TX,\tau} = \bigcap\{[\![\heartsuit]\!]_X([\![p_1]\!]_{X,\tau}, \ldots, [\![p_n]\!]_{X,\tau}) \mid \heartsuit(p_1, \ldots, p_n) \in \Gamma\}$$

where $p_1, \ldots, p_n \in \mathsf{V} \cup \overline{\mathsf{V}}$ and $\heartsuit \in \Lambda \cup \overline{\Lambda}$.

The announced coherence conditions now take the following form:

Definition 11. Suppose that T is a Λ-structure and R is a set of one-step tableau rules. We say that R is *one-step tableau sound* (resp. *one-step tableau* *complete*) with respect to T if, for all $\Gamma \in \mathcal{S}((\Lambda \cup \overline{\Lambda})(V \cup \overline{V}))$, all sets X and valuations $\tau : V \to \mathcal{P}(X)$:

$[\![\Gamma]\!]_{TX,\tau} \neq \emptyset$ only if (if) for all rules $\Gamma_0/\Gamma_1 \ldots \Gamma_n \in \mathsf{R}$ and all renamings $\sigma : V \to V$ with $\Gamma_0\sigma \subseteq \Gamma$, we have that $[\![\Gamma_i\sigma]\!]_{X,\tau} \neq \emptyset$ for some $1 \leq i \leq n$.

This means that a rule set is both sound and complete if a modalised sequent is satisfiable iff every one-step rule applicable to it has at least one satisfiable conclusion. Soundness follows immediately from one-step soundness.

Proposition 12 (Soundness). *Suppose $\Gamma, \Delta \in \mathcal{S}(\Lambda)$ and Γ, Δ has a closed tableau in the skeletal system given by R with global assumptions Δ. Then Γ is unsatisfiable in $\mathsf{Mod}(\Delta)$.*

For completeness, we show that the existence of a winning strategy for $\exists$ from Γ, Δ implies that Γ is satisfiable in $\mathsf{Mod}(\Delta)$ via suitable truth and existence lemmas that account for possibly non-monotone modal operators.

Definition 13. If $A \in \mathcal{F}(\Lambda)$ then $\mathsf{spec}(A) = \{\Sigma \in \mathsf{State}(\Lambda) \mid \exists \Sigma' \in \mathsf{sat}(A).\Sigma' \subseteq \Sigma\}$ are the *specified states* of A.

If we think of of $\mathsf{sat}(A)$ as the disjunctive normal form of A, a state $\Sigma \in \mathsf{State}(\Lambda)$ satisfies A if Σ contains all formulas of an element of $\mathsf{sat}(A)$. Thus $\mathsf{spec}(A)$ is the collection of states where A is required to hold, and non-monotonicity forces us to sandwich the interpretation of A between $\mathsf{spec}(A)$ and the complement of $\mathsf{spec}(\overline{A})$ in a syntactic model based on Λ-states. This will be a consequence of coherence, introduced next.

Definition 14 (Coherence). Suppose $W \subseteq \mathsf{State}(\Lambda)$. A coalgebra structure $w : W \to TW$ is *coherent*, if

$$w(\Gamma) \in [\![\heartsuit]\!]_W(X_1, \ldots, X_n)$$

whenever $\heartsuit(A_1, \ldots, A_n) \in \Gamma$ and $W \cap \mathsf{spec}(A_i) \subseteq X_i \subseteq W \setminus \mathsf{spec}(A_i)$ for all $i = 1, \ldots, n$. A valuation $\pi : V \to \mathcal{P}(W)$ is *coherent* if $\mathsf{spec}(p) \cap W \subseteq \pi(p) \subseteq W \setminus \mathsf{spec}(\overline{p})$ for all $p \in V$. Finally, a T-model (W, w, π) is coherent, if both (W, w) and π are coherent.

Given that $\exists$ has a winning strategy in the skeletal system, the next lemma asserts the existence of a coherent structure, that we will use later to prove satisfiability, given that the underlying set of one-step rules admits contraction:

Definition 15. A set R of one-step rules *admits contraction* if, for all rules $\Gamma_0/\Gamma_1, \ldots, \Gamma_n \in \mathsf{R}$ and all renamings $\sigma : V \to V$ we can find a rule $\Sigma_0/\Sigma_1 \ldots \Sigma_k \in \mathsf{R}$ and an injective renaming $\rho : V \to V$ such that $\Sigma_0\rho \subseteq \Gamma_0\sigma$ and, for all $j = 1, \ldots, k$ there exists $1 \leq i \leq n$ such that $\Sigma_j\rho \supseteq \Gamma_i\sigma$.

That is to say, an application of contraction to the premise of a modal rule (via a substitution that identifies propositional variables) can always be replaced by a different rule for which this is not the case, and moreover the conclusions of this rule are even harder to satisfy. The existence lemma now takes the following form:

Lemma 16 (Existence Lemma). *Suppose that* R *is one-step tableau complete and admits contraction. If* ∃ *has a winning strategy* f *in the game induced by the skeletal tableau system with global assumptions* Δ, *then there exists a coherent coalgebra structure* $w : W \to TW$ *on the set of states that are* f-*reachable from* Γ, Δ.

Given coherence, we can now prove:

Lemma 17 (Truth Lemma). *Suppose that* $M = (W, w, \pi)$ *is coherent. Then* $\mathsf{spec}(A) \cap W \subseteq [\![A]\!]_M \subseteq W \setminus \mathsf{spec}(\overline{A})$ *for all* $A \in \mathcal{F}(\Lambda)$.

Completeness is now an immediate consequence of the Truth Lemma and the Existence Lemma.

Proposition 18. *If* ∃ *has a winning strategy from* $\Gamma, \Delta \in \mathsf{State}(\Lambda)$ *in the skeletal game with global assumptions* Δ, *then* Γ *is satisfiable in* $\mathsf{Mod}(\Delta)$.

In summary, we have the following result that lays the semantical foundation of the algorithms in the following section.

Theorem 19. *Suppose that* R *is one-step sound and complete with respect to a* Λ-*structure* T. *The following are equivalent for* $\Gamma, \Delta \in \mathcal{S}(\Lambda)$:

1. Γ *is satisfiable in* $\mathsf{Mod}(\Delta)$
2. Γ *does not have a closed skeletal tableau with global assumptions* Δ
3. ∃ *has a winning strategy in the skeletal tableau game with global assumptions* Δ *from position* Γ, Δ.

As a by-product of this theorem, we obtain admissibility of cut (via semantical completeness) and the small model property, which is implicit in the proof of Proposition 18. We remark that the rules given in Example 7 are both one-step sound and complete [24].

5   Global Caching

In this section, we show that global caching [10] is applicable to coalgebraic logics, and give a feasible algorithm to decide satisfiability of a sequent Γ over a set Δ of global assumptions. The idea behind global caching is very simple: every sequent is expanded at most once, and sequents are not expanded unnecessarily. We begin our discussion of global caching in the context of a generic tableau system that we then subsequently specialise to coalgebraic logics to prove optimality.

Definition 20. *Suppose that* (S, R) *is a tableau system. A* caching graph *for* (S, R) *is a quintuple* $G = (A, U, E, X, L)$ *where* $A, U, E, X \subseteq S$ *and* $L \subseteq S \times \mathcal{P}(S) \cup \mathcal{P}(S) \times S$. *The set* $\mathsf{supp}(G) = A \cup U \cup E$ *is called the* support *of* G. *A caching graph* $G = (A, U, E, X, L)$ *is* expanded *if*

$$L = \bigcup_{\Gamma \in \mathsf{supp}(G)} \{(\Gamma, \Psi) \mid \Gamma/\Psi \in R\} \cup \{(\Psi, \Sigma) \mid \Gamma/\Psi \in R, \Sigma \in \Psi\}$$

and $\Psi \subseteq \mathsf{supp}(G) \cup X$ *for all* $\Gamma/\Psi \in R$ *with* $\Gamma \in \mathsf{supp}(G)$.

In other words, a caching graph is a concrete data structure that not only stores sequents, but also links every sequent in its support to each conclusion of a rule applicable to it, and every conclusion to each of its elements. We think of A as the set of winning positions of $\forall$ in the associated tableau game, and similarly E represents $\exists$'s winning positions. The set L (of links) represents the collection of all rules that can be applied to a sequent in the support of a caching graph. The status of sequents in U is undecided, but they are expanded, in the sense that L contains all rules that are applicable to elements in U. The conclusions of such rules that are not already contained in the support of a caching graph are collected in the set X, the set of sequents that are still unexpanded.

Definition 21. We define two transition relations $\rightarrow_E$ ("expand") and $\rightarrow_P$ ("propagate") on caching graphs. We put $(A, U, E, X, L) \rightarrow_E (A', U', E', X', L')$ if $A' = A$, $E' = E$ and there exists $\Gamma \in X$ such that

$$U' = U \cup \{\Gamma\} \qquad X' = X \cup \left(\bigcup \{\Psi \mid \Gamma/\Psi \in R\} \right) \setminus (A' \cup E' \cup U')$$
$$L' = L \cup \{(\Psi, \Sigma) \mid \Sigma \in \Psi, \Gamma/\Psi \in R\} \cup \{(\Gamma, \Psi) \mid \Gamma/\Psi \in R\}.$$

Moreover, $(A, U, E, X, L) \rightarrow_P (A', U', E', X', L')$ in case $X' = X$, $L = L'$ and

$$A' = A \cup \mu M^L \qquad E' = E \cup \nu W^L \qquad U' = U \setminus (A' \cup E')$$

where μM^L and νW^L are, respectively, the least and greatest fixpoints of the operators $W^L : \mathcal{P}(U) \rightarrow \mathcal{P}(U)$ and $M^L : \mathcal{P}(U) \rightarrow \mathcal{P}(U)$ given by

$$W^L(X) = \{\Gamma \in U \mid \forall(\Gamma, \Psi) \in L. \exists(\Psi, \Sigma) \in L. \Sigma \in X \cup E\}$$
$$M^L(X) = \{\Gamma \in U \mid \exists(\Gamma, \Psi) \in L. \forall(\Psi, \Sigma) \in L. \Sigma \in X \cup A\}$$

for $X \subseteq U$. We write $\rightarrow_{PE}$ for the union of $\rightarrow_P$ and $\rightarrow_E$ and $\rightarrow_{PE}^*$ for its reflexive-transitive closure.

In an expansion step, an unexpanded sequent $\Gamma \in X$ is chosen, all rules that are applicable to Γ are recorded in L and Γ is moved to U. To ensure that the ensuing caching graph is expanded, new conclusions that arise from expanding Γ that are not yet contained in the support are added to X, the set of unexpanded sequents. The (deterministic) propagation steps update the set of winning positions of $\forall$ and $\exists$ in the tableau game. For $\forall$, this amounts to recursively adding a sequent to A if we can apply a tableau rule whose conclusions are contained in A – this is achieved by the least fixpoint construction above. The winning positions of $\exists$ are computed by means of a greatest fixpoint, and we extend E by the largest set Ψ of sequents so that for every tableau rule applied to Ψ, at least one conclusion is contained in $\Psi \cup E$, in other words, the construction of a closed tableau for elements of $\Psi \cup E$ is impossible, provided that E already enjoys this property.

If we interleave expansion and propagation steps until all sequents are expanded ($X = \emptyset$), we update the winning positions in a final propagation step, and all elements not known to be either satisfiable or unsatisfiable (the elements of U) are declared to be satisfiable, since any tableau rule applied to a sequent in U necessarily has at least one conclusion in $E \cup U$, since this sequent would otherwise have been moved to A by propagation.

Lemma 22. *Suppose that (S, R) is a tableau system and (A, U, E, X, L) is an expanded caching graph for (S, R) for which all $\Gamma \in A$ but none of the $\Gamma \in E$, have a closed tableau. If $(A, U, E, X, L) \rightarrow^*_{PE} (A', U', E', \emptyset, L) \rightarrow_P (\hat{A}, \hat{U}, \hat{E}, \emptyset, \hat{L})$ then all $\Gamma \in \hat{A}$, but none of the $\Gamma \in \hat{U} \cup \hat{E}$ have a closed tableau.*

Correctness of global caching induces the following (nondeterministic) algorithm.

Algorithm 23. Decide whether $\Gamma \in S$ has a closed tableau.

1. initialise: Put $G = (A, U, E, X, L)$ where
   - $A = E = \emptyset$, $U = \{\Gamma\}$ and $X = \bigcup \{\Psi \mid \Gamma/\Psi \in R\}$
   - $L = \{(\Gamma, \Psi) \mid \Gamma/\Psi \in R\} \cup \{(\Psi, \Sigma) \mid \Sigma \in \Psi, \Gamma/\Psi \in R\}$
2. while $(X \neq \emptyset)$ do
   (a) choose G' with $G \rightarrow_E G'$ and put $G := G'$
   (b) (optional)
       - find G' with $G \rightarrow_P G'$ and put $G := G'$
       - return "yes" if $\Gamma \in A$ and "no" if $\Gamma \in E$
3. find G' with $G \rightarrow_P G'$ and put $G := G'$
4. return "yes" if $\Gamma \in E$ and "no" otherwise.

Correctness of this algorithm follows from Lemma 22, and termination is clear as every expand-transition adds one sequent to the support of a caching graph, as long as (S, R) is finite. Since transitions between caching graphs preserve the property that all elements in A, but none of the elements in E, have a closed tableau, we may in fact terminate earlier if we find the initial sequent in $E \cup A$.

Theorem 24. *Suppose that (S, R) is a finite tableau system and $\Gamma \in S$. Then every execution terminates in at most $3 \cdot |S| + 1$ steps and returns "yes" if and only if Γ has a closed tableau.*

We remark that – although Algorithm 23 is non-deterministic – we just need to check *one* particular execution, i.e. there is no inherent non-determinism, but room for heuristics. We now specialise Algorithm 23 to the case of coalgebraic logics and establish an (optimal) EXPTIME bound. In the general (coalgebraic) setting, we can not expect that satisfiability of a sequent Γ under global assumptions Δ is even decidable unless we make additional assumptions about the underlying set of one-step rules (which may in general be non-recursive). However, all rule sets that we are aware of, in particular the rule sets that completely axiomatise the logics introduced in Example 1 satisfy an additional assumption: the set of conclusions of a rule can be polynomially encoded in terms of the size of the premise. This was used in [24] and applied to fixpoint logics in [4].

To be precise, we assume that the underlying similarity type Λ is equipped with a size measure $s : \Lambda \to \mathbb{N}$ and measure the size of a formula A in terms of the number of subformulas of A adding $s(\heartsuit)$ for every occurrence of a modal operator $\heartsuit$ or $\overline{\heartsuit}$ in A. For the logics in our running example, we code numbers in binary, that is $\langle p/q \rangle = [p/q] = \lceil \log_2 p \rceil + \lceil \log_2 q \rceil$ for probabilistic modal logic and $s([C]) = 1$ for operators of coalition logic, as the overall set of agents is fixed. The definition of size is extended to sequents by $\mathsf{size}(\Gamma) = \sum_{A \in \Gamma} \mathsf{size}(A)$ for $\Gamma \in \mathcal{S}(\Lambda)$. In particular, the size of the closure of a sequent is polynomially bounded.

Lemma 25. *Suppose* $\Gamma \in \mathcal{S}(\Lambda)$. *Then* $\mathsf{size}(\Sigma) \leq 2\mathsf{size}(\Gamma)^2$ *for all* $\Sigma \subseteq \mathsf{cl}(\Gamma)$.

The notion of size allows us to formulate polynomial encodings.

Definition 26. A set R of tableau rules is *exponentially tractable*, if there exists an alphabet Σ and two functions $f : \mathcal{S}(\Lambda) \to \mathcal{P}(\Sigma^*)$ and $g : \Sigma^* \to \mathcal{P}(\mathcal{S}(\Lambda))$ together with a polynomial p such that $|x| \leq p(\mathsf{size}(\Gamma))$ for all $x \in f(\Gamma)$, $\mathsf{size}(\Delta) \leq p(|y|)$ for all $\Delta \in g(y)$, so that, for $\Gamma \in \mathcal{S}(\Lambda)$,

$$\{g(x) \mid x \in f(\Gamma_0)\} = \{\{\Gamma_1, \ldots, \Gamma_n\} \mid \Gamma_0/\Gamma_1, \ldots, \Gamma_n \in R\}$$

and both relations $x \in f(\Gamma)$ and $\Gamma \in g(x)$ are decidable in EXPTIME.

Tractability of the set $\mathsf{S}(R)$ of tableau rules follows from tractability of the substitution instances of rules in R, as both propositional rules and saturation can be encoded easily. At this point, we use the fact that the modal rules in the skeletal system are defined in terms of injective substitutions as otherwise a rule can be generated through infinitely many substitution instances.

Lemma 27. *Suppose* R *is a set of one-step rules. Then* $\mathsf{S}(R)$ *is exponentially tractable iff the set* $\{\Gamma_0\sigma/\Gamma_1\sigma, \ldots, \Gamma_n\sigma \mid \Gamma_0/\Gamma_1, \ldots, \Gamma_n \in R, \sigma : V \to \mathcal{F}(\Lambda)$ *injective} of substituted one-step rules is exponentially tractable.*

Tractability ensures that we can encode the data on which Algorithm 23 operates as strings of at most polynomial length in terms of the initial sequent and the global assumptions.

Lemma 28. *Suppose that* R *is exponentially tractable and* $\Gamma, \Delta \in \mathcal{S}(\Lambda)$. *Then every* $\Psi \subseteq \mathsf{cl}(\Gamma, \Delta)$ *that appears as the conclusion of a rule* $\Sigma/\Psi \in \mathsf{S}(R)$ *for which* $\Sigma \in \mathsf{cl}(\Gamma, \Delta)$ *can can be encoded as a string of polynomial length (in* $\mathsf{size}(\Gamma, \Delta)$). *Under this coding, the relations* $\{(\Sigma_0, \{\Sigma_1, \ldots, \Sigma_n\}) \mid \Sigma_0/\Sigma_1 \ldots \Sigma_n \in \mathsf{S}(R),$ $\Sigma_0 \subseteq \mathsf{cl}(\Gamma, \Delta)$ *and* $\{(\{\Sigma_1, \ldots, \Sigma_n\}, \Sigma_i) \mid 1 \leq i \leq n, \exists \Sigma_0 \subseteq \mathsf{cl}(\Gamma/\Delta).$ $\Sigma_0/\Sigma_1 \ldots \Sigma_n \in R\}$ *are decidable in exponential time.*

Tractability of rule sets guarantees that Algorithm 23 runs in EXPTIME.

Theorem 29. *Suppose that* Λ *is a modal similarity type and* T *is a* Λ-*structure. If* R *is a one-step tableau sound and complete set of one-step rules that admits contraction, then Algorithm 23 decides satisfiability of* Γ *in* $\mathsf{Mod}(\Delta)$ *in at most exponential time (w.r.t.* $\mathsf{size}(\Gamma, \Delta)$), *if* R *is exponentially tractable.*

In our examples, the situation is as follows:

Example 30. All logics mentioned in Example 1 can be captured by a one-step sound and complete rule set that is exponentially tractable [20,24], and we briefly discuss the case for those logics that we have singled out in Example 1 and Example 7.

1. For coalition logic, no coding is needed at all, as the size of sequents decreases when we move from the premise to the conclusion of a rule, and EXPTIME decidability of the rule set is clear.

2. For the conclusions of the rule schema that axiomatises probabilistic modal logic, we take the linear inequality $\sum_{j=1}^{m} s_j \bar{q}_j - \sum_{i=1}^{n} r_i p_i < k$ itself as a code for the associated set of conclusions. Tractability was shown in [24] using the fact that the (binary) size of the coefficients r_i can be polynomially bounded.

3. For rule sets that arise as combinations, tractability follows from tractability of the individual components, which is most conveniently made explicit in a multi-sorted setting [23].

As the modal logic K can be encoded into all logics mentioned in Example 1 with the exception of classical and monotone modal logic, global satisfiability for these logics is EXPTIME hard, and hence optimality of Algorithm 23.

6 Conclusions

We have given a sound and complete tableau calculus for coalgebraic modal logics in the presence of global assumptions. Based on the completeness of the tableau calculus, we have then described a concrete tableau algorithm to decide satisfiability in presence of global assumptions, based on global caching. In particular, this algorithm meets the (in nearly all cases optimal) EXPTIME bound, while avoiding the unnecessary overhead of computing least fixpoints naively. This showcases not only the wide applicability of global caching, but also demonstrates that automated reasoning with coalgebraic logics in the presence of global assumptions is also in practice not (much) harder than for modal logics with an underlying relational semantics. We have demonstrated by means of examples, that the general (coalgebraic) framework specialises to a large class of modal logics, and have thus not only described the first tableau algorithm for deciding e.g. probabilistic modal logic, but an algorithm that is also worst-case optimal that we plan to implement and evaluate experimentally in the future.

References

1. Baader, F., Calvanese, D., McGuinness, D., Nardi, D., Patel-Schneider, P. (eds.): The Description Logic Handbook: Theory, Implementation and Applications. Cambridge University Press, Cambridge (2003)
2. Chellas, B.: Modal Logic, Cambridge (1980)
3. Cîrstea, C.: A compositional approach to defining logics for coalgebras. Theoret. Comput. Sci. 327, 45–69 (2004)
4. Cîrstea, C., Kupke, C., Pattinson, D.: EXPTIME tableaux for the coalgebraic μ-calculus. In: Grädel, E., Kahle, R. (eds.) CSL 2009. LNCS, vol. 5771, pp. 179–193. Springer, Heidelberg (2009)
5. Cîrstea, C., Pattinson, D.: Modular proof systems for coalgebraic logics. Theor. Comp. Sci. 388, 83–108 (2007)
6. Donini, F., Massacci, F.: Exptime tableaux for $\mathcal{ALC}$. Artif. Intell. 124(1), 87–138 (2000)

7. Fagin, R., Halpern, J., Moses, Y., Vardi, M.: Reasoning about Knowledge. The MIT Press, Cambridge (1995)
8. Fine, K.: In so many possible worlds. Notre Dame J. Formal Logic 13, 516–520 (1972)
9. Goré, R.: Tableau methods for modal and temporal logics. In: D'Agostino, et al. (eds.) Handbook of Tableau Methods, pp. 297–396. Kluwer, Dordrecht (1999)
10. Goré, R., Nguyen, L.: EXPTIME tableaux for $\mathcal{ALC}$ using sound global caching. In: Calvanese, D., Franconi, E., Haarslev, V., Lembo, D., Motik, B., Turhan, A., Tessaris, S. (eds.) Proc. Description Logics 2007. CEUR Workshop Proceedings. CEUR-WS.org, vol. 250 (2007)
11. Goré, R., Nguyen, L.: EXPTIME tableaux with global caching for description logics with transitive roles, inverse roles and role hierarchies. In: Olivetti, N. (ed.) TABLEAUX 2007. LNCS (LNAI), vol. 4548, pp. 133–148. Springer, Heidelberg (2007)
12. Goré, R., Postniece, L.: An experimental evaluation of global caching for $\mathcal{ALC}$ (system description). In: Armando, A., Baumgartner, P., Dowek, G. (eds.) IJCAR 2008. LNCS (LNAI), vol. 5195, pp. 299–305. Springer, Heidelberg (2008)
13. Goré, R., Widmann, F.: Sound global state caching for $\mathcal{ALC}$ with inverse roles. In: Giese, M., Waaler, A. (eds.) TABLEAUX 2009. LNCS (LNAI), vol. 5607, pp. 205–219. Springer, Heidelberg (2009)
14. Haarslev, V., Möller, R.: RACER system description. In: Goré, R.P., Leitsch, A., Nipkow, T. (eds.) IJCAR 2001. LNCS (LNAI), vol. 2083, pp. 701–705. Springer, Heidelberg (2001)
15. Harel, D., Kozen, D., Tiuryn, J.: Dynamic Logic. The MIT Press, Cambridge (2000)
16. Heifetz, A., Mongin, P.: Probabilistic logic for type spaces. Games and Economic Behavior 35, 31–53 (2001)
17. Horrocks, I., Patel-Schneider, P.: Optimising description logic subsumption. J. Logic Comput. 9, 267–293 (1999)
18. Mazala, R.: Infinite games. In: Grädel, E., Thomas, W., Wilke, T. (eds.) Automata, Logics, and Infinite Games. LNCS, vol. 2500, pp. 23–42. Springer, Heidelberg (2002)
19. Pattinson, D.: Coalgebraic modal logic: Soundness, completeness and decidability of local consequence. Theoret. Comput. Sci. 309, 177–193 (2003)
20. Pattinson, D., Schröder, L.: Admissibility of cut in coalgebraic logics. Electr. Notes Theor. Comput. Sci. 203(5), 221–241 (2008)
21. Pauly, M.: A modal logic for coalitional power in games. J. Logic Comput. 12(1), 149–166 (2002)
22. Schröder, L.: A finite model construction for coalgebraic modal logic. J. Log. Algebr. Program. 73(1-2), 97–110 (2007)
23. Schröder, L., Pattinson, D.: Compositional algorithms for heterogeneous modal logics. In: Arge, L., Cachin, C., Jurdziński, T., Tarlecki, A. (eds.) ICALP 2007. LNCS, vol. 4596, pp. 459–471. Springer, Heidelberg (2007)
24. Schröder, L., Pattinson, D.: PSPACE bounds for rank-1 modal logics. ACM Transactions on Computational Logics 10(2) (2009)
25. Schröder, L., Pattinson, D., Kupke, C.: Nominals for everyone. In: Boutilier, C. (ed.) Proc. IJCAI 2009, pp. 917–922 (2009)
26. Stirling, C.: Modal and temporal logics. In: Handbook of logic in computer science. Background: computational structures, vol. 2, pp. 477–563. Oxford University Press, Inc., Oxford (1992)
27. Tsarkov, D., Horrocks, I.: FaCT++ description logic reasoner: System description. In: Furbach, U., Shankar, N. (eds.) IJCAR 2006. LNCS (LNAI), vol. 4130, pp. 292–297. Springer, Heidelberg (2006)

Blocked Clause Elimination

Matti Järvisalo[1], Armin Biere[2], and Marijn Heule[3]

[1] Department of Computer Science, University of Helsinki, Finland
[2] Institute for Formal Models and Verification, Johannes Kepler University, Linz, Austria
[3] Algorithmics Group, Delft University of Technology, The Netherlands

Abstract. Boolean satisfiability (SAT) and its extensions are becoming a core technology for the analysis of systems. The SAT-based approach divides into three steps: encoding, preprocessing, and search. It is often argued that by encoding arbitrary Boolean formulas in conjunctive normal form (CNF), structural properties of the original problem are not reflected in the CNF. This should result in the fact that CNF-level preprocessing and SAT solver techniques have an inherent disadvantagecompared to related techniques applicable on the level of more structural SAT instance representations such as Boolean circuits. In this work we study the effect of a CNF-level simplification technique called blocked clause elimination (BCE). We show that BCE is surprisingly effective both in theory and in practice on CNFs resulting from a standard CNF encoding for circuits: without explicit knowledge of the underlying circuit structure, it achieves the same level of simplification as a combination of circuit-level simplifications and previously suggested polarity-based CNF encodings. Experimentally, we show that by applying BCE in preprocessing, further formula reduction and faster solving can be achieved, giving promise for applying BCE to speed up solvers.

1 Introduction

Boolean satisfiability (SAT) solvers and their extensions, especially satisfiability modulo theories (SMT) solvers, are becoming a core technology for the analysis of systems, ranging from hardware to software. SAT solvers are in the heart of SMT solvers, and in some cases such as the theory of bit-vectors, state-of-the-art SMT solvers are based on bit-blasting and use pure SAT solvers for actual solving. This gives motivation for developing even more efficient SAT techniques.

SAT-based approaches typically consist of three steps: encoding, preprocessing, and search. These steps, however, are tightly intertwined. For example, efficient propagation techniques applied in search (unit propagation as a simple example) are also applicable in preprocessing for simplifying the input formula. Furthermore, preprocessing and simplifications can be applied both on the conjunctive normal form (CNF) level—which still is the most typical input form for state-of-the-art SAT solvers–and on higher-level, more structural formula representations, such as Boolean circuits. Indeed, SAT encodings often go though a circuit-level formula representation, which is then translated into CNF. This highlights the importance of good CNF representations of Boolean circuits.

It is often argued that by encoding arbitrary Boolean formulas in CNF, structural properties of the original problem are not reflected in the resulting CNF. This should

J. Esparza and R. Majumdar (Eds.): TACAS 2010, LNCS 6015, pp. 129–144, 2010.

result in the fact that CNF-level preprocessing and SAT solver techniques have an inherent disadvantage compared to related techniques that can be applied on the level of more structural SAT instance representations such as Boolean circuits. Motivated by this, various simplification techniques and intricate CNF encoders for circuit-level SAT instance descriptions have been proposed [1,2,3,4,5]. On the other hand, based on the highly efficient CNF-level clause learning SAT solvers and CNF simplification techniques such as [6,7,8,9,10,11], there is also strong support for the claim that CNF is sufficient as an input format for SAT solvers.

In this work we study the effect of a CNF-level simplification technique called blocked clause elimination (BCE), based on the concept of blocked clauses [12]. We show that BCE is surprisingly effective both in theory and in practice on CNFs resulting from the standard "Tseitin" CNF encoding [13] for circuits: without explicit knowledge of the underlying circuit structure, BCE achieves the same level of simplification as a combination of circuit-level simplifications, such as *cone of influence*, *non-shared input elimination*, and *monotone input reduction*, and previously suggested polarity-based CNF encodings, especially the Plaisted-Greenbaum encoding [14]. This implies that, without losing simplification achieved by such specialized circuit-level techniques, one can resort to applying BCE after the straightforward Tseitin CNF encoding, and hence implementing these circuit-level techniques is somewhat redundant. Moreover, since other related circuit level optimizations for *sequential* problems—in particular, the *bounded cone of influence reduction* [15] and using functional instead of relational representations of circuits [16]—can be mapped to cone of influence, these can also be achieved by BCE purely on the CNF-level. Additionally, as regards CNF-level simplification techniques, BCE achieves the simplification resulting from, e.g., *pure literal elimination*. In addition to the more theoretical analysis in this paper, we present an experimental evaluation of the effectiveness of BCE combined with SatElite-style variable eliminating CNF preprocessing [10], comparing our implementation with the standard Tseitin and Plaisted-Greenbaum encodings and the more recent NiceDAG [4,5] and Minicirc [3] CNF encoders.

The rest of this paper is organized as follows. After background on Boolean circuits and CNF encodings of circuits (Sect. 2) and on resolution-based CNF preprocessing (Sect. 3), we introduce blocked clause elimination (Sect. 4). Then the effectiveness of BCE is analyzed w.r.t. known circuit-level simplification techniques and CNF encodings (Sect. 5) and resolution-based preprocessing (Sect. 6). Finally, our implementation of BCE is briefly described (Sect. 7) and experimental results are reported on the practical effectiveness of BCE (Sect. 8).

2   Boolean Circuits and CNF SAT

This section reviews the needed background related to Boolean circuits and CNF-level satisfiability, and well-known CNF encodings of circuits.

Given a Boolean variable x, there are two *literals*, the positive literal, denoted by x, and the negative literal, denoted by $\bar{x}$, the *negation of* x. As usual, we identify $\bar{\bar{x}}$ with x. A *clause* is a disjunction ($\vee$, or) of distinct literals and a CNF formula is a conjunction ($\wedge$, and) of clauses. When convenient, we view a clause as a finite set of literals and a

CNF formula as a finite set of clauses; e.g. the formula $(a \lor \bar{b}) \land (\bar{c})$ can be written as $\{\{a, \bar{b}\}, \{\bar{c}\}\}$. A clause is a *tautology* if it contains both x and $\bar{x}$ for some variable x.

2.1 Boolean Circuits

A Boolean circuit over a finite set G of *gates* is a set $\mathcal{C}$ of equations of form $g :=$ $f(g_1, \ldots, g_n)$, where $g, g_1, \ldots, g_n \in G$ and $f : \{\mathbf{t}, \mathbf{f}\}^n \to \{\mathbf{t}, \mathbf{f}\}$ is a Boolean function, with the additional requirements that (i) each $g \in G$ appears at most once as the left hand side in the equations in $\mathcal{C}$, and (ii) the underlying directed graph

$$\langle G, E(\mathcal{C}) = \{\langle g', g \rangle \in G \times G \mid g := f(\ldots, g', \ldots) \in \mathcal{C}\}\rangle$$

is acyclic. If $\langle g', g \rangle \in E(\mathcal{C})$, then g' is a *child* of g and g is a *parent* of g'. If $g :=$ $f(g_1, \ldots, g_n)$ is in $\mathcal{C}$, then g is an f-gate (or of type f), otherwise it is an *input gate*. A gate with no parents is an *output gate*. The fanout (fanin, resp.) of a gate is the number of parents (children, resp.) the gate has.

A (partial) assignment for $\mathcal{C}$ is a (partial) function $\tau : G \to \{\mathbf{t}, \mathbf{f}\}$. An assignment τ is *consistent* with $\mathcal{C}$ if $\tau(g) = f(\tau(g_1), \ldots, \tau(g_n))$ for each $g := f(g_1, \ldots, g_n)$ in $\mathcal{C}$.

A *constrained Boolean circuit* $\mathcal{C}^\tau$ is a pair $\langle \mathcal{C}, \tau \rangle$, where $\mathcal{C}$ is a Boolean circuit and τ is a partial assignment for $\mathcal{C}$. With respect to a $\mathcal{C}^\tau$, each $\langle g, v \rangle \in \tau$ is a *constraint*, and g is *constrained* to v if $\langle g, v \rangle \in \tau$.

An assignment τ' *satisfies* $\mathcal{C}^\tau$ if (i) it is consistent with $\mathcal{C}$, and (ii) it respects the constraints in τ, meaning that for each gate $g \in G$, if $\tau(g)$ is defined, then $\tau'(g) = \tau(g)$. If some assignment satisfies $\mathcal{C}^\tau$, then $\mathcal{C}^\tau$ is *satisfiable* and otherwise *unsatisfiable*.

The following Boolean functions are some which often occur as gate types.

- NOT(v) is $\mathbf{t}$ if and only if v is $\mathbf{f}$.
- OR$(v_1, \ldots, v_n)$ is $\mathbf{t}$ if and only if at least one of $v_1, \ldots, v_n$ is $\mathbf{t}$.
- AND$(v_1, \ldots, v_n)$ is $\mathbf{t}$ if and only if all $v_1, \ldots, v_n$ are $\mathbf{t}$.
- XOR$(v_1, \ldots, v_n)$ is $\mathbf{t}$ if and only if an odd number of v_i's are $\mathbf{t}$.
- ITE(v_1, v_2, v_3) is $\mathbf{t}$ if and only if (i) v_1 and v_2 are $\mathbf{t}$, or (ii) v_1 is $\mathbf{f}$ and v_3 is $\mathbf{t}$.

As typical, we inline gate definitions of type $g := $ NOT(g'). In other words, each occurrence of g as $\hat{g} := f(\ldots, g, \ldots)$ is expected to be rewritten as $\hat{g} := f(\ldots, \text{NOT}(g'), \ldots)$.

2.2 Well-Known CNF Encodings

The standard satisfiability-preserving "Tseitin" encoding [13] of a constrained Boolean circuit $\mathcal{C}^\tau$ into a CNF formula TST$(\mathcal{C}^\tau)$ works by introducing a Boolean variable for each gate in $\mathcal{C}^\tau$, and representing for each gate $g := f(g_1, \ldots g_n)$ in $\mathcal{C}^\tau$ the equivalence $g \Leftrightarrow f(g_1, \ldots g_n)$ with clauses. Additionally, the constraints in τ are represented as unit clauses: if $\tau(g) = \mathbf{t}$ ($\tau(g) = \mathbf{f}$, resp.), introduce the clause (g) $((\bar{g})$, resp.). A well-known fact is that unit propagation[1] on TST$(\mathcal{C}^\tau)$ behaves equivalently to standard Boolean constraint propagation on the original circuit $\mathcal{C}^\tau$ (see, e.g., [17] for details).

---

[1] Given a CNF formula F, while there is a unit clause $\{l\}$ in F, unit propagation removes from F (i) all clauses in F in which l occurs, and (ii) the literal $\bar{l}$ from each clause in F.

A well-known variant of the Tseitin encoding is the Plaisted-Greenbaum encoding [14] which is based on *gate polarities*. Given a constrained Boolean circuit C^τ, a *polarity function* $\mathsf{pol}_C^\tau : G \to 2^{\{\mathbf{t},\mathbf{f}\}}$ assigns polarities to each gate in the circuit. Here $\mathbf{t}$ and $\mathbf{f}$ stand for the *positive* and *negative* polarities, respectively. Any polarity function must satisfy the following requirements.

- If $\langle g, v \rangle \in \tau$, then $v \in \mathsf{pol}_C^\tau(g)$.
- If $g := f(g_1, \ldots, g_n)$, then:
  - If $f = \text{NOT}$, then $v \in \mathsf{pol}_C^\tau(g)$ implies $\bar{v} \in \mathsf{pol}_C^\tau(g_1)$.
  - If $f \in \{\text{AND}, \text{OR}\}$, then $v \in \mathsf{pol}_C^\tau(g)$ implies $v \in \mathsf{pol}_C^\tau(g_i)$ for each i.
  - If $f = \text{XOR}$, then $\mathsf{pol}_C^\tau(g) \neq \emptyset$ implies $\mathsf{pol}_C^\tau(g_i) = \{\mathbf{t}, \mathbf{f}\}$.
  - If $f = \text{ITE}$, then $v \in \mathsf{pol}_C^\tau(g)$ implies $\mathsf{pol}_C^\tau(g_1) = \{\mathbf{t}, \mathbf{f}\}$ and $v \in \mathsf{pol}_C^\tau(g_i)$ for $i = 2, 3$.

The Plaisted-Greenbaum encoding [14] uses the polarity function minpol_C^τ that assigns for each gate the subset-minimal polarities from $2^{\{\mathbf{t},\mathbf{f}\}}$ respecting the requirements above. In other words, for each gate g,

$$\mathsf{minpol}_C^\tau(g) := \{v \mid \tau(g) = v \text{ or } v \in \mathsf{minpol}_C^\tau(g') \text{ for some parent } g' \text{ of } g\}.$$

The Tseitin encoding, on the other hand, can be seen as using the subset-maximal polarity assigning polarity function $\mathsf{maxpol}_C^\tau(g) := \{\mathbf{t}, \mathbf{f}\}$ for each gate g. For the gate types considered in this paper, the clauses introduced based on gates polarities are listed in Table 1.

Table 1. CNF encoding for constrained Boolean circuits based on gate polarities. In the table, $\mathbf{g}_i$ is $\bar{g}_i'$ if $g_i := \text{NOT}(g_i')$, and g_i otherwise.

gate g	$\mathbf{t} \in \mathsf{pol}_C^\tau(g)$	$\mathbf{f} \in \mathsf{pol}_C^\tau(g)$
$g := \text{OR}(g_1, \ldots, g_n)$	$(\bar{g} \vee \mathbf{g}_1 \vee \cdots \vee \mathbf{g}_n)$	$(g \vee \bar{\mathbf{g}}_1), \ldots, (g \vee \bar{\mathbf{g}}_n)$
$g := \text{AND}(g_1, \ldots, g_n)$	$(\bar{g} \vee \mathbf{g}_1), \ldots, (\bar{g} \vee \mathbf{g}_n)$	$(g \vee \bar{\mathbf{g}}_1 \vee \cdots \vee \bar{\mathbf{g}}_n)$
$g := \text{XOR}(g_1, g_2)$	$(\bar{g} \vee \bar{\mathbf{g}}_1 \vee \bar{\mathbf{g}}_2), (\bar{g} \vee \mathbf{g}_1 \vee \mathbf{g}_2)$	$(g \vee \bar{\mathbf{g}}_1 \vee \mathbf{g}_2), (g \vee \mathbf{g}_1 \vee \bar{\mathbf{g}}_2)$
$g := \text{ITE}(g_1, g_2, g_3)$	$(\bar{g} \vee \bar{\mathbf{g}}_1 \vee \mathbf{g}_2), (\bar{g} \vee \mathbf{g}_1 \vee \mathbf{g}_3)$	$(g \vee \bar{\mathbf{g}}_1 \vee \bar{\mathbf{g}}_2), (g \vee \mathbf{g}_1 \vee \bar{\mathbf{g}}_3)$
$\langle g, \mathbf{t} \rangle \in \tau$		(g)
$\langle g, \mathbf{f} \rangle \in \tau$		$(\bar{g})$

Given a constrained Boolean circuit C^τ, we denote the CNF resulting from the Plaisted-Greenbaum encoding of C^τ by $\text{PG}(C^\tau)$.

Relevant concepts additional concepts related to polarities are

- *monotone gates*: gate g is monotone if $|\mathsf{minpol}_C^\tau(g)| = 1$; and
- *redundant gates*: gate g is redundant if $\mathsf{minpol}_C^\tau(g) = \emptyset$.

3   Resolution and CNF-Level Simplification

The resolution rule states that, given two clauses $C_1 = \{x, a_1, \ldots, a_n\}$ and $C_2 = \{\bar{x}, b_2, \ldots, b_m\}$, the implied clause $C = \{a_1, \ldots, a_n, b_1, \ldots, b_m\}$, called the *resolvent* of C_1 and C_2, can be inferred by *resolving* on the variable x. We write $C = C_1 \otimes C_2$.

This notion can be lifted to sets of clauses: For two sets S_x and $S_{\bar{x}}$ of clauses which all contain x and $\bar{x}$, respectively, we define

$$S_x \otimes S_{\bar{x}} = \{C_1 \otimes C_2 \mid C_1 \in S_x, C_2 \in S_{\bar{x}}, \text{ and } C_1 \otimes C_2 \text{ is not a tautology}\}.$$

Following the Davis-Putnam procedure [18] (DP), a basic simplification technique, referred to as *variable elimination by clause distribution* in [10], can be defined. The elimination of a variable x in the whole CNF can be computed by pair-wise resolving each clause in S_x with every clause in $S_{\bar{x}}$. Replacing the original clauses in $S_x \cup S_{\bar{x}}$ with the set of *non-tautological* resolvents $S = S_x \otimes S_{\bar{x}}$ gives the CNF $(F \setminus (S_x \cup S_{\bar{x}})) \cup S$ which is satisfiability-equivalent to F.

Notice that DP is a complete proof procedure for CNFs, with exponential worst-case space complexity. Hence for practical applications of variable elimination by clause distribution as a simplification technique for CNFs, variable elimination needs to be bounded. Closely following the heuristics applied in the SatElite preprocessor [10] for applying variable elimination, in this paper we study as a simplification technique the bounded variant of variable elimination by clause distribution, VE, under which a variable x can be eliminated only if $|S| \leq |S_x \cup S_{\bar{x}}|$, i.e., when the resulting CNF formula $(F \setminus (S_x \cup S_{\bar{x}})) \cup S$ will not contain more clauses as the original formula F.[2]

It should be noted that the result of VE can vary significantly depending on the order in which variables are eliminated. In more detail, VE doesn't have a unique fixpoint for all CNF formulas, and the fixpoint reached in practice is dependent on variable elimination ordering heuristics. Hence VE is not *confluent*.

Proposition 1. VE *is not confluent.*

4 Blocked Clause Elimination

The main simplification technique studied in this paper is what we call *blocked clause elimination* (BCE), which removes so called *blocked clauses* [12] from CNF formulas.

Definition 1 (Blocking literal). *A literal l in a clause C of a CNF F blocks C (w.r.t. F) if for every clause $C' \in F$ with $\bar{l} \in C'$, the resolvent $(C \setminus \{l\}) \cup (C' \setminus \{\bar{l}\})$ obtained from resolving C and C' on l is a tautology.*

With respect to a fixed CNF and its clauses we have:

Definition 2 (Blocked clause). *A clause is blocked if it has a literal that blocks it.*

Example 1. Consider the formula $F_{\text{blocked}} = (a \lor b) \land (a \lor \bar{b} \lor \bar{c}) \land (\bar{a} \lor c)$. Only the first clause of F_{blocked} is not blocked. Both of the literals a and $\bar{c}$ block the second clause. The literal c blocks the last clause. Notice that after removing either $(a \lor \bar{b} \lor \bar{c})$ or $(\bar{a} \lor c)$, the clause $(a \lor b)$ becomes blocked. This is actually an extreme case in which BCE can remove all clauses of a formula, resulting in a trivially satisfiable formula. $\square$

---

[2] More precisely, the SatElite preprocessor [10] applies a variant of VE called *variable elimination by substitution*. The analysis on VE in this paper applies to this variant as well.

As a side-remark, notice that a literal l cannot block any clause in a CNF formula F if F contains the unit clause $\{\bar{l}\}$, and hence in this case no clause containing l can be blocked w.r.t. F.

An important fact is that BCE preserves satisfiability.

Proposition 2 ([12]). *Removal of an arbitrary blocked clause preserves satisfiability.*

Additionally, we have the following.

Proposition 3. *Given a CNF formula F, let clause $C \in F$ be blocked w.r.t. F. Any clause $C' \in F$, where $C' \neq C$, that is blocked w.r.t. F is also blocked w.r.t. $F \setminus \{C\}$.*

Therefore the result of blocked clause elimination is independent of the order in which blocked clauses are removed, and hence blocked clause elimination has a unique fixpoint for any CNF formula, i.e., BCE is confluent.

Proposition 4. BCE *is confluent.*

It should be noted that, from a proof complexity theoretic point of view, there are CNF formulas which can be made easier to prove unsatisfiable with resolution (and hence also with clause learning SAT solvers) by *adding* blocked clauses [12]. In more detail, there are CNF formulas for which minimal resolution proofs are guaranteed to be of exponential length originally, but by adding instance-specific blocked clauses to the formulas, the resulting formulas yield short resolution proofs. The effect of adding (instance-specific) blocked clauses has also been studied in different contexts [19,20,21]. However, in a more general practical sense, we will show that removal of blocked clauses by BCE yields simplified CNF formulas which are both smaller in size and easier to solve.

As a final remark before proceeding to the main contributions of this paper, we note that this is not the first time removing blocked clauses is proposed for simplifying CNFs [6]. However, in contrast to this paper, the work of [6] does not make the connection between blocked clauses and circuit-level simplifications and CNF encodings and, most importantly, [6] concentrates on extracting underlying circuit gate definitions for applying this knowledge in CNF simplification; blocked clause removal in [6] is actually *not* applied in the case any underlying gate definitions can be extracted, but rather as an auxiliary simplification over those clauses which cannot be associated with gate definitions.

5   Effectiveness of Blocked Clause Elimination

The main results of this section show the surprising effectiveness of blocked clause elimination when applied until fixpoint. We will apply the following definition of the relative effectiveness of CNF encodings and both circuit and CNF-level simplification techniques.

Definition 3. *Assume two methods T_1 and T_2 that take as input an arbitrary constrained Boolean circuit C^τ and output CNF formulas $T_1(C^\tau)$ and $T_2(C^\tau)$, respectively, that are satisfiability-equivalent to C^τ. We say that T_1 is at least as effective as T_2 if, for any C^τ, $T_1(C^\tau)$ contains at most as many clauses and variables as $T_2(C^\tau)$ does. If T_1 is at least as effective as T_2 and vice versa, then T_1 and T_2 are equally effective.*

Notice that, considering BCE, a stricter variant of this definition, based on clause elimination, could be applied: T_1 is at least as effective as T_2 , if for every circuit C^τ we have
$T_1(C^\tau) \subseteq T_2(C^\tau)$. However, for VE this stricter definition cannot be naturally applied,
since in general VE produces non-tautological resolvents which are not subsumed by
the original clauses. Because of this inherent property of VE, we will for simplicity in
the following use the "weaker" version, as in Definition 3. All the results presented not
concerning VE also hold under the stricter version of the definition. Also notice that the
"at least as effective" relation is analogously defined for two CNF-level simplification
methods which, instead of Boolean circuits, take CNF formulas as input.

When considering the effectiveness of VE in this paper, we apply a non-deterministic
interpretation which allows for *any* variable elimination order, i.e., we say that VE can
achieve the effectiveness of another simplification technique, if there is some elimination order for which VE achieves the same effectiveness. Finally, note that in the
following we always assume that Boolean circuits (CNF formulas, resp.) are closed
under standard circuit-level Boolean constraint propagation (unit propagation, resp.).

An overview of the main results of this section is presented in Fig. 1. An edge from
X to Y implies that X is as least as effective as Y; for further details, see the caption.

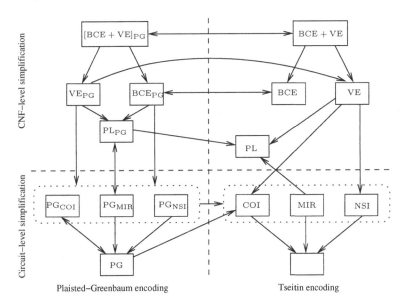

Fig. 1. Relative effectiveness of combinations of CNF encodings with both circuit and CNF-level
simplification techniques. An edge from X to Y implies that X is as least as effective as Y. Notice that transitive edges are omitted. On the left side, X_{PG} means the combination of first applying the Plaisted-Greenbaum and then the CNF-level simplification technique X on the resulting
CNF. Analogously, PG_X means the combination of first applying the circuit-level simplification
X and then the Plaisted-Greenbaum encoding. On the right side the standard Tseitin encoding is
always applied. The pointed circles around COI, MIR, and NSI on the left and right represent
applying the combination of these three simplifications and then the Plaisted-Greenbaum (left) or
Tseitin encoding (right). Additionally, BCE + VE refers to all possible ways of alternating BCE
and VE until fixpoint.

Notice that transitive edges are omitted: for example, BCE is at least as effective as the combination of PG, COI, NSI, and MIR.

5.1 Pure Literal Elimination by BCE

Before turning to the main results, relating BCE with circuit-level simplification techniques, we begin by first arguing that both BCE and VE actually achieve the same simplifications as the well-known *pure literal elimination*. Given a CNF formula F, a literal l occurring in F is *pure* if $\bar{l}$ does not occur in F.

Pure Literal Elimination (PL): While there is a pure literal l in F, remove all clauses containing l from F.

Notice that the following two lemmas apply for all CNF formulas, and is not restricted to CNFs produced by the TST or PG encodings.

Lemma 1. BCE *is at least as effective as* PL.

Proof sketch. A pure literal blocks all clauses which contain it by definition, and hence clauses containing a pure literal are blocked.   □

Lemma 2. VE *is at least as effective as* PL.

Proof sketch. Let l be a pure literal. By definition, $S_{\bar{l}}$ (the set of clauses containing $\bar{l}$) is empty. Hence $S_l \otimes S_{\bar{l}} = \emptyset$, and therefore VE removes the clauses in S_l.   □

5.2 Effectiveness of BCE on Circuit-Based CNFs

In this section we will consider several circuit-level simplification techniques—*non-shared input elimination, monotone input elimination,* and *cone of influence reduction* [17]—and additionally the Plaisted-Greenbaum CNF encoding.

For the following, we consider an arbitrary constrained Boolean circuit C^τ.

Non-shared input elimination (NSI): While there is a (non-constant) gate g with the definition $g := f(g_1, \ldots, g_n)$ such that each g_i is an input gate with fanout one (non-shared) in C^τ, remove the gate definition $g := f(g_1, \ldots, g_n)$ from C^τ.

Monotone input reduction (MIR): While there is a monotone input gate g in C^τ, assign g to $\text{minpol}_C^\tau(g)$.

Cone of influence reduction (COI): While there is a redundant gate g in C^τ, remove the gate definition $g := f(g_1, \ldots, g_n)$ from C^τ.

First, we observe that the Plaisted-Greenbaum encoding actually achieves the effectiveness of COI.

Lemma 3. $\text{PG}(C^\tau)$ *is at least as effective as* $\text{PG}(\text{COI}(C^\tau))$.

Proof sketch. For any redundant gate g, $\text{minpol}_C^\tau(g) = \emptyset$ by definition. Hence the Plaisted-Greenbaum encoding does not introduce any clauses for such a gate.   □

On the other hand, blocked clause elimination can achieve the Plaisted-Greenbaum encoding starting with the result of the Tseitin encoding.

Lemma 4. $\mathrm{BCE}(\mathrm{TST}(\mathcal{C}^{\tau}))$ *is at least as effective as* $\mathrm{PG}(\mathcal{C}^{\tau})$.

Proof sketch. We claim that BCE removes all clauses in $\mathrm{TST}(\mathcal{C}^{\tau}) \setminus \mathrm{PG}(\mathcal{C}^{\tau})$ from $\mathrm{TST}(\mathcal{C}^{\tau})$. There are two cases to consider: redundant and monotone gates. For both cases, BCE works implicitly in a top-down manner, starting from the output gates (although BCE has no explicit knowledge of the circuit $\mathcal{C}^{\tau}$ underlying $\mathrm{TST}(\mathcal{C}^{\tau})$).

Consider an arbitrary redundant output gate definition $g := f(g_1, \ldots, g_n)$. Since g is not constrained under τ, all clauses in $\mathrm{TST}(\mathcal{C}^{\tau})$ in which g occurs are related to this definition. Now it is easy to see that the literals associated with g (recall Table 1) block each of these clauses, and hence the clauses are blocked. On the circuit level, this is equivalent to removing the definition $g := f(g_1, \ldots, g_n)$.

Now consider an arbitrary monotone output gate definition $g := f(g_1, \ldots, g_n)$ with $\mathrm{minpol}_{\mathcal{C}}^{\tau}(g) = \{v\}$, where $v \in \{\mathbf{t}, \mathbf{f}\}$. Then g must be constrained: $\tau(g) = v$. Hence unit propagation on g removes all clauses produced by TST for the case "if $\bar{v} \in \mathrm{pol}_{\mathcal{C}}^{\tau}(g)$" in Table 1 and removes the occurrences of g from the clauses produced for the case "if $v \in \mathrm{pol}_{\mathcal{C}}^{\tau}(g)$". To see how BCE removes in a top-down manner those clauses related to monotone gate definitions which are not produced by PG, consider the gate definition $g_i := f'(g_1', \ldots, g_{n'}')$. Assume that unit propagation on g has no effect on the clauses produced by TST for this definition, that $\mathrm{minpol}_{\mathcal{C}}^{\tau}(g_i) = \{v\}$, and that BCE has removed all clauses related to the parents of g_i in $\mathrm{TST}(\mathcal{C}^{\tau}) \setminus \mathrm{PG}(\mathcal{C}^{\tau})$. Now one can check that the literals associated with g_i block each of the clauses produced by TST for the case "if $\bar{v} \in \mathrm{pol}_{\mathcal{C}}^{\tau}(g_i)$". This is because all the clauses produced by TST for the definitions of g_i's parents and in which g_i occurs have been already removed by BCE (or by unit propagation). Hence all the clauses produced by TST for the case "if $\bar{v} \in \mathrm{pol}_{\mathcal{C}}^{\tau}(g_i)$" in Table 1 are blocked. □

Combining Lemmas 3 and 4, we have

Lemma 5. $\mathrm{BCE}(\mathrm{TST}(\mathcal{C}^{\tau}))$ *is at least as effective as* $\mathrm{PG}(\mathrm{COI}(\mathcal{C}^{\tau}))$.

Next, we consider non-shared input elimination.

Lemma 6. $\mathrm{BCE}(\mathrm{TST}(\mathcal{C}^{\tau}))$ *is at least as effective as* $\mathrm{PG}(\mathrm{NSI}(\mathcal{C}^{\tau}))$.

Proof sketch. Assume a gate definition $g := f(g_1, \ldots, g_n)$ such that each g_i is a non-shared input gate. It is easy to check from Table 1 that for each g_i, each clause produced by TST for $g := f(g_1, \ldots, g_n)$ is blocked by $\mathbf{g}_i$. The result now follows from Lemma 4 and Proposition 3 (notice that $\mathrm{PG}(\mathcal{C}^{\tau})$ is always a subset of $\mathrm{TST}(\mathcal{C}^{\tau})$). □

On the other hand, PL cannot achieve the effectiveness of NSI when applying PG: since PG produces the same set of clauses as TST for any gate g with $\mathrm{minpol}_{\mathcal{C}}^{\tau}(g) = \{\mathbf{t}, \mathbf{f}\}$, no literal occurring in these clauses can be pure.

We now turn to the monotone input reduction. Notice that MIR is a proper generalization of PL: given a CNF formula F, any pure literal in F is monotone in the straight-forward circuit representation of F where each clause $C \in F$ is represented as an output OR-gate the children of which are the literals in C. On the other hand, a monotone input gate in a circuit $\mathcal{C}^{\tau}$ is not necessarily a pure literal in $\mathrm{TST}(\mathcal{C}^{\tau})$: TST introduces clauses which together contain both positive and negative occurrences of all gates, including monotone ones. However, it actually turns out that, when applying the Plaisted-Greenbaum encoding, PL and MIR are equally effective.

Lemma 7. $\mathrm{PL}(\mathrm{PG}(\mathcal{C}^\tau))$ *and* $\mathrm{PG}(\mathrm{MIR}(\mathcal{C}^\tau))$ *are equally effective.*

Proof sketch. Assume a gate definition $g := f(g_1, \ldots, g_n)$, where some g_i is a monotone input gate. To see that $\mathrm{PL}(\mathrm{PG}(\mathcal{C}^\tau))$ is at least as effective as $\mathrm{PG}(\mathrm{MIR}(\mathcal{C}^\tau))$, first notice that since g_i is monotone, g is monotone. Now, it is easy to check (recall Table 1) that g_i occurs only either negatively or positively in the clauses introduced by PG for $g := f(g_1, \ldots, g_n)$, and hence $\mathbf{g}_i$ is pure.

To see that $\mathrm{PG}(\mathrm{MIR}(\mathcal{C}^\tau))$ is at least as effective as $\mathrm{PL}(\mathrm{PG}(\mathcal{C}^\tau))$, notice that in order to be a pure literal in $\mathrm{PG}(\mathcal{C}^\tau)$, a gate has to be both monotone and an input. $\square$

Using this lemma, we arrive at the fact that BCE on TST can achieve the combined effectiveness of MIR and PG.

Lemma 8. $\mathrm{BCE}(\mathrm{TST}(\mathcal{C}^\tau))$ *is at least as effective as* $\mathrm{PG}(\mathrm{MIR}(\mathcal{C}^\tau))$.

Proof sketch. Since BCE can remove all clauses in $\mathrm{TST}(\mathcal{C}^\tau) \setminus \mathrm{PG}(\mathcal{C}^\tau)$ by Lemma 4, after this BCE can remove all clauses containing some monotone input gate g_i since BCE is at least as effective as PL (Lemma 1). The result then follows by Lemma 7. $\square$

Combining Lemmas 4, 5, 6, and 8, we finally arrive at

Theorem 1. $\mathrm{BCE}(\mathrm{TST}(\mathcal{C}^\tau))$ *is at least as effective as first applying the combination of* COI, MIR, *and* NSI *on* $\mathcal{C}^\tau$ *until fixpoint, and then applying* PG *on the resulting circuit.*

As an interesting side-remark, we have

Proposition 5. *The combination of* NSI, MIR, *and* COI *is confluent.*

Moreover, BCE is more effective than applying the combination of COI, MIR, and NSI on $\mathcal{C}^\tau$ until fixpoint, and then applying PG on the resulting circuit. To see this, consider for example a gate definition $g := \mathrm{OR}(g_1, \ldots, g_n)$, where g has $\mathrm{minpol}_C^\tau(g) = \{\mathbf{t}, \mathbf{f}\}$ and only a single g_i is an input gate with fanout one (non-shared), i.e. it occurs only in the definition of g. In this case the clauses in $\mathrm{TST}(\mathcal{C}^\tau)$ in which g_i occurs are blocked.

6   Benefits of Combining BCE and VE

We will now consider aspects of applying BCE in combination with VE. As implemented in the SatElite CNF preprocessor, VE has proven to be an extremely effective preprocessing technique in practice [10].

First, we show that VE, using an optimal elimination ordering, can also achieve the effectiveness of many of the considered circuit-level simplifications.

Theorem 2. *The following claims hold.*

1. $\mathrm{VE}(\mathrm{TST}(\mathcal{C}^\tau))$ *is at least as effective as (i)* $\mathrm{TST}(\mathrm{COI}(\mathcal{C}^\tau))$*; (ii)* $\mathrm{TST}(\mathrm{NSI}(\mathcal{C}^\tau))$.
2. $\mathrm{VE}(\mathrm{PG}(\mathcal{C}^\tau))$ *is at least as effective as* $\mathrm{VE}(\mathrm{TST}(\mathcal{C}^\tau))$.
3. $\mathrm{VE}(\mathrm{PG}(\mathcal{C}^\tau))$ *is at least as effective as*
   (i) $\mathrm{PG}(\mathrm{COI}(\mathcal{C}^\tau))$*; (ii)* $\mathrm{PG}(\mathrm{NSI}(\mathcal{C}^\tau))$*; and (iii)* $\mathrm{PG}(\mathrm{MIR}(\mathcal{C}^\tau))$.

Proof sketch.

1. (i) Assume a redundant output gate definition $g := f(g_1, \ldots, g_n)$. Now $S_g \otimes S_{\bar{g}} = \emptyset$ since all resolvents are tautologies when resolving on g (recall Table 1).

   (ii) Assume a gate definition $g := f(g_1, \ldots, g_n)$ such that each g_i is an non-shared input gate. For OR (similarly for AND), $S_{g_1} \otimes S_{\bar{g}_1} = \emptyset$. After resolving on g_1 we are left with the clauses $\cup_{i=2}^{k}\{g \vee \bar{g}_i\}$, where each $\bar{g}_i$ is then a pure literal. For XOR, simply notice that $S_{g_1} \otimes S_{\bar{g}_1} = \emptyset$. For ITE, notice that $S_{g_1} \otimes S_{\bar{g}_1} = \{\bar{g} \vee \mathbf{g_2} \vee \mathbf{g_3}\}$, and then $\mathbf{g_2}$ and $\mathbf{g_3}$ are both pure literals.

2. Follows from $\mathrm{PG}(\mathcal{C}^\tau) \subseteq \mathrm{TST}(\mathcal{C}^\tau)$

3. (i) Follows directly from Lemma 3.

   (ii) By a similar argument as in Item 1 (ii).

   (iii) Follows directly from Lemmas 2 and 7.   □

However, there are cases in which VE is not as effective as BCE. Namely, VE cannot achieve the effectiveness of MIR when applying TST, in contrast to BCE. To see this, notice that an input gate can have arbitrarily large finite fanout and still be monotone. On the other hand, VE cannot be applied on gates which have arbitrarily large fanout and fanin, since the elimination bound of VE can then be exceeded (number of clauses produced would be greater than the number of clauses removed). In general, a main point to notice is that for VE, in order to achieve the effectiveness of BCE (on the standard Tseitin encoding), one has to apply the Plaisted-Greenbaum encoding before applying VE. In addition, since VE is not confluent in contrast to BCE, in practice the variable elimination ordering heuristics for VE has to be good enough so that it forces the "right" elimination order. In addition, there are cases in which BCE is more effective than VE_{PG}. For some intuition on this, consider a clause C with blocking literal l. Notice that the result of performing VE on l is not dependent on whether C is removed. However, for any non-blocking literal $l' \in C$ the number of non-tautological clauses after applying VE on l' would be smaller if BCE would first remove C.

On the other hand, there are also cases in which the combination of BCE and VE can be more effective than applying BCE only. For instance, by applying VE on a CNF, new blocked clauses may arise. For more concreteness, consider a circuit with an XOR-gate $g := \mathrm{XOR}(g_1, g_2)$ where g_1 and g_2 are input gates with fanout one (non-shared). Assume that $g := \mathrm{XOR}(g_1, g_2)$ is rewritten as an AND-OR circuit structure $g := \mathrm{AND}(a, b)$, $a := \mathrm{OR}(g_1, g_2)$, $b := \mathrm{OR}(\mathrm{NOT}(g_1), \mathrm{NOT}(g_2))$, where a and b are newly introduced gates with fanout one. Notice that g_1 and g_2 now have fanout two. In the Tseitin encoding of this structure, BCE cannot see the non-sharedness of g_1 and g_2 in the underlying XOR. However, by first eliminating the OR-gates a and b with VE, BCE can then remove the clauses containing the variables g_1 and g_2 (the gates become implicitly "non-shared" again). In other words, there are cases in which variable elimination results in additional clauses to be blocked.

7 Implementation

In short, BCE can be implemented in a similar way as VE in the SatElite preprocessor [10]: first "touch" all literals. Then, as long as there is a touched literal l: find clauses that are blocked by l, mark l as not touched any more, remove these blocked clauses, and touch the negation of all literals in these clauses. The priority list of touched literals can be ordered by the number of occurrences. Literals with few occurrences of their negations are to be tried first. This algorithm is implemented in PrecoSAT version 465 (http://fmv.jku.at/precosat) and can be used to run BCE until completion.

In principle, the result is unique. However, as in our implementation of VE [10] in PrecoSAT, we have a heuristic cut-off limit in terms of the number of occurrences of a literal. If the number of occurrences of a literal is too large, then we omit trying to find blocked clauses for its negation. This may prevent the actual implementation from removing some blocked clauses. In general, however, as also witnessed by the results of using BCE on the CNFs generated with the Tseitin and Plaisted-Greenbaum encodings, this cut-off heuristic does not have any measurable effect.

8   Experiments

We evaluated how much reduction can be achieved using BCE in combination with VE and various circuit encoding techniques. Reduction is measured in the size of the CNF before and after preprocessing, and on the other hand, as gain in the number of instances solved.

We used all formulas of SMT-Lib (http://smtlib.org) over the theory of bit-vectors (QF_BV) made available on July 2, 2009, as a practice benchmark set for the SMT competition 2009. From these we removed the large number of mostly trivial SAGE examples. The remaining 3672 SMT problems were bit-blasted to And-Inverter Graphs (AIGs) in the AIGER format (http://fmv.jku.at/aiger) using our SMT solver Boolector [22]. Furthermore, we used the AIG instances used in [5], consisting of two types of instances: (i) AIGs representing BMC problems (with step bound $k = 45$) obtained from all the 645 sequential HWMCC'08 (http://fmv.jku.at/hwmcc08) model checking problems, and (ii) 62 AIGs from the structural SAT track of the SAT competition. We have made the SMT-Lib instances publicly available at http://fmv.jku.at/aiger/smtqfbv-aigs.7z (260MB); the others cannot be distributed due to license restrictions. However, the HWMCC'08 instances can easily be regenerated using publicly available tools [3] and the model checking benchmarks available at http://fmv.jku.at/hwmcc08. We encoded these 4379 structural SAT instances with four algorithms: the standard Tseitin encoding [13], the Plaisted-Greenbaum polarity-based encoding [14], the Minicirc encoder based on technology mapping [3] and VE, and the most recent NiceDAG encoder [4,5]. The NiceDAG implementation was obtained from the authors. For Minicirc, we used an improved implementation of Niklas Eén.

In order to additionally experiment with application benchmarks already in CNF, we also included 292 CNFs of the application track of the SAT competition 2009 to our benchmark set. All resulting CNFs were preprocessed with VE alone (further abbreviated e), and separately first with BCE (b), followed by VE (e), and both repeated again, which altogether gives 6 versions of each CNF (no BCE or VE, e, b, be, beb, bebe). We call such an application of one preprocessing algorithm, either BCE or VE, which is run to completion, a *preprocessing phase*.

---

[3] Notice that COI is performed already in the generation process by these tools. However, we did not implement the non-trivial NSI or MIR for the experiments.

Table 2. Effectiveness of BCE in combination with VE using various encoders

	encoding			b			be			beb			bebe			e		
	t	V	C	t	V	C	t	V	C	t	V	C	t	V	C	t	V	C
S U	0	46	256	2303	29	178	1042	11	145	1188	11	145	569	11	144	2064	11	153
A T	12	9	27	116	7	18	1735	1	8	1835	1	6	34	1	6	244	1	9
A P	10	9	20	94	7	18	1900	1	6	36	1	6	34	1	6	1912	1	6
A M	190	1	8	42	1	7	178	1	7	675	1	7	68	1	7	48	1	8
A N	9	3	10	50	3	10	1855	1	6	36	1	6	34	1	6	1859	1	6
H T	147	121	347	1648	117	277	2641	18	118	567	18	118	594	18	116	3240	23	140
H P	130	121	286	1398	117	277	2630	18	118	567	18	118	595	18	116	2835	19	119
H M	6961	16	91	473	16	84	621	12	78	374	12	77	403	12	76	553	15	90
H N	134	34	124	573	34	122	1185	17	102	504	17	101	525	17	100	1246	17	103
B T	577	442	1253	5799	420	1119	7023	57	321	1410	56	310	1505	52	294	8076	64	363
B P	542	442	1153	5461	420	1119	7041	57	321	1413	56	310	1506	52	294	7642	57	322
B M	10024	59	311	1252	58	303	1351	53	287	1135	53	286	1211	52	280	1435	55	303
B N	13148	196	643	2902	193	635	4845	108	508	2444	107	504	2250	105	500	5076	114	518

The results are presented in Table 2. The first column lists the benchmark family: S = SAT'09 competition, A = structural SAT track, H = HWMCC'08, B = bit-blasted bit-vector problems from SMT-Lib. These are all AIGs except for the CNF instances in S. The next column gives the encoding algorithm used: T = Tseitin, P = Plaisted-Greenbaum, M = Minicirc, N = NiceDAG, and U = unknown for the S family already in CNF. The t columns give the sum of the time in seconds spent in one encoding/preprocessing phase. The columns V and C list in millions the sum of numbers of variables and clauses over all produced CNFs in each phase.

The results show that the combination "be" of BCE and VE always gives better results than VE (e) alone, with comparable speed. Using a second phase (beb) of BCE gives further improvements, even more if VE is also applied a second time (bebe). The CNF sizes after applying BCE (b) for the P encoder and the T encoder are equal, as expected. Further preprocessing, however, diverges: since clauses and literals are permuted, VE is not confluent, and thus VE phases can produce different results.

We applied a time limit of 900 seconds and a memory limit of 4096 MB for each encoder and each preprocessing phase. Thus 139 out of $106848 = 6 \cdot (4 \cdot 4379 + 292)$ CNFs were not generated: HM encoding ran out of memory on 5 very large BMC instances, one large CNF in S could not be preprocessed at all, and there was a problem with the parser in NiceDAG, which could not parse 14 actually rather small AIGs in BN. Furthermore, there were 10 timeouts for various preprocessing phases in the A family: 2 in AT/beb, 2 in AN/be, 2 in AN/e, 2 in AP/be, and 2 in AP/e. However, except for the one large CNF, where also VE run out of memory, there is not a single case where BCE did not run until completion within the given time and memory limits.

Reducing the size of a CNF by preprocessing does not necessarily lead to faster running times. Since it was impossible to run all structural instances with an appropriate time limit, we only performed preliminary experiments with a very small time limit of 90 seconds. We used PrecoSAT v236, the winner of the application track of the SAT competition 2009, and PicoSAT v918, a fast clause learning solver which does not use sophisticated preprocessing algorithms, in contrast to PrecoSAT. In both cases the results were inconclusive. Running preprocessing until completion takes a considerable portion of the 90 seconds time limit, even if restricted to VE. In addition, the success of PrecoSAT shows that not running preprocessing until completion is a much better strategy, particularly if the preprocessor is run repeatedly again, with enough time spent on search in-between. However, this strategy is hard to evaluate when many preprocessing techniques are combined.[4] Therefore we decided to stick with the run-to-completion approach, which also gives some clear indication of how much CNF size reduction can be achieved through BCE.

For the 292 SAT competition instances we were able to run PrecoSAT with a more reasonable timeout of 900 seconds. The cluster machines used for the experiments, with Intel Core 2 Duo Quad Q9550 2.8 GHz processor, 8 GB main memory, running Ubuntu Linux version 9.04, are around two times as fast as the ones used in the first phase of the 2009 SAT competition. In the first phase of the competition, with a similar time limit, PrecoSAT solved many more instances than competitors. Nevertheless, using BCE we can improve the number of solved instances considerable: PrecoSAT solves 176 original instances, 177 preprocessed by BCE and VE alone (b and e), 179 be instances, 180 beb instances, and 183 bebe instances. If we accumulate the time for all the preprocessing phases and add it to the actual running time, then 181 instances can be solved in the last case. For the other cases the number of solved instances does not change.

It would be interesting to compare our results to pure circuit-level solvers. To our understanding, however, such solvers have not proven to be more efficient than running CNF solvers in combination with specialized circuit to CNF encodings.

9   Conclusions

We study a CNF-level simplification technique we call BCE (blocked clause elimination). We show that BCE, although a simple concept, is surprisingly effective: without any explicit knowledge of the underlying circuit structure, BCE achieves the same simplifications as combinations of circuit-level simplifications and the well-known polarity-based Plaisted-Greenbaum CNF encoding. This implies that the effect of such specialized circuit-level techniques can actually be accomplished directly on the CNF-level. To our best knowledge, these connections have not been known before. Furthermore, in contrast to specialized circuit-level techniques, BCE can be naturally applied on any CNF formula, regardless of its origin. Experimental results with an implementation of a CNF-level preprocessor combining BCE and SatElite-style variable elimination are presented, showing the effectiveness and possible benefits of applying BCE.

Acknowledgements. The authors thank Niklas Eén and Pete Manolios for providing up-to-date versions of the Minicirc and NiceDAG encoders used in the experiments. The first author is financially supported by Academy of Finland under the project "Extending the Reach of Boolean Constraint Reasoning" (#132812). The third author is supported by the Dutch Organization for Scientific Research under grant 617.023.611.

---

[4] In PrecoSAT v465, we have failed literal preprocessing, various forms of equivalence reasonsing, explicit pure literal pruning, BCE, VE, combined with on-the-fly subsumption.

References

1. Jackson, P., Sheridan, D.: Clause form conversions for Boolean circuits. In: Hoos, H.H., Mitchell, D.G. (eds.) SAT 2004. LNCS, vol. 3542, pp. 183–198. Springer, Heidelberg (2005)
2. Mishchenko, A., Chatterjee, S., Brayton, R.K.: DAG-aware AIG rewriting: A fresh look at combinational logic synthesis. In: DAC 2006, pp. 532–535. ACM, New York (2006)
3. Eén, N., Mishchenko, A., Sörensson, N.: Applying logic synthesis for speeding up SAT. In: Marques-Silva, J., Sakallah, K.A. (eds.) SAT 2007. LNCS, vol. 4501, pp. 272–286. Springer, Heidelberg (2007)
4. Manolios, P., Vroon, D.: Efficient circuit to CNF conversion. In: Marques-Silva, J., Sakallah, K.A. (eds.) SAT 2007. LNCS, vol. 4501, pp. 4–9. Springer, Heidelberg (2007)
5. Chambers, B., Manolios, P., Vroon, D.: Faster SAT solving with better CNF generation. In: DATE 2009, pp. 1590–1595. IEEE, Los Alamitos (2009)
6. Ostrowski, R., Grégoire, É., Mazure, B., Sais, L.: Recovering and exploiting structural knowledge from CNF formulas. In: Van Hentenryck, P. (ed.) CP 2002. LNCS, vol. 2470, pp. 185–199. Springer, Heidelberg (2002)
7. Brafman, R.I.: A simplifier for propositional formulas with many binary clauses. IEEE Transactions on Systems, Man, and Cybernetics, Part B 34(1), 52–59 (2004)
8. Bacchus, F.: Enhancing Davis Putnam with extended binary clause reasoning. In: AAAI 2002, pp. 613–619. AAAI Press, Menlo Park (2002)
9. Subbarayan, S., Pradhan, D.K.: NiVER: Non-increasing variable elimination resolution for preprocessing SAT instances. In: Hoos, H.H., Mitchell, D.G. (eds.) SAT 2004. LNCS, vol. 3542, pp. 276–291. Springer, Heidelberg (2005)
10. Eén, N., Biere, A.: Effective preprocessing in SAT through variable and clause elimination. In: Bacchus, F., Walsh, T. (eds.) SAT 2005. LNCS, vol. 3569, pp. 61–75. Springer, Heidelberg (2005)
11. Gershman, R., Strichman, O.: Cost-effective hyper-resolution for preprocessing CNF formulas. In: Bacchus, F., Walsh, T. (eds.) SAT 2005. LNCS, vol. 3569, pp. 423–429. Springer, Heidelberg (2005)
12. Kullmann, O.: On a generalization of extended resolution. Discrete Applied Mathematics 96-97, 149–176 (1999)
13. Tseitin, G.S.: On the complexity of derivation in propositional calculus. In: Siekmann, J., Wrightson, G. (eds.) Automation of Reasoning 2: Classical Papers on Computational Logic 1967–1970, pp. 466–483. Springer, Heidelberg (1983)
14. Plaisted, D.A., Greenbaum, S.: A structure-preserving clause form translation. Journal of Symbolic Computation 2(3), 293–304 (1986)
15. Biere, A., Clarke, E.M., Raimi, R., Zhu, Y.: Verifiying safety properties of a power PC microprocessor using symbolic model checking without BDDs. In: Halbwachs, N., Peled, D.A. (eds.) CAV 1999. LNCS, vol. 1633, pp. 60–71. Springer, Heidelberg (1999)
16. Jussila, T., Biere, A.: Compressing BMC encodings with QBF. Electronic Notes in Theoretical Computer Science 174(3), 45–56 (2007)
17. Drechsler, R., Junttila, T., Niemelä, I.: Non-clausal SAT and ATPG. In: Biere, A., Heule, M.J.H., van Maaren, H., Walsh, T. (eds.) Handbook of Satisfiability. Frontiers in Artificial Intelligence and Applications, vol. 185, pp. 655–694. IOS Press, Amsterdam (2009)
18. Davis, M., Putnam, H.: A computing procedure for quantification theory. Journal of the ACM 7(3), 201–215 (1960)
19. Purdom, P.W.: Solving satisfiability with less searching. IEEE Transactions on Pattern Analysis and Machine Intelligence 6(4), 510–513 (1984)

20. Kautz, H.A., Ruan, Y., Achlioptas, D., Gomes, C.P., Selman, B., Stickel, M.E.: Balance and filtering in structured satisfiable problems. In: IJCAI 2001, pp. 351–358. Morgan Kaufmann, San Francisco (2001)
21. Heule, M.J.H., Verwer, S.: Using a satisfiability solver to identify deterministic finite state automata. In: BNAIC 2009, pp. 91–98 (2009)
22. Brummayer, R., Biere, A.: Boolector: An efficient SMT solver for bit-vectors and arrays. In: Kowalewski, S., Philippou, A. (eds.) TACAS 2009. LNCS, vol. 5505, pp. 174–177. Springer, Heidelberg (2009)

BOOM: Taking Boolean Program Model Checking One Step Further*

Gerard Basler, Matthew Hague, Daniel Kroening, C.-H. Luke Ong,
Thomas Wahl, and Haoxian Zhao

Oxford University Computing Laboratory, Oxford, United Kingdom

Abstract. We present BOOM, a comprehensive analysis tool for Boolean programs. We focus in this paper on model-checking non-recursive concurrent programs. BOOM implements a recent variant of *counter abstraction*, where thread counters are used in a program-context aware way. While designed for bounded counters, this method also integrates well with the Karp-Miller tree construction for vector addition systems, resulting in a reachability engine for programs with *unbounded thread creation*. The concurrent version of BOOM is implemented using BDDs and includes partial order reduction methods. BOOM is intended for model checking system-level code via predicate abstraction. We present experimental results for the verification of Boolean device driver models.

1 Introduction

Over the past decade, *predicate abstraction* has evolved into a viable strategy for model checking software, witnessed by the success of device driver verification in Microsoft's SLAM project. The input program is converted into a finite-state *Boolean program*, whose paths overapproximate the original behavior.

Recently, *concurrent* software has gained tremendous stimulus due to the advent of multi-core computing architectures. The software is executed by asynchronous parallel threads, communicating, in the most general case, through fully shared variables. Bugs in such programming environments are known to be subtle and hard to detect by means of testing, strongly motivating formal analysis techniques for concurrent programs.

In this paper, we present BOOM, a model checker for Boolean programs. While BOOM has many features that make it useful for sequential programs [4], we focus here on analyzing the set of reachable states of a *replicated* non-recursive Boolean program. Replication often induces symmetry, which can and must be exploited for the analysis to scale. We present our implementation of a context-aware form of bounded *counter abstraction* [3], and compare its performance to alternative reduction techniques also implemented in BOOM, and to other tools.

Replication materializes in practice as dynamic thread creation. Even without a bound on the number of running threads, the reachability problem for non-recursive concurrent Boolean programs is decidable. We have extended BOOM by

---

* Supported by the Swiss National Science Foundation (200021-109594) and the Engineering and Physical Sciences Research Council (EP/G026254/1,EP/D037085/1).

J. Esparza and R. Majumdar (Eds.): TACAS 2010, LNCS 6015, pp. 145–149, 2010.

a variant of the *Karp-Miller tree*, which operates directly on Boolean programs. We demonstrate that our implementation performs much better in practice than the worst-case complexity of the construction seems to suggest. The result is a practically useful and **exact** reachability analysis for realistic concurrent Boolean programs with arbitrarily many threads.

2   Concurrent Boolean Program Analysis with BOOM

BOOM is capable of analyzing the reachable state space of *replicated* programs, where threads may dynamically create other threads during the execution. The Boolean variables are declared either *local* or *shared*. Each thread has its own private copy of the local variables. The shared variables, in contrast, are fully accessible to every thread. Shared-variable concurrency is very powerful and able to simulate many other communication primitives, such as locks.

Concurrent Boolean programs with replicated threads are naturally *symmetric*: the set of transitions of a derived Kripke model is invariant under permutations of the threads. BOOM exploits this property using a form of *counter abstraction*: global states are represented as vectors of counters, one per local state. Each counter tracks the number of threads in the corresponding local state. A transition by a thread translates into an update of the counters for the source and target local state.

The suggested rewriting of program transitions into counter updates can *in principle* be performed at the program text level. In practice, this is usually infeasible due to the *local state explosion problem*: the number of statically determined local states is exponential in the program text size. We recently proposed **context-awareness** as a solution [3]: at exploration time, the context in which a statement is executed is known and exposes the local-state counters that need to be updated. As a natural optimization, a global state in BOOM only keeps counters for *occupied* local states, where at least one thread resides in. Their number is obviously bounded by the number of running threads, which tends to be a tiny fraction of all local states.

Extending BOOM to Unbounded Thread Creation

If there is no limit to how many threads may be running, the thread counters become unbounded non-negative integers. The induced transition system is an instance of a *vector addition system with [control] states* (VASS); the control state represents the values of the shared program variables. The reachability of a *thread state* (s, l) (combination of shared and local state) in a concurrent Boolean program is reducible to a VASS *coverability* problem. The latter problem is decidable, using a tree construction proposed by Karp and Miller [8].

BOOM uses the Karp-Miller construction as the starting point for an algorithm to decide thread-state reachability. The local state explosion problem materializes here as the *dimensionality problem* for VASSes. Fortunately, our earlier solution of a context-aware, on-the-fly translation is instrumental in the unbounded case as well. Our version of the Karp-Miller procedure operates directly on Boolean programs. Bypassing the VASS allows us to avoid the blowup that a static translation into any type of addition system invariably entails. To ameliorate the exponential-space complexity of the Karp-Miller construction, we exploit the special form of vector-addition systems derived from Boolean programs. For example, our implementation keeps a copy of those tree nodes that are *maximal* with respect to the covering relation as partial order. Newly discovered nodes are compared against these maximal nodes only.

3 Results

BOOM and our benchmarks are available at `http://www.cprover.org/boom`; we refer the reader to this website for more details on the tool and the benchmarks.

The left chart below compares a plain symbolic exploration of the concurrent Boolean program against BOOM's implementation of **bounded** counter abstraction. Each data point specifies the numbers of threads running. The message of this chart is obvious. The right chart compares plain exploration against BOOM's implementations of partial-order reduction. Comparing left and right, we see that counter abstraction performs somewhat better. In other experiments (not shown), we observed that combining the two gives yet better performance.

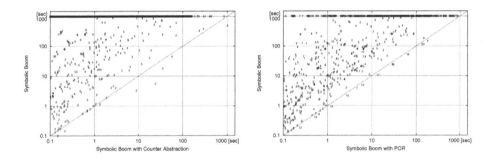

The chart on page 148 (left) compares the bounded version of BOOM with counter abstraction against the *lazy* version of GETAFIX [9] (which performs better than eager). GETAFIX targets *recursive* Boolean programs with a bounded number of context-switches. To compare with BOOM, we chose a non-recursive example from the GETAFIX website. The time for GETAFIX to convert the example into a sequential program is tiny and omitted. The table illustrates the time to explore the sequentialized program using MOPED-1, for different context-switch bounds. Note that BOOM explores *all* interleavings.

The graph on page 148 (right) shows our preliminary thread-state analysis of Boolean programs with unbounded thread creation. We see that for many examples, the running times are very small. On the other hand, 301 of 570 cases did not terminate within 60 min. We observed no more than 43 non-zero counters in any global state, despite millions of conceivable local states.

n	BOOM [sec]	GETAFIX/cont. bd. [sec]					
		1	2	3	4	5	6
2	< 0.1	0.1	0.4	2.0	8.7	41	139
3	0.1	0.1	1.0	0.6	4.8	30	187
4	1.2	0.1	1.9	1.2	12.2	146	1318
5	12.1	0.14	2.8	2.3	30.6	426	—
6	88.8	0.2	3.9	3.1	51.7	901	—

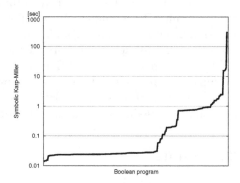

Benchmarks on Intel 3GHz, with timeout 60 mins, memory-out 4 GB.

4   Related Work and Conclusion

There are a few tools for the analysis of sequential Boolean programs [2,6]. When extended to multiple threads, the problem becomes undecidable. To allow a complete solution, BOOM disallows recursion. There are many tools available for the analysis of VASS. Closest to our work are the applications of these tools to Java [5,7] and to Boolean programs [1]. These tools compile their input into an explicit-state transition system, which will result in a high-dimensional VASS. Our experiments with explicit-state encodings (not shown) indicate that encoding Boolean programs symbolically is mandatory. We believe BOOM to be the first **exact** tool able to analyze non-recursive concurrent Boolean programs with *bounded* replication efficiently, and to extend the underlying technique to the *unbounded* case with encouraging performance.

References

1. Ball, T., Chaki, S., Rajamani, S.: Parameterized verification of multithreaded software libraries. In: Margaria, T., Yi, W. (eds.) TACAS 2001. LNCS, vol. 2031, p. 158. Springer, Heidelberg (2001)
2. Ball, T., Rajamani, S.: Bebop: A symbolic model checker for Boolean programs. In: Havelund, K., Penix, J., Visser, W. (eds.) SPIN 2000. LNCS, vol. 1885, pp. 113–130. Springer, Heidelberg (2000)
3. Basler, G., Kroening, D., Mazzucchi, M., Wahl, T.: Symbolic counter abstraction for concurrent software. In: Bouajjani, A., Maler, O. (eds.) Computer Aided Verification. LNCS, vol. 5643, pp. 64–78. Springer, Heidelberg (2009)
4. Basler, G., Kroening, D., Weissenbacher, G.: SAT-based summarization for boolean programs. In: Bošnački, D., Edelkamp, S. (eds.) SPIN 2007. LNCS, vol. 4595, pp. 131–148. Springer, Heidelberg (2007)
5. Delzanno, G., Raskin, J.-F., Begin, L.V.: Towards the automated verification of multithreaded Java programs. In: Katoen, J.-P., Stevens, P. (eds.) TACAS 2002. LNCS, vol. 2280, p. 173. Springer, Heidelberg (2002)
6. Esparza, J., Schwoon, S.: A BDD-based model checker for recursive programs. In: Berry, G., Comon, H., Finkel, A. (eds.) CAV 2001. LNCS, vol. 2102, p. 324. Springer, Heidelberg (2001)

7. Geeraerts, G., Raskin, J.-F., Begin, L.V.: Expand, enlarge and check.. made efficient. In: Etessami, K., Rajamani, S.K. (eds.) CAV 2005. LNCS, vol. 3576, pp. 394–407. Springer, Heidelberg (2005)
8. Karp, R., Miller, R.: Parallel program schemata. Computer and System Sciences (1969)
9. Torre, S.L., Madhusudan, P., Parlato, G.: Reducing context-bounded concurrent reachability to sequential reachability. In: Bouajjani, A., Maler, O. (eds.) Computer Aided Verification. LNCS, vol. 5643, pp. 477–492. Springer, Heidelberg (2009)

The OpenSMT Solver

Roberto Bruttomesso[1], Edgar Pek[2], Natasha Sharygina[1],
and Aliaksei Tsitovich[1]

[1] Università della Svizzera Italiana, Formal Verification Group, Lugano, Switzerland
[2] University of Illinois at Urbana-Champaign, Department of Computer Science, USA

Abstract. This paper describes OPENSMT, an incremental, efficient, and open-source SMT-Solver. OPENSMT has been specifically designed to be easily extended with new theory-solvers, in order to be accessible for non-experts for the development of customized algorithms. We sketch the solver's architecture and interface. We discuss its distinguishing features w.r.t. other state-of-the-art solvers.

1 Introduction

Satisfiability Modulo Theories [2] (SMT) is commonly understood as the problem of checking the satisfiability of a quantifier-free formula, usually defined in a decidable fragment of first order logic (e.g., linear arithmetic, bit-vectors, arrays).

In the context of formal verification, SMT-Solvers are every day gaining more importance as robust proof engines. They allow a more expressive language than propositional logic by supporting a set of decision procedures for arithmetic, bit-vectors, arrays, and they are faster then generic first-order theorem provers on quantifier-free formulæ.

Most verification frameworks are integrating SMT-Solvers as the main decision engine. With most off-the-shelf SMT-Solvers, the integration can be performed either via file or with a set of APIs, supported on the SMT-Solver's side, in such a way that it can be used as a black box by the calling environment.

OPENSMT is an attempt of providing an incremental, open-source SMT-Solver[1] that is easy to extend and, at the same time, efficient in performance. Our philosophy is to provide an open and comprehensive framework for the community, in the hope that it will facilitate the use and understanding of SMT-Solvers, in the same way as it was done for SAT-solvers and theorem provers.

OPENSMT participated in the last two SMTCOMP [1], the annual competition for SMT-Solvers, and it was the fastest open-source solver for the categories QF_UF (2008 and 2009), QF_IDL, QF_RDL, QF_LRA (2009). It also supports QF_BV, QF_UFIDL, and QF_UFLRA logics (the reader may refer to www.smtlib.org for more details about SMT logics and theories).

---

[1] OPENSMT is written in C++ and released under the GNU GPL license. It is available at http://verify.inf.usi.ch/opensmt

J. Esparza and R. Majumdar (Eds.): TACAS 2010, LNCS 6015, pp. 150–153, 2010.
© Springer-Verlag Berlin Heidelberg 2010

2   Tool Architecture

2.1   Overview

The architecture of OPENSMT implements the well-consolidated *lazy* or DPLL(T) approach [2], where a SAT-Solver is used as a Boolean enumerator, while a $\mathcal{T}$-solver, a decision procedure for the background theory $\mathcal{T}$, is used to check the consistency of the conjunction of the enumerated atoms. The architecture of OPENSMT is depicted in Figure 1, and it can be divided into three main blocks.

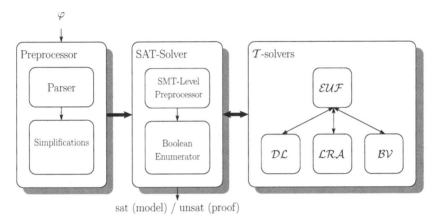

Fig. 1. OPENSMT functional architecture. $\mathcal{EUF}$, $\mathcal{DL}$, $\mathcal{LRA}$, and $\mathcal{BV}$ are the solvers for equality with uninterpreted functions, difference logic, linear real arithmetic, and bit-vectors respectively.

Preprocessor. The formula is parsed[2] and stored inside the *Egraph* [6], a DAG-like data structure whose vertexes, the *Enodes*, represent (sub)terms. Some static rewriting steps are then applied, in order to simplify and prepare the formula for solving. A commonly used and effective technique is, for instance, the elimination of variables by exploiting equalities appearing as top-level conjuncts of the formula.

SAT-Solver. The simplified formula is converted into CNF by means of the Tseitin encoding, and then given to the SAT-Solver. OPENSMT is built on top of the MINISAT2 incremental solver [7]. SATELITE preprocessing is applied to Boolean atoms only. We adapted the solver to include some recent optimizations, such as frequent restarts and phase caching.

$\mathcal{T}$-solvers. The organization of the theory solvers is the same proposed by the Simplify prover [6] (see Figure 1). The $\mathcal{EUF}$-solver acts as a layer and dispatcher for the $\mathcal{T}$-solvers for the other theories. $\mathcal{T}$-solvers communicates conflicts, deductions, and hints for guiding the search back to the SAT-solver.

---

[2] OPENSMT supports both SMT-LIB and Yices input formats.

2.2   The $\mathcal{T}$-solver Interface

Figure 2 shows the minimalistic interface API that a $\mathcal{T}$-solver is required to implement. *inform* is used to communicate the existence of a new $\mathcal{T}$-atom to the $\mathcal{T}$-solver. *assertLit* asserts a (previously informed) $\mathcal{T}$-atom in the $\mathcal{T}$-solver with the right polarity; it may also perform some cheap form of consistency check. *check* determines the $\mathcal{T}$-satisfiability of the current set of asserted $\mathcal{T}$-atoms. *pushBktPoint* and *popBktPoint* are used respectively to save and to restore the state of the $\mathcal{T}$-solver, in order to cope with backtracking within the

```
class T Solver
{
    void   inform          ( Enode * );
    bool   assertLit       ( Enode * );
    bool   check           ( bool );
    void   pushBktPoint    ( );
    void   popBktPoint     ( );
    bool   belongsToT      ( Enode * );
    void   computeModel    ( );

    vector< Enode * > & explanation;
    vector< Enode * > & deductions;
    vector< Enode * > & suggestions;
}
```

Fig. 2. The $\mathcal{T}$-solver interface

SAT-Solver. *belongsToT* is used to determine if a given $\mathcal{T}$-atom belongs to the theory solved by the $\mathcal{T}$-solver. Finally *computeModel* forces $\mathcal{T}$-solver to save the model (if any) inside *Enode*'s field.

Three vectors, explanation, deductions, suggestions, are shared among the $\mathcal{T}$-solvers, and they are used to simplify the communication of conflicts, $\mathcal{T}$-atoms to be deduced and "suggested" $\mathcal{T}$-atoms. Suggestions are atoms consistent with the current state of the $\mathcal{T}$-solver, but that they cannot be directly deduced. Suggestions are used to perform decisions in the SAT-Solver.

Explanations for deductions are computed on demand. When an explanation for a deduction l is required, the literal $\neg l$ is pushed in the $\mathcal{T}$-solver[3], and the explanation is computed by calling *check*. This process is completely transparent for the $\mathcal{T}$-solver thus avoiding any burden for generating and tracking explanations for deductions on the $\mathcal{T}$-solver side.

2.3   Customizing $\mathcal{T}$-solvers

SMT-Solvers are commonly used as black-box tools, either by passing a formula in a file, or by means of calls to an interface API. In some cases, however, the domain knowledge on the particular problem under consideration can be exploited to derive a more efficient procedure by customizing an existing one, or by deriving a new one from scratch.

This is for instance the case for the recent approach of [8], where properties of the execution of concurrent threads in a program are encoded as Boolean combinations of precedence relations of the form $x < y$. The problem can be encoded as QF_IDL formulæ, (i.e., by means of $\mathcal{T}$-atoms of the form $x - y <= c$, c being an integer constant), since $x < y$ and $\neg(x < y)$ can be encoded as $x - y <= -1$ and $y - x <= 0$ respectively. A graph-based encoding, such as the

---

[3] After having restored an appropriate $\mathcal{T}$-solver context.

one described in [5], allows to solve the problem in $O(nlog(n) + m)$, n being the number of vertices and m being the number of edges of the graph.

However, it is possible to devise a specialized procedure that deals directly with "precedence" atoms: instead of looking for an arbitrary negative cycle as in [5], it is enough to look for a cycle that contains at least an edge with constant -1. The complexity of the $\mathcal{T}$-solver decreases to $O(n + m)^4$.

OPENSMT provides an easy infrastructure for the addition of $\mathcal{T}$-solvers by means of an automatic script.

3 Other Features

Word-Level decision procedure for $\mathcal{BV}$. OPENSMT implements a word-level decision procedure for bit-vector extraction and concatenation and equalities [4]. The procedure is embedded in a congruence closure algorithm by means of an incremental and backtrackable data structure (CBE) that represents bit-vector slices modulo equivalence classes.

SMT-based preprocessor for linear arithmetic. Preprocessing is a crucial preliminary step to improve the solver performance. Traditional approaches tend to consider only top-level atoms to trigger simplifications. OPENSMT supports a preprocessing technique for linear arithmetic at the clause level, by means of a mixed Boolean-theory resolution rule [3].

Incremental solving support. OPENSMT, as well as other state-of-the-art solvers, supports a rich C API, which allows the incremental addition and removal of constraints in a stack-based manner.

Models and proofs. OPENSMT is able to generate a model if the formula is satisfiable and to construct a proof of unsatisfiability otherwise.

References

1. SMT-COMP, http://www.smtcomp.org
2. Barrett, C., Sebastiani, R., Seshia, S., Tinelli, C.: Satisfiability Modulo Theories. In: Handbook on Satisfiability, vol. 185. IO Press (2009)
3. Bruttomesso, R.: An Extension of the Davis-Putnam Procedure and its Application to Preprocessing in SMT. In: SMT (2009)
4. Bruttomesso, R., Sharygina, N.: A Scalable Decision Procedure for Fixed-Width Bit-Vectors. In: ICCAD (2009)
5. Cotton, S., Maler, O.: Fast and Flexible Difference Constraint Propagation for DPLL(T). In: Biere, A., Gomes, C.P. (eds.) SAT 2006. LNCS, vol. 4121, pp. 170–183. Springer, Heidelberg (2006)
6. Detlefs, D., Nelson, G., Saxe, J.B.: Simplify: a theorem prover for program checking. Journal of ACM 52(3), 365–473 (2005)
7. Eén, N., Sörensson, N.: An extensible SAT-solver. In: Giunchiglia, E., Tacchella, A. (eds.) SAT 2003. LNCS, vol. 2919, pp. 502–518. Springer, Heidelberg (2004)
8. Wang, C., Chaudhuri, S., Gupta, A., Yang, Y.: Symbolic pruning of concurrent program executions. In: ESEC/FSE, pp. 23–32 (2009)

---

[4] The problem reduces to finding strongly connected components in a graph.

STRANGER: An Automata-Based String Analysis Tool for PHP*

Fang Yu, Muath Alkhalaf, and Tevfik Bultan

Department of Computer Science
University of California, Santa Barbara, CA, USA
{yuf,muath,bultan}@cs.ucsb.edu

Abstract. STRANGER is an automata-based string analysis tool for finding and eliminating string-related security vulnerabilities in PHP applications. STRANGER uses symbolic forward and backward reachability analyses to compute the possible values that the string expressions can take during program execution. STRANGER can automatically (1) prove that an application is free from specified attacks or (2) generate vulnerability signatures that characterize all malicious inputs that can be used to generate attacks.

1   Introduction

Web applications provide critical services over the Internet and frequently handle sensitive data. Unfortunately, Web application development is error prone and results in applications that are vulnerable to attacks by malicious users. The global accessibility of critical Web applications make this an extremely serious problem. According to the Open Web Application Security Project (OWASP)'s top ten list that identifies the most serious web application vulnerabilities [6], the top three vulnerabilities are: 1) Cross Site Scripting (XSS), 2) Injection Flaws (such as SQL Injection) and 3) Malicious File Execution (MFE). A XSS vulnerability results from the application inserting part of the user's input in the next HTML page that it renders. Once the attacker convinces a victim to click on a URL that contains malicious HTML/JavaScript code, the user's browser will then display HTML and execute JavaScript that can result in stealing of browser cookies and other sensitive data. An SQL Injection vulnerability results from the application's use of user input in constructing database statements. The attacker can invoke the application with a malicious input that is part of an SQL command that the application executes. This permits the attacker to damage or get unauthorized access to data stored in a database. MFE vulnerabilities occur if developers directly use or concatenate potentially hostile input with file or stream functions, or improperly trust input files. All these vulnerabilities involve string manipulation operations and they occur due to inadequate sanitization and inappropriate use of input strings provided by users.

We present a new tool called STRANGER (STRing AutomatoN GEneratoR) that can be used to check the correctness of string manipulation operations in web applications. STRANGER implements an automata-based approach [9, 8] for automatic verification of string manipulating programs based on symbolic string analysis. String analysis is a

---

* This work is supported by NSF grants CCF-0916112 and CCF-0716095.

J. Esparza and R. Majumdar (Eds.): TACAS 2010, LNCS 6015, pp. 154–157, 2010.

static analysis technique that determines the values that a string expression can take during program execution at a given program point.

STRANGER encodes the set of string values that string variables can take as deterministic finite automata (DFAs). STRANGER implements both the *pre-* and *post-*image computations of common string functions on DFAs, including a novel algorithm for *language-*based replacement [9]. This replacement function takes three DFAs as arguments and outputs a DFA and can be used to model PHP replacement commands, e.g., `preg_replace()` and `str_replace()`, as well as many PHP sanitization routines, e.g., `addslashes()`, `htmlspecialchars()` and `mysql_real_escape_string()`. STRANGER implements all string manipulation functions using a symbolic automata representation (MBDD representation from the MONA automata package [2]) and leverages efficient manipulations on MBDDs such as determinization and minimization. This symbolic encoding also enables STRANGER to deal with large alphabets.

STRANGER combines forward and backward reachability analyses [8] and is capable of (1) checking the correctness of sanitization routines and proving that programs are free from specified attacks, and (2) identifying vulnerable programs, as well as generating non-trivial vulnerability signatures. Using forward reachability analysis, STRANGER computes an over-approximation of all possible values that string variables can take at each program point. If this conservative approximation does not include any attack pattern, STRANGER concludes that the program does not contain any vulnerabilities. Otherwise, intersecting these with attack patterns yields the potential attack strings. Using backward analysis STRANGER automatically generates string-based vulnerability signatures, i.e., a characterization that includes all malicious inputs that can be used to generate attack strings. In addition to identifying existing vulnerabilities and their causes, these vulnerability signatures can be used to filter out malicious inputs.

2   Tool Description

STRANGER uses Pixy [4] as a front end and MONA [2] automata package for automata manipulation. STRANGER takes a PHP program as input and automatically analyzes it and outputs the possible XSS, SQL Injection, or MFE vulnerabilities in the program. For each input that leads to a vulnerability, it also outputs the vulnerability signature, i.e., an automaton (in a dot format) that characterizes all possible string values for this input which may exploit the vulnerability. The architecture of STRANGER is shown in Figure 1. The tool consists of the following parts.

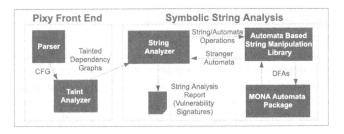

Fig. 1. The Architecture of STRANGER

PHP Parser and Taint Analyzer. The first step in our analysis is to parse the PHP program and construct the control flow graph (CFG). This is done by Pixy. PHP programs do not have a single entry point as in some other languages such as C and Java, so we process each script by itself along with all files included by that script. The CFG is passed to the taint analyzer in which alias and dependency analyses are performed to generate dependency graphs. A dependency graph specifies how the inputs flow to a sensitive sink with respect to *string operations*. The number of its nodes is linear to the number of the string operations in the program under a static single assignment environment. Loop structures contribute cyclic dependency relations. If no tainted data flow to the sink, taint analysis reports the dependency graph to be secure; otherwise, the dependency graph is tainted and passed to the string analyzer for more inspection.

String Analyzer. The string analyzer implements our vulnerability (forward and backward) analysis [8] on the tainted dependency graphs found by taint analysis. The dependency graphs are pre-processed to optimize the reachability analyses. First, a new acyclic dependency graph is built where all the nodes in a cycle (identifying cyclic dependency relations) are replaced by a single strongly connected component (SCC) node. The vulnerability analysis is conducted on the acyclic graph so that the nodes that are not in a cycle are processed only once. In the forward analysis, we propagate the post images to nodes in the topological order, initializing input nodes to DFAs accepting arbitrary strings. Upon termination, we intersect the language of the DFA of the sink node with the attack pattern. If the intersection is empty, we conclude that the sink is not vulnerable with respect to the attack pattern. Otherwise, we perform the backward analysis and propagate the pre images to nodes in the reverse topological order, initializing the sink node to a DFA that accepts the intersection of the result of the forward analysis and the attack pattern. Upon termination, the vulnerability signatures are the results of the backward analysis for each input node. For both analyses, when we hit an SCC node, we switch to a work queue fixpoint computation [8] on nodes that are part of the SCC represented by the SCC node. During the fixpoint computation we apply automata widening [1] on reachable states to accelerate the convergence of the fixpoint computation. We added the ability to choose when to apply the widening operator. This option enables computation of the precise fixpoint in cases where the fixpoint computations converges after a certain number of iterations without widening. We also incorporate a coarse widening operator [1] that guarantees the convergence to avoid potential infinite iterations of the fixpoint computation.

String Manipulation Library. String manipulation library (SML) handles all core string and automata operations such as replacement, concatenation, prefix, suffix, intersection, union, and widen. During the vulnerability analysis, all string and automata manipulation operations that are needed to decorate a node in a dependency graph are sent to SML along with the string and/or automata parameters. SML, then, executes the operation and returns back the result as an automaton. A Java class called *StrangerAutomaton* has been used as the type of the parameters and results. The class follows a well defined interface so that other automata packages can be plugged in and used with the string analyzer instead of SML. SML is also decoupled from the vulnerability analysis component so that it can be used with other string analysis tools.

StrangerAutomaton encapsulates *libstranger.so* shared library that has the actual string manipulation code implemented in C to get a faster computation and a tight control on memory. We used JNA (Java Native Access) to bridge the two languages.

3   Experiments and Conclusions

We have experimented with STRANGER on several benchmarks extracted from known vulnerable web applications [9]. For each vulnerable benchmark, we also generated a modified version where string manipulation errors are fixed. STRANGER took less than few seconds to analyze each benchmark. It successfully reported all known vulnerabilities, generated the vulnerability signatures, and verified that the modified version is secure and free from the previously reported vulnerabilities. We have also conducted a case study on `SimpGB-1.49.0` - a PHP guestbook web application. `SimpGB` consists of 153 php files containing 44000+ lines of code. Using a machine with Intel Core 2 Due 2.5 GHz with 4GB of memory running Linux Ubuntu 8.04, STRANGER took 231 minutes to check XSS vulnerabilities for all entries of executable PHP scripts and concluded 304 possible vulnerabilities out of 15115 sinks. STRANGER took 175 minutes to reveal 172 possible SQL Injection vulnerabilities from 1082 sinks, and 151 minutes to reveal 26 possible MFE vulnerabilities from 236 sinks.

In sum, we presented a string analysis tool for verification of web applications, focusing on SQLI, XSS and MFE attacks. In addition to identifying vulnerabilities and generating vulnerability signatures of vulnerable applications, STRANGER can also verify the absence of vulnerabilities in applications that use proper sanitization. Compared to grammar-based string analysis tools [3, 5, 7], STRANGER features specific automata-based techniques including automata widening [1], language-based replacement [9] and symbolic automata encoding and manipulation [2]. STRANGER and several benchmarks are available at `http://www.cs.ucsb.edu/~vlab/stranger`.

References

1. Bartzis, C., Bultan, T.: Widening arithmetic automata. In: Alur, R., Peled, D.A. (eds.) CAV 2004. LNCS, vol. 3114, pp. 321–333. Springer, Heidelberg (2004)
2. BRICS. The MONA project, `http://www.brics.dk/mona/`
3. Christensen, A., Møller, A., Schwartzbach, M.: Precise analysis of string expressions. In: Cousot, R. (ed.) SAS 2003. LNCS, vol. 2694, pp. 1–18. Springer, Heidelberg (2003)
4. Jovanovic, N., Krügel, C., Kirda, E.: Pixy: A static analysis tool for detecting web application vulnerabilities (short paper). In: S&P, pp. 258–263 (2006)
5. Minamide, Y.: Static approximation of dynamically generated web pages. In: WWW, pp. 432–441 (2005)
6. OWASP. Top ten project (May 2007), `http://www.owasp.org/`
7. Wassermann, G., Su, Z.: Sound and precise analysis of web applications for injection vulnerabilities. In: PLDI, pp. 32–41 (2007)
8. Yu, F., Alkhalaf, M., Bultan, T.: Generating vulnerability signatures for string manipulating programs using automata-based forward and backward symbolic analyses. In: ASE (2009)
9. Yu, F., Bultan, T., Cova, M., Ibarra, O.H.: Symbolic string verification: An automata-based approach. In: Havelund, K., Majumdar, R., Palsberg, J. (eds.) SPIN 2008. LNCS, vol. 5156, pp. 306–324. Springer, Heidelberg (2008)

When Simulation Meets Antichains

(On Checking Language Inclusion of Nondeterministic Finite (Tree) Automata)*

Parosh Aziz Abdulla[1], Yu-Fang Chen[1], Lukáš Holík[2], Richard Mayr[3], and Tomáš Vojnar[2]

[1] Uppsala University
[2] Brno University of Technology
[3] University of Edinburgh

Abstract. We describe a new and more efficient algorithm for checking universality and language inclusion on nondeterministic finite word automata (NFA) and tree automata (TA). To the best of our knowledge, the antichain-based approach proposed by De Wulf et al. was the most efficient one so far. Our idea is to exploit a simulation relation on the states of finite automata to accelerate the antichain-based algorithms. Normally, a simulation relation can be obtained fairly efficiently, and it can help the antichain-based approach to prune out a large portion of unnecessary search paths. We evaluate the performance of our new method on NFA/TA obtained from random regular expressions and from the intermediate steps of regular model checking. The results show that our approach significantly outperforms the previous antichain-based approach in most of the experiments.

1 Introduction

The language inclusion problem for regular languages is important in many application domains, e.g., formal verification. Many verification problems can be formulated as a language inclusion problem. For example, one may describe the actual behaviors of an implementation in an automaton $\mathcal{A}$ and all of the behaviors permitted by the specification in another automaton $\mathcal{B}$. Then, the problem of whether the implementation meets the specification is equivalent to the problem $L(\mathcal{A}) \subseteq L(\mathcal{B})$.

Methods for proving language inclusion can be categorized into two types: those based on *simulation* (e.g., [7]) and those based on the *subset construction* (e.g., [6,10,11,12]). Simulation-based approaches first compute a simulation relation on the states of two automata $\mathcal{A}$ and $\mathcal{B}$ and then check if all initial states of $\mathcal{A}$ can be simulated by some initial state of $\mathcal{B}$. Since simulation can be computed in polynomial time, simulation-based methods are usually very efficient. Their main drawback is that they are incomplete. Simulation preorder implies language inclusion, but not vice-versa.

On the other hand, methods based on the subset construction are complete but inefficient because in many cases they will cause an exponential blow up in the number

---

* This work was supported in part by the Royal Society grant JP080268, the Czech Science Foundation (projects P103/10/0306, 102/09/H042), the Czech COST project OC10009 associated with the ESF COST action IC0901, the Czech Ministry of Education by the project MSM 0021630528, the UPMARC project, the CONNECT project, and the ESF project Games for Design and Verification.

J. Esparza and R. Majumdar (Eds.): TACAS 2010, LNCS 6015, pp. 158–174, 2010.
© Springer-Verlag Berlin Heidelberg 2010

of states. Recently, De Wulf et al. [13] proposed the *antichain-based* approach. To the best of our knowledge, it was the most efficient one among all of the methods based on the subset construction. Although the antichain-based method significantly outperforms the classical subset construction, in many cases, it still sometimes suffers from the exponential blow up problem.

In this paper, we describe a new approach that nicely combines the simulation-based and the antichain-based approaches. The computed simulation relation is used for pruning out unnecessary search paths of the antichain-based method.

To simplify the presentation, we first consider the problem of checking universality for a word automaton $\mathcal{A}$. In a similar manner to the classical subset construction, we start from the set of initial states and search for sets of states (here referred to as *macro-states*) which are not accepting (i.e., we search for a counterexample of universality). The key idea is to define an "easy-to-check" ordering $\preceq$ on the states of $\mathcal{A}$ which implies language inclusion (i.e., $p \preceq q$ implies that the language of the state p is included in the language of the state q). From $\preceq$, we derive an ordering on macro-states which we use in two ways to optimize the subset construction: (1) searching from a macro-state needs not continue in case a smaller macro-state has already been analyzed; and (2) a given macro-state is represented by (the subset of) its maximal elements. In this paper, we take the ordering $\preceq$ to be the well-known maximal simulation relation on the automaton $\mathcal{A}$. In fact, the anti-chain algorithm of [13] coincides with the special case where the ordering $\preceq$ is the identity relation.

Subsequently, we describe how to generalize the above approach to the case of checking language inclusion between two automata $\mathcal{A}$ and $\mathcal{B}$, by extending the ordering to pairs each consisting of a state of $\mathcal{A}$ and a macro-state of $\mathcal{B}$.

In the second part of the paper, we extend our algorithms to the case of tree automata. First, we define the notion of *open trees* which we use to characterize the languages defined by tuples of states of the tree automaton. We identify here a new application of the so called upward simulation relation from [1]. We show that it implies (open tree) language inclusion, and we describe how we can use it to optimize existing algorithms for checking the universality and language inclusion properties.

We have implemented our algorithms and carried out an extensive experimentation using NFA obtained from several different sources. These include NFA from random regular expressions and also 1069 pairs of NFA generated from the intermediate steps of abstract regular model checking [5] while verifying the correctness of the bakery algorithm, a producer-consumer system, the bubble sort algorithm, an algorithm that reverses a circular list, and a Petri net model of the readers/writers protocol. We have also considered tree-automata derived from intermediate steps of abstract regular tree model checking. The experiments show that our approach significantly outperforms the previous antichain-based approach in almost all of the considered cases. (Furthermore, in those cases where simulation is sufficient to prove language inclusion, our algorithm has polynomial running time.)

The remainder of the paper is organized as follows. Section 2 contains some basic definitions. In Section 3, we begin the discussion by applying our idea to solve the universality problem for NFA. The problem is simpler than the language inclusion problem and thus we believe that presenting our universality checking algorithm first makes it easier for the reader to grasp the idea. The correctness proof of our universality check-ing algorithm is given in Section 4. In Section 5 we discuss our language inclusion checking algorithm for NFA. Section 6 defines basic notations for tree automata and in Section 7, we present the algorithms for checking universality and language inclu-sion for tree automata. The experimental results are described in Section 8. Finally, in Section 9, we conclude the paper and discuss further research directions.

2 Preliminaries

A *Nondeterministic Finite Automaton (NFA)* $\mathcal{A}$ is a tuple $(\Sigma, Q, I, F, \delta)$ where: Σ is an alphabet, Q is a finite set of states, $I \subseteq Q$ is a non-empty set of *initial* states, $F \subseteq Q$ is a set of *final* states, and $\delta \subseteq Q \times \Sigma \times Q$ is the transition relation. For convenience, we use $p \xrightarrow{a} q$ to denote the transition from the state p to the state q with the label a.

A word $u = u_1 \ldots u_n$ is accepted by $\mathcal{A}$ from the state q_0 if there exists a sequence $q_0 u_1 q_1 u_2 \ldots u_n q_n$ such that $q_n \in F$ and $q_{j-1} \xrightarrow{u_j} q_j$ for all $0 < j \leq n$. Define $L(\mathcal{A})(q) := \{u \mid u \text{ is accepted by } \mathcal{A} \text{ from the state } q\}$ (the language of the state q in $\mathcal{A}$). Define the language $L(\mathcal{A})$ of $\mathcal{A}$ as $\bigcup_{q \in I} L(\mathcal{A})(q)$. We say that $\mathcal{A}$ is *universal* if $L(\mathcal{A}) = \Sigma^*$. Let $\mathcal{A} = (\Sigma, Q_{\mathcal{A}}, I_{\mathcal{A}}, F_{\mathcal{A}}, \delta_{\mathcal{A}})$ and $\mathcal{B} = (\Sigma, Q_{\mathcal{B}}, I_{\mathcal{B}}, F_{\mathcal{B}}, \delta_{\mathcal{B}})$ be two NFAs. Define their union automaton $\mathcal{A} \cup \mathcal{B} := (\Sigma, Q_{\mathcal{A}} \cup Q_{\mathcal{B}}, I_{\mathcal{A}} \cup I_{\mathcal{B}}, F_{\mathcal{A}} \cup F_{\mathcal{B}}, \delta_{\mathcal{A}} \cup \delta_{\mathcal{B}})$. We define the post-image of a state $Post(p) := \{p' \mid \exists a \in \Sigma : (p, a, p') \in \delta\}$.

A *simulation* on $\mathcal{A} = (\Sigma, Q, I, F, \delta)$ is a relation $\preceq \subseteq Q \times Q$ such that $p \preceq r$ only if (i) $p \in F \implies r \in F$ and (ii) for every transition $p \xrightarrow{a} p'$, there exists a transition $r \xrightarrow{a} r'$ such that $p' \preceq r'$. It can be shown that for each automaton $\mathcal{A} = (\Sigma, Q, I, F, \delta)$, there exists a unique maximal simulation which can be computed in $O(|\Sigma||\delta|)$ [8].

Lemma 1. *Given a simulation $\preceq$ on an NFA $\mathcal{A}$, $p \preceq r \implies L(\mathcal{A})(p) \subseteq L(\mathcal{A})(r)$.*

For convenience, we call a set of states in $\mathcal{A}$ a *macro-state*, i.e., a macro-state is a subset of Q. A macro-state is *accepting* if it contains at least one accepting state, otherwise it is *rejecting*. For a macro-state P, define $L(\mathcal{A})(P) := \bigcup_{p \in P} L(\mathcal{A})(p)$. We say that a macro-state P is universal if $L(\mathcal{A})(P) = \Sigma^*$. For two macro-states P and R, we write $P \preceq^{\forall \exists} R$ as a shorthand for $\forall p \in P. \exists r \in R : p \preceq r$. We define the post-image of a macro-state $Post(P) := \{P' \mid \exists a \in \Sigma : P' = \{p' \mid \exists p \in P : (p, a, p') \in \delta\}\}$. We use $\mathcal{A}^{\subseteq}$ to denote the set of relations over the states of $\mathcal{A}$ that imply language inclusion, i.e., if $\preceq \in \mathcal{A}^{\subseteq}$, then we have $p \preceq r \implies L(\mathcal{A})(p) \subseteq L(\mathcal{A})(r)$.

3 Universality of NFAs

The *universality problem* for an NFA $\mathcal{A} = (\Sigma, Q, I, F, \delta)$ is to decide whether $L(\mathcal{A}) = \Sigma^*$. The problem is PSPACE-complete. The classical algorithm for the problem first determinizes $\mathcal{A}$ with the subset construction and then checks if every reachable macro-state is accepting. The algorithm is inefficient since in many cases the determinization will cause a very fast growth in the number of states. Note that for universality checking, we can stop the subset construction immediately and conclude that $\mathcal{A}$ is not universal whenever a rejecting macro-state is encountered. An example of a run of this algorithm

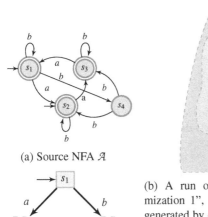

(a) Source NFA $\mathcal{A}$

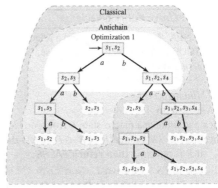

(c) Optimization 1 and 2

(b) A run of the algorithms. The areas labeled "Optimization 1", "Antichain", "Classical" are the macro-states generated by our approach with the maximal simulation and Optimization 1, the antichain-based approach, and the classical approach, respectively.

Fig. 1. Universality Checking Algorithms

is given in Fig. 1. The automaton $\mathcal{A}$ used in Fig. 1 is universal because all reachable macro-states are accepting.

In this section, we propose a more efficient approach to universality checking. In a similar manner to the classical algorithm, we run the subset construction procedure and check if any rejecting macro-state is reachable. However, our algorithm augments the subset construction with two optimizations, henceforth referred to as *Optimization 1* and *Optimization 2*, respectively.

Optimization 1 is based on the fact that if the algorithm encounters a macro-state R whose language is a superset of the language of a visited macro-state P, then there is no need to continue the search from R. The intuition behind this is that if a word is not accepted from R, then it is also not accepted from P. For instance, in Fig. 1(b), the search needs not continue from the macro-state $\{s_2, s_3\}$ since its language is a superset of the language of the initial macro-state $\{s_1, s_2\}$. However, in general it is difficult to check if $L(\mathcal{A})(P) \subseteq L(\mathcal{A})(R)$ before the resulting DFA is completely built. Therefore, we suggest to use an easy-to-compute alternative based on the following lemma.

Lemma 2. *Let P, R be two macro-states, $\mathcal{A}$ be an NFA, and $\preceq$ be a relation in $\mathcal{A}^{\subseteq}$. Then, $P \preceq^{\forall \exists} R$ implies $L(\mathcal{A})(P) \subseteq L(\mathcal{A})(R)$.*

Note that in Lemma 2, $\preceq$ can be any relation on the states of $\mathcal{A}$ that implies language inclusion. This includes any simulation relation (Lemma 1). When $\preceq$ is the maximal simulation or the identity relation, it can be efficiently obtained from $\mathcal{A}$ before the subset construction algorithm is triggered and used to prune out unnecessary search paths.

An example of how the described optimization can help is given in Fig. 1(b). If $\preceq$ is the identity, the universality checking algorithm will not continue the search from the macro-state $\{s_1, s_2, s_4\}$ because it is a superset of the initial macro-state. In fact,

---

Algorithm 1. *Universality Checking*

Input: An NFA $\mathcal{A} = (\Sigma, Q, I, F, \delta)$ and a relation $\preceq \in \mathcal{A}^{\subseteq}$.
Output: TRUE if $\mathcal{A}$ is universal. Otherwise, FALSE.

1 **if** *I is rejecting* **then return** *FALSE*;
2 *Processed*:=∅;
3 *Next*:={*Minimize*(*I*)};
4 **while** *Next* $\neq$ ∅ **do**
5 | Pick and remove a macro-state *R* from *Next* and move it to *Processed*;
6 | **foreach** $P \in \{Minimize(R') \mid R' \in Post(R)\}$ **do**
7 | | **if** *P is rejecting* **then return** *FALSE*;
8 | | **else if** $\nexists S \in Processed \cup Next$ s.t. $S \preceq^{\forall\exists} P$ **then**
9 | | | Remove all *S* from *Processed* ∪ *Next* s.t. $P \preceq^{\forall\exists} S$;
10 | | | Add *P* to *Next*;

11 **return** *TRUE*

---

the antichain-based approach [13] can be viewed as a special case of our approach when $\preceq$ is the identity. Notice that, in this case, only 7 macro-states are generated (the classical algorithm generates 13 macro-states). When $\preceq$ is the maximal simulation, we do not need to continue from the macro-state $\{s_2, s_3\}$ either because $s_1 \preceq s_3$ and hence $\{s_1, s_2\} \preceq^{\forall\exists} \{s_2, s_3\}$. In this case, only 3 macro-states are generated. As we can see from the example, a better reduction of the number of generated states can be achieved when a weaker relation (e.g., the maximal simulation) is used.

Optimization 2 is based on the observation that $L(\mathcal{A})(P) = L(\mathcal{A})(P \setminus \{p_1\})$ if there is some $p_2 \in P$ with $p_1 \preceq p_2$. This fact is a simple consequence of Lemma 2 (note that $P \preceq^{\forall\exists} P \setminus \{p_1\}$). Since the two macro-states P and $P \setminus \{p_1\}$ have the same language, if a word is not accepted from P, it is not accepted from $P \setminus \{p_1\}$ either. On the other hand, if all words in Σ^* can be accepted from P, then they can also be accepted from $P \setminus \{p_1\}$. Therefore, it is safe to replace the macro-state P with $P \setminus \{p_1\}$.

Consider the example in Fig. 1. If $\preceq$ is the maximal simulation relation, we can remove the state s_2 from the initial macro-state $\{s_1, s_2\}$ without changing its language, because $s_2 \preceq s_1$. This change will propagate to all the searching paths. With this optimization, our approach will only generates 3 macro-states, all of which are singletons. The result after apply the two optimizations are applied is shown in Fig. 1(c).

Algorithm 1 describes our approach in pseudocode. In this algorithm, the function *Minimize*(*R*) implements Optimization 2. The function does the following: it chooses a new state r_1 from R, removes r_1 from R if there exists a state r_2 in R such that $r_1 \preceq r_2$, and then repeats the procedure until all of the states in R are processed. Lines 8–10 of the algorithm implement Optimization 1. Overall, the algorithm works as follows. Till the set *Next* of macro-states waiting to be processed is non-empty (or a rejecting macro-state is found), the algorithm chooses one macro-state from *Next*, and moves it to the *Processed* set. Moreover, it generates all successors of the chosen macro-state, minimizes them, and adds them to *Next* unless there is already some $\preceq^{\forall\exists}$-smaller macro-state in *Next* or in *Processed*. If a new macro-state is added to *Next*, the algorithm at the same time removes all $\preceq^{\forall\exists}$-bigger macro-states from both *Next* and *Processed*. Note that the pruning of the *Next* and *Processed* sets together with checking whether a new macro-state should be added into *Next* can be done within a single iteration through *Next* and *Processed*. We discuss correctness of the algorithm in the next section.

4   Correctness of the Optimized Universality Checking

In this section, we prove correctness of Algorithm 1. Due to the space limitation, we only present an overview. A more detailed proof can be found in [2]. Let $\mathcal{A} = (\Sigma, Q, I, F, \delta)$ be the input automaton. We first introduce some definitions and notations that will be used in the proof. For a macro-state P, define $Dist(P) \in \mathbb{N} \cup \{\infty\}$ as the length of the shortest word in Σ^* that is not in $L(\mathcal{A})(P)$ (if $L(\mathcal{A})(P) = \Sigma^*$, $Dist(P) = \infty$). For a set of macro-states *MStates*, the function $Dist(MStates) \in \mathbb{N} \cup \{\infty\}$ returns the length of the shortest word in Σ^* that is not in the language of some macro-state in *MStates*. More precisely, if $MStates = \emptyset$, $Dist(MStates) = \infty$, otherwise, $Dist(MStates) = min_{P \in MStates} Dist(P)$. The predicate $Univ(MStates)$ is true if and only if all the macro-states in *MStates* are universal, i.e., $\forall P \in MStates : L(\mathcal{A})(P) = \Sigma^*$.

Lemma 3 describes the invariants used to prove the partial correctness of Alg. 1.

Lemma 3. *The below two loop invariants hold in Algorithm 1:*

1. $\neg Univ(Processed \cup Next) \implies \neg Univ(\{I\})$.
2. $\neg Univ(\{I\}) \implies Dist(Processed) > Dist(Next)$.

Due to the finite number of macro-states, we can show that Algorithm 1 eventually terminates. Algorithm 1 returns FALSE only if either the set of initial states is rejecting, or the minimized version of some successor R' of a macro-state R chosen from *Next* on line 5 is found to be rejecting. In the latter case, due to Lemma 2, R' is also rejecting. Then, R is non-universal, and hence $Univ(Processed \cup Next)$ is false. By Lemma 3 (Invariant 1), we have $\mathcal{A}$ is not universal. The algorithm returns TRUE only when *Next* becomes empty. When *Next* is empty, $Dist(Processed) > Dist(Next)$ is not true. Therefore, by Lemma 3 (Invariant 2), $\mathcal{A}$ is universal. This gives the following theorem.

Theorem 1. *Algorithm 1 always terminates, and returns TRUE iff the input automaton $\mathcal{A}$ is universal.*

5   The Language Inclusion Problem

The technique described in Section 3 can be generalized to solve the *language-inclusion problem*. Let $\mathcal{A}$ and $\mathcal{B}$ be two NFAs. The *language inclusion problem* for $\mathcal{A}$ and $\mathcal{B}$ is to decide whether $L(\mathcal{A}) \subseteq L(\mathcal{B})$. This problem is also PSPACE-complete. The classical algorithm for solving this problem builds on-the-fly the product automaton $\mathcal{A} \times \overline{\mathcal{B}}$ of $\mathcal{A}$ and the complement of $\mathcal{B}$ and searches for an accepting state. A state in the product automaton $\mathcal{A} \times \overline{\mathcal{B}}$ is a pair (p, P) where p is a state in $\mathcal{A}$ and P is a macro-state in $\mathcal{B}$. For convenience, we call such a pair (p, P) a *product-state*. A product-state is accepting iff p is an accepting state in $\mathcal{A}$ and P is a rejecting macro-state in $\mathcal{B}$. We use $L(\mathcal{A}, \mathcal{B})(p, P)$ to

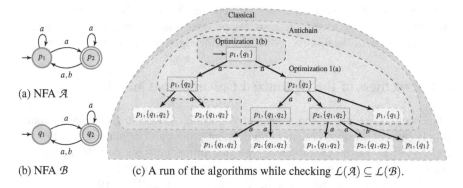

(a) NFA $\mathcal{A}$

(b) NFA $\mathcal{B}$

(c) A run of the algorithms while checking $L(\mathcal{A}) \subseteq L(\mathcal{B})$.

Fig. 2. Language Inclusion Checking Algorithms

denote the language of the product-state (p,P) in $\mathcal{A} \times \overline{\mathcal{B}}$. The language of $\mathcal{A}$ is not contained in the language of $\mathcal{B}$ iff there exists some accepting product-state (p,P) reachable from some initial product-state. Indeed, $L(\mathcal{A},\mathcal{B})(p,P) = L(\mathcal{A})(p) \setminus L(\mathcal{B})(P)$, and the language of $\mathcal{A} \times \overline{\mathcal{B}}$ consists of words which can be used as witnesses of the fact that $L(\mathcal{A}) \subseteq L(\mathcal{B})$ does not hold. In a similar manner to universality checking, the algorithm can stop the search immediately and conclude that the language inclusion does not hold whenever an accepting product-state is encountered. An example of a run of the classical algorithm is given in Fig. 2. We find that $L(\mathcal{A}) \subseteq L(\mathcal{B})$ is true and the algorithm generates 13 product-states (Fig. 2(c), the area labeled "Classical").

Optimization 1 that we use for universality checking can be generalized for language inclusion checking as follows. Let $\mathcal{A} = (\Sigma, Q_{\mathcal{A}}, I_{\mathcal{A}}, F_{\mathcal{A}}, \delta_{\mathcal{A}})$ and $\mathcal{B} = (\Sigma, Q_{\mathcal{B}}, I_{\mathcal{B}}, F_{\mathcal{B}}, \delta_{\mathcal{B}})$ be two NFAs such that $Q_{\mathcal{A}} \cap Q_{\mathcal{B}} = \emptyset$. We denote by $\mathcal{A} \cup \mathcal{B}$ the NFA $(\Sigma, Q_{\mathcal{A}} \cup Q_{\mathcal{B}}, I_{\mathcal{A}} \cup I_{\mathcal{B}}, F_{\mathcal{A}} \cup F_{\mathcal{B}}, \delta_{\mathcal{A}} \cup \delta_{\mathcal{B}})$. Let $\preceq$ be a relation in $(\mathcal{A} \cup \mathcal{B})^{\subseteq}$. During the process of constructing the product automaton and searching for an accepting product-state, we can stop the search from a product-state (p,P) if (a) there exists some visited product-state (r,R) such that $p \preceq r$ and $R \preceq^{\forall \exists} P$, or (b) $\exists p' \in P : p \preceq p'$. Optimization 1(a) is justified by Lemma 4, which is very similar to Lemma 2 for universality checking.

Lemma 4. *Let $\mathcal{A}$, $\mathcal{B}$ be two NFAs, (p,P), (r,R) be two product-states, where p, r are states in $\mathcal{A}$ and P, R are macro-states in $\mathcal{B}$, and $\preceq$ be a relation in $(\mathcal{A} \cup \mathcal{B})^{\subseteq}$. Then, $p \preceq r$ and $R \preceq^{\forall \exists} P$ implies $L(\mathcal{A},\mathcal{B})(p,P) \subseteq L(\mathcal{A},\mathcal{B})(r,R)$.*

By the above lemma, if a word takes the product-state (p,P) to an accepting product-state, it will also take (r,R) to an accepting product-state. Therefore, we do not need to continue the search from (p,P).

Let us use Fig. 2(c) to illustrate Optimization 1(a). As we mentioned, the antichain-based approach can be viewed as a special case of our approach when $\preceq$ is the identity. When $\preceq$ is the identity, we do not need to continue the search from the product-state $(p_2, \{q_1, q_2\})$ because $\{q_2\} \subseteq \{q_1, q_2\}$. In this case, the algorithm generates 8 product-states (Fig. 2(c), the area labeled "Antichain"). In the case that $\preceq$ is the maximal simulation, we do not need to continue the search from product-states $(p_1, \{q_2\})$, $(p_1, \{q_1, q_2\})$, and $(p_2, \{q_1, q_2\})$ because $q_1 \preceq q_2$ and the algorithm already visited the product-states $(p_1, \{q_1\})$ and $(p_2, \{q_2\})$. Hence, the algorithm generates only 6 product-states (Fig. 2(c), the area labeled "Optimization 1(a)").

If the condition of Optimization 1(b) holds, we have that the language of p (w.r.t. $\mathcal{A}$) is a subset of the language of P (w.r.t. $\mathcal{B}$). In this case, for any word that takes p to an accepting state in $\mathcal{A}$, it also takes P to an accepting macro-state in $\mathcal{B}$. Hence, we do not need to continue the search from the product-state (p, P) because all of its successor states are rejecting product-states. Consider again the example in Fig. 2(c). With Optimization 1(b), if $\preceq$ is the maximal simulation on the states of $\mathcal{A} \cup \mathcal{B}$, we do not need to continue the search from the first product-state $(p_1, \{q_1\})$ because $p_1 \preceq q_1$. In this case, the algorithm can conclude that the language inclusion holds immediately after the first product-state is generated (Fig. 2(c), the area labeled "Optimization 1(b)").

Observe that from Lemma 4, it holds that for any product-state (p, P) such that $p_1 \preceq p_2$ for some $p_1, p_2 \in P$, $L(\mathcal{A}, \mathcal{B})(p, P) = L(\mathcal{A}, \mathcal{B})(p, P \setminus \{p_1\})$ (as $P \preceq^{\forall\exists} P \setminus \{p_1\}$). Optimization 2 that we used for universality checking can therefore be generalized for language inclusion checking too.

We give the pseudocode of our optimized inclusion checking in Algorithm 2, which is a straightforward extension of Algorithm 1. In the algorithm, the definition of the *Minimize(R)* function is the same as what we have defined in Section 3. The function *Initialize(PStates)* applies Optimization 1 on the set of product-states *PStates* to avoid unnecessary searching. More precisely, it returns a maximal subset of *PStates* such that (1) for any two elements (p, P), (q, Q) in the subset, $p \not\preceq q \vee Q \not\preceq^{\forall\exists} P$ and (2) for any element (p, P) in the subset, $\forall p' \in P: p \not\preceq p'$. We define the post-image of a product-state $Post((p, P)) := \{(p', P') \mid \exists a \in \Sigma : (p, a, p') \in \delta, P' = \{p'' \mid \exists p \in P : (p, a, p'') \in \delta\}\}$.

Algorithm 2. *Language Inclusion Checking*

Input: NFA $\mathcal{A} = (\Sigma, Q_{\mathcal{A}}, I_{\mathcal{A}}, F_{\mathcal{A}}, \delta_{\mathcal{A}})$, $\mathcal{B} = (\Sigma, Q_{\mathcal{B}}, I_{\mathcal{B}}, F_{\mathcal{B}}, \delta_{\mathcal{B}})$. A relation $\preceq \in (\mathcal{A} \cup \mathcal{B})^{\subseteq}$.
Output: TRUE if $L(\mathcal{A}) \subseteq L(\mathcal{B})$. Otherwise, FALSE.

1 **if** *there is an accepting product-state in* $\{(i, I_{\mathcal{B}}) \mid i \in I_{\mathcal{A}}\}$ **then return** *FALSE*;
2 *Processed*:=$\emptyset$;
3 *Next*:= *Initialize*($\{(i, Minimize(I_{\mathcal{B}})) \mid i \in I_{\mathcal{A}}\}$);
4 **while** *Next* $\neq \emptyset$ **do**
5   Pick and remove a product-state (r, R) from *Next* and move it to *Processed*;
6   **foreach** $(p, P) \in \{(r', Minimize(R')) \mid (r', R') \in Post((r, R))\}$ **do**
7   **if** (p, P) *is an accepting product-state* **then return** *FALSE*;
8   **else if** $\nexists p' \in P$ *s.t.* $p \preceq p'$ **then**
9   **if** $\nexists (s, S) \in Processed \cup Next$ *s.t.* $p \preceq s \wedge S \preceq^{\forall\exists} P$ **then**
10   Remove all (s, S) from $Processed \cup Next$ s.t. $s \preceq p \wedge P \preceq^{\forall\exists} S$;
11   Add (p, P) to *Next*;

12 **return** *TRUE*

Correctness: Define $Dist(P) \in \mathbb{N} \cup \{\infty\}$ as the length of the shortest word in the language of the product-state P or ∞ if the language of P is empty. The value $Dist(PStates) \in \mathbb{N} \cup \{\infty\}$ is the length of the shortest word in the language of some product-state in *PStates* or ∞ if *PStates* is empty. The predicate *Incl(PStates)* is true iff for all product-states (p,P) in *PStates*, $L(\mathcal{A})(p) \subseteq L(\mathcal{B})(P)$. The correctness of Algorithm 2 can now be proved in a very similar way to Algorithm 1, using the invariants below:

1. $\neg Incl(Processed \cup Next) \implies \neg Incl(\{(i,I_{\mathcal{B}}) \mid i \in I_{\mathcal{A}}\})$.
2. $\neg Incl(\{(i,I_{\mathcal{B}}) \mid i \in I_{\mathcal{A}}\}) \implies Dist(Processed) > Dist(Next)$.

6   Tree Automata Preliminaries

To be able to present a generalization of the above methods for the domain of tree automata, we now introduce some needed preliminaries on tree automata.

A *ranked alphabet* Σ is a set of symbols together with a ranking function $\# : \Sigma \to \mathbb{N}$. For $a \in \Sigma$, the value $\#(a)$ is called the *rank* of a. For any $n \geq 0$, we denote by Σ_n the set of all symbols of rank n from Σ. Let ε denote the empty sequence. A *tree t* over a ranked alphabet Σ is a partial mapping $t : \mathbb{N}^* \to \Sigma$ that satisfies the following conditions: (1) $dom(t)$ is a finite, prefix-closed subset of $\mathbb{N}^*$ and (2) for each $v \in dom(t)$, if $\#(t(v)) = n \geq 0$, then $\{i \mid vi \in dom(t)\} = \{1, \ldots, n\}$. Each sequence $v \in dom(t)$ is called a *node* of t. For a node v, we define the ith *child* of v to be the node vi, and the ith *subtree* of v to be the tree t' such that $t'(v') = t(viv')$ for all $v' \in \mathbb{N}^*$. A *leaf* of t is a node v which does not have any children, i.e., there is no $i \in \mathbb{N}$ with $vi \in dom(t)$. We denote by $T(\Sigma)$ the set of all trees over the alphabet Σ.

A (finite, non-deterministic, bottom-up) *tree automaton* (abbreviated as TA in the sequel) is a quadruple $\mathcal{A} = (Q, \Sigma, \Delta, F)$ where Q is a finite set of states, $F \subseteq Q$ is a set of final states, Σ is a ranked alphabet, and Δ is a set of transition rules. Each transition rule is a triple of the form $((q_1, \ldots, q_n), a, q)$ where $q_1, \ldots, q_n, q \in Q$, $a \in \Sigma$, and $\#(a) = n$. We use $(q_1, \ldots, q_n) \xrightarrow{a} q$ to denote that $((q_1, \ldots, q_n), a, q) \in \Delta$. In the special case where $n = 0$, we speak about the so-called *leaf rules*, which we sometimes abbreviate as $\xrightarrow{a} q$.

Let $\mathcal{A} = (Q, \Sigma, \Delta, F)$ be a TA. A *run* of $\mathcal{A}$ over a tree $t \in T(\Sigma)$ is a mapping $\pi : dom(t) \to Q$ such that, for each node $v \in dom(t)$ of arity $\#(t(v)) = n$ where $q = \pi(v)$, if $q_i = \pi(vi)$ for $1 \leq i \leq n$, then Δ has a rule $(q_1, \ldots, q_n) \xrightarrow{t(v)} q$. We write $t \overset{\pi}{\Longrightarrow} q$ to denote that π is a run of $\mathcal{A}$ over t such that $\pi(\varepsilon) = q$. We use $t \Longrightarrow q$ to denote that $t \overset{\pi}{\Longrightarrow} q$ for some run π. The *language* accepted by a state q is defined by $L(\mathcal{A})(q) = \{t \mid t \Longrightarrow q\}$, while the *language* of $\mathcal{A}$ is defined by $L(\mathcal{A}) = \bigcup_{q \in F} L(\mathcal{A})(q)$.

7   Universality and Language Inclusion of Tree Automata

To optimize universality and inclusion checking on word automata, we used relations that imply language inclusion. For the case of universality and inclusion checking on tree automata, we now propose to use relations that imply inclusion of languages of the so called "open" trees (i.e., "leafless" trees or equivalently trees whose leaves are replaced by a special symbol denoting a "hole") that are accepted from tuples of tree automata states. We formally define the notion below. Notice that in contrast to the notion of a language accepted from a state of a word automaton, which refers to possible "futures" of the state, the notion of a language accepted at a state of a TA refers to possible "pasts" of the state. Our notion of languages of open trees accepted from tuples of tree automata states speaks again about the future of states, which turns out useful when trying to optimize the (antichain-based) subset construction for TA.

Consider a special symbol $\square \notin \Sigma$ with rank 0, called a *hole*. An *open tree* over Σ is a tree over $\Sigma \cup \square$ such that all its leaves are labeled[1] by $\square$. We use $T^{\square}(\Sigma)$ to denote the set of all open trees over Σ. Given states $q_1, \ldots, q_n \in Q$ and an open tree t with leaves $v_1, \ldots, v_n$, a run π of $\mathcal{A}$ on t from $(q_1, \ldots, q_n)$ is defined in a similar way as the run on a tree except that for each leaf v_i, $1 \leq i \leq n$, we have $\pi(v_i) = q_i$. We use $t(q_1, \ldots, q_n) \xRightarrow{\pi} q$ to denote that π is a run of $\mathcal{A}$ on t from $(q_1, \ldots, q_n)$ such that $\pi(\varepsilon) = q$. The notation $t(q_1, \ldots, q_n) \Longrightarrow q$ is explained in a similar manner to runs on trees. Then, the language of $\mathcal{A}$ accepted from a tuple $(q_1, \ldots, q_n)$ of states is $\mathcal{L}^{\square}(\mathcal{A})(q_1, \ldots, q_n) = \{t \in T^{\square} \mid t(q_1, \ldots, q_n) \Longrightarrow q \text{ for some } q \in F\}$. Finally, we define the language accepted from a tuple of macro-states $(P_1, \ldots, P_n) \subseteq Q^n$ as the set $\mathcal{L}^{\square}(\mathcal{A})(P_1, \ldots, P_n) = \bigcup\{\mathcal{L}^{\square}(\mathcal{A})(q_1, \ldots, q_n) \mid (q_1, \ldots, q_n) \in P_1 \times \ldots \times P_n\}$. We define $Post_a(q_1, \ldots, q_n) := \{q \mid (q_1, \ldots, q_n) \xrightarrow{a} q\}$. For a tuple of macro-states, we let $Post_a(P_1, \ldots, P_n) := \bigcup\{Post_a(q_1, \ldots, q_n) \mid (q_1, \ldots, q_n) \in P_1 \times \cdots \times P_n\}$.

Let us use $t^{\square}$ to denote the open tree that arises from a tree $t \in T(\Sigma)$ by replacing all the leaf symbols of t by $\square$ and let for every leaf symbol $a \in \Sigma$, $I_a = \{q \mid \xrightarrow{a} q\}$ is the so called a-initial macro-state. Languages accepted *at* final states of $\mathcal{A}$ correspond to the languages accepted *from* tuples of initial macro-states of $\mathcal{A}$ as stated in Lemma 5.

Lemma 5. *Let t be a tree over Σ with leaves labeled by $a_1, \ldots, a_n$. Then $t \in \mathcal{L}(\mathcal{A})$ if and only if $t^{\square} \in \mathcal{L}^{\square}(\mathcal{A})(I_{a_1}, \ldots, I_{a_n})$.*

7.1 Upward Simulation

We now work towards defining suitable relations on states of TA allowing us to optimize the universality and inclusion checking. We extend relations $\preceq \in Q \times Q$ on states to tuples of states such that $(q_1, \ldots, q_n) \preceq (r_1, \ldots, r_n)$ iff $q_i \preceq r_i$ for each $1 \leq i \leq n$. We define the set $\mathcal{A}^{\subseteq}$ of relations that imply inclusion of languages of tuples of states such that $\preceq \in \mathcal{A}^{\subseteq}$ iff $(q_1, \ldots, q_n) \preceq (r_1, \ldots, r_n)$ implies $\mathcal{L}^{\square}(\mathcal{A})(q_1, \ldots, q_n) \subseteq \mathcal{L}^{\square}(\mathcal{A})(r_1, \ldots, r_n)$.

We define an extension of simulation relations on states of word automata that satisfies the above property as follows. An *upward simulation* on $\mathcal{A}$ is a relation $\preceq \subseteq Q \times Q$ such that if $q \preceq r$, then (1) $q \in F \implies r \in F$ and (2) if $(q_1, \ldots, q_n) \xrightarrow{a} q'$ where $q = q_i$, then $(q_1, \ldots, q_{i-1}, r, q_{i+1}, \ldots, q_n) \xrightarrow{a} r'$ where $q' \preceq r'$. Upward simulations were discussed in [1], together with an efficient algorithm for computing them.[2]

Lemma 6. *For the maximal upward simulation $\preceq$ on $\mathcal{A}$, we have $\preceq \in \mathcal{A}^{\subseteq}$.*

The proof of this lemma can be obtained as follows. We first show that the maximal upward simulation $\preceq$ has the following property: If $(q_1, \ldots, q_n) \xrightarrow{a} q'$ in $\mathcal{A}$, then for

---

[1] Note that no internal nodes of an open tree can be labeled by $\square$ as $\#(\square) = 0$.

[2] In [1], upward simulations are parameterized by some downward simulation. However, upward simulations parameterized by a downward simulation greater than the identity cannot be used in our framework since they do not generally imply inclusion of languages of tuples of states.

every $(r_1,\ldots,r_n)$ with $(q_1,\ldots,q_n) \preceq (r_1,\ldots,r_n)$, there is $r' \in Q$ such that $q' \preceq r'$ and $(r_1,\ldots,r_n) \xrightarrow{a} r'$. From $(q_1,\ldots,q_n) \xrightarrow{a} q'$ and $q_1 \preceq r_1$, we have that there is some rule $(r_1,q_2,\ldots,q_n) \xrightarrow{a} s_1$ such that $q' \preceq s_1$. From the existence of $(r_1,q_2,\ldots,q_n) \xrightarrow{a} s_1$ and from $q_2 \preceq r_2$, we then get that there is some rule $(r_1,r_2,q_3,\ldots,q_n) \xrightarrow{a} s_2$ such that $s_1 \preceq s_2$, etc. Since the maximal upward simulation is transitive [1], we obtain the property mentioned above. This in turn implies Lemma 6.

7.2   Tree Automata Universality Checking

We now show how upward simulations can be used for optimized universality checking on tree automata. Let $\mathcal{A} = (\Sigma, Q, F, \Delta)$ be a tree automaton. We define $T_n^\square(\Sigma)$ as the set of all open trees over Σ with n leaves. We say that an n-tuple $(q_1,\ldots,q_n)$ of states of $\mathcal{A}$ is universal if $\mathcal{L}^\square(\mathcal{A})(q_1,\ldots,q_n) = T_n^\square(\Sigma)$, this is, all open trees with n leaves constructible over Σ can be accepted from $(q_1,\ldots,q_n)$. A set of macro-states $MStates$ is universal if all tuples in $MStates^*$ are universal. From Lemma 5, we can deduce that $\mathcal{A}$ is universal (i.e., $L(\mathcal{A}) = T(\Sigma)$) if and only if $\{I_a \mid a \in \Sigma_0\}$ is universal.

The following Lemma allows us to design a new TA universality checking algorithm in a similar manner to Algorithm 1 using Optimizations 1 and 2 from Section 3.

Lemma 7. *For any $\preceq \in \mathcal{A}^\subseteq$ and two tuples of macro-states of $\mathcal{A}$, we have $(R_1,\ldots,R_n) \preceq^{\forall\exists} (P_1,\ldots,P_n)$ implies $\mathcal{L}^\square(\mathcal{A})(R_1,\ldots,R_n) \subseteq \mathcal{L}^\square(\mathcal{A})(P_1,\ldots,P_n)$.*

Algorithm 3 describes our approach to checking universality of tree automata in pseudocode. It resembles closely Algorithm 1. There are two main differences: (1) The initial value of the *Next* set is the result of applying the function *Initialize* to the set $\{Minimize(I_a) \mid a \in \Sigma_0\}$. *Initialize* returns the set of all macro-states in $\{Minimize(I_a) \mid a \in \Sigma_0\}$, which are minimal w.r.t. $\preceq^{\forall\exists}$ (i.e., those macro states with the best chance of finding a counterexample to universality). (2) The computation of the *Post*-image of a set of macro-states is a bit more complicated. More precisely, for each symbol $a \in \Sigma_n, n \in \mathbb{N}$, we have to compute the post image of each n-tuple of macro-states

---

Algorithm 3. *Tree Automata Universality Checking*

Input: A tree automaton $\mathcal{A} = (\Sigma, Q, F, \Delta)$ and a relation $\preceq \in \mathcal{A}^\subseteq$.
Output: TRUE if $\mathcal{A}$ is universal. Otherwise, FALSE.

1 **if** $\exists a \in \Sigma_0$ *such that I_a is rejecting* **then return** *FALSE*;
2 *Processed*:=$\emptyset$;
3 *Next*:= *Initialize*$\{Minimize(I_a) \mid a \in \Sigma_0\}$;
4 **while** *Next* $\neq \emptyset$ **do**
5   Pick and remove a macro-state R from *Next* and move it to *Processed*;
6   **foreach** $P \in \{Minimize(R') \mid R' \in Post(Processed)(R)\}$ **do**
7   **if** *P is a rejecting macro-state* **then return** *FALSE*;
8   **else if** $\nexists Q \in Processed \cup Next$ *s.t.* $Q \preceq^{\forall\exists} P$ **then**
9   Remove all Q from $Processed \cup Next$ s.t. $P \preceq^{\forall\exists} Q$;
10   Add P to *Next*;

11 **return** *TRUE*

---

from the set. We design the algorithm such that we avoid computing the *Post*-image of a tuple more than once. We define the *Post*-image $Post(MStates)(R)$ of a set of macro-states *MStates* w.r.t. a macro-states $R \in MStates$. It is the set of all macro-states $P = Post_a(P_1, \ldots, P_n)$ where $a \in \Sigma_n, n \in \mathbb{N}$ and R occurs at least once in the tuple $(P_1, \ldots, P_n) \in MStates^*$. Formally, $Post(MStates)(R) = \bigcup_{a \in \Sigma}\{Post_a(P_1, \ldots, P_n) \mid n = \#(a), P_1, \ldots, P_n \in MStates, R \in \{P_1, \ldots, P_n\}\}$.

The following theorem states correctness of Algorithm 3, which can be proved using similar invariants as in the case of Algorithm 1 when the notion of distance from an accepting state is suitably defined (see [2] for more details).

Theorem 2. *Algorithm 3 always terminates, and returns* TRUE *if and only if the input tree automaton $\mathcal{A}$ is universal.*

7.3 Tree Automata Language Inclusion Checking

We are interested in testing language inclusion of two tree automata $\mathcal{A} = (\Sigma, Q_{\mathcal{A}}, F_{\mathcal{A}}, \Delta_{\mathcal{A}})$ and $\mathcal{B} = (\Sigma, Q_{\mathcal{B}}, F_{\mathcal{B}}, \Delta_{\mathcal{B}})$. From Lemma 5, we have that $L(\mathcal{A}) \subseteq L(\mathcal{B})$ iff for every tuple $a_1, \ldots, a_n$ of symbols from Σ_0, $L^\square(\mathcal{A})(I_{a_1}^{\mathcal{A}}, \ldots, I_{a_n}^{\mathcal{A}}) \subseteq L^\square(\mathcal{B})(I_{a_1}^{\mathcal{B}}, \ldots, I_{a_n}^{\mathcal{B}})$. In other words, for any $a_1, \ldots, a_n \in \Sigma_0$, every open tree that can be accepted from a tuple of states from $I_{a_1}^{\mathcal{A}} \times \ldots \times I_{a_n}^{\mathcal{A}}$ can also be accepted from a tuple of states from $I_{a_1}^{\mathcal{B}} \times \ldots \times I_{a_n}^{\mathcal{B}}$. This justifies a similar use of the notion of product-states as in Section 5. We define the language of a tuple of product-states as $L^\square(\mathcal{A}, \mathcal{B})((q_1, P_1), \ldots, (q_n, P_n)) := L^\square(\mathcal{A})(q_1, \ldots, q_n) \setminus L^\square(\mathcal{B})(P_1, \ldots, P_n)$. Observe that we obtain that $L(\mathcal{A}) \subseteq L(\mathcal{B})$ iff the language of every n-tuple (for any $n \in \mathbb{N}$) of product-states from the set $\{(i, I_a^{\mathcal{B}}) \mid a \in \Sigma_0, i \in I_a^{\mathcal{A}}\}$ is empty.

Our algorithm for testing language inclusion of tree automata will check whether it is possible to reach a product-state of the form (q, P) with $q \in F_{\mathcal{A}}$ and $P \cap F_{\mathcal{B}} = \emptyset$ (that we call accepting) from a tuple of product-states from $\{(i, I_a^{\mathcal{B}}) \mid a \in \Sigma_0, i \in I_a^{\mathcal{A}}\}$. The following lemma allows us to use Optimization 1(a) and Optimization 2 from Section 5.

Lemma 8. *Let $\preceq \in (\mathcal{A} \cup \mathcal{B})^\subseteq$. For any two tuples of states and two tuples of product-states such that $(p_1, \ldots, p_n) \preceq (r_1, \ldots, r_n)$ and $(R_1, \ldots, R_n) \preceq^{\forall \exists} (P_1, \ldots, P_n)$, we have $L^\square(\mathcal{A}, \mathcal{B})((p_1, P_1), \ldots, (p_n, P_n)) \subseteq L^\square(\mathcal{A}, \mathcal{B})((r_1, R_1), \ldots, (r_n, R_n))$.*

It is also possible to use Optimization 1(b) where we stop searching from product-states of the form (q, P) such that $q \preceq r$ for some $r \in P$. However, note that this optimization is of limited use for tree automata. Under the assumption that the automata $\mathcal{A}$ and $\mathcal{B}$ do not contain useless states, the reason is that for any $q \in Q_{\mathcal{A}}$ and $r \in Q_{\mathcal{B}}$, if q appears at a left-hand side of some rule of arity more than 1, then no reflexive relation from $\preceq \in (\mathcal{A} \cup \mathcal{B})^\subseteq$ allows $q \preceq r$.[3]

Algorithm 4 describes our method for checking language inclusion of TA in pseudocode. It closely follows Algorithm 2. It differs in two main points. First, the initial value of the *Next* set is the result of applying the function *Initialize* on the set

---

[3] To see this, assume that an open tree t is accepted from $(q_1, \ldots, q_n) \in Q_{\mathcal{A}}^n, q = q_i, 1 \leq i \leq n$. If $q \preceq r$, then by the definition of $\preceq$, $t \in L^\square(\mathcal{A} \cup \mathcal{B})(q_1, \ldots, q_{i-1}, r, q_{i+1}, \ldots, q_n)$. However, that cannot happen, as $\mathcal{A} \cup \mathcal{B}$ does not contain any rules with left hand sides containing both states from $\mathcal{A}$ and states from $\mathcal{B}$.

Algorithm 4. *Tree Automata Language Inclusion Checking*

Input: TAs $\mathcal{A}$ and $\mathcal{B}$ over an alphabet Σ. A relation $\preceq \in (\mathcal{A} \cup \mathcal{B})^{\subseteq}$.

Output: TRUE if $L(\mathcal{A}) \subseteq L(\mathcal{B})$. Otherwise, FALSE.

1 **if** *there exists an accepting product-state in* $\bigcup_{a \in \Sigma_0} \{(i, I_a^{\mathcal{B}}) \mid i \in I_a^{\mathcal{A}}\}$ **then return** *FALSE*;

2 *Processed*:=$\emptyset$;

3 *Next*:=*Initialize*($\bigcup_{a \in \Sigma_0} \{(i, Minimize(I_a^{\mathcal{B}})) \mid i \in I_a^{\mathcal{A}}\}$);

4 **while** *Next* $\neq \emptyset$ **do**

5 | Pick and remove a product-state (r, R) from *Next* and move it to *Processed*;

6 | **foreach** $(p, P) \in \{(r', Minimize(R')) \mid (r', R') \in Post(Processed)(r, R)\}$ **do**

7 | | **if** (p, P) *is an accepting product-state* **then return** *FALSE*;

8 | | **else if** $\nexists p' \in P$ *s.t.* $p \preceq p'$ **then**

9 | | | **if** $\nexists (q, Q) \in Processed \cup Next$ *s.t.* $p \preceq q \wedge Q \preceq^{\forall\exists} P$ **then**

10 | | | | Remove all (q, Q) from *Processed* $\cup$ *Next* s.t. $q \preceq p \wedge P \preceq^{\forall\exists} Q$;

11 | | | | Add (p, P) to *Next*;

12 **return** *TRUE*

$\{(i, Minimize(I_a^{\mathcal{B}})) \mid a \in \Sigma_0, i \in I_a^{\mathcal{A}}\}$, where *Initialize* is the same function as in Algorithm 2. Second, the computation of the *Post* image of a set of product-states means that for each symbol $a \in \Sigma_n, n \in \mathbb{N}$, we construct the $Post_a$-image of each n-tuple of product-states from the set. Like in Algorithm 3, we design the algorithm such that we avoid computing the $Post_a$-image of a tuple more than once. We define the post image $Post(PStates)(r, R)$ of a set of product-states *PStates* w.r.t. a product-state $(r, R) \in PStates$. It is the set of all product-states (q, P) such that there is some $a \in \Sigma, \#(a) = n$ and some n-tuple $((q_1, P_1), \ldots, (q_n, P_n))$ of product-states from *PStates* that contains at least one occurrence of (r, R), where $q \in Post_a(q_1, \ldots, q_n)$ and $P = Post_a(P_1, \ldots, P_n)$.

Theorem 3. *Algorithm 4 always terminates, and returns* TRUE *iff* $L(\mathcal{A}) \subseteq L(\mathcal{B})$.

8 Experimental Results

In this section, we describe our experimental results. We concentrated on experiments with inclusion checking, since it is more common than universality checking in various symbolic verification procedures, decision procedures, etc. We compared our approach, parameterized by maximal simulation (or, for tree automata, maximal upward simulation), with the previous pure antichain-based approach of [13], and with classical subset-construction-based approach. We implemented all the above in OCaml. We used the algorithm in [9] for computing maximal simulations. In order to make the figures easier to read, we often do not show the results of the classical algorithm, since in all of the experiments that we have done, the classical algorithm performed much worse than the other two approaches.

8.1 The Results on NFA

For language inclusion checking of NFA, we tested our approach on examples generated from the intermediate steps of a tool for abstract regular model checking [5]. In total,

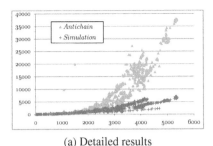

Size	Antichain	Simulation
0 - 1000	0.059	0.099
1000 - 2000	1.0	0.7
2000 - 3000	3.6	1.69
3000 - 4000	11.2	3.2
4000 - 5000	20.1	4.79
5000 -	33.7	6.3

(a) Detailed results

(b) Average execution time for different NFA pair sizes (in seconds)

Fig. 3. Language inclusion checking on NFAs generated from a regular model checker

we have 1069 pairs of NFA generated from different verification tasks, which included verifying a version of the bakery algorithm, a system with a parameterized number of producers and consumers communicating through a double-ended queue, the bubble sort algorithm, an algorithm that reverses a circular list, and a Petri net model of the readers/writers protocol (cf. [5,4] for a detailed description of the verification problems). In Fig. 3 (a), the horizontal axis is the sum of the sizes of the pairs of automata[4] whose language inclusion we check, and the vertical axis is the execution time (the time for computing the maximal simulation is included). Each point denotes a result from inclusion testing for a pair of NFA. Fig. 3 (b) shows the average results for different NFA sizes. From the figure, one can see that our approach has a much better performance than the antichain-based one. Also, the difference between our approach and the antichain-based approach becomes larger when the size of the NFA pairs increases. If we compare the average results on the smallest 1000 NFA pairs, our approach is 60% slower than the the antichain-based approach. For the largest NFA pairs (those with size larger than 5000), our approach is 5.32 times faster than the the antichain-based approach.

We also tested our approach using NFA generated from random regular expressions. We have two different tests: (1) language inclusion does not always hold and (2) language inclusion always holds[5]. The result of the first test is in Fig. 4(a). In the figure, the horizontal axis is the sum of the sizes of the pairs of automata whose language inclusion we check, and the vertical axis is the execution time (the time for computing the maximal simulation is included). From Fig. 4(a), we can see that the performance of our approach is much more stable. It seldom produces extreme results. In all of the cases we tested, it always terminates within 10 seconds. In contrast, the antichain-based approach needs more than 100 seconds in the worst case. The result of the second test is in Fig. 4(b) where the horizontal axis is the length of the regular expression and the vertical axis is the average execution time of 30 cases in milliseconds. From Fig. 4(b), we observe that our approach has a much better performance than the antichain-based approach if the language inclusion holds. When the length of the regular expression is 900, our approach is almost 20 times faster than the antichain-based approach.

---

[4] We measure the size of the automata as the number of their states.

[5] To get a sufficient number of tests for the second case, we generate two NFA $\mathcal{A}$ and $\mathcal{B}$ from random regular expressions, build their union automaton $\mathcal{C} = \mathcal{A} \cup \mathcal{B}$, and test $L(\mathcal{A}) \subseteq L(\mathcal{C})$.

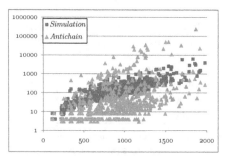
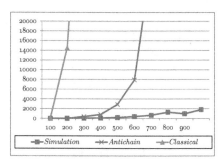

(a) Language inclusion does not always hold   (b) Language inclusion always holds

Fig. 4. Language inclusion checking on NFA generated from regular expressions

When the maximal simulation relation $\preceq$ is given, a natural way to accelerate the language inclusion checking is to use $\preceq$ to minimize the size of the two input automata by merging $\preceq$-equivalent states. In this case, the simulation relation becomes sparser. A question arises whether our approach has still a better performance than the antichain-based approach in this case. Therefore, we also evaluated our approach under this setting. Here again, we used the NFA pairs generated from abstract regular model checking [5]. The results show that although the antichain-based approach gains some speed-up when combined with minimization, it is still slower than our approach. The main reason is that in many cases, simulation holds only in one direction, but not in the other. Our approach can also utilize this type of relation. In contrast, the minimization algorithm merges only simulation equivalent states.

We have also evaluated the performance of our approach using backward language inclusion checking combined with maximal backward simulation. As De Wulf et al. [13] have shown in their paper, backward language inclusion checking of two automata is in fact equivalent to the forward version on the reversed automata. This can be easily generalized to our case. The result is very consistent to what we have obtained; our algorithm is still significantly better than the antichain-based approach.

8.2 The Results on TA

For language inclusion checking on TA, we tested our approach on 86 tree automata pairs generated from the intermediate steps of a regular tree model checker [3] while verifying the algorithm of re-balancing red-black trees after insertion or deletion of a leaf node. The results are given in Table 1. Our approach has a much better performance when the size of a TA pair is large. For TA pairs of size smaller than 200, our approach is on average 1.39 times faster than the antichain-based approach.

Table 1. Language inclusion checking on TA

Size	Antichain (*sec.*)	Simulation (*sec.*)	Diff.	# of Pairs
0 - 200	1.05	0.75	140%	29
200 - 400	11.7	4.7	246%	15
400 - 600	65.2	19.9	328%	14
600 - 800	3019.3	568.7	531%	13
800 - 1000	4481.9	840.4	533%	5
1000 - 1200	11761.7	1720.9	683%	10

However, for those of size above 1000, our approach is on average 6.8 times faster than the antichain-based approach.

9 Conclusion

We have introduced several original ways to combine simulation relations with antichains in order to optimize algorithms for checking universality and inclusion on NFA. We have also shown how the proposed techniques can be extended to the domain of tree automata. This was achieved by introducing the notion of languages of open trees accepted from tuples of tree automata states and using the maximal upward simulations parameterized by the identity proposed in our earlier work [1]. We have implemented the proposed techniques and performed a number of experiments showing that our techniques can provide a very significant improvement over currently known approaches. In the future, we would like to perform even more experiments, including, e.g., experiments where our techniques will be incorporated into the entire framework of abstract regular (tree) model checking or into some automata-based decision procedures. Apart from that, it is also interesting to develop the described techniques for other classes of automata (notably Büchi automata) and use them in a setting where the transitions of the automata are represented not explicitly but symbolically, e.g., using BDDs.

References

1. Abdulla, P.A., Bouajjani, A., Holík, L., Kaati, L., Vojnar, T.: Computing Simulations over Tree Automata. In: Ramakrishnan, C.R., Rehof, J. (eds.) TACAS 2008. LNCS, vol. 4963, pp. 93–108. Springer, Heidelberg (2008)
2. Abdulla, P.A., Chen, Y.-F., Holík, L., Mayr, R., Vojnar, T.: When Simulation Meets Antichains (On Checking Language Inclusion of Nondeterministic Finite (Tree) Automata). Technical report, FIT-TR-2010-001, FIT, Brno University of Technology, Czech Republic (2010)
3. Bouajjani, A., Habermehl, P., Holík, L., Touili, T., Vojnar, T.: Antichain-Based Universality and Inclusion Testing over Nondet. Finite Tree Automata. In: Ibarra, O.H., Ravikumar, B. (eds.) CIAA 2008. LNCS, vol. 5148, pp. 57–67. Springer, Heidelberg (2008)
4. Bouajjani, A., Habermehl, P., Moro, P., Vojnar, T.: Verifying Programs with Dynamic 1-Selector-Linked Structures in Regular Model Checking. In: Halbwachs, N., Zuck, L.D. (eds.) TACAS 2005. LNCS, vol. 3440, pp. 13–29. Springer, Heidelberg (2005)
5. Bouajjani, A., Habermehl, P., Vojnar, T.: Abstract Regular Model Checking. In: Alur, R., Peled, D.A. (eds.) CAV 2004. LNCS, vol. 3114, pp. 372–386. Springer, Heidelberg (2004)
6. Brzozowski, J.A.: Canonical Regular Expressions and Minimal State Graphs for Definite Events. In: Mathematical Theory of Automata (1962)
7. Dill, D.L., Hu, A.J., Wong-Toi, H.: Checking for Language Inclusion Using Simulation Preorders. In: Larsen, K.G., Skou, A. (eds.) CAV 1991. LNCS, vol. 575. Springer, Heidelberg (1992)
8. Henzinger, M.R., Henzinger, T.A., Kopke, P.W.: Computing simulations on finite and infinite graphs. In: Proc. 36th FOCS (1995)
9. Holík, L., Šimáček, J.: Optimizing an LTS-Simulation Algorithm. In: Proc. of MEMICS 2009 (2009)

10. Hopcroft, J.E.: An n.log n Algorithm for Minimizing States in a Finite Automaton. Technical Report CS-TR-71-190, Stanford University (1971)
11. Meyer, A.R., Stockmeyer, L.J.: The Equivalence Problem for Regular Expressions with Squaring Requires Exponential Space. In: Proc. of the 13th Annual Symposium on Switching and Automata Theory. IEEE CS, Los Alamitos (1972)
12. Møller, F. (2004), http://www.brics.dk/automaton
13. De Wulf, M., Doyen, L., Henzinger, T.A., Raskin, J.-F.: Antichains: A New Algorithm for Checking Universality of Finite Automata. In: Ball, T., Jones, R.B. (eds.) CAV 2006. LNCS, vol. 4144, pp. 17–30. Springer, Heidelberg (2006)

On Weak Modal Compatibility, Refinement, and the MIO Workbench

Sebastian S. Bauer, Philip Mayer, Andreas Schroeder, and Rolf Hennicker

Institut für Informatik, Ludwig-Maximilians-Universität München, Germany
{bauerse,mayer,schroeda,hennicker}@pst.ifi.lmu.de

Abstract. Building on the theory of modal I/O automata (MIOs) by
Larsen et al. we introduce a new compatibility notion called weak modal
compatibility. As an important property of behavioral interface theories
we prove that weak modal compatibility is preserved under weak modal
refinement. Furthermore, we organize and compare different notions of
refinement and compatibility to give an easily-accessible overview. Finally, we describe the MIO Workbench, an Eclipse-based editor and verification tool for modal I/O automata, which implements various refinement, compatibility and composition notions and is able to depict the
results of verification directly on the graphical representation of MIOs –
relations or state pairs in the positive and erroneous paths in the negative
case.

1 Introduction

Interface design has been a long-standing and important issue in the design of
software systems. Various methods of interface specifications, both static and
behavioral, have been suggested for software components [3,4]. We believe that
behavioral specifications for components are of particular importance, and focus
on such specifications in this paper.

Among the most widely accepted methods for specifying behavioral properties
of interfaces are I/O automata [15,16], which have been introduced to specify the
temporal ordering of events involving a component, explicitly taking communication aspects such as sending or receiving messages into consideration. Many
variations of these automata have been introduced over the years; for example
interface automata [5], timed interface automata [6], or resource automata [2].
At the same time, another aspect of interface behavior has been studied: Modal
automata [13] explicitly address the difference between required and optional
actions by using must and may transitions, which allow protocols and implementations to differ with regard to non-compulsory actions. Recently, both the
input/output and the may/must aspects of behavioral specifications have been
integrated [11], giving rise to modal I/O automata (MIOs).

Building on the basic formalisms for behavioral specifications such as MIOs,
we can use notions of interface compatibility and correct interface implementation (refinement) to verify component behavior; for a survey on compatibility
notions see [3]. Interface theories [4] are commonly used to precisely define these

J. Esparza and R. Majumdar (Eds.): TACAS 2010, LNCS 6015, pp. 175–189, 2010.
© Springer-Verlag Berlin Heidelberg 2010

requirements. Interface theories are tuples $(\mathcal{A}, \leq, \sim, \otimes)$ of a semantic domain $\mathcal{A}$, a refinement relation $\leq \subseteq \mathcal{A} \times \mathcal{A}$, a (symmetric) compatibility relation $\sim \subseteq \mathcal{A} \times \mathcal{A}$, and a (possibly partial) composition function $\otimes : \mathcal{A} \times \mathcal{A} \to \mathcal{A}$ satisfying the following three properties: Let $S, T, T', T'' \in \mathcal{A}$.

(1) Preservation of compatibility: If $S \sim T$ and $T' \leq T$ then $S \sim T'$.
(2) Compositional refinement: If $T' \leq T$ then $S \otimes T' \leq S \otimes T$.
(3) Transitivity of refinement: If $T'' \leq T'$ and $T' \leq T$ then $T'' \leq T$.

These three properties imply *independent implementability*, which is the basis for top-down component-based design.

Independent implementability states that in order to refine a given composed interface $S \otimes T$ towards an implementation, it suffices to independently refine S and T, say, to S' and T', respectively; then the refinements S' and T' are compatible and their composition refines the interface $S \otimes T$. More formally, let $(\mathcal{A}, \leq, \sim, \otimes)$ be an interface theory. Independent implementability means that if $S \sim T$, $S' \leq S$ and $T' \leq T$ hold, both $S' \sim T'$ and $S' \otimes T' \leq S \otimes T$ follow.

In this paper, we elaborate on the challenges of component behavior specification. We introduce new interface theories in the same line as in de Alfaro and Henzinger [4] for modal I/O automata with appropriate refinement and compatibility notions. We introduce the notion of *weak modal compatibility* which allows for loose coupling between interfaces and prove its preservation under weak modal refinement.

Another result of this paper is the organization and comparison of different existing and new notions of refinement and compatibility. We give an easily-accessible overview of these notions and their relationships.

Although I/O automata and modal automata have a long history, there is little tool support. Therefore, another major contribution of this paper is a verification tool and editor for MIOs – the MIO Workbench – which includes implementations of various refinement and compatibility notions, including but not limited to the ones which are part of our interface theories. We believe that the ability to automatically verify these properties is useful for both discussing the theory of MIOs as well as a foundation for practical applications.

This paper is structured as follows. We discuss modal I/O transition systems in Sect. 2. In Sect. 3, we introduce our notion of weak modal compatibility, followed by an overview of the different notions of refinement and compatibility in Sect. 4. Tool support for MIOs is discussed in Sect. 5. We conclude in Sect. 6.

2 Modal (I/O) Transition Systems

This first section is devoted to a short introduction to modal transition systems, and in particular modal *input/output* transition systems. A modal transition system is characterized by the fact that it has *two* transition relations, indicating allowed (*may*) and required (*must*) behavior. In this paper, we consider an extended version of the original modal transition systems [13] by including a signature which distinguishes between *internal* and *external* actions.

Definition 1 (Modal Transition System). *A modal transition system (MTS) $S = (states_S, start_S, (ext_S, int_S), \dashrightarrow_S, \longrightarrow_S)$ consists of a set of states $states_S$, an initial state $start_S \in states_S$, disjoint sets ext_S and int_S of external and internal actions where $act_S = ext_S \cup int_S$ denotes the set of (all) actions, a may-transition relation $\dashrightarrow_S \subseteq states_S \times act_S \times states_S$, and a must-transition relation $\longrightarrow_S \subseteq states_S \times act_S \times states_S$. The pair (ext_S, int_S) is called the signature of S.*

An MTS S is called *syntactically consistent* if every required transition is also allowed, i.e. it holds that $\longrightarrow_S \subseteq \dashrightarrow_S$. From now on we only consider syntactically consistent MTSs. Moreover, we call an MTS S an *implementation* if the two transition relations coincide, i.e. $\longrightarrow_S = \dashrightarrow_S$.

Modal I/O transition systems [11] further differentiate between two kinds of external actions, namely *input* and *output* actions.

Definition 2 (Modal I/O Transition System). *A modal I/O transition system (MIO) S is an MTS with the set of external actions ext_S partitioned into two disjoint sets in_S, out_S of input and output actions, respectively. The triple (in_S, out_S, int_S) is called the signature of S.*

The notions of syntactic consistency and implementation also apply for MIOs.

Example 1. Our running example in this paper is the specification (and implementation) of a flight booking service. In Fig. 1, the MIO T_0 specifying the service provider is depicted. For improving readability, output actions are suffixed with an exclamation mark (*!*) whereas input actions are suffixed with a question mark (*?*). Internal actions do not have any suffix.

In the initial state (indicated by a filled circle) the session is initiated by receiving *bookTicket?*, followed by the reception of the data of requested tickets in *ticketData?*. Then, a service implementation may ask the client for choosing a seat number (*seat!*) which it must be able to receive afterwards (*seatNo?*). The reservation of the tickets may be cancelled by the service provider (*fail!*) if the requested flight is fully booked, or the request is confirmed by sending *ok!*, which is followed by receiving the account data (*accountData?*) of the client. ∎

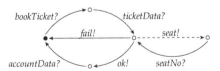

Fig. 1. Specification T_0 of a flight booking service

In the following, we recall the standard definition of refinement for modal transition systems, cf. [13]. The notion of refinement aims at capturing the relation between an abstract specification of an interface and a more detailed one, possibly an implementation of that interface. Thus, it allows for a stepwise refinement of an abstract specification towards an implementation.

The basic idea of *modal* refinement is that any required (*must*) transition in the abstract specification must also occur in the concrete specification. Conversely, any allowed (*may*) transition in the concrete specification must be allowed by the abstract specification. Moreover, in both cases the target states must conform to each other. Modal refinement has the following consequences: A concrete specification may leave out allowed transitions, but is required to keep all must transitions, and moreover, it is not allowed to perform more transitions than the abstract specification admits. The following definition of modal refinement is called *strong* since every transition that is taken into account must be simulated "immediately", i.e. without performing internal actions before.

Definition 3 (Strong Modal Refinement [13]). *Let S and T be MTSs (MIOs, resp.) with the same signature. A relation $R \subseteq states_S \times states_T$ is called strong modal refinement for S and T iff for all $(s,t) \in R$ and for all $a \in acts_S$ it holds that*

1. *if $t \xrightarrow{a}_T t'$ then there exists $s' \in states_S$ such that $s \xrightarrow{a}_S s'$ and $(s',t') \in R$,*
2. *if $s \dashrightarrow_S s'$ then there exists $t' \in states_T$ such that $t \dashrightarrow_T t'$ and $(s',t') \in R$.*

We say that S strongly modally refines T, written $S \leq_m T$, iff there exists a strong modal refinement for S and T containing $(start_S, start_T)$.

If both S and T are implementations, i.e. the must-transition relation coincides with the may-transition relation, then strong modal refinement coincides with (strong) bisimulation; if $\longrightarrow_T = \emptyset$ then it corresponds to simulation [17].

Example 2. In Fig. 2, a (possible) implementation T_1 of the flight booking service specified by the MIO T_0 in Fig. 1 is shown. In this particular implementation of the specification T_0, the optional output for asking the client for a particular seat number is never taken. However, all must-transitions of T_0 are retained in the implementation T_1, hence we have $T_1 \leq_m T_0$.   ∎

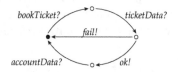

Fig. 2. Implementation T_1 of T_0

Next, we introduce a binary (synchronous) composition operator on MIOs. When two protocols (implementations), each one describing a particular component, can communicate by synchronous message passing, we are interested in computing the resulting protocol (implementation) of the composed system. Although composition can obviously be defined for MTSs, we directly give a definition for MIOs as this is our main interest.

It is convenient to restrict the composition operator to *composable* MIOs by requiring that overlapping of actions only happens on complementary types.

Definition 4 (Composability [11]). *Two MIOs S and T are called composable if $(in_S \cup int_S) \cap (in_T \cup int_T) = \emptyset$ and $(out_S \cup int_S) \cap (out_T \cup int_T) = \emptyset$.*

We now define composition of MIOs in a straightforward way by a binary partial function $\otimes$ synchronizing on matching (shared) actions.

Definition 5 (Composition [11]). *Two composable MIOs S_1 and S_2 can be composed to a MIO $S_1 \otimes S_2$ defined by states $_{S_1 \otimes S_2} = states_{S_1} \times states_{S_2}$, the initial state is given by $start_{S_1 \otimes S_2} = (start_{S_1}, start_{S_2})$, $in_{S_1 \otimes S_2} = (in_{S_1} \backslash out_{S_2}) \cup (in_{S_2} \backslash out_{S_1})$, $out_{S_1 \otimes S_2} = (out_{S_1} \backslash in_{S_2}) \cup (out_{S_2} \backslash in_{S_1})$, $int_{S_1 \otimes S_2} = int_{S_1} \cup int_{S_2} \cup (in_{S_1} \cap out_{S_2}) \cup (in_{S_2} \cap out_{S_1})$. The transition relations $\dashrightarrow_{S_1 \otimes S_2}$ and $\longrightarrow_{S_1 \otimes S_2}$ are given by, for each $\rightsquigarrow \in \{\dashrightarrow, \longrightarrow\}$,*

- *for all $i,j \in \{1,2\}, i \neq j$, for all $a \in (act_{S_1} \cap act_{S_2})$, if $s_i \overset{a}{\rightsquigarrow}_{S_i} s_i'$ and $s_j \overset{a}{\rightsquigarrow}_{S_j} s_j'$ then $(s_1, s_2) \overset{a}{\rightsquigarrow}_{S_1 \otimes S_2} (s_1', s_2')$,*
- *for all $a \in act_{S_1}$, if $s_1 \overset{a}{\rightsquigarrow}_{S_1} s_1'$ and $a \notin act_{S_2}$ then $(s_1, s_2) \overset{a}{\rightsquigarrow}_{S_1 \otimes S_2} (s_1', s_2)$,*
- *for all $a \in act_{S_2}$, if $s_2 \overset{a}{\rightsquigarrow}_{S_2} s_2'$ and $a \notin act_{S_1}$ then $(s_1, s_2) \overset{a}{\rightsquigarrow}_{S_1 \otimes S_2} (s_1, s_2')$.*

Composition of MIOs only synchronizes transitions with matching shared actions and same type of transition, i.e. a must-transition labeled with a shared action only occurs in the composition if there exist corresponding matching must-transitions in the original MIOs.

A well-known problem occurs when composing arbitrary MIOs S and T: If for a reachable state (s,t) in $S \otimes T$, S in state s is able to send out a message a shared with T, and T in state t is not able to receive a then this is considered as a compatibility problem since S may get stuck in this situation. We want to rule out this erroneous behavior by requiring that S and T must be *compatible*.

The following definition of strong compatibility is strongly influenced by [5] and [11]. Intuitively, two MIOs S and T are compatible if for every reachable state in the product $S \otimes T$, if S is able to provide an output which is shared with T, i.e. is in the input alphabet of T, then T must "immediately" be able to receive this message (and vice versa).

Definition 6 (Strong Modal Compatibility). *Let S and T be composable MIOs. S and T are called strongly modally compatible, denoted by $S \sim_{sc} T$, iff for all reachable states (s,t) in $S \otimes T$,*

1. *for all $a \in (out_S \cap in_T)$, if $s \overset{a}{\dashrightarrow}_S s'$ then there exists $t' \in states_T$ such that $t \overset{a}{\longrightarrow}_T t'$,*
2. *for all $a \in (out_T \cap in_S)$, if $t \overset{a}{\dashrightarrow}_T t'$ then there exists $s' \in states_S$ such that $s \overset{a}{\longrightarrow}_S s'$.*

Example 3. In Fig. 3, a specification S of a client of the flight booking service is shown. It is easily provable that indeed S and T_0 and also S and T_1 are strongly modally compatible, i.e. $S \sim_{sc} T_0$ and $S \sim_{sc} T_1$.   ■

For MIOs equipped with $\sim_{sc}$ and $\leq_m$, we obtain a valid interface theory.

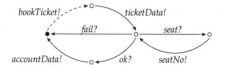

Fig. 3. Protocol S

Theorem 1. *Let S, T, T', T'' be MIOs, and let S and T be composable.*

1. *(Preservation) If $S \sim_{sc} T$ and $T' \leq_m T$ then $S \sim_{sc} T'$.*
2. *(Compositionality) If $T' \leq_m T$ then $S \otimes T' \leq_m S \otimes T$.*
3. *(Transitivity) If $T'' \leq_m T'$ and $T' \leq_m T$ then $T'' \leq_m T$.*

The proof of statement 1 is given in [1]; statement 2 is a consequence of a result in [13] (where it has been proved that every static construct – for which $\otimes$ is a special case – is compositional for $\leq_m$) and statement 3 follows directly from the definition of $\leq_m$.

Remark 1. The compatibility notions used in this paper follow a *pessimistic* approach: two MIOs S and T are only compatible if no communication error between S and T can occur in *any* environment of $S \otimes T$. A different approach to compatibility is the *optimistic* one, cf. [11,5]: two MIOs S and T are compatible if they are compatible for any "helpful" environment in the sense that the environment never provides outputs that would cause the product $S \otimes T$ to run in a state (s, t) with incompatible states s and t.

3   Weak Modal Compatibility

The refinement presented in the last section is strong in the sense that every must-transition in the protocol must be *immediately* simulated in the implementation and conversely, every may-transition in the implementation must be *immediately* simulated in the protocol. This definition can be weakened by including the notion of *weak transitions*.

For denoting weak transitions, given a MIO S and an action $a \in ext_S$, we write $s \xrightarrow{a}{}^*_S s'$ iff there exist states $s_1, s_2 \in states_S$ such that

$$s(\xrightarrow{\tau}_S)^* s_1 \xrightarrow{a}_S s_2 (\xrightarrow{\tau}_S)^* s'$$

where $t(\xrightarrow{\tau}_T)^* t'$ stands for finitely many transitions with internal actions leading from t to t'; including no transition and in this case $t = t'$. The label τ always denotes an arbitrary internal action. Moreover, we write

$$s \xrightarrow{\hat{a}}{}^*_S s' \text{ iff either } s \xrightarrow{a}{}^*_S s' \text{ and } a \in ext_S, \text{ or } s(\xrightarrow{\tau}_S)^* s' \text{ and } a \notin ext_S.$$

Both notations are analogously used for may-transitions.

Similar to the generalization of bisimulation to weak bisimulation [17], one can introduce a notion of modal refinement in a weak form: Every (non-weak) must-transition in the protocol must be simulated in the implementation by a weak must-transition, and conversely, every (non-weak) may-transition in the implementation must be simulated by a weak may-transition in the protocol. This form of weak modal refinement was originally introduced in [10].

Definition 7 (Weak Modal Refinement [10]). *Let S and T be MTSs (MIOs, resp.) with the same signature.[1] A relation $R \subseteq states_S \times states_T$ is called a weak modal refinement for S and T iff for all $(s,t) \in R$, for all $a \in acts_S$ it holds that*

1. *if $t \xrightarrow{a}_T t'$ then there exists $s' \in states_S$ such that $s \xrightarrow{\hat{a}}{}^*_S s'$ and $(s',t') \in R$,*

2. *if $s \dashrightarrow{a}_S s'$ then there exists $t' \in states_T$ such that $t \dashrightarrow{\hat{a}}{}^*_T t'$ and $(s',t') \in R$.*

We say that S weakly modally refines T, denoted by $S \leq^*_m T$, iff there exists a weak modal refinement for S and T containing $(start_S, start_T)$.

Example 4. In Fig. 4, another implementation T_2 of T_0 is presented which, after receiving *bookTicket?*, performs an internal action *log* with the meaning of executing an internal logging operation. T_0 does not specify any internal actions, so we have $T_2 \not\leq_m T_0$, but weak modal refinement allows to postpone the further execution of *ticketData?* (according to protocol T_0) until some internal (must)-transitions are passed through. It follows that $T_2 \leq^*_m T_0$.   ∎

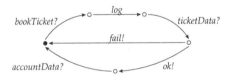

Fig. 4. Implementation T_2 of T_0

Let us recall our goal. We want to find appropriate notions of refinement and compatibility for component behavior specifications. In order to obtain a valid interface theory involving weak modal refinement we have to make sure that, given a suitable compatibility notion, compatibility is preserved under refinement. The following example shows that strong compatibility is *not* preserved by weak modal refinement.

Example 5. S and T_0 are strongly compatible and $T_2 \leq^*_m T_0$. But S and T_2 are not strongly compatible, since S is able to send out the message *ticketData* to T_2, but T_2, being in the state before performing *log*, is not able to receive the message immediately.   ∎

---

[1] More generally, in the weak case, one could also allow that S and T have arbitrary (non related) internal actions.

Obviously, internal actions are not adequately considered in the definition of compatibility. Dealing with this problem requires a new definition of compatibility, which we call *weak modal compatibility*. The intuition behind weak modal compatibility follows from the previous example: If a MIO *may* send out a certain message to its partner, we consider this transaction as compatible if the other MIO *must* be able to receive it, possibly performing some internal must steps in between. Note that the *must* modality is essential here: If internal *may* transitions would be allowed then this path could be omitted in further refinements and therefore compatibility of implementations would not be ensured anymore.

In the following, given a MIO S and an action $a \in ext_S$, we write $s \xrightarrow{a}_S^{\triangleleft} s'$ iff there exists a state $s'' \in states_S$ such that

$$s(\xrightarrow{\tau}_S)^* s'' \xrightarrow{a}_S s'.$$

Moreover, $s \xrightarrow{\hat{a}}_S^{\triangleleft} s'$ denotes $s \xrightarrow{a}_S^{\triangleleft} s'$ if $a \in ext_S$, otherwise $s(\xrightarrow{\tau}_S)^* s'$. Both notations are analogously used for may-transitions.

Definition 8 (Weak Modal Compatibility). *Let S and T be composable MIOs. S and T are called weakly modally compatible, denoted by $S \sim_{wc} T$, iff for all reachable states (s, t) in $S \otimes T$,*

1. *for all $a \in (out_S \cap in_T)$, if $s \dashrightarrow_S^a s'$ then there exists $t' \in states_T$ such that $t \xrightarrow{a}_T^{\triangleleft} t'$,*

2. *for all $a \in (out_T \cap in_S)$, if $t \dashrightarrow_T^a t'$ then there exists $s' \in states_S$ such that $s \xrightarrow{a}_S^{\triangleleft} s'$.*

Obviously, it holds that $S \sim_{sc} T$ implies $S \sim_{wc} T$.

Example 6. Looking back to our examples, it can be easily verified that S is weakly modally compatible with both T_0 and T_2 since the reception of *ticketData* in T_2 must take place after the internal must transition labeled with *log*. ∎

Based on the MIO formalism, weak modal compatibility $\sim_{wc}$ and weak modal refinement $\leq_m^*$ satisfy the desired properties of an interface theory.

Theorem 2. *Let S, T, T', T'' be MIOs, and let S and T be composable.*

1. *(Preservation) If $S \sim_{wc} T$ and $T' \leq_m^* T$ then $S \sim_{wc} T'$.*
2. *(Compositionality) If $T' \leq_m^* T$ then $S \otimes T' \leq_m^* S \otimes T$.*
3. *(Transitivity) If $T'' \leq_m^* T'$ and $T' \leq_m^* T$ then $T'' \leq_m^* T$.*

The proof of statement 1 is given in [1]; statement 2 is a consequence of a result in [10] (where it has been proved that $\otimes$ is a binary, τ-insensitive operator on MTSs with input/output labels and therefore $\otimes$ is compositional for $\leq_m^*$) and statement 3 follows directly from the definition of $\leq_m^*$.

4   Overview of Refinement and Compatibility Notions

In order to complete the picture of existing notions of modal refinements for modal transition systems and their relationships to the notions of compatibility defined here, we also consider may-weak modal refinement, which has been defined in [12] (and, under the name of observational modal refinement, in [11]) to generalize alternating simulation [5]. May-weak modal refinement keeps the strong requirement for required (must-)transitions (as in strong modal refinement, but restricted to external actions), but has a weak condition for allowed (may-)transitions: every allowed transition in the more concrete MTS must be simulated by an allowed transition in the abstract MTS, possibly preceded by finitely many internal transitions.

Definition 9 (May-Weak Modal Refinement [12]). *Let S and T be MTSs (MIOs, resp.) with the same signature. A relation $R \subseteq states_S \times states_T$ is called may-weak modal refinement for S and T iff for all $(s,t) \in R$ it holds that*

1. *for all $a \in ext_T$, if $t \xrightarrow{a}_T t'$ then there exists $s' \in states_S$ such that $s \xrightarrow{a}_S s'$ and $(s',t') \in R$,*

2. *for all $a \in act_S$, if $s \dashrightarrow^{a}_S s'$ then there exists $t' \in states_T$ such that $t \dashrightarrow^{\hat{a}}{}^{\triangleleft}_T t'$ and $(s',t') \in R$.*

We say that S may-weakly modally refines T, denoted by $S \leq^{\triangleleft}_m T$, iff there exists a may-weak modal refinement for S and T containing $(start_S, start_T)$.

Given MIOs as the underlying formalism, may-weak modal refinement together with strong modal compatibility forms a valid interface theory.

Theorem 3. *Let S, T, T', T'' be MIOs, and let S and T be composable.*

1. *(Preservation) If $S \sim_{sc} T$ and $T' \leq^{\triangleleft}_m T$ then $S \sim_{sc} T'$.*
2. *(Compositionality) If $T' \leq^{\triangleleft}_m T$ then $S \otimes T' \leq^{\triangleleft}_m S \otimes T$.*
3. *(Transitivity) If $T'' \leq^{\triangleleft}_m T'$ and $T' \leq^{\triangleleft}_m T$ then $T'' \leq^{\triangleleft}_m T$.*

The proof of Thm. 3 is given in [1].

So far, we have considered three modal refinement notions. Obviously, for any two modal transition systems (or MIOs) S and T we have

Fact 1. if $S \leq_m T$ then $S \leq^*_m T$;
Fact 2. if $S \leq_m T$ then $S \leq^{\triangleleft}_m T$.

The converses of the above implications do obviously not hold; moreover, it is also obvious that weak modal refinement does not imply may-weak modal refinement. However, also may-weak modal refinement does not imply weak modal refinement since condition 1 in Def. 9 only considers external actions; for instance, for T and T' in Fig. 5, $T' \leq^{\triangleleft}_m T$ but $T' \not\leq^*_m T$ since the internal must transition of T is not respected by T' which would be required for weak modal refinement.

Table 1. Overview of preservation of compatibility under refinement

	Strong Compatibility $\sim_{sc}$	Weak Compatibility $\sim_{wc}$
Strong Refinement $\leq_m$	✓ (Thm. 1)	✓ (Fact 1 & Thm. 2)
Weak Refinement $\leq_m^*$	✗ (Ex. 5)	✓ (Thm. 2)
May-Weak Refinement $\leq_m^\lhd$	✓ (Thm. 3)	✗ (Ex. 7)

We have shown that all modal refinements are compositional w.r.t. $\otimes$, but they substantially differ when preservation of strong/weak compatibility is considered. Table 1 summarizes the relationships between modal refinement and compatibility notions; a checkmark indicates that compatibility is preserved under refinement.

Example 7. Weak compatibility is not preserved under may-weak modal refinement, as shown in Fig. 5. ∎

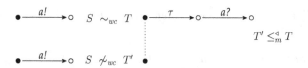

Fig. 5. Counterexample

5 The MIO Workbench

In the previous sections, we have illustrated the sometimes subtle distinctions between different definitions of refinement and compatibility. During our work, we have come to appreciate the help of implementations of our formal notions, which were an unflinching partner in finding inconsistencies and confirming counterexamples. To aid ourselves and others, we have implemented a complete set of verification notions and surrounding functionality for working with modal I/O automata – the MIO Workbench, an Eclipse-based editor and verification tool for modal I/O automata, which we present here for the first time.

Workbench Features. The most direct and intuitive way to work with MIOs is using a graphical editing facility based on a graph of nodes (states) and edges (transitions) as well as accompanying labels. The first feature provided by the workbench is thus a

(1) *Graphical Editor*, allowing to create new or change existing MIOs.

The implementation of the different notions of refinement and compatibility are the next features of the MIO Workbench:

(2) *Refinement Verification.* These include strong, may-weak, and weak modal refinement.

(3) *Compatibility Verification.* We support the notions of strong (with and without "helpful" environment, cf. [5]), and weak modal compatibility.

Furthermore, it is interesting to see an actual composition of composable MIOs:

(4) *Composition Operation* on MIOs.

The output of a composition operation is either the composed MIO or a list of problematic actions which caused the composition to fail.

Considering refinement and compatibility verification, we can get two very important, but very different results. First, if refinement or compatibility is possible, we get refinement relation(s) and matching states for compatibility, respectively. However – and this is even more important – if the verification fails, we get the error states and the error transitions in the two automata, i.e. the exact position(s) which led to the erroneous outcome.

Visualizing these results in a graphical way is very important. Therefore, the workbench also includes:

(5) *Refinement relation and state match view.* If a refinement or compatibility verification was successful, the workbench graphically displays the relation or the matching states side-by-side between the two input MIOs.

(6) *Problem view including error states and unmatched actions.* If a refinement or compatibility verification was not successful, the workbench graphically displays, side-by-side, the path which led to an erroneous state, and the transition possible in one automaton, but not in the other.

On the technical side, the MIO Workbench is based on the Eclipse platform. We use an Eclipse Modeling Framework (EMF)-based metamodel for MIOs, which enables persistence and simple access to concrete automata. The workbench integrates into Eclipse by adding MIO-specific file handling and the new MIO editor as well as the verification view. The MIO Workbench is extensible with regard to new notions of refinement, compatibility, and composition, by means of standard Eclipse extension points.

User Interface. Fig. 6 shows the MIO editor inside the Eclipse workbench. On the left-hand side, the project explorer shows MIOs stored on the file system as .mio files; on the right-hand side, the editor for one of these MIOs is displayed. A MIO is displayed in the classical way by using nodes as states and edges as transitions. Each transition has a type (must or may), which is indicated by a square or diamond, respectively. Furthermore, each transition also stands for an internal, input, or output action. An input action is colored green and is suffixed with a question mark (*?*). An output action is colored red and is suffixed with an exclamation mark (*!*). Finally, an internal action is gray and does not have a suffix. The MIO editor offers all the usual operations such as adding new nodes, moving them around, changing labels, types, and re-layouting.

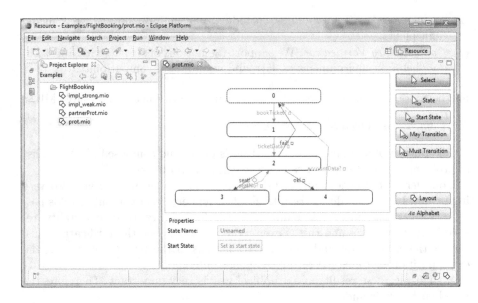

Fig. 6. MIO Workbench editor

The verification view of the MIO Workbench is the central access point to the verification functionality. It features a side-by-side view of two modal I/O automata, which can then be analyzed for refinement or compatibility, or composed.

Fig. 7 shows verification of the protocol T_0 (left) and implementation T_2 (right) from Ex. 4 using weak modal refinement, such that $T_2 \leq^*_m T_0$, which is indicated by the green top and the green arrows between related states.

As said above, the most interesting results are negative cases, i.e. if a refinement does not exist or compatibility does not hold. In this case, the MIO

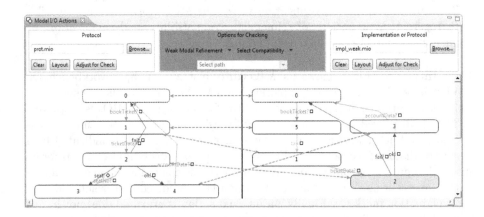

Fig. 7. MIO Workbench refinement view

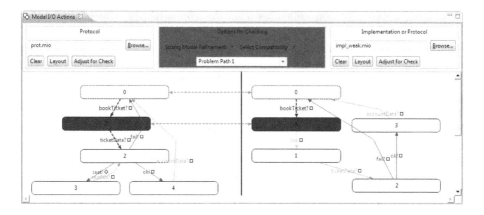

Fig. 8. MIO Workbench showing refinement problem

Workbench displays the possible error paths, each indicating a state pair in violation and the corresponding erroneous action.

Fig. 8 shows the visualization of Ex. 4 again, but this time using strong modal refinement. Thus, we can take the *bookTicket?* action on both sides, marked in dark red, arriving at the state pair *(1,5)*. Here, the protocol T_0 can take the *ticketData?* action, also marked in dark red, which the implementation T_2 is unable to follow. Since it is a *must*, there is no relation in this case, which is indicated by the red top and the dark red actions.

The MIO Workbench contains additional helpful features such as automatically laying out MIOs, adjusting an alphabet of a MIO by hiding non-shared labels for a compatibility or refinement check, and more.

The Workbench in Context. To our knowledge, the MIO Workbench is the first tool for modal I/O automata which includes a full set of refinement, compatibility, and composition notions as well as a (graphical) MIO editor.

Perhaps the closest related tool is MTSA [7], which includes a (text-based) editor and implementations of refinement as well as composition of modal automata. As the MIO Workbench is based on modal *input/output* automata as first class citizens, it differs by including compatibility verification based on I/O information; furthermore, it includes a graphical editor and a side-by-side graphical result view. There are also tools for I/O automata (i.e. without modality), for example the command-line based IOA toolset [9] for plain I/O automata or the Eclipse-based Tempo Toolkit [14] which deals with timed I/O automata; however, none of those considers both modality and communication aspects available in MIOs.

6   Conclusion

In this paper, we have presented an overview of modal I/O automata and various notions of modal refinement and compatibility. We have motivated the need for a new compatibility notion called *weak modal compatibility*, which allows the passing of internal actions. We have shown this compatibility notion to hold under weak modal refinement, and we have given an overview of the relationships between modal refinements and compatibility notions introduced in this paper.

On the practical side, we have presented a verification tool and graphical editor for modal I/O automata called the MIO Workbench, which implements various refinement and compatibility notions based on MIOs. We believe that tool support is of great help for discussing modal I/O automata and may serve in research, teaching, and as a prototype for industrial applications. The MIO Workbench can be freely downloaded from www.miowb.net.

As future work, we plan to extend our notions of compatibility to new use cases identified from practical service specifications and from distributed systems with asynchronous communication. It also looks interesting to investigate compatibility in the context of a new semantics for MTSs introduced recently in [8].

Acknowledgements. We would like to thank Alexander Knapp who has pointed out the need for a more flexible compatibility relation between interface specifications. This research has been partially supported by the GLOWA-Danube project 01LW0602A2 sponsored by the German Federal Ministry of Education and Research, the EC project SENSORIA, IST-2005-016004, and the EC project REFLECT, IST-2007-215893.

References

1. Bauer, S.S., Mayer, P., Schroeder, A., Hennicker, R.: On weak modal compatibility, refinement, and the MIO Workbench. Technical Report 1001, Institut für Informatik, Ludwig-Maximilians-Universität München (January 2010)
2. Chakrabarti, A., de Alfaro, L., Henzinger, T.A., Stoelinga, M.: Resource interfaces. In: Alur, R., Lee, I. (eds.) EMSOFT 2003. LNCS, vol. 2855, pp. 117–133. Springer, Heidelberg (2003)
3. Clarke, E.M., Sharygina, N., Sinha, N.: Program compatibility approaches. In: de Boer, F.S., Bonsangue, M.M., Graf, S., de Roever, W.-P. (eds.) FMCO 2005. LNCS, vol. 4111, pp. 243–258. Springer, Heidelberg (2006)
4. de Alfaro, L., Henzinger, T.A.: Interface theories for component-based design. In: Henzinger, T.A., Kirsch, C.M. (eds.) EMSOFT 2001. LNCS, vol. 2211, pp. 148–165. Springer, Heidelberg (2001)
5. de Alfaro, L., Henzinger, T.A.: Interface-based Design. In: Broy, M., Grünbauer, J., Harel, D., Hoare, C.A.R. (eds.) Engineering Theories of Software-intensive Systems. NATO Science Series: Mathematics, Physics, and Chemistry, vol. 195, pp. 83–104. Springer, Heidelberg (2005)
6. de Alfaro, L., Henzinger, T.A., Stoelinga, M.: Timed interfaces. In: Sangiovanni-Vincentelli, A.L., Sifakis, J. (eds.) EMSOFT 2002. LNCS, vol. 2491, pp. 108–122. Springer, Heidelberg (2002)
7. D'Ippolito, N., Fischbein, D., Foster, H., Uchitel, S.: MTSA: Eclipse support for modal transition systems construction, analysis and elaboration. In: Cheng, L.-T., Orso, A., Robillard, M.P. (eds.) ETX, pp. 6–10. ACM, New York (2007)

8. Fischbein, D., Braberman, V.A., Uchitel, S.: A sound observational semantics for modal transition systems. In: Leucker, M., Morgan, C. (eds.) Theoretical Aspects of Computing - ICTAC 2009. LNCS, vol. 5684, pp. 215–230. Springer, Heidelberg (2009)

9. Garland, S.J., Lynch, N.: Using I/O automata for developing distributed systems. In: Leavens, G.T., Sitaraman, M. (eds.) Foundations of Component-Based Systems, pp. 285–312. Cambridge University Press, Cambridge (2000)

10. Hüttel, H., Larsen, K.G.: The use of static constructs in a modal process logic. In: Meyer, A.R., Taitslin, M.A. (eds.) Logic at Botik 1989. LNCS, vol. 363, pp. 163–180. Springer, Heidelberg (1989)

11. Larsen, K.G., Nyman, U., Wasowski, A.: Modal I/O automata for interface and product line theories. In: De Nicola, R. (ed.) ESOP 2007. LNCS, vol. 4421, pp. 64–79. Springer, Heidelberg (2007)

12. Larsen, K.G., Nyman, U., Wasowski, A.: On modal refinement and consistency. In: Caires, L., Vasconcelos, V.T. (eds.) CONCUR 2007. LNCS, vol. 4703, pp. 105–119. Springer, Heidelberg (2007)

13. Larsen, K.G., Thomsen, B.: A modal process logic. In: LICS, pp. 203–210. IEEE Computer Society, Los Alamitos (1988)

14. Lynch, N., Michel, L., Shvartsman, A.: Tempo: A toolkit for the timed input/output automata formalism. In: SIMUTools. Industrial Track: Simulation Works. Conference Proc. CD, paper 3105, Marseille, France, 8 pages (2008)

15. Lynch, N.A., Tuttle, M.R.: Hierarchical correctness proofs for distributed algorithms. In: PODC, pp. 137–151 (1987)

16. Lynch, N.A., Tuttle, M.R.: An introduction to input/output automata. CWI Quarterly 2, 219–246 (1989)

17. Milner, R.: Communication and Concurrency. International Series in Computer Science. Prentice Hall, Englewood Cliffs (1989)

Rational Synthesis

Dana Fisman[1], Orna Kupferman[1], and Yoad Lustig[2]

[1] School of Computer Science and Engineering, Hebrew University, Jerusalem 91904, Israel
[2] Rice University, Houston Texas 77005, USA

Abstract. *Synthesis* is the automated construction of a system from its specification. The system has to satisfy its specification in all possible environments. Modern systems often interact with other systems, or agents. Many times these agents have objectives of their own, other than to fail the system. Thus, it makes sense to model system environments not as hostile, but as composed of *rational agents*; i.e., agents that act to achieve their own objectives.

We introduce the problem of synthesis in the context of rational agents (*rational synthesis*, for short). The input consists of a temporal-logic formula specifying the system, temporal-logic formulas specifying the objectives of the agents, and a solution concept definition. The output is an implementation T of the system and a profile of strategies, suggesting a behavior for each of the agents. The output should satisfy two conditions. First, the composition of T with the strategy profile should satisfy the specification. Second, the strategy profile should be an equilibrium in the sense that, in view of their objectives, agents have no incentive to deviate from the strategies assigned to them, where "no incentive to deviate" is interpreted as dictated by the given solution concept. We provide a method for solving the rational-synthesis problem, and show that for the classical definitions of equilibria studied in game theory, rational synthesis is not harder than traditional synthesis. We also consider the multi-valued case in which the objectives of the system and the agents are still temporal logic formulas, but involve payoffs from a finite lattice.

1 Introduction

Synthesis is the automated construction of a system from its specification. The basic idea is simple and appealing: instead of developing a system and verifying that it adheres to its specification, we would like to have an automated procedure that, given a specification, constructs a system that is correct by construction. The first formulation of synthesis goes back to Church [8]; the modern approach to synthesis was initiated by Pnueli and Rosner, who introduced LTL (linear temporal logic) synthesis [24]. The *LTL synthesis problem* receives as input a specification given in LTL and outputs a reactive system modeled by a finite-state transducer satisfying the given specification — if such exists. It is important to distinguish between system outputs, controlled by the system, and system inputs, controlled by the environment. A system should be able to cope with all values of the input signals, while setting the output signals to desired values [24]. Therefore, the quantification structure on input and output signals is different. Input signals are universally quantified while output signals are existentially quantified.

Modern systems often interact with other systems. For example, the clients interacting with a server are by themselves distinct entities (which we call agents) and are

J. Esparza and R. Majumdar (Eds.): TACAS 2010, LNCS 6015, pp. 190–204, 2010.

many times implemented by systems. In the traditional approach to synthesis, the way in which the environment is composed of its underlying agents is abstracted. In particular, the agents can be seen as if their only objective is to conspire to fail the system. Hence the term "hostile environment" that is traditionally used in the context of synthesis. In real life, however, many times agents have goals of their own, other than to fail the system. The approach taken in the field of algorithmic game theory [21] is to assume that agents interacting with a computational system are *rational*, i.e., agents act to achieve their own goals. Assuming agents rationality is a restriction on the agents behavior and is therefore equivalent to restricting the universal quantification on the environment. Thus, the following question arises: can system synthesizers capitalize on the rationality and goals of agents interacting with the system?

Consider for example a peer-to-peer network with only two agents. Each agent is interested in downloading infinitely often, but has no incentive to upload. In order, however, for one agent to download, the other agent must upload. More formally, for each $i \in \{0, 1\}$, Agent i controls the bits u_i ("Agent i tries to upload") and d_i ("Agent i tries to download"). The objective of Agent i is *always eventually* $(d_i \wedge u_{1-i})$. Assume that we are asked to synthesize the protocol for Agent 0. It is not hard to see that the objective of Agent 0 depends on his input signal, implying he cannot ensure his objective in the traditional synthesis sense. On the other hand, suppose that Agent 0, who is aware of the objective of Agent 1, declares and follows the following TIT FOR TAT strategy: I will upload at the first time step, and from that point onward I will reciprocate the actions of Agent 1. Formally, this amounts to initially setting u_0 to **True** and for every time $k > 0$, setting u_0 at time k to equal u_1 at time $k - 1$. It is not hard to see that, against this strategy, Agent 1 can only ensure his objective by satisfying Agent 0 objective as well. Thus, assuming Agent 1 acts rationally, Agent 0 can ensure his objective.

The example above demonstrates that a synthesizer can capitalize on the rationality of the agents that constitute its environment. When synthesizing a protocol for rational agents, we still have no control on their actions. We would like, however, to generate a strategy for each agent (a *strategy profile*) such that once the strategy profile is given to the agents, then a rational agent would have no incentive to deviate from the strategy suggested to him and would follow it. Such a strategy profile is called in game theory a *solution* to the game. Accordingly, the *rational synthesis* problem gets as input temporal-logic formulas specifying the objective φ_0 of the system, the objectives $\varphi_1, \ldots, \varphi_n$ of the agents that constitute the environment, and a solution concept definition. The desired output is a system and a strategy profile for the agents such that the following hold. First, if all agents adhere to their strategies, then the result of the interaction of the system and the agents satisfies φ_0. Second, once the system is in place, and the agent are playing a game among themselves, the strategy profile is a solution to this game according to the given solution concept.[1]

A well known solution concept is *Nash equilibrium* [19]. A strategy profile is in Nash equilibrium if no agent has an incentive to deviate from his assigned strategy, provided that the other agents adhere to the strategies assigned to them. For example, if the TIT FOR TAT strategy for Agent 0 is suggested to both agents in the peer-to-peer example,

---

[1] For a formal definition of *rational synthesis*, see Definition 1.

then the pair of strategies is a Nash equilibrium. Indeed, for all $i \in \{0, 1\}$, if Agent i assumes that Agent $1 - i$ adheres to his strategy, then by following the strategy, Agent i knows that his objective would be satisfied, and he has no incentive to deviate from it. The stability of a Nash equilibrium depends on the players assumption that the other players adhere to the strategy. In some cases this is a reasonable assumption. Consider, for example, a standard protocol published by some known authority such as IEEE. When a programmer writes a program implementing the standard, he tends to assume that his program is going to interact with other programs that implement the same standard. If the published standard is a Nash equilibrium, then there is no incentive to write a program that deviates from the standard. Game theory suggests several *solution concepts*, all capturing the idea that the participating agents have no incentive to deviate from the protocol (or strategy) assigned to them. We devise a method to solve rational synthesis for the suggested solution concepts. In fact, our method works for all solution concept that can be defined in Extended Strategy Logic (see Section 4). We show that for the well-studied solution concepts [21] of dominant-strategies solution, Nash equilibrium, and subgame-perfect Nash equilibrium, rational synthesis is not harder than traditional synthesis (both are 2EXPTIME-complete).

An important facet in the task of a rational synthesizer is to synthesize a system such that once it is in place, the game played by the agents has a solution with a favorable outcome. *Mechanism design*, studied in game theory and economy [20,21], is the study of designing a game whose outcome (assuming players rationality) achieves some goal. Rational synthesis can be viewed as a variant of mechanism design in which the game is induced by the objective of the system, and the objectives of both the system and the agents refer to their on-going interaction and are specified by temporal-logic formulas.

Having defined rational synthesis, we turn to solve it. In [5], the authors introduced *strategy logic* – an extension of temporal logic with first order quantification over strategies. The rich structure of strategy logic enables it to specify properties like the existence of a Nash-equilibrium. While [5] does not consider the synthesis problem, the technique suggested there can be used in order to solve the rational-synthesis problem for Nash equilibrium and dominant strategies. Strategy logic, however, is not sufficiently expressive in order to specify subgame-perfect-Nash equilibrium [26] which, as advocated in [28] (see also Section 3), is the most suited for infinite multiplayer games — those induced by rational synthesis. The weakness of strategy logic is its inability to quantify over game histories. We extend strategy logic with history variables, and show that the extended logic is sufficiently expressive to express rational synthesis for the traditional solution concepts. Technically, adding history variables to strategy logic results in a *memoryful logic* [16], in which temporal logic formulas have to be evaluated not along paths that start at the present, but along paths that start at the root and go through the present.

Classical applications of game theory consider games with real-valued payoffs. For example, agents may bid on goods or grade candidates. In the peer-to-peer network example, one may want to refer to the amount of data uploaded by each agent, or one may want to add the possibility of pricing downloads. The full quantitative setting is undecidable already in the context of model checking [1]. Yet, several special cases for which the problem is decidable have been studied [2]. We can distinguish between cases in which decidability is achieved by restricting the type of systems [1], and cases in which it is achieved by restricting the domain of values [11]. We solve the quantitative rational synthesis problem for the case the domain of values is a finite distributive De Morgan lattice. The lattice setting is a good starting point to the quantitative setting. First, lattices have been successfully handled for easier problems, and in particular, multi-valued synthesis [12,13]. In addition, lattices are sufficiently rich to express interesting quantitative properties. This is sometime immediate (for example, in the peer-to-peer network, one can refer to the different attributions of the communication channels, giving rise to the lattice of the subsets of the attributions), and sometimes thanks to the fact that real values can often be abstracted to finite linear orders. From a technical point of view, our contribution here is a solution of a latticed game in which the value of the game cannot be obtained by joining values obtained by different strategies, which is unacceptable in synthesis.

Related Work. Already early work on synthesis has realized that working with a hostile environment is often too restrictive. The way to address this point, however, has been by adding assumptions on the environment, which can be part of the specification (c.f., [3]). The first to consider the game-theoretic approach to dealing with rationality of the environment in the context of LTL synthesis were Chatterjee and Henzinger [6]. The setting in [6], however, is quite restricted; it considers exactly three players, where the third player is a fair scheduler, and the notion of *secure equilibria* [4]. Secure equilibrium, introduced in [4], is a Nash equilibria in which each of the two players prefers outcomes in which only his objective is achieved over outcomes in which both objectives are achieved, which he still prefers over outcomes in which his objective is not achieved. It is not clear how this notion can be extended to multiplayer games, and to the distinction we make here between controllable agents that induce the game (the system) and rational agents (the environment). Also, the set of solution concepts we consider is richer.

Ummels [28] was the first to consider subgame perfect equilibria in the context of infinite multiplayer games. The setting there is of turn-based games and the solution goes via a reduction to 2-player games. Here, we consider concurrent games and therefore cannot use such a reduction. Another difference is that [28] considers parity winning conditions whereas we use LTL objectives. In addition, the fact that the input to the rational synthesis problem does not include a game makes the memoryful nature of subgame perfect equilibria more challenging, as we cannot easily reduce the LTL formulas to memoryless parity games.

To the best of our knowledge, we are the first to handle the multi-valued setting. As we show, while the lattice case is decidable, its handling required a nontrivial extension of both the Boolean setting and the algorithms known for solving latticed games [13].

2   Preliminaries

We consider *infinite concurrent multiplayer games* (in short, *games*) defined as follows. A *game arena* is a tuple $\mathcal{G} = \langle V, v_0, I, (\Sigma_i)_{i \in I}, (\Gamma_i)_{i \in I}, \delta \rangle$, where V is a set of nodes, v_0 is an initial node, I is a set of players, and for $i \in I$, the set Σ_i is the set of actions of Player i and $\Gamma_i : V \to 2^{\Sigma_i}$ specifies the actions that Player i can take at each node.

Let $I = \{1, \ldots, n\}$. Then, the transition relation $\delta : V \times \Sigma_1 \times \cdots \times \Sigma_n \to V$ is a deterministic function mapping the current node and the current choices of the agents to the successor node. The transition function may be restricted to its relevant domain. Thus, $\delta(v, \sigma_1, \ldots, \sigma_n)$ is defined for $v \in V$ and $\langle \sigma_1, \ldots, \sigma_n \rangle \in \Gamma_1(v) \times \cdots \times \Gamma_n(v)$.

A *position* in the game is a tuple $\langle v, \sigma_1, \sigma_2, \ldots, \sigma_n \rangle$ with $v \in V$ and $\sigma_i \in \Gamma_i(v)$ for every $i \in I$. Thus, a position describes a state along with possible choices of actions for the players in this state. Consider a sequence $p = p_0 \cdot p_1 \cdot p_2 \cdots$ of positions. For $k \geq 0$, we use $node(p_k)$ to denote the state component of p_k, and use $p_k[i]$, for $i \in I$, to denote the action of Player i in p_k. The notations extend to p in the straightforward way. Thus, $node(p)$ is the projection of p on the first component. We say that p is a *play* if the transitions between positions is consistent with δ. Formally, p is a *play starting at node* v if $node(p_0) = v$ and for all $k \geq 0$, we have $node(p_{k+1}) = \delta(p_k)$. We use $\mathcal{P}_{\mathcal{G}}$ (or simply $\mathcal{P}$ when $\mathcal{G}$ is clear from the context) to denote all possible plays of $\mathcal{G}$.

Note that at every node $v \in V$, each player i chooses an action $\sigma_i \in \Gamma_i(v)$ simultaneously and independently of the other players. The game then proceeds to the successor node $\delta(v, \sigma_1, \ldots, \sigma_n)$. A *strategy* for Player i is a function $\pi_i : V^+ \mapsto \Sigma_i$ that maps histories of the game to an action suggested to Player i. The suggestion has to be consistent with Γ_i. Thus, for every $v_0 v_1 \cdots v_k \in V^+$, we have $\pi_i(v_0 v_1 \cdots v_k) \in \Gamma_i(v_k)$. Let Π_i denote the set of possible strategies for Player i. For a set of players $I = \{1, \ldots, n\}$, a *strategy profile* is a tuple of strategies $\langle \pi_1, \pi_2, \ldots, \pi_n \rangle \in \Pi_1 \times \Pi_2 \times \cdots \times \Pi_n$. We denote the strategy profile by $(\pi_i)_{i \in I}$ (or simply π, when I is clear from the context). We say that p is an *outcome* of the profile π if for all $k \geq 0$ and $i \in I$, we have $p_k[i] = \pi_i(node(p_0) \cdot node(p_1) \cdots node(p_k))$. Thus, p is an outcome of π if all the players adhere to their strategies in π. Note that since δ is deterministic, π fixes a single play from each state of the game. Given a profile π we denote by $outcome(\pi)^{\mathcal{G}}$ (or simply $outcome(\pi)$) the one play in $\mathcal{G}$ that is the outcome of π when starting in v_0. Given a strategy profile π and a nonempty sequence of nodes $h = v_0 v_1 \ldots v_k$, we define the *shift of π by h* as the strategy profile $(\pi_i^h)_{i \in I}$ in which for all $i \in I$ and all histories $w \in V^*$, we have $\pi_i^h(w) = \pi_i(h \cdot w)$. We denote by $outcome(\pi)_h^{\mathcal{G}}$ (or simply $outcome(\pi)_h$) the concatenation of $v_0 v_1 \ldots v_{k-1}$ with the one play in $\mathcal{G}$ that is the outcome of π^h when starting in v_k. Thus, $outcome(\pi)_h$ describes the outcome of a game that has somehow found itself with history h, and from that point, the players behave if the history had been h. Given a profile $(\pi_i)_{i \in I}$, an index $j \in I$, and a strategy π_j' for Player j, we use (π_{-j}, π_j') to refer to the profile of strategies in which the strategy for all players but j is as in π, and the strategy for Player j is π_j'. Thus, $(\pi_{-j}, \pi_j') = \langle \pi_1, \pi_2, \ldots, \pi_{j-1}, \pi_j', \pi_{j+1}, \ldots, \pi_n \rangle$.

3   Rational Synthesis

In this section we define the problem of rational synthesis. We work with the following model: the world consists of the *system* and a set of n agents *Agent 1, ..., Agent n*. For uniformity we refer to the system as *Agent 0*. We assume that Agent i controls a set X_i of variables, and the different sets are pairwise disjoint. At each point in time, each agent sets his variables to certain values. Thus, an action of *Agent i* amounts to assigning values to his variables. Accordingly, the set of actions of *Agent i* is given by 2^{X_i}. We use X to denote $\bigcup_{0 \leq i \leq n} X_i$. We use X_{-i} to denote $X \setminus X_i$ for $0 \leq i \leq n$.

Each of the agents (including the system) has an objective. The objective of an agent is formulated via a linear temporal logic formula (LTL [23]) over the set of variables of all agents.[2] We use φ_i to denote the objective of *Agent i*.

This setting induces the game arena $\mathcal{G} = \langle V, v_0, I, (\Sigma_i)_{i \in I}, (\Gamma_i)_{i \in I}, \delta \rangle$ defined as follows. The set of players $I = \{0, 1, \ldots, n\}$ consists of the system and the agents. The moves of agent i are all the possible assignments to its variables. Thus, $\Sigma_i = 2^{X_i}$. We use Σ, Σ_i, and Σ_{-i} to denote the sets 2^X, 2^{X_i}, and $2^{X_{-i}}$, respectively. An agent can set his variables as he wishes throughout the game. Thus $\Gamma_i(v) = \Sigma_i$ for every $v \in V$. The game records in its vertices all the actions taken by the agents so far. Hence, $V = \Sigma^*$ and for all $v \in \Sigma^*$ and $\langle \sigma_0, \ldots, \sigma_n \rangle \in \Sigma$, we have $\delta(v, \sigma_0, \ldots, \sigma_n) = v \cdot \langle \sigma_0, \ldots, \sigma_n \rangle$.

At each moment in time, the system gets as input an assignment in Σ_{-0} and it generates as output an assignment in Σ_0. For every possible history $h \in (\Sigma_{-0} \cup \Sigma_0)^*$ the system should decide what $\sigma_0 \in \Sigma_0$ it outputs next. Thus, a strategy for the system is a function $\pi_0 : \Sigma^* \to \Sigma_0$ (recall that $\Sigma = \Sigma_{-0} \cup \Sigma_0$ and note that indeed $V^+ = \Sigma^*$). In the standard synthesis problem, we say that π_0 realizes φ_0 if all the computations that π_0 generates satisfy φ_0. In rational synthesis, on the other hand, we also generate strategies for the other agents, and the single computation that is the outcome of all the strategies should satisfy φ_0. That is, we require $outcome(\pi)^{\mathcal{G}} \models \varphi_0$ where $\mathcal{G}$ is as defined above. In addition, we should generate the strategies for the other agents in a way that would guarantee that they indeed adhere to their strategies.

Recall that while we control the system, we have no control on the behaviors of *Agent 1*, ..., *Agent n*. Let $\pi_0 : \Sigma^* \to \Sigma_0$ be a strategy for the system in $\mathcal{G}$. Then, π_0 induces the game $\mathcal{G}_{\pi_0} = \langle \Sigma^*, \epsilon, I, (\Sigma_i)_{i \in I}, (\Gamma_i')_{i \in I}, \delta \rangle$, where for $i \in I \setminus \{0\}$, we have $\Gamma_i' = \Gamma_i$, and $\Gamma_0'(w) = \{\pi_0(w_{-0})\}$, where w_{-0} is obtained from w by projecting its letters on Σ_{-0}. Recall that δ is restricted to the relevant domain. Thus, as Γ_0' is deterministic, we can regard $\mathcal{G}_{\pi_0}$ as an n-player (rather than $n + 1$-player) game. Note that $\mathcal{G}_{\pi_0}$ contains all the possible behaviors of *Agent 1*, ..., *Agent n*, when the system adheres to π_0.

Definition 1 (Rational Synthesis). *Consider a solution concept γ. The problem of rational synthesis (with solution concept γ) is to return, given LTL formulas $\varphi_0, \varphi_1, \ldots, \varphi_n$, specifying the objectives of the system and the agents constituting its environment, a strategy profile $\pi = \langle \pi_0, \pi_1, \ldots, \pi_n \rangle \in \Pi_0 \times \Pi_1 \times \cdots \times \Pi_n$ such that both (a) $outcome(\pi)^{\mathcal{G}} \models \varphi_0$ and (b) the strategy profile $\langle \pi_1, \ldots, \pi_n \rangle$ is a solution in the game $\mathcal{G}_{\pi_0}$ with respect to the solution concept γ.*

The rational-synthesis problem gets a solution concept as a parameter. As discussed in Section 1, the fact $\langle \pi_1, \ldots, \pi_n \rangle$ is a solution with respect to the concept guarantees that it is not worthwhile for the agents constituting the environment to deviate from the strategies assigned to them. Several solution concepts are studied and motivated in game theory. We focus on three leading concepts, and we first recall their definitions and motivations in game theory. The common setting in game theory is that the objective for each player is to maximize his *payoff* – a real number that is a function of the play. We use $payoff_i : \mathcal{P} \to \mathbb{R}$ to denote the payoff function of player i. That is, $payoff_i$

---

[2] We could have worked with any other ω-regular formalism for specifying the objectives. We chose LTL for simplicity of the presentation.

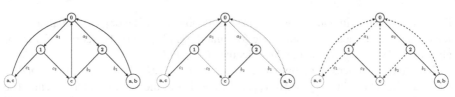

assigns to each possible play p a real number $payoff_i(p)$ expressing the payoff of i on p. For a strategy profile π we use (with a slight abuse of notation) $payoff_i(\pi)$ to abbreviate $payoff_i(outcome(\pi))$.

The simplest and most appealing solution concept is dominant-strategies solution. A *dominant strategy* is a strategy that a player can never lose by adhering to, regardless of the strategies of the other players. Therefore, if there is a profile of strategies π in which all strategies π_i are dominant, then no player has an incentive to deviate from the strategy assigned to him in π. Formally, π is a *dominant strategy profile* if for every $1 \le i \le n$ and for every (other) profile π', we have that $payoff_i(\pi') \le payoff_i(\pi'_{-i}, \pi_i)$. Consider, for example, a game played by three players: Alice, Bob and Charlie whose actions are $\{a_1, a_2\}$, $\{b_1, b_2\}$ and $\{c_1, c_2\}$, respectively. The game is played on the game arena depicted in the left of Figure above. The labels on the edges are marked by the possible action moves. Each player wants to visit infinitely often a node marked by his initial letter. In this game, Bob's strategy of choosing b_1 from Node 2 is a dominant strategy. All of the strategies of Charlie are dominating. Alice, though, has no dominating strategy. Unfortunately, in many games some agents do not have dominant strategies, thus no dominant-strategy solution exists. Naturally, if no dominant strategy solution exists, one would still like to consider other solution concepts.

Another well known solution concept is Nash equilibrium [19]. A strategy profile is *Nash equilibrium* if no player has an incentive to deviate from his strategy in π provided he assumes the other players adhere to the strategies assigned to them in π. Formally, π is a *Nash equilibrium profile* if for every $1 \le i \le n$ and for every (other) strategy π'_i for player i, we have that $payoff_i(\pi_{-i}, \pi'_i) \le payoff_i(\pi)$. For example, the strategy profile depicted in the middle of Figure above by dotted edges is a Nash equilibrium of the game to its left. Knowing the strategy of the other players, each player cannot gain by deviating from his strategy.

An important advantage of Nash equilibrium is that a Nash equilibrium exists in almost every game [22].[3] A weakness of Nash equilibrium is that it is not nearly as stable as a dominant-strategy solution: if one of the other players deviates from his assigned strategy, nothing is guaranteed.

Nash equilibrium is suited to a type of games in which the players make all their decisions without knowledge of other players choices. The type of games considered in rational synthesis, however, are different, as players do have knowledge about the choices of the other players in earlier rounds of the game. To see the problem that this setting poses for Nash equilibrium, let us consider the ULTIMATUM game. In ULTIMATUM, Player 1 chooses a value $x \in [0, 1]$, and then Player 2 chooses whether to accept the choice, in which case the payoff of Player 1 is x and the payoff of Player 2 is $1 - x$, or to reject the choice, in which case the payoff of both players is 0. One Nash

---

[3] In particular, all n-player turn-based games with ω-regular objectives have Nash equilibrium [7].

equilibrium in ULTIMATUM is $\pi = \langle \pi_1, \pi_2 \rangle$ in which π_1 advises Player 1 to always choose $x = 1$ and π_2 advises Player 2 to always reject. It is not hard to see that π is indeed a Nash equilibrium. In particular, if Player 2 assumes that Player 1 follows π_1, he has no incentive to deviate from π_2. Still, the equilibrium is unstable. The reason is that π_2 is inherently not credible. If Player 1 chooses x smaller than 1, it is irrational for Player 2 to reject, and Player 1 has no reason to assume that Player 2 adheres to π_2. This instability of a Nash equilibrium is especially true in a setting in which the players have information about the choices made by the other players. In particular, in ULTIMATUM, Player 1 knows that Player 2 would make his choice after knowing what x is.

To see this problem in the setting of infinite games, consider the strategy profile depicted in the right of Figure above by dashed edges. This profile is also a Nash equilibrium of the game in the left of the figure. It is, however, not very rational. The reason is that if Alice deviates from her strategy by choosing a_2 rather than a_1 then it is irrational for Bob to stick to his strategy. Indeed, if he sticks to his strategy he does not meet his objective, yet if he deviates and chooses b_1 he does meet his objective.

This instability of Nash equilibrium has been addressed in the definition of subgame-perfect equilibrium [26]. A strategy profile π is in *subgame-perfect equilibrium (SPE)* if for every possible history of the game, no player has an incentive to deviate from his strategy in π provided he assumes the other players adhere to the strategies assigned to them in π. Formally, π is an SPE profile if for every possible history h of the game, player $1 \le i \le n$, and strategy π_i' for player i, we have that $payoff_i(\pi_{-i}, \pi_i')_h \le payoff_i(\pi)_h$. The dotted strategy depicted in the middle of Figure above is a subgame-perfect equilibrium. Indeed, it is a Nash equilibrium from every possible node of the arena, including non-reachable ones.

In the context of on-going behaviors, real-valued payoffs are a big challenge and most works on reactive systems use Boolean temporal-logic as a specification language. Below we adjust the definition of the three solution concepts to the case the objectives are LTL formulas.[4] Essentially, the adjustment is done by assuming the following simple payoffs: If the objective φ_i of Agent i holds, then his payoff is 1; otherwise his payoff is 0. The induced solution concepts are then as followed. Consider a strategy profile $\pi = \langle \pi_1, \ldots, \pi_n \rangle$.

- We say that π is a *dominant strategy profile* if for every $1 \le i \le n$ and profile π', if $outcome(\pi') \models \varphi_i$, then $outcome(\pi_{-i}', \pi_i) \models \varphi_i$.
- We say that π is a *Nash equilibrium profile* if for every $1 \le i \le n$ and strategy π_i', if $outcome(\pi_{-i}, \pi_i') \models \varphi_i$, then $outcome(\pi) \models \varphi_i$.
- We say that π is a *subgame-perfect equilibrium profile* if for every history $h \in \Sigma^*$, $1 \le i \le n$, and strategy π_i', if $outcome(\pi_{-i}, \pi_i')_h \models \varphi_i$, then $outcome(\pi)_h \models \varphi_i$.

4   Solution in the Boolean Setting

In this section we solve the rational-synthesis problem. Let $I = \{0, 1, \ldots, n\}$ denote the set of agents. Recall that $\Sigma_i = 2^{X_i}$ and $\Sigma = 2^X$, where $X = \cup_{i \in I} X_i$, and that the partition of the variables among the agents induces a game arena with states in

---

[4] In Section 5, we make a step towards generalizing the framework to the multi-valued setting and consider the case the payoffs are taken from a finite distributive lattice.

Σ^*. Expressing rational synthesis involves properties of strategies and histories. *Strategy Logic* [5] is a logic that treats strategies in games as explicit first-order objects. Given an LTL formula ψ and strategy variables $z_0, \ldots, z_n$ ranging over strategies of the agents, the strategy logic formula $\psi(z_0, \ldots, z_n)$ states that ψ holds in the outcome of the game in which Agent i adheres to the strategy z_i. The use of existential and universal quantifiers on strategy variables enables strategy logic to state that a given profile consists of dominant strategies or is a Nash equilibrium. However, strategy logic is not strong enough to state the existence of a subgame perfect equilibrium. The reason is that a formula $\varphi(z_0, \ldots, z_n)$ in strategy logic assumes that the strategies $z_0, \ldots, z_n$ are computed from the initial vertex of the game, and it cannot refer to histories that diverge from the strategies. We therefore extend strategy logic with first order variables that range over arbitrary histories of the game.

Extended Strategy Logic.   Formulas of *Extended Strategy Logic* (ESL) are defined with respect to a game $\mathcal{G} = \langle V, v_0, I, (\Sigma_i)_{i \in I}, (\Gamma_i)_{i \in I}, \delta \rangle$, a set $\mathbb{H}$ of history variables, and sets $\mathbb{Z}_i$ of strategy variables for $i \in I$. Let $I = \{0, \ldots, n\}$, $\Sigma = \Sigma_0 \times \cdots \times \Sigma_n$, and let ψ be an LTL formula over Σ. Let h be a history variable in $\mathbb{H}$, and let $z_0, \ldots, z_n$ be strategy variables in $\mathbb{Z}_0, \ldots, \mathbb{Z}_n$, respectively. We use z as an abbreviation for $(z_0, \ldots, z_n)$. The set of ESL formulas is defined inductively as follows.[5]

$$\Psi ::= \psi(z) \mid \psi(z; h) \mid \Psi \vee \Psi \mid \neg \Psi \mid \exists z_i . \Psi \mid \exists h . \Psi$$

We use the usual abbreviations $\wedge, \rightarrow$, and $\forall$. We denote by *free*(Ψ) the set of strategy and history variables that are *free* (not in a scope of a quantifier) in Ψ. A formula Ψ is *closed* if *free*$(\Psi) = \emptyset$. The *alternation depth* of a variable of a closed formula is the number of quantifier switches ($\exists \forall$ or $\forall \exists$, in case the formula is in positive normal form) that bind the variable. The *alternation depth* of closed formula Ψ is the maximum alternation depth of a variable occurring in the formula.

We now define the semantics of ESL. Intuitively, an ESL formula of the form $\psi(z; h)$ is interpreted over the game whose prefix matches the history h and the suffix starting where h ends is the outcome of the game that starts at the last vertex of h and along which each agent $i \in I$ adheres to his strategy in z. Let $\mathbb{X} \subseteq \mathbb{H} \cup \bigcup_{i \in I} \mathbb{Z}_i$ be a set of variables. An assignment $\mathcal{A}_{\mathbb{X}}$ assigns to every history variable $h \in \mathbb{X} \cap \mathbb{H}$, a history $\mathcal{A}_{\mathbb{X}}(h) \in V^+$ and assigns to every strategy variable $z_i \in \mathbb{X} \cap \mathbb{Z}_i$, a strategy $\mathcal{A}_{\mathbb{X}}(z_i) \in \Pi_i$. Given an assignment $\mathcal{A}_{\mathbb{X}}$ and a strategy $\pi_i \in \Pi_i$, we denote by $\mathcal{A}_{\mathbb{X}}[z_i \leftarrow \pi_i]$ the assignment $\mathcal{A}'_{\mathbb{X} \cup \{z_i\}}$ in which $\mathcal{A}'_{\mathbb{X} \cup \{z_i\}}(z_i) = \pi_i$ and for a variable $x \neq z_i$ we have $\mathcal{A}'_{\mathbb{X} \cup \{z_i\}}(x) = \mathcal{A}_{\mathbb{X}}(x)$. For histories of the game $w \in V^+$ we define $\mathcal{A}_{\mathbb{X}}[h \leftarrow w]$ similarly.

We now describe when a given game $\mathcal{G}$ and a given assignment $\mathcal{A}_{\mathbb{X}}$ satisfy an ESL formula Ψ, where $\mathbb{X}$ is such that *free*$(\Psi) \subseteq \mathbb{X}$. For LTL, the semantics is as usual [17].

---

[5] We note that strategy logic as defined in [5] allows the application of LTL path operators ($\bigcirc$ and $\mathcal{U}$) on strategy logic closed formulas. Since we could not come up with a meaningful specification that uses such applications, we chose to ease the presentation and do not allow them in ESL. Technically, it is easy to extend ESL and allow such applications.

$(\mathcal{G},\mathcal{A}_{\mathbb{X}}) \models \psi(z)$ iff $outcome(\mathcal{A}_{\mathbb{X}}(z))^{\mathcal{G}} \models \psi$ $(\mathcal{G},\mathcal{A}_{\mathbb{X}}) \models \Psi_1 \vee \Psi_2$ iff $(\mathcal{G},\mathcal{A}_{\mathbb{X}}) \models \Psi_1$ or $(\mathcal{G},\mathcal{A}_{\mathbb{X}}) \models \Psi_2$

$(\mathcal{G},\mathcal{A}_{\mathbb{X}}) \models \psi(z;h)$ iff $outcome(\mathcal{A}_{\mathbb{X}}(z))^{\mathcal{G}}_{\mathcal{A}_{\mathbb{X}}(h)} \models \psi$ $(\mathcal{G},\mathcal{A}_{\mathbb{X}}) \models \exists z_i.\Psi$ iff $\exists \pi_i \in \Pi_i.(\mathcal{G},\mathcal{A}_{\mathbb{X}}[z_i \leftarrow \pi_i]) \models \Psi$

$(\mathcal{G},\mathcal{A}_{\mathbb{X}}) \models \neg \Psi$ iff $(\mathcal{G},\mathcal{A}_{\mathbb{X}}) \not\models \Psi$ $(\mathcal{G},\mathcal{A}_{\mathbb{X}}) \models \exists h.\Psi$ iff $\exists w \in V^+.(\mathcal{G},\mathcal{A}_{\mathbb{X}}[h \leftarrow w]) \models \Psi$

Let Ψ be an ESL formula. We use $[\![\Psi]\!]$ to denote its set of satisfying assignments; that is, $[\![\Psi]\!] = \{(\mathcal{G}, \mathcal{A}_{\mathbb{X}}) \mid \mathbb{X} = free(\Psi) \text{ and } (\mathcal{G},\mathcal{A}_{\mathbb{X}}) \models \Psi\}$. Given a game graph $\mathcal{G}$, we denote by $[\![\Psi]\!]_{\mathcal{G}}$ the assignment $\mathcal{A}_{\mathbb{X}}$ to the free variables in Ψ such that $(\mathcal{G}, \mathcal{A}_{\mathbb{X}}) \in [\![\Psi]\!]$.

Expressing Rational Synthesis.   We now show that the rational synthesis problem for the three traditional solution concepts can be stated in ESL. We first state that a given strategy profile $y = (y_i)_{i \in I}$ is a solution concept on the game $\mathcal{G}_{y_0}$, that is, the game induced by $\mathcal{G}$ when Agent 0 adheres to his strategy in y. We use I_{-0} to denote the set $\{1, \ldots, n\}$, that is, the set of all agents except for the system, which is Agent 0. Given a strategy profile $z = (z_i)_{i \in I}$, we use $(z_{-\{i,0\}}, y_i, y_0)$ to denote the strategy profile where all agents but i and 0 follow z and agents i and 0 follow y_i and y_0, respectively. For $i \in I$, let φ_i be the objective of Agent i. For a solution concept $\gamma \in \{\text{DS, NASH, SPE}\}$ and a strategy profile $y = (y_i)_{i \in I}$, the formula $\Psi^\gamma(y)$, expressing that the profile $(y_i)_{i \in I_{-0}}$ is a solution with respect to γ in $\mathcal{G}_{y_0}$, is defined as follows.

- $\Psi^{\text{DS}}(y) := \bigwedge_{i \in I_{-0}} \forall z. (\varphi_i(z_{-0}, y_0) \rightarrow \varphi_i(z_{-\{i,0\}}, y_i, y_0))$.
- $\Psi^{\text{NASH}}(y) := \bigwedge_{i \in I_{-0}} \forall z_i. (\varphi_i(y_{-i}, z_i) \rightarrow \varphi_i(y))$.
- $\Psi^{\text{SPE}}(y) := \forall h. \bigwedge_{i \in I_{-0}} \forall z_i. ((\varphi_i(y_{-i}, z_i, h) \rightarrow (\varphi_i(y, h))$.

We can now state the existence of a solution to the rational-synthesis problem with input $\varphi_0, \ldots, \varphi_n$ by the closed formula $\Phi^\gamma := \exists (y_i)_{i \in I}.(\varphi_0((y_i)_{i \in I}) \wedge \Psi^\gamma((y_i)_{i \in I}))$. Indeed, the formula specifies the existence of a strategy profile whose outcome satisfies φ_0 and for which the strategies for the agents in I_{-0} constitute a solution with respect to γ in the game induced by y_0.

ESL Decidability.   In order to solve the rational-synthesis problem we are going to use automata on infinite trees. Given a set D of directions, a D-*tree* is the set D^*. The elements in D^* are the *nodes* of the tree. The node ϵ is the root of the tree. For a node $u \in D^*$ and a direction $d \in D$, the node $u \cdot d$ is the *successor* of u with *direction d*. Given D and an alphabet Σ, a Σ-labeled D-tree is a pair $\langle D^*, \tau \rangle$ such that $\tau : D^* \rightarrow \Sigma$ maps each node of D^* to a letter in Σ.

An *alternating parity tree automaton (APT)* is a tuple $\mathcal{A} = \langle \Sigma, D, Q, \delta_0, \delta, \chi \rangle$, where Σ is the input alphabet, D is the directions set, Q is a finite set of states, δ_0 is the initial condition, δ is the transition relation and $\chi : Q \mapsto \{1, \ldots, k\}$ is the parity condition. The initial condition δ_0 is a positive boolean formula over Q specifying the initial condition. For example, $(q_1 \vee q_2) \wedge q_3$ specifies that the APT accepts the input tree if it accepts it from state q_3 as well as from q_1 or q_2. The transition function δ maps each state and letter to a boolean formula over $D \times Q$. Thus, as with δ_0, the idea is to allow the automaton to send copies of itself in different states. In δ, the copies are sent to the successors of the current node, thus each state is paired with the direction to which the copy should proceed. Due to lack of space, we refer the reader to [9] for the definition of runs and acceptance.

Base ESL formulas, of the form $\psi(z, h)$, refer to exactly one strategy variable for each agent, and one history variable. The assignment for these variables can be described by a $(\Sigma \times \{\bot, \top\})$-labeled Σ-tree, where the Σ-component of the labels is used in order to describe the strategy profile π assigned to the strategy variable, and the $\{\bot, \top\}$-component of the labels is used in order to label the tree by a unique finite path corresponding to the history variable. We refer to a $(\Sigma \times \{\bot, \top\})$-labeled Σ-tree as a *strategy-history tree*. The labeling function τ of a strategy-history tree $\langle \Sigma^*, \tau \rangle$ can be regarded as two labeling functions τ_s and τ_h mapping nodes of the tree to action tuples in Σ and history information in $\{\top, \bot\}$, respectively. A node $u = d_0 d_1 \ldots d_k$ in a strategy-history tree $\langle \Sigma^*, \tau \rangle$ corresponds to a history of the play in which at time $0 \le j \le k$, the agents played as recorded in d_j. A label $\tau_s(u) = (\sigma_0, \ldots, \sigma_n)$ of node u describes for each agent i, an action σ_i that the strategy π_i advises Agent i to take when the history of the game so far is u. A label $\tau_h(u)$ describes whether the node u is along the path corresponding to the history (where $\top$ signifies that it does and $\bot$ that it does not). Among the $|\Sigma|$ successors of u in the strategy-history tree, only the successor $u \cdot \tau_s(u)$ corresponds to a scenario in which all the agents adhere to their strategies in the strategy profile described in $\langle \Sigma^*, \tau \rangle$. We say that a path ρ in a strategy-history tree $\langle \Sigma^*, (\tau_s, \tau_h) \rangle$ is *obedient* if for all nodes $u \cdot d \in \rho$, for $u \in \Sigma^*$ and $d \in \Sigma$, we have $d = \tau_s(u)$. Note that there is a single obedient path in every strategy-history tree. This path corresponds to the single play in which all agents adhere to their strategies. The $\{\top, \bot\}$ labeling is legal if there is a unique finite prefix of a path starting at the root, all of whose node are marked with $\top$. Note that there is a single path in the tree whose prefix is marked by $\top$'s and whose suffix is obedient.

An ESL formula Ψ may contain several base formulas. Therefore, Ψ may contain, for each $i \in I$, several strategy variables in $\mathbb{Z}_i$ and several history variables in $\mathbb{H}$. For $i \in I$, let $\{z_i^1, \ldots, z_i^{m_i}\}$ be the set of strategy variables in $\Psi \cap \mathbb{Z}_i$. Recall that each strategy variable $z_i^j \in \mathbb{Z}_i$ corresponds to a strategy $\pi_i^j : \Sigma^* \to \Sigma_i$. Let $\{h_1, \ldots, h_m\}$ be the set of history variables in Ψ. Recall that each history variable h corresponds to a word in Σ^*, which can be seen as a function $w_h : \Sigma^* \to \{\top, \bot\}$ labeling only that word with $\top$'s. Thus, we can describe an assignment to all the variables in Ψ by a Υ-labeled Σ-tree, with $\Upsilon = \Sigma_0^{m_0} \times \Sigma_1^{m_1} \times \cdots \times \Sigma_n^{m_n} \times \{\bot, \top\}^m$.

We solve the rational synthesis problem using tree automata that run on Υ-labeled Σ-trees. Note that the specification of rational synthesis involves an external quantification of a strategy profile. We construct an automaton $\mathcal{U}$ that accepts all trees that describe a strategy profile that meets the desired solution. A witness to the nonemptiness of the automaton then induces the desired strategies.

We define $\mathcal{U}$ as an APT. Consider an ESL formula $\psi(z, h)$. Consider a strategy-history tree $\langle \Sigma^*, (\tau_s, \tau_h) \rangle$. Recall that ψ should hold along the path that starts at the root of the tree, goes through h, and then continues to $outcome(z)_h$. Thus, adding history variables to strategy logic results in a *memoryful logic* [16], in which LTL formulas have to be evaluated not along a path that starts at the present, but along a path that starts at the root and goes through the present. The memoryful semantics imposes a real challenge on the decidability problem, as one has to follow all the possible runs of a nondeterministic automaton for ψ, which involves a satellite implementing the subset construction of this automaton [16]. Here, we use instead the τ_h labeling of the node with $\{\top, \bot\}$ elements.

The definition of the APT $\mathcal{A}_\Psi$ for $\llbracket \Psi \rrbracket_\mathcal{G}$ works by induction on the structure of Ψ. At the base level, we have formulas of the form $\psi(z, h)$, where ψ is an LTL formula, z is a strategy profile, and h is a history variable. The constructed automaton then has three tasks. The first task is to check that the $\{\bot, \top\}$ labeling is legal; i.e. there is a unique path in the tree marked by $\top$'s. The second task is to detect the single path that goes through h and continues from h according to the strategy profile z. The third task is to check that this path satisfies ψ. The inductive steps then built on APT complementation, intersection, union and projection [18]. In particular, as in strategy logic, quantification over a strategy variable for agent i is done by "projecting out" the corresponding Σ_i label from the tree. That is, given an automaton $\mathcal{A}$ for Ψ, the automaton for $\exists z_i.\Psi$ ignores the Σ_i component that refers to z_i and checks $\mathcal{A}$ on a tree where this component is guessed. The quantification over history variables is similar. Given an automaton $\mathcal{A}$ for Ψ the automaton for $\exists h.\Psi$ ignores the $\{\bot, \top\}$ part of the label that corresponds to h and checks $\mathcal{A}$ on a tree where the $\{\bot, \top\}$ part of the label is guessed.

Theorem 1. *Let Ψ be an ESL formula over $\mathcal{G}$. Let d be the alternation depth of Ψ. We can construct an APT $\mathcal{A}_\Psi$ such that $\mathcal{A}_\Psi$ accepts $\llbracket \Psi \rrbracket_\mathcal{G}$ and its emptiness can be checked in time $(d + 1)$-EXPTIME in the size of Ψ.*

Solving Rational Synthesis   We can now reduce rational-synthesis to APT emptiness. The following theorem states that the complexity of solving rational synthesis for the three common solution concepts is not more expensive than traditional synthesis.

Theorem 2. *LTL rational-synthesis is 2EXPTIME-complete for the solution concepts of dominant strategy, Nash equilibrium, and subgame-perfect equilibrium.*

5   Solution in the Multi-valued Setting

As discussed in Section 1, classical applications of game theory consider games with quantitative payoffs. The extension of the synthesis problem to the rational setting calls also for an extension to the quantitative setting. Unfortunately, the full quantitative setting is undecidable already in the context of model checking [1]. In this section we study a decidable fragment of the quantitative rational synthesis problem: the payoffs are taken from *finite De-Morgan lattices*. A lattice $\langle A, \leq \rangle$ is a partially ordered set in which every two elements $a, b \in A$ have a least upper bound (*a join b*, denoted $a \vee b$) and a greatest lower bound (*a meet b*, denoted $a \wedge b$). A lattice is *distributive* if for every $a, b, c \in A$, we have $a \wedge (b \vee c) = (a \wedge b) \vee (a \wedge c)$. De-Morgan lattices are distributive lattices in which every element a has a unique complement element $\neg a$ such that $\neg\neg a = a$, De-Morgan rules hold, and $a \leq b$ implies $\neg b \leq \neg a$. Many useful payoffs are taken from finite De-Morgan lattices: all payoffs that are linearly ordered, payoffs corresponding to subsets of some set, payoffs corresponding to multiple view-points, and more [12,13].

We specify quantitative specifications using the temporal logic *latticed LTL* (LLTL, for short), where the truth value of a specification is an element in a lattice. For a strategy profile π and an LLTL objective φ_i of Agent i, the payoff of Agent i in π is the truth value of φ_i in $outcome(\pi)$. A synthesizer would like to find a profile π in which $payoff_0(\pi)$ is as high as possible. Accordingly, we define the latticed rational synthesis as follows.

Definition 2 (Latticed Rational Synthesis). *Consider a solution concept γ. The problem of latticed rational synthesis (with solution concept γ) is to return, given LLTL formulas $\varphi_0, \ldots, \varphi_n$ and a lattice value $v \in \mathcal{L}$, a strategy profile $\pi = \langle \pi_0, \pi_1, \ldots, \pi_n \rangle \in \Pi_0 \times \Pi_1 \times \cdots \times \Pi_n$ such that (a) $payoff_0(\pi) \geq v$ and (b) the strategy profile $\langle \pi_1, \ldots, \pi_n \rangle$ is a solution in the game $\mathcal{G}_{\pi_0}$ with respect to the solution concept γ.*

In the Boolean setting, we reduced the rational-synthesis problem to decidability of ESL. The decision procedure for ESL is based on the automata-theoretic approach, and specifically on APT's. In the lattice setting, automata-theoretic machinery is not as developed as in the Boolean case. Consequently, we restrict attention to LLTL specifications that can be translated to deterministic latticed Büchi word automata (LDBW), and to the solution concept of Nash equilibrium.[6]

An LDBW can be expanded into a deterministic latticed Büchi tree automata (LDBT), which is the key behind the analysis of strategy trees. It is not hard to lift to the latticed setting almost all the other operations on tree automata that are needed in order to solve rational synthesis. An exception is the problem of emptiness. In the Boolean case, tree-automata emptiness is reduced to deciding a two-player game [10]. Such games are played between an $\vee$-player, who has a winning strategy iff the automaton is not empty (essentially, the $\vee$-player chooses the transitions with which the automaton accepts a witness tree), and a $\wedge$-player, who has a winning strategy otherwise (essentially, the $\wedge$-player chooses a path in the tree that does not satisfy the acceptance condition). A winning strategy for the $\vee$-player induces a labeled tree accepted by the tree automaton.

In latticed games, deciding a game amounts to finding a lattice value l such that the $\vee$-player can force the game to computations in which his payoff is at least l. The value of the game need not be achieved by a single strategy and algorithms for analyzing latticed games consider values that emerge as the join of values obtained by following different strategies [13,27]. A labeled tree, however, relates to a single strategy. Therefore, the emptiness problem for latticed tree automata, to which the latticed rational synthesis is reduced, cannot be reduced to solving latticed games. Instead, one has to consider the *single-strategy* variant of latticed games, namely the problem of finding values that the $\vee$-player can ensure by a single strategy. We address this problem below.

Theorem 3. *Consider a latticed Büchi game G. Given a lattice element l, we can construct a Boolean generalized-Büchi game G_l such that the $\vee$-player can achieve value greater or equal l in G using a single strategy iff the $\vee$-player wins in G_l. The size of G_l is bounded by $|G| \cdot |\mathcal{L}|^2$ and G_l has at most $|\mathcal{L}|$ acceptance sets.*

Using Theorem 3, we can solve the latticed rational synthesis problem in a fashion similar to the one we used in the Boolean case. We represent strategy profiles by Σ-labeled Σ-trees, and sets of profiles by tree automata. We construct two Boolean generalized-Büchi tree automata. The first, denoted $\mathcal{A}_0$, for the language of all profiles π in which $payoff_0(\pi) \geq v$, and the second, denoted $\mathcal{A}_N$, for the language of all Nash equilibria. The intersection of $\mathcal{A}_0$ and $\mathcal{A}_N$ then contains all the solutions to the latticed rational

---

[6] A *Büchi* acceptance conditions specifies a subset F of the states, and an infinite sequence of states satisfies the condition if it visits F infinitely often. A *generalized Büchi condition* specifies several such sets, all of which should be visited infinitely often.

synthesis problem. Thus, solving the problem amounts to returning a witness to the nonemptiness of the intersection, and we have the following.

Theorem 4. *Latticed rational-synthesis for objectives in LDBW and the solution concept of Nash equilibrium is in EXPTIME.*

We note that the lower complexity with respect to the Boolean setting (Theorem 2) is only apparent, as the objectives are given in LDBWs, which are less succinct than LLTL formulas [12,15].

6 Discussion

While various solution concepts have been studied in the context of formal verification and infinite concurrent games [3,4,5,6,7,28], this is the first paper to introduce the natural problem of *rational synthesis*. Rational Synthesis asks whether and how one can synthesize a system that functions in a rational (self-interest) environment. As in traditional synthesis, one cannot control the agents that constitute the environment. Unlike traditional synthesis, the agents have objectives and will follow strategies that best guarantee their objectives are met.

Both the question and solution separate the game-theoretic considerations from the synthesis technique, and can be generalized to other/new solution concepts. We showed that for the common solution concepts of dominant strategies equilibrium, Nash equilibrium, and subgame perfect equilibrium, rational synthesis has the same complexity as traditional synthesis. We also took a first step in addressing the question in the quantitative setting.

Acknowledgement.   We thank Roderick Bloem for helpful comments on an earlier draft of this paper.

References

1. Chakrabarti, A., Chatterjee, K., Henzinger, T.A., Kupferman, O., Majumdar, R.: Verifying quantitative properties using bound functions. In: Borrione, D., Paul, W. (eds.) CHARME 2005. LNCS, vol. 3725, pp. 50–64. Springer, Heidelberg (2005)
2. Chatterjee, K., Doyen, L., Henzinger, T.: Quantative languages. In: Proc. 17th Annual Conf. of the European Association for Computer Science Logic (2008)
3. Chatterjee, K., Henzinger, T., Jobstmann, B.: Environment assumptions for synthesis. In: 19th Int. Conf. on Concurrency Theory, pp. 147–161 (2008)
4. Chatterjee, K., Henzinger, T., Jurdzinski, M.: Games with secure equilibria. Theoretical Computer Science (2006)
5. Chatterjee, K., Henzinger, T.A., Piterman, N.: Strategy logic. In: 18th Int. Conf. on Concurrency Theory, pp. 59–73 (2007)
6. Chatterjee, K., Henzinger, T.A.: Assume-guarantee synthesis. In: Grumberg, O., Huth, M. (eds.) TACAS 2007. LNCS, vol. 4424, pp. 261–275. Springer, Heidelberg (2007)
7. Chatterjee, K., Majumdar, R., Jurdzinski, M.: On Nash equilibria in stochastic games. In: Marcinkowski, J., Tarlecki, A. (eds.) CSL 2004. LNCS, vol. 3210, pp. 26–40. Springer, Heidelberg (2004)
8. Church, A.: Logic, arithmetics, and automata. In: Proc. Int. Congress of Mathematicians, 1962, pp. 23–35. Institut Mittag-Leffler (1963)

9. Grädel, E., Thomas, W., Wilke, T. (eds.): Automata, Logics, and Infinite Games. LNCS, vol. 2500. Springer, Heidelberg (2002)
10. Gurevich, Y., Harrington, L.: Trees, automata, and games. In: Proc. 14th ACM Symp. on Theory of Computing, pp. 60–65 (1982)
11. Gurfinkel, A., Chechik, M.: Multi-valued model-checking via classical model-checking. In: 14th Int. Conf. on Concurrency Theory, pp. 263–277 (2003)
12. Kupferman, O., Lustig, Y.: Lattice automata. In: Cook, B., Podelski, A. (eds.) VMCAI 2007. LNCS, vol. 4349, pp. 199–213. Springer, Heidelberg (2007)
13. Kupferman, O., Lustig, Y.: Latticed simulation relations and games. In: Namjoshi, K.S., Yoneda, T., Higashino, T., Okamura, Y. (eds.) ATVA 2007. LNCS, vol. 4762, pp. 316–330. Springer, Heidelberg (2007)
14. Kupferman, O., Vardi, M.Y.: Weak alternating automata and tree automata emptiness. In: Proc. 30th ACM Symp. on Theory of Computing, pp. 224–233 (1998)
15. Kupferman, O., Vardi, M.Y.: From linear time to branching time. ACM Transactions on Computational Logic 6(2), 273–294 (2005)
16. Kupferman, O., Vardi, M.Y.: Memoryful branching-time logics. In: Proc. 21st IEEE Symp. on Logic in Computer Science, pp. 265–274 (2006)
17. Manna, Z., Pnueli, A.: The Temporal Logic of Reactive and Concurrent Systems: Specification. Springer, Heidelberg (1992)
18. Muller, D.E., Schupp, P.E.: Alternating automata on infinite trees. Theoretical Computer Science 54, 267–276 (1987)
19. Nash, J.F.: Equilibrium points in n-person games. In: Proceedings of the National Academy of Sciences of the United States of America (1950)
20. Nisan, N., Ronen, A.: Algorithmic mechanism design. In: Proc. 31st ACM Symp. on Theory of Computing, pp. 129–140 (1999)
21. Nisan, N., Roughgarden, T., Tardos, E., Vazirani, V.V.: Algorithmic Game Theory. Cambridge University Press, Cambridge (2007)
22. Osborne, M.J., Rubinstein, A.: A Course in Game Theory. The MIT Press, Cambridge (1994)
23. Pnueli, A.: The temporal logic of programs. In: Proc. 18th IEEE Symp. on Foundations of Computer Science, pp. 46–57 (1977a)
24. Pnueli, A., Rosner, R.: On the synthesis of a reactive module. In: Proc. 16th ACM Symp. on Principles of Programming Languages, pp. 179–190 (1989)
25. Rosner, R.: Modular Synthesis of Reactive Systems. PhD thesis, Weizmann Institute of Science (1992)
26. Selten, R.: Reexamination of the perfectness concept for equilibrium points in extensive games. International Journal of Game Theory 4(1), 25–55 (1975)
27. Shoham, S., Grumberg, O.: Multi-valued model checking games. In: Peled, D.A., Tsay, Y.-K. (eds.) ATVA 2005. LNCS, vol. 3707, pp. 354–369. Springer, Heidelberg (2005)
28. Ummels, M.: Rational behaviour and strategy construction in infinite multiplayer games. In: Proc. 26th Conf. on Foundations of Software Technology and Theoretical Computer Science, pp. 212–223 (2006)
29. Vardi, M.Y., Wolper, P.: Reasoning about infinite computations. Information and Computation 115(1), 1–37 (1994)

Efficient Büchi Universality Checking*

Seth Fogarty and Moshe Y. Vardi

Department of Computer Science, Rice University, Houston, TX
{sfogarty,vardi}@cs.rice.edu

Abstract. The complementation of Büchi automata, required for checking automata universality, remains one of the outstanding automata-theoretic challenges in formal verification. Early constructions using a Ramsey-based argument have been supplanted by rank-based constructions with exponentially better bounds. The best rank-based algorithm for Büchi universality, by Doyen and Raskin, employs a subsumption technique to minimize the size of the working set. Separately, in the context of program termination, Lee et al. have specialized the Ramsey-based approach to size-change termination (SCT) problems. In this context, Ramsey-based algorithms have proven to be surprisingly competitive. The strongest tool, from Ben-Amram and Lee, also uses a subsumption technique, although only for the special case of SCT problems.

We extend the subsumption technique of Ben-Amram and Lee to the general case of Büchi universality problems, and experimentally demonstrate the necessity of subsumption for the scalability of the Ramsey-based approach. We then empirically compare the Ramsey-based tool to the rank-based tool of Doyen and Raskin over a terrain of random Büchi universality problems. We discover that the two algorithms exhibit distinct behavior over this problem terrain. As expected, on many of the most difficult areas the rank-based approach provides the superior tool. Surprisingly, there also exist several areas, including the area most difficult for rank-based tools, on which the Ramsey-based solver scales better than the rank-based solver. This result demonstrates the pitfalls of using worst-case complexity to evaluate algorithms. We suggest that a portfolio approach may be the best approach to checking the universality of Büchi automata.

1 Introduction

The complementation problem for nondeterministic automata over infinite words is a vital step in the automata-theoretic approach to formal verification. The automata-theoretic approach reduces questions about program adherence to a specification to questions about language containment [19]. Representing liveness, fairness, or termination properties requires finite automata that operate on infinite words. One automaton, $\mathcal{A}$, encodes the behavior of the program, while another automaton, $\mathcal{B}$, encodes the formal specification. To ensure adherence, verify that the intersection of $\mathcal{A}$ with the complement of $\mathcal{B}$ is empty. The most difficult step is constructing the complementary automaton $\overline{\mathcal{B}}$. When addressing this problem, the formal verifications community

---
* Work supported in part by NSF grants CCF-0613889, ANI-0216467, OISE-0913807, and CCF-0728882, by BSF grant 9800096, and by gift from Intel. Proofs and additional figures available at http://www.cs.rice.edu/~vardi/papers/tacas10rj.pdf

J. Esparza and R. Majumdar (Eds.): TACAS 2010, LNCS 6015, pp. 205–220, 2010.

has focused on universality testing [6,18,20]. This is the simplest case of containment checking: checking if the universal language is contained in the language of the automaton. Finite automata on infinite words are classified by their acceptance condition and transition structure. We consider here nondeterministic Büchi automata, in which a run is accepting when it visits at least one accepting state infinitely often [2].

The first complementation constructions for nondeterministic Büchi automata employed a Ramsey-based combinatorial argument to partition infinite words into a finite set of regular languages. Proposed by Büchi in 1962 [2], this construction was shown in 1987 by Sistla, Vardi, and Wolper to be implementable with a blow-up of $2^{O(n^2)}$ [17]. This brought the complementation problem into singly-exponential blow-up, but left a gap with the $2^{\Omega(n \log n)}$ lower bound proved by Michel [13].

The gap was tightened one year later in 1988, when Safra described a $2^{O(n \log n)}$ construction [15]. Because of this, the Ramsey-based approach has never been implemented. Work since then has focused on improving the practicality of $2^{O(n \log n)}$ constructions, either by providing simpler constructions, further tightening the bound [16], or improving the derived algorithms. In 2001, Kupferman and Vardi employed a rank-based analysis of Büchi automata to simplify complementation [12]. Recently, Doyen and Raskin have demonstrated the necessity of using a subsumption technique in the rank-based approach, providing a direct universality checker that scales to automata several orders of magnitude larger than previous tools [6].

Separately, in the context of of program termination analysis, Lee, Jones, and Ben-Amram presented the size-change termination (SCT) principle in 2001 [5]. Lee et al. describe a method of size-change termination analysis and reduce this problem to the containment of two Büchi automata. Stating the lack of efficient Büchi containment solvers, they also propose a direct Ramsey-based combinatorial solution. The Lee, Jones, and Ben-Amram (LJB) algorithm was provided as a practical alternative to reducing the SCT problems to Büchi containment, but bears a striking resemblance to the 1987 Ramsey-based complementation construction. In a previous paper, we showed that the LJB algorithm for deciding SCT is a specialized realization of the Ramsey-based construction [9]. When examined empirically, Ramsey-based tools proved to be surprisingly competitive to their rank-based counterparts. The best Ramsey-based tool employs a subsumption technique for the specific case of SCT problems [1].

This paper extends the subsumption technique of Ben-Amram and Lee to the general case of Büchi universality. By doing so we provide a direct algorithm, derived from the Ramsey-based complementation construction, for checking the universality of Büchi automata. We note that subsumption is a heuristic technique and, even with this improvement, there is still an exponential gap between the $2^{O(n^2)}$ Ramsey-based approach and the $2^{O(n \log n)}$ rank-based approach. Motivated by the Ramsey-based approach's strong performance on the domain of SCT problems, we investigate the empirical performance of these two algorithms. Due to a paucity of real-world universality problems, we compare the algorithms over a terrain of random universality problems [6,18] characterized by transition density, acceptance density, and size.

Our empirical results first demonstrate that, as with rank-based algorithms, subsumption is necessary for scalability in Ramsey-based tools. Further, we observe that the two algorithms exhibit significantly different behavior. The terrain points that pose difficulty for each algorithm, while overlapping, are distinct. In terms of scalability, we show that in many areas the rank-based universality tool performs exponentially better than the Ramsey-based universality tool. However, there also exist several areas where the Ramsey-based tool is more scalable than the rank-based tool, despite the massive difference between $2^{O(n \log n)}$ and $2^{O(n^2)}$. Finally, we discover that the Ramsey-based tool is better at demonstrating non-universality by finding a counterexample, while the rank-based tool is superior when proving universality. This final difference can be attributed to the manner in which each approaches explores the state space of the complemented automaton, but does not explain the other behaviors of the two approaches. We are thus forced to conclude that worst-case complexity is a poor predictor of an algorithms performance, and no substitute for empirical analysis. We suggest that a portfolio approach [10,14] may be employed when checking the universality of Büchi automata. Failing that, run both algorithms in parallel, and see which terminates first.

2 Preliminaries

In this section we review the relevant details of Büchi automata, introducing along the way the notation used throughout this paper. An *nondeterministic Büchi automaton on infinite words* is a tuple $B = \langle \Sigma, Q, Q^{in}, \rho, F \rangle$, where Σ is a finite nonempty alphabet, Q a finite nonempty set of states, $Q^{in} \subseteq Q$ a set of initial states, $F \subseteq Q$ a set of accepting states, and $\rho : Q \times \Sigma \rightarrow 2^Q$ a nondeterministic transition function. We lift the ρ function to sets of states and words of arbitrary length in the usual fashion.

A *run* of a Büchi automaton B on a word $w \in \Sigma^\omega$ is a infinite sequence of states $q_0 q_1 ... \in Q^\omega$ such that $q_0 \in Q^{in}$ and, for every $i \geq 0$, we have $q_{i+1} \in \rho(q_i, w_i)$. A run is *accepting* iff $q_i \in F$ for infinitely many $i \in \mathbb{N}$. A word $w \in \Sigma^\omega$ is accepted by B if there is an accepting run of B on w. The words accepted by B form the *language* of B, denoted by $L(B)$. A *path* in B from q to r is a finite subsequence of a run beginning in q and ending in r. A path is *accepting* if some state in the path is in F.

A Büchi automaton A is contained in a Büchi automaton B iff $L(A) \subseteq L(B)$, which can be checked by verifying that the intersection of A with the complement $\overline{B}$ of B is empty: $L(A) \cap L(\overline{B}) = \emptyset$. We know that the language of an automaton is nonempty iff there are states $q \in Q^{in}$, $r \in F$ such that there is a path from q to r and a path from r to itself. The initial path is called the prefix, and the combination of the prefix and cycle is called a *lasso* [19]. Further, the intersection of two automata can be constructed, having a number of states proportional to the product of the number states of the original automata [3]. Thus the most computationally demanding step is constructing the complement of B. In the formal verification field, existing empirical work has focused on the simplest form of containment testing, *universality* testing, where A is the universal automaton [6,18].

For algorithms that compute sets of states, a subsumption technique can sometimes be employed to limit the size of working sets. This technique ignores certain states when their behavior is subsumed by other states. A *subsumption* relation is a partial order over the state space of an automaton, such that if a state q subsumes a state r, then r can be removed from any set containing q.

2.1   Ramsey-Based Universality

When Büchi introduced these automata in 1962, he described a complementation construction involving a Ramsey-based combinatorial argument. We describe a universality testing algorithm based on an improved implementation presented in 1987. To construct the complement of $\mathcal{B}$, where $Q = \{q_0, ..., q_{n-1}\}$, we construct a set $\widetilde{Q}_\mathcal{B}$ whose elements capture the essential behavior of $\mathcal{B}$. Each element corresponds to an answer to the following question. Given a finite nonempty word w, for every two states $q, r \in Q$: is there a path in $\mathcal{B}$ from q to r over w, and is some such path accepting?

Define $Q' = Q \times \{0, 1\} \times Q$, and $\widetilde{Q}_\mathcal{B}$ to be the subset of $2^{Q'}$ whose elements do not contain both $\langle q, 0, r \rangle$ and $\langle q, 1, r \rangle$ for any q and r. Each element of $\widetilde{Q}_\mathcal{B}$ is a $\{0, 1\}$-arc-labeled graph on Q. An arc represents a path in $\mathcal{B}$, and the label is 1 if the path is accepting. Note that there are 3^{n^2} such graphs. With each graph $\widetilde{g} \in \widetilde{Q}_\mathcal{B}$ we associate a language $L(\widetilde{g})$, the set of words for which the answer to the posed question is the graph encoded by $\widetilde{g}$.

Definition 1. [2,17] *Let $\widetilde{g} \in \widetilde{Q}_\mathcal{B}$ and $w \in \Sigma^+$. Say $w \in L(\widetilde{g})$ iff for all $q, r \in Q$:*
(1) $\langle q, a, r \rangle \in \widetilde{g}$, $a \in \{0, 1\}$, iff there is a path in $\mathcal{B}$ from q to r over w
(2) $\langle q, 1, r \rangle \in \widetilde{g}$ iff there is an accepting path in $\mathcal{B}$ from q to r over w

The languages $L(\widetilde{g})$ for the graphs $\widetilde{g} \in \widetilde{Q}_\mathcal{B}$, form a partition of Σ^+. With this partition of Σ^+ we can devise a finite family of ω-languages that cover Σ^ω. For every $\widetilde{g}, \widetilde{h} \in \widetilde{Q}_\mathcal{B}$, let Y_{gh} be the ω-language $L(\widetilde{g}) \cdot L(\widetilde{h})^\omega$. We say that a language Y_{gh} is *proper* if Y_{gh} is non-empty, $L(\widetilde{g}) \cdot L(\widetilde{h}) \subseteq L(\widetilde{g})$, and $L(\widetilde{h}) \cdot L(\widetilde{h}) \subseteq L(\widetilde{h})$. There are a finite, if exponential, number of such languages. A Ramsey-based argument shows that every infinite string belongs to a language of this form, and that $\overline{L(\mathcal{B})}$ can be expressed as the union of languages of this form.

Lemma 1. [2,17]
(1) $\Sigma^\omega = \bigcup \{Y_{gh} \mid Y_{gh} \text{ is proper}\}$
(2) For $\widetilde{g}, \widetilde{h} \in \widetilde{Q}_\mathcal{B}$, either $Y_{gh} \cap L(\mathcal{B}) = \emptyset$ or $Y_{gh} \subseteq L(\mathcal{B})$
(3) $\overline{L(\mathcal{B})} = \bigcup \{Y_{gh} \mid Y_{gh} \text{ is proper and } Y_{gh} \cap L(\mathcal{B}) = \emptyset\}$

To obtain the complementary Büchi automaton $\overline{\mathcal{B}}$, Sistla et al. construct, for each $\widetilde{g} \in \widetilde{Q}_\mathcal{B}$, a deterministic automata on finite words, $\mathcal{B}_g$, that accepts exactly $L(\widetilde{g})$ [17]. Using the automata $\mathcal{B}_g$, one could construct the complementary automaton $\overline{\mathcal{B}}$ and use a lasso-finding algorithm to prove the emptiness of $\overline{\mathcal{B}}$, and thus the universality of $\mathcal{B}$. However, we can avoid an explicit lasso search by employing the rich structure of the graphs in $\widetilde{Q}_\mathcal{B}$. For every two graphs $\widetilde{g}, \widetilde{h} \in \widetilde{Q}_\mathcal{B}$, determine if Y_{gh} is proper. If Y_{gh} is proper, test if it is contained in $L(\mathcal{B})$ by looking for a lasso with a prefix in $\widetilde{g}$ and a cycle in $\widetilde{h}$. In order to test if a proper language Y_{gh} is contained in $L(\mathcal{B})$, search for a $q \in Q^{in}$, $r \in Q$, $a \in \{0, 1\}$ such that the arc $\langle q, a, r \rangle \in \widetilde{g}$ and the arc $\langle r, 1, r \rangle \in \widetilde{h}$. We call this test of a pair of graphs the *two-arc test*.

Lemma 2. [17] *A Büchi automaton $\mathcal{B}$ is universal iff every proper pair $\langle \widetilde{g}, \widetilde{h} \rangle$ of graphs from $\widetilde{Q}_\mathcal{B}$ passes the two-arc test.*

Lemma 2 yields a PSPACE algorithm to determine universality [17]. Simply check each $\widetilde{g}, \widetilde{h} \in \widetilde{Q}_{\mathcal{B}}$. If Y_{gh} is both proper and not contained in $L(\mathcal{B})$, then the pair $\langle \widetilde{g}, \widetilde{h} \rangle$ provide a counterexample to the universality of $\mathcal{B}$. If no such pair exists, the automaton must be universal. This algorithm faces difficulty on two fronts. First, the number of graphs is 3^{n^2}. Second, checking language nonemptiness is an exponentially difficult problem. To address these problems we construct only graphs with non-empty languages. We borrow the notion of composition from [5], allowing us to use exponential space to compute exactly the needed graphs. Given a graph $\widetilde{g}$ whose language contains the word w_1 and a graph $\widetilde{h}$ whose language contains the word w_2, their composition $\widetilde{g}; \widetilde{h}$ can be defined such that $w_1 w_2 \in L(\widetilde{g}; \widetilde{h})$.

Definition 2. [5] *Given two graphs $\widetilde{g}, \widetilde{h} \in \widetilde{Q}_{\mathcal{B}}$, define their composition $\widetilde{g}; \widetilde{h}$ to be:*

$$\{\langle q, 1, r \rangle \mid q, r, s \in Q, \ \langle q, b, s \rangle \in \widetilde{g}, \ \langle s, c, r \rangle \in \widetilde{h}, \ b = 1 \text{ or } c = 1\}$$
$$\cup \{\langle q, 0, r \rangle \mid q, r, s \in Q, \ \langle q, 0, s \rangle \in \widetilde{g}, \ \langle s, 0, r \rangle \in \widetilde{h}, \ and$$
$$\forall t \in Q, \ b, c \in \{0, 1\} . \ \langle q, a, t \rangle \in \widetilde{g} \wedge \langle t, b, r \rangle \in \widetilde{h} \text{ implies } a = b = 0\}$$

Using composition, we can define a concrete algorithm that explores the space of graphs on-the-fly, searching for a counterexample. Given a Büchi automaton $\mathcal{B}$, for every $\sigma \in \Sigma$, define $\widetilde{g}_\sigma$ to be $\{\langle q, 0, r \rangle \mid q \in Q \setminus F, \ r \in \rho(q, \sigma) \setminus F\} \cup \{\langle q, 1, r \rangle \mid q \in Q, \ r \in \rho(q, \sigma), \ q \text{ or } r \in F\}$. Let $\widetilde{Q}_{\mathcal{B}}^1$ be the set $\{\widetilde{g}_\sigma \mid \sigma \in \Sigma\}$. To generate the non-empty graphs, compose graphs from $\widetilde{Q}_{\mathcal{B}}^1$ until we reach closure. The resulting subset of $\widetilde{Q}_{\mathcal{B}}$, written $\widetilde{Q}_{\mathcal{B}}^f$, contains exactly the graphs with non-empty languages. In addition to non-emptiness, properness requires testing language containment. Recall that a pair of graphs $\langle \widetilde{g}, \widetilde{h} \rangle$ with non-empty languages is proper when both $L(\widetilde{g}) \cdot L(\widetilde{h}) \subseteq L(\widetilde{g})$, and $L(\widetilde{h}) \cdot L(\widetilde{h}) \subseteq L(\widetilde{h})$. We employ composition to provide a novel polynomial time test for the containment of graph languages.

Lemma 3. *For any $\widetilde{g}, \widetilde{h}, \widetilde{k} \in \widetilde{Q}_{\mathcal{B}}^f$, it holds that $L(\widetilde{g}) \cdot L(\widetilde{h}) \subseteq L(\widetilde{k})$ iff $\widetilde{g}; \widetilde{h} = \widetilde{k}$*

Algorithm 1 employs composition to search for proper pairs of graphs and check the universality of a Büchi automaton $\mathcal{B}$. On non-universal automaton, this algorithm can terminate as soon as it finds a counterexample, and thus sometimes avoid computing the entire set of graphs.

Algorithm 1. `RamseyUniversality(`$\mathcal{B}$`)`

Initialize $\widetilde{Q}_{\mathcal{B}}^f \Leftarrow \widetilde{Q}_{\mathcal{B}}^1$
repeat
    Take two graphs $\widetilde{g}, \widetilde{h} \in \widetilde{Q}_{\mathcal{B}}^f$
    Include $\widetilde{g}; \widetilde{h}$ in $\widetilde{Q}_{\mathcal{B}}^f$
    if $\widetilde{g}; \widetilde{h} = \widetilde{g}$ and $\widetilde{h}; \widetilde{h} = \widetilde{h}$ **then**
        if $\langle \widetilde{g}, \widetilde{h} \rangle$ *fails the two-arc test* **then return** *Not Universal*
until $\widetilde{Q}_{\mathcal{B}}^f$ *reaches fixpoint*
return *Universal*

2.2 Rank-Based Complementation

If a Büchi automaton $\mathcal{B}$ does not accept a word w, then every run of $\mathcal{B}$ on w must eventually cease visiting accepting states. The rank-based construction uses a notion of ranks to track the progress of each possible run towards this fair termination. The rank-based construction accepts w precisely if all runs cease visiting accepting states, and so defines a automaton for the complement of $L(\mathcal{B})$. For a definition of this construction, see [12].

An algorithm seeking to refute the universality of $\mathcal{B}$ can look for a lasso in the state-space of the rank-based complement of $\mathcal{B}$. A classical approach is Emerson-Lei backward-traversal nested fixpoint $\nu Y.\mu X.(X \cup (Y \cap F))$ [8]. This nested fixpoint employs the observation that a state in a lasso can reach an arbitrary number of accepting states. The outer fixpoint iteratively computes sets $Y_0, Y_1, \ldots$ such that Y_i contains all states with a path visiting i accepting states. Universality is checked by testing if Y_∞, the set of all states with a path visiting arbitrarily many accepting states, intersects Q^{in}. In contrast to the Ramsey-based approach, this rank-based approach can terminate early on some *universal* automaton, when some Y_i is already disjoint from Q^{in}. If no initial state has a path to i accepting states, then no initial state can lead to a lasso. In this case we already know the complemented automaton is empty, and the original automaton is universal. In consequence, extracting a counter-example from the Emerson-Lei algorithm is non-trivial, and requires that the algorithm fully terminates. Doyen and Raskin implemented this algorithm using a subsumption relation, providing a universality checker that scales to automata an orders of magnitude larger than previous approaches [6].

3   Subsumption in the Ramsey-Based Algorithm

Subsumption has proven to be very effective in the rank-based approach [6] and in the Ramsey-based approach specialized to SCT problems [1]. To use subsumption in the special case of SCT problems, Ben-Amram and Lee replaced a test for an arc in idempotent graphs with a test for strongly-connected components in all graphs. To use subsumption in the general Ramsey-based approach, we need to replace the two-arc test over proper pairs of graphs. We simplify Algorithm 1 by removing the requirement that pairs of graphs should be proper. Instead of examining only pairs $\langle \widetilde{g}, \widetilde{h} \rangle$ where $\widetilde{g}; \widetilde{h} = \widetilde{g}$ and $\widetilde{h}; \widetilde{h} = \widetilde{h}$, we examine every pair $\langle \widetilde{g}, \widetilde{h} \rangle$ of non-empty graphs. When examining a proper pair of graphs, we used the two-arc test: search for a $q \in Q^{in}$, $r \in Q$, $a \in \{0, 1\}$ such that $\langle q, a, r \rangle \in \widetilde{g}$ and $\langle r, 1, r \rangle \in \widetilde{h}$. When examining a pair of graphs that may not be proper, we cannot limit our search to single arcs. We must test for a path from q to r, and a path from r to itself. We test for this path by computing the strongly connected components of $\widetilde{h}$, and testing if some strongly connected component of $\widetilde{h}$ both contains a 1-labeled arc and is reachable from a start state in $\widetilde{g}$.

A *strongly connected component* (SCC) of a graph $\widetilde{g}$ is a maximal set S of nodes, so that for every $q, r \in S$ there is a path from q to r, and a path from r to q. Computing the strongly connected components of a graph can be done in linear time with a depth-first search [4]. An SCC S in a graph $\widetilde{g}$ is 1-labeled when there are $q, r \in S$ with an arc $\langle q, 1, r \rangle \in \widetilde{g}$. We say there is a path from a state q to an SCC S when there is a path from q to an element of S. Once we partition the nodes into strongly connected components, we can simply search for a reachable 1-labeled SCC.

Definition 3. *A pair $\langle \widetilde{g}, \widetilde{h} \rangle$ of graphs passes the* lasso-finding *test when there exists: $q \in Q^{in}$, $r \in Q$, $a \in \{0,1\}$ and $S \subseteq Q$ such that, $\langle q, a, r \rangle \in \widetilde{g}$, there is a path from r to S in $\widetilde{h}$, and S is a 1-labeled SCC of $\widetilde{h}$.*

Lemma 4. $\widetilde{Q}_\mathcal{B}^f$ *contains a pair $\langle \widetilde{g}, \widetilde{h} \rangle$ that fails the lasso-finding test iff $\widetilde{Q}_\mathcal{B}^f$ contains a pair of graphs $\langle \widetilde{g}', \widetilde{h}' \rangle$ that fails the two-arc test.*

In [9], we demonstrated that the Lee, Jones, and Ben-Amram algorithm for size-change termination is a specialized realization of the Ramsey-based containment test. In [1], Ben-Amram and Lee optimize this specialized algorithm, removing certain graphs when computing the closure under composition. Using the lasso-finding test, we now show how to employ Ben-Amram and Lee's subsumption relation for the general case of Büchi universality. Doing so allows us to ignore graphs when they are approximated by other graphs.

Intuitively, a graph $\widetilde{g}$ approximates another graph $\widetilde{h}$ when the arcs of $\widetilde{g}$ are a subset of, or less strict than, the arcs of $\widetilde{h}$. In this case, finding an arc or SCC in $\widetilde{g}$ is strictly harder than finding one in than $\widetilde{h}$. When the right arc can be found in $\widetilde{g}$, then it also occurs in $\widetilde{h}$. When $\widetilde{g}$ does not have a satisfying arc, then we already have a counterexample. Thus we need not consider $\widetilde{h}$.

Formally, given two graphs $\widetilde{g}, \widetilde{h} \in \widetilde{Q}_\mathcal{B}$, we say that $\widetilde{g}$ *approximates* $\widetilde{h}$, written $\widetilde{g} \preceq \widetilde{h}$, when for every arc $\langle q, a, r \rangle \in \widetilde{g}$ there is an arc $\langle q, a', r \rangle \in \widetilde{h}$, $a \leq a'$. Note that approximation is a transitive relation. Using the notion of approximation, we present an algorithm that computes a subset of $\widetilde{Q}_\mathcal{B}^f$, called $\widetilde{Q}_\mathcal{B}^{\preceq}$. A set of graphs $\widetilde{Q}$ is $\preceq$-*closed under composition* when for every $\widetilde{g}, \widetilde{h} \in \widetilde{Q}$, there exists $\widetilde{k} \in \widetilde{Q}$ such that $\widetilde{k} \preceq \widetilde{g}; \widetilde{h}$. Given a set $\widetilde{Q}_\mathcal{B}^1$ of graphs, Algorithm 2 computes a set $\widetilde{Q}_\mathcal{B}^{\preceq}$ by keeping only the minimal elements under the $\preceq$ relation. $\widetilde{Q}_\mathcal{B}^{\preceq}$ will be $\preceq$-closed under composition, but not closed under composition in the normal sense.

Note that the lasso-finding test is required to safely limit our search to graphs in $\widetilde{Q}_\mathcal{B}^{\preceq}$. Since we are now removing elements from $\widetilde{Q}_\mathcal{B}^{\preceq}$, it is possibly that the proper pair of graphs in $\widetilde{Q}_\mathcal{B}^f$ that fails the two-arc test may never be computed: a graph in the pair may be approximated by another graph, one that does not satisfy the conditions of properness. When using the lasso-finding test, on the other hand, we examine all pairs of graphs. As an example, consider the set containing the single graph $\widetilde{g} = \{\langle q, 0, q \rangle, \langle q, 0, r \rangle, \langle r, 0, q \rangle\}$. We leave it to the reader to verify that this set is $\preceq$-closed under composition, and that $\langle \widetilde{g}, \widetilde{g} \rangle$ fails the lasso-finding test, but that $\langle \widetilde{g}, \widetilde{g} \rangle$ is not proper. Similarly, if we consider the graph $\widetilde{g} = \{\langle q, 1, r \rangle, \langle r, 1, q \rangle\}$, we find that $\langle \widetilde{g}, \widetilde{g} \rangle$ fails the two-arc test, but passes the lasso-finding test.

Theorem 1. *Given an initial set $\widetilde{Q}_\mathcal{B}^1$ of graphs, the set $\widetilde{Q}_\mathcal{B}^f$ contains a proper pair $\langle \widetilde{g}, \widetilde{h} \rangle$ of graphs that fails the two-arc test if and only if the set $\widetilde{Q}_\mathcal{B}^{\preceq}$ computed in Algorithm 2 contains a pair $\langle \widetilde{g}', \widetilde{h}' \rangle$ of graphs that fails the lasso-finding test.*

Algorithm 2. `RamseyUniversality(`$\mathcal{B}$`)`

Construct the set $\widetilde{Q}_{\mathcal{B}}^1$ of all single-character graphs
Initialize the worklist $\widetilde{W} \Leftarrow \widetilde{Q}_{\mathcal{B}}^1$
Initialize the set $\widetilde{Q}_{\mathcal{B}}^{\preceq} \Leftarrow \emptyset$
while $\widetilde{W} \neq \emptyset$ **do**
    Remove an element $\widetilde{g}$ from $\widetilde{W}$
    for $\widetilde{h} \in \widetilde{Q}_{\mathcal{B}}^{\preceq}$ **do**
        if $\widetilde{h} \preceq \widetilde{g}$ **then**
           └ Discard $\widetilde{g}$ and exit **for**
        else if $\widetilde{g} \preceq \widetilde{h}$ **then**
           └ Remove $\widetilde{h}$ from $\widetilde{Q}_{\mathcal{B}}^{\preceq}$
        else if $\langle \widetilde{g}, \widetilde{h} \rangle$ *or* $\langle \widetilde{h}, \widetilde{g} \rangle$ *fails the lasso-finding test* **then**
           └ **return** *Not Universal*
    if $\widetilde{g}$ *has not been discarded* **then**
        Add $\widetilde{g}$ to $\widetilde{Q}_{\mathcal{B}}^{\preceq}$
        └ **for** $\widetilde{h} \in \widetilde{Q}_{\mathcal{B}}^1$ **do** Add $\widetilde{g}; \widetilde{h}$ to $\widetilde{W}$
return *Universal*

Based on the algorithm used by Ben-Amram and Lee, Algorithm 2 extends Algorithm 1 to exploit subsumption and avoid computing the entirety of $\widetilde{Q}_{\mathcal{B}}^{f,1}$. To make the algorithm more concrete, a worklist is used to keep track of which graphs have yet to be considered. Further, instead of composing arbitrary pairs of graphs, we compose each graph only with graphs from $\widetilde{Q}_{\mathcal{B}}^1$. Since any composition can be phrased as a sequence of compositions of graphs from $\widetilde{Q}_{\mathcal{B}}^1$, this is sufficient to generate the entirety of $\widetilde{Q}_{\mathcal{B}}^{\preceq}$ while reducing the size of the worklist considerably. To achieve reasonable performance, our implementation memoizes the strongly connected components of graphs and implements the lasso-finding test as an intersection test over two sets of states.

4   Empirical Analysis

The subsumption technique employed in Algorithm 2 is purely a heuristic improvement: the worst-case complexity of the algorithm does not change. Thus the Ramsey-based algorithm has a worst-case running time exponentially slower than that of the rank-based algorithm. Motivated by the strong performance of Ramsey-based algorithms on SCT problems [9], we compare Ramsey and rank based solvers on a terrain of random automata.

To evaluate the performance of various tools on Büchi universality problems, we employ the random model proposed by Tabakov and Vardi and later used by Doyen and Raskin [6,18]. This model fixes the input alphabet as $\Sigma = \{0, 1\}$ and considers the containment of Σ^ω in, and thus the *universality* of, the language of a random automata.

---

[1] This algorithm does not prune $\widetilde{Q}_{\mathcal{B}}^1$ for subsumed graphs. As our alphabet consists of two characters, and $\widetilde{Q}_{\mathcal{B}}^1$ contains two elements, this is acceptable for our use. For larger alphabets, $\widetilde{Q}_{\mathcal{B}}^1$ could be checked for subsumed graphs.

Each automaton $\mathcal{B} = \langle \Sigma, Q, Q^{in}, \rho, F \rangle$ is constructed with a given *size* n, *transition density* r, and *acceptance density* f. Q is simply the set $\{0...n-1\}$, and $Q^{in} = \{0\}$. For each letter $\sigma \in \Sigma$, we choose $\lceil n * r \rceil$ pairs of states $(s, s') \in Q^2$ uniformly at random and the transitions $\langle s, \sigma, s' \rangle$ are included in ρ. We impose one exception to avoid trivial cases of non-universality: the initial node must have at least one outgoing transition for each letter of the alphabet. The set F of accepting states comprises $\lceil n * f \rceil$ states, likewise chosen uniformly at random.

Data points are derived from 100 or more[2] random automata with the given n, r, and f. Each tool is given one hour to solve each problem. When possible, we compute the median running time [6,18]. This allows us to plot the data on a logarithmic scale and easily judge exponential behavior. However, in many cases interesting behavior emerges after a significant percentage of the runs time out. In these cases we measure the timeout percentage instead of median running time.

Our rank-based tool, simply called RANK, is a slightly modified version of the **Mh** tool developed by Doyen and Raskin [6]. Our Ramsey-based tool, called RAMSEY, is based on the **sct/scp** program– an optimized C implementation of the SCT algorithm from Ben-Amram and Lee [1]. We have modified the RAMSEY tool to solve arbitrary Büchi universality problems by implementing Algorithm 2. Both tools can be configured to not employ their subsumption techniques. In this case, we append (ns) to the program name.

All experiments were performed on the Shared University Grid at Rice (SUG@R)[3], a cluster of Sunfire x4150 nodes, each with two 2.83GHz Intel Xeon quad-core processors and 16GB of RAM. Each run is given a dedicated node.

4.1 Subsumption

We know that subsumption is vital to the performance of rank-based solvers [6]. Further, we have observed subsumption's utility on the domain of SCT problems [9]. This motivates us to extend the subsumption technique of [1] to the case of general Büchi universality, resulting in Algorithm 2. Employing observations from Section 4.2 below, we check the practical utility of subsumption on the most difficult terrain point for RAMSEY, where transition density $r = 1.5$ and acceptance density $f = 0.5$. Figure 1 displays RAMSEY's performance as size increases, on a logarithmic scale. If more than 50% of the problems timed out, the median is displayed at 3600 seconds, which flattens the RAMSEY (ns) line at the last data point. We observe that the RAMSEY (ns) line has a higher slope than the RAMSEY line. As this graph uses a logarithmic scale, this difference in the slope indicates an exponential improvement in scalability when subsumption is used. Similar results held for every terrain point we measured, demonstrating that although a heuristic technique, subsumption is required for the scalability of our Ramsey-based approach. We also note that the curves appear to be linear on the logarithmic scale, suggesting that the median running time for this terrain point is $2^{O(n)}$, rather than the $2^{O(n^2)}$ of the worst-case complexity bound.

---

[2] When the results from 100 automata appear anomalous, additional automata are generated and tested to improve the fidelity of the results. No data are ever excluded.

[3] http://rcsg.rice.edu/sugar/

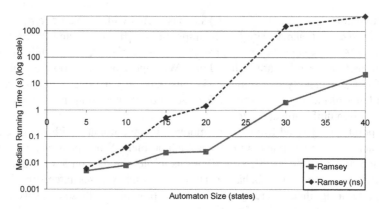

Fig. 1. Subsumption exponentially improves RAMSEY median running times ($r = 1.5, f = 0.5$)

4.2 Behavior over the Terrain

As stated above, randomly generated automata of a given size can vary in two parameters. By changing the transitions and acceptance density, we can observe the behavior of each tool over a variety of terrain points. Automata with a high transition density tend to be universal, while automata with low transition density tend to be non-universal. Acceptance density has a smaller, but still noticeable, affect on universality [6,18]. To map out the behavior of the two tools over this terrain, we hold size constant at $n = 100$, and examined a variety of terrain points. We generate data points for each combination of transition density $r \in \{0.02, 0.26, 0.50, 0.74, 0.98\}$ and acceptance density $f \in \{0.5, 1.5, 2.0, 2.5, 3.0\}$.

Figure 2(a) displays the percentage of cases in which the RANK tool timed out in each terrain point. As observed in [6], there is a sharp spike in timeouts at transitions density $r = 1.5$, acceptance density of 0.26. This spike trails off quickly as transition density changes, and only slightly more gradually as acceptance density changes. There is a subtler high point at $r = 2.0$, $f = 0.02$, where the timeouts rise to 50%. This is

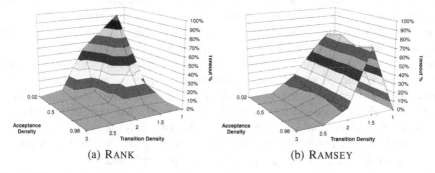

(a) RANK   (b) RAMSEY

Fig. 2. Differences in behavior between RANK and RAMSEY over problem terrain, measured as percentage of problems that timeout when size $n = 100$

consistent with other rank-based tools, even those using different algorithms [18]. Figure 2(b) displays the percentage of cases in which the RAMSEY tool timed out in each terrain point. Like RANK, $r = 1.5$, $f = 0.26$ is a difficult terrain point for RAMSEY. However, RAMSEY continues to time out frequently along all terrain points with transition density $r = 1.5$, and has no significant timeouts at any other terrain points.

Simply glancing at the terrain graphs, it appears that RANK may perform better than RAMSEY in most terrain points. On the other hand, RAMSEY does not exhibit a second high point at $r = 2.0$, $f = 0.02$, and at least for this size of automata RAMSEY beats RANK at the hardest point for RANK. What these graphs clearly show is that those attributes that make a problem hard for RANK to handle are not necessarily the same as those attributes of a problem that cause difficulty for RAMSEY.

4.3 Scalability

We explore some interesting terrain points by measuring the scalability of each algorithm: we hold the transition and acceptance densities constant, and increase size. We choose to investigate three terrain points: a point $r = 1.5$, $f = 0.5$, where RANK seems to perform better than RAMSEY; the main spike $r = 1.5$, $f = 0.26$, where both tools exhibited difficulty solving problems; and a final point $r = 2.0$, $f = 0.05$ near RANK's second high point, where RAMSEY seems to perform better.

Figure 3 displays the median running time for problems with the transition density at $r = 1.5$ and the acceptance density at $f = 0.5$, on a logarithmic scale. If more than 50% of the problems timed out, the median is displayed at 3600 seconds, cutting off RAMSEY's line. As the scale is logarithmic, the difference in the slope between RANK's line and RAMSEY's indicates that, on this terrain point, RANK clearly scales exponentially better than RAMSEY. The third line, labeled "Parallel", displays the behavior of running both tools in parallel on separate machines, and terminating as soon as either tool gives an answer. Is is notable that this line, while having the same slope as RANK's, is lower; indicating there are a number of cases even at this terrain point where RAMSEY terminates before RANK.

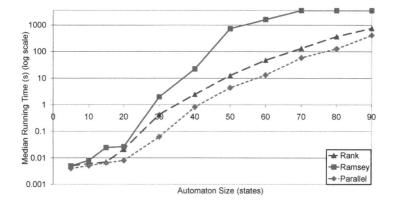

Fig. 3. RANK scales exponentially better than RAMSEY when $r = 1.5$ and $f = 0.5$ (log scale)

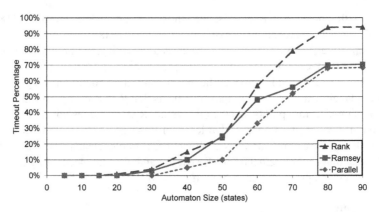

Fig. 4. RAMSEY scales better than RANK at the most difficult terrain point ($r = 1.5$, $f = 0.26$)

The most difficult terrain points for both tools lie near $r = 1.5$, $f = 0.26$. Up to $n = 50$, median running times (see addendum) indicate that RAMSEY performs better than RANK only by a constant factor. Past this this size, the percentage of timeouts is too high for median measurements to be meaningful. However, a gap in the timeout percentage appears as the automata grow larger than 50 states. Figure 4 displays the percentage of runs that timed out for each size n at this terrain point. It does appear that, past $n = 50$, RAMSEY begins to scale significantly better than RANK. We again display the behavior of running both tools in parallel on separate machines using the third line, labeled "Parallel." We again find that even at a terrain point that favors one tool, RAMSEY, we benefit from running both tools simultaneously.

At size $n = 100$, RANK exhibited difficulty when the transition density was 2.0 and the acceptance density was low. We measured the scalability of RAMSEY and RANK

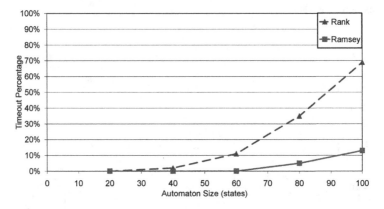

Fig. 5. RAMSEY scales much better than RANK when $r = 2$ and $f = 0.05$

on problems with $r = 2.0$ and $f = 0.05$. At this terrain point the median running times do not increase exponentially for either RANK or RAMSEY. As a large number of problems still did not complete, Figure 5 displays the timeout percentages as size grows. At this terrain point, RAMSEY does appear to scale better than RANK. However the gap is not the exponential improvement we observed when RANK performed better than RAMSEY. At this configuration, running the tools in parallel was only a slight improvement over running RAMSEY alone.

4.4 Universal vs. Non-universal Automata

Section 2 reviews the algorithms used by RANK and RAMSEY to explore the state space of the complemented automaton. Of note is that in certain cases each tools can terminate before computing the entirety of their fixpoints: RANK on universal automata, and RAMSEY on non-universal automata. This suggests that RANK may perform better on universal automata, and RAMSEY may perform better on non-universal automata.

To confirm this hypothesis, we compare RANK and RAMSEY on a corpus of universal and non-universal automata. Our corpus is derived from 1000 automata with size $n = 50$, transition density $r = 1.8$, and acceptance density $f = 0.2$. This point was chosen because of the relatively equal proportion of universal and non-universal automata. Table 1 summarizes the results. RANK does indeed perform better on universal automata. Universal automata were solved in a median time of 108.3 seconds, while on non-universal automata, the median running time was 177.8 seconds. We observe the inverse behavior in RAMSEY: on non-universal automata RAMSEY had a median running time of only 33.1 seconds, while on universal automata the median running time was 253.4 seconds. The universality or non-universality of a problem does affect the performance of each approach.

Table 1. RANK performs better on universal problems, RAMSEY on non-universal problems, measured by median running time ($n = 50, r = 1.8, f = 0.2$)

	Count	RANK	RAMSEY
Universal	460	108.3	253.4
Non-Universal	527	177.8	33.1
Unknown	13		

The question naturally arises: does the difference in performance on universal vs. non-universal automata fully explain the different behaviors of RAMSEY and RANK. This is not the case. As previously noted in Figure 3, RANK performs exponentially better than RAMSEY on automata with a transition density of 1.5 and an acceptance density of 0.5. More than 80% of the solved automata at this terrain point are non-universal: a distribution that should favor RAMSEY. Further, Figure 5 shows a terrain point where RAMSEY scales significantly better than RANK. At this terrain point, more than two-thirds of solved automata with $n > 50$ were universal, and should have favored RANK. Therefore we cannot conclude that the difference in behavior between RANK and RAMSEY is truly attributed to the gap in performance between universal and non-universal automata.

5   Conclusion

This paper tells two stories. The first story is about subsumption. In general, subsumption is a trade off: there is a benefit to reducing the working sets of the algorithms, but checking for subsumed states can be computationally expensive. In the domain of CNF satisfiability solvers, subsumption is generally regarded as an ineffective technique: the overhead of checking for subsumed clauses outweighs any benefit gained from removing them. For checking Büchi automata universality, it has previously been shown that subsumption is not only useful, but vital for the scalability of the rank-based approach [6]. In this paper, we demonstrate that this also holds for the Ramsey-based approach, which use not only a different construction but also a different algorithm to explore the state space of this construction. These results suggest the use of subsumption relations in other constructions, such as the slice-based construction of Kähler and Wilke [11].

The second story is that neither the rank-based approach nor the Ramsey-based approach to Büchi universality testing is clearly superior. This is true despite the massive gap in worst-case complexity between the two approaches. Each approach exhibits distinct behavior on the terrain of random universality problems. Due to these differences, we do not believe a winner takes all approach is best for universality checking. The current best approach is to run both tools in parallel, and see which terminates first. Doing so improves performance by a constant factor, relative to the best tool for any given terrain point.

Preferable to running the algorithms in parallel would be to employ a *portfolio approach*. A portfolio approach attempts to predict which algorithm would perform better on a given problem [10]. To do this, we would have to examine the space of universality problems and discover significant attributes of problems. Transition and acceptance density are not the only observable attributes of an automaton, or even necessarily the most important ones. While they are significant for randomly generated problems, there is no reason to expect that transition and acceptance density are good indicators of difficulty for real-world problems. In the case of SAT solvers, over ninety pertinent attributes were found [7]. Machine-learning techniques were used to identify which features suggest which approach to SAT solving. The challenge that now faces us is discovering a similar body of features with which to characterize Büchi automata, and to create a corpus of automata to characterize. In addition to transition and acceptance density, attributes could include the density of initial states, the number of strongly connected components in the automata, and the density of strongly connecting components containing an accepting state[4]. One point that is well demonstrated in our investigation is that theoretical worst-case analysis often yields little information on actual algorithmic performance; an algorithm running in $2^{O(n^2)}$ can perform better in practice than an algorithm running in $2^{O(n \log n)}$. We do note RAMSEY, the program running in $2^{O(n^2)}$ time and space, sometimes consumed on the order of 20 GB of memory, where RANK rarely consumed more than 300 megabytes.

Finally, in this paper we focus on universality as a special case of Büchi containment that encapsulates its algorithmically difficult aspects. To actually verify that an

---

[4] We thank the reviewers for suggestions on possible criteria.

implementation $\mathcal{A}$ adheres to a specification $\mathcal{B}$, we need to lift our universality testing algorithms to the general case of containment testing. Computing the intersection of two automata uses the product of the state spaces. For the rank-based approach, this results in pairing a state $\mathcal{A}$ with a state in in $\mathrm{KV}(\mathcal{B})$. The theory of rank-based containment testing with subsumption is described in [6] and implemented in RANK. Ramsey-based universality, however, avoids directly exploring the state space of the automata. A theory of Ramsey-based containment was developed for [9], but without subsumption. To add containment testing to RAMSEY requires the extension of the theory developed in this paper for universality testing.

References

1. Ben-Amram, A.M., Lee, C.S.: Program termination analysis in polynomial time. TOPLAS 29(1) (2007)
2. Büchi, J.R.: On a decision method in restricted second order arithmetic. In: ICLMPS (1962)
3. Choueka, Y.: Theories of automata on ω-tapes: A simplified approach. In: JCSS (1974)
4. Cormen, T.H., Leiserson, C.E., Rivest, R.L.: Introduction to Algorithms. MIT Press/McGraw-Hill (1990)
5. Jones, N.D., Lee, C.S., Ben-Amram, A.M.: The size-change principle for program termination. In: POPL, pp. 81–92 (2001)
6. Doyen, L., Raskin, J.-F.: Antichains for the automata-based approach to model-checking. LMCS 1(5), 1–20 (2009)
7. Devkar, A., Shoham, Y., Nudelman, E., Leyton-Brown, K., Hoos, H.: Understanding random SAT: Beyond the clauses-to-variables ratio. In: Wallace, M. (ed.) CP 2004. LNCS, vol. 3258, pp. 438–452. Springer, Heidelberg (2004)
8. Emerson, E.A., Lei, C.-L.: Efficient model checking in fragments of the propositional μ-calculus. In: LICS, pp. 267–278 (1986)
9. Fogarty, S., Vardi, M.Y.: Büchi complementation and size-change termination. In: Kowalewski, S., Philippou, A. (eds.) TACAS 2009. LNCS, vol. 5505, pp. 16–30. Springer, Heidelberg (2009)
10. Andrew, G., McFadden, J., Leyton-Brown, K., Nudelman, E., Shoham, Y.: A portfolio approach to algorithm selection. In: IJCAI, pp. 1542–1543 (2003)
11. Kähler, D., Wilke, T.: Complementation, disambiguation, and determinization of Büchi automata unified. In: Aceto, L., Damgård, I., Goldberg, L.A., Halldórsson, M.M., Ingólfsdóttir, A., Walukiewicz, I. (eds.) ICALP 2008, Part I. LNCS, vol. 5125, pp. 724–735. Springer, Heidelberg (2008)
12. Kupferman, O., Vardi, M.Y.: Weak alternating automata are not that weak. ACM Transactions on Computational Logic 2(2), 408–429 (2001)
13. Michel, M.: Complementation is more difficult with automata on infinite words. CNET, Paris (1988)
14. Rozier, K.Y., Vardi, M.Y.: LTL satisfiability checking. In: Bošnački, D., Edelkamp, S. (eds.) SPIN 2007. LNCS, vol. 4595, pp. 149–167. Springer, Heidelberg (2007)
15. Safra, S.: On the complexity of ω-automata. In: Proc. 29th IEEE Symp. on Foundations of Computer Science, pp. 319–327 (1988)
16. Schewe, S.: Büchi complementation made tight. In: STACS, pp. 661–672 (2009)
17. Sistla, A.P., Vardi, M.Y., Wolper, P.: The complementation problem for Büchi automata with applications to temporal logic. In: Brauer, W. (ed.) ICALP 1985. LNCS, vol. 194, pp. 465–474. Springer, Heidelberg (1985)

18. Tabakov, D., Vardi, M.Y.: Model checking Büchi specifications. In: LATA (2007)
19. Vardi, M.Y.: Automata-theoretic model checking revisited. In: Cook, B., Podelski, A. (eds.) VMCAI 2007. LNCS, vol. 4349, pp. 137–150. Springer, Heidelberg (2007)
20. Wulf, M.D., Doyen, L., Henzinger, T.A., Raskin, J.-F.: Antichains: A new algorithm for checking universality of finite automata. In: Ball, T., Jones, R.B. (eds.) CAV 2006. LNCS, vol. 4144, pp. 17–30. Springer, Heidelberg (2006)

Automated Termination Analysis for Programs with Second-Order Recursion

Markus Aderhold

Technische Universität Darmstadt, Germany
aderhold@informatik.tu-darmstadt.de

Abstract. Many algorithms on data structures such as *terms* (finitely branching trees) are naturally implemented by second-order recursion: A first-order procedure f passes itself as an argument to a second-order procedure like *map*, *every*, *foldl*, *foldr*, etc. to recursively apply f to the direct subterms of a term. We present a method for automated termination analysis of such procedures. It extends the approach of *argument-bounded functions* (i) by inspecting type components and (ii) by adding a facility to take care of second-order recursion. Our method has been implemented and automatically solves the examples considered in the literature. This improves the state of the art of inductive theorem provers, which (without our approach) require user interaction even for termination proofs of simple second-order recursive procedures.

1   Introduction

Functional programs frequently use higher-order procedures such as *map* and *every* that expect functions as parameters [7,12]. For instance, *map* applies a function to each element of a list and returns the list of the result values. Similarly, *every*(p, k) yields *true* iff $p(x)$ evaluates to *true* for all elements x of a list k. If a procedure f calls a higher-order procedure g using f as an argument for g, e. g., $g(f, \ldots)$, we say that f is defined by *higher-order recursion* [8,14].

In this paper, we consider the automated termination analysis of functional programs that may use *second-order recursion*.[1] Typical examples arise in algorithms on finitely branching trees such as terms; e. g., applying a substitution to a term or collecting variables in a term. Termination analysis for such programs is non-trivial: In the higher-order theorem provers Isabelle [8,10,14] and PVS [11], the user needs to assist the system to prove termination in these cases. In contrast, the method we propose solves typical termination problems automatically. Furthermore, our method supplies information that allows a theorem prover to generate useful induction axioms for proofs about such programs.

Figure 1 shows an example program. In Fig. 1(a), data types *bool*, $\mathbb{N}$, and *list*[@A] are defined by enumerating the respective data constructors *true*, *false*, 0, *succ*, ø, and "::". Each argument position of a data constructor is assigned a

---

[1] As in [3], we define the order $o(\tau)$ of base types τ like $\mathbb{N}$ or *list*[$\mathbb{N}$] as 0; the order of a functional type $\tau_1 \times \ldots \times \tau_n \to \tau$ is $1 + \max_i o(\tau_i)$ for a base type τ.

J. Esparza and R. Majumdar (Eds.): TACAS 2010, LNCS 6015, pp. 221–235, 2010.

(a) **structure** *bool* <= *true, false*
     structure $\mathbb{N}$ <= 0, *succ*(*pred* : $\mathbb{N}$)
     structure *list*[@*A*] <= ø, ::(*hd* : @*A*, *tl* : *list*[@*A*])
     procedure *last*(*k* : *list*[@*A*]) : @*A* <=
     assume *k* ≠ ø; *if* *tl*(*k*) = ø *then* *hd*(*k*) *else* *last*(*tl*(*k*)) *end*

(b) **structure** *variable.symbol* <= *variable*(*varID* : $\mathbb{N}$)
     structure *function.symbol* <= *func*(*funcID* : $\mathbb{N}$)
     structure *term* <=
       var(*vsym* : *variable.symbol*),
       apply(*fsym* : *function.symbol*, *args* : *list*[*term*])

     procedure *every*(*p* : @*A* → *bool*, *k* : *list*[@*A*]) : *bool* <=
     if *k* = ø *then* *true* *else* *if* *p*(*hd*(*k*)) *then* *every*(*p*, *tl*(*k*)) *else* *false* *end* *end*
     procedure *groundterm*(*t* : *term*) : *bool* <=
     if ?*var*(*t*) *then* *false* *else* *every*(*groundterm*, *args*(*t*)) *end*

Fig. 1. A functional program with (a) the first-order procedure *last* and (b) the second-order procedure *every* and second-order recursion in procedure *groundterm*

selector function; e. g., selector *pred* denotes the predecessor function. Expressions of the form ?*cons*(*t*) check if *t* denotes a value of the form *cons*(...). In Fig. 1(b), procedure *every* is a second-order procedure that gets a first-order function *p* as argument. Procedure *groundterm* uses *second-order recursion* to check if a term *t* (modeled by data type *term*) does not contain any variables.

Our approach extends the method of *argument-bounded functions* [15,18] that is used, for instance, in the semi-automated verifier √eriFun [17] for termination analysis and the synthesis of suitable induction axioms. Using this approach, termination of *every* can be easily proved: Selector *tl* is *argument-bounded*, which intuitively means $\#(k) \geq \#(tl(k))$ for all lists $k \neq ø$, where $\#(k)$ counts the occurrences of *list*-constructors ø and :: in *k* (and thus corresponds to the length of list *k* plus 1). A system-generated *difference procedure* [15,18] Δ_{tl} : *list*[@*A*] → *bool* decides if this inequality is strict for a given list *k*, which is the case if $k \neq ø$. To prove that the second argument of procedure *every* gets strictly smaller in the recursive call *every*(*p*, *tl*(*k*)), it suffices to show the trivial *termination hypothesis* $\forall k : list[@A].\ k \neq ø \wedge p(hd(k)) \rightarrow \Delta_{tl}(k)$.

Proving termination of *groundterm*, however, is challenging and hence is the main problem we tackle in this paper. The key observation is that *every* applies *p* only to members *x* of list *k*. While in Isabelle the user needs to state and prove this knowledge explicitly as a *congruence theorem*, our approach automatically extracts such information from the definition of *every*. More specifically, our approach detects that for any instantiation of type variable @*A* with a type τ, the number of τ-constructors in each value $x : \tau$ that *p* is applied to by *every* is bounded by the number of τ-constructors in the elements *e* of list *k*: $\sum_{e \in k} \#(e) \geq \#(x)$. We say that *every* is *call-bounded* wrt. *p*. For the second-order recursion in *groundterm* and *args*(*t*) = t_1 :: ... :: t_n :: ø this means $\#(t_1) + ... + \#(t_n) \geq \#(x)$. Since $t = apply(fsym(t), args(t))$ contains one *term*-constructor more than

$args(t)$, we have $\#(t) > \#(t_1) + \ldots + \#(t_n) \geq \#(x)$, so *groundterm* is only called recursively with arguments x that are smaller than t, which ensures termination.

Formally, we parameterize the size measure $\#$ by a type position so that for $args(t) : list[term]$ we can separately count the *list*- and *term*-constructors. This allows us to consider $args : term \rightarrow list[term]$ as argument-bounded wrt. type component *term* (i.e., $args(t)$ contains no more *term*-constructors than t).

The contributions of this paper are:

(1) An extended notion of *argument-boundedness* that also considers *components* of types (Sect. 2), along with a corresponding extension of the *estimation calculus* to automate size estimation proofs (Sect. 3). These extensions allow our approach to prove termination of several purely first-order procedures that cannot be handled by the original approach in [15,18].

(2) The novel notion of *call-boundedness* to automatically prove termination of procedures with second-order recursion (Sect. 4). This extension maintains the advantage that "optimized" induction axioms can be synthesized.

We discuss related work and experimental results in Sect. 5. Proofs of the theorems in this paper are given in [1] and [2] along with further details and examples.

2   Size Estimation for Polymorphic Data Types

In this section we define the basic ingredients for size estimation proofs. We begin with a brief account of the programming language $\mathcal{L}$ (which is the input language of ✓eriFun [17] and roughly corresponds to the second-order fragment of Haskell with strict evaluation); see [1,2,16] for formal details on $\mathcal{L}$.

2.1   Programming Language

The input language $\mathcal{L}$ of ✓eriFun consists of definition principles for freely generated polymorphic data types, for first-order and second-order procedures (based on non-mutual recursion,[2] case analyses via *if*-expressions, and functional composition) that operate on these data types, and for statements about the data types and procedures. Each function symbol can be associated with a so-called *context requirement*, which is stipulated explicitly for procedures (as for *last* in Fig. 1) and implicitly for all selectors. ✓eriFun enforces via proof obligations that the context requirement be satisfied for each function call [13]; e.g., *last*, *hd*, and *tl* may only be called on non-empty lists.

A *base type* is a type variable $@A$ or an expression of the form $str[\tau_1, \ldots, \tau_k]$, where $\tau_1, \ldots, \tau_k$ are base types and *str* is a k-ary type constructor ($k \geq 0$). A *type* is a base type or an expression of the form $\tau_1 \times \ldots \times \tau_k \rightarrow \tau$ for types $\tau_1, \ldots, \tau_k, \tau$. *Type constructors* are defined by expressions of the following form:

$$\texttt{structure } str[@A_1, \ldots, @A_k] <= \ldots, \; cons(sel_1 : \tau_1, \ldots, sel_n : \tau_n), \; \ldots \quad (1)$$

---

[2] Our approach can be extended to handle mutual recursion without much difficulty.

The τ_j are base types, and str may only occur as $str[@A_1, \ldots, @A_k]$ in the τ_j. Each $cons$ is called a *data constructor* and the sel_j are called *selectors*.

We will address *type symbols* (i.e., type constructors and type variables) in a base type by their *position* $\pi \in \mathbb{N}^*$: $@A|_\epsilon := @A$, $str[\tau_1, \ldots, \tau_k]|_\epsilon := str$, and $str[\tau_1, \ldots, \tau_k]|_{h\pi'} := \tau_h|_{\pi'}$ for $h \in \{1, \ldots, k\}$. $Pos(\tau) \subseteq \mathbb{N}^*$ denotes the set of all valid positions in type τ. For a data constructor $cons(sel_1 : \tau_1, \ldots, sel_n : \tau_n)$ and a type symbol S, the set

$$Pos_S(cons) := \{(j, \pi) \in \{1, \ldots, n\} \times \mathbb{N}^* \mid \pi \in Pos(\tau_j), \tau_j|_\pi = S\} \qquad (2)$$

contains the positions of all occurrences of S in the selector types of $cons$, given by a selector number j and a position π in τ_j. Data constructor $cons$ is called *reflexive* if $Pos_{str}(cons) \neq \emptyset$, and *irreflexive* otherwise.

Subsequently, we let $\Sigma(P)$ denote the signature of all function symbols defined by an $\mathcal{L}$-program P. As usual, $\mathcal{T}(\Sigma(P), \mathcal{V})$ denotes the set of all *terms* over $\Sigma(P)$ and a set $\mathcal{V}$ of variables. We write $\mathcal{T}(\Sigma(P))$ instead of $\mathcal{T}(\Sigma(P), \emptyset)$ for the set of all *ground terms* over $\Sigma(P)$. $\Sigma(P)^c \subset \Sigma(P)$ contains all data constructors of P. $\mathcal{CL}(\Sigma(P), \mathcal{V})$ is the set of *clauses* over $\Sigma(P)$, i.e., sets of literals. A *literal* is an if-free Boolean term or the negation $if(b, false, true)$ of such a term.

For a ground type[3] τ, $\mathbb{V}(P)_\tau$ denotes the "values" of type τ: If τ is a ground base type, $\mathbb{V}(P)_\tau := \mathcal{T}(\Sigma(P)^c)_\tau$, and for each ground type $\tau = \tau_1 \times \ldots \times \tau_k \to \tau_{k+1}$, $\mathbb{V}(P)_\tau$ contains all closed (i.e., no free variables) λ-expressions of type τ; e.g., $\lambda t : term.\ groundterm(t) \in \mathbb{V}(P)_{term \to bool}$.

The call-by-value interpreter $eval_P : \mathcal{T}(\Sigma(P)) \mapsto \mathbb{V}(P)$ is a partial function that defines the operational semantics of $\mathcal{L}$ [2]. The evaluation of a ground term t either (i) succeeds and yields a value $eval_P(t) \in \mathbb{V}(P)$ or (ii) diverges, because a procedure called in t does not terminate.

A procedure **procedure** $f(x_1 : \tau_1, \ldots, x_n : \tau_n) : \tau \mathrel{<=}$ **assume** $c_f;\ B_f$ of a program P *terminates* iff the interpreter $eval_P$ returns a value for each procedure call $f(q_1, \ldots, q_n)$. The q_i are either constructor ground terms or λ-expressions that contain only calls of arbitrary, but *terminating* functions. Program P *terminates* iff all procedures f defined in P terminate.

A universally quantified formula of the form $\forall x_1 : \tau_1, \ldots, x_n : \tau_n.\ b$, where $b \in \mathcal{T}(\Sigma(P), \mathcal{V})_{bool}$, is *true* iff P terminates and $eval_{P'}(b[\vec{q}]) = true$ for each terminating program $P' \supseteq P$ and all $q_1, \ldots, q_n \in \mathbb{V}(P')$.[4]

2.2   A Size Measure for Values of Base Types

Our size measure $\#(t, \pi)$ for terms t is parameterized with a type position π so that we can precisely specify which data constructors are to be counted. Figure 2 sketches an implementation of Mergesort: Procedure $split$ splits list k into two lists that are recursively sorted and then merged together by some procedure $merge$. To prove termination of $msort$, we need to show that $split$ is strictly argument-bounded: $\#(k, \epsilon) > \#(split(k), \mathbf{1})$ and $\#(k, \epsilon) > \#(split(k), \mathbf{2})$. The type position distinguishes between the *list*-constructors of the pair of lists.

---

[3] A *ground (base) type* is a (base) type without type variables; e.g., $list[\mathbb{N}]$.

[4] Program P' may define additional data types and procedures.

```
structure pair[@A, @B] <= mkpair(fst : @A,  snd : @B)
procedure split(k : list[@A]) : pair[list[@A], list[@A]] <= ...
procedure msort(k : list[N]) : list[N] <=
if k = ø then ø else if tl(k) = ø then k
  else merge(msort(fst(split(k))), msort(snd(split(k)))) end end
procedure filter(k : list[@A], p : @A → bool) : list[@A] <=
if k = ø then ø else if p(hd(k)) then hd(k) :: filter(tl(k), p)
                          else filter(tl(k), p)  end end
procedure qsort(k : list[N]) : list[N] <=
if k = ø then ø else qsort(filter(tl(k), λn : N. n ≤ hd(k))) <> hd(k) ::
                     qsort(filter(tl(k), λn : N. n > hd(k)))  end
```

Fig. 2. Implementation of Mergesort (sketch) and Quicksort

Definition 1. *For each ground base type* $\tau = str[\tau'_1, \ldots, \tau'_k]$ *as in* (1) *the* size measure $\#_\tau : T(\Sigma(P)^c)_\tau \times Pos(\tau) \to \mathbb{N}$ *is defined by* $\#_\tau(cons(t_1, \ldots, t_n), \pi) :=$

$$
\begin{cases}
1 & \text{if } \pi = \epsilon \text{ and cons is irreflexive,} \\
2 + \sum_{(j,\pi') \in Pos_{str}(cons)} \#_{\theta(\tau_j)}(t_j, \pi') & \text{if } \pi = \epsilon \text{ and cons is reflexive,} \\
\sum_{(j,\pi') \in Pos_{@A_h}(cons)} \#_{\theta(\tau_j)}(t_j, \pi'\pi'') & \text{if } \pi = h\pi'',
\end{cases}
$$

where $\theta := \{@A_1/\tau'_1, \ldots, @A_k/\tau'_k\}$ *instantiates the type variables of* str. *If type* τ *is obvious from the context, we will usually omit the type index in* $\#_\tau$.

Intuitively, the size $\#(t, \pi)$ of a term $t \in T(\Sigma(P)^c)_\tau$ is computed as follows: We replicate the type (and data) constructor definitions so that each type constructor occurs at most once in type τ. Then $\#(t, \pi)$ counts the $\tau|_\pi$-constructors in t. For example, $list[list[N]]$ is transformed into $listA[listB[N]]$, so $\#(t, \epsilon)$ counts the $listA$-constructors in t and $\#(t, 1)$ counts the $listB$-constructors in t.

The formal definition of the size measure above directly uses the type position without needing to replicate any type constructors. Irreflexive data constructors get weight 1. A reflexive data constructor $cons(sel_1 : \tau_1, \ldots, sel_n : \tau_n)$ in a term $cons(t_1, \ldots, t_n)$ is counted with weight[5] 2 and we recurse into those $t_j : \theta(\tau_j)$ that *by definition of cons* may also contain str-constructors ($\tau_j|_{\pi'} = str$). For instance, for $\tau := list[list[N]]$ and $\pi := \epsilon$ we recursively add the size $\#(t_2, \epsilon)$ of the tl-component of $t_1 :: t_2$, whereas we do *not* recurse into the hd-component t_1. Finally, for $\pi = h\pi''$ we recursively add up the sizes of those t_j that contain $\tau'_h|_{\pi''}$-constructors, so we recurse into the occurrences of the h-th type parameter $@A_h$ in τ_j. For example, for $\tau := list[list[N]]$, term $t_1 :: t_2$, and $\pi := 1$, $\#_{list[N]}(t_1, \epsilon) + \#_{list[list[N]]}(t_2, 1)$ counts the $list$-constructors of the *inner* lists.

Example 1. For type $\tau := list[N]$, $\#_{list[N]}(t, \epsilon) = 2R + I$ for the numbers R and $I = 1$ of occurrences of :: and ø in t, respectively, whereas $\#_{list[N]}(t, 1)$ is the

---

[5] This simplifies some size estimation proofs; e. g., one can prove that $apply(f, l)$ is greater than $var(v)$ without having to check if the argument list l is non-empty.

sum of the sizes of the elements in list t. Note that $\#_{list[\mathbb{N}]}(\emptyset, 1) = 0$, whereas $\#_{list[\mathbb{N}]}(0 :: \emptyset, 1) = \#_{\mathbb{N}}(0, \epsilon) = 1 \neq 0$. Thus $\#_{list[\mathbb{N}]}(t, 1) = 0$ iff $t = \emptyset$. This a useful property, cf. the end of Sect. 2.4. $\diamondsuit$

Example 2. For terms $t \in \mathcal{T}(\Sigma(P)^c)_{term}$, $\#_{term}(t, \epsilon)$ counts the occurrences of *term*-constructors *var* (with weight 1) and *apply* (with weight 2) in t. $\diamondsuit$

2.3   Argument-Bounded Functions

A function f is called *argument-bounded* iff the result $f(\ldots, t, \ldots)$ of a function call is bounded by argument t of the call wrt. the size measure (provided that the function may be applied to t); e.g., $\#(tl(k), \epsilon) \leq \#(k, \epsilon)$ for each $k \neq \emptyset$. Such facts are used to show that some parameter x of a procedure p decreases in recursive calls if f is used in the argument of a recursive call; e.g., $p(f(x))$. For the sake of readability we consider only unary functions here, which can be easily generalized to arbitrary arity [1].

Definition 2. *A function $f : \tau \to \tau'$ with context requirement c_f is (π, ϱ)-argument-bounded for $\pi \in Pos(\tau)$ and $\varrho \in Pos(\tau')$ iff (i) τ is a base type with $\tau|_\pi = \tau'|_\varrho$ and (ii) $\#(q, \pi) \geq \#(eval_P(f(q)), \varrho)$ for all $q \in \mathbb{V}(P)$ with $eval_P(c_f[q]) = true.$*[6]

Example 3. Procedure *last* (Fig. 1) is $(1, \epsilon)$-argument-bounded: The size of the last element of list k is bounded by the sum of the sizes of k's elements.

Procedure *filter* (Fig. 2) is (ϵ, ϵ)-argument-bounded wrt. k, because the list of all elements x in k that satisfy $p(x)$ is not longer than k. $\diamondsuit$

Selectors are argument-bounded, as they return a component of their input:

Theorem 1. *Let $sel_j : \tau \to \tau_j$ be a selector as in (1), $\tau = str[@A_1, \ldots, @A_k]$, $\pi \in Pos(\tau)$, and $\varrho \in Pos(\tau_j)$. If $\tau|_\pi = \tau_j|_\varrho$, then sel_j is (π, ϱ)-argument-bounded.*

Example 4. $pred(\ldots) : \mathbb{N} \to \mathbb{N}$ is (ϵ, ϵ)-argument-bounded. $hd : list[@A] \to @A$ is $(1, \epsilon)$-argument-bounded: The size of the first element of a non-empty list k is bounded by the sum of the sizes of all elements in k. $tl : list[@A] \to list[@A]$ is (ϵ, ϵ)-argument-bounded, as $tl(k)$ contains fewer *list*-constructors "::" than k. tl is also $(1, 1)$-argument-bounded, because $tl(k)$ contains a subset of the elements in k. Finally, selector $args : term \to list[term]$ is $(\epsilon, 1)$-argument-bounded. $\diamondsuit$

2.4   Difference Procedures

Using argument-bounded functions, we can establish inequalities like $\#(k, \epsilon) \geq \#(tl(k), \epsilon)$ to ensure that the second argument of procedure *every* does not increase in the recursive call (cf. Fig. 1). However, this inequality needs to be strict to guarantee termination of *every*. Strictness of such inequalities is expressed by so-called *difference procedures*; e.g., $\Delta_{tl}^{\epsilon, \epsilon} : list[@A] \to bool$ returns *true* iff $\#(k, \epsilon) > \#(tl(k), \epsilon)$.

---

[6] "$q \in \mathbb{V}(P)$" implicitly means that τ is instantiated to a ground base type.

(a) procedure $\Delta^{\epsilon,\epsilon}_{pred(...)}(x : \mathbb{N})$: $bool$ <= assume $?succ(x)$; $true$
    procedure $\Delta^{\epsilon,\epsilon}_{tl}(k : list[@A])$: $bool$ <= assume $?{::}(k)$; $true$
    procedure $\Delta^{\epsilon,1}_{args}(t : term)$: $bool$ <= assume $?apply(t)$; $true$

(b) procedure $\Delta^{1,\epsilon}_{hd}(k : list[@A])$: $bool$ <= assume $?{::}(k)$; $?{::}(tl(k))$
    procedure $\Delta^{1,1}_{tl}(k : list[@A])$: $bool$ <= assume $?{::}(k)$; $true$

Fig. 3. Some automatically synthesized difference procedures for selectors

Definition 3. *For a* (π, ϱ)-*argument-bounded function* $f : \tau \to \tau'$ *with context requirement* c_f, $\Delta^{\pi,\varrho}_f : \tau \to bool$ *is a* (π, ϱ)-*difference function for* f *iff (i)* $\Delta^{\pi,\varrho}_f$ *also has context requirement* c_f *and (ii) for all* $q \in \mathbb{V}(P)$ *with* $eval_P(c_f[q]) = true$

$$eval_P\big(\Delta^{\pi,\varrho}_f(q)\big) = true \iff \#(q, \pi) > \#(eval_P(f(q)), \varrho) \ .$$

(ϵ, ϱ)-argument-bounded selectors have quite simple difference procedures, because the selector cancels the leading data constructor, cf. Fig. 3(a):

Theorem 2. *Let* $sel_j : \tau \to \tau_j$ *be an* (ϵ, ϱ)-*argument-bounded selector for some* ϱ. *Then a* (ϵ, ϱ)-*difference procedure for* sel_j *is given by*

procedure $\Delta^{\epsilon,\varrho}_{sel_j}(x : \tau)$: $bool$ <= assume $?cons(x)$; $true$.

The synthesis of (π, ϱ)-difference procedures for selectors with $\pi \neq \epsilon$ is a bit more involved and described in [1,2]. Figure 3(b) illustrates the idea by examples. $\Delta^{1,\epsilon}_{hd}$ returns $true$ iff list k contains at least two elements: Since the size of each element in k is ≥ 1, the size of the first element $hd(k)$ is smaller than the sum of the sizes of all elements in k. The uniform synthesis of such procedures uses the fact that $\#(hd(k) :: tl(k), 1) > \#(hd(k), \epsilon)$ iff $\#(tl(k), 1) > 0$, i.e., iff $?{::}(tl(k))$.

3   Estimation Proofs

So-called estimation proofs can be used to verify that a procedure computes an argument-bounded function. We obtain estimation proofs from the estimation calculus, which is also used to synthesize difference procedures for argument-bounded procedures and to generate termination hypotheses for recursively defined procedures.

3.1   The Estimation Calculus

The estimation calculus is used to prove inequalities $\#(t_1, \pi_1) \geq \#(t_2, \pi_2)$. The inequalities to be shown are given by some set E. When proving an inequality, a clause Δ (called a *difference equivalent of* E) is synthesized such that the proved inequality is strict iff one of the literals in Δ holds.

Definition 4. *For a terminating program* P, *let* $\Gamma_{\pi,\varrho}$ *be a family of* (π, ϱ)-*argument-bounded function symbols in* P. *Given a* call context $C \in \mathcal{CL}(\Sigma(P), \mathcal{V})$, *the estimation calculus is defined by:*

Language: *Estimation tuples of the form* $\langle \Delta, E \rangle$, *where* $\Delta \in \mathcal{CL}(\Sigma(P), \mathcal{V})$ *and* $E \subseteq_{fin} \mathcal{E}(\Sigma(P), \mathcal{V}) := \{(t_1, \pi_1) \succcurlyeq (t_2, \pi_2) \mid t_i \in \mathcal{T}(\Sigma(P), \mathcal{V})_{\tau_i}$ *for some base types* $\tau_1, \tau_2, \ \pi_i \in Pos(\tau_i)$ *for* $i = 1, 2$ *and* $\tau_1|_{\pi_1} = \tau_2|_{\pi_2}\}$.

Inference Rules: *The following estimation rules are given for each type constructor str and data constructors cons, rcons, ircons, ircons$_1$, and ircons$_2$ of str, where rcons is* reflexive *and all ircons$_i$ are* irreflexive:[7]

Identity

(1) $\dfrac{\langle \Delta, E \uplus \{(t, \pi) \succcurlyeq (t, \pi)\} \rangle}{\langle \Delta, E \rangle}$

Equivalence

(2) $\dfrac{\langle \Delta, E \uplus \{(t_1, \epsilon) \succcurlyeq (t_2, \epsilon)\} \rangle}{\langle \Delta, E \rangle}$ *if* $C \vdash ?ircons_1(t_1)$ *and* $C \vdash ?ircons_2(t_2)$

Strong Estimation

(3) $\dfrac{\langle \Delta, E \uplus \{(t_1, \epsilon) \succcurlyeq (t_2, \epsilon)\} \rangle}{\langle \Delta \cup \{true\}, E \rangle}$ *if* $C \vdash ?rcons(t_1)$ *and* $C \vdash ?ircons(t_2)$

Strong Embedding

(4) $\dfrac{\langle \Delta, E \uplus \{(t_1, \epsilon) \succcurlyeq (t_2, \pi_2)\} \rangle}{\langle \Delta \cup \{true\}, E \cup \{(SEL_j(t_1), \pi_1) \succcurlyeq (t_2, \pi_2)\} \rangle}$ *if* $C \vdash ?rcons(t_1)$ *and* $(j, \pi_1) \in Pos_{str}(rcons)$

Argument Estimation

(5) $\dfrac{\langle \Delta, E \uplus \{(t', \pi') \succcurlyeq (f(t, t_1, \ldots, t_n), \varrho)\} \rangle}{\langle \Delta \cup \{\Delta_f^{\pi, \varrho}(t, t_1, \ldots, t_n)\}, E \cup \{(t', \pi') \succcurlyeq (t, \pi)\} \rangle}$ *if* $f \in \Gamma_{\pi, \varrho}$

Weak Embedding

(6) $\dfrac{\langle \Delta, E \uplus \{(t_1, \epsilon) \succcurlyeq (t_2, \epsilon)\} \rangle}{\langle \Delta, E \cup \{(SEL_j(t_1), \pi) \succcurlyeq (SEL_j(t_2), \pi) \mid (j, \pi) \in Pos_{str}(rcons)\} \rangle}$
if $C \vdash ?rcons(t_1)$ *and* $C \vdash ?rcons(t_2)$

Constructor Wrapping

(7) $\dfrac{\langle \Delta, E \uplus \{(t, \varrho) \succcurlyeq (cons(t_1, \ldots, t_n), h\pi')\} \rangle}{\langle \Delta, E \cup \{(t, \varrho) \succcurlyeq (t_j, \pi\pi')\} \rangle}$ *if* $Pos_{@A_h}(cons) = \{(j, \pi)\}$

Minimum

(8) $\dfrac{\langle \Delta, E \uplus \{(t_1, \epsilon) \succcurlyeq (t_2, \epsilon)\} \rangle}{\langle \Delta \cup \{?rcons(t_1) \mid rcons \in R\}, E \rangle}$
if $C \vdash ?ircons(t_2)$ *and* R *is the set of all reflexive constructors of str*

Deduction: *We write* $\langle \Delta_0, E_0 \rangle \Rightarrow_{\Gamma, C} \langle \Delta_1, E_1 \rangle$ *iff* $\langle \Delta_1, E_1 \rangle$ *results from* $\langle \Delta_0, E_0 \rangle$ *by applying some estimation rule.* $\Rightarrow^*_{\Gamma, C}$ *denotes the reflexive and transitive closure of* $\Rightarrow_{\Gamma, C}$. $\langle \Delta_0, E_0 \rangle \Rightarrow^*_{\Gamma, C} \langle \Delta_n, E_n \rangle$ *is called a* deduction *of* $\langle \Delta_n, E_n \rangle$ *from* $\langle \Delta_0, E_0 \rangle$. *We use the notation* $\vdash_{\Gamma, C} \langle \Delta, (t_1, \pi_1) \succcurlyeq (t_2, \pi_2) \rangle$ *iff* $\langle \emptyset, \{(t_1, \pi_1) \succcurlyeq (t_2, \pi_2)\} \rangle \Rightarrow^*_{\Gamma, C} \langle \Delta, \emptyset \rangle$. $(t_1, \pi_1) \succcurlyeq_{\Gamma, C} (t_2, \pi_2)$ *denotes the existence of a* difference equivalent Δ *with* $\vdash_{\Gamma, C} \langle \Delta, (t_1, \pi_1) \succcurlyeq (t_2, \pi_2) \rangle$.

---

[7] The rules are applied from top to bottom. We write $C \vdash ?cons(t)$ iff (i) $t = cons(\ldots)$ or (ii) $?cons(t) \in C$ or (iii) $\neg ?cons'(t) \in C$ for all str-constructors $cons' \neq cons$. $SEL_j(t)$ stands for t_j if $t = cons(\ldots, t_j, \ldots)$, and abbreviates $sel_j(t)$ otherwise.

Definition 4 extends the calculus from [15,18] by type positions π and rule (7) for data constructors such as *mkpair* (Fig. 2) that just wrap the item of interest; e. g., to show $\#(t, \varrho) \geq \#(mkpair(t_1, t_2), 1)$ it suffices to show $\#(t, \varrho) \geq \#(t_1, \epsilon)$.

Example 5. We get the following estimation proof for call context $C := \{k \neq \emptyset\}$:

$$\langle \emptyset, \ \{(k, \epsilon) \succcurlyeq (filter(tl(k), g), \epsilon)\} \rangle$$
$$\Rightarrow_{\Gamma, C} \langle \{\Delta_{filter}^{\epsilon, \epsilon}(tl(k), g)\}, \ \{(k, \epsilon) \succcurlyeq (tl(k), \epsilon)\} \rangle \qquad \qquad \text{by (5)}$$
$$\Rightarrow_{\Gamma, C} \langle \{true, \ \Delta_{filter}^{\epsilon, \epsilon}(tl(k), g)\}, \ \{(tl(k), \epsilon) \succcurlyeq (tl(k), \epsilon)\} \rangle \qquad \text{by (4)}$$
$$\Rightarrow_{\Gamma, C} \langle \{true, \ \Delta_{filter}^{\epsilon, \epsilon}(tl(k), g)\}, \ \emptyset \rangle \qquad \qquad \text{by (1)} \qquad \diamond$$

In the following, we use expressions of the form (i) $(t_1, \pi_1) \geqslant_\# (t_2, \pi_2)$ and (ii) $(t_1, \pi_1) >_\# (t_2, \pi_2)$ for terms $t_i \in \mathcal{T}(\Sigma(P), V)_{\tau_i}$ and positions $\pi_i \in Pos(\tau_i)$, $i = 1, 2$, with $\tau_1|_{\pi_1} = \tau_2|_{\pi_2}$. Such expressions are *true* iff (i) $\#(eval_P(t_1), \pi_1) \geq \#(eval_P(t_2), \pi_2)$ or (ii) $\#(eval_P(t_1), \pi_1) > \#(eval_P(t_2), \pi_2)$, respectively.

Theorem 3. *The estimation calculus is sound: If* $\vdash_{\Gamma, C} \langle \Delta, (t_1, \pi_1) \succcurlyeq (t_2, \pi_2) \rangle$, *then the following formulas are true (where* $x_1, \dots, x_n$ *are all variables in* C, t_1, *and* t_2 *such that* $x_i \in V_{\tau_i}$ *for all* $i \in \{1, \dots, n\}$*):*

(1) $\forall x_1 : \tau_1, \dots, x_n : \tau_n. \ \bigwedge C \rightarrow (t_1, \pi_1) \geqslant_\# (t_2, \pi_2)$

(2) $\forall x_1 : \tau_1, \dots, x_n : \tau_n. \ \bigwedge C \rightarrow [\bigvee \Delta \leftrightarrow (t_1, \pi_1) >_\# (t_2, \pi_2)]$

Theorem 4. *The set* $\{ (t_1, \pi_1) \succcurlyeq (t_2, \pi_2) \in \mathcal{E}(\Sigma(P), V) \mid (t_1, \pi_1) \geqslant_{\Gamma, C} (t_2, \pi_2) \}$ *of provable size estimation problems is decidable.*

Thus whenever a proof procedure for the estimation calculus finds a proof of $(t_1, \pi_1) \geqslant_{\Gamma, C} (t_2, \pi_2)$, we know that t_1 is at least as big as t_2 by Theorem 3. If no estimation proof exists, the inequality might still hold, because the estimation calculus is incomplete. However, it is powerful enough to solve termination problems that are relevant in practice, see Sect. 5.

3.2   Proving Argument-Boundedness of Procedures

Using the estimation calculus, we can prove argument-boundedness of a procedure f by analyzing the *result terms* $t_1, \dots, t_n$ of f (these are maximal *if*-free terms outside an *if*-condition in the body B_f). The *call context* $C_i \in \mathcal{CL}(\Sigma(P), V)$ of a result term t_i consists of the conditions in B_f that lead to t_i.

Theorem 5. *Let* procedure $f(x : \tau) : \tau' <=$ assume c_f; B_f *be a terminating procedure,* $\pi \in Pos(\tau)$, *and* $\varrho \in Pos(\tau')$ *such that (i)* τ *is a base type with* $\tau|_\pi = \tau'|_\varrho$ *and (ii)* $\vdash_{\Gamma, C_i}^f \langle \Delta_i, (x, \pi) \succcurlyeq (t_i, \varrho) \rangle$ *for each result term* t_i *of* f *under call context* C_i *and some* Δ_i, *where* $\vdash_{\Gamma, C_i}^f$ *differs from* $\vdash_{\Gamma, C_i}$ *in that the* Argument Estimation *rule (5) may also be used for each recursive call* $f(t')$ *in* t_i.
   Then f *is* (π, ϱ)*-argument-bounded and* procedure $\Delta_f^{\pi, \varrho}(x : \tau) : bool <= B_{\Delta_f}$ *is a* (π, ϱ)*-difference procedure for* f, *where* B_{Δ_f} *is derived from* B_f *by replacing each result term* t_i *with the disjunction* $\bigvee \Delta_i$ *(represented by if-conditionals).*

```
procedure Δ₁,ₑ_last(k : list[@A]) : bool <=
assume k ≠ ø;  if tl(k) = ø then false else true end

procedure Δᵉ,ₑ_filter(k : list[@A], p : @A → bool) : bool <=
if k = ø then false else if p(hd(k)) then Δᵉ,ₑ_filter(tl(k), p) else true end end
```

Fig. 4. Difference procedures for argument-bounded procedures

Example 6. Procedure *last* shown in Fig. 1(a) is $(1, \epsilon)$-argument-bounded, because $\vdash^{last}_{\Gamma, C_1} \langle \Delta_1, (k, 1) \rangle \succcurlyeq (hd(k), \epsilon) \rangle$ for $C_1 := \{k \neq \emptyset, tl(k) = \emptyset\}$, $\Delta_1 := \{\Delta^{1,\epsilon}_{hd}(k)\}$, and $\vdash^{last}_{\Gamma, C_2} \langle \Delta_2, (k, 1) \rangle \succcurlyeq (last(tl(k)), \epsilon) \rangle$ for $C_2 := \{k \neq \emptyset, tl(k) \neq \emptyset\}$, $\Delta_2 := \{\Delta^{1,1}_{tl}(k), \Delta^{1,\epsilon}_{last}(tl(k))\}$. $\bigvee \Delta_1$ simplifies to *false* and $\bigvee \Delta_2$ simplifies to *true* using the definition of the difference procedures (Fig. 3) and call contexts C_1 and C_2. Difference procedure $\Delta^{1,\epsilon}_{last}$ is shown in Fig. 4: The last element of list k is smaller than the sum of the sizes of all list elements if the length of k is ≥ 2.◇

Example 7. For procedure *filter* (Fig. 2), the difference procedure $\Delta^{\epsilon,\epsilon}_{filter}$ wrt. parameter k (Fig. 4) reflects the intuition that the returned sublist of k is shorter than k iff at least one element x of k does *not* satisfy $p(x)$.   ◇

4   Automated Termination Proofs

We implicitly assume procedure bodies to be in η-long form to clearly exhibit *indirect* function calls; e.g., $every(p, tl(k))$ abbreviates $every(\lambda x : @A.\ p(x), tl(k))$ in Fig. 1, because $p =_\eta \lambda x : @A.\ p(x)$. Subterm $p(x)$ is an *indirect* function call, whereas $p(hd(k))$ and $every(\lambda x : @A.\ p(x), tl(k))$ are *direct* function calls:

Definition 5. *A direct call of a function f in a term t is a subterm $f(t_1, \ldots, t_n)$ of t that occurs outside a λ-expression. A subterm $f(t_1, \ldots, t_n)$ of t inside a λ-expression is an indirect call of f.*

Definition 6. *For a procedure or λ-expression f with body B_f and parameters $x_1, \ldots, x_n$, a procedure or λ-expression g, and $q_1, \ldots, q_n, q'_1, \ldots, q'_m \in \mathbb{V}(P)$, we write $f(q_1, \ldots, q_n) \triangleright g(q'_1, \ldots, q'_m)$ iff B_f contains a subterm $h(t'_1, \ldots, t'_m)$ under some call context C such that for $\sigma := \{x_1/q_1, \ldots, x_n/q_n\}$, $\sigma(h) =_\eta g$, $eval_P(\sigma(c)) = true$ for all $c \in C$, and $q'_i = eval_P(\sigma(t'_i))$ for all $i = 1, \ldots, m$.*

Intuitively, relation $\triangleright$ means "requires evaluation of". For instance, we have $every(groundterm, var(q) :: \emptyset) \triangleright groundterm(var(q))$.

Now we are ready to state a termination criterion for procedures *without* second-order recursion. The formulas *(ii)* of Theorem 6 are so-called *termination hypotheses*; if these formulas are true, the procedure terminates.

Theorem 6. *A procedure* procedure $f(x : \tau) : \tau' <=$ assume c_f; B_f *terminates if all procedures $g \neq f$ occurring in B_f and c_f terminate and if there is some $\pi \in Pos(\tau)$ such that each recursive call $f(t)$ in B_f under some call context $C \in \mathcal{CL}(\Sigma(P), \mathcal{V})$ is a direct procedure call such that (i) $\vdash_{\Gamma, C} \langle \Delta, (x, \pi) \rangle \succcurlyeq (t, \pi) \rangle$ for some Δ, and (ii) $\forall x : \tau.\ \bigwedge C \to \bigvee \Delta$ is true.*

Example 8. Procedure *qsort* (Fig. 2) terminates. For $\pi := \epsilon$, $C := \{k \neq \emptyset\}$, and any g, $(k, \epsilon) \geqslant_{\Gamma, C} (filter(tl(k), g), \epsilon)$ with $\bigvee \Delta = true$, cf. Example 5.   ◇

Example 9. Procedure *termlist.size* terminates according to Theorem 6:

> **procedure** *termlist.size*$(k : list[term]) : \mathbb{N} <=$
> *if* $k = \emptyset$ *then* 0
>   *else if* ?*var*$(hd(k))$
>   *then* $1 + termlist.size(tl(k))$
>   *else* $1 + termlist.size(tl(k)) + termlist.size(args(hd(k)))$
> *end   end*

For position $\pi := 1$ it is easy to show $(k, 1) \geqslant_{\Gamma, C_1} (tl(k), 1)$ and $(k, 1) \geqslant_{\Gamma, C_2}$ $(args(hd(k)), 1)$ for the respective call contexts C_1 and C_2. The resulting termination hypotheses $\forall k : list[term].\ k \neq \emptyset \wedge \ldots \rightarrow \Delta_{tl}^{1,1}(k)$ and $\forall k : list[term].\ k \neq \emptyset \wedge \neg\, ?var(hd(k)) \rightarrow (\Delta_{hd}^{1,\epsilon}(k) \vee \Delta_{args}^{\epsilon,1}(hd(k)))$ are obviously true, cf. Fig. 3.   ◇

Example 9 cannot be solved by the original method in [15,18], because there a list is always measured by its *length* (the special case $\pi = \epsilon$ of our theorem).

4.1   Call-Bounded Procedures

Call-bounded procedures f are well-behaved in the sense that they call their functional parameter only with arguments of a bounded size: For each sequence $f(g, q) \rhd^* g(q')$ of procedure calls, the size of q is a bound of the size of q'. We consider only procedures with two parameters in the following definition for readability reasons; the straightforward generalization is given in [1].

Definition 7. *A procedure* **procedure** $f(F : \tau' \rightarrow \tau'',\ x : \tau) : \tau''' <= $ **assume** c_f; B_f *is* (π, ϱ)-*call-bounded for* $\pi \in Pos(\tau)$ *and* $\varrho \in Pos(\tau')$ *iff* τ *is a base type with* $\tau|_\pi = \tau'|_\varrho$ *such that* $\#(q, \pi) \geq \#(q', \varrho)$ *for all* $g \in \mathbb{V}(P)_{\tau' \rightarrow \tau''}$ *and* $q \in \mathbb{V}(P)_\tau$ *with* $f(g, q) \rhd h_1(\ldots) \rhd \ldots \rhd h_n(\ldots) \rhd g(q')$, *where* $h_i \neq g$ *for all* $i = 1, \ldots, n$.

Example 10. *every* is $(1, \epsilon)$-call-bounded, because parameter p will only be called with an argument x with $\#(k, 1) \geq \#(x, \epsilon)$. More formally, $\#(q, 1) \geq \#(q', \epsilon)$ whenever $every(g, q) \rhd every(g, q_1) \rhd \ldots \rhd every(g, q_n) \rhd g(q')$ for some $n \geq 0$. For the same reason, *filter* is also $(1, \epsilon)$-call-bounded.   ◇

The next theorem allows us to easily identify many call-bounded procedures.

Theorem 7. *A procedure* **procedure** $f(F : \tau' \rightarrow \tau'',\ x : \tau) : \tau''' <= $ **assume** c_f; B_f *is* (π, ϱ)-*call-bounded for* $\pi \in Pos(\tau)$ *and* $\varrho \in Pos(\tau')$ *if* τ *is a base type with* $\tau|_\pi = \tau'|_\varrho$ *and* F *occurs in* B_f *only*

(1) in direct function calls $F(t)$ *under some call context* C *such that* $\vdash_{\Gamma, C} \langle \Delta, (x, \pi) \succcurlyeq (t, \varrho) \rangle$ *for some* Δ, *or*
(2) in direct recursive calls $f(F, t')$ *under some call context* C' *such that* $\vdash_{\Gamma, C'} \langle \Delta', (x, \pi) \succcurlyeq (t', \pi) \rangle$ *for some* Δ'.

Example 11. Procedure *every* (Fig. 1) is easily proved $(1, \epsilon)$-call-bounded:

(1) $\vdash_{\Gamma, C} \langle \{\Delta_{hd}^{1,\epsilon}(k)\}, (k, 1) \succcurlyeq (hd(k), \epsilon) \rangle$, where $C = \{k \neq \emptyset\}$
(2) $\vdash_{\Gamma, C'} \langle \{\Delta_{tl}^{1,1}(k)\}, (k, 1) \succcurlyeq (tl(k), 1) \rangle$, where $C' = \{k \neq \emptyset,\ p(hd(k))\}$ ◇

Generalized Detection of Call-Bounded Procedures. Theorem 7 handles the frequently occurring special case of Definition 7 where $h_1 = \ldots = h_n = f$, i.e., the functional parameter F is either called directly or passed to the recursive call $f(F, t')$ without modification. The theorem can be generalized (i) to allow f to pass F to another call-bounded procedure $h_i \neq f$, (ii) to allow modification of F in recursive calls by encapsulating it in a λ-expression $\lambda x'. \ldots F(t'') \ldots$, and (iii) to allow F to occur in *indirect* recursive calls as well, see [1].

4.2 Proving Termination of Procedures

The concept of call-bounded procedures allows us to prove termination of procedures that pass themselves to a call-bounded second-order procedure: In the following theorem, the arguments t of *direct* recursive calls need to decrease, cf. requirements *(1)* and *(2)*. Indirect recursive calls need to occur via a call-bounded procedure g, cf. *(3)*. This procedure g must be called with a bounding argument t' that is strictly smaller than the argument x of f, cf. *(4)* and *(5)*.

Theorem 8. *A procedure $f(x : \tau) : \tau' <=$ assume c_f; B_f terminates if all procedures $g \neq f$ occurring in B_f and c_f terminate and if there is some $\pi \in Pos(\tau)$ such that for each direct recursive call $f(t)$ in B_f under some call context C*

(1) $\vdash_{\Gamma,C} \langle \Delta, (x, \pi) \succcurlyeq (t, \pi) \rangle$ for some Δ and
(2) $\forall x : \tau. \bigwedge C \rightarrow \bigvee \Delta$ is true

and for each indirect recursive call $g(f, t')$ in B_f under some call context C'

(3) procedure g is (π', π)-call-bounded for some π',
(4) $\vdash_{\Gamma,C'} \langle \Delta', (x, \pi) \succcurlyeq (t', \pi') \rangle$ for some Δ', and
(5) $\forall x : \tau. \bigwedge C' \rightarrow \bigvee \Delta'$ is true.

Example 12. Procedure *groundterm* of Fig. 1 terminates by Theorem 8:

(3) *every* is $(\mathbf{1}, \epsilon)$-call-bounded, see Example 11 (i.e., $\pi := \epsilon$)
(4) $\vdash_{\Gamma,C'} \langle \{\Delta^{\epsilon,\mathbf{1}}_{args}(t)\}, (t, \epsilon) \succcurlyeq (args(t), \mathbf{1}) \rangle$, where $C' := \{\neg ? var(t)\}$
(5) $\forall t : term.\ \neg ? var(t) \rightarrow \Delta^{\epsilon,\mathbf{1}}_{args}(t)$ is trivially true, see Fig. 3 $\Diamond$

Similarly to [15,18], Theorem 8 can be generalized in a straightforward way from a single parameter and type position to a set of parameter indices and positions (e.g., for a lexicographic combination of size orders to prove termination of procedures like the Ackermann function). Furthermore, indirect recursive calls $f(t'')$ may be (deeply) nested within λ-expressions; e.g., in $g(\lambda y. \ldots f(t'') \ldots, t')$, see [1] for details and examples.

Induction Axioms. From a terminating procedure one can uniformly synthesize a sound induction axiom. Our method maintains the advantage of the original approach [15,18] that the induction axiom(s) can be optimized by analyzing the termination proof: Some variables can be universally quantified in the induction hypotheses (as in [9]) and irrelevant premises are removed [2].

5   Related Work and Experimental Results

Our method is intended to be used in inductive theorem provers: In this setting it is important that many procedures can be proved terminating without user interaction so that the user can quickly move on to the actual verification task.

In Isabelle 2009 [8,10,14] a termination proof of a procedure with second-order recursion requires the user to state and prove a *congruence theorem* about the second-order procedure involved. For instance, Isabelle can only prove termination of *groundterm* when the user has proved and explicitly tagged $k = k' \wedge (\forall x : @A.\ x \in k \rightarrow p(x) = p'(x)) \rightarrow every(p, k) = every(p', k')$ as a *congruence rule* about procedure *every*. Our approach with call-bounded procedures can be considered as *automatically* discovering and proving congruence theorems such as $k = k' \wedge (\forall x : @A.\ \#(x, \epsilon) < \#(k, \mathbf{1}) \rightarrow p(x) = p'(x)) \rightarrow every(p, k) = every(p', k')$.

In PVS [11] the user needs to supply a measure function that computes the size of a data object, so there is no automation as in our approach.

Since Coq does not offer automated termination analysis either, Barthe et al. [4] suggest an approach that ensures termination by typing. Their system uses *sized types*, i.e., types that contain information about the size of values. For instance, argument-boundedness of procedure *split* (cf. Fig. 2) is expressed by assigning type $list^{\ell}[@A] \rightarrow pair[list^{\ell}[@A], list^{\ell}[@A]]$ to *split*, where $list^{\ell}[@A]$ represents lists of length $\leq \ell$. This analysis is less detailed than ours, because it does not detect the cases when the resulting lists are strictly smaller than the input list. Thus the termination proof of Mergesort fails in this approach, whereas our method succeeds using difference procedures that identify these cases [1]. In the terminology of sized types, call-boundedness of *every* could be expressed by assigning type $(@A^{\ell} \rightarrow bool) \times list[@A^{\ell}] \rightarrow bool$ to *every*, thus constraining the *items* of the list to be of size $\leq \ell$. The approach by Barthe et al. has *not* been integrated into Coq.

ACL2 [5,9] offers heuristics for automated termination proofs, but procedures cannot be defined by second-order recursion.

There are also several stand-alone approaches for termination analysis, which are useful if only termination of a procedure is to be proved (i.e., if there is no need to synthesize induction axioms for subsequent proofs about the procedure). As an example, we mention the Haskell termination analyzer by Giesl et al. [6].

Experimental Results.   Our approach has been integrated into the verifier ✓eriFun, which allows us to compare its performance with Isabelle.[8] Table 1 shows the results of our experiments: We evaluated our approach on 16 representative procedures with second-order recursion, including all examples from [8,10,11,14]. These procedures are based on 8 common second-order procedures without second-order recursion (e.g., *map*, *foldl*, and *every*). The set of first-order examples comprises auxiliary procedures for the examples of second-order recursion as

---

[8] See http://www.informatik.tu-darmstadt.de/pm/~aderhold for an experimental version of ✓eriFun and a list of the example procedures.

Table 1. Termination proving capabilities of inductive provers

number and category of examples	Isabelle	✓eriFun
16 procedures with second-order recursion	0	15
8 second-order procedures without second-order recursion	8	8
40 first-order procedures without second-order recursion	24	38
64 procedures in total	32	61

well as the examples from [15,18], which we included to make sure that our approach properly subsumes the original approach. Indeed, our approach only fails on procedures that the original approach already fails on (e. g., because a parameter is *increased* in recursive calls).

Isabelle fails on the examples of second-order recursion, because we only supplied the raw definition of the procedures. When the user states and proves the required congruence theorems, 15 procedures can be shown terminating as well. The remaining procedure is an artificial example (computing the constant zero function) by Krauss [8] that our approach also fails on, because we would need information about the procedure's semantics before proving its termination.

We did not base our method on the *sized types* approach [4] (although this would be feasible in principle), because the latter cannot solve many naturally occurring examples; e. g., it succeeds on only 21 of 40 first-order procedures in the example set and fails on several common sorting algorithms from [15].

In summary, the experimental results show that the extended estimation calculus (though incomplete) is powerful enough to prove termination of the everyday examples of second-order recursion that frequently occur in practice.

6   Conclusion

We extended the concept of argument-bounded functions [15,18] in two respects: Firstly, we parameterized the size measure to also consider *components* of types. This facilitates automated termination proofs (e. g., for the Mergesort implementation in Fig. 2) that were impossible with the original method. Secondly, we identified the new notion of *call-boundedness* to automate termination proofs for procedures with second-order recursion, which the original method could not cope with at all.

Our method has been integrated into ✓eriFun [17]. It *automatically* solves the typical examples of second-order recursion considered in the literature [8,10,11,14] and in this paper within few seconds, whereas other state-of-the-art theorem provers require guidance by the user.

Information gathered from termination analysis is among the most important keys for guiding highly automated verifiers such as ACL2 and ✓eriFun when selecting useful induction axioms. In all examples of second-order recursion, ✓eriFun synthesizes optimal induction axioms using the results of our method for termination analysis. Although the examples are not overly difficult, such procedures using second-order recursion via *map, every, filter, foldl, foldr,* and similar procedures on other data types (e. g., trees) are widely used in functional programming. Hence our method significantly improves the state of the art in automated theorem proving by reducing the need for user interaction.

Acknowledgment. I am grateful to Jürgen Giesl, Alexander Krauss, Simon Siegler, and Christoph Walther for helpful discussions, to Nathan Wasser for implementing the approach, and to the anonymous referees for valuable feedback.

References

1. Aderhold, M.: Automated termination analysis for programs with second-order recursion. Technical report, TU Darmstadt (2009)
2. Aderhold, M.: Verification of Second-Order Functional Programs. Doctoral dissertation, TU Darmstadt (2009)
3. Andrews, P.B.: An Introduction to Mathematical Logic and Type Theory: To Truth Through Proof. Kluwer Academic Publishers, Dordrecht (2002)
4. Barthe, G., Grégoire, B., Pastawski, F.: CIC⁻: Type-based termination of recursive definitions in the calculus of inductive constructions. In: Hermann, M., Voronkov, A. (eds.) LPAR 2006. LNCS (LNAI), vol. 4246, pp. 257–271. Springer, Heidelberg (2006)
5. Boyer, R.S., Goldschlag, D.M., Kaufmann, M., Moore, J.S.: Functional instantiation in first-order logic. In: Lifschitz, V. (ed.) Papers in Honor of John McCarthy, pp. 7–26. Academic Press, London (1991)
6. Giesl, J., Swiderski, S., Schneider-Kamp, P., Thiemann, R.: Automated termination analysis for Haskell: From term rewriting to programming languages. In: Pfenning, F. (ed.) RTA 2006. LNCS, vol. 4098, pp. 297–312. Springer, Heidelberg (2006)
7. Peyton Jones, S. (ed.): Haskell 98 Language and Libraries: The Revised Report. Cambridge University Press, Cambridge (2003)
8. Krauss, A.: Automating Recursive Definitions and Termination Proofs in Higher-Order Logic. Doctoral dissertation, TU München, Germany (2009)
9. Manolios, P., Turon, A.: All-termination(T). In: Kowalewski, S., Philippou, A. (eds.) TACAS 2009. LNCS, vol. 5505, pp. 398–412. Springer, Heidelberg (2009)
10. Nipkow, T., Paulson, L.C., Wenzel, M. (eds.): Isabelle/HOL — A Proof Assistant for Higher-Order Logic. LNCS, vol. 2283. Springer, Heidelberg (2002)
11. Owre, S., Shankar, N., Rushby, J.M., Stringer-Calvert, D.W.J.: PVS Language Reference. Computer Science Laboratory, SRI International (November 2001)
12. Paulson, L.C.: ML for the Working Programmer, 2nd edn. Cambridge University Press, Cambridge (1996)
13. Schlosser, A., Walther, C., Gonder, M., Aderhold, M.: Context dependent procedures and computed types in √eriFun. In: Proc. of 1st Workshop Programming Languages meet Program Verification. ENTCS, vol. 174, pp. 61–78 (2007)
14. Slind, K.: Reasoning about Terminating Functional Programs. PhD thesis, TU München, Germany (1999)
15. Walther, C.: On proving the termination of algorithms by machine. Artificial Intelligence 71(1), 101–157 (1994)
16. Walther, C., Aderhold, M., Schlosser, A.: The $\mathcal{L}$ 1.0 Primer. Technical Report VFR 06/01, Technische Universität Darmstadt (2006)
17. Walther, C., Schweitzer, S.: Verification in the classroom. Journal of Automated Reasoning 32(1), 35–73 (2004)
18. Walther, C., Schweitzer, S.: Automated termination analysis for incompletely defined programs. In: Baader, F., Voronkov, A. (eds.) LPAR 2004. LNCS (LNAI), vol. 3452, pp. 332–346. Springer, Heidelberg (2005)

Ranking Function Synthesis
for Bit-Vector Relations[*]

Byron Cook[1], Daniel Kroening[2], Philipp Rümmer[2],
and Christoph M. Wintersteiger[3]

[1] Microsoft Research, UK
[2] Oxford University, UK
[3] ETH Zurich, Switzerland

Abstract. Ranking function synthesis is a key aspect to the success of modern termination provers for imperative programs. While it is well-known how to generate linear ranking functions for relations over (mathematical) integers or rationals, efficient synthesis of ranking functions for machine-level integers (bit-vectors) is an open problem. This is particularly relevant for the verification of low-level code. We propose several novel algorithms to generate ranking functions for relations over machine integers: a complete method based on a reduction to Presburger arithmetic, and a template-matching approach for predefined classes of ranking functions based on reduction to SAT- and QBF-solving. The utility of our algorithms is demonstrated on examples drawn from Windows device drivers.

1   Introduction

Modern termination provers for imperative programs compose termination arguments by repeatedly invoking ranking function synthesis tools. Such synthesis tools are available for numerous domains, including linear and non-linear systems, and data structures. Thus, complex termination arguments can be constructed that reason simultaneously about the heap as well as linear and non-linear arithmetic.

Efficient synthesis of ranking functions for machine-level bit-vectors, however, has remained an open problem. Today, the most common approach to create ranking functions over machine integers is to use tools actually designed for rational arithmetic. Because such tools do not faithfully model all properties of machine integers, it can happen that invalid ranking functions are generated (both for terminating and for non-terminating programs), or that existing ranking functions are not found. Both phenomena can lead to incompleteness of termination provers: verification of actually terminating programs might fail.

[*] Supported by the Swiss National Science Foundation grant no. 200021-111687, by the Engineering and Physical Sciences Research Council (EPSRC) under grant no. EP/G026254/1, by the EU FP7 STREP MOGENTES, and by the EU ARTEMIS CESAR project.

J. Esparza and R. Majumdar (Eds.): TACAS 2010, LNCS 6015, pp. 236–250, 2010.

This paper considers the termination problem as well as the synthesis of ranking functions for programs written in languages like ANSI-C, C++, or Java. Such languages typically provide bit-vector arithmetic over 16, 32, or 64 bit words, and usually support both unsigned and signed datatypes (represented using the 2's complement). We present two new algorithms to generate ranking functions for bit-vectors: (i) a complete method based on a reduction to Presburger arithmetic, and (ii) a template-matching approach for predefined classes of ranking functions, including an extremely efficient SAT-based method. We quantify the performance of these new algorithms using examples drawn from Windows device drivers. Our algorithms are compared to the linear ranking function synthesis engine Rankfinder, which uses rational arithmetic.

Programs using *only* machine integers can also be proved terminating without ranking functions. Therefore, we also compare the performance of our methods with one approach not based on ranking functions, the rewriting of termination properties to safety properties according to Biere et al. [5].

Our results indicate that, on practical examples, the presented new methods clearly surpass the known methods in terms of precision and performance.

This paper is organised as follows: in Sect. 2, we provide motivating examples, briefly explain the architecture of termination provers and define the set of considered programs. In Sect. 3, a known, linear programming based approach for ranking function synthesis is analysed. Subsequently, a new extension to this method is presented that handles bit-vector programs soundly. Sect. 3.3 presents two approaches based on template-matching for predefined classes of ranking functions. In Sect. 4, the results of an experimental evaluation of all new methods are given and compared to results obtained through known approaches.

2   Termination of Bit-Vector Programs

We start by discussing two examples extracted from Windows device drivers that illustrate the difficulty of termination checking for low-level code. Both examples will be used in later sections to illustrate our methods.

The first example (Fig. 1) iterates for as many times as there are bits set in i. Termination of the loop can be proven by finding a *ranking function*, which is a function into a well-founded domain that monotonically decreases in each loop iteration. To find a ranking function for this example, it is necessary to take the semantics of the bit-wise AND operator & into account, which is not easily possible in arithmetic-based ranking function synthesis tools (see Sect. 3.1). A possible ranking function is the linear function $m(\mathtt{i}) = \mathtt{i}$, because the result of i & (i-1) is always in the range $[0, \mathtt{i} - 1]$: the value of $m(\mathtt{i})$ decreases with every iteration, but it can not decrease indefinitely as it is bounded from below.

The second program (Fig. 2) is potentially non-terminating, because the variable nLoop might be initialised with a value that is not a multiple of 4, so that the loop condition is never falsified. For a correct analysis, it is necessary to know that integer underflows do not change the remainder modulo 4. Ignoring overflows, but given the information that the variable nLoop is in the

```
unsigned char i;
while (i!=0)
    i = i & (i-1);
```

Fig. 1. Code fragment of Windows driver kernel/agplib/init.c (#40 in our benchmarks)

```
unsigned long ulByteCount;
for (int nLoop = ulByteCount;
     nLoop; nLoop -= 4) { [...] }
```

Fig. 2. Code fragment of Windows device driver audio/gfxswap.xp/filter.cpp (#14 in our benchmarks)

range $[-2^{31}, 2^{31} - 1]$ and is decremented in every iteration, a ranking function synthesis tool might incorrectly produce the ranking function nLoop.

2.1 Syntax and Semantics of Bit-Vector Programs

In order to simplify presentation, we abstract from the concrete language and datatypes and introduce a simpler category of bit-vector programs. Real-world programs can naturally be reduced to our language, which is in practice done by the Model Checker (possibly also taking care of data abstractions, etc).

We assume that bit-vector programs consist of only a single loop (endlessly repeating its body), possibly preceded by a sequence of statements (the *stem*).[1] Apart from this, our program syntax permits guards (assume (t)), sequential composition $(\beta; \gamma)$, choice $(\beta \square \gamma)$, and assignments $(x := t)$. Programs operate on global variables $x \in \mathcal{X}$, each of which ranges over a set $\mathbb{B}^{\alpha(x)}$ of bit-vectors of width $\alpha(x) > 0$. The syntactic categories of programs, statements, and expressions are defined by the following grammar:

$\langle Prog \rangle ::= \langle Stmt \rangle \text{ repeat } \{ \langle Stmt \rangle \}$

$\langle Stmt \rangle ::= \text{skip} \mid \text{assume} (\langle Expr \rangle) \mid \langle Stmt \rangle; \langle Stmt \rangle \mid \langle Stmt \rangle \square \langle Stmt \rangle \mid x := \langle Expr \rangle$

$\langle Expr \rangle ::= 0_n \mid 1_n \mid \cdots \mid *_n \mid x \mid \text{cast}_n(\langle Expr \rangle) \mid \neg \langle Expr \rangle \mid \langle Expr \rangle \circ \langle Expr \rangle$

Because the width of variables is fixed and does not change during program execution, it is not necessary to introduce syntax for variable declarations. Expressions $0_n, 1_n, \ldots$ are bit-vector literals of width n, the expression $*_n$ non-deterministically returns an arbitrary bit-vector of width n, and the operator cast_n changes the width of a bit-vector (cutting off the highest-valued bits, or filling up with zeros as highest-valued bits). The semantics of bitwise negation $\neg$, and of the binary operators $\circ \in \{+, \times, \div, =, <_s, <_u, \&, \mid, \ll, \gg\}$ is as

---

[1] This is not a restriction, as will become clear in the next section.

usual.[2] When evaluating the arithmetic operators $+, \times, \div, \ll, \gg$, both operands are interpreted as unsigned integers. In the case of the strict ordering relation $<_s$ (resp., $<_u$) the operands are interpreted as signed integers in 2's complement format (resp., as unsigned integers).

We write $t : n$ to denote that the expression t is correctly typed and denotes a bit-vector of width n. In the rest of the paper, we always assume that programs are type-correct.

The state space of programs defined over a (finite) set $\mathcal{X}$ of bit-vector variables with widths α is denoted by $\mathcal{S}$, and consists of all mappings from $\mathcal{X}$ to bit-vectors of the correct width: $\mathcal{S} = \{f \in \mathcal{X} \to \mathbb{B}^+ \mid f(x) \in \mathbb{B}^{\alpha(x)} \text{ for all } x \in \mathcal{X}\}$. The transition relation defined by a statement β is denoted by $R_\beta \subseteq \mathcal{S} \times \mathcal{S}$. In particular, we define the transition relation for sequences as $R_{\beta_1;\beta_2}(s, s') \equiv \exists s'' . R_{\beta_1}(s, s'') \wedge R_{\beta_2}(s'', s')$.

Example. We consider the program given in Fig. 2. Using unsigned arithmetic (and $-4 \equiv 2^{32} - 4 \mod 2^{32}$), the bit-vector program for a single loop iteration is

$$\mathsf{assume}\ (nLoop \neq 0);\ nLoop := nLoop + (2^{32} - 4) \tag{1}$$

Complexity. We say that a bit-vector program β repeat $\{\gamma\}$ *terminates* if there is no infinite sequence of states $a_0, a_1, a_2, \ldots \in \mathcal{S}$ with $R_\beta(a_0, a_1)$ and $R_\gamma(a_i, a_{i+1})$ for all $i > 0$. The termination problem for bit-vector programs is decidable:

Lemma 1. *Deciding termination of bit-vector programs is PSPACE-complete in the program length[3] plus $\sum_{x \in \mathcal{X}} \alpha(x)$, i.e., the size of the program's available memory.*

Practically, the most successful termination provers are based on incomplete methods that try to avoid this high complexity, by such means as the generation of specific kinds of ranking functions (like functions that are linear in program variables). The general strategy of such provers is described in the next section.

2.2   Binary Reachability Analysis and Ranking Functions

Definition 1 (Ranking function). *Suppose $(D, \prec)$ is a well-founded, strictly partially ordered set, and $R \subseteq U \times U$ is a relation over a non-empty set U. A ranking function for R is a function $m : U \to D$ such that:*

$$\textit{for all } a, b \in U : R(a, b) \textit{ implies } m(b) \prec m(a).$$

Of particular interest in the context of this paper is the well-founded domain of natural numbers $(\mathbb{N}, <)$. In general, we can directly conclude:

Lemma 2. *If a (global) ranking function exists for the transition relation R of a program β, then β terminates.*

---

[2] Adding further operations, e.g., bit-vector concatenation, is straightforward.

[3] The number of characters in the program text. We assume that a unary representation is used for the index n of the operators $0_n, 1_n, \ldots, *_n$, and cast_n.

The problem of deciding termination of a program may thus be stated as a problem of ranking function synthesis. By the disjunctive well-foundedness theorem [15], this is simplified to the problem of finding a ranking function for every *path* through the program. The ranking functions found for all n paths are used to construct a global, disjunctive ranking relation $M(a, b) = \bigvee_{i=1}^{n} m_i(b) \prec m_i(a)$.

A technique that puts this theorem to use is *Binary Reachability Analysis* [8,9]. In this approach, termination of a program is first expressed as a *safety* property [5], initially assuming that the program does *not* terminate. Consequently, a (software) Model Checker is applied to obtain a counterexample to termination, i.e., an example of non-termination. This counterexample contains a *stem* that describes how to reach a loop in the program, and a *cycle* that follows a path π through the loop, finally returning to the entry location of the loop. What follows is an analysis solely concerned with the stem and π, which is why we may safely restrict ourselves to single-loop programs here.

The next step in the procedure is to synthesise a ranking function for π, which can be seen as a new, smaller, and loop-free program that does not contain choice operators. Semantically, π is interpreted as a relation $R_\pi(x, x')$ between program states x, x'. If a ranking function m_π is found for this relation, the original safety property is weakened to exclude all paths of the program that satisfy the ranking relation $m_\pi(x') \prec m_\pi(x)$, and the process starts over. If no further non-terminating paths are found, termination of the program is proven.

3   Ranking Functions for Bit-Vector Programs

We introduce new methods based on integer linear programming, SAT-solving, and QBF-solving to synthesise ranking functions for paths in a bit-vector program. Before that, we give a short overview of the derivation of ranking functions using linear programming, which is the starting point for our methods.

3.1   Synthesis of Ranking Functions by Linear Programming

The approach to generate ranking functions that is used in binary reachability engines like Terminator [9] and ARMC [16] was developed by Podelski et al. [14]. In this setting, ranking functions are generated for transition relations $R \subseteq \mathbb{Q}^n \times \mathbb{Q}^n$ that are described by systems of linear inequalities:

$$R(x, x') \equiv Ax + A'x' \leq b \qquad (A, A' \in \mathbb{Q}^{k \times n}, b \in \mathbb{Q}^k)$$

where $x, x' \in \mathbb{Q}^n$ range over vectors of rationals. Bit-vector relations have to be encoded into such systems, which usually involves an over-approximation of program behaviour. The derived ranking functions are linear and have the codomain $D = \{z \in \mathbb{Q} \mid z \geq 0\}$, which is ordered by $y \prec z \equiv y + \delta \leq z$ for some rational $\delta > 0$. Ranking functions $m : \mathbb{Q}^n \to D$ are represented as $m(x) = rx + c$, with $r \in \mathbb{Q}^n$ a row vector and $c \in \mathbb{Q}$. Such a function m is a ranking function with the domain $(D, \prec)$ if and only if the following condition holds:

for all $x, x' \in \mathbb{Q}^n$: $R(x, x')$ implies $rx + c \geq 0 \wedge rx' + c \geq 0 \wedge rx' + \delta \leq rx$ (2)

Coefficients r for which this implication is satisfied can be constructed using Farkas' lemma, of which the 'affine' form given in [19] is appropriate. Using this lemma, a necessary and sufficient criterion for the existence of linear ranking functions can be formulated:

Theorem 1 (Existence of linear ranking functions [14]). *Suppose that $R(x, x') \equiv Ax + A'x' \leq b$ is a satisfiable transition relation. R has a linear ranking function $m(x) = rx + c$ iff there are non-negative vectors $\lambda_1, \lambda_2 \in \mathbb{Q}^k$ s.t.:*

$$\lambda_1 A' = 0, \quad (\lambda_1 - \lambda_2)A = 0, \quad \lambda_2(A + A') = 0, \quad \lambda_2 b < 0.$$

In this case, m can be chosen as $\lambda_2 A'x + (\lambda_1 - \lambda_2)b$.

This criterion for the existence of linear ranking functions is necessary and sufficient for linear inequalities on the rationals, but only sufficient over the integers or bit-vectors: there are relations $R(x, x') \equiv Ax + A'x' \leq b$ for which linear ranking functions exist, but the criterion fails, e.g.:

$$R(x, x') \equiv x \in [0, 4] \wedge x' \geq 0.2x + 0.9 \wedge x' \leq 0.2x + 1.1 .$$

Restricting x and x' to the integers, this is equivalent to $x = 0 \wedge x' = 1$ and can be ranked by $m(x) = -x + 1$. Over the rationals, the program defined by the inequalities does not terminate, which implies that no ranking function exists and the criterion of Theorem 1 fails.

3.2   Synthesis of Ranking Functions by Integer Linear Programming

To extend the approach from Sect. 3.1 and fully support bit-vector programs, we first generalise Theorem 1 to disjunctions of systems of inequalities over the integers. We then define an algorithm to synthesise linear ranking functions for programs defined in Presburger arithmetic, which subsumes bit-vector programs.

Linear ranking functions over the integers. In order to faithfully encode bit-vector operations like addition with overflow (describing non-convex transition relations), it is necessary to consider also disjunctive transition relations R:

$$R(x, x') \equiv \bigvee_{i=1}^{l} A_i x + A_i' x' \leq b_i \tag{3}$$

where $l \in \mathbb{N}$, $A_i, A_i' \in \mathbb{Z}^{k \times n}$, $b_i \in \mathbb{Z}^k$, and $x, x' \in \mathbb{Z}^n$ range over integer vectors. Linear ranking functions for such relations can be constructed by solving an implication like (2) for each disjunct of the relation, as shown below. There is one further complication, however: Farkas' lemma, which is the main ingredient for Theorem 1, is in general not complete for inequalities over the integers.

Farkas' lemma is complete for *integral* systems, however: $Ax + A'x' \leq b$ is called integral if the polyhedron $\{\binom{x}{x'} \in \mathbb{Q}^{2n} \mid Ax + A'x' \leq b\}$ coincides with its integral hull (the convex hull of the integer points contained in it). Every system of inequalities can be transformed into an integral system with the same integer solutions, although this might increase the size of the system exponentially [19].

Lemma 3. *Suppose $R(x, x') \equiv \bigvee_{i=1}^{l} A_i x + A_i' x' \leq b_i$ is a transition relation in which each disjunct is satisfiable and integral. R has a linear ranking function $m(x) = rx + c$ if and only if there are non-negative vectors $\lambda_1^i, \lambda_2^i \in \mathbb{Q}^k$ for $i \in \{1, \ldots, l\}$ such that:*

$$\lambda_1^i A_i' = 0, \quad \lambda_2^i (A_i + A_i') = 0, \quad \lambda_2^i b_i < 0, \quad (\lambda_1^i - \lambda_2^i) A_i = 0, \quad \lambda_2^i A_i' = r. \quad (4)$$

Ranking functions for Presburger arithmetic. Presburger arithmetic (PA) is the first-order theory of integer arithmetic without multiplication [17]. We describe a complete procedure to generate linear ranking functions for PA-defined transition relations by reduction to Lem. 3.[4]

Suppose a transition relation $R(x, x')$ is defined by a Presburger formula. Because PA allows quantifier elimination [17], it can be assumed that $R(x, x')$ is a quantifier-free Boolean combination of equations, inequalities, and divisibility constraints $\epsilon \mid (cx + dx' + e)$. Divisibility constraints are introduced during quantifier elimination and state that the value of the term $cx + dx' + e$ (with $c, d \in \mathbb{Z}^n, e \in \mathbb{Z}$) is a multiple of the positive natural number $\epsilon \in \mathbb{N}^+$.

In order to apply Lem. 3, we eliminate divisibility constraints from $R(x, x')$ as explained in detail below. This is possible by introducing auxiliary program variables y, y': we will transform $R(x, x')$ to a formula $R'(x, y, x', y')$ without divisibility constraints, such that $\exists y, y'. R'(x, y, x', y') \equiv R(x, x')$. The transformation increases the size of the PA formula only polynomially.

By rewriting to disjunctive normalform, replacing equations $s = t$ with inequalities $s \leq t \wedge t \leq s$, the relation $R'(x, y, x', y')$ can be stated as in (3):

$$R'(x, y, x', y') \equiv \bigvee_{i=1}^{l} A_i \binom{x}{y} + A_i' \binom{x'}{y'} \leq b_i$$

We can then apply Lem. 3 to R' to derive a linear ranking function $m'(x, y)$. To ensure that no auxiliary variables y occur in $m'(x, y)$ (i.e., $m'(x, y) = m(x)$), equations are added to (4) that constrain the corresponding entries of r to zero.

Replacing divisibility constraints by disjunctions of equations. The following equivalences are used in the transformation from $R(x, x')$ to $R'(x, y, x', y')$:

$$\epsilon \mid (cx + dx' + e) \equiv \epsilon \mid \left(cx - \epsilon \left\lfloor \frac{cx}{\epsilon} \right\rfloor + dx' - \epsilon \left\lfloor \frac{dx'}{\epsilon} \right\rfloor + e \right) \quad (5)$$

$$\equiv \bigvee_{\substack{i \in \mathbb{Z} \\ 0 \leq i \cdot \epsilon - e < 2\epsilon}} i \cdot \epsilon - e = cx - \epsilon \left\lfloor \frac{cx}{\epsilon} \right\rfloor + dx' - \epsilon \left\lfloor \frac{dx'}{\epsilon} \right\rfloor \quad (6)$$

$$\equiv \exists y_c, y_d'. \left(\begin{array}{l} 0 \leq cx - \epsilon y_c < \epsilon \wedge 0 \leq dx' - \epsilon y_d' < \epsilon \\ \wedge (\bigvee_{0 \leq i \cdot \epsilon - e < 2\epsilon} i \cdot \epsilon - e = cx - \epsilon y_c + dx' - \epsilon y_d') \end{array} \right) \quad (7)$$

---

[4] The procedure can also derive ranking functions that contain integer division expressions $\lfloor \frac{t}{\epsilon} \rfloor$ for some $\epsilon \in \mathbb{Z}$, but it is not complete for such functions. Assuming that a polynomial method is used to solve (4), the complexity of our procedure is singly exponential.

Equivalence (5) holds because divisibility is not affected by subtracting multiples of ϵ on the right-hand side, while (6) expresses that the value of the term $cx - \epsilon\lfloor\frac{cx}{\epsilon}\rfloor + dx' - \epsilon\lfloor\frac{dx'}{\epsilon}\rfloor$ lies in the right-open interval $[0, 2\epsilon)$. Therefore, the divisibility constraints of (5) are equivalent to a disjunction of exactly two equations. Finally, the integer division expressions $\lfloor\frac{cx}{\epsilon}\rfloor$ can equivalently be expressed using existential quantifiers in (7).

To avoid the introduction of new quantifiers, the quantified variables y_c, y_d' are treated as program variables. Whenever a constraint $\epsilon \mid (cx + dx' + e)$ occurs in $R(x, x')$, we introduce new pre-state variables y_c, y_d and post-state variables y_c', y_d' that are defined by adding conjuncts to $R(x, x')$:

$$R'(x, y_c, y_d, x', y_c', y_d') \equiv R(x, x') \wedge 0 \le cx - \epsilon y_c < \epsilon \wedge 0 \le dx - \epsilon y_d < \epsilon$$
$$\wedge 0 \le cx' - \epsilon y_c' < \epsilon \wedge 0 \le dx' - \epsilon y_d' < \epsilon$$

In $R'(x, y_c, y_d, x', y_c', y_d')$, the constraint $\epsilon \mid (cx + dx' + e)$ can then be replaced with a disjunction $\bigvee_{0 \le i \cdot \epsilon - e < 2\epsilon} i \cdot \epsilon - e = cx - \epsilon y_c + dx' - \epsilon y_d'$ as in (7). Iterating this procedure eventually leads to a transition relation $R'(x, y, x', y')$ without divisibility judgements, such that $\exists y, y'. R'(x, y, x', y') \equiv R(x, x')$.

Representation of bit-vector operations in PA. Presburger arithmetic is expressive enough to capture the semantics of all bit-vector operations defined in Sect. 2, so that ranking functions for bit-vector programs can be generated using the method from the previous section. For instance, the semantics of a bit-vector addition $s + t$ can be defined in weakest-precondition style as:

$$wp(x := s + t, \phi) = wp\left(\begin{matrix} y_1 := s; \ y_2 := t, \\ \exists x. (0 \le x < 2^n \wedge 2^n \mid (x - y_1 - y_2) \wedge \phi) \end{matrix}\right)$$

where $s : n, t : n$ denote bit-vectors of length n, and y_1, y_2 are fresh variables. The existentially quantified formula assigns to x the remainder of $y_1 + y_2$ modulo 2^n.

A precise translation of non-linear operations like $\times$ and $\&$ can be done by case analysis over the values of their operands, which in general leads to formulae of exponential size, but is well-behaved in many cases that are practically relevant (e.g., if one of the operands is a literal). Such an encoding is only possible because the variables of bit-vector programs range over finite domains of fixed size.

Example. We encode the bit-vector program (1) corresponding to Fig. 2 in PA:

$$nLoop \ne 0 \wedge 2^{32} \mid (nLoop' - nLoop - 2^{32} + 4)$$
$$\wedge \ 0 \le nloop < 2^{32} \wedge 0 \le nloop' < 2^{32}$$

From the side conditions, we can read off that the term $nLoop' - nLoop - 2^{32} + 4$ has the range $[5 - 2^{33}, 3]$, so that the divisibility constraint can directly be split into two equations (auxiliary variables as in (7) are unnecessary in this particular example). With further simplifications, we can express the transition relation as:

$$\left(nLoop' = nLoop - 4 \wedge 0 \le nloop' \wedge nloop < 2^{32}\right)$$
$$\vee \left(nLoop' = nLoop + 2^{32} - 4 \wedge 0 < nloop \wedge nloop' < 2^{32}\right)$$

It is now easy to see that each disjunct is satisfiable and integral, which means that Lem. 3 is applicable. Because the conditions (4) are not simultaneously satisfiable for all disjuncts, no linear ranking function exists for the program.

3.3   Synthesis of Ranking Functions from Templates

A subset of the ranking functions for bit-vector programs can be identified by templates of a desired class of functions with undetermined coefficients. In order to find the coefficients, we consider two methods: (i) an encoding into quantified Boolean formulas (QBF) to check all suitable values, and (ii) a propositional SAT-solver to check likely values.

We primarily consider linear functions of the program variables. Let $x = (x_1, \ldots, x_{|\mathcal{X}|})$ be a vector of program variables and associate a coefficient c_i with each $x_i \in \mathcal{X}$. The coefficients constitute the vector $c = (c_1, \ldots, c_{|\mathcal{X}|})$. We can then construct the template polynomial

$$p(c, x) := \sum_{i=1}^{|\mathcal{X}|} (c_i \times \mathsf{cast}_w(x_i))$$

with the bit-width $w \geq \max_i(\alpha(x_i)) + \lceil \log_2(|\mathcal{X}| + 1) \rceil$ and $\alpha(c_i) = w$, chosen such that no overflows occur during summation. The following theorem provides a bound on w that guarantees that ranking functions can be represented for all programs that have linear ranking functions.

Theorem 2. *There exists a linear ranking function on path π with transition relation $R_\pi(x, x')$, if*

$$\exists c \, \forall x, x' \, . \, R_\pi(x, x') \Rightarrow p(c, x') <_s p(c, x) \, . \tag{8}$$

Vice versa, if there exists a linear ranking function for π, then Eq. (8) must be valid whenever

$$w \geq \max_i(\alpha(x_i)) \cdot (|\mathcal{X}| - 1) + |\mathcal{X}| \cdot \log_2 |\mathcal{X}| + 1 \, .$$

It is straightforward to flatten Eq. (8) into QBF. Thus, a QBF solver that returns an assignment for the top-level existential variables is able to compute suitable coefficients. Examples of such solvers are Quantor [4], sKizzo [3], and Squolem [13]. In our experiments, we use an experimental version of QuBE [11].

Despite much progress, the capacity of QBF solvers has not yet reached the level of propositional SAT solvers. We therefore consider the following simplistic way to enumerate coefficients: we restrict all coefficients to $\alpha(c_i) = 2$ and we fix a concrete assignment $\gamma(c) \in \{0, 1, 3\}$ to the coefficients (corresponding to $\{-1, 0, 1\}$ in 2's complement). Negating and applying γ transforms Equation 8 into

$$\neg \exists x, x' \, . \, R_\pi(x, x') \wedge \neg(p(\gamma(c), x') <_s p(\gamma(c), x)) \, , \tag{9}$$

which is a bit-vector (or SMT-$\mathcal{BV}$) formula that may be flattened to a purely propositional formula in the straightforward way. The formula is satisfiable iff p is *not* a genuine ranking function. Thus, we enumerate all possible γ until we find one for which Equation 9 is unsatisfiable, which means that $p(\gamma(c), x)$ must be a genuine ranking function on π. Even though there are $3^{|\mathcal{X}|}$ possible combinations of coefficient values to test, this method performs surprisingly well in practice, as demonstrated by our experimental evaluation in Sect. 4.

Example. We consider the program given in Fig. 1. The only variable in the program is i, and it is 8 bits wide. We construct the polynomial $p(c, i) = c \times \mathsf{cast}_9(i)$ with $\alpha(c) = 9$. For the only path through the loop in this example, the transition relation $R_\pi(i, i')$ is $i \neq 0 \wedge i' = i ~\&~ (i - 1)$. Solving the resulting formula

$$\exists c \forall i, i' . R_\pi(i, i') \Rightarrow p(c, i') <_s p(c, i)$$

with a QBF-Solver does not return a result within an hour. We thus rewrite the formula according to Equation 9 and obtain

$$\neg \exists i, i' . R_\pi(i, i') \wedge \neg(p(c, i') <_s p(c, i))$$

which we solve (in a negligible amount of runtime) for all choices of $c \in \{0, 1, 3\}$. The formula is unsatisfiable for $c = 1$, and we conclude that $\mathsf{cast}_9(i)$ is a suitable ranking function. In this particular example, it is possible to omit the cast.

4   Experiments

4.1   Large-Scale Benchmarks

Following Cook et al. [9], we implemented a binary reachability analysis engine to evaluate our ranking synthesis methods. Our implementation uses SATABS as the reachability checker [7], which implements SAT-based predicate abstraction. Our benchmarks are device drivers from the Windows Driver Development Kit (WDK).[5] The WDK already includes verification harnesses for the drivers. We use GOTO-CC[6] to extract model files from a total of 87 drivers in the WDK.

Most of the drivers contain loops over singly and doubly-linked lists, which require an arithmetic abstraction. This abstraction can be automated by existing shape analysis methods (e.g., the one recently presented by Yang et al. [20]).

Slicing the input. Just like Cook et al. [9], we find that most of the runtime is spent in the reachability checker (more than 99%), especially after all required ranking functions have been synthesised and no more counterexamples exist. To reduce the resource requirements of the Model Checker, our binary reachability engine analyses each loop separately and generates an inter-procedural slice [12] of the program, slicing backwards from the termination assertion. In addition, we

---

[5] Version 6, available at http://www.microsoft.com/whdc/devtools/wdk/
[6] http://www.cprover.org/goto-cc/

Table 1. The behaviour on the loops of a keyboard driver

1	2	3	4	5	6	7	8	9	10	11	12	13	Loop
list	list	unr.	i++	unr.	unr.	unr.	unr.	wait	unr.	unr.	i++	list	Type
126	85	687	248	340	298	253	844	109	375	333	3331	146	CE Time [sec]
0.5	0.1	–	0.7	–	–	–	–	0.4	–	–	2.2	0.4	Synth. Time [sec]
×	×	✓	MO	✓	✓	✓	✓	×	✓	✓	MO	×	Terminates?

rewrite the program into a single-loop program, abstracting from the behaviour of all other loops.[7] With this (abstracting) slicer in place, we find that absolute runtime and memory requirements are reduced dramatically.

As our complete data on Windows drivers is voluminous, we present a typical example in detail. The full dataset is available online.[8] The keyboard class driver in the WDK (KBDCLASS) contains a total of 13 loops in a harness (SDV_FLAT_ HARNESS) that calls all dispatch functions nondeterministically.

Table 1 describes the behaviour of our engine on this driver. For every loop we list the type (list iteration, i++, unreachable, or 'wait for device'), the time it takes to find a potentially non-terminating path ('CE Time'), the time required to find a ranking function using our SAT template from Sect. 3.3 ('Synth. Time', where applicable), and the final result. In the last row, 'MO' indicates a memory-out after consuming 2 GB of RAM while proving that no further counterexamples to termination exist. The entire analysis of this driver requires 2 hours.[9]

We were able to isolate a possible termination problem in the USB driver bulkusb that may result in the system being blocked. The driver requests an interface description structure for every device available by calling an API function. It increments the loop counter if this did not return an error. The API function, however, may return NULL if no interface matches the search criteria, resulting in the loop counter not being incremented. Since numberOfInterfaces is a local (non-shared) variable of the loop, the problem would persist in a concurrent setting, where a device may be disconnected while the loop is executed.

4.2 Experiments on Smaller Examples

The predominant role of the reachability engine on our large-scale experiments prevents a meaningful comparison of the utility of the various techniques for ranking function synthesis. For this reason, we conducted further experiments on smaller programs, where the behaviour of the reachability engine has less

---

[7] Following the hypothesis that loop termination seldom depends on complex variables that are possibly calculated by other loops, our slicing algorithm replaces all assignments that depend on five or more variables with non-deterministic values, and all loops other than the analysed one with program fragments that havoc the program state (non-deterministic assignments to all variables that might change during the execution of the loop).

[8] http://www.cprover.org/termination/

[9] All experiments were run on 8-core Intel Xeon 3 GHz machines with 16 GB of RAM.

Table 2. Experimental results on 61 benchmarks drawn from Windows device drivers

#	1	2	3	4	5	6	7	8	9	10	11	12	13	14	15	16	17	18	19	20	21	22	23	24	25	26	27	28	29	30	31
Manual Insp.	L	L	L	L	N	N	N	L	T	N	T	L	L	N	T	L	L	L	L	T	L	L	L	L	L	L	L	N	T	L	T
SAT	●	●	●	●	○	○	○	●	○	○	○	●	●	○	○	●	●	●	●	●	○	●	●	●	●	●	●	○	○	●	○
Seneschal	●	●	●	●	○	○	–	●	○	○	○	●	●	○	○	●	●	●	●	●	○	–	●	●	●	●	●	○	○	○	–
Rankfinder	○	●	○	●	○	○	○	●	◐	○	○	●	○	◐	◐	●	○	●	●	○	○	○	●	●	●	●	◐	○	○	–	○
QBF [-1,+1]	–	–	●	●	○	○	–	–	–	○	–	●	–	–	–	–	–	–	–	–	●	–	–	–	–	–	○	–	●	–	○
QBF $P(c,x)$	–	–	●	●	○	–	–	–	–	–	–	●	–	–	–	–	–	–	–	–	●	–	–	–	–	–	–	–	–	–	–
Biere et al. [5]	–	–	–	●	–	–	–	–	–	○	–	●	●	–	–	–	–	–	●	–	–	●	–	–	–	–	–	○	–	–	●

#	32	33	34	35	36	37	38	39	40	41	42	43	44	45	46	47	48	49	50	51	52	53	54	55	56	57	58	59	60	61
Manual Insp.	T	L	N	L	T	L	L	L	L	L	L	L	N	T	L	L	T	T	T	L	T	T	N	L	L	L	L	L	N	T
SAT	○	●	○	○	●	○	●	●	●	●	●	●	○	○	●	●	○	○	○	●	○	○	○	●	●	●	●	●	○	○
Seneschal	○	●	○	○	●	○	●	●	●	●	●	●	○	○	●	●	○	○	○	●	○	○	○	●	●	●	●	–	○	–
Rankfinder	○	●	○	○	●	◐	●	◐	○	○	●	○	●	○	○	●	○	○	○	●	○	–	○	–	●	○	●	●	○	○
QBF [-1,+1]	○	–	–	–	–	–	–	–	●	–	–	●	–	–	●	–	–	○	○	●	○	–	–	–	–	–	–	–	○	–
QBF $P(c,x)$	–	–	–	–	–	–	–	–	–	–	–	–	○	–	–	–	–	–	–	●	–	–	–	–	–	–	–	–	–	–
Biere et al. [5]	–	–	–	●	–	–	–	–	●	–	–	–	–	●	●	●	–	–	●	●	–	–	–	–	–	–	–	–	○	●

● – Termination was proven   T – Terminating (non-linear)
○ – (Possibly) Non-terminating   L – Terminating, and linear
◐ – Incorrect under bit-vector semantics   ranking functions exist.
– – Memory or time limits exhausted   N – Non-terminating

impact. We manually extracted 61 small benchmark programs from the WDK drivers. Most of them contain bit-vector operations, including multiplication, and some of them contain nested loops. All benchmarks were manually sliced by removing all source code that does not affect program termination (much like an automated slicer, but more thoroughly). We also employ the same abstraction technique as described in the previous section. All but ten of the benchmark programs terminate. The time limit in these benchmarks was 3600 s, and the memory consumption was limited to 2 GB.

To evaluate the integer linear programming method described in Sect. 3.2, we developed the prototype Seneschal.[10] It is based on the prover Princess [18] for Presburger arithmetic with uninterpreted predicates and works by (i) translating a given bit-vector program into a PA formula, (ii) eliminating the quantifiers in the formula, (iii) flattening the formula to a disjunction of systems of inequalities, and (iv) applying Lem. 3 to compute ranking functions. Seneschal does currently not, however, transform systems of inequalities to integral systems, which means that it is a sound but incomplete tool; the experiments show that transformation to integral systems is unnecessary for the majority of the considered programs.

Table 2 summarizes the results. The first column indicates the result obtained by manual inspection, i.e., if a specific benchmark is terminating, and if so whether there is a linear ranking function to prove this. The other columns represent the following ranking synthesis approaches: SAT is the coefficient enumeration approach from Sect. 3.3; Seneschal is the integer linear programming approach from Sect. 3.2; Rankfinder is the linear programming approach over rationals from Sect. 3.1; QBF [-1,+1] is a QBF template approach from Sect. 3.3 with coefficients restricted to $[-1,+1]$, such that the template represents the same ranking functions as the one used for the SAT enumeration approach. QBF

---

[10] http://www.philipp.ruemmer.org/seneschal.shtml

$P(c, x)$ is the unrestricted version of this template. Note that two benchmarks (#27 and #34) are negatively affected by our slicer: due to the abstraction, no linear ranking functions are found. On the original programs, the SAT-based approach and Seneschal find suitable ranking functions, on benchmark #34 however, the Model Checker times out afterwards.

Comparing the various techniques, we conclude that the simple SAT-based enumeration is most successful in synthesising useful ranking functions. It is able to prove 34 out of 51 terminating benchmarks and reports 27 as non-terminating. It does not time out on any instance.

Seneschal shows the second best performance: it proves 31 programs as terminating, almost as many as the SAT-based template approach. It reports 25 benchmarks as non-terminating and times out on 5.

For the experiments using Rankfinder[11], the bit-vector operators $+$, $\times$ with literals, $=$, $<_s$ and $<_u$ are approximated by the corresponding operations on the rationals, whereas nonexistence of ranking functions is reported for programs that use any other operations. Furthermore, we add constraints of the form $0 \leq v < 2^n$, where n is the bit-width of v, restricting the range of pre-state variables. This results in 23 successful termination proofs, and 35 cases of alleged non-termination. In three cases, the Model Checker times out on proving the final property, and in 5 cases Rankfinder returns an unsuitable ranking function.

For the two QBF techniques we used an experimental version of QuBE, which performed better than sKizzo, Quantor, and Squolem. The constrained template $(QBF[-1, +1])$ is still able to synthesise some useful ranking functions within the time limit. It proves 9 benchmarks terminating and reports 11 as non-terminating. The unconstrained approach (QBF $P(c, x)$), however, proves only 5 programs terminating and one non-terminating, with the QBF-Solver timing out on all other benchmarks.

We also implemented the approach suggested by Biere et al. [5] (bottom row of Table 2), which does not require ranking functions, but instead proves that an entry state of the loop is never revisited. Generally, these assertions are difficult for SATABS. While this method is able to show only 14 programs terminating, there are 4 benchmarks (#31, #45, #50, and #61) that none of the other methods can handle as they require non-linear ranking functions.

Our benchmark suite, all results with added detail, and additional experiments are available online at http://www.cprover.org/termination/.

5   Related Work

Numerous efficient methods are now available for the purpose of finding ranking functions (e.g., [6, 10, 14, 1]). Some tools are complete for the class of ranking functions for which they are designed (e.g., [14]), others employ a set of heuristics (e.g., [1]). Until now, no known tool supported machine-level integers.

Bradley et al. [6] give a complete search-based algorithm to generate linear ranking functions together with supporting invariants for programs defined in

---

[11] http://www.mpi-inf.mpg.de/~rybal/rankfinder/

Presburger arithmetic. We propose a related constraint-based method to synthesise linear ranking functions for such programs. It is worth noting that our method is a decision procedure for the existence of linear ranking functions in this setting, while the procedure in [6] is sound and complete, but might not terminate when applied to programs that lack linear ranking functions. An experimental comparison with Bradley et al.'s method is future work.

Ranking function synthesis is not required if the program is purely a finite-state system. In particular, Biere, Artho and Schuppan describe a reduction of liveness properties to safety by means of a monitor construction [5]. The resulting safety checks require a comparison of the entire state vector whereas the safety checks for ranking functions refer only to few variables. Our experimental results indicate that the safety checks for ranking functions are in most cases easier. Another approach for proving termination of large finite-state systems was proposed by Ball et al. [2]; however, we would need to develop a technique to find suitable abstractions. Furthermore, since neither one of these techniques leads to ranking functions, it is not clear how they can be integrated into systems whose aim is to prove termination of programs that mix machine integers with data-structures, recursion, and/or numerical libraries with arbitrary precision.

6 Conclusion

The development of efficient ranking function synthesis tools has led to more powerful automatic program termination provers. While synthesis methods are available for a number of domains, efficient procedures for programs over machine integers have until now not been known. We have presented two new algorithms solving the problem of ranking function synthesis for bit-vectors: (i) a complete method based on a reduction to quantifier-free Presburger arithmetic, and (ii) a template-matching method for finding ranking functions of specified classes. Through experimentation with examples drawn from Windows device drivers we have shown their efficiency and applicability to systems-level code. The bottleneck of the methods is the reachability analysis engine. We will therefore consider optimizations for this engine specific to termination analysis as future work.

Acknowledgements. We would like to thank M. Narizzano for providing us with an experimental version of the QuBE QBF-Solver that outputs an assignment for the top-level existentials and H. Samulowitz for discussions about QBF encodings of the termination problem and for evaluating several QBF solvers. Besides, we are grateful for useful comments from Vijay D'Silva, Georg Weissenbacher, and the anonymous referees.

References

1. Babic, D., Hu, A.J., Rakamaric, Z., Cook, B.: Proving termination by divergence. In: SEFM, pp. 93–102. IEEE, Los Alamitos (2007)
2. Ball, T., Kupferman, O., Sagiv, M.: Leaping loops in the presence of abstraction. In: Damm, W., Hermanns, H. (eds.) CAV 2007. LNCS, vol. 4590, pp. 491–503. Springer, Heidelberg (2007)

3. Benedetti, M.: sKizzo: A suite to evaluate and certify QBFs. In: Nieuwenhuis, R. (ed.) CADE 2005. LNCS (LNAI), vol. 3632, pp. 369–376. Springer, Heidelberg (2005)

4. Biere, A.: Resolve and expand. In: Hoos, H.H., Mitchell, D.G. (eds.) SAT 2004. LNCS, vol. 3542, pp. 59–70. Springer, Heidelberg (2005)

5. Biere, A., Artho, C., Schuppan, V.: Liveness checking as safety checking. In: FMICS. ENTCS, vol. 66, pp. 160–177. Elsevier, Amsterdam (2002)

6. Bradley, A.R., Manna, Z., Sipma, H.B.: Termination analysis of integer linear loops. In: Abadi, M., de Alfaro, L. (eds.) CONCUR 2005. LNCS, vol. 3653, pp. 488–502. Springer, Heidelberg (2005)

7. Clarke, E.M., Kroening, D., Sharygina, N., Yorav, K.: Predicate abstraction of ANSI-C programs using SAT. FMSD 25(2-3), 105–127 (2004)

8. Cook, B., Podelski, A., Rybalchenko, A.: Abstraction refinement for termination. In: Hankin, C., Siveroni, I. (eds.) SAS 2005. LNCS, vol. 3672, pp. 87–101. Springer, Heidelberg (2005)

9. Cook, B., Podelski, A., Rybalchenko, A.: Termination proofs for systems code. In: PLDI, pp. 415–426. ACM, New York (2006)

10. Encrenaz, E., Finkel, A.: Automatic verification of counter systems with ranking functions. In: INFINITY. ENTCS, pp. 85–103. Elsevier, Amsterdam (2009)

11. Giunchiglia, E., Narizzano, M., Tacchella, A.: QuBE++: an efficient QBF solver. In: Hu, A.J., Martin, A.K. (eds.) FMCAD 2004. LNCS, vol. 3312, pp. 201–213. Springer, Heidelberg (2004)

12. Horwitz, S., Reps, T.W., Binkley, D.: Interprocedural slicing using dependence graphs. In: PLDI, pp. 35–46. ACM, New York (1988)

13. Jussila, T., Biere, A., Sinz, C., Kroening, D., Wintersteiger, C.M.: A first step towards a unified proof checker for QBF. In: Marques-Silva, J., Sakallah, K.A. (eds.) SAT 2007. LNCS, vol. 4501, pp. 201–214. Springer, Heidelberg (2007)

14. Podelski, A., Rybalchenko, A.: A complete method for the synthesis of linear ranking functions. In: Steffen, B., Levi, G. (eds.) VMCAI 2004. LNCS, vol. 2937, pp. 239–251. Springer, Heidelberg (2004)

15. Podelski, A., Rybalchenko, A.: Transition invariants. In: LICS, pp. 32–41. IEEE, Los Alamitos (2004)

16. Podelski, A., Rybalchenko, A.: ARMC: The logical choice for software model checking with abstraction refinement. In: Hanus, M. (ed.) PADL 2007. LNCS, vol. 4354, pp. 245–259. Springer, Heidelberg (2006)

17. Presburger, M.: Über die Vollständigkeit eines gewissen Systems der Arithmetik ganzer Zahlen, in welchem die Addition als einzige Operation hervortritt. In: Sprawozdanie z I Kongresu metematyków słowiańskich, Warsaw 1929, pp. 92–101 (1930)

18. Rümmer, P.: A constraint sequent calculus for first-order logic with linear integer arithmetic. In: Cervesato, I., Veith, H., Voronkov, A. (eds.) LPAR 2008. LNCS (LNAI), vol. 5330, pp. 274–289. Springer, Heidelberg (2008)

19. Schrijver, A.: Theory of Linear and Integer Programming. Wiley, Chichester (1986)

20. Yang, H., Lee, O., Berdine, J., Calcagno, C., Cook, B., Distefano, D., O'Hearn, P.W.: Scalable shape analysis for systems code. In: Gupta, A., Malik, S. (eds.) CAV 2008. LNCS, vol. 5123, pp. 385–398. Springer, Heidelberg (2008)

Fairness for Dynamic Control

Jochen Hoenicke[2], Ernst-Rüdiger Olderog[1], and Andreas Podelski[2]

[1] Department für Informatik, Universität Oldenburg, 26111 Oldenburg, Germany
[2] Institut für Informatik, Universität Freiburg, 79110 Freiburg, Germany

Abstract. Already in Lamport's bakery algorithm, integers are used for fair schedulers of concurrent processes. In this paper, we present the extension of a fair scheduler from 'static control' (the number of processes is fixed) to 'dynamic control' (the number of processes changes during execution). We believe that our results shed new light on the concept of fairness in the setting of dynamic control.

1 Introduction

In Lamport's bakery algorithm [8], integers are used to express the urgency to schedule a process (the goal being to prevent the starvation of each single process by ensuring fairness). The same basic idea, though in a different realization, underlies the explicit fair scheduler of [10]. Here, the urgency to schedule a process is expressed by a possibly negative integer. The urgency increases (and the integer value decreases) if the process is enabled and not taken. The non-starvation of the process apparently relies on a lower-bound invariant: the value cannot decrease below $-n$ if n is the number of all processes. This lower bound becomes void when we move from 'static control' (the number of processes is fixed) to 'dynamic control' (the number of processes changes during execution). Indeed, the first contribution of this paper is to show that the scheduler of [10] does not ensure fairness for dynamic control; in our counterexample a process starves in an execution where it is enabled in every second step; each time when it is enabled again, its urgency has already been overtaken by some new process. This negative result opens the problem of the existence of a fair scheduler for dynamic control. We present two solutions.

The main contribution of this paper is a fair scheduler for dynamic control. The originality of this scheduler lies in a heresy. We deviate from the generally accepted believe that the non-starvation of a process relies on the well-foundedness of the corresponding sequence of integer values.

The third contribution of this paper is a different kind of fair scheduler for dynamic control. The originality of our second solution to the problem lies again in a heresy. We reformulate the problem. By dropping one of the conditions in the original definition of a fair scheduler, we arrive at a weaker notion of a scheduler (a "monitor"). The difference between a scheduler and a monitor lies in the fact that a 'monitored' execution may block. Each infinite 'monitored' execution is fair; in comparison, each 'scheduled' execution is infinite and fair. In the context of verification based on the automata-theoretic approach of Vardi-Wolper [15],

J. Esparza and R. Majumdar (Eds.): TACAS 2010, LNCS 6015, pp. 251–265, 2010.

where one checks for the existence of infinite fair executions, the weaker notion of a monitor is sufficient.

In the remainder of the paper, we will present the results described above, along with a thorough investigation of a number of annexed questions. We believe that our results provide a new understanding of fairness in the context of dynamic control.

Why use explicit scheduling. There may be situations where one would like to "get rid of fairness". For example, in program analysis (whose formal foundation can be given by abstract interpretation [5]), one may want to define the semantics in terms of a (pure) transition system, i.e., a graph. Here, a popular approach is to take one of the fair schedulers used in operating systems, and to consider a new system which is composed of the original one and the scheduler, and whose semantics can be given in terms of a transition system. The objection to this approach is that the analysis result is valid only for one particular fair scheduler; i.e., it does not extend to another fair scheduler. To remove this objection, one has to take a *universal* scheduler, i.e., one that encompasses all possible fair schedulers. In contrast with schedulers implemented in operating systems, a universal scheduler is not meant to be practical. Universality holds if the scheduler is sufficiently permissive, i.e., if every possible fair execution can be scheduled (by letting the scheduler choose an appropriate sequence of alternatives at all non-deterministic choices). In order to be correct (sound), it must not be too permissive, i.e., no unfair execution can be scheduled.

Motivation of our work. Our interest for fairness in the setting of dynamic control stems from three directions.

Networked transportation systems (e.g., cars driving in groups called *platoons*) are modeled as concurrent systems (see, e.g., [2]). The fact that a traffic participant can appear and join a platoon is modeled by the creation of a new concurrent process. Fairness needs to be added as an assumption for the model for the validity of liveness properties (e.g., the termination of a merge manoeuvre between platoons).

Operating systems are typical examples of reactive systems where threads are created specifically for individual tasks. Although the execution of the overall system may be infinite, those threads must terminate in order to keep the overall system reactive. For recent automatic proof techniques addressing the termination of such threads see [13,14,12,4]. All these techniques are specifically designed to cope with fairness. Presently, however, they are restricted to the setting of static control, i.e., to the setting where the number of processes is statically fixed.

Perhaps surprisingly, recent work on model checking *safety* properties of operating systems code involve fairness [9]. Fairness is used essentially to eliminate useless (unfair) paths in the state space (i.e., paths that can be pruned without affecting the reachability of error states). This work uses explicit scheduling of the model checker for the "fair" exploration of the state space. Although the explicit scheduler in [9] is inspired by [10], it chooses a different idea for the representation of the relative urgency of processors.

Roadmap. In Section 2 we state the definitions on which we build in this paper. We formulate the classical notion of (strong) fairness not for Dijkstra's guarded command programs but, instead, for *infinitary* guarded command programs, i.e., with infinitely many branches in the **do** loops. These programs formalize the setting of *infinitary control* where infinitely many processes can be active at the same moment. In *dynamic control* only finitely many processes can be active at each moment. Then we adapt the notion of explicit scheduling and the specific scheduler for (strong) fairness from [10], which we call here $\mathbb{S}_{88}$ to the setting of infinitary control. In Section 3 we show that $\mathbb{S}_{88}$ is not valid for dynamic control. In the following we present two solutions to overcome this problem. In Section 4 we present a new scheduler $\mathbb{S}_{10}$ that is valid for dynamic control. In Section 5 we give up the requirement for a scheduler that the transition relation is total and introduce a monitor $\mathbb{M}_{88}$ derived from $\mathbb{S}_{88}$. This monitor is also valid for dynamic control. In Section 6 we investigate which of the previous results remains true in the setting of infinitary control. Section 7 concludes this paper.

2   Definitions

Though the motivation for considering fairness stems from concurrency, it is easier and more elegant to study it in terms of structured nondeterministic programs such as Dijkstra's guarded commands [7]. We follow this approach in this paper. In this section, we carry the classical definitions of fairness from Dijkstra's guarded command language over to an infinitary guarded command language, i.e., with infinitely many branches in **do** loops. It is perhaps a surprise that the definitions carry over directly. We then immediately have the definitions of fairness of programs with dynamically created processes because we will define those formally as a subclass of infinitary guarded command programs.

2.1   Dynamic Control

Our goal is a minimalistic model that allows us the study of fairness for programs with dynamically created processes. As a starting point we introduce programs with *infinitary control* by extending Dijkstra's language of guarded command programs [6] with **do** loops that have infinitely many branches. Syntactically, these **do** loops are statements of the form

$$S \equiv \textbf{do} \; [\!]_{i=0}^{\infty} \; B_i \rightarrow S_i \; \textbf{od} \tag{1}$$

where for each $i \in \mathbb{N}$ the *component* $B_i \rightarrow S_i$ consists of a Boolean expression B_i, its *guard*, and the statement S_i, its *command*. Therefore a component $B_i \rightarrow S_i$ is called a *guarded command* and S is called an *infinitary guarded command*.

We define the class of programs with dynamic control as a subclass of programs with infinitary control. At each moment each of the infinitely many processes "exists" (whether is has been created or not). Each process is modeled by a branch in the infinitary **do** loop. However, at each moment, only finitely many processes have been created (or activated or allocated). All others are dormant.

Processes are referred to by natural numbers. The process (with number) i is represented by the guarded command $B_i \rightarrow S_i$. To model processes creation we use a Boolean expression cr_i for each process i such that this process is considered as being created if cr_i evaluates to true. All other processes are treated as not being created yet. It is an important assumption that a created process can disappear but not reappear, i.e., once the value of the expression cr_i has changed from true to false it cannot go back to true.

We define a structural operational semantics in the sense of Plotkin [11] for infinitary guarded commands. As usual, it is defined in terms of transitions between configurations. A *configuration* K is a pair $<S, \sigma>$ consisting a statement S that is to be executed and a state σ that assigns a value to each program variable. A *transition* is written as a step $K \rightarrow K'$ between configurations. To express termination we use the empty statement E: a configuration $<E, \sigma>$ denotes termination in the state σ. For a Boolean expression B we write $\sigma \models B$ if B evaluates to true in the state σ. Process i is *created* in a state σ if $\sigma \models cr_i$ and it is *enabled* in state σ if it is created and its guard B_i evaluates to true, formally, $\sigma \models cr_i \wedge B_i$.

For the infinitary **do** loop S as in (1) we have two cases of transitions:

1. $<S, \sigma> \rightarrow <S_i; S, \sigma>$ if $\sigma \models cr_i \wedge B_i$ for each $i \in \mathbb{N}$,

2. $<S, \sigma> \rightarrow <E, \sigma>$ if $\sigma \models \bigwedge_{i=1}^{\infty} \neg(cr_i \wedge B_i)$.

Case 1 states that each *enabled* component $B_i \rightarrow S_i$ of S, i.e., with both the expression cr_i and the guard B_i evaluating to true in the current state σ, can be entered. If more than one component of S is enabled, one of them will be chosen nondeterministically. The successor configuration $<S_i; S, \sigma>$ formalizes the repetition of the **do** loop: once the command S_i is executed the whole loop S has to be executed again. Formally, the transitions of the configuration $<S_i; S, \sigma>$ are determined by the transition rules for the other statements of the guarded command language. For further details see, e.g., [1]. Case 2 states that the **do** loop terminates if none of the components is enabled any more, i.e, if all expressions $cr_i \wedge B_i$ evaluate to false in the state σ.

In this paper we investigate programs with only *one* infinitary **do** loop S of the form (1). This simplifies its definition of fairness and is sufficient for modeling dynamic control. An *execution* of S starting in a state σ_0 is a sequence of transitions

$$K_0 \rightarrow K_1 \rightarrow K_2 \rightarrow \ldots, \tag{2}$$

with $K_0 = <S, \sigma_0>$ as the initial configuration, which is either infinite or maximally finite, i.e., the sequence cannot be extended further by some transition.

Consider a program S of the form (1). Then for S having *infinitary control* there is no further requirement on the set of created processes. A program S has *dynamic control* if for every execution (2) of S the set of created processes is finite in every state of a configuration in (2).

A program S has *bounded control* if for every execution (2) there exists some $n \in \mathbb{N}$ such that the number of created processes is bounded by n in every state of a configuration in (2). A program S has *static control* if there is a fixed finite set F of processes such that for every execution (2) the set of created processes is contained in F in every state of a configuration in (2).

Note that we have the following hierarchy: programs with static control are a special case of programs with bounded control, which are a special case of programs with dynamic control, which in turn are a special case of programs with infinitary control.

2.2   Fairness

In this paper we extend the definition of fairness[1] of [10] from programs with static control to programs with process creation and infinitary control. Since fairness can be expressed in terms of created, enabled, and selected processes only, we abstract from all other details in executions and define it on runs.

We now fix an execution as in (2) and define the corresponding run. A transition $K_j \rightarrow K_{j+1}$ with $j \in \mathbb{N}$ is a *select transition* if it consists of the selection of an enabled process of S, formally, if $K_j = <S, \sigma>$ and $K_{j+1} = <S_i; S, \sigma>$ with $\sigma \models cr_i \wedge B_i$ for some $i \in \mathbb{N}$, so process i has been *selected* for execution in this transition. We define the *selection* of the transition $K_j \rightarrow K_{j+1}$ as the triple (C_j, E_j, i_j), where C_j is the set of all created processes, i.e.,

$$C_j = \{i \in \mathbb{N} \mid \sigma \models cr_i\},$$

and E_j is the subset of all enabled processes, i.e.,

$$E_j = \{i \in C_j \mid \sigma \models B_i\},$$

and i_j is the (index of the) selected process, i.e., $i_j = i$. Obviously, the selected command is among the enabled components. A *run of the execution* (2) is the sequence of all its selections, formally, the sequence

$$(C_{j_0}, E_{j_0}, i_{j_0})(C_{j_1}, E_{j_1}, i_{j_1}) \ldots$$

such that $C_{j_0} C_{j_1} \ldots$ is the subsequence of configurations with outgoing select transitions. Computations that do not pass through any select transition yield the empty run. A *run of a program* S is the run of one of its executions.

A run

$$(C_0, E_0, i_0)(C_1, E_1, i_1)(C_2, E_2, i_2) \ldots \tag{3}$$

is called *fair* if it satisfies the condition

$$\forall i \in \mathbb{N} : (\overset{\infty}{\exists} j \in \mathbb{N} : i \in E_j \rightarrow \overset{\infty}{\exists} j \in \mathbb{N} : i = i_j).$$

---

[1] In the literature, this notion of fairness is qualified as *strong fairness* (or *compassion*). For brevity, we simply refer to this notion without the qualifier in this paper.

where the quantifier $\overset{\infty}{\exists}$ denotes "there exist infinitely many". By our assumption (see Subsection 2.1), the fact that the process i is infinitely often enabled, formally $\overset{\infty}{\exists} j \in \mathbb{N} : i \in E_j$, implies by $E_j \subseteq C_j$ that process i is created at some moment and stays created forever, formally $\exists j_0 \in \mathbb{N}\ \forall j \geq j_0 : i \in C_j$.

In a fair run, every process i which is enabled infinitely often, is selected infinitely often. Note that every finite run is trivially fair. An *execution* of a program S of the form (1) is *fair* if its run is fair. Thus for fairness only select transitions are relevant; transitions inside the commands S_i of S do not matter. Again, every finite execution is trivially fair. Thus we concentrate on infinite executions throughout this paper.

Although we are not interested in the case where infinitely many processes can be enabled at the same time (continuously or infinitely often) and although this case is perhaps not practically relevant, the definition of fairness still makes sense, i.e., there exist fair executions in this case.

2.3   Explicit Scheduling

We extend the definition of a scheduler from [10] to the setting of infinitary control. In a given state σ the scheduler inputs a set C of created processes and a subset $E \subseteq C$ of enabled processes. It outputs some process $i \in E$ and transitions to a new state σ'. We require that the scheduler is totally defined, i.e., for every scheduler state and every input set E the scheduler will produce an output $i \in E$ and update its scheduler state. Thus a scheduler can never block the execution of a program but only influence its direction. Summarizing, we arrive at the following definition.

Definition 1 ([10]). *A* scheduler *is a triple* $\mathbb{S} = (\Sigma, \Sigma_0, \delta)$, *where*

- Σ *is a set of* states *with typical element* σ,
- $\Sigma_0 \subseteq \Sigma$ *is the set of* initial states, *and*
- δ *is a* transition relation *of the form*

$$\delta \subseteq \Sigma \times 2^{\mathbb{N}} \times 2^{\mathbb{N}} \times \mathbb{N} \times \Sigma$$

which is total *in the following sense:*

$$\forall \sigma \in \Sigma\ \forall C \in 2^{\mathbb{N}}\ \forall E \in 2^{C} \setminus \{\emptyset\}\ \exists i \in E\ \exists \sigma' \in \Sigma : (\sigma, C, E, i, \sigma') \in \delta.$$

Thus for every state σ, *every set* C *of created processes, and every nonempty subset* $E \subseteq C$ *of enabled processes there exists a process* $i \in E$ *and an the updated state* σ' *such that the tuple* $(\sigma, C, E, i, \sigma')$ *satisfies the transition relation* δ.

A run $(C_0, E_0, i_0)(C_1, E_1, i_1)(C_2, E_2, i_2)\dots$ *is* produced by a scheduler $\mathbb{S}$ *if there exists an infinite sequence* $\sigma_0\sigma_1\sigma_2\dots \in \Sigma^{\omega}$ *with* $\sigma_0 \in \Sigma_0$ *such that*

$$(\sigma_j, C_j, E_j, i_j, \sigma_{j+1}) \in \delta$$

holds for all $j \in \mathbb{N}$. *A scheduler* $\mathbb{S}$ *is* sound *if every run that is produced by* $\mathbb{S}$ *is fair. A scheduler* $\mathbb{S}$ *is* universal *if every fair run is produced by* $\mathbb{S}$. *A scheduler* $\mathbb{S}$ *is* valid *if it is both sound and universal.*

2.4   The Scheduler $\mathbb{S}_{88}$

The explicit schedulers given in [10] use auxiliary integer-valued variables (so-called *scheduling variables*), one for each process, to keep track of the relative urgency of each process (relative to the other processes). Making it more urgent is implemented by decrementing its scheduling value. Thus, scheduling values can become negative. The crucial step is the non-deterministic update to a *non-negative* integer each time after the process has been selected. Then, the process is not necessarily less urgent than all other processes. However, it is definitely less urgent than those that already have a negative scheduling value. This fact is used to prove (by induction) the *scheduling invariant*: the scheduling value will never decrease below $-n$, where n is the number of all processes [10]. This again means that a process cannot become "arbitrarily urgent"; i.e., it has to be selected after it has been made more urgent a finite (though unboundedly large) number of times, which is exactly what fairness means.

In [10] a scheduler for fairness of programs with static control was proposed. We extend it here to the case of infinitely many components and call it $\mathbb{S}_{88}$. With each process i it associates a *scheduling variable* $z[i]$ representing a priority assigned to that process. A process i has a higher priority than a process j if $z[i] < z[j]$ holds.

Definition 2 ([10]). *The scheduler* $\mathbb{S}_{88} = (\Sigma, \Sigma_0, \delta)$ *is defined as follows:*

- *The states* $\sigma \in \Sigma$ *are given by the values of an infinitary array* z *of type* $\mathbb{N} \to \mathbb{Z}$*, i.e.,* $z[i]$ *is a positive or negative integer for each* $i \in \mathbb{N}$*.*
- *The initial states in* Σ_0 *are those where each scheduler variable* $z[i]$ *has some nonnegative integer value.*
- *The relation* $(\sigma, C, E, i, \sigma') \in \delta$ *holds for states* $\sigma, \sigma' \in \Sigma$*, a set* C *of created processes, a set* $E \subseteq C$ *of enabled processes, and a process* $i \in E$ *if the value of* $z[i]$ *is minimal in* σ*, i.e., if*

$$z[i] = min\{z[k] \mid k \in E\}$$

holds in σ*, and* σ' *is obtained from* σ *by executing the following statement:*

$$UPDATE_i \equiv z[i] := ?;$$
$$\textbf{for all} \quad j \in E \setminus \{i\} \textbf{ do } z[j] := z[j] - 1 \textbf{ od}.$$

Note that the transition relation δ is total as required by Definition 1. The update of the scheduling variables guarantees that the priorities of all enabled but not selected processes j are increased. The priority of the selected process i, however, is reset arbitrarily. The idea is that by gradually increasing the priority of enabled processes, their activation cannot be refused forever.

3   The Scheduler $\mathbb{S}_{88}$ and Dynamic Control

For static control the scheduler $\mathbb{S}_{88}$ is valid, i.e., sound and universal as shown in [10]. A closer examination of the proof shows that this result extends to bounded control. However, for dynamic control this does not hold any more.

Theorem 1. *The scheduler $\mathbb{S}_{88}$ is not valid for dynamic control.*

Proof. We show that $\mathbb{S}_{88}$ is *not sound* for programs with dynamic control. To this end, we construct a run produced by $\mathbb{S}_{88}$ in which process 0 is treated unfair, i.e., it is infinitely often enabled but never selected. The idea is that in each step a new process is created, which is enabled all the time. The process 0 is only enabled in every second step. The scheduling variable of the other processes will decrease more rapidly than the scheduling variable of process 0 and thus will overtake it. The values of scheduling variables will force $\mathbb{S}_{88}$ to activate the newly created processes rather than process 0.

Table 1. A run where process 0 is treated unfair

i	σ_0	σ_1	σ_2	σ_3	σ_4	σ_5	σ_6	σ_7	σ_8	σ_9	...
0	(0)	0	(-1)	-1	(-2)	-2	(-3)	-3	(-4)	-4	...
1	0*	0	-1*	0	-1	-2	-3*	0	-1	-2	...
2	0	-1*	0	-1	-2*	0	-1	-2	-3	-4	...
3		0	-1	-2*	0	-1	-2	-3	-4*	0	...
4			0	-1	-2	-3*	0	-1	-2	-3	...
5				0	-1	-2	-3	-4*	0	-1	...
$\vdots$				$\ddots$							...

Table 1 shows an initial segment of this run in detail. In the column denoted by i the process numbers are shown. The other columns show the values of the scheduling variables $z[i]$ in the scheduler states $\sigma_0, \sigma_1, \sigma_2, \ldots$. A star $*$ after a value indicates that in this state the process in the corresponding row is selected. For example, in state σ_0 process 1 is selected. An entry in parenthesis indicates that in this state the corresponding process is not enabled. This is the case only for process 0. If process 0 is not enabled its scheduling variable $z[0]$ is not decremented in the next step. Empty boxes in the table indicate that in this state the corresponding process is *not yet created*, otherwise the process is created. Thus in state σ_0 only the processes 0, 1, and 2 are created. Note that in each step a newly created process appears in the successor state.

In general, in each state σ_{2n} process 0 is not enabled, its priority is $-n$, and for each $z \in \{-n, \ldots, 0\}$ there are exactly two processes different from process 0 with priority z. In state each σ_{2n+1} process 0 is enabled, its priority is still $-n$, there is one process with priority $-n-1$, and for each $z \in \{-n, \ldots, 0\}$ there are again exactly two processes different from process 0 with priority z: the process scheduled in the previous step and the new process have priority 0 and the two processes with priority $z+1$ in the previous step have now priority z. Then the single process with priority $-n-1$ is scheduled and we arrive at state σ_{2n+2}, where process 0 has priority $-n-1$ and there are two processes different from 0 for each priority $z \in \{-n-1, \ldots, 0\}$. This concludes the proof. $\square$

It is interesting to notice the following.

Remark 1. The scheduler $\mathbb{S}_{88}$ is universal for dynamic control.

The proof idea is that at each moment the value of the scheduling variable $z[i]$ of process i is set to the number of times process i is enabled before i is selected or disappears or gets disabled forever. In this construction the variables $z[i]$ have at each moment nonnegative values. The selected process i has the scheduling value $z[i] = 0$. All other enabled processes j have scheduling values $z[j] \geq 1$.

An alternative scheduler for fairness was proposed in [3], Chapter 6. There it is shown that this scheduler is, in our terminology, valid for static control. However, by a variant of the counterexample in Table 1 it can be shown that also this scheduler is unsound for dynamic control.

4   The Scheduler $\mathbb{S}_{10}$

We obtain the scheduler $\mathbb{S}_{10}$ from $\mathbb{S}_{88}$ by the applying the decrement of the scheduling variable to all created processes $j \in C \setminus \{i\}$ and not only to the enabled processes $j \in E \setminus \{i\}$.

Definition 3. *The scheduler $\mathbb{S}_{10}$ results from $\mathbb{S}_{88}$ by replacing UPDATE$_i$ with*

$$S\text{-}UPDATE_i \equiv z[i] := ?;$$
$$\textbf{for all} \quad j \in C \setminus \{i\} \textbf{ do } z[j] := z[j] - 1 \textbf{ od}.$$

Theorem 2. *The scheduler $\mathbb{S}_{10}$ is valid for dynamic control.*

Proof. We show that $\mathbb{S}_{10}$ is both sound and universal for dynamic control.

Soundness. Consider a run

$$(C_0, E_0, i_0)\ldots(C_j, E_j, i_j)\ldots \tag{4}$$

of a program of the form (1) with dynamic control that is produced by $\mathbb{S}_{10}$ using the sequence $\sigma_0 \sigma_1 \ldots \sigma_j \sigma_{j+1} \ldots$ of scheduler states. We claim that (4) is fair.

Suppose the contrary holds. Then there exists some process i that is enabled infinitely often, but from some moment on never selected. Formally, for some $j_0 \geq 0$

$$(\overset{\infty}{\exists} j \in \mathbb{N} : i \in E_j) \wedge (\forall j \geq j_0 : i \neq i_j)$$

holds in (4). Then the variable $z[i]$ of $\mathbb{S}_{10}$, which gets decremented whenever the process i is not selected, becomes arbitrarily small. Thus we can choose j_0 large enough so that $z[i] < 0$ holds in σ_{j_0}. Consider the set

$$Cr_{i,j} = \{k \in \mathbb{N} \mid k \in C_j \wedge \sigma_j \models z[k] \leq z[i]\}$$

of all created processes in C_j whose priority is least that of the neglected process i, formally, whose scheduling variable has at most the value of the scheduling variable of i. Since we consider dynamic control, Cr_{i,j_0} is finite in σ_{j_0}.

We show that for all $j \geq j_0$:

$$Cr_{i,j+1} \subseteq Cr_{i,j} \quad \text{and} \quad Cr_{i,j+1} \neq Cr_{i,j} \text{ if } i \in E_j. \tag{5}$$

Consider a process p that was not in $Cr_{i,j}$. We show $p \notin Cr_{i,j+1}$ to prove the inclusion. If p was scheduled in step j, then $\sigma_{j+1} \models z[i] < 0 \leq z[p]$, thus $p \notin Cr_{i,j+1}$.

If process p is newly created in step j we exploit two facts. (1) By the definition of $S\text{-}UPDATE_i$, its scheduling variable $z[p]$ is not decremented as long as p is not created. (2) The process p has not been created before by the assumption that a created process can disappear but not reappear, stated in Subsection 2.1. By (1) and (2), $z[p]$ has still its initial nonnegative value in state σ_{j+1}, thus $\sigma_{j+1} \models z[p] \geq 0$. So $p \notin Cr_{i,j+1}$.

If we take a process p different from the selected process then in the successor state σ_{j+1} the validity of the inequality $z[p] \leq z[i]$ is preserved (both p and i have their scheduling variable decremented by the definition of $S\text{-}UPDATE_i$).

If process i is enabled in step j, the scheduler needs to select a process p from $Cr_{i,j}$. As seen before, the scheduled process is not in $Cr_{i,j+1}$, thus $Cr_{i,j} \neq Cr_{i,j+1}$. This proves property (5).

By assumption i is enabled infinitely often, so by (5) the set $Cr_{i,j}$ is strictly decreasing infinitely often. This contradicts the fact that Cr_{i,j_0} is finite.

Universality. Consider a fair run

$$(C_0, E_0, i_0)(C_1, E_1, i_1)(C_2, E_2, i_2)\ldots\ldots \tag{6}$$

We show that (6) can be produced by $\mathbb{S}_{10}$ by constructing a sequence $\sigma_0 \ldots \sigma_j \ldots$ of scheduler states satisfying $(\sigma_j, C_j, E_j, i_j, \sigma_{j+1}) \in \delta$ for every $j \in \mathbb{N}$. The construction proceeds by assigning appropriate values to the scheduling variables $z[i]$ of $\mathbb{S}_{10}$. For $i, j \in \mathbb{N}$ we put

$$\sigma_j(z[i]) = |\{k \in \mathbb{N} \mid j \leq k < m_{i,j} \wedge i \in C_k\}| - |\{k \in \mathbb{N} \mid m_{i,j} \leq k < j \wedge i \in C_k\}|,$$

where

$$m_{i,j} = min\left\{ m \in \mathbb{N} \;\middle|\; \begin{array}{c} (1)\ (j \leq m \wedge i_m = i) \\ \vee \\ (2)\ (\forall n \geq m : i \notin E_n) \end{array} \right\}.$$

Note that $m_{i,j}$ is the minimum of a non-empty subset of $\mathbb{N}$ because the run (6) is fair. In case (1) of the definition of $m_{i,j}$, i.e., when i is eventually selected, the value $\sigma_j(z[i])$ is nonnegative. However, in case (2) of the definition of $m_{i,j}$, i.e., when i is not enabled any more, the value $\sigma_j(z[i])$ can denote arbitrarily negative values.

This construction of values $\sigma_j(z[i])$ is possible with the assignments in $\mathbb{S}_{10}$. In the constructed run the selected process i has the scheduling value $z[i] = 0$. All other enabled processes j have scheduling values $z[j] \geq 1$. So i is the unique enabled process with the minimum of all scheduling values, which is 0. $\qquad\square$

5   The Monitor $\mathbb{M}_{88}$

The scheduler $\mathbb{S}_{88}$ does not decrease the scheduling variables of processes that are not enabled. So these scheduling variables cannot become arbitrarily negative. However, $\mathbb{S}_{88}$ it not valid for dynamic control. The new scheduler $\mathbb{S}_{10}$ is valid for dynamic control but the scheduling variables can become arbitrarly negative for created processes that are from some moment on never enabled any more.

In this section we shall propose a variant of $\mathbb{S}_{88}$ where the scheduling variables are prevented from becoming negative. The price we pay for this property is that this may lead to a blocking behaviour. Schedulers are required to be nonblocking, i.e., they should have a totally defined transition relation. We now drop this requirement and call the resulting device a *monitor*.

Definition 4. *A monitor is a triple* $\mathbb{M} = (\Sigma, \Sigma_0, \delta)$, *where*

- Σ *is a set of* states *with typical element* σ,
- $\Sigma_0 \subseteq \Sigma$ *is the set of* initial *states, and*
- δ *is a* transition relation *of the form*

$$\delta \subseteq \Sigma \times 2^{\mathbb{N}} \times 2^{\mathbb{N}} \times \mathbb{N} \times \Sigma$$

(without totality requirement as for schedulers).

A run $(C_0, E_0, i_0)(C_1, E_1, i_1)(C_2, E_2, i_2)\ldots$ *is* accepted *by a monitor* $\mathbb{M}$ *if there exists an infinite sequence* $\sigma_0 \sigma_1 \sigma_2 \ldots \in \Sigma^{\omega}$ *with* $\sigma_0 \in \Sigma_0$ *such that*

$$(\sigma_j, C_j, E_j, i_j, \sigma_{j+1}) \in \delta$$

holds for all $j \in \mathbb{N}$. *A monitor* $\mathbb{M}$ *is* sound *if every run that is accepted by* $\mathbb{M}$ *is fair. A monitor* M *is* universal *if every fair run is accepted by* $\mathbb{M}$. *A monitor* $\mathbb{M}$ *is* valid *if it is both sound and universal.*

Since the totality requirement is dropped for the transition relation δ, the monitor cannot be used to produce a fair run step-by-step because for a given scheduler state σ, a set C of created processes, and a set E of enabled processes there may not be a process $i \in E$ and an updated scheduler state σ' with $(\sigma, C, E, i, \sigma') \in \delta$. However, a monitor can be used as an acceptor of given runs. Then the question of being able to stepwise produce the run is not relevant. We modify the scheduler $\mathbb{S}_{88}$ of Definition 2 to a monitor called $\mathbb{M}_{88}$.

Definition 5. *The monitor* $\mathbb{M}_{88}$ *is obtained from the scheduler* $\mathbb{S}_{88}$ *by changing the type of the infinitary array* z *of scheduling variables to* $\mathbb{N} \to \mathbb{N}$, *i.e., for each process* $i \in \mathbb{N}$ *the scheduling variable* $z[i]$ *can store only* nonnegative *integers. As a consequence, inside the statement* $UPDATE_i$ *each decrement operation*

$$z[j] := z[j] - 1$$

is defined only if $z[j] > 0$ *holds. Otherwise the operation will cause a failure, which blocks any further execution.*

As in the scheduler $\mathbb{S}_{88}$ the process i with the minimal value of the scheduling variables among the enabled processes is selected. However, in contrast to $\mathbb{S}_{88}$ and $\mathbb{S}_{10}$ the transition relation of the monitor $\mathbb{M}_{88}$ is not totally defined any more. Nevertheless, we have the following result.

Theorem 3. *The monitor $\mathbb{M}_{88}$ is valid for dynamic control.*

Proof. We show that $\mathbb{M}_{88}$ is both sound and universal for dynamic control.

Soundness. Consider a run

$$(C_0, E_0, i_0)\ldots(C_j, E_j, i_j)\ldots \tag{7}$$

of a program of the form (1) with dynamic control that is accepted by $\mathbb{M}_{88}$, and let $\sigma_0\ldots\sigma_j\ldots$ be a sequence of states with $(\sigma_j, C_j, E_j, i_j, \sigma_{j+1}) \in \delta$ for every $j \in \mathbb{N}$. We claim that (7) is fair.

Suppose the contrary holds. Then there exists some process i which is infinitely often enabled, but from some moment on never selected. Note that whenever process i is enabled but not selected, the monitor $\mathbb{M}_{88}$ decrements its scheduling variable $z[i]$ *provided* $z[i] > 0$ holds. However, $z[i]$ cannot be decremented infinitely often without raising a failure, *Contradiction.*

Universality. Let the (7) be fair. Then we can proceed as in the proof outlined for Remark 1 because according to that construction in each step of the run exactly the selected process i has the scheduling value $z[i] = 0$. All other enabled processes have scheduling values $z[j] \geq 1$. Thus the monitor $\mathbb{M}_{88}$ can simulate the scheduler $\mathbb{S}_{88}$. □

The scheduling variables of the scheduler $\mathbb{S}_{88}$ when applied to programs with n processes (static control) can become arbitrarily positive but *not arbitrarily negative*, i.e., they do not assume values below $-n$ due to an execution invariant of $\mathbb{S}_{88}$(see [10]). By contrast, the scheduling variables of $\mathbb{S}_{10}$ *can become arbitrarily negative* even when it is applied to programs with static comtrol only. By definition, the scheduling variables of the monitor $\mathbb{M}_{88}$ stay nonnegative. The price for this is that the monitor *can block* the computation.

Other Monitors

The monitor $\mathbb{M}_{88}$ selects a process i with the minimal value of the scheduling variables among the enabled processes. We discuss two variants of this choice. Let $\mathbb{M}_{88}{}^{*}$ result from $\mathbb{M}_{88}$ by selecting an enabled process i with $z[i] = 0$, and $\mathbb{M}_{88}{}^{**}$ result from $\mathbb{M}_{88}$ by selecting an *arbitrary* enabled process.

Remark 2. The monitors $\mathbb{M}_{88}{}^{*}$ and $\mathbb{M}_{88}{}^{**}$ are valid for dynamic control.

Proof. A closer inspection of the proof of Theorem 3 shows that the soundness argument is independent of how an enabled process is selected. For the universality argument we notice that in the construction of the monitor state sequence always an enabled process i with $z[i] = 0$ is selected. □

Surprisingly, an attempt to modify the scheduler $\mathbb{S}_{10}$ to a corresponding monitor $\mathbb{M}_{10}$ fails because we can show that this monitor is not valid. Indeed, let us define the monitor $\mathbb{M}_{10}$ analogously to Definition 5 by changing in the scheduler $\mathbb{S}_{10}$ the type of the infinitary array z of scheduling variables to $\mathbb{N} \to \mathbb{N}$, i.e., for each process $i \in \mathbb{N}$ the scheduling variable $z[i]$ can store *only nonnegative* integers. Again, the transition relation of the monitor $\mathbb{M}_{10}$ is not totally defined because the decrement operations $z[j] := z[j] - 1$ can fail.

In contrast to the monitor $\mathbb{M}_{88}$, we have the following negative result.

Remark 3. The monitor $\mathbb{M}_{10}$ is not valid for dynamic control, not even for static control.

Proof. We show that $\mathbb{M}_{10}$ is *not universal* for programs with *static control*. Consider a fair run of a program where from some moment on a created process j is not enabled any more. Then the corresponding variable $z[j]$ gets decremented whenever another process i is selected. So $z[j] = 0$ will eventually hold and thus the run cannot be accepted by $\mathbb{M}_{10}$ without blocking. □

6 Infinitary Fairness

In this section we investigate which of our previous results actually relies on the restriction to dynamic control. We shall see that some hold even in the setting of infinitary control and others do not.

Since the scheduler $\mathbb{S}_{88}$ is not valid for dynamic control, it is not valid for infinitary control either. More precisely, $\mathbb{S}_{88}$ is not sound for infinitary control. This follows trivially from the corresponding argument in the proof of Theorem 1 for dynamic control. On the other hand, $\mathbb{S}_{88}$ is universal for infinitary control. Indeed, the proof idea presented for Remark 1 does not rely on the restriction to dynamic control.

For the scheduler $\mathbb{S}_{10}$ we have analogous results for infinitary control.

Theorem 4. *The scheduler $\mathbb{S}_{10}$ is not valid for infinitary control.*

Proof. The soundness argument in the proof of Theorem 2 exploits the assumption of dynamic control. We show now that $\mathbb{S}_{10}$ is *not sound* for programs with infinitary control. To this end, we construct a run produced by $\mathbb{S}_{10}$ where *every* process is treated unfair. More precisely, every process is always enabled but selected *only once*, in the ith selection of the run: $(\mathbb{N}, \mathbb{N}, 0)(\mathbb{N}, \mathbb{N}, 1)(\mathbb{N}, \mathbb{N}, 2) \ldots$ This is possible by choosing the corresponding sequence $\sigma_0 \sigma_1 \sigma_3 \ldots$ of scheduler states as follows:

i	σ_0	σ_1	σ_2	σ_3	σ_4	$\ldots$
0	0*	0	-1	-2	-3	$\ldots$
1	0	-1*	0	-1	-2	$\ldots$
2	0	-1	-2*	0	-1	$\ldots$
3	0	-1	-2	-3*	0	$\ldots$
4	0	-1	-2	-3	-4*	$\ldots$
$\ldots$	$\ldots$	$\ldots$	$\ldots$	$\ldots$	$\ldots$	$\ldots$

$$\sigma_j(z[i]) = \begin{cases} i + 1 - j & \text{if } i < j \\ -j & \text{if } i \geq j \end{cases}$$

The table on the previous page shows an initial segment of this sequence in detail. As in Table 1, in the column denoted by i the process numbers are shown. The other columns in the table show the values of the scheduling variables $z[i]$ in the scheduler states $\sigma_0, \sigma_1, \sigma_2, \ldots$. A star $*$ after a value indicates that in this state the process in the corresponding row is selected. For example, in state σ_0 process 0 is selected.   □

On the other hand, the universality of $\mathbb{S}_{10}$ still holds for infinitary control. Indeed, the universality argument in the proof of Theorem 2 does not use the assumption of dynamic control. What about the monitor $\mathbb{M}_{88}$? Interestingly, it can also be used for infinitary control.

Remark 4. The monitor $\mathbb{M}_{88}$ is valid for infinitary control.

This result follows from a closer examination of the proof of Theorem 3 which does not use the assumption of dynamic control.

7   Conclusion

The results presented in this paper provide a new understanding of fairness in the context of dynamic control. Fairness means the non-starvation of each single process. I.e, it must not happen that a process, say i, is enabled infinitely often but not taken. Thus, at each state σ of an execution, there is only a finite number of positions where process i is enabled before it is taken. The difficulty of scheduling a dynamically growing number of processes stems from the need to prioritize "fairly" among the processes.

Our first result says that correlating the priority to the number of times that a process was enabled but not taken does not guarantee fairness. Since more and more newly created processes can increase their priority, it is possible that one of them overtakes process i in its priority.

Our second result says that correlating the priority to the number of times that a process was not taken (regardless of whether it was enabled or not) prevents this kind of overtaking and succeeds in guaranteeing fairness. As a consequence, the priority of a process that is never enabled again can get arbitrarily high, and in particular higher than the priority of every enabled process. This fact, although it contradicts the original intuition about explicit scheduling, does not impede the functioning of the scheduler.

The third result says that correlating the priority to the number of times that a process was enabled but not taken does guarantee fairness *if* this can happen only a finite number of times. Which itself is enforced by a bound on its priority; i.e., the priority cannot increase indefinitely. As a result, one obtains blocked executions (the execution gets blocked if the bound is reached). Although one needs to overcome a conceptual barrier (since blocking contradicts the philosophy that underlies the very concept of scheduling), one arrives at the concept of a monitor which fullfills the purpose of a scheduler in the context of verification.

This leads to a new line of future research: explore the potential of the monitor for automated verification methods for termination and liveness properties. Tools for programs that have terminating, though unboundedly long executions, in general use integer arithmetic to deal with ranking functions. The concept of the integer variable that measures the priority of a process is related to the concept of a rank and requires the same kind of reasoning; i.e., adding an integer-based monitor to deal with fairness does not add a foreign element as far as the reasoning method is concerned. For this reason, the potential of the monitor for automated verification methods seems promising.

We have left open the following question. Does there exists an explicit scheduler for infinitary control?

Acknowledgements. This work was partly supported by the German Research Council (DFG) as part of the Transregional Collaborative Research Center "Automatic Verification and Analysis of Complex Systems" (SFB/TR 14 AVACS). We thank Andrey Rybalchenko for helpful comments on this paper.

References

1. Apt, K.-R., Olderog, E.-R.: Verification of Sequential and Concurrent Programs, 2nd edn. Springer, Heidelberg (1997)
2. Bauer, J., Schaefer, I., Toben, T., Westphal, B.: Specification and verification of dynamic communication systems. In: Goossens, K., Petrucci, L. (eds.) ACSD, Turku, Finland. IEEE, Los Alamitos (2006)
3. Best, E.: Semantics of Sequential and Parallel Programs. Prentice Hall, Englewood Cliffs (1996)
4. Cook, B., Podelski, A., Rybalchenko, A.: Proving thread termination. In: PLDI. ACM Press, New York (2007)
5. Cousot, P., Cousot, R.: Abstract interpretation: A unified lattice model for static analysis of programs by construction or approximation of fixedpoints. In: POPL, pp. 238–252. ACM, New York (1977)
6. Dijkstra, E.W.: Guarded commands, nondeterminacy and formal derivation of programs. Comm. of the ACM 18, 453–457 (1975)
7. Francez, N.: Fairness. Springer, New York (1986)
8. Lamport, L.: A new solution of Dijkstra's concurrent programming problem. Comm. of the ACM 17(8), 453–455 (1974)
9. Musuvathi, M., Quadeer, S.: Fair stateless model checking. In: PLDI (June 2008)
10. Olderog, E.R., Apt, K.R.: Fairness in parallel programs, the transformational approach. ACM TOPLAS 10, 420–455 (1988)
11. Plotkin, G.: A structural approach to operational semantics. J. of Logic and Algebraic Programming 60-61, 17–139 (2004)
12. Pnueli, A., Podelski, A., Rybalchenko, A.: Separating fairness and well-foundedness for the analysis of fair discrete systems. In: Halbwachs, N., Zuck, L.D. (eds.) TACAS 2005. LNCS, vol. 3440, pp. 124–139. Springer, Heidelberg (2005)
13. Podelski, A., Rybalchenko, A.: Transition invariants. In: LICS 2004, pp. 32–41. IEEE Computer Society, Los Alamitos (2004)
14. Podelski, A., Rybalchenko, A.: Transition predicate abstraction and fair termination. In: POPL, pp. 132–144. ACM, New York (2005)
15. Vardi, M.Y., Wolper, P.: An automata-theoretic approach to automatic program verification. In: LICS, pp. 332–344. IEEE Computer Society, Los Alamitos (1986)

JTorX: A Tool for On-Line Model-Driven Test Derivation and Execution

Axel Belinfante

Formal Methods and Tools, University of Twente, The Netherlands
Axel.Belinfante@cs.utwente.nl

Abstract. We introduce JTORX, a tool for model-driven test derivation and execution, based on the ioco theory. This theory, originally presented in [12], has been refined in [13] with test-cases that are input-enabled. For models with underspecified traces [3] introduced uioco.

JTORX improves over its predecessor TORX [14] by using uioco and this newer ioco theory. By being much easier to deploy, due to improved installation, configuration and usage. And by integrating additional functionality, next to testing: checking for (u)ioco between models [6]; checking for underspecified traces in a model; interactive or guided simulation of a model. This makes JTORX an excellent vehicle for educational purposes in courses on model-based testing, as experience has shown – and its usefulness is not limited to education, as experience has shown too.

1 Introduction

Ten years ago we presented TORX, a tool for model-based testing. Its main focus was on *on line* test derivation and execution, i.e. a test is derived on demand while it is being executed (for *off line* execution a test case was treated as a special kind of model; only much later TORX was extended with (experimental) *off line* test derivation). As we wrote in [1], important features of TORX are flexibility and openness. However, it turned out that in our attempt to obtain these features we sacrificed ease of deployment, in particular ease of configuration, and, on Windows, ease of installation. For case studies that was not an issue because 1) usually one can choose where to run them (on a Unix system), 2) typically they were done by TORX-experts, and 3) the configuration overhead was small compared to the overall effort of setting up a case study anyway. However, it was an issue for transfer of the tool to non-TORX-experts, like students who have to install and use the tool to do tool-based exercises, or staff members who want to use it to show the idea of model-based testing.

JTORX is our answer to this problem. JTORX is a re-implementation of the main functionality of TORX in Java. As a consequence, installation of JTORX is rather simple, also on Windows. Configuration is much simpler than in TORX, because all of it can be done via the JTORX Graphical User Interface (GUI).

Not only is JTORX easier to deploy, we also used the opportunity to catch up with theoretical progress, and to add features that are helpful for education and for quick impromptu demonstrations. These are discussed in the next section.

JTORX is, under BSD-style license, available for free at [17].

J. Esparza and R. Majumdar (Eds.): TACAS 2010, LNCS 6015, pp. 266–270, 2010.

2   Features

Catching up with theoretical progress led to the following. The initial design of TORX, based on the *ioco* theory of [12], made use of the fact that in that theory test cases are non input-enabled (once the tester has decided to apply a stimulus it will not look at output that might be produced by the system under test (SUT) until the stimulus has been applied). This was already revised when we started to experiment with timed testing [5]. The design of JTORX is based on the refined *ioco* theory of [13] in which test cases are input-enabled. In addition, JTORX allows testing for *uioco* (introduced in [3]), a weaker relation than *ioco* developed for models that contain underspecified traces. In JTORX the ability to support off line test derivation has been taken into account from the start.

The following features were added in JTORX to ease educational use, next to the functionality for on line test derivation and execution: a checker to find underspecified traces in a given model; a checker that checks (instead of tests) whether two models are (u)ioco-related [6]; a simulator for manual exploration of a model (or *suspension automaton*, see Section 3) or guided simulation of a given trace, e.g. produced by one of the checkers. The test run can be guided, using such trace, or a test purpose. To access models, JTORX has built-in support for: GRAPHML [8] (to allow the use of graph editor yEd [15] to draw a model as automaton), the Aldebaran (.aut) file format, the Jararaca [16] file format (to allow a regular expression-style specification of traces to guide a test run), and the TORX Explorer protocol to allow model access via the mcrl2 [9], LTSmin [4] and CADP [7] tool environments. To connect to a SUT JTORX has built-in support for: use of a simulated model; use of a real program that communicates using labels of the model, either on its standard input and output, or over a single TCP connection; use of the TORX Adapter protocol (for backwards compatibility). Each test run is reported in a (text) log shown in the GUI (and as in TORX visualized in a dynamically updated *message sequence chart*). During a test run (as in TORX), and during simulation, progress through models and suspension automaton is visualized in dynamically updated automaton viewers.

3   Architecture

The flexibility and openness of TORX were obtained by having a modular tool architecture. JTORX inherits this architecture (but not the deployment issues, by having a different implementation). A typical (J)TORX configuration, depicted in Fig. 1, contains at least the following components. (Components that are only used in guided test runs appear dotted in this figure.)   An Explorer provides uniform access to the (labelled transition system) state space of the Model (or Test Purpose, in case of a guided test run). A Primer provides access to the *suspension automaton* (see [13]) of the Model (or Test Purpose) accessed via its Explorer, i.e. it determinizes and marks *quiescent* states (in which the SUT is expected to stay silent) with δ-labelled selfloops. It does this on demand. To avoid storing states unnecessarily Primer and Driver tell their resp. Explorer

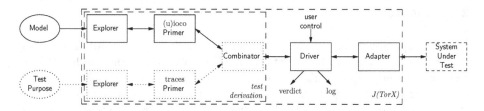

Fig. 1. Tool components of a typical (J)TorX configuration. Items TP, Explorer, Primer and Combinator in the dotted boxes are only present in a guided test run.

and Primer which states (reached by stimulus or observation not in the test run) to forget. An Adapter provides uniform access to the SUT. The Driver controls a test run, and decides whether to obtain and apply a stimulus, whether to obtain and check an observation, or to stop the test run. Additional components, like the Combinator, are used e.g. to guide a test run using a Test Purpose. Typically, an Explorer is modeling-formalism dependent, but model-independent; an Adapter is model-dependent, and specific for a particular (family of) SUT. The other tool components are model-, formalism- and SUT-independent.

4   Usage

At four universities students have used JTorX in courses on testing techniques, to compare models, and to test a real program w.r.t. a model that they developed themselves. Doing these exercises gave the students a deeper understanding of the ioco theory and its test derivation algorithm, and allowed them to experience model-based testing in practice. For the tutors, the use of JTorX greatly reduced the effort needed to set up the exercise class, compared to the use of TorX in previous years. Moreover, it encouraged developing more elaborate exercises – for example, testing of a real program (now facilitated by JTorX built-in standard i/o Adapter) was not done in previous years. For the students, JTorX clearly provided a better user experience – with TorX there typical were complaints, e.g. about the GUI, but with JTorX there were none. As a result, JTorX will continue to be used in these courses.

JTorX found a real, unintended error in a Java program developed as SUT for one of the courses. The program occasionally lost inputs, because its input handling was initialized *inside* (instead of before) its main input-processing loop.

In an internship a student used Unit Testing and then JTorX to test the program he developed. JTorX found five errors, some of which rather subtle – these might not have been found without JTorX, even when the time invested in model-based testing would have been spent on manual testing instead [11].

5   Future Work

We foresee improvements to JTorX in two directions: improvement of the user experience e.g. by professionalization of the user interface, and extension of the functionality. Implementation in JTorX of TorX' ability to deal with parameterized action labels will enable use of its real-time Explorer [5] and its Explorer for Promela models. Also, connection to TorXakis [10] is planned.

6 Related Work

We are aware of existing tools for model-based testing like those discussed in [2], but to our knowledge, none of them posseses a similar suitability for education.

Acknowledgements

Our gratitude goes to Mark Timmer for helping with the testing techniques practical exercises at University of Twente, to Jan Tretmans for trying JTorX and providing feedback, and to Jaco van de Pol for feedback on this article.

References

1. Belinfante, A., et al.: Formal test automation: A simple experiment. In: 12th Int. Workshop on Testing of Communicating Systems, pp. 179–196. Kluwer, Dordrecht (1999)
2. Belinfante, A.F.E., Frantzen, L., Schallhart, C.: Tools for test case generation. In: Broy, M., Jonsson, B., Katoen, J.-P., Leucker, M., Pretschner, A. (eds.) Model-Based Testing of Reactive Systems. LNCS, vol. 3472, pp. 391–438. Springer, Heidelberg (2005)
3. van der Bijl, H.M., Rensink, A., Tretmans, J.: Compositional testing with ioco. In: Petrenko, A., Ulrich, A. (eds.) FATES 2003. LNCS, vol. 2931, pp. 86–100. Springer, Heidelberg (2004)
4. Blom, S.C.C., van de Pol, J.C., Weber, M.: Bridging the gap between enumerative and symbolic model checkers. Technical Report TR-CTIT-09-30, Centre for Telematics and Information Technology, University of Twente, Enschede (2009)
5. Bohnenkamp, H.C., Belinfante, A.F.E.: Timed testing with TorX. In: Fitzgerald, J.S., Hayes, I.J., Tarlecki, A. (eds.) FM 2005. LNCS, vol. 3582, pp. 173–188. Springer, Heidelberg (2005)
6. Frantzen, L.: iocoChecker (2008), http://www.cs.ru.nl/~lf/tools/iocochecker
7. Garavel, H., et al.: Cadp 2006: A toolbox for the construction and analysis of distributed processes. In: Damm, W., Hermanns, H. (eds.) CAV 2007. LNCS, vol. 4590, pp. 158–163. Springer, Heidelberg (2007)
8. GraphML work group: GraphML file format, http://graphml.graphdrawing.org
9. Groote, J.F., et al.: The mcrl2 toolset. In: Proc. International Workshop on Advanced Software Development Tools and Techniques, WASDeTT 2008 (2008)
10. Mostowski, W., Poll, E., Schmaltz, J., Tretmans, J., Schreur, R.W.: Model-based testing of electronic passports. In: Alpuente, M. (ed.) FMICS 2009. LNCS, vol. 5825, pp. 207–209. Springer, Heidelberg (2009)
11. Sijtema, M.: Developing XBus2 — a software bus, that is maintainable, testable and backwards-compatible. Internship Report, University of Twente (2009)
12. Tretmans, J.: Test generation with inputs, outputs, and repetitive quiescence. Software - Concepts and Tools 17(3) (1996)

13. Tretmans, J.: Model Based Testing with Labelled Transition Systems. In: Hierons, R.M., Bowen, J.P., Harman, M. (eds.) FORTEST. LNCS, vol. 4949, pp. 1–38. Springer, Heidelberg (2008)

14. Tretmans, J., Brinksma, H.: TorX: Automated model-based testing. In: Hartman, A., Dussa-Ziegler, K. (eds.) First European Conference on Model-Driven Software Engineering, Nuremberg, Germany, Nuremberg, Germany, December 2003, pp. 13–43 (2003)

15. yWorks: yEd, http://www.yworks.com/en/products_yed_about.html

16. Jararaca manual, http://fmt.cs.utwente.nl/tools/torx/jararaca.1.html

17. JTorX website, http://fmt.cs.utwente.nl/tools/jtorx/

SLAB: A Certifying Model Checker for Infinite-State Concurrent Systems*

Klaus Dräger[1], Andrey Kupriyanov[1], Bernd Finkbeiner[1], and Heike Wehrheim[2]

[1] Universität des Saarlandes, Saarbrücken, Germany
[2] Universität Paderborn, Germany

Abstract. Systems and protocols combining concurrency and infinite state space occur quite often in practice, but are very difficult to verify automatically. At the same time, if the system is correct, it is desirable for a verifier to obtain not a simple "yes" answer, but some independently checkable certificate of correctness. We present SLAB — the first certifying model checker for infinite-state concurrent systems. The tool uses a procedure that interleaves automatic abstraction refinement using Craig interpolation with slicing, which removes irrelevant states and transitions from the abstraction. Given a transition system and a safety property to check, SLAB either finds a counterexample or produces a certificate of system correctness in the form of inductive verification diagram.

1 Slicing Abstractions

SLAB (for *sl*icing *ab*stractions) is an automatic certifying model checker that implements the *abstraction refinement* loop presented in [1]. It interleaves refinement steps with *slicing*, which tracks the dependencies between variables and transitions in a system and removes irrelevant parts.

SLAB maintains an explicit graph representation of the abstract model: each node represents a set of concrete states, identified by a set of predicates; each edge represents a set of concrete transitions, identified by their transition relations.

Starting with the initial abstraction, the abstract model is transformed by refinement and slicing steps until the system is proved correct or a concretizable error path is found.

A *refinement step* increases the precision of the abstraction by introducing a new predicate, which is obtained by Craig interpolation from the unsatisfiable formula corresponding to some spurious error path. To minimize the increase in the size of the graph, the new predicate is only applied to one specific node on the error path. This node is split into two copies, the labels of which now additionally contain the new predicate and its negation, respectively.

A *slicing step* reduces the size of the abstraction while maintaining all error paths. *Elimination rules* drop nodes and edges from the abstraction if they have

---

* This work was partly supported by the German Research Council (DFG) as part of the Transregional Collaborative Research Center "Automatic Verification and Analysis of Complex Systems" (SFB/TR 14 AVACS, www.avacs.org).

become unreachable or if their label has become unsatisfiable. *Simplification rules* remove constraints from transition relations that have become irrelevant and simplify the graph structure of the abstraction.

2   Certifying Model Checker

If SLAB proves a concurrent system correct, then it produces from the final abstraction an efficiently and independently checkable certificate of the correctness. Such a certificate is much more useful than the usual binary response "correct"/"incorrect" (see e.g. [6]): it provides higher *degree of confidence* in the results of the verification run; it can be employed in *automated theorem proving* by importing it into a theorem prover and composing with certificates from other subgoals into a single proof; finally, it can be used to obtain *proof-carrying code*.

SLAB produces certificates in the form of inductive verification diagrams [5]: directed graphs in which nodes n are labeled with state predicates φ_n, and edges — with sets of transition relations. They satisfy the following properties (where we use Φ for the disjunction over all φ_n):

- Every initial state is represented by some node, i.e., *init* implies Φ;
- If a state s is represented by a node and has an outgoing transition $s \xrightarrow{\tau} s'$, then s' is also represented by some node. Equivalently, for each transition relation τ, the Hoare triple $\{\Phi\}\tau\{\Phi\}$ must be valid.
- Every node label precludes the error condition, i.e. Φ implies $\neg error$.

Thus the disjunction of the certificate node labels forms an inductive invariant which ensures that an error can never occur, and checking the correctness of the certificate boils down to verifying the above conditions on Φ.

The edge labels provide an alternative set of simpler Hoare triples for the second condition: For each node n and transition τ, $\{\varphi_n\}\tau\{\bigvee_m \varphi_m\}$ must hold, where the disjunction is over all m with $n \xrightarrow{\tau} m$.

As an example, Fig. 2 shows the specification of a simplified ring-buffer for a double-ended queue, consisting of cells (represented by integer variables) which can be either free (0) or occupied (1). Starting with a single occupied cell x_1, we can toggle a cell's state if the states of its neighbors differ.

$init$	$x_1 = 1 \wedge x_2 = 0 \wedge \cdots \wedge x_n = 0$
$error$	$x_1 = 1 \wedge x_2 = 1 \wedge \cdots \wedge x_n = 1$
τ_1	$x_n + x_2 = 1 \wedge x_1' = 1 - x_1 \wedge \Delta(\{x_1\})$
τ_2	$x_1 + x_3 = 1 \wedge x_2' = 1 - x_2 \wedge \Delta(\{x_2\})$
$\vdots$	$\vdots$
τ_n	$x_1 + x_{n-1} = 1 \wedge x_n' = 1 - x_n \wedge \Delta(\{x_n\})$

Fig. 1. Initial condition, error condition, and transitions of the deque example. $\Delta(S)$ denotes the frame condition that all variables $x \notin S$ remain unchanged.

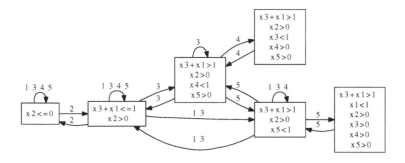

Fig. 2. A certificate of correctness for the deque example

The certificate produced by SLAB for an instance with 5 cells is shown on Fig. 2. The inductivity of the diagram guarantees that no error state is reachable.

3 Results

SLAB is written in C++, and is available for the Linux platform. As an underlying mechanism for satisfiability checking and Craig interpolation, SLAB uses the MathSAT 4 SMT solver [2].

The model checker produces certificates both in graphical format as in Fig. 2 for visual inspection by the user, and in the SMT-LIB format, which can be checked by any of a large number of standard SMT solvers.

Table 1. Experimental results of SLAB, comparing its performance on a range of benchmarks to the tools ARMC, BLAST and NuSMV. Running times are given in seconds, with a timeout of 1 hour. All benchmarks were measured on AMD Opteron 2.6Ghz processors.

Benchmark	ARMC time	BLAST time	NuSMV time (10)	NuSMV time (100)	SLAB time	SLAB certificate size
Deque 5	1.81	0.55	0.03	5.64	0.06	6
Deque 10	776.33	2.32	0.05	13.89	0.18	11
Deque 15	timeout	6.40	0.08	22.71	0.40	16
Deque 20	timeout	13.41	0.14	36.08	0.69	20
Bakery 2	2.26	21.71	0.03	0.72	0.43	25
Bakery 3	33.44	134.72	0.04	6.44	1.45	35
Bakery 4	753.15	error	0.17	293.65	4.00	45
Bakery 5	timeout	879.71	0.33	timeout	10.26	55
Philosophers 3	125.82	15.02	0.24	7.82	0.76	11
Philosophers 4	timeout	92.04	0.89	25.16	3.05	26
Philosophers 5	timeout	658.80	4.36	554.86	11.50	57
Philosophers 6	timeout	timeout	9.24	timeout	42.57	120
Fischer 2	1.45	N/A	N/A	N/A	0.65	24
Fischer 3	48.68	N/A	N/A	N/A	9.16	170
Fischer 4	1842.85	N/A	N/A	N/A	122.77	1014

The user can customize several parameters of the abstraction refinement loop:

- The *initial abstraction*: The user can choose either a simple 4-state abstraction, based on the initial and error conditions, or a control flow graph.
- The *trace selection strategy*: The user can choose between random and deterministic selection of traces.
- The *node splitting strategy*: The user may allow several nodes to be split along any unsatisfiable trace of the abstraction.

Table 1 shows the performance of SLAB on a range of benchmarks. For comparison, we also give the running times of the *Abstraction Refinement Model Checker* ARMC [7], the *Berkeley Lazy Abstraction Software Verification Tool* BLAST [4] and the *New Symbolic Model Checker* NuSMV [3], where applicable. The benchmarks include a finite-state concurrent systems (Deque and Philosophers), an infinite-state discrete system (Bakery), and a real-time system (Fisher). BLAST and NuSMV are not applicable to the real-time system Fischer. Because NuSMV is able to verify only finite state systems, the running times for this tool are given for two cases: when all integer variables are bounded to 10 and 100 values.

Availability. SLAB is available online at http://react.cs.uni-sb.de/slab, including documentation and the benchmarks used in this paper.

Acknowledgements. We would like to thank Alberto Griggio for fruitful discussions about the MathSAT 4 SMT solver.

References

1. Brückner, I., Dräger, K., Finkbeiner, B., Wehrheim, H.: Slicing abstractions. In: Arbab, F., Sirjani, M. (eds.) FSEN 2007. LNCS, vol. 4767, pp. 17–32. Springer, Heidelberg (2007)
2. Bruttomesso, R., Cimatti, A., Franzén, A., Griggio, A., Sebastiani, R.: TheMathSAT 4 SMT solver. In: Gupta, A., Malik, S. (eds.) CAV 2008. LNCS, vol. 5123, pp. 299–303. Springer, Heidelberg (2008)
3. Cimatti, A., Clarke, E., Giunchiglia, E., Giunchiglia, F., Pistore, M., Roveri, M., Sebastiani, R., Tacchella, A.: NuSMV 2: An OpenSource tool for symbolic model checking. In: Brinksma, E., Larsen, K.G. (eds.) CAV 2002. LNCS, vol. 2404, pp. 241–268. Springer, Heidelberg (2002)
4. Henzinger, T., Jhala, R., Majumdar, R., Sutre, G.: Software verification with BLAST. In: Ball, T., Rajamani, S.K. (eds.) SPIN 2003. LNCS, vol. 2648, pp. 235–239. Springer, Heidelberg (2003)
5. Manna, Z., Pnueli, A.: Temporal Verification of Reactive Systems: Safety. Springer, Heidelberg (1995)
6. Namjoshi, K.: Certifying model checkers. In: Berry, G., Comon, H., Finkel, A. (eds.) CAV 2001. LNCS, vol. 2102, pp. 2–13. Springer, Heidelberg (2001)
7. Podelski, A., Rybalchenko, A.: ARMC: The logical choice for software model checking with abstraction refinement. In: Hanus, M. (ed.) PADL 2007. LNCS, vol. 4354, pp. 245–259. Springer, Heidelberg (2006)

Tracking Heaps That Hop with Heap-Hop

Jules Villard[1], Étienne Lozes[1], and Cristiano Calcagno[2,3]

[1] LSV, ENS Cachan, CNRS
[2] Monoidics Ltd
[3] Imperial College, London

Abstract. Heap-Hop is a program prover for concurrent heap-manipulating programs that use Hoare monitors and message-passing synchronization. Programs are annotated with pre and post-conditions and loop invariants, written in a fragment of separation logic. Communications are governed by a form of session types called *contracts*. Heap-Hop can prove safety and race-freedom and, thanks to contracts, absence of memory leaks and deadlock-freedom. It has been used in several case studies, including concurrent programs for copyless list transfer, service provider protocols, and load-balancing parallel tree disposal.

1 Introduction

Copyless message passing is an alternative to lock-based concurrency. Unlike message-passing in a context of distributed memory, copyless message passing programs can lead to efficient implementations, as only pointers to the contents of the message in memory are transferred. To avoid bugs, and in particular races, the programmer has to make sure that the ownership of the heap region representing the contents of a message is lost upon sending.

Heap-Hop [1] is a program prover that checks concurrent programs that manipulate the heap, in particular list and tree structures, and synchronize using Hoare monitors and copyless message passing. Heap-Hop supports asynchronous communications on *channels*, each consisting of two endpoints which are dynamically allocated on the heap. Each endpoint can send to, and receive from, the other endpoint (its *peer*). Endpoints can be passed around as any other heap objects, and channels can be explicitly closed. Upon closure, no message should be pending for either peer, as this would result in a memory leak. Heap-Hop is based on verification conditions generation and checking, so the user only has to provide pre and post-conditions and loop invariants.

The proof system used by Heap-Hop [9] is based on separation logic [7], a logic that provides a local and modular analysis: the specification of a program p is *small*, in that it focuses on the resources actually needed by p to execute correctly, hopefully leading to concise proofs. The locality principle of separation logic is usually a strength, but for message passing it is also a weakness, since memory leaks and progress properties need to be checked on a global view of the program. To ensure these global properties, we rely on *contracts*. Contracts are a form of session types [8], or communicating

J. Esparza and R. Majumdar (Eds.): TACAS 2010, LNCS 6015, pp. 275–279, 2010.

finite state machines, that dictate which sequences of messages are admissible on a channel.

Heap-Hop provides strong guarantees: memory safety, meaning that the program does not fault on memory accesses; race freedom; contract obedience; and compliance with user specifications (pre and post-conditions). Moreover, depending on the contract, Heap-Hop can also ensure deadlock-freedom and absence of memory leaks. We have tested Heap-Hop on several case studies, including concurrent programs for copyless list transfer, service providers, communication protocols, and parallel tree disposal.

We first introduce the programming language and annotations with a few examples of increasing complexity, and then give some insights on Heap-Hop's internals. We conclude with some related works.

2   Heap-Hop

Programming Language. In our setting, channels are bidirectional FIFO and always consist of exactly two endpoints (e and f in the examples below). Communications are asynchronous, sending never fails, and receiving may block until the right message has arrived. The first argument of send/receive instructions is a *message identifier* which indicates what kind of message is communicated, and the second one is the endpoint that is used. Other arguments are optional depending on the number of parameters of the message. open and close respectively allocate and deallocate a channel and its two endpoints.[1] open takes one parameter: the contract identifier explained below.

The following program, with logical annotations in square brackets, exchanges a memory cell between two threads put and get by passing a message cell.

```
main() { local x,e,f; x=new(); (e,f)=open(C); put(e,x) || get(f); }
put(e,x) [e|->C{a} * x|->] { send(cell,e,x); } [e|->C{a}]
get(f) [f|->~C{a}] { y = receive(cell,f); } [f|->~C{a} * y|->]
```

The logical annotations are spatial conjunctions ($*$) of "points to" predicates that denote ownership of a cell ($x \mapsto$) or of an endpoint ($e \mapsto C\{a\}$ for contract C in state a). Notice how the ownership of the cell is transferred from the precondition of put to the postcondition of get. For Heap-Hop to accept this example, we will annotate the cell message with the formula $val \mapsto$,[2] to specify that the transmitted value corresponds indeed to a cell, and we will define the *contract C* for the channel (e, f).

Contracts are finite state machines that describe the protocol followed by the channel, *i.e.* which sequences of sends and receives are admissible on the channel. A contract C is written from one of the endpoints' point-of-view, the other one following the dual contract $\bar{C}$ (~c in source code), where sends ! and receives ? have been swapped.

Before giving a contract for the previous example, we make it more interesting by sending e over itself after sending x, so that get can then close the channel (e, f). We need a second message close_me whose invariant uses the special *src* variable which refers to the sending endpoint, just as *val* refers to the sent value.

---

[1] We have chosen a close primitive where both ends of a channel are closed together.

[2] A message can have several parameters, in which case they are referred to as *val0*, *val1*, ...

```
message cell [val|->]
message close_me [val|->C{b} * val==src]
contract C { initial state a { !cell -> a; !close_me -> b; }
             final state b {} }

put(e,x) [e|->C{a} * x|->] {       get(f) [f|->~C{a}] {
  send(cell,e,x);                    y = receive(cell,f);
  send(close_me,e,e); } [emp]        ee = receive(close_me,f);
                                     close(ee,f); } [y|->]
```

Notice how the postcondition of `put` is now emp (the empty heap). After the receive of `close_me`, and with the help of its invariant, Heap-Hop can prove that e and f form a channel and that they are both in the same final state, which permits the closing of (e, f). This would not be the case had we omitted $val = src$ in the invariant.

Let us give a final version of the program that sends a whole linked list starting at x (denoted by list(x) in the annotations) cell by cell through the channel. Our contract C already allows this: we can send an unbounded number of cells before we leave the state a. `get` cannot know when the `close_me` message will come anymore, so a `switch receive` between messages `cell` and `close_me` is used, which in general selects either message from the receive queue, whichever comes first.

```
put(e,x) [e|->C{a} * list(x)] {    get(f) [f|->~C{a}] {
  local t;                           local x, ee = 0;
  while(x != 0)                      while(ee == 0) [(†)] {
  [e|->C{a} * list(x)] {               switch receive {
    t = x->tl;                           x=receive(cell,f): {dispose(x);}
    send(cell,e,x);                      ee=receive(close_me,f): {}
    x = t; }                           }}
  send(close_me,e,e); } [emp]        close(ee,f); } [emp]
```

$(†) \triangleq$ `if ee==0 then f|->~C{a} else (ee|->C{b} * f|->~C{b},pr:ee)`[3]

A particularity of the copyless message passing setting is that doing the sending of the cell before dereferencing x in the example above (*i.e.* placing the `send(cell,e,x);` one line earlier) would result in a fault, as the cell pointed to by x is not owned by this thread anymore after it has been sent.

Usage. Heap-Hop takes annotated programs as input, and outputs a diagnosis for every function of the program: either a successful check, or an error report showing the incriminated program lines and formulas where the check failed. It also outputs a graphical representation of the contracts declared in the file. Contracts play a fundamental role in the analysis. Heap-Hop checks whether the following three conditions hold:

Deterministic From every state of the contract, there should be at most one transition labeled by a given message name and a given direction.
Positional Every state of the contract must allow either only sends or only receives.
Synch All cycles in the contract that go through a final state must contain at least one send and one receive.

These conditions are sufficient to ensure the absence of memory leak on channel closure [9]; Heap-Hop will issue a warning if they are not met. If moreover there is only one

---

[3] In `f|->~C{b},pr:ee`, `pr:ee` means that ee is the peer of f.

channel used in the whole program, without Hoare monitors, and if all `switch receive` statements are exhaustive with respect to the contract, then the program is also guaranteed to be deadlock-free. Currently, Heap-Hop does not report on deadlock-freedom since we expect simpler proofs of it to be available using other methods [6].

3   Internals

Heap-Hop is an extension of a previous tool called Smallfoot [2], and uses the same principles: it first converts the annotated program into verification conditions, then checks each condition by applying symbolic forward execution, eventually checking that the computed symbolic heap entails the targeted one. However, in case of non-deterministic contracts, fundamental changes are needed in the symbolic execution mechanism. Consider the following example:

```
contract ND { initial state a { !m -> b; !m -> c; }
              state b {} final state c {} }
foo() { (e,f) = open(ND); send(m,e); receive(m,f); close(e,f); }
```

Starting from state a, symbolic execution could then proceed to state b or c. Notice that only the choice of state c, which is the final state, allows to close the channel in the end, and this choice is not evident when the send is executed. For this reason, our symbolic execution mechanism explores all the possibilities in parallel, by operating on sets of symbolic heaps and pruning wrong choices along the way.

4   Related Work and Conclusion

As already mentioned, Heap-Hop is an extension of Smallfoot based on a fully formalized proof theory [9]. Another extension of Smallfoot is SmallfootRG [3], that combines Separation Logic with Rely-Guarantee reasoning. Typical case studies of SmallfootRG are non-blocking concurrent algorithms, but it does not support message passing. Chalice [6] is a program prover that has been recently extended to support copyless message passing, and allows to prove deadlock-freedom using credits and lock levels. Both SmallfootRG and Chalice could encode our contracts and `switch receive` constructs, but this encoding, as well as being tedious, would be incomplete for non-deterministic contracts. SessionJ [5] and Sing# [4] are realistic programming languages that rely on contracts. The Sing# compiler uses a static analyzer to check some restricted form of copyless message-passing, but seemingly does not support ownership transfer of recursive data structures.

References

1. http://www.lsv.ens-cachan.fr/~villard/heaphop/
2. Berdine, J., Calcagno, C., O'Hearn, P.: Smallfoot: Modular Automatic Assertion Checking with Separation Logic. In: de Boer, F.S., Bonsangue, M.M., Graf, S., de Roever, W.-P. (eds.) FMCO 2005. LNCS, vol. 4111, pp. 115–137. Springer, Heidelberg (2006)

3. Calcagno, C., Parkinson, M., Vafeiadis, V.: Modular Safety Checking for Fine-Grained Concurrency. In: Riis Nielson, H., Filé, G. (eds.) SAS 2007. LNCS, vol. 4634, p. 233. Springer, Heidelberg (2007)
4. Fähndrich, M., Aiken, M., Hawblitzel, M., Hodson, O., Hunt, G., Larus, J., Levi, S.: Language Support for Fast and Reliable Message-Based Communication in Singularity OS. In: EuroSys (2006)
5. Hu, R., Yoshida, N., Honda, K.: Session-Based Distributed Programming in Java. In: Vitek, J. (ed.) ECOOP 2008. LNCS, vol. 5142, pp. 516–541. Springer, Heidelberg (2008)
6. Leino, K., Müller, P., Smans, J.: Deadlock-free Channels and Locks. To appear in ESOP 2010 (2010)
7. Reynolds, J.C.: Separation Logic: A Logic for Shared Mutable Data Structures. In: LICS 2002 (2002)
8. Takeuchi, K., Honda, K., Kubo, M.: An Interaction-Based Language and Its Typing System. In: Halatsis, C., Philokyprou, G., Maritsas, D., Theodoridis, S. (eds.) PARLE 1994. LNCS, vol. 817, pp. 398–413. Springer, Heidelberg (1994)
9. Villard, J., Lozes, É., Calcagno, C.: Proving Copyless Message Passing. In: Hu, Z. (ed.) APLAS 2009. LNCS, vol. 5904, pp. 194–209. Springer, Heidelberg (2009)

Automatic Analysis of Scratch-Pad Memory Code for Heterogeneous Multicore Processors*

Alastair F. Donaldson, Daniel Kroening, and Philipp Rümmer

Oxford University Computing Laboratory, Oxford, UK

Abstract. Modern multicore processors, such as the Cell Broadband Engine, achieve high performance by equipping accelerator cores with small "scratch-pad" memories. The price for increased performance is higher programming complexity – the programmer must manually orchestrate data movement using direct memory access (DMA) operations. Programming using asynchronous DMAs is error-prone, and *DMA races* can lead to nondeterministic bugs which are hard to reproduce and fix. We present a method for DMA race analysis which automatically instruments the program with assertions modelling the semantics of a memory flow controller. To enable automatic verification of instrumented programs, we present a new formulation of k-induction geared towards software, as a proof rule operating on loops. We present a tool, SCRATCH, which we apply to a large set of programs supplied with the IBM Cell SDK, in which we discover a previously unknown bug. Our experimental results indicate that our k-induction method performs extremely well on this problem class. To our knowledge, this marks both the first application of k-induction to software verification, and the first example of software model checking for heterogeneous multicore processors.

1 Introduction

Heterogeneous multicore processors such as the Cell Broadband Engine (BE) circumvent the shared memory bottleneck by equipping cores with small "scratch-pad" memories [16,18]. These fast, private memories are not coherent with main memory, and allow independent calculations to be processed in parallel by separate cores without contention. While this can boost performance,[1] it places heterogeneous multicore programming at the far end of the concurrent programming spectrum. The programmer can no longer rely on the hardware and operating system to seamlessly transfer data between the levels of the memory hierarchy, and must instead manually orchestrate data movement between memory spaces using *direct memory access* (DMA). Low-level data movement code is error-prone: misuse of DMA operations can lead to *DMA races*, where concurrent DMA operations refer to the same portion of memory, and at least one modifies the memory. There is an urgent need for techniques and tools to

---

* Alastair F. Donaldson is supported by EPSRC grant EP/G051100. Daniel Kroening and Philipp Rümmer are supported by EPSRC grant EP/G026254/1, the EU FP7 STREP MOGENTES, and the EU ARTEMIS CESAR project.
[1] A supercomputer comprised of Cell processors recently assumed #1 spot on the Top 500 list.

J. Esparza and R. Majumdar (Eds.): TACAS 2010, LNCS 6015, pp. 280–295, 2010.

analyse DMA races, which, if undetected, can lead to nondeterministic bugs that are difficult to reproduce and fix.

We present a method for DMA race analysis which automatically instruments the program with assertions modelling the semantics of a memory flow controller. The instrumented programs are amenable to automatic verification by state-of-the-art model checkers. Recent dramatic advances in SAT/SMT techniques have led to widespread use of Bounded Model Checking (BMC) [3,5] for finding bugs in software. As well as detecting DMA races, we are interested in proving their *absence*. However, BMC is only complete if the bound exceeds a completeness threshold [19] for the property, which is often prohibitively large. We overcome this limitation by presenting a novel formulation of k-induction [24]. The k-induction method has been shown effective for verifying safety properties of hardware designs. In principle, k-induction can be applied to software by encoding a program as a monolithic transition function. This approach has not proven successful due to the loss of control-flow structure associated with such a naïve encoding, and because important refinements of k-induction (*e.g.* restriction to loop-free paths) are not useful for software where the state-vector is very large.

We present a general proof rule for k-induction that is applicable to imperative programs with loops, and prove correctness of this rule. In contrast to the naïve encoding discussed above, our method preserves the program structure by operating at the loop level. Furthermore, it allows properties to be expressed through assertion statements rather than as explicit invariants. Our experimental results indicate that this method of k-induction performs very well when applied to realistic DMA-based programs, which use double- and triple-buffering schemes for efficient data movement: such programs involve regularly-structured loops for which k-induction succeeds with a relatively small k. We investigate heuristics to further boost the applicability of k-induction when checking for DMA races, and discuss limitations of k-induction in this application domain.

We have implemented our techniques as a tool, SCRATCH, which checks programs written for the Synergistic Processor Element (SPE) cores of the Cell BE processor. We present an evaluation of SCRATCH using a set of 22 example programs provided with the IBM Cell SDK for Multicore Acceleration [18], in which we discover a previously unknown bug, which has been independently confirmed. Our experiments show the effectiveness of our methods in comparison to predicate abstraction: k-induction allows us to prove programs correct that cannot be verified using current predicate abstraction tools, and bug-finding is orders of magnitude faster. Additionally, SCRATCH is able to find bugs which go undetected by a runtime race-detection tool for the Cell processor.

In summary, our major contributions are:

- an automatic technique for instrumenting programs with assertions to check for DMA races, enabling verification of multicore programs with scratch-pad memory.
- a new proof rule for k-induction operating on programs with loops, which we show to be effective when applied to a large set of realistic DMA-based programs.

To our knowledge, this marks the first application of k-induction to software verification, and of software model checking to heterogeneous multicore programs.

2   Direct Memory Access Operations

We consider heterogeneous multicore processors consisting of a host core, connected to main memory, and a number of accelerator cores with private scratch-pad memory. A DMA operation[2] specifies that a contiguous chunk of memory, of a given size, should be transferred between two memory addresses l and h. The address l refers to accelerator memory (*local store*), and h to main memory (*host memory*). A *tag* (typically an integer value) must also be specified with a DMA; the operation is said to be *identified* by this tag. It is typical for DMA operations to be initiated by the accelerator cores: an accelerator *pulls* data into local store, rather than having the host *push* data. We assume this scenario throughout the paper.

DMA operations are non-blocking – an accelerator thread which issues a DMA continues executing while the operation is handled by a specialised piece of hardware called a *memory flow controller*. An accelerator thread can issue a *wait* operation, specifying a tag t, which causes execution to block until all DMAs identified by t have completed. A DMA with tag t is *pending* until a wait operation with tag t is issued.

Although a DMA *may* complete before an explicit wait operation is issued, this cannot be guaranteed, thus access by the host or accelerator to memory that is due to be modified by a pending DMA should be regarded as a bug. Failure to issue a wait operation may result in nondeterministic behaviour: it may *usually* be the case that the required data has arrived, but occasionally the lack of a wait may result in reading from uninitialised memory, leading to incorrect computation. This nondeterminism means that bugs arising due to misuse of DMA can be extremely difficult to reproduce and fix.

2.1   DMA Primitives and Properties of Interest

We consider the following primitives for DMA operations:

- put(l, h, s, t): issues a transfer of s bytes from local store address l to host address h, identified by tag t
- get(l, h, s, t): issues a transfer of s bytes from host address h to local store address l, identified by tag t
- wait(t): blocks until completion of all pending DMA operations identified by tag t

For each accelerator core, we assume hardware-imposed maximum values D and M for the number of DMAs that may be pending simultaneously and the number of bytes that may be transferred by a single DMA, respectively. We assume that tags are integers in the range $[0, D - 1]$. On the Cell processor, $D = 32$ and $M = 16384$ (16K).

We have informally described the notion of memory being corrupted by DMA operations. A special case of memory corruption is where two pending DMAs refer to overlapping regions of memory, and at least one of the DMAs modifies the region of memory. We call this a *DMA race*, and focus our attention on the detection of DMA races for the remainder of the paper. This focus is for reasons of space only: our techniques can be readily adapted to detect races where the buffer referred to by a pending DMA is accessed by non-DMA statements.

---

[2] For brevity, we sometimes write "DMA" rather than "DMA operation."

```
#define CHUNK 16384 // Process data in 16K chunks

float buffers[3][CHUNK/sizeof(float)]; // Triple-buffering requires 3 buffers

void process_data(float* buf) { ... }

void triple_buffer(char* in, char* out, int num_chunks) {
    unsigned int tags[3] = { 0, 1, 2 }, tmp, put_buf, get_buf, process_buf;

(1) get(buffers[0], in, CHUNK, tags[0]); // Get triple-buffer scheme rolling
    in += CHUNK;
(2) get(buffers[1], in, CHUNK, tags[1]);
    in += CHUNK;
(3) wait(tags[0]); process_data(buffers[0]); // Wait for and process first buffer
    put_buf = 0; process_buf = 1; get_buf = 2;
    for(int i = 2; i < num_chunks; i++) {
(4)     put(buffers[put_buf], out, CHUNK, tags[put_buf]); // Put data processed
        out += CHUNK;                                     //    last iteration
(5)     get(buffers[get_buf], in, CHUNK, tags[get_buf]); // Get data to process
        in += CHUNK;                                      //    next iteration
(6)     wait(tags[process_buf]);                 // Wait for and process data
        process_data(buffers[process_buf]);      //    requested last iteration

        tmp = put_buf; put_buf = process_buf; // Cycle the buffers
        process_buf = get_buf; get_buf = tmp;
    }
    ... // Handle data processed/fetched on final loop iteration
}
```

Fig. 1. Triple-buffering example, adapted from an example provided with the IBM Cell SDK [18]

Definition 1. *Let* $\text{op}_1(l_1, h_1, s_1, t_1)$ *and* $\text{op}_2(l_2, h_2, s_2, t_2)$ *be a pair of simultaneously pending DMA operations, where* $\text{op}_1, \text{op}_2 \in \{\text{put}, \text{get}\}$. *The pair is said to be* race free *if the following holds:*

$$((\text{op}_1 = \text{put} \wedge \text{op}_2 = \text{put}) \vee (l_1 + s_1 \leq l_2) \vee (l_2 + s_2 \leq l_1)) \wedge$$
$$((\text{op}_1 = \text{get} \wedge \text{op}_2 = \text{get}) \vee (h_1 + s_1 \leq h_2) \vee (h_2 + s_2 \leq h_1)).$$

The first conjunct in Definition 1 asserts that the local store regions referred to by op_1 and op_2 do not overlap, *unless* both are put operations (which do not modify local store); the second conjunct asserts that the host memory regions do not overlap, unless both op_1 and op_2 are get operations (which do not modify host memory). We say there is a *DMA race* when some pair of pending DMA operations is not race free.

2.2   Illustrative Example: Triple-Buffering

Figure 1, adapted from an example provided with the IBM Cell SDK [18], illustrates the use of DMA operations to stream data from host memory to local store to be processed, and to stream results back to host memory. Triple-buffering is used to overlap communication with computation: each iteration of the loop in triple_buffer puts results computed during the previous iteration to host memory, gets input to be processed next iteration from host memory, and processes data which has arrived in local memory.

If num_chunks is greater than three, this example exhibits a local store DMA race, which we can observe by logging the first six DMA operations. To the right of each operation we record its source code location and, if appropriate, its loop iteration. We omit host address parameters as they are not relevant to the data race.

```
        get(buffers[0], ..., CHUNK, tags[0])   (1)
        get(buffers[1], ..., CHUNK, tags[1])   (2)
        wait(tags[0])                          (3)
(*)     put(buffers[0], ..., CHUNK, tags[0])   (4), i=2
        get(buffers[2], ..., CHUNK, tags[2])   (5), i=2
        wait(tags[1])                          (6), i=2
        put(buffers[1], ..., CHUNK, tags[2])   (4), i=3
(*)     get(buffers[0], ..., CHUNK, tags[0])   (5), i=3
```

At this point in execution the operations marked (*) are both pending, since the only intervening wait operation uses a distinct tag. The operations are not race free according to Definition 1 since they use the same region of local store and one is a get. The race can be avoided by inserting a wait with tag tags[get_buf] before the get at (5).

We discovered this bug using SCRATCH, our automatic DMA analysis tool, described in §6, which can also show that the fix is correct. The bug occurs in an example provided with the IBM Cell SDK, and was, to our knowledge, previously unknown. Our bug report via the Cell BE forum has been independently confirmed. In the remainder of the paper, we present the new techniques of SCRATCH that enable these results.

3   Goto Programs

We present our results in terms of a simple goto language, which is minimal, but general enough to uniformly translate C programs like the one in Figure 1. The syntax of the goto language is shown in the following grammar, in which $x \in X$ ranges over integer variables, $a \in A$ over arrays variables, ϕ and e over boolean and integer expressions (for which we do not define syntax, assuming the standard operations), and $l_1, \ldots, l_k \in \mathbb{Z}$ over integers:

$$Prog ::= Stmt; \ldots; Stmt \qquad\qquad VarRef ::= x \mid a[e]$$

$$Stmt ::= VarRef := * \mid assume\ \phi \mid assert\ \phi \mid goto\ l_1, \ldots, l_k$$

A goto program is a list of statements numbered from 1 to n.

The language includes assertions, nondeterminisic assignment ($VarRef := *$), assumptions (which can constrain variables to specific values), and nondeterministic gotos. Execution of a goto statement, which is given a sequence of integer values as argument (the *goto targets*), causes the value of one of these (possibly negative) integers to be added to the instruction pointer. We use $x := e$ and $a[i] := e$ as shorthands for assignments to variables and array elements, respectively, which can be expressed in the syntax above via a sequence of nondeterministic assignments and assumptions. For simplicity, we assume variables and array elements range over the mathematical integers, $\mathbb{Z}$; when translating C programs into the goto language the actual range of variables will always be bounded, so SAT-based analysis of goto programs by means of bit-blasting is possible.

The transition system described by a program $\alpha = \alpha_1; \ldots; \alpha_n$ is the graph (S, E_α). $S = \{(\sigma, pc) \mid \sigma : (X \cup (A \times \mathbb{Z})) \to \mathbb{Z}, pc \in \mathbb{Z}\} \cup \{\frac{1}{4}\}$ is the set of program states, where σ is a store mapping variables and array locations to integer values, pc is the instruction pointer, and $\frac{1}{2}$ is a distinguished state that designates erroneous termination of a program. E_α is the set of transitions (we write t^σ for the value of an expression given the variable assignment σ, denote the set of all storage locations by $L = X \cup (A \times \mathbb{Z})$, and define tt, ff to be the truth values of boolean expressions):

$$
\begin{aligned}
E_\alpha = \ & \{(\sigma, pc) \to (\sigma', pc + 1) \mid \alpha_{pc} = x := *, \; \forall l \in L \setminus \{x\}. \; \sigma(l) = \sigma'(l)\} \\
& \cup \{(\sigma, pc) \to (\sigma', pc + 1) \mid \alpha_{pc} = a[e] := *, \; \forall l \in L \setminus \{(a, e^\sigma)\}. \; \sigma(l) = \sigma'(l)\} \\
& \cup \{(\sigma, pc) \to (\sigma, pc + 1) \mid \alpha_{pc} = assume \; \phi, \; \phi^\sigma = tt\} \\
& \cup \{(\sigma, pc) \to (\sigma, pc + 1) \mid \alpha_{pc} = assert \; \phi, \; \phi^\sigma = tt\} \\
& \cup \{(\sigma, pc) \to \tfrac{1}{2} \mid \alpha_{pc} = assert \; \phi, \; \phi^\sigma = ff\} \\
& \cup \{(\sigma, pc) \to (\sigma, pc + l_i) \mid \alpha_{pc} = goto \; l_1, \ldots, l_k, \; i \in \{1, \ldots, k\}\}
\end{aligned}
$$

Proper termination of α in a state s is denoted by $s \downarrow$ and occurs if the instruction pointer of s does not point to a valid statement: $s \downarrow \; \equiv \; s = (\sigma, pc) \land pc \notin [1, n]$. Note that no transitions exist from states s with $s \downarrow$.

The set $traces(\alpha)$ of (finite and infinite) traces of a program α is defined in terms of its transition system:

$$
\begin{aligned}
traces(\alpha) = \ & \left\{ s_1 s_2 \cdots s_k \; \middle| \; \begin{array}{l} \exists \sigma. \; s_1 = (\sigma, 1), \; s_k \downarrow \; \text{or} \; s_k = \tfrac{1}{2}, \\ \forall i \in \{1, \ldots, k - 1\}. \; s_i \to s_{i+1} \end{array} \right\} \\
& \cup \{s_1 s_2 \cdots \mid \exists \sigma. \; s_1 = (\sigma, 1), \; \forall i \in \mathbb{N}. \; s_i \to s_{i+1}\}
\end{aligned}
$$

In particular, no traces exist on which assumptions fail.[3] A program α is considered *correct* if no trace in $traces(\alpha)$ terminates erroneously, *i.e.* no trace contains $\tfrac{1}{2}$.

4   Encoding DMA Operations in Goto Programs

We now consider the goto language extended with the DMA primitives of §2.1:

$$
Stmt ::= \ \ldots \mid \mathsf{get}(e, e, e, e) \mid \mathsf{put}(e, e, e, e) \mid \mathsf{wait}(e)
$$

For a goto program with DMAs, we introduce a series of array variables with size D (see §2.1), which we call *tracker arrays*. These "ghost variables" log the state of up to D pending DMA operations during program execution. The tracker arrays are as follows, with $0 \leq j < D$:

- *valid*: $valid[j] = 1$ if values at position j in the other arrays are being used to track a DMA operation, otherwise $valid[j] = 0$ and values at position j in the other arrays are meaningless
- *is_get*: $is\_get[j] = 1$ if j-th tracked DMA is a get, otherwise $is\_get[j] = 0$
- *local, host, size, tag*: element j records local store address, host address, size, tag of j-th tracked DMA, respectively

---

[3] In our context, this is preferable to modelling failed assumptions via a distinguished "blocked program" state: it simplifies the notion of sequential composition of programs (*cf.* §5.1).

Statement	Translated form
start of program	$\forall_{0 \leq j < D}$ *assume valid*$[j] = 0;$
get(l, h, s, t)	*assert* $0 \leq s \leq M \wedge 0 \leq t < D;$ $\forall_{0 \leq j < D}$ *assert* $\neg valid[j] \vee (disjoint(l, s, local[j], size[j]) \wedge$ $\quad\quad (is\_get[j] \vee disjoint(h, s, host[j], size[j])));$ *assert* $\neg(valid[0] \wedge valid[1] \wedge \cdots \wedge valid[D - 1]);$ $i := *;$ *assume* $0 \leq i < D \wedge \neg valid[i];$ $valid[i] := 1;$ $is\_get[i] := 1;$ $local[i] := l;$ $host[i] := h;$ $size[i] := s;$
put(l, h, s, t)	*assert* $0 \leq s \leq M \wedge 0 \leq t < D;$ $\forall_{0 \leq j < D}$ *assert* $\neg valid[j] \vee (disjoint(h, s, host[j], size[j]) \wedge$ $\quad\quad (\neg is\_get[j] \vee disjoint(l, s, local[j], size[j])));$ *assert* $\neg(valid[0] \wedge valid[1] \wedge \cdots \wedge valid[D - 1]);$ $i := *;$ *assume* $0 \leq i < D \wedge \neg valid[i];$ $valid[i] := 1;$ $is\_get[i] := 0;$ $local[i] := l;$ $host[i] := h;$ $size[i] := s;$
wait(t)	*assert* $0 \leq t < D;$ $\forall_{0 \leq j < D}$ $valid[j] := valid[j] \wedge \neg(t = tag[j])$

Fig. 2. Rules to translate DMA operations into assertions and assignments to tracker arrays. We use $disjoint(a_1, s_1, a_2, s_2)$ as shorthand for $a_1 + s_1 \leq a_2 \vee a_2 + s_2 \leq a_1$.

To check properties of DMA operations we translate a program with DMA primitives into a standard goto program, where get, put and wait operations are replaced with assertions about and assignments to the tracker arrays. The translation rules are given in Figure 2. We use $\forall_{0 \leq j < D}$ to indicate that the following statement should be duplicated D times with increasing values for j. Since the rules of Figure 2 replace single statements with multiple statements, it is necessary to perform a re-numbering of program statements and goto targets after translation; we omit details of this re-numbering.

The encoding of DMAs is based on Definition 1, and is designed to ensure that correct programs cannot issue DMA operations that are simultaneously pending but not race free. Note that in our simple goto language we do not model actual movement of data via DMA. In practice, to achieve soundness, we must set the memory locations written to by a DMA operation to nondeterministic values. The Cell processor supports further DMA primitives involving *fences* and *barriers*. Our implementation (§6) supports these operations via extensions of the rules in Figure 2; we do not present the extended rules due to lack of space.

5 k-Induction for Goto Programs

Our encoding of DMA programs is directly amenable to Bounded Model Checking [3] as an effective method to discover DMA races. However, BMC alone cannot be used to verify the (unbounded) *absence* of DMA races in programs with loops.

The k-induction procedure [24], proposed as a method to allow verification of hardware designs (represented as finite state machines) using a SAT solver, is a stronger version of the standard invariant approach to verify safety properties. Using normal invariants, proving that a program satisfies a safety property ϕ requires showing that

(i) some formula I (which often is identical to ϕ) holds in all initial states, (ii) I is preserved by all state transitions of the program (I is *inductive*), and (iii) I implies ϕ. The main difficulty of this method is the construction of inductive formulae I. The k-induction principle addresses this difficulty by weakening (ii) to the property that I has to be preserved only if it held in the previous k states of program execution. In return, (i) has to be strengthened appropriately.

We describe the principle using the notation of [9]. Let $\mathbf{I}(s)$ and $\mathbf{T}(s, s')$ be formulae encoding the initial states and transition relation for a finite state system, and $\mathbf{P}(s)$ a formula representing states satisfying a safety property. For $k \geq 0$, to prove $\mathbf{P}$ by k-induction it is required first to show that $\mathbf{P}$ holds in all states reachable from an initial state within k steps, *i.e.* that the following formula (the base case) is unsatisfiable:

$$\mathbf{I}(s_1) \wedge \mathbf{T}(s_1, s_2) \wedge \cdots \wedge \mathbf{T}(s_{k-1}, s_k) \wedge (\overline{\mathbf{P}(s_1)} \vee \cdots \vee \overline{\mathbf{P}(s_k)}) \ .$$

Secondly, it is required to show that whenever $\mathbf{P}$ holds in k consecutive states $s_1, \ldots, s_k$, $\mathbf{P}$ also holds in the next state s_{k+1} of the system. This is established by checking that the following formula (the step case) is unsatisfiable:

$$\mathbf{P}(s_1) \wedge \mathbf{T}(s_1, s_2) \wedge \cdots \wedge \mathbf{P}(s_k) \wedge \mathbf{T}(s_k, s_{k+1}) \wedge \overline{\mathbf{P}(s_{k+1})} \ .$$

In principle, k-induction can be used for SAT-based software model checking "out-of-the-box." A program can be encoded as a monolithic transition function, where the program counter is an explicit variable. Assertions appearing in the original program can be gathered together into a single invariant. The encoded program and invariant can be represented as a SAT formula, to which k-induction can be applied.

This naïve encoding has not shown success in practice due to the loss of structure associated with the translation process. Furthermore, important refinements which boost the applicability of k-induction to hardware designs, such as the restriction to loop-free paths [24], are not useful when dealing with software where the state-vector is large.

To verify absence of DMA races in goto programs, we present a novel formulation of k-induction, which operates at the loop level, and prove its correctness.

5.1   A Proof Rule for k-Induction with Loops

To present our proof rule for k-induction we require some additional machinery and notation. Given programs $\alpha = \alpha_1; \ldots; \alpha_m$ and $\beta = \beta_1; \ldots; \beta_n$, the *size* of α, denoted $|\alpha|$, is m, and we define the sequential composition of α and β as follows:

$$\alpha \,\mathring{,}\, \beta \ =_{\mathrm{def}} \ \alpha_1; \ldots; \alpha_m; \ \beta_1; \ldots; \beta_n \ .$$

For $i > 0$, we use α^i to denote the sequential composition of i copies of α, and α^0 to denote the empty program. For a single-statement program of the form α_1, we drop the leading 1:, writing simply α_1.

A program α is *self-contained*, denoted $contained(\alpha)$, if, for each goto statement $goto \ldots, l, \ldots$ appearing in α, we have $(i + l) \in \{1, \ldots, |\alpha| + 1\}$. In other words, goto statements can only change the instruction pointer to the locations of statements inside α, or to the location immediately following α.

We define a function that replaces all assertions in a program with assumptions. Given a program $\alpha = \alpha_1; \ldots; \alpha_n$, the corresponding program $\alpha_{assume} = \alpha'_1; \ldots; \alpha'_n$ is defined by: $\alpha'_i = assume \ \phi$ if $\alpha_i = assert \ \phi$, and $\alpha'_i = \alpha_i$ otherwise.

Finally, we present k-induction as a proof rule operating on distinguished loops in a goto program of the following form:

$$\alpha \ \text{\textfractionsolidus}\ goto\ 1, (|\beta| + 2)\ \text{\textfractionsolidus}\ \beta\ \text{\textfractionsolidus}\ goto\ (-|\beta| - 1)\ \text{\textfractionsolidus}\ \gamma$$

where α, β and γ are self-contained. The program consists of a prelude α, a loop with body β and a tail γ. Other than self-containedness, we do not make any assumptions about the shape of components α, β and γ, which may contain further (nested) loops and arbitrary control structure. We do not demand the presence of an explicit loop condition: a loop condition b can be simulated by choosing *assume b* as the first statement of the loop body, and *assume ¬b* as the first statement of the tail. Note that the restriction to self-contained components is mild, *e.g.* early exit from the loop via a break statement can be simulated by a flag together with an appropriate loop condition.

Proof rule for k-induction

$$\cfrac{\begin{array}{cccc} contained(\alpha) & contained(\beta) & contained(\gamma) & k \geq 0 \\ \alpha\ \text{\textfractionsolidus}\ \gamma \text{ is correct} & \{\alpha_{assume}\ \text{\textfractionsolidus}\ \beta^{i-1}_{assume}\ \text{\textfractionsolidus}\ \beta\ \text{\textfractionsolidus}\ \gamma \text{ is correct}\}_{i \in \{1,\dots,k\}} \\ \beta^k_{assume}\ \text{\textfractionsolidus}\ \beta \text{ is correct} & \beta^k_{assume}\ \text{\textfractionsolidus}\ \gamma \text{ is correct} \end{array}}{\alpha\ \text{\textfractionsolidus}\ goto\ 1, (|\beta| + 2)\ \text{\textfractionsolidus}\ \beta\ \text{\textfractionsolidus}\ goto\ (-|\beta| - 1)\ \text{\textfractionsolidus}\ \gamma \text{ is correct}}$$

In this rule, the assertions present in the program (*e.g.* the formulae in Figure 2) take the role of the inductive invariant needed for verification. The premises include base cases requiring the program to be shown correct when the prelude, followed by between zero and k loop iterations, are executed. The premises $\beta^k_{assume}\ \text{\textfractionsolidus}\ \beta$ *is correct* and $\beta^k_{assume}\ \text{\textfractionsolidus}\ \gamma$ *is correct* form the induction step, establishing that if it is possible to execute k loop iterations from an arbitrary state without violating any assertions then it is possible to successfully execute a further loop iteration, or the loop tail.

Theorem 2 (Correctness). *The above proof rule is sound.*

By presenting k-induction using a general proof rule, we do not restrict the method to a SAT-based implementation. Although our practical implementation is SAT-based, the rule could as well be used in any (possibly interactive) deductive verification system.

5.2 Heuristics to aid k-Induction for DMA Programs

Through our experiments in §6 we observe that k-induction works extremely well for checking assertions representing DMA race-freeness, generated by the rules in Figure 2. For realistic example programs written for the Cell processor, the generated assertions are inductive already for small k, with no further annotations required to verify correctness. The result is a verification method that is fully automatic and efficient on a large range of Cell programs. Intuitively, k-induction works well in this application domain because DMA operations in loops are typically designed to be pending for only a bounded number of loop iterations, allowing k-induction to succeed with a value of k proportional to the bound. This is analogous to the intuition that k-induction works well for sequential hardware circuits with pipelines, where the k required for induction to succeed is proportional to the pipeline depth [1].

For less regular examples, our practical experience has led to the following heuristics which can be applied to help k-induction succeed, or to quickly determine when the technique is unlikely to work. These heuristics are merely optimisations to our technique; we are able to verify all benchmarks presented in §6 *without* use of heuristics.

Bounded lifetimes. In practice, the programmer often knows that no DMA operation should pend for more than a small number (Z, say) of loop iterations. To take advantage of this domain specific information, the tracker arrays can be extended with a component to record the number x of enclosing loop iterations for which a DMA has been pending, asserting that x never exceeds Z. When proving the step case for $k > Z$, this allows the assumption that only DMAs issued within the last Z iterations are tracked, eliminating many unreachable states which might otherwise cause the step case to fail.

Free slots. While it is legal for up to D operations to be pending simultaneously, most practical applications require significantly fewer simultaneous DMAs. Adding an assertion to the start of the loop body requiring at least Z free slots in the tracker arrays (for some $Z > 0$) can help k-induction to succeed when it otherwise would not.

Bounded periods of inactivity. Generally, to prove that a DMA operation is race free, it is necessary to be able to assume that the operation was race free on a previous loop iteration. If a DMA statement might not to be executed for an *arbitrary* number of loop iterations then k-induction is unlikely to work. By introducing extra instrumentation to check that each DMA statement is executed at least once every Z iterations (for some $Z > 0$) we can set up reasonable conditions under which k-induction "gives up," resulting in a base case failure identifying a problematic DMA statement.

6   Experimental Evaluation

We have implemented a prototype tool, SCRATCH,[4] built on top of the CBMC model checker [5]. SCRATCH accepts an arbitrary C program written for an SPE core of the Cell BE processor, and checks for DMA races involving local memory. The translation described in §4 is applied to transform the input program into a form where DMAs are replaced with assertions and assignments to tracker arrays. BMC can be applied to the resulting program to check for DMA races up to a certain depth, and combined with k-induction, using the formulation of §5, to prove absence of races. Although our k-induction method is, in principle, applicable to arbitrary nested loops, for implementation convenience SCRATCH currently applies k-induction only to single loops. We are able to analyse many interesting examples with this restriction, in some cases by converting a nest of two loops into a single loop.

We evaluate SCRATCH using a set of 22 benchmarks adapted from examples supplied with the IBM Cell SDK for Multicore Acceleration [18], categorized as follows:

- x-**buf** ($x \in \{1, 2, 3\}$) Data processing programs which use single-, double- or triple-buffering for data-movement (*cf.* Figure 1). I/O indicates that separate buffers are used for input and output. Some variants of these programs use fences/barriers

---

[4] SCRATCH is available online at http://www.cprover.org/scratch/.

Benchmark	Correct			Buggy			Benchmark	Correct			Buggy		
	k	D	time	D	time	depth		k	D	time	D	time	depth
race check 1	0	2	0.35	1	0.94	34	cpaudio	3	4	5.83	1	0.99	57
race check 2	0	4	0.35	3	0.95	65	3-buf I/O	3	4	12.29	2	0.67	133
sync atomic op	1	1	0.39	1	0.33	64	2-buf + barrier	3	4	3.23	2	0.56	130
sync mutex	1	1	0.43	1	0.34	74	2-buf I/0	3	4	3.53	3	0.76	137
simple dma	1	1	0.39	1	0.36	80	3-buf + fence	3	5	35.94	3	0.7	184
1-buf	1	1	0.41	1	0.43	100	normalize	3	8	71.74	12	2.34	549
1-buf I/O	1	1	0.44	2	0.54	109	Euler complex	3	10	420.54	8	3.91	273
2-buf	1	2	0.66	2	0.54	87	3-buf I/O + barrier	4	2	9.65	3	0.68	160
2-buf + fence	2	4	1.39	2	0.37	130	3-buf I/O + fence	4	4	12.99	3	0.68	159
Euler simple	2	5	4.79	3	1.32	167	checksum	4	4	3.49	4	0.59	53
3-buf	3	3	15.84	3	0.65	160	Julia 2	7	3	32.75	32	2783.4	1955

Fig. 3. Results using SCRATCH for proving correctness via k-induction, and for bug-finding, on Cell SDK benchmarks

- **race check, simple dma** Examples which illustrate data races and use of DMA
- **sync atomic/mutex** Programs illustrating the use of SDK synchronization primitives for atomic operations and mutexes, in conjunction with DMA operations
- **cpaudio, normalize** Applications which copy one channel of a stereo audio file to the other, and normalize the volume of a mono audio file, respectively
- **checksum** Computes a checksum on data in host memory. Multiple buffers are used to coordinate data-movement efficiently
- **Euler simple/complex** Particle simulation using Euler integration. The simple version uses separate individual buffers for position, velocity and mass data; the complex version uses double-buffering
- **Julia** n Quaternion Julia set ray-tracing, where an SPE renders n columns of output

Manual program slicing has been applied to each benchmark to remove portions of code that do not affect DMA operations. This routine slicing could be automated: the sliced code uses vector datatypes and intrinsic functions specific to the Cell processor, which the slicer would need to understand.

Figure 3 shows results applying SCRATCH to correct and buggy versions of the benchmarks.[5] With the exception of *3-buf* and *cpaudio*, bugs are injected into the examples, either by removing a wait operation, changing the tag used to identify a DMA, or switching an operation from get to put (or vice-versa). The *3-buf* benchmark is the triple-buffering example discussed in §2.2, in which SCRATCH uncovered an existing bug. A DMA race occurs when the *cpaudio* benchmark is executed with zero frames of audio. This is arguably a bug since the precondition that the number of frames should be positive is not specified. For each benchmark, we give the smallest value of k for which correctness can be proved using k-induction (*without* employing the heuristics of §5.2); the minimum number D of DMAs which it was necessary to track (setting D to a low value reduces the size of the tracker arrays, which can significantly reduce verification complexity; we compute the optimum value for D iteratively for each benchmark,

---

[5] Experiments are performed on a 3GHz Intel Xeon machine running Linux 2.6 (64-bit).

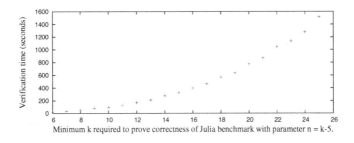

Fig. 4. Verification time for the *Julia* benchmark increases cubically with k

starting with $D = 1$), and the time, in seconds, taken for verification. We also show the smallest depth of execution required for bug-finding. Results are ordered with respect to k, Correct-D and Buggy-D. MiniSat 1.14, compiled with full optimisations, is used as back-end SAT solver. It has been reported to perform comparatively to state-of-the-art SMT solvers for SMT-$\mathcal{BV}$ [7] on this type of workload.

The results of Figure 3 indicate that k-induction provides a tractable method for proving correctness for this set of benchmarks: verification is achieved in under 10 seconds for 15 of the 22 examples, with only *Euler complex* taking longer than two minutes to check. The *normalize* and *Euler complex* benchmarks require the largest values for D, and result in the largest SAT instances for the correct programs, taking the longest time to verify. The *Julia* benchmark contains a loop for which the number of iterations is a fixed parameter n, the columns of a raytraced image to be computed by one SPE. For this example, k-induction succeeds with $k = n + 5$ (the results in Figure 3 are for the case where $n = 2$). In Figure 4, we illustrate the scalability of k-induction by plotting the time taken for verification of the Julia benchmark against the size of k when we vary parameter n between 1 and 25. Growth is less than cubic, showing that our k-induction method scales well.

With the exception of *Julia*, bug-finding is fast, taking less than 4 seconds. The *Julia* benchmark is the only example where the bug leads to unbounded issuing of non-interfering DMAs. Thus an assertion fails only when an attempt is made to issue a DMA operation when 32 operations are already pending. This situation requires a large search depth to detect, resulting in a SAT instance with more than 1.5 million variables which takes considerable time to solve. The "bounded lifetimes" heuristic of §5.2 can be used to short-circuit the bug-finding process for this example. Requiring that no DMA pends for more than three loop iterations (which is the case for the correct version of this benchmark), bug-finding takes just $1.88\,s$, requiring a search depth of 901.

Comparison with predicate abstraction The translation implemented by SCRATCH operates at the level of control flow graphs. In order to compare with other tools, we have hand-translated three of our benchmarks, *1-buf*, *2-buf* and *3-buf*, into C programs that track DMA operations as described in §4. We aimed to compare with BLAST [2] and SATABS [6] but were unable to obtain results using BLAST due to a bug in the tool, which we have reported to the BLAST developers.

Figure 5 shows results for proving correctness and finding bugs using SATABS, with Cadence SMV as a back-end model checker. For each example, we show the number

Benchmark	Correct			Buggy		
	iterations	time	SCRATCH speedup	iterations	time	SCRATCH speedup
1-buf	15	9.49	23.14 ×	3	1.25	2.91 ×
2-buf	>100	>1352.43	>417.78 ×	20	33.62	59.97 ×
3-buf	>100	>4344.98	>120.9 ×	69	4969.03	6641.47 ×

Fig. 5. Results applying CEGAR-based verification to three of the Cell SDK examples using SatAbs, in comparison to bounded model checking with k-induction using CBMC

of refinement iterations required (*iterations*), the time taken for verification (*time*), and the speed-up factor obtained by using SCRATCH over SATABS (obtained by comparing with the results of Figure 3). For all three examples, SATABS is eventually able to find the bug, but is three orders of magnitude slower than SCRATCH when applied to *3-buf*. The abstraction-refinement process leads to a conclusive verification result when applied to the correct version of *1-buf*, but is an order of magnitude slower than our k-induction technique. SATABS was not able to prove correctness for correctness of *2-buf* or *3-buf* within 100 refinement iterations.

Comparison with IBM Race Check library. The IBM Cell SDK [18] comes with a library for detecting DMA races [17] at runtime. The library maintains a log of pending operations, checking each new operation against entries in the log. If a DMA race is detected, then an error message is written to the console.

Using a Sony PlayStation 3 console, which is equipped with a Cell processor, we tested the Race Check library on each of our buggy examples. DMA races are detected for all but three benchmarks, and race detection takes less than $0.1\ s$ in each case. The bug in *cpaudio* was not detected since the example runs on a specific input file that does not expose the bug. The *Julia* bug, where more than 32 DMA operations may be simultaneously pending, is beyond the scope of the library. Although the buggy version of *1-buf I/O* crashes when executed on the Cell hardware, the Race Check library does not detect the DMA race responsible for this crash. This false negative appears to be a bug rather than a fundamental limitation, since *1-buf I/O* is similar to examples where the Race Check library successfully detects DMA races. Note that runtime race detection cannot be used to prove *absence* of DMA races, unlike our k-induction method.

7   Related Work

The concept of k-induction was first published in [24,4], targeting the verification of hardware designs represented by transition relations (although the basic idea had already been used in earlier implementations [20] and a version of one-induction used for BDD-based model checking [8]). A major emphasis of these two papers is on the restriction to loop-free or shortest paths, which we do not consider in our k-induction rule due to the size of state vectors and the high degree of determinism in software programs. Several optimisations and extensions to the technique have been proposed, including property strengthening to reduce induction depth [25], improving performance via incremental SAT solving [9], and supporting verification of temporal properties [1]. Applications of k-induction have focused exclusively on hardware designs [24,4,20] and synchronous programs [14,13]. A principle related to k-induction has also been used for circular reasoning about liveness properties [21]. To the best of our knowledge, there has been no previous work on applying k-induction to imperative programs comparable to our procedure in §5.

Techniques for detecting data races in shared memory multithreaded applications have been extensively studied. Notable static methods are based on formal type systems [11], or use classic pointer-analysis techniques; the latter approach is used by tools such as RACERX [10] and CHORD [22]. The ERASER tool [23] uses binary rewriting to monitor shared variables and to find failures of the locking discipline at runtime. Other dynamic techniques include [12], which is based on state-less search with partial-order reduction, and [15] which is based on a partial-order reduction technique for SystemC similar to the method of Flanagan and Godefroid [12].

None of these race detection techniques are applicable to software for heterogeneous multicore processors with multiple memory spaces. The only race detection tool we are aware of which is geared towards heterogeneous multicore is the IBM Race Check library [17], which we compare with in §6. The speed of runtime race detection with this library is attractive, but requires access to commodity hardware and can only be used to find bugs which are revealed by a particular set of inputs. In contrast, our k-induction technique can prove absence of DMA races, and BMC is able to detect potential races by assuming that input parameters may take *any* value.

8 Summary and Future Work

We have contributed an automatic technique for analysing DMA races in heterogeneous multicore programs which manage scratch-pad memory. At the heart of our method is a novel formulation of k-induction. We have demonstrated the effectiveness of this technique experimentally via a prototype tool, SCRATCH.

We plan to extend this work in the following ways. We intend to generalise and make precise our intuitions as to why k-induction works well for DMA-based programs. Our vision is a set of conditions for identifying classes of programs amenable to verification by k-induction, thus making the technique more broadly applicable for software analysis. SCRATCH focuses on analysing DMA races for accelerator memory by analysing accelerator source code in isolation. It is not possible to check meaningful properties of host memory without some knowledge of how this memory is structured. To check DMA races for host memory we plan to design a method which analyses host and accelerator source code side-by-side. A further challenge is the problem of DMA race checking between concurrently executing accelerator cores in a heterogeneous system. A starting point towards this goal could involve combining our methods with adapted versions of race checking techniques for shared memory concurrent software (*cf.* §7).

Acknowledgement. We are grateful to Matko Botinčan, Leopold Haller and the anonymous reviewers for their comments on an earlier draft of this work.

References

1. Armoni, R., Fix, L., Fraer, R., Huddleston, S., Piterman, N., Vardi, M.Y.: SAT-based induction for temporal safety properties. Electr. Notes Theor. Comput. Sci. 119(2), 3–16 (2005)
2. Beyer, D., Henzinger, T.A., Jhala, R., Majumdar, R.: The software model checker Blast. STTT 9(5-6), 505–525 (2007)
3. Biere, A., Cimatti, A., Clarke, E.M., Strichman, O., Zhu, Y.: Bounded model checking. Advances in Computers 58, 118–149 (2003)
4. Bjesse, P., Claessen, K.: SAT-based verification without state space traversal. In: Johnson, S.D., Hunt Jr., W.A. (eds.) FMCAD 2000. LNCS, vol. 1954, pp. 372–389. Springer, Heidelberg (2000)
5. Clarke, E., Kroening, D., Lerda, F.: A tool for checking ANSI-C programs. In: Jensen, K., Podelski, A. (eds.) TACAS 2004. LNCS, vol. 2988, pp. 168–176. Springer, Heidelberg (2004)
6. Clarke, E., Kroening, D., Sharygina, N., Yorav, K.: SATABS: SAT-based predicate abstraction for ANSI-C. In: Halbwachs, N., Zuck, L.D. (eds.) TACAS 2005. LNCS, vol. 3440, pp. 570–574. Springer, Heidelberg (2005)
7. Cordeiro, L., Fischer, B., Marques-Silva, J.: SMT-based bounded model checking for embedded ANSI-C software. In: ASE (2009)
8. Déharbe, D., Moreira, A.M.: Using induction and BDDs to model check invariants. In: CHARME. IFIP Conference Proceedings, vol. 105, pp. 203–213. Chapman & Hall, Boca Raton (1997)
9. Eén, N., Sörensson, N.: Temporal induction by incremental SAT solving. Electr. Notes Theor. Comput. Sci. 89(4) (2003)
10. Engler, D., Ashcraft, K.: RacerX: Effective, static detection of race conditions and deadlocks. In: SOSP, pp. 237–252. ACM, New York (2003)
11. Flanagan, C., Freund, S.N.: Type-based race detection for Java. In: PLDI, pp. 219–232. ACM, New York (2000)
12. Flanagan, C., Godefroid, P.: Dynamic partial-order reduction for model checking software. In: POPL, pp. 110–121. ACM, New York (2005)
13. Franzén, A.: Using satisfiability modulo theories for inductive verification of Lustre programs. Electr. Notes Theor. Comput. Sci. 144(1), 19–33 (2006)
14. Hagen, G., Tinelli, C.: Scaling up the formal verification of Lustre programs with SMT-based techniques. In: FMCAD, pp. 109–117. IEEE, Los Alamitos (2008)
15. Helmstetter, C., Maraninchi, F., Maillet-Contoz, L., Moy, M.: Automatic generation of schedulings for improving the test coverage of systems-on-a-chip. In: FMCAD, pp. 171–178. IEEE, Los Alamitos (2006)
16. Hofstee, H.P.: Power efficient processor architecture and the Cell processor. In: HPCA, pp. 258–262. IEEE Computer Society, Los Alamitos (2005)
17. IBM: Example Library API Reference, version 3.1 (July 2008)
18. IBM: Cell BE resource center (2009), http://www.ibm.com/developerworks/power/cell/
19. Kroening, D., Strichman, O.: Efficient computation of recurrence diameters. In: Zuck, L.D., Attie, P.C., Cortesi, A., Mukhopadhyay, S. (eds.) VMCAI 2003. LNCS, vol. 2575, pp. 298–309. Springer, Heidelberg (2002)
20. Lillieroth, C.J., Singh, S.: Formal verification of FPGA cores. Nord. J. Comput. 6(3), 299–319 (1999)

21. McMillan, K.L.: Circular compositional reasoning about liveness. In: Pierre, L., Kropf, T. (eds.) CHARME 1999. LNCS, vol. 1703, pp. 342–346. Springer, Heidelberg (1999)
22. Naik, M., Aiken, A., Whaley, J.: Effective static race detection for Java. In: PLDI, pp. 308–319. ACM, New York (2006)
23. Savage, S., Burrows, M., Nelson, G., Sobalvarro, P., Anderson, T.: Eraser: A dynamic data race detector for multithreaded programs. ACM Trans. Comput. Syst. 15(4), 391–411 (1997)
24. Sheeran, M., Singh, S., Stålmarck, G.: Checking safety properties using induction and a SAT-solver. In: Johnson, S.D., Hunt Jr., W.A. (eds.) FMCAD 2000. LNCS, vol. 1954, pp. 108–125. Springer, Heidelberg (2000)
25. Vimjam, V.C., Hsiao, M.S.: Explicit safety property strengthening in SAT-based induction. In: VLSID, pp. 63–68. IEEE, Los Alamitos (2007)

Simplifying Linearizability Proofs with Reduction and Abstraction

Tayfun Elmas[1], Shaz Qadeer[2], Ali Sezgin[1], Omer Subasi[1], and Serdar Tasiran[1]

[1] Koç University, İstanbul, Turkey
{telmas,asezgin,osubasi,stasiran}@ku.edu.tr
[2] Microsoft Research, Redmond, WA
qadeer@microsoft.com

Abstract. The typical proof of linearizability establishes an abstraction map from the concurrent program to a sequential specification, and identifies the commit points of operations. If the concurrent program uses fine-grained concurrency and complex synchronization, constructing such a proof is difficult. We propose a sound proof system that significantly simplifies the reasoning about linearizability. Linearizability is proved by transforming an implementation into its specification within this proof system. The proof system combines reduction and abstraction, which increase the granularity of atomic actions, with variable introduction and hiding, which syntactically relate the representation of the implementation to that of the specification. We construct the abstraction map incrementally, and eliminate the need to reason about the location of commit points in the implementation. We have implemented our method in the QED verifier and demonstrated its effectiveness and practicality on several highly-concurrent examples from the literature.

1 Introduction

Linearizability is a well-known correctness criterion for concurrent data-structure implementations [1]. A concurrent implementation, denoted *Impl*, is said to be linearizable with respect to a sequential specification, denoted *Spec*, if every concurrent operation *op* of *Impl* takes effect atomically between its call and return points, where the correct effect is described by a sequential operation *op′* in *Spec*.

The typical proof of linearizability establishes an *abstraction map*, from *Impl*-states to *Spec*-states [2], and shows that only one action of *op*, called the *commit action*, is mapped to *op′*, and other actions are mapped to stuttering (identity) transitions in *Spec*. Under fine-grained concurrency control, constructing such a proof requires considerable expertise. First, identifying the commit action becomes nontrivial when *op* is written in terms of many small actions that make visible changes to the state. It further complicates the analysis when the commit point is determined at runtime depending on thread interleavings. Second, while the abstraction map relates *Impl*-states to *Spec*-states, it must also filter out the effects of the partially completed operations of *Impl* on the state except for the

J. Esparza and R. Majumdar (Eds.): TACAS 2010, LNCS 6015, pp. 296–311, 2010.
© Springer-Verlag Berlin Heidelberg 2010

commit action. This includes completing partial operations or rolling back the effects of these operations back to a clean state [3].

In this paper, we present a new method for proving linearizability of programs with fine-grained concurrency. Our method permits more tractable proofs by eliminating the above difficulties of constructing an abstraction map and not requiring the identification of the commit points. In [4], we showed that by interleaving reduction with abstraction, we can increase atomicity to the point that assertions in a concurrent program can be verified by sequential (local) reasoning. In this work, we argue that program rewriting guided by atomicity is an effective method for proving linearizability and present a sound proof system and a supporting tool that realize this method in a formal and practical setting.

We prove that *Impl* is linearizable with respect to *Spec*, by transforming *Impl* to *Spec* via a sequence of phases. In a *reduction* phase, we alternate reduction and abstraction to mark a set of sequentially composed actions as atomic. These actions are collected together, and the effects of thread interleavings are eliminated. In a *refinement* phase, we couple variable introduction and variable hiding, in order to make the code closer to the specification. These techniques provide us with the ability to *syntactically* relate implementation of a data structure to a specification with a different representation. We also provide the soundness guarantee that, the proof transformations preserve the behaviors of the original program. Thus, one can simplify the program by growing atomic blocks and continue the linearizability proof with another method, e.g., separation logic [5].

Interleaving reduction and refinement phases supports the incremental construction of the abstraction map. By increasing atomicity, a reduction phase enables a following refinement phase to implicitly establish a simple and clean abstraction map towards the specification. A refinement phase also helps to improve a following reduction phase by eliminating *superficial conflicts*: Two equivalent operations might conflict on low-level (implementation) variables but this does not necessarily correspond to real conflicts in terms of the final specification. Our solution to this issue indirectly introduces a semantic hierarchy into mover checks in reduction, which is not particular to linearizability and is likely to be useful in any kind of reduction proof.

We have implemented our method in the QED verifier. We demonstrate the effectiveness and practicality of our method by proving linearizability of several tricky examples from the literature. All proofs are available online and reproducible using QED.

1.1 Related Work

Refinement between a concurrent program and its sequential specification is well-studied [2,6,7,8]. Previous work showed that, under certain conditions, auxiliary variables enable construction of an abstraction map to prove refinement [2,6]. However, in practice writing an abstraction map for programs with fine-grained concurrency remains a challenge since there are a large number of cases to consider. [3] used a complex abstraction map, called *aggregation function*, that completes the atomic transactions that are committed but not yet finished. The refinement proofs in [1,9,10,11], despite being supported by automated proof checkers, all require manual guidance for the derivation of the proof, requiring the user to manage low-level logical reasoning. On the other hand, in our method the user guides the proof via code transformations at the programming language level. Recently, [5] provided a tool that automates the derivation of the proof using shape abstraction. To our knowledge, its automating ability is limited to linked-list based data structures and it still requires identification of the possible commit points.

Owicki-Gries [12,1] and rely-guarantee [13] methods have been used in refinement proofs. However, in the case of fine-grained concurrency, deriving the proof obligations in both approaches requires expertise. The idea of local reasoning is exploited by separation logic [14] which is not particularly useful for shared objects with high level of interference. In these cases, we show that abstraction is an important tool to reduce the effects of interference.

Wang and Stoller [15] statically prove linearizability of the program using its sequentially executed version as the specification. Their notion of atomicity is defined over a fixed set of primitives, which is limited in the case of superficial conflicts. On the other hand, our notion of atomicity is more general and supported by abstraction to prove atomicity even under high level of interference. They provided hand-crafted proofs for several non-blocking algorithms, and our proofs are mechanically checked. In [16], Groves gives a hand-proof of the linearizability of the nonblocking queue, by reducing executions the fine-grained program to its sequential version. His use of reduction is non-incremental, and must consider the commutativity of each action by doing a global reasoning, while our reasoning is local.

2   Motivation and Overview

Our running example is a multiset of integers. Figure 1 shows the concurrent implementation (*Impl*), and the sequential specification (*Spec*), of InsertPair and LookUp operations[1]. The instruction assume ϕ blocks until ϕ becomes true, and havoc x assigns a nondeterminstic value to x. Our goal is to verify linearizability of *Impl* with respect to *Spec*.

Spec uses the variable S, which maps each integer to its cardinality in the multiset. Initially, S is empty, so S[x]==0 for every integer x.

Impl contains an array M of N slots. For each slot, the elt field stores an integer, and the stt field indicates the status of the slot. The atomic FindSlot operation[2] allocates an empty slot by setting its stt field to reserved, and returns its index. FindSlot fails and returns -1 if it cannot find any empty slot. The lock of each slot is acquired and released separately by lock and unlock operations, respectively.

---

[1] We omit the Insert operation to simplify the explanation.

[2] The original implementation of FindSlot uses fine-grain locking, and traverses the array using a loop similar to that of LookUp. In order to simplify the explanation, we use a version of FindSlot that has already been transformed using our proof steps.

Implementation (*Impl*)

```
enum Status = { empty,reserved,full };
record Slot { elt: int, stt: Status };
var M: array[0..N-1] of Slot

LookUp(x:int) returns(r:bool)
  var i: int;
1 for (i := 0; i < N; i++) {
2   lock(M[i]);
3   if (M[i].elt==x && M[i].stt==full){
4     unlock(M[i]);
5     r := true; return;
6   } else unlock(M[i]);
7 }
8 r := false;

atomic FindSlot(x:int) returns (r:int)
1 if (forall 0<=i<N. M[i].stt != empty) {
2   r := -1;
3 } else {
4   assume (0<=r<N && M[r].stt==empty);
5   M[r].stt := reserved;
6 }
```

```
InsertPair(x:int, y:int) returns (r:bool)
   var i,j: int;
1  i := FindSlot(x);
2  if (i == -1) {
3    r := false; return;
4  }
5  j := FindSlot(y);
6  if (j == -1) {
7    M[i].stt := empty;
8    r := false; return;
9  }

10 M[i].elt := x;
11 M[j].elt := y;

12 lock(M[i]);
13 lock(M[j]);
14 M[i].stt := full;
15 M[j].stt := full;
16 unlock(M[i]);
17 unlock(M[j]);
18 r := true;
```

Specification (*Spec*)

```
var S: array [int] of int;
atomic LookUp(x:int) returns (r:bool)
  r := (S[x] > 0);
```

```
atomic InsertPair(x:int, y:int) returns (r:bool)
  if(r) { S[x] := S[x] + 1; S[y] := S[y] + 1; }
```

Fig. 1. The concurrent implementation and the sequential specification of multiset

A typical linearizability proof establishes an abstraction map that relates the slots M of *Impl* to the map S of *Spec*. Let |A| denote the cardinality of the set A. The following abstraction map expresses the programmer's design intent clearly:

```
S[x]==|{ i | 0<=i<N && M[i].elt==x && M[i].stt==full }|
```

In words, for each integer x, the number of slots i in *Impl* with M[i].elt==x and M[i].stt==full represents S[x] in *Spec*. When the proof is done at finest granularity of concurrency, more complicated variants of this abstraction map has to be used. In the following, we envision such a proof, and highlight common difficulties. We then illustrate how our proposed approach alleviates these difficulties and allows the proof to use the above map.

2.1   Challenges in a Typical Refinement Proof for Multiset

Abstraction maps and commit points. Many techniques work by first selecting a commit point in every operation. The most likely choice for the commit point for InsertPair is line 16, since releasing the first lock makes the inserted element M[i].elt visible to other threads. Consider an abstraction map from *Impl* to *Spec* and suppose that line 16 of InsertPair is executed by *Impl*. This transition must be mapped to a single transition that increments S[x] and S[y] atomically. As a first try, let us consider the simple abstraction map introduced above:

```
S[x]==|{ i | 0<=i<N && M[i].elt==x && M[i].stt==full }|
```

This map does not work with this choice of commit point, because when lines 14 and 15 of `InsertPair` are executed, `S[x]` and `S[y]` are incremented, but the execution has not reached the commit point yet. In addition, the updates that are propagated to `S` are not atomic. Our next, slightly more sophisticated map below does not update `S[x]` and `S[y]` while the locks to these cells are held. (`HeldBy(M[i],t)` is true when thread `t` is holding the lock of `M[i]`):

`S[x]==|{ i | 0<=i<N && M[i].elt==x && M[i].stt==full && !HeldBy(M[i],t)}|`

The problem with this map is that every slot locked by a thread would be excluded from `S`. As a result, at line 16 (the commit point) the map would increment `S[x]` but not `S[y]` since `M[j]` is still locked. Thus, this map still does not accomplish the atomic specification state update we are after. The right map has to complete this partial update at the commit point by incrementing `S[y]` as well although the lock of `M[j]` is still held.

We next try different selections of commit points: lines 14, 15 or 17. For each of these choices, in order to produce the intended specification state and avoid non-atomic updates to it, an abstraction map must "roll back" effects of executions of `InsertPair` that have not reached their commit point, and must "complete" the effects of others that are past their commit point but have not yet finished. To accomplish this, the map must refer to not only the locking state but also the program counters of all threads.

Non-fixed commit points. Another issue that complicates the linearizability proof for multiset is that the commit action of `LookUp` is not fixed, but depends on the concurrently executing insertions by other threads. If `LookUp(x)` returns true its commit action is at line 3, where it finds out that the slot being visited contains x and is valid. When `LookUp(x)` fails, its commit point must be chosen as the first read of a slot it performs or earlier. This is because, in the absence of a `Delete` operation, it is possible that x gets inserted into a slot `M[i]`, after `LookUp` visits the ith slot and fails to find x, therefore, the commit point cannot be past the first read of a slot. Techniques that depend on the existence of a fixed commit point would be ineffective in such situations [13].

2.2 Proof by Reduction and Abstraction

Observe that the code blocks between lines 12-17 of `InsertPair` is *atomic*, i.e., any execution in which the actions of this block are interleaved with actions from other threads can be transformed into one in which actions of the commit block are contiguous. The technique we present allows us to express this fact and use it in a sound manner in a refinement or linearizability proof. Being able to treat the commit block as a single atomic action eliminates all of the potential difficulties outlined above.

In our method the proof is constructed by transforming *Impl* to *Spec*, both shown in Figure 1. This is done through a reduction phase followed by a refinement phase. In the reduction phase, we reduce the bodies of `InsertPair` and

LookUp to single atomic actions. This phase is guided by a simple hint about the locking discipline (see [17] for details of automating reduction).

In order to handle the non-fixed commit points of LookUp, we apply a transformation to separate its succeeding and failing executions. Since each failing iteration of LookUp is a left-mover, the failing branch of LookUp trivially reduces to a single action. For the successful branch, we apply an abstraction to the failing iterations that makes them also right-movers, and combine the abstracted iterations with the final, successful iteration. This reduces the successful branch into an atomic action. At the end, we obtain LookUp as a single atomic action that summarizes both successful and failing executions of the original code.

After transforming InsertPair and LookUp to single atomic actions, the locking state becomes unnecessary. We use variable hiding to clean up the calls to lock and unlock. Finally, we arrive at the representation of the multiset in *Spec* in three proof steps. First, we introduce the *Spec* variable S to the current version of the program. Then, we add (and prove) the following invariant, which links the new variable to the array M:

`S[x]==|{ i | 0<=i<N && M[i].elt==x && M[i].stt==full }|`

Recall that the above invariant establishes the simplest abstraction map that reflects the programmer's design intent. The invariant allows us to add the assignments S[x] := S[x] + 1; and S[y] := S[y] + 1; at the end of InsertPair. We follow the introduction of S with a variable hiding step in which we replace the bodies of InsertPair and LookUp with the corresponding bodies in *Spec* (Figure 1). Our soundness theorems given in Section 5 guarantee that transforming *Impl* to *Spec* using our rules implies the linearizability of *Impl*.

What is noteworthy about the proof we outlined is that it handles two separate concerns in separate proof steps: 1) concurrency control using locking and the stt field, and 2) relating the array-based representation of *Impl* to the representation in *Spec*. This example does not illustrate the use of variable hiding to eliminate superficial conflicts. In Section 6 we provide an example that does.

3   Concurrent Programs: Syntax and Semantics

Program. A program P is a tuple $P = \langle Global_P, Proc_P \rangle$. $Global_P$ is the set of uniquely-named global variables. $Proc_P$ is a set of procedures. A procedure is a tuple $\langle \rho, local_\rho, body_\rho \rangle$, where ρ is the *name*, $local_\rho$ is the set of *local variables*, and $body_\rho$ is the *body* of the procedure.

We distinguish the input variables $\overrightarrow{in}_\rho \subseteq local_\rho$ and the output variables $\overrightarrow{out}_\rho \subseteq local_\rho$. The tuple $\langle \rho, \overrightarrow{in}_\rho, \overrightarrow{out}_\rho \rangle$ is called the *signature* of the procedure. The signatures of the procedures in *Proc* form the signature of the program, denoted $\mathsf{Sig}(P)$. We employ the convention that the variables in $\overrightarrow{in}_\rho$ and $\overrightarrow{out}_\rho$ are read-only and write-only, respectively, while the rest of the variables in $local_\rho$ can be both read and updated.

We use Var_P to denote $Global_P \cup \bigcup_{\rho \in Proc} local_\rho$. We assume that each local variable is used in a unique procedure. Var'_P consisting of the primed version of each variable in Var_P. We omit the subscripts when the program and the procedure are clear from the context.

Execution model. Let Tid be the set of all thread identifiers. For simplicity of presentation, we assume that procedure calls are inlined properly, assuming no recursion in the call chain. In general, our method applies to the inter-procedural case allowing recursion [4].

Without loss of generality, each thread calls one procedure ρ from $Proc$, and terminates when ρ returns. Statements of the procedures may refer to the current thread id through the special variable $tid \in Global$, whose domain is Tid.

Syntax. We assume that each atomic statement α, which we call an *(atomic) action*, is in the form: assert $a; p$. Let ρ be the procedure whose body contains α, and $V = Global \cup local_\rho$. The *assert predicate* a be over only unprimed variables from V. The *transition predicate* p is over both primed and unprimed variables in $V \cup V'$. For any action α, let ϕ_α and τ_α denote its assert and transition predicates. For instance, $\phi_\alpha = a$ and $\tau_\alpha = p$, for α given above.

We use sequential composition ($;$), choice ($\square$) and loop ($\circlearrowright$) operators to form *compound statements*. We also define the *nullary action* stop, which appears only at runtime and intuitively marks the end of fully executing a statement.

Program states. A program state s is a pair consisting of
  - a *variable valuation* σ_s that maps a thread id and a variable to a value, such that $\sigma_s(t, g) = \sigma_s(u, g)$ for all states s and thread id's t, u, whenever g is a global variable.
  - a *code map* ϵ_s that keeps track of a (compound) statement for each thread, such that $\epsilon_s(t) = c$ means that at program state s, the remaining part of the program to be executed by thread t is given by c.

A program state s is called *initial* if $\forall t \in Tid. \exists \rho \in Proc. \epsilon_s(t) = body_\rho$, i.e. every thread is about to call a procedure. State s is called *final* if $\epsilon_s(t) = $ stop, for all $t \in Tid$. We write $Initial(s)$ (resp. $Final(s)$) to denote that s is an initial (resp. final) state.

Let $\sigma_s|_V$ denote the projection of valuation σ_s on $V \subseteq Var$. Define $s|_V$ to be the program state $(\sigma_s|_V, \epsilon_s)$. This definition also pointwise applies to collections of states.

Predicates over program variables. For an assert predicate x, let $x[t]$ denote the predicate in which all free occurrences of tid is replaced with t. We say that a program state s satisfies $x[t]$, denoted as $s \vDash x[t]$ or as $x[t](s)$, if $x[t]$ evaluates to true when all free occurrences of each unprimed variable v is replaced with $\sigma_s(t, v)$. An assert predicate is called a *state predicate* if it does not contain any free occurrence of tid.

Similarly, the pair of program states (s_1, s_2) satisfies a transition predicate $p[t]$, denoted as $(s_1, s_2) \vDash p[t]$ or as $p[t](s_1, s_2)$, if $p[t]$ evaluates to true when each unprimed variable v (resp. v') is replaced with $\sigma_{s_1}(t, v)$ (resp. $\sigma_{s_2}(t, v)$).

Let $\mathsf{fv}(p)$ be the set of free variables in the (state or transition) predicate p.

Execution semantics. We assume a sequentially-consistent memory model. For thread t and $\gamma \in Atom$, (t, γ) is called a *transition label*. We say $s \xrightarrow{(t,\alpha)} s'$ holds when t can execute α next (in which case s' is a (t, α) successor[3] of s), all other threads do not update their control flow, all local variables of other threads remain the same, the global variables and local variables of t are updated so that the transition predicate of α is satisfied. Formally, $s \xrightarrow{(t,\alpha)} s'$ if $(s, s') \vDash \tau_\alpha[t]$ and for all $u \neq t$ and for any local variable x, $\sigma_s(u, x) = \sigma_{s'}(u, x)$.

Run. A run r of the program is a sequence of state transitions:

$$r = r_1 \xrightarrow{(t_1, \alpha_1)} r_2 \xrightarrow{(t_2, \alpha_2)} \cdots \xrightarrow{(t_{n-1}, \alpha_{n-1})} r_n$$

For the definitions that follow, we fix the run r above. Let $Tid(r)$ denote the set of threads occurring in r. Let r_i denote the ith program state, and $r(i)$, the ith transition label (t_i, α_i) in r. For a state predicate ϕ, we say that r is a run of P from ϕ if $Initial(r_1)$ and $r_1 \vDash \phi$.

The run is *maximal* if r_n cannot make any transition. Henceforth, we will only consider maximal runs.

Trace. A *trace* is a sequence of transition labels, $\mathbf{l} = l_1 \ldots l_k$. The trace moves a state s_1 to s_{k+1}, written $s_1 \xrightarrow{\mathbf{l}} s_{k+1}$, if there is a run r of P over $\mathbf{l}$, such that $r_j = s_j$, for all $1 \leq j \leq k+1$ and $r_i \xrightarrow{l_i} r_{i+1}$.

Violation-freedom. A run r of P from ϕ is called a *violation* if $\neg\phi_\alpha[t](r_k)$ evaluates to true for some $(t, \alpha) \in \mathsf{next}(r_k)$. Intuitively, a violation is a run of P that starts from an initial program state s_1 and reaches a program state s_k which violates the assert predicate, ϕ_α, of an action α which thread t can execute at state s_k. A run is said to be *successful* if it is not a violation. We indicate a successful run as $s_1 \xrightarrow{\mathbf{l}} s_2$ and a violation as $s_1 \xrightarrow{\mathbf{l}} \mathsf{error}$.

4   Program Transformations

In this section, we formalize our notion of proof and introduce the rules for the proof calculus. A *proof state* is the pair $(P, \mathcal{I})$, where P is a program, and $\mathcal{I}$ is a state predicate, called the *inductive invariant* of the program. We require that for every proof state $(P, \mathcal{I})$, all the atomic actions of P preserve $\mathcal{I}$. An atomic action α preserves $\mathcal{I}$, written $\alpha \leftrightarrows \mathcal{I}$, if $s_1 \xrightarrow{(t,\alpha)} s_2$ and $s_1 \vDash \mathcal{I}$ imply $s_2 \vDash \mathcal{I}$.

A proof consists of rewriting the input program, denoted P_1, iteratively so that, in the limit, one arrives at a program, denoted P_n, that can be verified by sequential reasoning methods. Formally, the proof is expressed as $(P_1, \mathsf{true}) \dashrightarrow (P_2, \mathcal{I}_2) \dashrightarrow \cdots \dashrightarrow (P_n, \mathcal{I}_n)$ Each proof step is governed by a proof rule, which we present below.

---

[3] Our technical report [18] contains a more elaborate discussion of the operational semantics of our formal language.

The following proof rule states the general form of updating $\mathcal{I}$, replacing it with a stronger invariant.

Rule 1 (Invariant). *Replace invariant $\mathcal{I}_1$ with $\mathcal{I}_2$ if $\alpha \leftrightarroweq \mathcal{I}_2$ for all the actions α in P, and $\mathcal{I}_2 \Rightarrow \mathcal{I}_1$.*

The basic idea in reduction and abstraction is to replace an action with another action that simulates the former.

Definition 1 (Simulation). *Let α, β be actions, t be an arbitrary thread id. We say β simulates α at proof state $(P, \mathcal{I})$, written $(P, \mathcal{I}) \vdash \alpha \preceq \beta$, if both of the following hold:*

$$\textbf{S1.} \quad (\mathcal{I} \wedge \neg \phi_\alpha) \Rightarrow \neg \phi_\beta \qquad \textbf{S2.} \quad (\mathcal{I} \wedge \tau_\alpha) \Rightarrow (\neg \phi_\beta \vee \tau_\beta)$$

Intuitively, **S1** states that if there is a violation with α, there has to be a violation with β substituted in place of α. **S2** states that for each violation-free run, replacing α with β results in either a violation, or a violation-free run with the same end state.

4.1   Reduction

Reduction, due to Lipton [19], creates coarse-grained atomic statements by combining fine-grained actions. An action α can be combined with another action if α is a certain kind of mover. A mover is an action that can commute over actions of other threads in any run. We write $(P, \mathcal{I}) \vdash \alpha : m$ to indicate that α is $m-$mover in the proof state $(P, \mathcal{I})$, where $m \in \{\mathbb{L}, \mathbb{R}\}$.

We decide that an action α is a mover by statically checking a simulation relation, that states that commuting α with every β can lead to the same state or goes wrong. An assert predicate x is p-stable, if $\forall s, s'. x(s) \wedge p(s, s') \Rightarrow x(s')$.

Let $\mathsf{wp}(p, x)$, the *weakest (liberal) pre-condition* of predicate x for transition predicate p, stand for all states which cannot reach a state where x evaluates to false after executing p. Formally, $\mathsf{wp}(p, x) = \{s \mid \forall s'. p(s, s') \Rightarrow x(s')\}$. For two transition predicates p and q, define their composition $p \cdot q$, as the transition predicate $p \cdot q = \{(s_1, s_2) \mid \exists s_3. p(s_1, s_3) \wedge q(s_3, s_2)\}$. The operator $[\![\ ]\!]$ expresses the result of combining two actions to one atomic action.[4]

$$[\![\alpha; \beta]\!] = \mathsf{assert}\,(\phi_\alpha \wedge \mathsf{wp}(\tau_\alpha, \phi_\beta)); (\tau_\alpha \cdot \tau_\beta) \qquad [\![\alpha \square \beta]\!] = \mathsf{assert}\,(\phi_\alpha \wedge \phi_\beta); (\tau_\alpha \vee \tau_\beta)$$

Definition 2 (Left-mover). *Action α is a left-mover in proof state $(P, \mathcal{I})$, denoted $(P, \mathcal{I}) \vdash \alpha : \mathbb{L}$, if the following holds for every action β in P and every pair of distinct thread ids t and u: $(P, \mathcal{I}) \vdash [\![\beta[u]\ ;\ \alpha[t]]\!] \preceq [\![\alpha[t]\ ;\ \beta[u]]\!]$.*

Definition 3 (Right-mover). *Action α is a right-mover in proof state $(P, \mathcal{I})$, denoted $(P, \mathcal{I}) \vdash \alpha : \mathbb{R}$, if, for every action β in P, and every pair of distinct thread ids t and u: $(P, \mathcal{I}) \vdash [\![\alpha[t]\ ;\ \beta[u]]\!] \preceq [\![\beta[u]\ ;\ \alpha[t]]\!]$ and $\phi_\beta[u]$ is $\tau_\alpha[t]$-stable.*

---

[4] We assume that a transition predicate $\tau_\alpha[t]$ can only change the variables in the scope of t and that if t and u are running the same procedure, local variables are suitably renamed to prevent false conflicts.

The reduction rules below define the conditions under which non-atomic statements are transformed to atomic actions. We omit the rules about procedure calls and parallel composition which are similar to those of [4].

Rule 2 (Reduce-Sequential). *Replace occurrences of $\alpha \; ; \; \gamma$ with $[\![\alpha \; ; \; \gamma]\!]$ if either $(P, \mathcal{I}) \vdash \alpha : \mathbb{R}$ or $(P, \mathcal{I}) \vdash \gamma : \mathbb{L}$.*

Rule 3 (Reduce-Choice). *Replace occurrences of $\alpha \; \Box \; \gamma$ with $[\![\alpha \; \Box \; \gamma]\!]$.*

Rule 4 (Reduce-Loop). *Replace occurrences of $\alpha^{\circlearrowleft}$ with β if the following hold:*

L1. $(P, \mathcal{I}) \vdash \alpha : m$ *s.t.* $m \in \{\mathbb{R}, \mathbb{L}\}$ **L2.** $\beta \leftrightarrows \mathcal{I}$

L3. $\phi_\beta \Rightarrow \tau_\beta[\mathit{Var}/\mathit{Var}']$ **L4.** $(P, \mathcal{I}) \vdash [\![\beta \; ; \; \alpha]\!] \preceq \alpha$

4.2 Abstraction

The purpose of the abstraction rule is to replace an action with another action An abstraction step consists of replacing an action α with another action β, which in principle leads to less interference with other actions.

Rule 5 (Abstraction). *Replace the action α with action β if $\beta \leftrightarrows \mathcal{I}$ and $(P, \mathcal{I}) \vdash \alpha \preceq \beta$.*

This rule is usually applied for an action $\mathsf{assert}\, a; p$ by replacing it with 1) $\mathsf{assert}\, b; p$ such that $b \Rightarrow a$ or 2) with $\mathsf{assert}\, a; q$ such that $p \Rightarrow q$. While the former corresponds to adding extra assertions to the action, the latter adds more (non-deterministic) transitions.

4.3 Variable Introduction and Hiding

Intuitively, variable introduction rewrites some actions in the program so that these can refer to a new (*history*) variable. Variable hiding is the dual of variable introduction; each action is rewritten so that it does no longer refer to the hidden variable. Hiding a variable also requires quantifying out the variable in the invariant.

In order to ensure soundness, in both cases, we need a relation between actions over different sets of variables. For this, we extend our simulation relation ($\preceq$) for each rule. In addition, we require that the input and output variables of the procedures ($\overrightarrow{in}_\rho, \overrightarrow{out}_\rho$) are fixed during the proof; the rules below are not applicable to these variables.

Rule 6 (Add-Variable). *Add the new variable v to Var_P, and replace every action α with β whenever $(P, \mathcal{I}) \vdash \alpha \preceq_{+v} \beta$, which holds if the following are both valid:*

A1. $(\mathcal{I} \wedge \neg \phi_\alpha) \Rightarrow (\forall v.\ \neg \phi_\beta)$ **A2.** $(\mathcal{I} \wedge \tau_\alpha) \Rightarrow (\forall v.\ \neg \phi_\beta \vee (\exists v'.\ \tau_\beta))$

Rule 7 (Hide-Variable). *Remove the existing variable v from the program, and replace the invariant $\mathcal{I}$ with $\exists v. \mathcal{I}$. Replace every action α with β whenever $(P,\mathcal{I}) \vdash \alpha \preceq_{-v} \beta$, which holds if the following are both valid:*

H1. $(\exists v. \mathcal{I} \wedge \neg\phi_\alpha) \Rightarrow \neg\phi_\beta$ $\qquad$ **H2.** $(\exists v, v'. \mathcal{I} \wedge \tau_\alpha) \Rightarrow (\neg\phi_\beta \vee \tau_\beta)$

Fix a thread t and a state s. In both of the rules, the first condition (**A1**, **H1**) states that violations are preserved. The second condition (**A2**, **H2**) states that transitions (over the common variables of α and β) are either preserved or additional violations are introduced.

5   Soundness Theorems

Given a proof $(P_1, \mathcal{I}_1) \dashrightarrow \cdots \dashrightarrow (P_n, \mathcal{I}_n)$, we now provide the soundness theorems. Each theorem relates P_n to P_1, providing a soundness guarantee for a particular use of our method. Due to lack of space, we provide the proofs in our technical report [18].

5.1   Proving Assertions

The first theorem is an extension of the main soundness theorem in [4]. Intuitively, the theorem states that proof steps preserve violations, and initial-final state pairs when the output program is good from the final invariant.

Good and Bad. In the following, we define $Good(P, \mathcal{I})$ as the set of pre- and post-state pairs associated with succeeding (maximal) runs of program P from states satisfying $\mathcal{I}$. $Bad(P, \mathcal{I})$ is the set of pre-states associated with violations. Formally,

$$Good(P, \mathcal{I}) = \{(s_1, s_2) \mid Initial(s_1),\ s_1 \vDash \mathcal{I},\ \exists l.\ s_1 \xrightarrow{l} s_2,\ Final(s_2)\}$$
$$Bad(P, \mathcal{I}) \ = \{s_1 \mid Initial(s_1),\ s_1 \vDash \mathcal{I},\ \exists l.\ s_1 \xrightarrow{l} \mathsf{error}\}$$

P is said to be *good* from $\mathcal{I}$ if $Bad(P, \mathcal{I}) = \emptyset$; it is called *bad* from $\mathcal{I}$, otherwise.

Theorem 1. *Let $(P_1, \mathcal{I}_1) \dashrightarrow \cdots \dashrightarrow (P_n, \mathcal{I}_n)$ be a sequence of proof steps. Let $V = Var_{P_1} \cap Var_{P_n}$ and $X = (Var_{P_1} \cup Var_{P_n}) \backslash V$. The following hold:*

C1. $Bad|_V(P_1, \exists X.\ \mathcal{I}_n) \subseteq Bad|_V(P_n, \exists X.\ \mathcal{I}_n)$
C2. $\forall (s_1, s_n) \in Good|_V(P_1, \exists X.\ \mathcal{I}_n) :$
$\qquad$ **a.** $s_1 \in Bad|_V(P_n, \exists X.\ \mathcal{I}_n)$ $\quad$ or $\quad$ **b.** $(s_1, s_n) \in Good|_V(P_n, \exists X.\ \mathcal{I}_n)$

Note that, since the input and output variables of procedures are fixed during the proof, so the set V above will always be nonempty. A corollary of the above theorem is that, if P_n is good from $\mathcal{I}_n$, then P_1 is good from $\mathcal{I}_n$. This means that, one can prove the assertions in P_1 by gradually obtaining programs with coarser-grained concurrency using our proof rules.

5.2 Proving Linearizability

In this section, we establish a link between P_1 and P_n in the context of proving linearizability. For this, we first define *behavioral simulation*, a special kind of simulation that relates two programs through their observable behaviors over procedure input and output values.

Behavioral simulation. Let $r = s_1 \xrightarrow{1} s_n$ be a (maximal) run of the program. Let ρ be the procedure executed by t. We call the tuple $(t, \rho, \sigma_{s_1}(t, \overrightarrow{in}_\rho), \sigma_{s_n}(t, \overrightarrow{out}_\rho))$ the behavior of t in r and denote it by $\mathsf{beh}(r, t)$. The behavior includes the name of the procedure called by t, along with the values of the input and the output variables of the procedure[5]. We write $\mathsf{Beh}(r)$ to denote $\{\mathsf{beh}(r, t) \mid t \in Tid(r)\}$.

We define $\mathsf{fst}(r, t)$ and $\mathsf{lst}(r, t)$ be the indices of first and the last actions of t in r. Formally, with $L = \{i \mid r(i) = (t, \alpha)\}$, $\mathsf{fst}(r, t) = \min(L)$ and $\mathsf{lst}(r, t) = \max(L)$. Let $\ll_r$ be a partial order over $Tid(r)$ ordering threads that do not execute concurrently: $t \ll_r u$ if $\mathsf{lst}(r, t) < \mathsf{fst}(r, u)$.

Definition 4. *Let P and P' be two programs with $\mathsf{Sig}(P) = \mathsf{Sig}(P')$, and let $\mathcal{I}$ be a state predicate. Let $X_1 = \mathsf{fv}(\mathcal{I}) \backslash Var_P$ and $X_2 = \mathsf{fv}(\mathcal{I}) \backslash Var_{P'}$. P' behaviorally-simulates P from $\mathcal{I}$, denoted $P \lhd_\mathcal{I} P'$ if for each maximal run r of program P from $\exists X_1.\mathcal{I}$, there exists a maximal run r' of P' from $\exists X_2.\mathcal{I}$ such that 1) $\mathsf{Beh}(r) = \mathsf{Beh}(r')$ and 2) $\ll_r \subseteq \ll_{r'}$*

The following theorem connects behavioral simulation to the generic notion of linearizability. We say P *is linearizable to P' from $\mathcal{I}$* to restrict the definition of linearizability to runs of P and P' from $\mathcal{I}$. A program P is called an *atomic program* if for every $\rho \in Proc_P$, $body_\rho$ is an atomic action.

Theorem 2. *Let P' be an atomic program that is good from $\mathcal{I}$. A program P is linearizable to P' from $\mathcal{I}$ iff $P \lhd_\mathcal{I} P'$.*

The following theorem states that each good program reached during the proof behaviorally simulates the initial program.

Theorem 3 (Soundness). *Let $(P_1, \mathcal{I}_1) \dashrightarrow \cdots \dashrightarrow (P_n, \mathcal{I}_n)$ be a sequence of proof steps such that P_n is good from $\mathcal{I}_n$. Then for all $1 \le i \le n$, $P_1 \lhd_{\mathcal{I}_n} P_i$ holds.*

Theorems 2 and 3 provide two options for proving linearizability of P_1 to the intended specification from $\mathcal{I}$, represented by an atomic program P_n. First, one can complement another proof method with ours, by first performing the proof $(P_1, \mathsf{true}) \dashrightarrow \cdots \dashrightarrow (P_k, \mathcal{I})$, and then applying her method to prove that P_k is linearizable to P_n. Once the proof passes, this implies that P_1 is also linearizable to P_n, since our transformations preserve all the behaviors of the program relevant to linearizability. Alternatively, s/he can keep transforming $(P_k, \mathcal{I})$ up to $(P_n, \mathcal{I})$, and complete the full proof of linearizability in our system. Note that, for the theorems to ensure soundness in these cases, s/he must also prove that P_k (resp. P_n) is good from $\mathcal{I}$. The latter is formalized by the following.

---

[5] Notice that the first and the last states of the run provide us the values of $\overrightarrow{in}_\rho$ and $\overrightarrow{out}_\rho$, respectively.

Corollary 1. *Let* $(P_1, \text{true}) \dashrightarrow \cdots \dashrightarrow (P_n, \mathcal{I})$ *be a sequence of proof steps, such that* P_n *is an atomic program that is good from* $\mathcal{I}$. *Then,* P_1 *is linearizable to* P_n *from* $\mathcal{I}$.

6   Implementation and Experience

We implemented our proof method in the QED verifier. QED accepts as input a multithreaded program written in an extension of the Boogie programming language and a proof script. All the transformations are applied automatically, and when necessary, the preconditions of the transformations are checked, by generating verification conditions and feeding them to the Z3 SMT solver. Using QED, we mechanically proved the linearizability of the following programs:

- Lock-coupling linked list [13]
- Treiber's non-blocking stack [20]
- Non-blocking and two-lock queues [21]
- Non-blocking mutex lock implementation adapted from [22]

For each data structure, we chose a generic specification as the target of the proof, and were able to transform the program to the specification program through few reduction and refinement phases. The QED tool and the proof scripts of the above programs are available at **http://qed.codeplex.com**.

In the rest of the section, we overview the proof of the non-blocking queue, and describe how coupling variable introduction and hiding helps us to cope with superficial conflicts. This is an important limitation for reduction, and interestingly, our standard notion of abstraction on the existing variables (Section 4.2) does not help in this situation. Our solution to eliminating the conflict is to hide the variables on which the conflict happens; but, differently from the standard abstraction, introducing new variables, which will carry enough (semantic) information from the hidden variables and will not cause conflicts.

6.1   Non-Blocking Queue

Figure 2 shows the version of the non-blocking queue [21] after applying a reduction phase on the original implementation. Atomic action Do_Dequeue removes an element from the queue, and Do_Enqueue appends a new element to the queue. The implementation is lazy in that Do_Enqueue does not update the Tail variable after adding the new node. As a result, at any time Tail may point to any node between Head and null. The actions labeled Move_Tail and Update_Tail try to move the Tail towards the end of the list. This resembles relaxed balancing in concurrent implementation of tree-like data structures, in which restructuring the data structure is separated from actual operations, and delayed.

The predicate Reach(next,k,l,m) expresses that, from node k, following zero or more next pointers, we first reach l and then m [23]. The Reach predicate gives us the ability to do simple abstractions on actions accessing the list nodes. For

Implementation (*Impl*)

```
record Node { data: int; next: Node; }
var Head, Tail: Node;

Dequeue() returns (x: int)
 var tail: Node;
 while(true) {
Move_Tail: atomic {
    havoc tail;
    assume Reach(next, Tail, tail, null)
            && tail != null;
    Tail := tail;
    }
} // end while
Do_Dequeue: atomic {
  if (Head.next == null) {
    x := null;
  } else {
    assume (Head != Tail);
    Head := Head.next;  x := Head.data;
  }
}
```

```
Enqueue(x: int)
  var node, tail: Node;
  atomic {
    node := new Node(x);
    node.next := null;
  }
  while(true) {
Move_Tail:atomic {
    havoc tail;
    assume Reach(next, Tail, tail, null)
              && tail != null;
    Tail := tail;
  }
} // end while
Do_Enqueue: atomic {
    assume (Tail.next == null);
    Tail.next := node;  tail := Tail;
}
Update_Tail: atomic {
    if (Tail == tail) Tail := node;
}
```

Specification (*Spec*)

```
atomic Dequeue() returns (x: int)
  if (Head.next == null) {
    return null;
  } else {
    Head := Head.next; x := Head.data;
  }
```

```
atomic Enqueue(x: int)
  node := new Node(x);
  node.next := null;
  _Tail.next := node;
  _Tail := _Tail.next;
```

Fig. 2. The reduced implementation of the non-blocking queue and its specification

example, a former abstraction step in the reduction phase replaces the action n
:= tail.next with the action havoc n; assume Reach(next,tail,n,n); while the
former is not mover, the latter is.

In order to apply reduction, the only option is to show that Move_Tail is
a right-mover, since Do_Enqueue and Do_Dequeue perform the actual operations,
thus are not movers. Move_Tail conflicts with Do_Enqueue and Do_Dequeue on Tail.
Notice that Move_Tail performs an internal operation that does not affect the
semantics of the queue. Thus, these conflicts are superficial. Havocing Tail in
the conflicting actions, or hiding Tail are a valid proof steps, and would make
reduction pass. However, the resulting code would perform incorrect operation.

We eliminate the conflict by coupling the hiding of Tail with introducing
the history variable _Tail of the same type. Differently from Tail, _Tail always
points to the end of the queue. We then associate the existing variables with the
new variable _Tail by the following invariant.

Reach(next, Head, Tail, Tail) && Reach(next, Tail, _Tail, null)
                        && (_Tail != null) && (_Tail.next == null)

In order to satisfy the invariant, we add to the end of Do_Enqueue the assignment _Tail := _Tail.next. Once there is _Tail to keep track of the end of the list,
we are ready to hide Tail. This is done by replacing the actions in the program
with actions that do not refer to Tail, but now uses _Tail to access the end of the
linked list. Figure 3 shows the version of the program after hiding Tail. Notice

```
record Node { data: int; next: Node; }          procedure Enqueue(x: int)
var Head, _Tail: Node;                            var node, tail: Node;
                                                  atomic {
procedure Dequeue()                                 node := new Node(x);
 var tail: Node;                                     node.next := null;
                                                  }
 while(true) {
Move_Tail: atomic { havoc tail; }                 while(true) {
 } // end while                                   Move_Tail: atomic { havoc tail; }
                                                  } // end while
Do_Dequeue: atomic {
  if (Head.next == null) {                        Do_Enqueue: atomic {
   x := null;                                       _Tail.next := node;
  } else {                                          _Tail := _Tail.next;
   Head := Head.next;  x := Head.data;              havoc tail;
  }                                               }
}                                                 Update_Tail: atomic { assume true; }
```

Fig. 3. The version of the non-blocking queue after hiding `Tail`

that the new form of `Move_Tail` does not perform any semantic operation in the new program, and does not conflict with other actions. In addition, the actions `Do_Enqueue` and `Do_Dequeue` now use `_Tail` to correctly perform their operations.

The hiding step also includes existentially quantifying `Tail` in the invariant given above. This produces the following invariant for the new program.

`Reach(next, Head, _Tail, null) && (_Tail != null) && (_Tail.next == null)`

We proceed with a reduction phase that combines the blocks into a single action for each operation. The combined operations, together with the above invariant (for simplicity, we omit parts of the representation invariant), give the correct behavior of a sequential queue implementation. Corollary 1 ensures that the original implementation in [21] is linearizable to this final program from the invariant. Note that it also possible to continue the proof with an extra refinement phase to prove the linearizability to a more generic specification of the queue.

References

1. Herlihy, M.P., Wing, J.M.: Linearizability: a correctness condition for concurrent objects. ACM Trans. Program. Lang. Syst. 12, 463–492 (1990)
2. Abadi, M., Lamport, L.: The existence of refinement mappings. Theor. Comput. Sci. 82, 253–284 (1991)
3. Park, S., Dill, D.L.: Protocol verification by aggregation of distributed transactions. In: Alur, R., Henzinger, T.A. (eds.) CAV 1996. LNCS, vol. 1102, pp. 300–310. Springer, Heidelberg (1996)
4. Elmas, T., Qadeer, S., Tasiran, S.: A calculus of atomic actions. In: POPL 2009: ACM Symposium on Principles of Programming Languages. ACM, New York (2009)
5. Vafeiadis, V.: Shape-value abstraction for verifying linearizability. In: Jones, N.D., Müller-Olm, M. (eds.) VMCAI 2009. LNCS, vol. 5403, pp. 335–348. Springer, Heidelberg (2009)

6. Hesselink, W.H.: Eternity variables to prove simulation of specifications. ACM Trans. Comput. Logic 6, 175–201 (2005)
7. Jonsson, B., Pnueli, A., Rump, C.: Proving refinement using transduction. Distrib. Comput. 12, 129–149 (1999)
8. Kesten, Y., Pnueli, A., Shahar, E., Zuck, L.D.: Network invariants in action. In: Brim, L., Jančar, P., Křetínský, M., Kucera, A. (eds.) CONCUR 2002. LNCS, vol. 2421, pp. 101–115. Springer, Heidelberg (2002)
9. Hendler, D., Shavit, N., Yerushalmi, L.: A scalable lock-free stack algorithm. In: SPAA 2004: ACM symposium on Parallelism in algorithms and architectures, pp. 206–215. ACM, New York (2004)
10. Gao, H., Groote, J.F., Hesselink, W.H.: Lock-free dynamic hash tables with open addressing. Distrib. Comput. 18, 21–42 (2005)
11. Colvin, R., Groves, L., Luchangco, V., Moir, M.: Formal verification of a lazy concurrent list-based set algorithm. In: Ball, T., Jones, R.B. (eds.) CAV 2006. LNCS, vol. 4144, pp. 475–488. Springer, Heidelberg (2006)
12. Owicki, S., Gries, D.: Verifying properties of parallel programs: an axiomatic approach. Commun. ACM 19, 279–285 (1976)
13. Vafeiadis, V., Herlihy, M., Hoare, T., Shapiro, M.: Proving correctness of highly-concurrent linearisable objects. In: PPoPP 2006 ACM Symposium on Principles and practice of parallel programming, pp. 129–136. ACM, New York (2006)
14. Amit, D., Rinetzky, N., Reps, T.W., Sagiv, M., Yahav, E.: Comparison under abstraction for verifying linearizability. In: Damm, W., Hermanns, H. (eds.) CAV 2007. LNCS, vol. 4590, pp. 477–490. Springer, Heidelberg (2007)
15. Wang, L., Stoller, S.D.: Static analysis for programs with non-blocking synchronization. In: ACM SIGPLAN 2005 Symposium on Principles and Practice of Parallel Programming (PPoPP). ACM Press, New York (2005)
16. Groves, L.: Verifying michael and scott's lock-free queue algorithm using trace reduction. In: CATS 2008: Symposium on Computing: the Australasian theory, Darlinghurst, Australia, pp. 133–142. Australian Computer Society, Inc. (2008)
17. Elmas, T., Sezgin, A., Tasiran, S., Qadeer, S.: An annotation assistant for interactive debugging of programs with common synchronization idioms. In: Workshop on Parallel and Distributed Systems: Testing, Analysis, and Debugging (2009)
18. Elmas, T., Qadeer, S., Sezgin, A., Subasi, O., Tasiran, S.: Simplifying the proof of linearizability with reduction and abstraction. Technical Report, Koc University (2009), http://theorem.ku.edu.tr/tacas10tr.pdf
19. Lipton, R.J.: Reduction: a method of proving properties of parallel programs. Commun. ACM 18, 717–721 (1975)
20. Treiber, R.K.: Systems programming: Coping with parallelism. rj5118 (1986)
21. Michael, M.M., Scott, M.L.: Simple, fast, and practical non-blocking and blocking concurrent queue algorithms. In: PODC 1996: ACM symposium on Principles of distributed computing, pp. 267–275. ACM, New York (1996)
22. Krieger, O., Stumm, M., Unrau, R., Hanna, J.: A fair fast scalable reader-writer lock. In: ICPP 1993: The International Conference on Parallel Processing, Washington, DC, USA, pp. 201–204. IEEE Computer Society, Los Alamitos (1993)
23. Lahiri, S., Qadeer, S.: Back to the future: revisiting precise program verification using smt solvers. In: POPL 2008: ACM symposium on Principles of programming languages, pp. 171–182. ACM, New York (2008)

A Polymorphic Intermediate Verification Language: Design and Logical Encoding

K. Rustan M. Leino[1] and Philipp Rümmer[2]

[1] Microsoft Research, Redmond
leino@microsoft.com
[2] Oxford University Computing Laboratory
philr@comlab.ox.ac.uk

Abstract. Intermediate languages are a paradigm to separate concerns in software verification systems when bridging the gap between programming languages and the logics understood by theorem provers. While such intermediate languages traditionally only offer rather simple type systems, this paper argues that it is both advantageous and feasible to integrate richer type systems with features like (higher-ranked) polymorphism and quantification over types. As a concrete solution, the paper presents the type system of Boogie 2, an intermediate verification language that is used in several program verifiers. The paper gives two encodings of types and formulae in simply typed logic such that SMT solvers and other theorem provers can be used to discharge verification conditions.

1 Introduction

Building a program verifier is a complex task that requires understanding of many domains. Designing its foundation draws from domains like semantics, specifications, and decision procedures, and constructing its implementation involves knowledge of compilers and software engineering. The task can be made manageable by breaking it into smaller pieces, each of which is simpler to understand. A successful practice (*e.g.*, [11,4,5]) is to make use of an *intermediate verification language* [16,1,10].

The intermediate verification language serves as a thinking tool in the design of the verifier front end for each particular source language. As such, it must provide a level of abstraction that is high enough to give leverage to the front end. At the same time, there is a risk that the general translations of higher-leverage features become too cumbersome to sustain good decision procedure performance. Some higher-leverage features, like a fancy type system, provide safety to the front end by restricting what intermediate programs are admissible. At the same time, there is a risk that such restrictions lead to cumbersome encodings in the front end, especially compared to the encodings that are possible by directly using the more coarse-grained type system of a decision procedure.

In this paper, we introduce the type system of the intermediate verification language *Boogie 2* developed by the authors, the successor of BoogiePL [8,1]. Unlike its untyped predecessor, whose type annotations were mainly used for some consistency checks, Boogie 2 features an actual type system. Going beyond the Hindley-Milner style types in the intermediate verification language Why [10], Boogie 2 features polymorphic

J. Esparza and R. Majumdar (Eds.): TACAS 2010, LNCS 6015, pp. 312–327, 2010.

maps, higher-rank polymorphism, and impredicativity, which are useful in modeling the semantics of a type-safe object store (as in Spec# or Java).

In addition to introducing the polymorphic features of Boogie, we describe our translation of Boogie's polymorphic logic into simply typed logic, which is used by many satisfiability modulo theories (SMT) solvers that support the SMT-LIB format [2]. In fact, we give two different translations into simply typed logic, and we present performance figures from substantial benchmarks that compare these. The benchmarks come from the Spec# program verifier [1], the VCC [5] and HAVOC [4] verifiers for C, and Dafny [14], all of which build on Boogie. All of the benchmarks make extensive use of so-called triggers required for e-matching [9], and our experiments give evidence to that the triggers are properly maintained by our translations.

The contributions of our work are: (i) An impredicative type system for an intermediate verification language, featuring full higher-ranked polymorphism, (ii) two translations of the verification language, and especially its polymorphic maps, into simply typed logic suitable for SMT solvers, (iii) experimental data comparing the performance of the two translations with each other and with an (unsound) translation ignoring types.

2   Boogie 2 Types and Expressions

A Boogie program consists of a set of mathematical and imperative declarations that define a set of execution sequences. The Boogie program is correct if none of those execution sequences contains an error state [13]. Programs can be written by hand, but most Boogie programs are machine generated by various program verifiers to encode the semantics of given source programs. For example, the source-language declaration in Fig. 1 can be modeled in Boogie as shown in Fig. 2, where the object store is represented explicitly by a variable *Heap* whose type is a map from object references and field names to values (we explain this example in more detail later).

For the purposes of this paper, one can think of the imperative features of Boogie as convenient syntactic shorthands for writing Boogie expressions. Hence, we focus on Boogie's expressions and their types. For further details of the language, we refer to the Boogie 2 language reference manual [13].

2.1   Type Declarations

The built-in types of Boogie are booleans (**bool**), mathematical integers (**int**), and bit-vector types of every size (**bv0, bv1, bv2,** ...). In addition, there are map types, which we describe below, and user-defined type constructors. A program can also declare parameterized *type synonyms*, which are essentially like macros, thus providing syntactic convenience but not adding to the expressiveness of the type system. A type denotes a nonempty set of individuals, and the sets denoted by different types are disjoint. Each different parameterization of a type constructor yields a distinct type, each denoting an uninterpreted set of individuals. For example, the type declarations in Fig. 2 introduce a nullary type constructor *Ref* and a unary type constructor *Field*. The sets of individuals denoted by *Ref*, *Field* **int**, and *Field Ref* are all disjoint.

```
class Person { int age; bool isMarried; }
```

Fig. 1. An example code snippet from a source program

type *Ref*;   **const unique** *age* : *Field* **int**;
type *Field* α;   **const unique** *isMarried* : *Field* **bool**;
type *HeapType* $= \langle\alpha\rangle[Ref, Field\ \alpha]\ \alpha$;   **var** *Heap* : *HeapType*;
function *IsWellFormed*(*HeapType*) **returns** (**bool**);
const unique *snapshot* : *Field HeapType*;

Fig. 2. An example of how object-oriented program features, like those in Fig. 1, can be modeled in Boogie (the language features used are introduced in detail in Section 2). *Ref* is a type and *Field* is a unary type constructor. Type synonym *HeapType* is defined as the polymorphic map type that represents the heap. *IsWellFormed* demonstrates that functions can take polymorphic maps as arguments. For any *r* of type *Ref*, *Heap*[*r*, *snapshot*] has type *HeapType*, illustrating that polymorphic maps can be arbitrarily nested (an instance of impredicativity). The modifier **unique** is used to say that the constant declared has a different value than all other **unique** constants, which for the 3 constants here also follows from the fact that their types are different.

2.2 Expressions

Boogie expressions include variables and constants, function applications, logical, arithmetic, and relational operators, as well as logical quantifiers, type coercions, and map operations. All expressions are total: every well-typed expression yields some appropriately typed value that is a function of its subexpressions. For the most part, typing of expressions is obvious and straightforward. Let us describe the more salient features.

Polymorphic Functions, Quantifications over Types. Functions can be polymorphic, that is, they can take type parameters. Analogously, the bound variables in universal and existential quantifiers can range over both individuals (of specified types) and types. Polymorphism is useful because it allows a user to provide an axiomatization of, say, pairs that is independent of the pair element types, while maintaining the type guarantee that different types of pairs are not mixed up.

For example, Fig. 3 declares a binary type constructor *Pair*, along with a function *Cons* for constructing a pair and a function *Left* that extracts the left element of a pair. Type parameters and bound type variables are introduced inside angle brackets, like in C# or Java. A function declaration in Boogie only defines the signature of the function; properties of functions can be defined by axioms. The figure includes an axiom that defines the relationship between *Cons* and *Left*. Note that the quantification is over any element types α and β and any elements a and b of those types. Hence, the axiom applies generically to pairs with any element types.

The meaning of a function depends on its type-parameter instantiation. That is, a polymorphic function f is really a family of functions $\bar{f}$, one for each possible instantiation (*e.g.*, f_{int}, f_{Ref}).

Type Coercions. Boogie infers instantiations for type parameters of function applications. Usually, they can be inferred from the types of the function's arguments, but

type *Pair* α β;
function $Cons\langle\alpha,\beta\rangle(\alpha,\beta)$ **returns** $(Pair\ \alpha\ \beta)$;
function $Left\langle\alpha,\beta\rangle(Pair\ \alpha\ \beta)$ **returns** (α);
axiom $(\forall\,\langle\alpha,\beta\rangle\ a\colon\alpha,\ b\colon\beta\bullet Left(Cons(a,b))=a\ )$;

type *Sequence* α;
function $Length\langle\alpha\rangle(Sequence\ \alpha)$ **returns** (**int**);
function $EmptySequence\langle\alpha\rangle()$ **returns** $(Sequence\ \alpha)$;
axiom $(\forall\,\langle\alpha\rangle\bullet Length(EmptySequence()\colon Sequence\ \alpha)=0\ )$;

Fig. 3. Examples of polymorphic functions and quantifications over types in Boogie. In the last line, the quantifier ranges only over types, not over any individuals, and the type coercion makes the application *EmptySequence*() well-typed.

sometimes it is also necessary to consider the context of the function application. In particular, if a type parameter is used among the domain types in the function's signature, then its instantiation in a function application can be inferred from the arguments. But in the case that a type parameter is used only in the return type, then type inference needs to consult the context. Type parameters that are not used in either the domain types or the result type are not allowed.

For example, Fig. 3 declares a function that gives the length of a generic sequence. Function *EmptySequence* returns a zero-length sequence of any type. Type parameter α is used only in the return type of *EmptySequence*, which is common and useful for this and similar functions. Hence, to infer the type parameter in an application *EmptySequence*(), the context surrounding the application must be used.

An error is reported if an instantiation for type parameters cannot be determined uniquely. To deal with such cases, the language offers a type coercion expression $e : t$, which has type t, provided t is a possible typing for expression e. For example, the expression $Length(EmptySequence())$ is ill-formed because of the ambiguous type-parameter instantiation; but with the type coercion in Fig. 3, the ambiguity is resolved.

Because the meaning of a polymorphic function is really that of a family of functions, note that $EmptySequence_{\mathbf{int}}()$ has a different value than $EmptySequence_{Ref}()$.

Maps. In addition to functions, Boogie offers *maps*. Like functions, maps have a list of domain types and a result type and can be polymorphic. The difference is that maps are themselves expressions (they are "first class"), unlike functions, which can appear in an expression only when applied to arguments. This means that program variables can hold maps (like *Heap* in Fig. 2).

Though they may have the appearance of higher-order values, maps are but first-order individuals, and to "apply" them to arguments, one applies Boogie's built-in map-select operator, written with square brackets (to be suggestive of retrieving an element at a given index of an array) [19]. For example, if m is a map of type $[\mathbf{int},\mathbf{bool}]Ref$, that is, a map type with domain types **int** and **bool** and result type Ref, then the expression $m[5,\mathbf{false}]$ denotes a value of type Ref. Due to maps, Boogie can in many situations be used like a higher-order language (where functions can be passed around as values), but still allows the use of efficient first-order reasoners.

If m is an expression denoting a map, i is a list of expressions whose types correspond to the domain types of m, and x is an expression of the result type of m, then the map-update expression $m[i := x]$ denotes the map that is like m, except that it maps i to x [19]. Using common notation for arrays, the imperative part of Boogie allows the assignment statement $m[i] := x$; as a shorthand for $m := m[i := x]$;.

Boogie does not promise *extensionality* of maps, that is, the property that maps with all the same elements are equal; for example, m and $m[i := m[i]]$ are not provably equal, but they are provably equal at all values of the domains. From our experience, extensionality is not required for most applications; the motivation to exclude extensionality by default is the better performance of decision procedures for non-extensional maps. Where extensionality is needed, users can supply the required axioms themselves.

A novel and key feature of maps in Boogie is that they can be polymorphic. To motivate this feature, let us consider one of the most important modeling decisions that the designer of a program verifier faces: how to model the memory operated on by the source language. For example, for a type-safe object-oriented language, one may choose to model the object store (the *heap*) as a two-dimensional map from object references and field names to values [23,1,14]. Since the result type of such a map depends on the selected field name, it is natural to declare the heap to be of a polymorphic map type. (Without polymorphic maps, one either needs to introduce explicit cast functions or split the one heap variable into several.)

As we already alluded to, Fig. 2 shows by example some Boogie declarations that a verifier might use to encode the semantics of the object-oriented program in Fig. 1 (*cf.* [1,14]). In the example, *Ref* is used to denote the type of all object references, *Field* α denotes the type of field names that in the heap retrieve values of type α, and $\langle \alpha \rangle [Ref, Field\ \alpha]\ \alpha$ is the polymorphic map type of the heap itself. For instance, if r is a reference, then $Heap[r, age]$ is an integer and $Heap[r, isMarried]$ is a boolean.

Boogie's type system allows advanced uses of polymorphic maps, which is useful for the kind of semantic models one defines in a program verifier. For example, it is common to want to define properties of heaps, for example distinguishing heaps that satisfy some sort of well-formedness condition from heaps that do not. A natural way to do that is to start by defining a function on heaps, like *IsWellFormed* in Fig. 2. This is an example of a higher-rank type.

Type parameters of maps are like those of functions: each type parameter must be used in either the domain types or the result type of the map type, and it is an error if type inference cannot uniquely determine the instantiations of type parameters. And as for functions, a polymorphic map is really a family of maps, one for each possible type-parameter instantiation. For example, a map m of type $\langle \alpha \rangle [int] \alpha$ really denotes a family of maps $\bar{m}$, and $m_{int}[E]$ has a different value than $m_{bool}[E]$. It should also be noted that the types $[\alpha]\ T$ and $\langle \alpha \rangle [\alpha]\ T$ are different: the first is a type with a free type parameter α and can be instantiated to any (monomorphic) map type $[s]\ T$, while the second describes polymorphic maps from *any* type to T.

Equality among map types does not depend on the names or order of type parameters. For example, the type $\langle \alpha, \beta \rangle [\alpha, \beta] int$ is equal to $\langle \gamma, \delta \rangle [\delta, \gamma] int$. Polymorphism, however, is significant: the types $[int] \mathbf{bool}$ and $\langle \alpha \rangle [\alpha] \mathbf{bool}$ are incompatible.

Equality. Equality in Boogie is standard mathematical equality, but the typing of equality expressions in Boogie is more liberal than is absolutely the standard. The equality expression $E = F$ is allowed if there is some instantiation of enclosing type parameters that makes the types of E and F equal. Let us motivate this typing rule.

A common way to specify the effects of a source-language procedure is to use a **modifies** clause that lists the object-field locations in the heap that the procedure is allowed to modify. The **modifies** clause is then encoded into Boogie as a procedure postcondition that specifies a relation between the procedure's heap on entry, written $\mathbf{old}(Heap)$, and its heap on return, written $Heap$ (see, *e.g.*, [14]). For instance, to encode that a procedure's effect on the heap in the source language is limited to $p.age$ and $p.isMarried$, one can in Boogie use a postcondition like

$$(\forall \langle \alpha \rangle \; r \colon \mathit{Ref}, \; f \colon \mathit{Field} \; \alpha \; \bullet \; Heap[r, f] = \mathbf{old}(Heap[r, f]) \; \vee$$
$$(r = p \wedge f = age) \vee (r = p \wedge f = isMarried) \;)$$

In order to type check this expression, it is necessary for the type system to consider the possible instantiation $\alpha := \mathbf{int}$ for $f = age$ and $\alpha := \mathbf{bool}$ for $f = isMarried$, and Boogie does exactly that. Being liberal in this typing rule does not cause any semantic problems in Boogie: because different types represent disjoint sets of individuals, an equation simply evaluates to **false** if the two sides of the equation evaluate to individuals of different types. For example, for the f in the quantifier above, $f = age \wedge f = isMarried$ type checks but always evaluates to **false**.

2.3   Formalization of the Type System and Type Checking

The abstract syntactic category of types is described by the following grammar:

$$Type \; ::= \; \alpha \; | \; C \; Type^* \; | \; \langle \alpha^* \rangle \, [Type^*] \, Type$$

in which $C \in \mathcal{C}$ ranges over type constructors (with a fixed arity $arity(C)$) and $\alpha \in \mathcal{A}$ over an infinite set of type variables. We assume that $\mathcal{C}$ always contains the pre-defined nullary constructors $\mathbf{bool}, \mathbf{int}, \mathbf{bv0}, \mathbf{bv1}, \mathbf{bv2}, \ldots$ Only those types are well-formed in which type constructors receive the correct number of argument types, and in which type parameters of polymorphic map types occur in the map domain or result types.

For two types $s, t \in Type$, we write $s \equiv t$ iff s and t are equal modulo renaming or reordering of bound type parameters. A *type substitution* is a mapping $\sigma : \mathcal{A} \to Type$ from type variables to types. Substitutions are canonically extended on all types, assuming that variable capture is avoided by renaming bound type variables when necessary.

Formalizing the typing of expressions, the judgment $\mathcal{V} \Vdash E : t$ says that in a context with variable-type bindings $\mathcal{V}$, expression E can be typed as type t. Figure 4 shows the most important typing rules. All other operators are typed as in the rule for function application. In the figure and the whole paper, $\mathcal{F}$ denotes the set of declared functions and constants, whereas $\mathcal{X}$ denotes an infinite set of variables.

Note that for any type-correct program, all type-parameter instantiations have been resolved. But this does not mean that the application of a polymorphic function or map can easily be replaced by a specific monomorphic instance, because of quantifications over types. For example, the application of $EmptySequence$ in Fig. 3 is resolved to $EmptySequence_\alpha$, but α is a quantified type variable that refers to any type; hence, the axiom says something about every member of the $EmptySequence$ family.

$$\frac{x \mapsto t \in \mathcal{V}}{\mathcal{V} \Vdash x : t} \qquad \frac{\mathcal{V} \Vdash E : t}{\mathcal{V} \Vdash E{:}t : t}$$

$$\frac{f\langle\bar{\alpha}\rangle(\bar{s}) \textbf{ returns } (t) \in \mathcal{F}}{\mathcal{V} \Vdash E_i : \sigma(s_i) \quad (\text{for } (E_i, s_i) \in (\bar{E}, \bar{s}))}{\mathcal{V} \Vdash f(\bar{E}) : \sigma(t)} \ *$$

$$\frac{\mathcal{V} \Vdash E : s \qquad \mathcal{V} \Vdash F : t}{\sigma(s) \equiv \sigma(t)}{\mathcal{V} \Vdash E = F : \textbf{bool}}$$

$$\frac{(\mathcal{V}, \bar{x} \mapsto \bar{t}) \Vdash E : \textbf{bool} \qquad Q \in \{\forall, \exists\}}{\mathcal{V} \Vdash (Q \langle\bar{\alpha}\rangle \, \bar{x} : \bar{t} \bullet E) : \textbf{bool}}$$

$$\frac{\mathcal{V} \Vdash m : \langle\bar{\alpha}\rangle[\bar{s}]t}{\mathcal{V} \Vdash E_i : \sigma(s_i) \quad (\text{for } (E_i, s_i) \in (\bar{E}, \bar{s}))}{\mathcal{V} \Vdash m[\bar{E}] : \sigma(t)} \ *$$

$$\frac{\mathcal{V} \Vdash m : \langle\bar{\alpha}\rangle[\bar{s}]t \qquad \mathcal{V} \Vdash F : \sigma(t)}{\mathcal{V} \Vdash E_i : \sigma(s_i) \quad (\text{for } (E_i, s_i) \in (\bar{E}, \bar{s}))}{\mathcal{V} \Vdash m[\bar{E} := F] : \langle\bar{\alpha}\rangle[\bar{s}]t} \ *$$

Fig. 4. The typing rules for Boogie expressions. The context of type judgments is a partial mapping $\mathcal{V} : \mathcal{X} \rightharpoonup \textit{Type}$ that assigns types to variables. The rules marked with '*' impose the side condition $dom(\sigma) = \{\bar{\alpha}\}$. The typing rules show what it means for expressions to be type correct; they abstract over how type inference is done.

2.4 Matching Triggers

We have one more thing to say about expressions in Boogie, and it concerns the way many SMT solvers handle universal quantifications, namely by selective instantiation. Instantiations are based on (user-supplied or inferred) *matching triggers*, which indicate which patterns of ground terms in the prover's state are to give rise to instantiations [9]. Boogie has support for specifying matching triggers for quantifications. For example,

axiom $(\forall x : t \bullet \{f(x)\} \, fInverse(f(x)) = x)$;

specifies the trigger $f(x)$ and says to instantiate the universally quantified variable with any value appearing among the ground terms as an argument of function f. In an SMT solver based solely on triggers, these are the only instantiations there will ever be. All Boogie front ends make heavy use of triggers. (For an application that uses quantifiers and an explanation of the design of triggers for that application, see [15].)

A trigger is a set of expressions, each of which will undergo the encoding into the underlying logic that we are about to describe. However, it is important that the logical encoding not interfere with user-defined triggers or automatically inferred triggers, since that might lead to poor performance (too many instantiations) or incompleteness (too few instantiations).

3   Representation of Types as Terms

Automated theorem provers and SMT solvers typically offer only untyped or simple multi-sorted logics as their input language (with the notable exception of Alt-Ergo [3], which provides a polymorphic type system). With such a prover as the verification back end, the expressions from the richer language have to be translated into the simpler logic. We describe two approaches to this translation in Section 4: one that captures type information using logical guards and one that encodes type parameters of polymorphic functions as additional function arguments. In both cases, it is necessary to encode

Boogie's types as terms (so that typing conditions can be expressed as formulae), which is the subject of this section.

As a simply typed target language, we use a subset of the Boogie expression language, restricting the available types to (i) the built-in types **bool** and **int** (other types supported directly by the simply typed logic can be treated analogously to **int**), (ii) a type U for (non-**bool**, non-**int**) individuals, and (iii) a type T for (encoded) types. If necessary, expressions in this simply-typed language could be translated further to an untyped logic by adding domain predicates and guards for the types **bool**, **int**, U, and T. Because current SMT solvers are able to directly handle the four types, however, such a translation will usually not be required. Furthermore, we introduce a function symbol $type : U \rightarrow T$ that maps individuals to their type.

We encode types so that T forms an algebraic datatype. If the target logic has direct support for algebraic datatypes, one may be able to build on it; in the scope of this paper, we use functions and axioms to describe the encoding.

3.1 Type Constructors

Each type constructor $C \in \mathcal{C}$ gives rise to a function symbol $C^\# : T^{arity(C)} \rightarrow T$, as well as an axiomatization of a number of properties, including distinctness and injectivity. To formalize that the images of different type-constructor functions $C^\#$ are disjoint, we introduce a function $Ctor: T \rightarrow \textbf{int}$ and, for each type constructor C, a unique constant n_C. Injectivity is achieved by defining selector functions $C^{-1}, \ldots, C^{-n} : T \rightarrow T$ for each n-ary type constructor C:

$$(\forall \bar{x}: T \bullet Ctor(C^\#(\bar{x})) = n_C) \wedge \bigwedge_{i=1}^{arity(C)} (\forall \bar{x}: T \bullet C^{-i}(C^\#(\bar{x})) = x_i)$$

Theoretically, further axioms are needed for a faithful model of the type system. However, because these additional axioms are of a kind that cannot be expected to be useful for SMT solvers (e.g., statements about well-foundedness), we practically use only the axioms shown above in the Boogie implementation.

3.2 Reduction of Map Types to Ordinary Type Constructors

The encoding of Boogie's polymorphic map types is done by a reduction to normal type constructors: a map type t containing the free type variables $\alpha_1, \ldots, \alpha_n$ (and arbitrary bound variables) can be encoded like a type expression $C_t \alpha_1, \ldots, \alpha_n$, for some fresh constructor C_t. The access functions can then be seen and axiomatized as ordinary functions $select_t$, $store_t$, based on the axioms of the first-order theory of arrays [19].

There is a caveat in this construction: if two map types s, t have common instances $u = \sigma_s(s) = \sigma_t(t)$, then an encoding of u using either C_s or C_t will be overly restrictive. In particular, it might happen that u is encoded as C_s in one part, and as C_t in another part of the same formula, leading to incompleteness:

> **function** $f\langle\alpha\rangle(\alpha)$ **returns** (**int**);
> **axiom** $(\forall \langle\alpha\rangle\ m: [\alpha]\ \textbf{int} \bullet f(m) = 0)$; **axiom** $(\forall \langle\alpha\rangle\ m: [\textbf{int}]\ \alpha \bullet f(m) = 1)$;

If $s = [\alpha]$ **int** in the first axiom happens to be encoded as $C_s\,\alpha$, and $t = [\textbf{int}]\,\alpha$ in the second axiom as $C_t\,\alpha$, then the inconsistency of the two axioms will be lost: $C_s\,\alpha$ and $C_t\,\alpha$ do not have any common instances. The solution is to define larger classes of type constructors for map types: we abstract over map types and define constructors only for "most general" map types. Let us be more precise.

Given two types $s, t \in \textit{Type}$, we write $t \sqsubseteq s$ and say that t is an *instance* of s iff there is a substitution σ such that $\sigma(s) \equiv t$. Observe that $\sqsubseteq$ is a pre-order on types, but not a partial order because anti-symmetry is violated for types that differ only in the names of free variables. The induced equivalence relation is denoted with $\cong$: for $s, t \in \textit{Type}$, we define $s \cong t$ iff $s \sqsubseteq t$ and $t \sqsubseteq s$. It is the case that $\equiv\ \subseteq\ \cong$.

The pre-order $\sqsubseteq$ is canonically extended to $\textit{Type}\,C = \textit{Type}\,/\!\cong$ and partially orders the set. In fact, $(\textit{Type}\,C, \sqsubseteq)$ is a join-semi-lattice (*i.e.*, any two types have a least common upper bound) whose $\top$-element is the class of type variables α. The strict order $\sqsubset$ satisfies the *ascending chain condition (ACC)*: every ascending chain of types in $\textit{Type}\,C$ eventually becomes stationary. This is important, because it justifies the existence of most-general map types that are the basis for our map-type encoding.

Let $\mathcal{M}_C \subseteq \textit{Type}\,C$ be the set of $\sqsubseteq$-maximal type classes whose elements start with the map type constructor, and let $\mathcal{M}$ be a set of unique representatives for all classes in $\mathcal{M}_C$. The elements of $\mathcal{M}$ can be seen as skeletons of map types and determine the binding and occurrences of bound type variables. Examples of types in $\mathcal{M}$ are:

$$[\alpha]\,\beta \qquad [\alpha, \beta]\,\gamma \qquad [\alpha, \beta, \gamma]\,\delta \qquad \langle\alpha\rangle[\alpha]\,\alpha \qquad \langle\alpha\rangle[\alpha]\,\beta \qquad \langle\alpha\rangle[\alpha]\,(C\,\alpha)$$

For every type t that starts with a map type constructor, there is a unique type $m = \mathrm{skel}(t) \in \mathcal{M}$ with $t \sqsubseteq m$. For example, $\mathrm{skel}(\langle\alpha\rangle[C\,\alpha, \textbf{int}]\textbf{bool}) = \langle\alpha\rangle[C\,\alpha, \beta]\gamma$. This means that every map type t (also types containing free variables) can be represented in the form $\sigma(\mathrm{skel}(t))$, whereby the substitution σ is uniquely determined for all variables that occur free in $\mathrm{skel}(t)$. We write $\mathrm{flesh}(t)$ for the unique substitution satisfying $\mathrm{flesh}(t)(\mathrm{skel}(t)) = t$ whose domain is a subset of $\{\alpha_1, \ldots, \alpha_n\}$, where $\alpha_1, \ldots, \alpha_n$ are the free variables in $\mathrm{skel}(t)$. For example, $\mathrm{flesh}(\langle\alpha\rangle[C\,\alpha, \textbf{int}]\textbf{bool}) = (\beta \mapsto \textbf{int}, \gamma \mapsto \textbf{bool})$.

Translation of Types to Terms. In order to encode types, for each type $t \in \mathcal{M}$ that contains n free type variables $\alpha_1, \ldots, \alpha_n$, we introduce a new n-ary function symbol $\textsc{m}_t^{\#} : T^n \to T$. We will use the notation $\mathrm{Skel}^{\#}(s) := \textsc{m}_{\mathrm{skel}(s)}^{\#}$ for the skeleton symbol of an arbitrary map type s, and $\mathrm{Skel}^{-i}(s) := \textsc{m}_{\mathrm{skel}(s)}^{-i}$ for the selectors. Given an instantiation $\mu : \mathcal{A} \to \textit{Term}$ of type variables, types can then be translated to terms:

$$[\![\alpha]\!]_{\mu} = \mu(\alpha) \qquad\qquad [\![C\,t_1 \ldots t_n]\!]_{\mu} = C^{\#}([\![t_1]\!]_{\mu}, \ldots, [\![t_n]\!]_{\mu})$$
$$[\![m]\!]_{\mu} = \mathrm{Skel}^{\#}(m)([\![\mathrm{flesh}(m)(\beta_1)]\!]_{\mu}, \ldots, [\![\mathrm{flesh}(m)(\beta_n)]\!]_{\mu})$$

In the last equation, m is a map type $\langle\bar{\alpha}\rangle[\bar{s}]\,t$ such that $\mathrm{skel}(m)$ contains the free type variables $\beta_1, \ldots, \beta_n$ (in this order of occurrence). Some examples are:

$$[\![C\,T]\!]_{\mu} = C^{\#}(T^{\#}) \qquad\qquad [\![[\textbf{int}]\,T]\!]_{\mu} = \textsc{m}_{[\alpha]\beta}^{\#}(\textit{int}^{\#}, T^{\#})$$
$$[\![[T]\,S]\!]_{\mu} = \textsc{m}_{[\alpha]\beta}^{\#}(T^{\#}, S^{\#}) \qquad\qquad [\![\langle\alpha\rangle[\alpha]\,S]\!]_{\mu} = \textsc{m}_{\langle\alpha\rangle[\alpha]\beta}^{\#}(S^{\#})$$

Symbols and Axioms of Maps with Map Reduction. The access functions *select* and *store* can be seen and axiomatized as ordinary functions, based on the axioms of the first-order theory of arrays [19]. For each map type $m \in \mathcal{M}$, we introduce separate symbols $select_m$ and $store_m$. Suppose that $m = \langle \bar{\alpha} \rangle [\bar{s}]\, t \in \mathcal{M}$ contains the free type variables $\bar{\beta} = (\beta_1, \ldots, \beta_n)$ (in this order of occurrence). Then, the access functions have the following types:

$$select_m \langle \bar{\alpha}, \bar{\beta} \rangle (m, \bar{s}) \textbf{ returns } (t) \qquad store_m \langle \bar{\alpha}, \bar{\beta} \rangle (m, \bar{s}, t) \textbf{ returns } (m)$$

It is necessary to include both $\bar{\alpha}$ and $\bar{\beta}$ as type parameters, because m is parametric in the latter, and $\bar{s}$ and t might be parametric in both. The semantics of maps is defined by axioms similar to the standard axioms of non-extensional arrays [19] ($\bar{\alpha}'$ is a vector of fresh type variables, and $\bar{\alpha} \mapsto \bar{\alpha}'$ the substitution that replaces $\bar{\alpha}$ with $\bar{\alpha}'$):

$$(\forall \langle \bar{\alpha}, \bar{\beta} \rangle\ h\colon m,\ \bar{x}\colon \bar{s},\ z\colon t \bullet\ select_m(store_m(h, \bar{x}, z), \bar{x}) = z\ ) \wedge$$
$$(\forall \langle \bar{\alpha}, \bar{\alpha}', \bar{\beta} \rangle\ h\colon m,\ \bar{x}\colon \bar{s},\ \bar{y}\colon (\bar{\alpha} \mapsto \bar{\alpha}')\bar{s},\ z\colon t \bullet$$
$$\bar{x} = \bar{y} \vee select_m(store_m(h, \bar{x}, z), \bar{y}) = select_m(h, \bar{y})\ )$$

4   Translation of Expressions

We define two main approaches to translating typed Boogie expressions into equivalent simply typed expressions: one that captures type information using logical guards (Section 4.1) and one that encodes type parameters of polymorphic functions as ordinary (additional) arguments (Section 4.2). The second encoding relies on the usage of e-matching to instantiate quantifiers (in contrast to methods like superposition used in first-order theorem provers), because typing information is generated such that triggers can only match on expressions of the right type (also see [6]).

The following Boogie program is used as running example for the translations:

function $Mojo\langle \alpha \rangle (\alpha)$ **returns** (**int**); **axiom** $(\forall x\colon \textbf{int} \bullet Mojo(x) = x\ )$;
type *GuitarPlayer*; **axiom** $(\forall g\colon GuitarPlayer \bullet Mojo(g) = 68\ )$;

Note that it is essential to take the types of the quantified variables into account to not introduce inconsistent axioms.

4.1   Translation Using Type Guards

There is a long tradition of encoding type information using type guards, *e.g.*, [17,6,7]. As this translation is rather naive and has the disadvantage of complicating the propositional structure of formulae, it has been claimed [6] that its performance impact is prohibitive for many applications. We are able to show in Section 5, however, that this is no longer the case with state-of-the-art SMT solvers.

The Mojo example is complemented with type guards as follows. Because the quantified formulae are now guarded and only concern individuals of the right types, no contradiction is introduced. The function $i2u$ is defined below.

function $Mojo^{\#}(U)$ **returns** (U);   **const** $GuitarPlayer^{\#}\colon T$;
axiom $(\forall x\colon U \bullet type(Mojo^{\#}(x)) = int^{\#}\ )$;   // function axiom
axiom $(\forall x\colon U \bullet type(x) = int^{\#} \Rightarrow Mojo^{\#}(x) = x\ )$;
axiom $(\forall g\colon U \bullet type(g) = GuitarPlayer^{\#} \Rightarrow Mojo^{\#}(g) = i2u(68)\ )$;

Function Axioms. During the translation, user-defined Boogie functions are replaced with U-typed functions. For a function $f\langle\alpha_1,\ldots,\alpha_m\rangle(s_1,\ldots,s_n)$ **returns** (t) such that $\alpha_1,\ldots,\alpha_k$ do not occur in $s_1,\ldots,s_n$ (but only in t), while $\alpha_{k+1},\ldots,\alpha_m$ occur in $s_1,\ldots,s_n$ (and possibly in t), this post-translation function $f^{\#}$ has the type $T^k \times U^n \to U$. We will capture the original typing with an axiom of the shape:

$$(\forall \bar{x}\colon \bar{U}, \bar{y}\colon \bar{T} \bullet \ type(f^{\#}(\bar{y},\bar{x})) = [\![t]\!]_\mu) \tag{1}$$

This axiom does not contain any quantifiers corresponding to $\alpha_{k+1},\ldots,\alpha_m$ that occur in $s_1,\ldots,s_n$, which is advantageous for SMT solvers because the formula does not offer good triggers for $\alpha_{k+1},\ldots,\alpha_m$. Instead, the mapping $\mu : \mathcal{A} \to \mathit{Term}$ that determines the values of type parameters plays a prominent role. We define this mapping using *extractor terms*, which are recursively defined over types and describe how the type parameter values can be reconstructed from the actual arguments $\bar{x}$ with the help of the selector functions C^{-i} defined in Section 3.1.

Suppose that $\alpha \in \mathcal{A}$ is a type variable. Assuming that the term E encodes the type $t \in \mathit{Type}$, the set $\mathit{extractors}_\alpha(E, t)$ specifies terms that compute α's value:

$$\mathit{extractors}_\alpha(E, \beta) = \textbf{if } \alpha = \beta \textbf{ then } \{E\} \textbf{ else } \emptyset$$
$$\mathit{extractors}_\alpha(E,\, C\, t_1 \ldots t_n) = \textstyle\bigcup_{i=1}^n \mathit{extractors}_\alpha(C^{-i}(E),\ t_i) \qquad (C \in \mathcal{C})$$
$$\mathit{extractors}_\alpha(E, m) = \textstyle\bigcup_{i=1}^n \mathit{extractors}_\alpha(\mathrm{Skel}^{-i}(m)(E),\ \mathrm{flesh}(m)(\gamma_i))$$

In the last equation, m is a map type $\langle\bar{\beta}\rangle[\bar{s}]\, t$ such that $\mathit{skel}(m)$ contains the free type variables $\gamma_1,\ldots,\gamma_n$ (in this order of occurrence). Some examples are:

$$\mathit{extractors}_\alpha(x,\, C\, \beta\, \alpha) = \{C^{-2}(x)\}$$
$$\mathit{extractors}_\alpha(x,\, \langle\beta\rangle[C\,\beta\,\alpha]\,\alpha) = \{C^{-2}(\mathrm{M}^{-1}_{\langle\beta\rangle[C\,\beta\,\gamma]\,\delta}(x)),\ \mathrm{M}^{-2}_{\langle\beta\rangle[C\,\beta\,\gamma]\,\delta}(x)\}$$

The extractor $C^{-2}(x)$, for instance, can derive α's value from the instance C **int bool** of $C\,\beta\,\alpha$, resulting in $C^{-2}([\![C\text{ int bool}]\!]) = C^{-2}(C^{\#}(\textbf{int}^{\#}, \textbf{bool}^{\#})) = \textbf{bool}^{\#}$.

A simple optimization (that is implemented in Boogie but left out from this paper for reasons of presentation) is to keep argument or result types **int** and **bool** of functions, instead of replacing them with U. This can reduce the number of casts to and from U later needed in the translation.

Embedding of Built-in Types. SMT solvers offer built-in types like booleans, integers, and bit vectors, whose usage is crucial for performance. We define casts to and from the type U in order to integrate built-in types into our framework. For the built-in types **bool** and **int**, we introduce the cast functions $i2u : \textbf{int} \to U$, $u2i : U \to \textbf{int}$, $b2u : \textbf{bool} \to U$, $u2b : U \to \textbf{bool}$ and axiomatize them as:

$$(\forall x\colon \textbf{int} \bullet \ type(i2u(x)) = int^{\#} \wedge u2i(i2u(x)) = x\,) \wedge$$
$$(\forall x\colon U \bullet \ type(x) = int^{\#} \Rightarrow i2u(u2i(x)) = x\,)$$

and analogously for **bool**. The axioms imply that $i2u$ and $b2u$ are embeddings into U, and that $u2i$ and $u2b$ are their inverses. For simplicity, in the following translation we insert casts in each place where operators over **bool** or **int** occur, although many of the casts could directly be eliminated using the axioms. Such optimizations are present in the Boogie implementation as well.

Translation of Expressions. Given an instantiation $\mu : \mathcal{A} \to \textit{Term}$ of type variables, the main cases of the translation are:

$$
\begin{aligned}
[\![x]\!]_\mu &= x && (x \in \mathcal{X}) \\
[\![f(E_1, \dots, E_n)]\!]_\mu &= f^\#([\![E_1]\!]_\mu, \dots, [\![E_n]\!]_\mu) \\
[\![E = F]\!]_\mu &= b2u([\![E]\!]_\mu = [\![F]\!]_\mu) \\
[\![E + F]\!]_\mu &= i2u\big(u2i([\![E]\!]_\mu) + u2i([\![F]\!]_\mu)\big) && \cdots \\
[\![E \wedge F]\!]_\mu &= b2u\big(u2b([\![E]\!]_\mu) \wedge u2b([\![F]\!]_\mu)\big) && \cdots \\
[\![(\forall \langle \bar{\alpha}\rangle\, \bar{x} : \bar{t} \bullet E\,)]\!]_\mu &= b2u(\forall \bar{x} : \bar{U},\ \bar{y} : \bar{T} \bullet \textit{type}(\bar{x}) = [\![\bar{t}]\!]_{\mu'} \Rightarrow u2b([\![E]\!]_{\mu'})\,) \\
[\![(\exists \langle \bar{\alpha}\rangle\, \bar{x} : \bar{t} \bullet E\,)]\!]_\mu &= b2u(\exists \bar{x} : \bar{U},\ \bar{y} : \bar{T} \bullet \textit{type}(\bar{x}) = [\![\bar{t}]\!]_{\mu'} \wedge u2b([\![E]\!]_{\mu'})\,)
\end{aligned}
$$

In the last two equations, $\bar{y}$ is a vector of fresh variables, and $\mu' = (\mu, \bar{\alpha} \mapsto \bar{y})$. In the case that a type parameter α_i occurs in some of the types $\bar{t}$, a more efficient translation is possible by extracting the value of α_i from the bound variables $\bar{x}$:

$$
\mu'(\alpha_i) \in \bigcup_{j=1}^m \textit{extractors}_{\alpha_i}(\textit{type}(x_j), t_j)
$$

The optimization is particularly relevant with e-matching-based SMT solvers, because the formula resulting from the original translation often does not contain good triggers for the variables $\bar{y}$: type parameters $\bar{\alpha}$ are used only in types, which usually do not provide good discrimination for instantiation.

4.2   Translation Using Type Arguments

Our second translation works by explicitly passing the values of type parameters to functions. In the context of SMT solvers, this allows us to completely leave out type guards and leads to formulae with a simpler propositional structure, albeit functions have a higher arity and more terms occur in the formulae. It has to be noted that this second translation crucially depends on the usage of an SMT solver with e-matching: such solvers are not able to exploit missing type guards, because typing information is inserted in expressions in such a way that triggers can only match on expressions of the right type. The translation trades generality for performance: while it is not applicable with most first-order theorem provers (*e.g.*, superposition provers), the experimental evaluation in Section 5 shows a clear performance gain compared to the type guard translation from the previous section. A similar observation is made in [6].

When using type arguments, the Mojo example gets translated as follows:

function $\textit{Mojo}^\#(T, U)$ **returns** (U);   **axiom** $(\forall x : U \bullet \textit{Mojo}^\#(\textit{int}^\#, x) = x\,)$;
const $\textit{GuitarPlayer}^\# : T$;   **axiom** $(\forall g : U \bullet \textit{Mojo}^\#(\textit{GuitarPlayer}^\#, g) = i2u(68)\,)$;

The Typing of Functions. A function $f\langle \alpha_1, \dots, \alpha_m\rangle(s_1, \dots, s_n)$ **returns** $(t) \in \mathcal{F}$ is during the translation replaced by a function $f^\#$ with the type $T^m \times U^n \to U$, *i.e.*, the type parameters are given the status of ordinary function arguments. It is unnecessary to generate typing axioms for $f^\#$, since typing information is inserted everywhere in terms during the translation and does not have to be derived by the SMT solver.

		Type Guards	Type Arguments	No Types
Z3 2.0				
Boogie	(2598)	2002/595/1, 0.781s	2000/597/1, 0.651s	1984/613/1, 0.813s
VCC	(7840)	6999/839/2, 3.447s	6999/836/5, 2.181s	6999/836/5, 2.196s
HAVOC (385)		353/16/16, 0.709s	351/18/16, 0.524s	350/17/18, 0.367s
Z3 1.3				
Boogie	(2590)	1978/609/3 1.107	1974/611/5 1.212	1961/626/3 2.385

Fig. 5. Results for the different benchmark categories. In each cell, we give the number of times the outcome valid/invalid/timeout occurred, as well as the average time needed for successful proof attempts (*i.e.*, counting cases with the outcome valid or invalid).

Translation of Expressions. We maintain both an instantiation $\mu : \mathcal{A} \to Term$ and an environment $\mathcal{V} : \mathcal{X} \to Type$ that assigns types to variables during the translation:

$$
\begin{aligned}
[\![x]\!]_{\mu,\mathcal{V}} &= x & (x \in \mathcal{X}) \\
[\![f(\bar{E})]\!]_{\mu,\mathcal{V}} &= f^{\#}([\![\sigma(\bar{\alpha})]\!]_{\mu,\mathcal{V}}, [\![\bar{E}]\!]_{\mu,\mathcal{V}}) \\
[\![E = F]\!]_{\mu,\mathcal{V}} &= b2u([\![E]\!]_{\mu,\mathcal{V}} = [\![F]\!]_{\mu,\mathcal{V}} \wedge [\![t_E]\!]_\mu = [\![t_F]\!]_\mu) \\
[\![E + F]\!]_{\mu,\mathcal{V}} &= i2u(u2i([\![E]\!]_{\mu,\mathcal{V}}) + u2i([\![F]\!]_{\mu,\mathcal{V}})) \quad \cdots \\
[\![E \wedge F]\!]_{\mu,\mathcal{V}} &= b2u(u2b([\![E]\!]_{\mu,\mathcal{V}}) \wedge u2b([\![F]\!]_{\mu,\mathcal{V}})) \quad \cdots \\
[\![(Q \langle \bar{\alpha} \rangle \; \bar{x} : \bar{t} \bullet E)]\!]_{\mu,\mathcal{V}} &= b2u(Q \, \bar{x} : \bar{U}, \; \bar{y} : \bar{T} \bullet u2b([\![E]\!]_{(\mu, \bar{\alpha} \mapsto \bar{y}),(\mathcal{V}, \bar{x} \mapsto \bar{t})}))
\end{aligned}
$$

The second equation assumes f has typing $\langle \bar{\alpha} \rangle (\bar{s})$ **returns** (t) and that σ is the instantiation of the type parameters $\bar{\alpha}$ that is inferred when applying f to $\bar{E}$. The types t_E, t_F in the third equation are determined by $\mathcal{V} \Vdash E : t_E$ and $\mathcal{V} \Vdash F : t_F$. In the last equation, $\bar{y}$ is a vector of fresh variables, and $Q \in \{\forall, \exists\}$ is a quantifier.

5   Experimental Results and Related Work

We quantitatively evaluate the two different translations of Boogie expressions, together with a third unsound translation that simply erases all type information. The third translation is close to the translation used by the Boogie 1 tool, so that a comparison between Boogie 2 and Boogie 1 is possible. The evaluated Boogie programs are:

- *The Boogie and SscBoogie regression test suites:* A collection of correct and incorrect programs written in Boogie, Spec# [1], and Dafny [14] that make use of polymorphism; also parts of the Boogie tool itself (a Spec# program) are included.
- *Hyper-V verification conditions generated by VCC [5]:* Boogie programs that stem from a project to verify the Microsoft hypervisor Hyper-V.
- *Benchmarks from the HAVOC tool [4]:* Regression tests and verification conditions to prove memory safety and invariants of various C programs.

Because the programs of the last two categories do not use polymorphism, the overhead of our translations for simple problems (that could really be handled with the "No Types" translation) is measured.

For each of the categories, we used Boogie 2 to generate verification conditions with the different translations and write them to separate files. We then measured the performance of the state-of-the-art SMT solver Z3 2.0[1] on the altogether more than 10,000 verification conditions. The prover was run on each verification condition with a timeout of 120s (1800s for the Boogie tests), measuring the average time needed over three runs. All experiments were made on an Intel Core 2 Duo, 3.16GHz, with 4GB.

Figure 5 summarizes the results. The time difference between the type argument encoding and the translation without types is always very small, the argument encoding is even faster in two categories. The type guard encoding is close to the other translations on the Boogie tests, but is on average about 55% slower on the VCC examples, and performs similarly on the HAVOC examples. One explanation for this phenomenon is that (in particular) VCC generates a large number of Boogie functions, which leads to a large number of additional axioms in the type guard encoding.

Related Work. The intermediate verification language Boogie is most closely related to Why [10], which offers ML-style polymorphism [22]. ML-style polymorphism (or "let polymorphism") is more limited than the higher-rank polymorphism in Boogie; for example, it does not allow polymorphic map types nor general quantifications over types, both of which are used heavily by some Boogie front ends. Our typing rule for equality is similar to the "heterogeneous equality" introduced in [18]. Meanwhile, compilers have also explored the benefits of using typed intermediate languages [21].

Couchot and Lescuyer turn formulae with ML-style polymorphism into multi-sorted and untyped formulae [6], taking advantage of built-in theories. They have implemented their translations as modules of the Why tool [10] and report on some experiments. With Simplify [9], they measure a 200% slowdown with their version of a type guard translation, and a 300% slowdown with their other encoding (which is somewhat similar to our type argument encoding). In contrast, we measure a slowdown of at most 95% with the type guards encoding and at most 45% with the type arguments encoding.

Bobot et al. show how to incorporate ML-style polymorphism directly into an SMT solver [3]. Our type arguments translation is quite similar to the machinery they present. It would be interesting to put to test their conjecture that building polymorphism into a prover is a better solution than handling it through a pre-processing step.

There is a large body of work on the encoding of (typed) higher-order logic (HOL) in first-order logic (FOL). Such translations primarily target FOL provers, in contrast to SMT solvers as in our case. Meng and Paulson [20] enrich terms with type annotations in the form of first-order functions and describe different translations, some of which are sound, while others require proofs to be typechecked and possibly rejected afterwards. Similarly, Hurd [12] describes translations from HOL to FOL in which type information can be included in the operator for function application, which is similar to our type argument encoding (and in particular the handling of map types). Translations in the same spirit as our type guard encoding have been studied [7] for the Mizar language.

6   Conclusions

We have introduced the type system of Boogie 2, shown how its advanced type features are useful to program verifiers in encoding program semantics, and shown how to

---

[1] http://research.microsoft.com/projects/z3/

translate its polymorphic types and expressions into first-order formulae suitable for SMT solvers. Our experimental data support the idea that including such advanced features in an intermediate verification language is both desirable for verifier front ends and feasible for performance. Future work include further optimizations like monomorphization.

Acknowledgments. We thank Stephan Tobies and Shuvendu Lahiri for providing us with Boogie files from VCC and HAVOC for use as benchmarks. We also thank Michał Moskal, Nikolaj Bjørner, and Leonardo de Moura for help with Z3, and them, Alastair Donaldson, Shaz Qadeer, Andrei Voronkov for useful discussions and comments. Finally, we are grateful for valuable comments from the anonymous referees.

References

1. Barnett, M., Chang, B.Y.E., DeLine, R., Jacobs, B., Leino, K.R.M.: Boogie: A modular reusable verifier for object-oriented programs. In: de Boer, F.S., Bonsangue, M.M., Graf, S., de Roever, W.-P. (eds.) FMCO 2005. LNCS, vol. 4111, pp. 364–387. Springer, Heidelberg (2006)
2. Barrett, C., Ranise, S., Stump, A., Tinelli, C.: The Satisfiability Modulo Theories Library, SMT-LIB (2008), www.SMT-LIB.org
3. Bobot, F., Conchon, S., Contejean, E., Lescuyer, S.: Implementing polymorphism in SMT solvers. In: SMT 2008 (2008)
4. Chatterjee, S., Lahiri, S.K., Qadeer, S., Rakamarić, Z.: A reachability predicate for analyzing low-level software. In: Grumberg, O., Huth, M. (eds.) TACAS 2007. LNCS, vol. 4424, pp. 19–33. Springer, Heidelberg (2007)
5. Cohen, E., Moskal, M., Schulte, W., Tobies, S.: A practical verification methodology for concurrent programs. MSR-TR 2009-15, Microsoft Research (2009)
6. Couchot, J.F., Lescuyer, S.: Handling polymorphism in automated deduction. In: CADE-21, pp. 263–278 (2007)
7. Dahn, I.: Interpretation of a Mizar-like logic in first-order logic. In: Caferra, R., Salzer, G. (eds.) FTP 1998. LNCS (LNAI), vol. 1761, pp. 137–151. Springer, Heidelberg (2000)
8. DeLine, R., Leino, K.R.M.: BoogiePL: A typed procedural language for checking object-oriented programs. MSR-TR 2005-70, Microsoft Research (March 2005)
9. Detlefs, D., Nelson, G., Saxe, J.B.: Simplify: a theorem prover for program checking. J. ACM 52(3), 365–473 (2005)
10. Filliâtre, J.C.: Why: a multi-language multi-prover verification tool. Research Report 1366, LRI, Université Paris Sud (March 2003)
11. Flanagan, C., Leino, K.R.M., Lillibridge, M., Nelson, G., Saxe, J.B., Stata, R.: Extended static checking for Java. In: PLDI 2002. ACM, New York (2002)
12. Hurd, J.: First-order proof tactics in higher-order logic theorem provers. Technical Report NASA/CP-2003-212448, pp. 56–68 (2003)
13. Leino, K.R.M.: This is Boogie 2. Manuscript KRML 178 (2008), http://research.microsoft.com/~leino/papers.html
14. Leino, K.R.M.: Specification and verification of object-oriented software. In: Summer School Marktoberdorf 2008. NATO ASI Series F. IOS Press, Amsterdam (2009)
15. Leino, K.R.M., Monahan, R.: Reasoning about comprehensions with first-order SMT solvers. In: SAC 2009, pp. 615–622. ACM, New York (2009)
16. Leino, K.R.M., Saxe, J.B., Stata, R.: Checking Java programs via guarded commands. FTfJP 1999. Tech. Rep. 251, Fernuniversität Hagen (May 1999)

17. Manzano, M.: Extensions of First-Order Logic. Cambridge Tracts in Theoretical Computer Science. Cambridge University Press, Cambridge (1996)
18. McBride, C.: Elimination with a motive. In: Callaghan, P., Luo, Z., McKinna, J., Pollack, R. (eds.) TYPES 2000. LNCS, vol. 2277, pp. 197–216. Springer, Heidelberg (2002)
19. McCarthy, J.: Towards a mathematical science of computation. In: IFIP Congress 62, pp. 21–28. North-Holland, Amsterdam (1962)
20. Meng, J., Paulson, L.C.: Translating higher-order clauses to first-order clauses. J. Autom. Reason. 40(1), 35–60 (2008)
21. Morrisett, G., Walker, D., Crary, K., Glew, N.: From System F to typed assembly language. TOPLAS 21(3), 527–568 (1999)
22. Pierce, B.C.: Types and Programming Languages. The MIT Press, Cambridge (2002)
23. Poetzsch-Heffter, A.: Specification and verification of object-oriented programs. Habilitationsschrift, Technische Universität München (1997)

Trace-Based Symbolic Analysis for Atomicity Violations

Chao Wang[1], Rhishikesh Limaye[2], Malay Ganai[1], and Aarti Gupta[1]

[1] NEC Laboratories America, Princeton, NJ, USA
[2] University of California, Berkeley, CA, USA

Abstract. We propose a symbolic algorithm to accurately predict atomicity violations by analyzing a concrete execution trace of a concurrent program. We use both the execution trace and the program source code to construct a symbolic predictive model, which captures a large set of alternative interleavings of the events of the given trace. We use precise symbolic reasoning with a satisfiability modulo theory (SMT) solver to check the feasible interleavings for atomicity violations. Our algorithm differs from the existing methods in that all reported atomicity violations can appear in the actual program execution; and at the same time the feasible interleavings analyzed by our model are significantly more than other predictive models that guarantee the absence of false alarms.

1 Introduction

Atomicity, or *serializability*, is a semantic correctness condition for concurrent programs. Intuitively, a thread interleaving is serializable if it is equivalent to a serial execution, i.e. a thread interleaving which executes a transactional block without other threads interleaved in between. The transactional blocks are typically marked explicitly in the code. Much attention has recently been focused on *three-access* atomicity violations [1,2], which involves one shared variable and three consecutive accesses to the variable. Here we characterize consecutive accesses with respect to a shared variable; these accesses can be separated by events over possibly other shared variables. If two accesses in a local thread, which are inside a transactional block, are interleaved in between by an access in another thread, this interleaving may be unserializable if the remote access has data conflicts with the two local accesses. In practice, unserializable interleavings often indicate the presence of subtle concurrency bugs in the program.

Known techniques for detecting atomicity violations fall into the following three categories: static detection, runtime monitoring, and runtime prediction. Type-state or other static analysis based methods [3,4] try to identify potential violations at compile time. These methods typically ignore data and most of the synchronization primitives other than locks, and tend to report a large number of bogus errors. Runtime monitoring aims at identifying atomicity violations exposed by a given execution trace [5,1,6,7,8]. However, it is a challenging task during testing to trigger the erroneous thread schedule in the first place. In contrast, runtime prediction aims at detecting atomicity violations in all feasible interleavings of events of the given trace. In other words, even if no violation exists in that trace, but an alternative interleaving is erroneous, a predictive method [9,2,10,11,12,13] may be able to catch it without actually re-running the test.

Although there have been several predictive methods in the literature, they either suffer from imprecision as a result of conservative modeling (or no modeling at all) of the program data flow and consequently many false negatives [9,2,10], or suffer from a very

J. Esparza and R. Majumdar (Eds.): TACAS 2010, LNCS 6015, pp. 328–342, 2010.

Thread T_1	Thread T_2
atomic{	
t_1 : $a := x$	
t_2 : $x := a + 1$	
}	
	t_3 : $b := x$
	t_4 : if($b > 0$)
	t_5 : $x := 5$;

(a) first example

Thread T_1	Thread T_2
atomic{	
t_1 : $x := 1$	
t_2 : $a := x + 1$	
}	
t_3 : signal(c)	
	t_4 : wait(c)
	t_5 : $x := 3$;

(b) second example

Fig. 1. Ignoring data/synchronizations may lead to bogus errors. All variables are initialized to 0.

limited coverage of interleavings due to trace-based under-approximations [11,12,13]. Previous efforts [4,2,10], for instance, focus on the control paths and model only locks provided that they obey the nested locking discipline. Their model can be viewed as abstracting other synchronization primitives into NOPs, including semaphores, barriers, POSIX condition variables, and Java's wait-notify[1]. Because of such approximations, the reported atomicity violations may not exist in the actual program. Although *potential* atomicity violations can serve as good hints for subsequent analysis, they are often not immediately useful to programmers, because manually deciding whether such violations exist in the actual program execution itself is a very challenging task.

Fig. 1 provides two examples in which the transactions, marked by keyword *atomic*, are indeed serializable, but *atomizer* [9] or methods in [2,10] would report them as atomicity violations. In each example, there are two concurrent threads T_1, T_2 and a shared variable x. Variables a, b are thread-local and variable c is a condition variable, accessible through POSIX-style signal/wait. The given trace is denoted by event sequence $t_1 t_2 t_3 t_4 t_5$ and is a serial execution. If one ignores data and synchronizations, there seems to be alternative interleavings, $t_1 t_3 t_4 t_5 t_2$ in (a) and $t_1 t_4 t_5 t_2 t_3$ in (b), that are unserializable. However, these interleavings cannot occur in the actual program execution, because of the initial value $x = 0$ and the if-condition in the first example and the signal/wait in the second example.

Methods using happens-before causalities [11,12] often guarantee no bogus errors, but tend to miss many real ones. Fig. 2 shows a model in this category—the maximal causal model [12]—for the examples in Fig. 1. This model has been shown in [12] to subsume many earlier happens-before causal models. Here events accessing the shared variable x are represented by the actual values read/written in the given trace, and events involving thread-local variables only are abstracted into NOPs. The model admits all interleavings in which these *concrete events* are sequentially consistent. In Fig. 2, for example, the alternative sequences are deemed as sequentially inconsistent in both programs, because consecutive reads t_1, t_3 in the first example return different values, and in the second example t_2 reads in 1 from x immediately after t_5 writing 3. Therefore, this model can avoid reporting these two bogus errors. However, consider modifying the programs in Fig. 1 by changing t_4 in the first example into if(b≥0), and removing the signal/wait of t_3, t_4 in the second example. Now, the aforementioned alternative interleavings expose real atomicity violations, but in both examples, the concrete read/write events (Fig. 2) remain the same—these real violations will be missed.

---

[1] These synchronization primitives cannot be simulated using only nested locks.

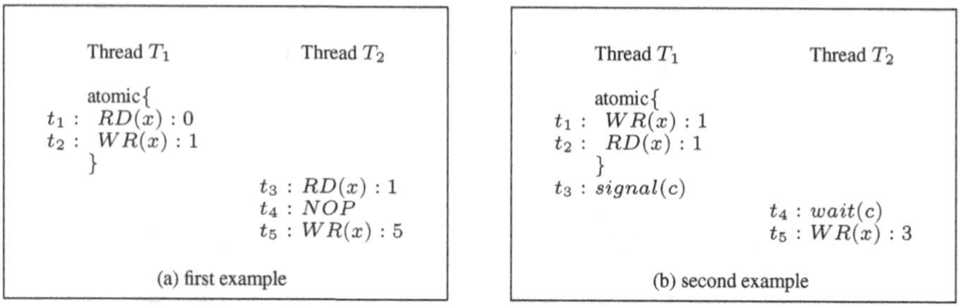

Fig. 2. Predictive models using under-approximations may miss real errors

In this paper, we propose a more precise algorithm for predicting atomicity viola-tions. Given an execution trace on which transactional blocks are explicitly marked, we check all alternative interleavings of the *symbolic events* of that trace for three-access atomicity violations. The symbolic events are constructed from both the concrete trace and the program source code. Compared to existing causal models, for example, [12], our model covers more interleavings while guaranteeing no false alarms. Since the al-gorithm is more precise than the methods in [9,2], we envision the following procedure in which it may be applied:

1. Run a test of the concurrent program to obtain an execution trace.
2. Run a sound but over-approximate algorithm [9,2] to detect all *potential* atomicity violations. If no violation is found, return.
3. Build the precise predictive model, and for each potential violation, check whether it is feasible. If it is feasible, create a concrete and replayable witness trace.

More specifically, we formulate the checking in Step 3 as a satisfiability problem, by constructing a formula which is satisfiable iff there exists a feasible and yet unseri-alizable interleaving of events of the given trace. The formula is in a quantifier-free first-order logic and is decided by a Satisfiability Modulo Theory (SMT) solver [14].

Our main contributions are applying the trace-based symbolic predictive model to analyzing atomicity and encoding the detection of three-access violations on its inter-leavings as an SMT problem, followed by the subsequent analysis using a SMT solver. Our model for predicting atomicity violations tracks the actual data flow and models all synchronization primitives precisely. The greater capability of covering interleav-ings by our method is due to the use of concrete trace as well as the program source code. Furthermore, using symbolic techniques rather than explicit enumeration makes the analysis less sensitive to the large number of interleavings.

The remainder of this paper is organized as follows. After establishing notation in Section 2 and Section 3, we present the SMT-based algorithm for detecting atomicity violations in Section 4. In Section 5, we explain how to search for an erroneous prefix as opposed to a complete interleaving. We present experimental results in Section 6, review related work in Section 7, and give our conclusions in Section 8.

2   Preliminaries

Programs and Traces. A *concurrent program* has a set of *threads* and a set SV of *shared variables*. Each thread T_i, where $1 \leq i \leq k$, has a set of *local variables* LV_i.

- Let $Tid = \{1, \ldots, k\}$ be the set of thread indices.
- Let $V_i = SV \cup LV_i$, where $1 \leq i \leq k$, be the set of variables accessible in T_i.

The remaining aspects of a concurrent program are left unspecified, to apply more generally to different programming languages. An *execution trace* is a sequence of events $\rho = t_1 \ldots t_n$. An *event* $t \in \rho$ is a tuple $\langle tid, action \rangle$, where $tid \in Tid$ and $action$ is a computation of the form $(\text{assume}(c), asgn)$, i.e. a *guarded assignment*, where

- $asgn$ is a set of assignments, each of the form $v := exp$, where $v \in V_i$ is a variable and exp is an expression over V_i.
- $\text{assume}(c)$ means the conditional expression c over V_i must be true for the assignments in $asgn$ to execute.

Each event t in ρ is a unique execution instance of a statement in the program. If a statement in the textual representation of the program is executed multiple times, e.g., in a loop or a recursive function, each execution instance is modeled as a separate event. By defining the expression syntax suitably, the trace representation can model executions of any multithreaded program[2].

The guarded assignment action has three variants: (1) when the guard $c = $ true, it models normal assignments in a basic block; (2) when the assignment set $asgn$ is empty, $\text{assume}(c)$ models the execution of a branching statement `if(c)`; and (3) with both the guard and the assignment set, it can model the atomic *check-and-set* operation, which is the foundation of all concurrency/synchronization primitives.

Synchronization Primitives. We use the guarded assignments in our implementation to model all synchronization primitives in POSIX Threads (or *PThreads*). This includes locks, semaphores, condition variables, barriers, etc. For example, acquire of a mutex lock l in the thread T_i, where $i \in Tid$, is modeled as event $\langle i, (\text{assume}(l = 0), \{l := i\}) \rangle$; here 0 means the lock is available and thread index i indicates the owner of the lock. Release of lock l is accurately modeled as $\langle i, (\text{assume}(l = i), \{l := 0\}) \rangle$. Similarly, acquire of a counting semaphore cs is modeled using $(\text{assume}(cs > 0), \{cs := cs - 1\})$, while release is modeled using $(\text{assume}(cs \geq 0), \{cs := cs + 1\})$. Fig. 3 shows the symbolic representations of traces in Fig. 1. Note that signal/wait in the second example are modeled using guarded assignments as well. Specifically, `wait(c)` is split into two events t_4 and $t_{4'}$, which first resets c to 0, then waits for c to become non-zero and in the same atomic action resets c back to 0. This modeling conforms to the POSIX standard, allowing t_3 :`signal(c)` to be interleaved in between.

Concurrent Trace Programs. The semantics of an execution trace is defined using a state transition system. Let $V = SV \cup \bigcup_i LV_i$, $1 \leq i \leq k$, be the set of all program variables and Val be a set of values of variables in V. A *state* is a map $s : V \to Val$ assigning a value to each variable. We also use $s[v]$ and $s[exp]$ to denote the values of $v \in V$ and expression exp in state s. We say that a *state transition* $s \xrightarrow{t} s'$ exists, where s, s' are states and t is an event in thread T_i, $1 \leq i \leq k$, iff

- $t = \langle i, (\text{assume}(c), asgn) \rangle$, $s[c]$ is true, and for each assignment $v := exp$ in $asgn$, $s'[v] = s[exp]$ holds; states s and s' agree on all other variables.

---

[2] Details on modeling generic language constructs, such as those in C/C++/Java, are not directly related to concurrency; for more information refer to recent efforts in [15,16].

$$
\begin{array}{l}
t_1 : \langle 1, (\text{assume}(\text{true}\ ), \{a := x \qquad\}\rangle\rangle \\
t_2 : \langle 1, (\text{assume}(\text{true}\ ), \{x := a + 1\ \}\rangle\rangle \\
\\
t_3 : \langle 2, (\text{assume}(\text{true}\ ), \{b := x \qquad\}\rangle\rangle \\
t_4 : \langle 2, (\text{assume}(b > 0), \{ \qquad\qquad\}\rangle\rangle \\
t_5 : \langle 2, (\text{assume}(\text{true}\ ), \{x := 5 \qquad\}\rangle\rangle
\end{array}
$$

(a) first example

$$
\begin{array}{l}
t_1 : \langle 1, (\text{assume}(\text{true}\ ), \{x := 1 \qquad\}\rangle\rangle \\
t_2 : \langle 1, (\text{assume}(\text{true}\ ), \{a := x + 1\ \}\rangle\rangle \\
t_3 : \langle 1, (\text{assume}(\text{true}\ ), \{c := 1 \qquad\}\rangle\rangle \\
\\
t_4 : \langle 2, (\text{assume}(\text{true}\ ), \{c := 0 \qquad\}\rangle\rangle \\
t_{4'} : \langle 2, (\text{assume}(c > 0), \{c := 0 \qquad\}\rangle\rangle \\
t_5 : \langle 2, (\text{assume}(\text{true}\ ), \{x := 3 \qquad\}\rangle\rangle
\end{array}
$$

(a) second example

Fig. 3. The symbolic representations of concurrent execution traces

Let $\rho = t_1 \dots t_n$ be an execution trace of program P. Then ρ can be viewed as a total order on the set of symbolic events in ρ. From ρ one can derive a partial order called the concurrent trace program (CTP). Previously, we have used CTPs [17,18] to predict assertion failures and to prune redundant interleavings in stateless model checking.

Definition 1. *The* concurrent trace program *with respect to* ρ, *denoted* CTP_ρ, *is a partially ordered set* $(T, \sqsubseteq)$ *such that,*

- $T = \{t \mid t \in \rho\}$ *is the set of events, and*
- $\sqsubseteq$ *is a partial order such that, for any* $t_i, t_j \in T$, $t_i \sqsubseteq t_j$ *iff* $tid(t_i) = tid(t_j)$ *and* $i < j$ *(in* ρ, *event* t_i *appears before* t_j*).*

Intuitively, CTP_ρ orders events from the same thread by their execution order in ρ; events from different threads are not *explicitly* ordered with each other. In the sequel, we will say $t \in CTP_\rho$ to mean that $t \in T$ is associated with the CTP.

We now define *feasible linearizations* of CTP_ρ. Let $\rho' = t'_1 \dots t'_n$ be a linearization of CTP_ρ, i.e. an interleaving of events of ρ. We say that ρ' is *feasible* iff there exist states $s_0, \dots, s_n$ such that, s_0 is the initial state of the program and for all $i = 1, \dots, n$, there exists a transition $s_{i-1} \xrightarrow{t'_i} s_i$. This definition captures the standard sequential consistency semantics for concurrent programs, where we modeled concurrency primitives such as locks by using auxiliary shared variables.

3   Three-Access Atomicity Violations

An execution trace ρ is *serializable* iff it is equivalent to a feasible linearization ρ' which executes the transactions without other threads interleaved in between. Informally, two traces are equivalent iff we can transform one into another by repeatedly swapping adjacent independent events. Here two events are considered as *independent* iff swapping their execution order always leads to the same program state.

Atomicity Violations. Three-access atomicity violation is a special case of serializability violations, involving an event sequence $t_c \dots t_r \dots t_{c'}$ such that:

1. t_c and $t_{c'}$ are in a transactional block of one thread, and t_r is in another thread;
2. t_c and t_r are data dependent; and t_r and $t_{c'}$ are data dependent.

The recent study in [1] shows that in practice atomicity violations account for a very large number of concurrency errors. Depending on whether each event is a *read* or *write*, there are eight combinations of the triplet $t_c, t_r, t_{c'}$. While R-R-R, R-R-W, and W-R-R are serializable, the remaining five may indicate atomicity violations.

Given the CTP_ρ and a transaction $trans = t_i \ldots t_j$, where $t_i \ldots t_j$ are events from a thread in ρ, we use the set PAV to denote all these potential atomicity violations. Conceptually, the set PAV can be computed by scanning the trace ρ once, and for each remote event $t_r \in CTP_\rho$, finding the two local events $t_c, t_{c'} \in trans$ such that $\langle t_c, t_r, t_{c'} \rangle$ forms a non-serializable pattern.

The crucial problem of deciding whether an event sequence $t_c \ldots t_r \ldots t_{c'}$ exists in the actual program execution is difficult. However, over-approximate algorithms, such as those based on Lipton's reduction theory [9] or [10,2], can be used to weed out event triplets in PAV that are definitely infeasible. For example, the method in [2] reduces the problem of checking (the existence of) $t_c \ldots t_r \ldots t_{c'}$ to *simultaneous reachability* under nested locking. That is, does there exist an event $t_{c''}$ such that (1) $t_{c''}$ is within the same thread and is located between t_c and $t_{c'}$ and (2) $t_{c''}, t_r$ are simultaneously reachable? Under nested locking, simultaneous reachability can be decided by a compositional analysis based on locksets and *acquisition histories* [19]. However, the analysis in [2] is over-approximate in that it ignores the data flow and synchronizations other than nested locks[3].

Guarded Independence. Sometimes, two events with data conflict may still be independent with each other, although they are *conflict-dependent*. A data conflict occurs when two events access the same variable and at least one of them is a *write*. In the literature, conflict-independence between two events is defined as: (1) executing one does not enable/disable another, and (2) they do not have data conflict. These conditions are sufficient but not necessary for two events to be *independent*. Consider event t_1:x=5 and event t_2:x=5, for example. They have a data conflict but are semantically independent. Here, we use a more precise *guarded independence* relation as follows (c.f. [20]).

Definition 2. *Two events t_1, t_2 are guarded independent with respect to a condition c_G, denoted $\langle t_1, t_2, c_G \rangle$, iff the guard $c_G(t_1, t_2)$ implies that the following properties:*

1. *if t_1 is enabled in s and $s \xrightarrow{t_1} s'$, then t_2 is enabled in s iff t_2 is enabled in s'; and*
2. *if t_1, t_2 are enabled in s, there is a unique state s' such that $s \xrightarrow{t_1 t_2} s'$ and $s \xrightarrow{t_2 t_1} s'$.*

The guard c_G is computed by a static traversal of the control flow structure [20]. For each event t, let $V_{RD}(t)$ be the set of variables read by t, and $V_{WR}(t)$ be the set of variables written by t. We define the *potential conflict set* between $t_1, t_2 \in CTP_\rho$ as

$$\mathcal{C}_{t_1,t_2} = V_{RD}(t_1) \cap V_{WR}(t_2) \cup V_{RD}(t_2) \cap V_{WR}(t_1) \cup V_{WR}(t_1) \cap V_{WR}(t_2) \ .$$

For programs with pointers ($*p$) and arrays ($a[i]$), we compute the guarded independence relation R_G as follows:

1. when $\mathcal{C}_{t_1,t_2} = \emptyset$, add $\langle t_1, t_2, true \rangle$ to R_G;
2. when $\mathcal{C}_{t_1,t_2} = \{a[i], a[j]\}$, add $\langle t_1, t_2, i \neq j \rangle$ to R_G;
3. when $\mathcal{C}_{t_1,t_2} = \{*p_i, *p_j\}$, add $\langle t_1, t_2, p_i \neq p_j \rangle$ to R_G;
4. when $\mathcal{C}_{t_1,t_2} = \{x\}$, consider the following cases:

---

[3] Programs with only nested locking can enforce mutual exclusion, but cannot coordinate thread interactions because nested locks cannot simulate powerful primitives such as semaphores.

   a. **RD-WR:** if $x \in V_{RD}(t_1)$ and $x := e$ is in t_2, add $\langle t_1, t_2, x = e \rangle$ to R_G;
   b. **WR-WR:** if $x := e_1$ is in t_1 and $x := e_2$ is in t_2, add $\langle t_1, t_2, e_1 = e_2 \rangle$ to R_G;
   c. **WR-C:** if x is in assume condition *cond* of t_1, and $x := e$ is in t_2, add $\langle t_1, t_2, cond = cond[x \rightarrow e] \rangle$ to R_G, in which $cond[x \rightarrow e]$ denotes the replacement of x with e.

This set of rules can be easily extended to handle a richer set of language constructs. Note that among these patterns, the syntactic conditions based on data conflict (conflict-independence) is able to catch the first pattern only. Also note that methods in [1,2,10] use conflict-independence (hence *conflict-serializable*), whereas our method is based on guarded independence. In symbolic search based on SMT/SAT solvers, the guarded independence relation can be compactly encoded as constraints in the problem formulation, as described in the next section.

4   Capturing the Feasible Interleavings

Given the CTP_ρ and a set PAV of event triplets as potential atomicity violations, we check whether a violation exists in any feasible linearization of CTP_ρ. For this, we create a formula Φ which is satisfiable iff there exists a feasible linearization of CTP_ρ that exposes the violation. Let $\Phi := \Phi_{CTP_\rho} \wedge \Phi_{AV}$, where Φ_{CTP_ρ} captures all feasible linearizations of CTP_ρ and Φ_{AV} encodes the condition that one event triplet exists.

4.1   Concurrent Static Single Assignment

Our encoding is based on transforming CTP_ρ into a concurrent static single assignment (CSSA) form. Our CSSA form, inspired by [21], has the property that each variable is defined exactly once. Here a *definition* of variable $v \in V$ is an event that modifies v, and a *use* of v is an event where it appears in a condition or in the right-hand side of an assignment. Unlike in the classic sequential SSA form, we need not add ϕ-functions to model the confluence of multiple if-else branches, because in CTP_ρ, each thread has a single control path. All the branching decisions in the program have already been made during the execution that generates the trace ρ in the first place.

   We differentiate the shared variables in SV from the thread-local variables in LV_i, $1 \le i \le k$. Each use of $v \in LV_i$ corresponds to a unique preceding event in the same thread T_i that defines v. Each use of $v \in SV$, in contrast, may map to multiple definitions in the same or other threads, and a π-function is added to model these definitions.

Definition 3. *A π-function, added for a shared variable v before its use, has the form $\pi(v_1, \ldots, v_l)$, where each v_i, $1 \le i \le l$, is either the most recent definition of v in the same thread as the use, or a definition of v in another concurrent thread.*

The construction of the CSSA form consists of the following steps:

1. Create unique names for local/shared variables in their definitions.
2. For each use of a local variable $v \in LV_i$, $1 \le i \le k$, replace v with the most recent (unique) definition v'.
3. For each use of a shared variable $v \in SV$, create a unique name v' and add the definition $v' \leftarrow \pi(v_1, \ldots, v_l)$. Then replace v with the new definition v'.

$$
\begin{aligned}
&t_0 : \langle 1, (\text{assume(true} \quad), \{a_0 := 0, b_0 := 0, x_0 := 0 \}) \rangle \\
&t_1 : \langle 1, (\text{assume(true} \quad), \{a_1 := \pi^1 \qquad\qquad\qquad \}) \rangle \text{ where } \pi^1 \leftarrow \pi(x_0, x_2) \\
&t_2 : \langle 1, (\text{assume(true} \quad), \{x_1 := a_1 + 1 \qquad\qquad \}) \rangle \\[6pt]
&t_3 : \langle 2, (\text{assume(true} \quad), \{b_1 := \pi^2 \qquad\qquad\qquad \}) \rangle \text{ where } \pi^2 \leftarrow \pi(x_0, x_1) \\
&t_4 : \langle 2, (\text{assume}(b_1 > 0), \{ \qquad\qquad\qquad\qquad \}) \rangle \\
&t_5 : \langle 2, (\text{assume(true} \quad), \{x_2 := 5 \qquad\qquad\qquad \}) \rangle
\end{aligned}
$$

Fig. 4. The CSSA form of the concurrent trace program

Fig. 4 shows the CSSA form of the CTP in Fig. 3(a). Note that event t_0 is added to model the initial values of all variables. We add names π^1 and π^2 for the shared variable uses. The assignment in t_1 becomes $a_1 := \pi^1$ because the value read from x can be defined as either x_0 or x_2, depending on the thread interleaving. The local variable a_1 in t_2, on the other hand, is uniquely defined as in t_1.

The semantics of π-functions are defined as follows. Let $v' \leftarrow \pi(v_1, \ldots, v_l)$ be defined in event t, and let each parameter v_i, $1 \leq i \leq l$, be defined in event t_i. The evaluation of π-function depends on the write-read consistency in a particular interleaving. Intuitively, $(v' = v_i)$ iff v_i is the most recent definition before the use in event t. More formally, $(v' = v_i)$, $1 \leq i \leq l$, iff the following conditions hold,

- event t_i, which defines v_i, is executed before event t; and
- any event t_j that defines v_j, $1 \leq j \leq l$ and $j \neq i$, is executed either before the definition in t_i or after the use in t.

4.2 Encoding Feasible Linearizations

We construct Φ_{CTP_ρ} based on the notion of feasible linearizations (defined in Section 2). It consists of the following subformulas:

$$\Phi_{CTP} := \Phi_{PO} \wedge \Phi_{VD} \wedge \Phi_{PI} ,$$

where Φ_{PO} encodes the program order, Φ_{VD} encodes the variable definitions, and Φ_{PI} encodes the π-functions.

To ease the presentation, we use the following notations.

- **Event t_{first}:** we add a dummy event t_{first} to be the first event executed in the CTP.
- **Event t_{first}^i:** for each $i \in Tid$, this is the first event of the thread T_i;
- **Preceding event:** for each event t, we define its thread-local preceding event t' as follows: $tid(t') = tid(t)$ and for any other event $t'' \in CTP$ such that $tid(t'') = tid(t)$, either $t'' \sqsubseteq t'$ or $t \sqsubseteq t''$.
- **HB-constraint:** we use $HB(t, t')$ to denote that event t is executed before t'.

The detailed encoding algorithm is given as follows:

- *Path Conditions.* For each event $t \in CTP_\rho$, we define the path condition $g(t)$ which is true iff t is executed.
  1. If $t = t_{\text{first}}$, or $t = t_{\text{first}}^i$ where $i \in Tid$, let $g(t) :=$ true.
  2. Otherwise, let $g(t) := c \wedge g(t')$, where $t' :$ (assume$(c), asgn$) is the thread-local preceding event.

- *Program Order (Φ_{PO}). Φ_{PO} captures the event order within threads. Let Φ_{PO} := true initially. For each event $t \in CTP_\rho$,
  1. if $t = t_{\text{first}}$, do nothing;
  2. if $t = t^i_{\text{first}}$, where $i \in Tid$, let $\Phi_{PO} := \Phi_{PO} \wedge HB(t_{\text{first}}, t^i_{\text{first}})$;
  3. otherwise, t has a thread-local preceding event t'; let $\Phi_{PO} := \Phi_{PO} \wedge HB(t', t)$.
- *Variable Definition (Φ_{VD}). Let Φ_{VD} := true initially. For each event $t \in CTP_\rho$,
  1. if t has action $(\text{assume}(c), asgn)$, for each assignment $v := exp$ in $asgn$, let $\Phi_{VD} := \Phi_{VD} \wedge (v = exp)$;
- *The π-Function (Φ_{PI}). Let Φ_{PI} := true initially. For each assignment $v' \leftarrow \pi(v_1, \ldots, v_l)$, where v' is used in event t, and each v_i, $1 \leq i \leq l$, is defined in event t_i; let

$$\Phi_{PI} := \Phi_{PI} \wedge \bigvee_{i=1}^{l} (v' = v_i) \wedge g(t_i) \wedge HB(t_i, t) \wedge \bigwedge_{j=1, j \neq i}^{l} (HB(t_j, t_i) \vee HB(t, t_j))$$

This encodes that the π-function evaluates to v_i iff it chooses the i-th definition in the π-set (indicated by $g(t_i) \wedge HB(t_i, t)$), such that any other definition v_j, $1 \leq j \leq l$ and $j \neq i$, is defined either before t_i, or after this use of v_i in t.

4.3   Encoding Atomicity Violations

Given a set PAV of potential violations, we build formula Φ_{AV} as follows: Initialize Φ_{AV} := false. Then for each event triplet $\langle t_c, t_r, t_{c'} \rangle \in PAV$, where t_c and t_r are guarded independent under $c_G(t_c, t_r)$, and t_r and $t_{c'}$ are guarded independent under $c_G(t_r, t_{c'})$, as defined in Section 3, let

$$\Phi_{AV} := \Phi_{AV} \vee (\, g(t_c) \wedge g(t_r) \wedge g(t_{c'}) \wedge \neg c_G(t_c, t_r) \wedge \neg c_G(t_r, t_{c'})$$
$$\wedge HB(t_c, t_r) \wedge HB(t_r, t_{c'})\,)$$

Recall that for two events t and t', the constraint $HB(t, t')$ denote that t must be executed before t'. Consider a model where we introduce for each event $t \in CTP$ a fresh integer variable $\mathcal{O}(t)$ denoting its position in the linearization (execution time). A satisfiable assignment to Φ_{CTP_ρ} therefore induces values of $\mathcal{O}(t)$, i.e., positions of all events in the linearization. $HB(t, t')$ is defined as follows:

$$HB(t, t') := \mathcal{O}(t) < \mathcal{O}(t')$$

In satisfiability modulo theory, $HB(t, t')$ corresponds to a special subset of *Integer Difference Logic (IDL)*, i.e. $\mathcal{O}(t) < \mathcal{O}(t')$, or simply $\mathcal{O}(t) - \mathcal{O}(t') \leq -1$. It is special in that the integer constant c in the IDL constraint $(x - y \leq c)$ is always -1. Deciding this fragment of IDL is easier because consistency can be reduced to cycle detection in the constraint graph, which has a linear complexity, rather than the more expensive negative-cycle detection [22].

Fig. 5 illustrates the CSSA-based encoding of CTP in Fig. 4. Note that it is common for many path conditions, variable definitions, and HB-constraints to be constants. For example, $HB(t_0, t_1)$ and $HB(t_0, t_5)$ in Fig. 4 are always true, while $HB(t_5, t_0)$ and $HB(t_1, t_0)$ are always false—such simplifications are frequent and will lead to significant reduction in formula size.

Path Conditions: Program Order: Variable Definitions:

$t_0:$ $g_0 = $ true $(a_0 = 0) \wedge (b_0 = 0) \wedge (x_0 = 0)$
$t_1:$ $g_1 = $ true $HB(t_0, t_1)$ $a_1 = \pi^1$
$t_2:$ $g_2 = g_1$ $HB(t_1, t_2)$ $x_1 = a_1 + 1$

$t_3:$ $g_3 = $ true $HB(t_0, t_3)$ $b_1 = \pi^2$
$t_4:$ $g_4 = g_3 \wedge (b_1 > 0)$ $HB(t_3, t_4)$
$t_5:$ $g_5 = g_4$ $HB(t_4, t_5)$ $x_2 = 5$

The π-Functions:

$t_1:$ $(\pi^1 = x_0) \wedge g_0 \wedge HB(t_0, t_1) \wedge (HB(t_5, t_0) \vee HB(t_1, t_5))$
$\vee$ $(\pi^1 = x_2) \wedge g_5 \wedge HB(t_5, t_1) \wedge (HB(t_0, t_5) \vee HB(t_1, t_0))$
$t_3:$ $(\pi^2 = x_0) \wedge g_0 \wedge HB(t_0, t_1) \wedge (HB(t_5, t_0) \vee HB(t_1, t_5))$
$\vee$ $(\pi^2 = x_1) \wedge g_2 \wedge HB(t_2, t_1) \wedge (HB(t_0, t_2) \vee HB(t_1, t_0))$

Fig. 5. The CSSA-based encoding of CTP_ρ in Fig. 4

For synchronization primitives such as locks, there are even more opportunities to simplify the formula. For example, if $\pi^1 \leftarrow \pi(l_1, \ldots, l_n)$ denotes the value read from a lock variable l during lock acquire, then we know that $(\pi^1 = 0)$ must hold, since the lock need to be available. This means for non-zero π-parameters, the constraint $(\pi^1 = l_i)$, where $1 \leq i \leq n$, always evaluates to false. And due to the mutex lock semantics, for all $1 \leq i \leq n$, we know $l_i = 0$ iff l_i is defined by a lock release.

The encoding of $\Phi = \Phi_{CTP_\rho} \wedge \Phi_{AV}$ closely follows our definitions of CTP, feasible linearizations, and the semantics of π-functions. We now state its correctness. The proof is straightforward and is omitted for brevity.

Theorem 1. *Formula $\Phi = \Phi_{CTP_\rho} \wedge \Phi_{AV}$ is satisfiable iff there exists a feasible linearization of the CTP that violates the given atomicity property.*

Let n be the number of events in CTP_ρ, let n_π be the number of shared variable uses, let l_π be the maximal number of parameters in any π-function, and let l_{trans} be the number of shared variable accesses in $trans$. We also assume that each event in ρ accesses at most one shared variable. The size of $(\Phi_{PO} \wedge \Phi_{VD} \wedge \Phi_{PI} \wedge \Phi_{AV})$ in the worst case is $O(n + n + n_\pi \times l_\pi^2 + n_\pi \times l_{trans})$. We note that shared variable accesses in typical concurrent programs are often few and far in between, especially when compared to computations within threads, to minimize the synchronization overhead. This means that l_π, n_π, and l_{trans} are typically much smaller than n, which significantly reduces the formula size[4]. In contrast, in conventional bounded model checking (BMC) algorithms for verifying concurrent programs, e.g. [20], which employ an explicit *scheduler variable* at each time frame, the BMC formula size quadratically depends on n, and cannot be easily reduced even if l_π, n_π, and l_{trans} are significantly smaller than n.

5   Capturing Erroneous Trace Prefixes

The algorithm presented so far aims at detecting atomicity violations in all feasible linearizations of a CTP. Therefore, a violation is reported iff (1) a three-access atomicity violation occurs in an interleaving, and (2) the interleaving is a feasible linearization

---

[4] Our experiments show that l_π is typically in the lower single-digit range (the average is 4).

of CTP_ρ. Sometimes, this may become too restrictive, because the existence of an atomicity violation often leads to the subsequent execution of a branch that is not taken by the given trace ρ (hence the branch is not in CTP_ρ).

Consider the example in Fig. 6. In this trace, event t_4 is guarded by $(a = 1)$. There is a real atomicity violation under thread schedule $t_1 t_5 t_2 \ldots$. However, this trace prefix invalidates the condition $(a = 1)$ in t_3—event t_4 will be skipped. In this sense, the trace $t_1 t_5 t_2 \ldots$ does not qualify as a linearization of CTP_ρ. In our aforementioned symbolic encoding, the π-constraint in t_6 will become invalid.

$$
\begin{aligned}
t_6 : \quad & (\pi^2 = x_1) \wedge g_1 \wedge HB(t_1, t_6) \wedge (HB(t_4, t_1) \vee HB(t_6, t_4)) \wedge (HB(t_5, t_1) \vee HB(t_6, t_5)) \\
\vee \ & (\pi^2 = x_2) \wedge g_4 \wedge HB(t_4, t_6) \wedge (HB(t_1, t_4) \vee HB(t_6, t_1)) \wedge (HB(t_5, t_4) \vee HB(t_6, t_5)) \\
\vee \ & (\pi^2 = x_3) \wedge g_5 \wedge HB(t_5, t_6) \wedge (HB(t_1, t_5) \vee HB(t_6, t_1)) \wedge (HB(t_4, t_5) \vee HB(t_6, t_4))
\end{aligned}
$$

Note that in the interleaving $t_1 t_5 t_2 \ldots$, we have g_4, $HB(t_4, t_1)$, $HB(t_6, t_4)$, $HB(t_4, t_5)$, $HB(t_6, t_4)$ all evaluated to false. This rules out the interleaving as a feasible linearization of CTP_ρ, although it has exposed a real atomicity violation.

Thread T_1	Thread T_2
atomic{	
$t_1:$ $x := 0$	
$t_2:$ $a := x + 1$	
}	
$t_3:$ if$(a = 1)$	
$t_4:$ $x := 2$	
	$t_5: x := 3$
	$t_6: b := x;$

(a) the given trace

$$
\begin{aligned}
t_1 &: \langle 1, (\text{assume(true)}, \ \{x_1 := 0 \ \}) \rangle \\
t_2 &: \langle 1, (\text{assume(true)}, \ \{a_1 := \pi^1 + 1 \}) \rangle \\
t_3 &: \langle 1, (\text{assume}(a_1 = 1), \{ \ \}) \rangle \\
t_4 &: \langle 1, (\text{assume(true)}, \ \{x_2 := 2 \ \}) \rangle \\
t_5 &: \langle 2, (\text{assume(true)}, \ \{x_3 := 3 \ \}) \rangle \\
t_6 &: \langle 2, (\text{assume(true)}, \ \{b_1 := \pi^2 \ \}) \rangle
\end{aligned}
$$

(b) erroneous prefix

Fig. 6. The atomicity violation leads to a previously untaken branch

We now extend our notion of feasible linearizations of a CTP to all prefixes of its feasible linearizations, or the *feasible linearization prefixes*. The extension is straightforward. Let $\mathsf{FeaLin}(CTP_\rho)$ be the set of feasible linearizations of CTP_ρ. We define the set $\mathsf{FeaPfx}(CTP_\rho)$ of feasible linearization prefixes as follows:

$$\mathsf{FeaPfx}(CTP_\rho) := \{w \mid w \text{ is a prefix of } \rho' \in \mathsf{FeaLin}(CTP_\rho)\}$$

We extend our symbolic encoding to capture these erroneous trace prefixes (as opposed to entire erroneous traces). We extend the symbolic encoding in Section 4 as follows. Let event triplet $\langle t_c, t_r, t_{c'} \rangle \in PAV$ be the potential violation. We modify the construction of Φ_{PI} (for the π-function in event t) as follows:

$$
\begin{aligned}
\Phi_{PI} := \Phi_{PI} \wedge (\ & HB(t_{c'}, t) \vee \\
& \textstyle\bigvee_{i=1}^{l} (v' = v_i) \wedge g(t_i) \wedge HB(t_i, t) \wedge \bigwedge_{j=1, j \neq i}^{l} (HB(t_j, t_i) \vee HB(t_i, t_j)))
\end{aligned}
$$

That is, if the atomicity violation has already happened in some prefix, as indicated by $HB(t_{c'}, t)$, i.e. when the event t associated with this π-function happens after $t_{c'}$, then we do not enforce any read-after-write consistency. Otherwise, read-after-write consistency is enforced as before, as shown in the second line in the formula above. The rest of the encoding algorithm remains the same. We now state the correctness of this encoding extension. The proof is straightforward and is omitted for brevity.

Theorem 2. *Formula* $\Phi = \Phi_{CTP_p} \wedge \Phi_{AV}$ *is satisfiable iff there exists a feasible linearization prefix of the CTP that violates the given atomicity property.*

6   Experiments

We have implemented the proposed algorithm in a tool called *Fusion*. Our tool is capable of handling execution traces generated by multi-threaded C programs using the Linux *PThreads* library. We use CIL [23] for instrumenting the C source code and use the *Yices* SMT solver [14] to solve the satisfiability formulas. Our experiments were conducted on a PC with 1.6 GHz Intel processor and 2GB memory running Fedora 8.

We have conducted preliminary experiments using the following benchmarks[5]: The first set of examples mimic two concurrency bug patterns from the Apache web server code (c.f. [1]). The original programs, *atom001* and *atom002*, have atomicity violations. We generated two additional programs, *atom001a* and *atom002a*, by adding code to the original programs to remove the violations. The second set of examples are Linux/Pthreads/C implementation of the parameterized *bank* example [24]. We instantiate the program with the number of threads being 2,3,…. The original programs (*bank-av*) have nested locks as well as shared variables, and have known bugs due to atomicity violations. We provided two different fixes, one of which (*bank-nav*) removes all atomicity violations while another (*bank-sav*) removes some of them. We used both condition variables and additional shared variables in our fixes. Although the original programs (*bank-av*) does not show the difference in the quality of various prediction methods (because violations detected by ignoring data and synchronizations are actually feasible), the precision differences show up on the programs with fixes. In these cases, some atomicity violations no longer exist, and yet methods based on over-approximate predictive models would still report violations.

Table 1. Experimental results of predicting atomicity violations

| Test Program | | | The Given Trace | | Symbolic Analysis | | | | w/o Data [2] |
name	thrds	svars	simplify/ original	regions	orig-pavs	hb-pavs	sym-avs	sym-time (s)	pavs
atom001	3	14	50 / 88	1	8	2	1	0.03	1
atom001a	3	16	58 / 100	1	8	2	**0**	0.03	1
atom002	3	24	349 / 462	1	212	34	33	20.4	33
atom002a	3	26	359 / 462	1	212	34	**0**	17.6	33
bank-av-2	3	109	278 / 748	2	24	8	8	0.1	8
bank-av-4	5	113	527 / 1213	4	48	16	16	0.6	16
bank-av-6	7	117	770 / 1672	6	72	24	24	2.3	24
bank-av-8	9	121	1016 / 2134	8	96	32	32	2.5	32
bank-sav-2	3	119	337 / 852	2	24	8	**4**	0.2	8
bank-sav-4	5	123	642 / 1410	4	48	16	**8**	0.9	16
bank-sav-6	7	127	941 / 1960	6	72	24	**12**	3.8	24
bank-sav-8	9	131	1243 / 2517	8	96	32	**16**	4.6	32
bank-nav-2	3	119	341 / 856	2	24	8	**0**	0.2	8
bank-nav-4	5	123	647 / 1414	4	48	16	**0**	0.2	16
bank-nav-6	7	127	953 / 1972	6	72	24	**0**	3.7	24
bank-nav-8	9	131	1163 / 2362	8	96	32	**0**	140.6	32

---

[5] Examples are available at http://www.nec-labs.com/~chaowang/pubDOC/atom.tar.gz

Table 1 shows the experimental results. The first three columns show the statistics of test cases, including the program name, the number of threads, and the number of shared variables that are accessed in the given trace. The next two columns show the length of the trace, in both the original and the simplified versions, and the number of transactions (*regions*). Our simplification consists of trace-based program slicing, dead variable removal, and constant folding; furthermore, variables defined as global, but not accessed by more than one thread in the given trace, are not counted as shared in the table (*svars*). The next four columns show the statistics of our symbolic analysis, including the size of PAV (*orig-pavs*), the number of violations after pruning using a simple static must-happen-before analysis (*hb-pavs*), the number of real violations (*sym-avs*) reported by our symbolic analysis, and the runtime in seconds. In the last column, we provide the number of (potential) atomicity violations if we ignore the data flow and synchronizations other than nested locking.

The results show that, if one relies on only static analysis, the number of reported violations (in *orig-pavs*) is often large, even for a prediction based on a single trace. Our simple must-happen-before analysis utilizes the semantics of thread *create* and *join*, and seems effective in pruning away event triplets that are definitely infeasible. In addition, if one utilizes the nested locking semantics, as in *w/o Data* [2], more spurious event triplets can be pruned away. However, note that the number of remaining violations can still be large. In contrast, our symbolic analysis prunes away all the spurious violations and reports much fewer atomicity violations. For each violation that we report, we also produce a concrete execution trace exposing the violation. This *witness* trace can be used by the thread scheduler in *Fusion*, to re-run the program and replay the actual violation. We also note that the runtime overhead of our symbolic analysis is modest. The algorithm can be used in the context of a post-mortem analysis.

7   Related Work

We have mentioned in Section 1 some of the static methods [3,4], runtime monitoring [5,1,6,7,8], and runtime prediction [9,2,10,11,12,13] for detecting atomicity violations. Lu *et al.* [1] used access interleaving invariants to capture patterns of test runs and then monitor production runs for detecting three-access atomicity violations. Xu *et al.* [5] used a variant of the two-phase locking algorithm to monitor and detect serializability violations. Both methods were aimed at detecting, not predicting, errors in the given trace. In [4], Farzan and Madhusudan introduced the notion of *causal atomicity* in a static program analysis focusing on the control paths; subsequently they used execution traces for predicting atomicity violations [10,2]. Wang and Stoller [6] also studied the prediction of serializability violations under the assumptions of deadlock-freedom and nested locking; their algorithms are precise for checking violations involving one or two transactions but incomplete for checking arbitrary runs.

Our symbolic encoding for detecting atomicity violations is related to, but is different from, the SSA-based SAT encoding [15], which is popular for *sequential* programs. Our analysis differs from the context-bounded analysis in [25,26,16] since they *a priori* fix the number of context switches in order to reduce concurrent programs to sequential programs. In contrast, our method in Section 4 is for the unbounded case, although context-bounding constraints may be added to further improve performance. We directly capture the partial order in *difference logic*, therefore differing from

CheckFence [27], which explicitly encodes ordering between all pairs of events in pure Boolean logic. In [28], a non-standard synchronous execution model is used to schedule multiple events simultaneously whenever possible instead of using the standard interleaving model. Furthermore, all the aforementioned methods were applied to whole programs and not to concurrent trace programs (CTPs). In previous works [17,18] we have used the notion of CTP, but the context was stateless model checking to prune redundant interleavings in the former, and predicting assertion failures in the later.

The quantifier-free formulas produced by our encoding are decidable due to the finite size of the CTP. When non-linear arithmetic operations appear in the symbolic execution trace, they are treated as bit-vector operations. This way, the rapid progress in SMT solvers can be directly utilized to improve performance in practice. In the presence of unknown functions, trace-based abstraction techniques as in [29], which uses concrete parameter/return values to model library functions, are employed to derive the predictive model, while ensuring that the analysis results remain precise.

8 Conclusions

In this paper, we propose a symbolic algorithm for detecting three-access atomicity violations in all feasible interleavings of events in a given execution trace. The new algorithm uses a succinct encoding to generate an SMT formula such that the violation of an atomicity property exists iff the SMT formula is satisfiable. It does not report bogus errors and at the same time achieves a better interleaving coverage than existing methods for predictive analysis.

References

1. Lu, S., Tucek, J., Qin, F., Zhou, Y.: AVIO: detecting atomicity violations via access interleaving invariants. In: Architectural Support for Programming Languages and Operating Systems, pp. 37–48 (2006)
2. Farzan, A., Madhusudan, P.: Meta-analysis for atomicity violations under nested locking. In: Bouajjani, A., Maler, O. (eds.) Computer Aided Verification. LNCS, vol. 5643, pp. 248–262. Springer, Heidelberg (2009)
3. Flanagan, C., Qadeer, S.: A type and effect system for atomicity. In: Programming Language Design and Implementation, pp. 338–349 (2003)
4. Farzan, A., Madhusudan, P.: Causal atomicity. In: Ball, T., Jones, R.B. (eds.) CAV 2006. LNCS, vol. 4144, pp. 315–328. Springer, Heidelberg (2006)
5. Xu, M., Bodík, R., Hill, M.D.: A serializability violation detector for shared-memory server programs. In: Programming Language Design and Implementation, pp. 1–14 (2005)
6. Wang, L., Stoller, S.D.: Runtime analysis of atomicity for multithreaded programs. IEEE Trans. Software Eng. 32(2), 93–110 (2006)
7. Farzan, A., Madhusudan, P.: Monitoring atomicity in concurrent programs. In: Gupta, A., Malik, S. (eds.) CAV 2008. LNCS, vol. 5123, pp. 52–65. Springer, Heidelberg (2008)
8. Flanagan, C., Freund, S.N., Yi, J.: Velodrome: a sound and complete dynamic atomicity checker for multithreaded programs. In: PLDI, pp. 293–303 (2008)
9. Flanagan, C., Freund, S.N.: Atomizer: A dynamic atomicity checker for multithreaded programs. In: Parallel and Distributed Processing Symposium (IPDPS). IEEE, Los Alamitos (2004)
10. Farzan, A., Madhusudan, P.: The complexity of predicting atomicity violations. In: Kowalewski, S., Philippou, A. (eds.) TACAS 2009. LNCS, vol. 5505, pp. 155–169. Springer, Heidelberg (2009)

11. Chen, F., Rosu, G.: Parametric and sliced causality. In: Damm, W., Hermanns, H. (eds.) CAV 2007. LNCS, vol. 4590, pp. 240–253. Springer, Heidelberg (2007)

12. Serbănută, T.F., Chen, F., Rosu, G.: Maximal causal models for multithreaded systems. Technical Report UIUCDCS-R-2008-3017, University of Illinois at Urbana-Champaign (2008)

13. Sadowski, C., Freund, S.N., Flanagan, C.: Singletrack: A dynamic determinism checker for multithreaded programs. In: Castagna, G. (ed.) ESOP 2009. LNCS, vol. 5502, pp. 394–409. Springer, Heidelberg (2009)

14. Dutertre, B., de Moura, L.: A fast linear-arithmetic solver for dpll(t). In: Ball, T., Jones, R.B. (eds.) CAV 2006. LNCS, vol. 4144, pp. 81–94. Springer, Heidelberg (2006)

15. Clarke, E., Kroening, D., Lerda, F.: A tool for checking ANSI-C programs. In: Jensen, K., Podelski, A. (eds.) TACAS 2004. LNCS, vol. 2988, pp. 168–176. Springer, Heidelberg (2004)

16. Lahiri, S., Qadeer, S., Rakamaric, Z.: Static and precise detection of concurrency errors in systems code using SMT solvers. In: Bouajjani, A., Maler, O. (eds.) Computer Aided Verification. LNCS, vol. 5643, pp. 509–524. Springer, Heidelberg (2009)

17. Wang, C., Chaudhuri, S., Gupta, A., Yang, Y.: Symbolic pruning of concurrent program executions. In: Foundations of Software Engineering, pp. 23–32. ACM, New York (2009)

18. Wang, C., Kundu, S., Ganai, M., Gupta, A.: Symbolic predictive analysis for concurrent programs. In: International Symposium on Formal Methods, pp. 256–272. ACM, New York (2009)

19. Kahlon, V., Ivancic, F., Gupta, A.: Reasoning about threads communicating via locks. In: Etessami, K., Rajamani, S.K. (eds.) CAV 2005. LNCS, vol. 3576, pp. 505–518. Springer, Heidelberg (2005)

20. Wang, C., Yang, Z., Kahlon, V., Gupta, A.: Peephole partial order reduction. In: Tools and Algorithms for Construction and Analysis of Systems, pp. 382–396. Springer, Heidelberg (2008)

21. Lee, J., Padua, D., Midkiff, S.: Basic compiler algorithms for parallel programs. In: Principles and Practice of Parallel Programming, pp. 1–12 (1999)

22. Wang, C., Gupta, A., Ganai, M.: Predicate learning and selective theory deduction for a difference logic solver. In: Design Automation Conference, pp. 235–240. ACM, New York (2006)

23. Necula, G., McPeak, S., Rahul, S., Weimer, W.: CIL: Intermediate language and tools for analysis and transformation of c programs. In: Horspool, R.N. (ed.) CC 2002. LNCS, vol. 2304, pp. 213–228. Springer, Heidelberg (2002)

24. Farchi, E., Nir, Y., Ur, S.: Concurrent bug patterns and how to test them. In: Parallel and Distributed Processing Symposium, p. 286 (2003)

25. Rabinovitz, I., Grumberg, O.: Bounded model checking of concurrent programs. In: Etessami, K., Rajamani, S.K. (eds.) CAV 2005. LNCS, vol. 3576, pp. 82–97. Springer, Heidelberg (2005)

26. Lal, A., Reps, T.W.: Reducing concurrent analysis under a context bound to sequential analysis. In: Gupta, A., Malik, S. (eds.) CAV 2008. LNCS, vol. 5123, pp. 37–51. Springer, Heidelberg (2008)

27. Burckhardt, S., Alur, R., Martin, M.: CheckFence: checking consistency of concurrent data types on relaxed memory models. In: PLDI, pp. 12–21. ACM, New York (2007)

28. Jussila, T., Heljanlo, K., Niemelä, I.: BMC via on-the-fly determinization. STTT 7(2), 89–101 (2005)

29. Beckman, N., Nori, A.V., Rajamani, S.K., Simmons, R.J.: Proofs from tests. In: International Symposium on Software Testing and Analysis, pp. 3–14. ACM, New York (2008)

ACS: Automatic Converter Synthesis for SoC Bus Protocols

Karin Avnit, Arcot Sowmya, and Jorgen Peddersen

The University of New South Wales,
Sydney, Australia
{kavnit,sowmya,jorgenp}@cse.unsw.edu.au

Abstract. In System-on-Chip (SoC) design, pre-designed and pre-verified modules are often integrated into the system. In the absence of a single interface standard for such modules, "plug-n-play style" integration is not likely, as the modules are often designed to comply with different interface protocols, and a protocol converter is required to mediate between them. ACS is a tool that allows for automatic checking of protocol compatibility and automatic converter synthesis for SoC bus based protocols. It is based on formal foundations and guarantees correct-by-construction deterministic solutions in VHDL, whenever it is physically possible to mediate between a given pair of protocols.

Keywords: System-on-Chip, Protocol converter, Protocol compatibility, Converter synthesis, Bus-based architecture.

1 Introduction

Reuse of Intellectual Property (IP) modules has become common practice in chip design. Aimed at accelerating the design phase and increasing system reliability, pre-designed and pre-verified modules are integrated into a single chip. As the integrated modules are often designed by different groups and for different purposes, they typically comply with different interface protocols. For such modules to communicate correctly there is a need for a protocol converter that mediates between them.

In a bus based SoC architecture, the system includes one or more common buses to which all modules interconnect, and all system communication is managed by the bus interface protocols. A general bus-based SoC architecture, including protocol converters for modules is illustrated in Figure 1. For an IP to be integrated into this architecture it needs to either employ an interface protocol that is compatible with the bus protocol, or use a protocol converter.

Automatic Converter Synthesis (ACS) is a tool implementation of methods and algorithms that were developed for provably-correct automatic synthesis of protocol converters for bus protocols of SoCs. It offers instantaneous generation of provably-correct converters for mediation between a given pair of protocols. The methods rely on a dedicated FSM-based formalism and formal definitions

J. Esparza and R. Majumdar (Eds.): TACAS 2010, LNCS 6015, pp. 343–348, 2010.
© Springer-Verlag Berlin Heidelberg 2010

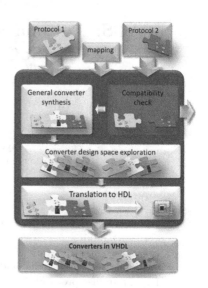

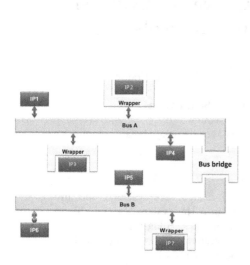

Fig. 1. A typical SoC architecture

Fig. 2. Tool description

of protocol compatibility and correct protocol conversion [1,2,3], and the derived algorithm for automatic converter synthesis has proofs of correctness and completeness [2].

The paper is organized as follows. An overview of the underlying methods and algorithms is presented in section 2. A description of the process flow of the tool is provided in section 3. Experiments with the tool are described in section 4 and the tool status and future work are discussed in section 5.

2   The Formal Foundations

Complete descriptions of the models and methods on which ACS relies are available [1,2,3]. A brief overview is provided here.

The algorithms implemented in ACS are derived from precise formal definition of protocol compatibility and correct protocol conversion that arose from an extensive study of SoC bus protocol characteristics.

The protocol model on which the methods rely distinguishes between control and data channels, and the IP modules are assumed to transfer data items from one to another based on control information, indicating when data items are available on the bus. It is assumed that a data item that is written to the bus may remain valid for more than a single clock cycle and can therefore be read from the bus more than once.

The notion of protocol compatibility, on which the definitions rely, includes three basic conditions. Two protocols are considered to be compatible if and only if:

1. Data is read by one protocol only when written by the other, ensuring that data items are read from the bus only when the bus is guaranteed to hold a valid value.

2. A given data item is read as distinct exactly once. This guarantees a mutual understanding between the communicating parties of the amount of data that is transferred and prevents loss of data and incorrect data duplication.
3. No deadlocks can occur and livelocks can always be avoided, ensuring that every transfer can terminate in a finite number of steps.

A protocol converter is defined as an FSM with bounded counters and finite buffers. The buffers store data items that were written to the bus by one protocol until the other protocol is ready to read them. The general notion of correct protocol conversion includes two conditions. A converter mediating between two protocols is correct if and only if:

1. The converter is compatible with each of the protocols, and thereby complies with the three conditions above.
2. The converter remains neutral in the conversation between the protocols. It transfers all and only data items that were provided to it by the protocols.

The definition of correct conversion was derived from these notions, and the algorithm for converter synthesis was designed to guarantee that the converters produced comply with this definition. Typically, more than one converter exists that guarantees correct mediation between protocols. In search of these converters, the first step in automatic synthesis of protocol converters produces a machine referred to as *the Most General Correct Converter (*MGC^2*)*, which is a nondeterministic converter that describes all possible behaviors a of a correct converter and restricts the design space for correct converters. The MGC^2 is computed using an iterative algorithm that starts with the construction of an initial converter that allows every possible sequence of transitions in both protocols (whether correct or not). This is achieved in two simple steps - the computation of the cross product of the protocols, and an inversion of channel actions of the protocols (according to a predefined inversion function). The converter synthesis algorithm then iteratively restricts the initial converter to only correct behaviors, until a fixed point is reached, in which none of the behaviors enabled by the converter causes a violation of the definition for correct conversion.

As the produced MGC^2 is potentially non-deterministic, an algorithm for design space exploration of the MGC^2 was also developed [3]. The algorithm extracts deterministic converters out of the MGC^2, that are guaranteed to comply with the definition of correct protocol conversion. This is achieved by the identification of input control conditions for which more than a single behavior is enabled, and the construction of sub-converters in which a priori choice is taken to include only one behavior under the identified conditions.

3   ACS Process Flow

The input to the tool consists of a pair of protocol models and mapping information. A protocol is specified as a directed graph in the DOT format [4]. The mapping information indicates the relation between the data channels of the two protocols (an output data channel of one protocol is mapped to each input data channel of the other protocol). The process flow of the tool, as described in this section, is illustrated in Figure 2.

After loading the input information, in which a syntax check is performed, and setting some basic parameters (the size of buffers to be used in the converter), the user can choose to perform an analysis, in which it is checked if a converter exists for the pair of protocols under the specified parameters. Based on the construction of the MGC^2, a partial analysis option reports on an upper bound for the number of unique converters that exist, while a full analysis reports on the exact number of converters that exist and produces a report on the number of states and transitions in each of the potential converters. A model of the MGC^2 is also provided in the DOT format.

The next step after the analysis of the MGC^2 is the converter synthesis. If specified by the user, the tool can export all converters into files in both the DOT format and VHDL, enabling instant simulation, comparison between the different converters, and direct integration into the SoC design.

For a given pair of protocols, the output of the tool is a list of deterministic, provably-correct converters in VHDL, the number of which depends on the given protocols and settings. A system designer at this point may choose which of the converters and integrate it into the system with the use of any standard hardware design IDE application (such as Xilinx ISE [5]). Comparisons between the different converters produced by the tool can be made based on the number of states and transitions in the converters, the size of buffers that each converter uses (a report of these parameters is produced by the tool), or if other criteria for comparisons are desired, the designer may wish to run simulations of the converters in standard hardware simulation tools and examine the converter performance as done with any VHDL design.

4   Experiments

The PC-based tool was used to generate converters for a number of simple examples, as well as full scale commercial protocols such as the AMBA protocol family [6,7,8] and the Open Core Protocol (OCP) [9]. Results of experiments with commercial protocols are reported in Table 1. The table shows the number of states and transitions in each MGC^2, the number of converters found relative to the number of different combinations of choices that exist in the MGC^2 (# column), and the execution time on a standard PC (Pentium 4 CPU 3.2GHZ, 2GB of RAM). It also lists the number of states and transitions in the minimal converter found in each experiment and the improvement it shows relative to the MGC^2.

The experiments illustrate a number of points regarding automatic converter synthesis. First, the significant difference between the potential number of choice combinations and the number of correct converters found implies that the likelihood of a successful manual or random search for a deterministic converter is low and a systematic search is needed. Taking for example the converters between

Table 1. Experimental results

Initiator	Reactor	Buffer	MGC^2 States	MGC^2 Trans	#	Time	Min States	Min Trans	Improvement States	Improvement Trans
		1	0	0	-	< 1sec	-	-	-	-
ASB	APB	2	10	19	4/96	< 1sec	8	13	20%	31%
		5	10	19	9/96	2sec	8	13	20%	31%
OCP	APB	2	4	15	4/1,024	3sec	2	3	50%	80%
		10	4	15	4/1,024	5sec	2	3	50%	80%
OCP	ASB	2	14	32	4/4,096	1min	7	10	56%	75%
(READ)	(READ)	10	14	32	4/4,096	1min	7	10	56%	75%
OCP	ASB	2	16	40	1102/65,536	15min	7	10	56%	75%
(WRITE)	(WRITE)	10	16	40	1102/65,536	30min	7	10	56%	75%

an OCP master and an APB slave, the design space of the converters include 1024 different combinations of choices between behaviors, and only 4 of these combinations yield valid unique converters. Second, the table shows that there can be dramatic differences between different converters for the same pair of protocols, by showing that the minimal converter found is significantly smaller than the MGC^2. In the example of OCP to APB converters, the MGC^2 has 4 states and 14 transitions, but the minimal converter has only 2 states and 3 transitions, which is a significant difference. In this case the measure for comparison was the physical size of the converters (number of states and transitions) but this comparison can be made for any other meaningful measure that can be estimated, such as buffer utilization, power consumption etc. The differences between converters emphasize the advantage of using automatic synthesis in improving system performance, and this difference appears to grow with the complexity of the protocols. This can be attributed to the flexibility of complex protocols, which allow for greater choices for the communicating party, and in this case the converter.

Converters that were produced by the tool were successfully synthesized to FPGAs and simulated with the use of standard commercial tools for hardware design (Xilinx ISE, Modelsim and Synplify simulators).

Note that it is not always possible to generate a converter for any pair of protocols or for any size of buffers. This limitation has to do with the characteristics of the protocols involved. For example, an AMBA2 APB master follows a very simple protocol that does not include any wait states and expects, for example, that any "read" request be serviced within one clock cycle. Such a protocol cannot be correctly converted to more complex slaves such as ASB or OCP, since these slaves do not guarantee an immediate response and may try and force wait states on the master. No converter can overcome such differences and guarantee correct conversion for any legal behavior of the protocols. In such cases where it is not possible to generate a converter the tool will report that the MGC^2 could not be produced.

5 Status and Future Work

ACS was implemented as a part of ongoing research in formal methods for hardware design automation, and as such it is evolving continuously, following advances in the research. The tool currently supports automatic converter synthesis for protocols with unidirectional data channels and matching data bus widths between protocols, although the algorithms for mismatched data widths have been already developed [2] and will soon be integrated into the tool. Other extensions that will be integrated into the tool in the coming months include automatic compatibility check [2] with counter examples on failure, and buffer size suggestions.

References

1. Avnit, K., D'Silva, V., Sowmya, A., Ramesh, S., Parameswaran, S.: A formal approach to the protocol converter problem. In: DATE 2008, March 10-14, pp. 294–299 (2008), doi:10.1109/DATE.2008.4484695
2. Avnit, K., D'Silva, V., Sowmya, A., Ramesh, S., Parameswaran, S.: Provably correct on-chip communication: A formal approach to automatic protocol converter synthesis. ACM Trans. Des. Autom. Electron. Syst. 14(2), 1–41 (2009)
3. Avnit, K., Sowmya, A.: A formal approach to design space exploration of protocol converters. In: Design, Automation & Test in Europe Conference & Exhibition. DATE 2009, April 2009, pp. 129–134 (2009)
4. Gansner, E., North, S.C.: Drawing graphs with dot. AT&T Bell Laboratories, Murray Hill (2002)
5. Xilinx, I.: Software Manuals and Help,
   http://www.xilinx.com/support/documentation/index.htm
6. ARM: AMBA2 specification IHI 0011A (May 1999),
   http://www.arm.com/products/solutions/AMBAHomePage.html
7. ARM: AMBA3 Advanced Peripheral Bus specification IHI 0024B (October 2004),
   http://www.arm.com/products/solutions/AMBAHomePage.html
8. ARM: AMBA3 AHB-lite specification IHI 0033A (June 2006),
   http://www.arm.com/products/solutions/AMBAHomePage.html
9. OCPIP: Open Core Protocol International Partnership (2005),
   http://www.ocpip.org

AlPiNA: An Algebraic Petri Net Analyzer[*]

Didier Buchs, Steve Hostettler, Alexis Marechal, and Matteo Risoldi

Software Modeling and Verification laboratory
University of Geneva, Route de Drize 7, CH-1227 Carouge, Switzerland
http://smv.unige.ch

Abstract. *AlPiNA* is a graphical editor and model checker for a class of high-level Petri nets called *Algebraic Petri Nets*. Its main purpose is to perform reachability checks on complex models. It performs symbolic model checking based on ΣDD, an efficient evolution in the Decision Diagrams field, using novel techniques such as *algebraic clustering* and *algebraic unfolding*. AlPiNA offers a user-friendly interface, and is easily extensible.

1 Introduction

This article introduces the AlPiNA model checking tool. AlPiNA allows checking reachability properties on Algebraic Petri Nets (APN) models, a class of High Level Petri Nets. It encodes state spaces symbolically as Decision Diagrams [6], which reduces memory consumption and computation time that are major obstacles to the practical use of model checking. Users can specify properties to verify using a dedicated language, and they can provide additional information on the model to improve model checking performance. In the current iteration of AlPiNA, we focus on reachability properties for several reasons – among others, the fact that many interesting properties can be expressed as reachability properties as proven in CPN Tools [7].

AlPiNA has two main goals. The first goal is improving model checking performance by leveraging the Decision Diagrams framework and the innovative concepts of *algebraic clustering* and *algebraic net unfolding*. Algebraic clustering reduces the memory footprint of state space calculation by semi-automatically decomposing the system in independent processes. Partial algebraic net unfolding allows reducing the complexity of the data type unfolding. The second goal of AlPiNA is coupling this high performance with a user friendly interface. The user can specify models and properties with a graphical and textual editor. We propose to separate the model and performance-related information. This gives the users a high-level view of the model, freeing them from the need to use low-level formalisms in a complex way.

The article is structured as follows. Section 2 quickly illustrates the theoretical foundations of AlPiNA. Section 3 describes the tool's architecture and shows some benchmarks. Finally, the tool's current status and perspectives are discussed.

---

[*] This project was partially funded by the COMEDIA project of the Hasler foundation, ManCom initiative project number 2107.

J. Esparza and R. Majumdar (Eds.): TACAS 2010, LNCS 6015, pp. 349–352, 2010.

2   Theoretical Foundations of AlPiNA

Concurrency and non-determinism are the major causes of exponential state space explosion [12]. This happens when model components have few causal dependencies with each other and therefore evolve almost independently. Because of the exponential nature of the model checking problem, the state space rapidly becomes intractable as the number of components increases. To overcome this, the state space encoding must have a lower complexity than the explicit enumeration of states. We extend the approach initiated by McMillan [4] called Symbolic Model Checking, which exploits maximal sharing of state elements. In APNs, values are instances of algebraic abstract data types (ADT), therefore they require a more powerful encoding of the state space than Binary Decision Diagrams [1]. Because of this, we defined an evolution of Decision Diagrams (DD) [6] called ΣDD [3].

Clusters (i.e. sets of states) maximize the sharing induced by encoding with DDs [6]. For example, all the places of a Petri net that represent a process and its resources are grouped together. In this case, the cluster is called a *topological cluster* [9] since it is solely based on the Petri net topology. In high-level Petri nets, because of the level of abstraction, places can represent *classes* of similar processes and resources. *Algebraic clusters* [2] allow the user to group process instances with their resources. AlPiNA automatically derives clustering from this grouping. The more independent the resulting clusters are, the more efficient the symbolic representation will be. In the best case, the memory consumption is logarithmic to the number of states.

Since AlPiNA uses APNs, it has to manipulate universally quantified variables. An interesting way of improving performance is to perform an *algebraic net unfolding* [2]. It instantiates the variables of the system in a pre-processing phase, before state space exploration. By doing this, it becomes possible to compile the model with bindings that satisfy the transition guards. Unfolding may significantly increase the speed of the state space construction when the data domains are finite or bounded. Still, it is not always possible or even desirable to perform unfolding for two reasons. The first reason is that a bound may be difficult to figure out: if the bound is too small, the validation becomes incorrect; if it is too large, unfolding may become very expensive and model checking itself intractable. The second reason is that sometimes it is useless to unfold a data domain if only a few of its values are effectively used.

To tackle this problem, we propose to perform *partial unfolding*, i.e. choosing only a subset of the domains. The choice whether a domain should be part of the unfolding is a trade-off between the possible speed gain and the cost of the unfolding itself. Its computational complexity is $O(n^c)$ where n is the size of the largest data domain and c the largest number of input arcs.

In AlPiNA we generate the state space using an algorithm called saturation [5]. The algorithm benefits from the clustering of the state space to *fire* all transitions local to a component before firing inter-component transitions. All the transitions local to a given cluster are only applied to the subset of the state space relevant to the cluster, avoiding superfluous computations. A detailed technical description of the encoding as well as the notion of *algebraic cluster* and *algebraic unfolding* has been given in [2].

3 Tool Description

AlPiNA's architecture can be seen in Fig. 1. AlPiNA is composed of a *Model Checker Engine* (1) and a *Graphical User Interface* (2) built on top of it.

AlPiNA's architecture can be seen in Fig. 1. AlPiNA is composed of the *Model Checker Engine* (1) and a *Graphical User Interface* (2) built on top of it.

The foundation of the *Model Checker Engine* is the symbolic representation offered by DD structures, as presented in the previous section. The first two layers of our engine refer to libraries that handle DD structures. The third layer is a bridge between the APN semantics and the underlying layers. It performs optimisations such as algebraic clustering and net unfolding. On top of the engine block, we find the property checker layer, that uses the state space generated by the previous layer to compute the properties satisfaction. These two layers communicate with the GUI block, they receive the models and return the generated state space and properties statisfaction results.

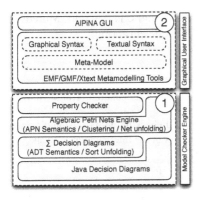

Fig. 1. Architecture Overview

Fig. 2. State space generation

		AlPiNA				Maria		Helena	
		Partial Unfold.		Total Unfold.					
Model Size	States #	Mem (MB)	Time (s)	Mem (MB)	Time (s)	Mem (MB)	Time (s)	Mem (MB)	Time (s)
Distributed Database									
10	197E3	10	0.8	12.4	1.3	47	44.3	24	9
15	7.2E7	33	2.6	41	5.8	-	-	1.4E3	7.5E3
35	5.8E17	544	69.4	789	278	-	-	-	-
Dining Philosophers									
10	186E4			1.9	0.15	375	141	11	5
15	2.5E9			2.6	0.18	-	-	409	822
300	1.2E188			162	48.5	-	-	-	-
Slotted Ring									
5	53856			4.9	0.2	23	4.3	10	5
10	8.3E9			55.6	1.7	-	-	-	-
15	1.5E15			330	9.8	-	-	-	-
Leader Election									
15	399E4			27.7	1.4	795	361	107	142
50	1.7E21			702	76	-	-	-	-

The second block of the AlPiNA architecture is the GUI. We used the Eclipse Tools from the Eclipse Modeling Project (EMP) [8] to create a user friendly interface, following the MDA directives. The first layer is the metamodels specifications, created with EMF. With these metamodels, we created a graphical concrete syntax using GMF for the Petri Nets editor, and a textual concrete syntax using XText for the textual editors. This schema allows us to create an extensible and modular tool.

AlPiNA has good memory consumption and processing time as shown in Fig. 2. It outperforms by an order of magnitude two widely used high level Petri nets model checkers, Maria [10] and Helena [11]. This figure shows the results obtained for some well known examples in the model checking field. The "–" symbol indicates that a result could not be computed[1]. Every example shows that the techniques we present in this tool can produce excellent results when applicable. The distributed database example

---

[1] These benchmarks were computed using a 4 GB ram, 2.5 GHz Core 2 Duo Macbook Pro. The source code can be downloaded at http://alpina.unige.ch

shows also that *partial net unfolding* can give better results than total unfolding. The blank cells indicate that the test has not been run. Indeed, *partial net unfolding* is not useful when the algebra are to small, which is the case for the *Dining Philosophers*, the *Slotted Ring* and the *Leader election*.

4   Current Status and Perspectives

Compared to other high-level model checkers, AlPiNA has the advantage of treating state spaces larger by orders of magnitude while being user friendly. Users benefit from the efficiency based on the Decision Diagrams technology in a transparent manner. They can also easily specify *algebraic clustering* and *algebraic net unfolding* to improve model checking performance. Thanks to this, AlPiNA outperforms Maria and Helena when the model has strong concurrency.

All the features mentioned in this paper have been implemented in AlPiNA. A public release can be found at *http://alpina.unige.ch*. The tool has a user-friendly interface, taking full advantage of the EMF tools features. We are currently working on the next version which should bring modularity to the formalism and CTL support. Moreover, we will improve user guidance while defining the algebraic clustering.

References

1. Bryant, R.E.: Graph-based algorithms for boolean function manipulation. Transactions on Computers C-35, 677–691 (1986)
2. Buchs, D., Hostettler, S.: Managing complexity in model checking with decision diagrams for algebraic petri net. In: Moldt, D. (ed.) Pre-proceedings of the International Workshop on Petri Nets and Software Engineering, pp. 255–271 (2009),
   http://smv.unige.ch/publications/pdfs/pnse09.pdf
3. Buchs, D., Hostettler, S.: Sigma Decision Diagrams: Toward efficient rewriting of sets of terms. In: Corradini, A. (ed.) TERMGRAPH 2009: Preliminary proceedings of the 5th International Workshop on Computing with Terms and Graphs, number TR-09-05 in TERMGRAPH workshops, Università di Pisa, pp. 18–32 (2009),
   http://smv.unige.ch/publications/pdfs/termgraph09.pdf
4. Burch, J.R., Clarke, E.M., McMillan, K.L., Dill, D.L., Hwang, L.J.: Symbolic model checking: 10^{20} states and beyond. Inf. Comput. 98(2), 142–170 (1992)
5. Ciardo, G., Lüttgen, G., Siminiceanu, R.: Efficient symbolic state-space construction for asynchronous systems. In: Nielsen, M., Simpson, D. (eds.) ICATPN 2000. LNCS, vol. 1825, pp. 103–122. Springer, Heidelberg (2000)
6. Couvreur, J.-M., Thierry-Mieg, Y.: Hierarchical decision diagrams to exploit model structure. In: Wang, F. (ed.) FORTE 2005. LNCS, vol. 3731, pp. 443–457. Springer, Heidelberg (2005)
7. CPN Group. CPN tools, http://wiki.daimi.au.dk/cpntools/cpntools.wiki
8. Eclipse. Eclipse modeling project, http://www.eclipse.org/modeling/
9. Hamez, A., Thierry-Mieg, Y., Kordon, F.: Hierarchical set decision diagrams and automatic saturation. In: Petri Nets, pp. 211–230 (2008)
10. Mäkelä, M.: Modular reachability analyzer, http://www.tcs.hut.fi/Software/maria/
11. Pajault, C., Evangelista, S.: High level net analyzer, http://helena.cnam.fr/
12. Valmari, A.: The state explosion problem. In: Lectures on Petri Nets I: Basic Models, Advances in Petri Nets, the volumes are based on the Advanced Course on Petri Nets, London, UK, pp. 429–528. Springer, Heidelberg (1998)

PASS: Abstraction Refinement for Infinite Probabilistic Models*

Ernst Moritz Hahn[1], Holger Hermanns[1], Björn Wachter[1], and Lijun Zhang[2]

[1] Saarland University, Saarbrücken, Germany
[2] Oxford University Computing Laboratory, UK

Abstract. We present PASS, a tool that analyzes concurrent probabilistic programs, which map to potentially infinite Markov decision processes. PASS is based on predicate abstraction and abstraction refinement
and scales to programs far beyond the reach of numerical methods which
operate on the full state space of the model. The computational engines
we use are SMT solvers to compute finite abstractions, numerical methods to compute probabilities and interpolation as part of abstraction
refinement. PASS has been successfully applied to network protocols and
serves as a test platform for different refinement methods.

1 Introducing PASS

Network protocols are subject to random phenomena like unreliable communication and employ randomization as a strategy for collision avoidance. Further,
they are often distributed and thus inherently concurrent. To account for both
randomness and concurrency, Markov decision processes (MDPs) are used as
a semantic foundation as they feature both non-deterministic and probabilistic
choice. Typically one is interested in computing (*maximal* or *minimal*) *reachability probabilities*, e.g., of delivering three messages after ten transmission attempts
(under *best-case* and *worst-case* assumptions concerning the environment).

Probabilistic reachability is expressible in terms of least fixed points of a system of recursive equations [1] where the unknowns correspond to the probability
of an individual state. For finite MDPs, probabilistic reachability can be reduced
to linear programming [2] or solved approximately by value iteration. Current
implementations, e.g., in the popular PRISM model checker [3], use numerical
methods like value iteration. However, the infamous state explosion problem is
even more severe than in the qualitative setting. Explicit-state methods do not
scale well in presence of expensive numerical computations. Symbolic techniques
are often not effective because the probabilities arising as intermediate results
of computations exhibit little structure or regularity to exploit.

* This work is supported by the NWO-DFG bilateral project ROCKS, by the DFG
as part of the Transregional Collaborative Research Center SFB/TR 14 AVACS and
the Graduiertenkolleg "Leistungsgarantien für Rechnersysteme", and has received
funding from the European Community's Seventh Framework Programme under
grant agreement n° 214755.

J. Esparza and R. Majumdar (Eds.): TACAS 2010, LNCS 6015, pp. 353–357, 2010.
© Springer-Verlag Berlin Heidelberg 2010

PASS[1] uses the same principal machinery, but aims at supporting infinite or very large models by resorting to counterexample-guided abstraction refinement (CEGAR): instead of exploring the state space of the model, PASS uses predicate abstraction to maintain a finite abstract model. Analysis of the abstract model is typically very efficient since it has few states. It yields probability intervals that are guaranteed to contain the probabilities in the original model. The difference between interval bounds quantifies the approximation error caused by abstraction. The abstraction is refined until the approximation error is small enough. Otherwise the abstract model provides diagnostic information to refine the abstraction. The process is described in [4,5]. A major difference to conventional CEGAR for predicate abstraction lies in the notion and interpretation of counterexamples: counterexamples are Markov chains rather than single paths.

Predicate abstraction for probabilistic models [6] and suitable refinement techniques [4] premiered in PASS. Preceding abstraction-refinement methods in the probabilistic setting like magnifying-lens abstraction [7] or RAPTURE [8] are restricted to finite models, since they locally unfold the state space of the original model. Our previous version PASS 1.0 has only been able to compute effective upper bounds on probabilities rather than probability intervals.

Kwiatkowska et al. pioneered game-based abstractions [9] which have the benefit of providing safe upper and lower bounds. The idea is that the abstraction distinguishes two kinds of non-determinism: non-determinism present in the original model and non-determinism that results from abstraction. This has been applied to a sequential C-like language with probabilistic choice but without concurrency [10]. In [11], concurrent probabilistic programs have been considered, but without refinement and only for finite models.

To be able to compute probability intervals, we have recently enhanced the PASS machinery with notions of game-based abstraction [5]. To this end, we have introduced a coarser game-based abstraction, called *parallel abstraction*. It can be efficiently computed for concurrent probabilistic programs and yields tight probability bounds, as shown by our experimental results [5]. Beside this feature, PASS has been improved in terms of robustness, efficiency and usability.

2 Architecture

The architecture of PASS, depicted in Figure 1, revolves around an abstraction refinement loop.

PASS reads programs in a concurrent, guarded-command language extending the one of PRISM. The semantics of a program is an MDP in which each state is a valuation of program variables. Initial states are specified by an expressions over program variables. The rest of the description consists of commands. Each command comprises a guard and a set of probabilistic alternatives. Each alternative is associated with a probability and an update formula. If a state fulfills the guard of a command, this state has a probabilistic choice to go to each state obtained by the respective update formula. Unlike PRISM, we allow variables

---

[1] The acronym stands for Predicate Abstraction for Stochastic Systems.

with infinite range. Probabilistic reachability properties are specified by giving an expression that defines the set of goal states. PASS then computes probability bounds to reach them.

We use the *predicate abstraction* method of [5] where probabilistic programs are abstracted to stochastic games [12]. The abstraction is implemented using SMT-based enumeration. The abstractions of the commands are stored in BDDs. Prior to the quantitative analysis, we perform a preprocessing step where we prune the abstract state space to the states that are both reachable from an initial abstract state and can reach a goal state. To this end, we employ a BDD-based forward and backward analysis respectively.

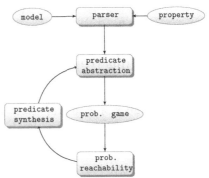

Fig. 1. Architecture of PASS

The stochastic game is first converted from a symbolic BDD-based representation to a sparse-matrix representation. Then the lower and upper bound probabilities are computed by *value iteration*. Value iteration also generates game strategies, a resolution of non-determinism in the game that witnesses the obtained probabilities. These strategies form the foundation for the notion of an abstract probabilistic counterexample [4], which can be used to either refute properties or provide diagnostic information to refine the abstraction.

PASS supports two different refinement methods: Probabilistic CEGAR [4], which analyzes probabilistic counterexamples based on the idea of strongest evidence [13], and the method in [5], which splits abstract states where certain strategies in the abstract game and the obtained bounds indicate a loss of precision. Both methods have their benefits. A comparison is given in [5].

3   Selected Features

Several new features have not been covered in previous publications [6,4,5].

Improved value iteration scheme. It is important to use an efficient value iteration scheme since this step has to be repeated after each refinement step. The order in which value iteration updates the probabilities at a state has a significant impact on the number of iterations. The value of a state depends on its successors. Following the dependencies in the evaluation order can significantly speed up value iteration [14]. PASS now performs value iteration according to a reversed depth-first order starting with the goal states.

Interpolation. PASS uses interpolation to analyze paths of the abstract model. We have written a wrapper to include different interpolation tools with implemented bindings for MathSAT [15], CSIsat [16] and FOCI [17].

On-the-fly Abstraction. To only compute transitions of abstract states that are actually reachable, PASS computes the abstraction layer-wise starting with the initial states interleaving state exploration with SMT-based abstraction. In order to benefit from learned clauses and avoid a repetitive build up of the SMT problem, on-the-fly abstraction employs incremental SMT solving across layers.

4   Concluding Remarks

PASS consists of approximately 18.000 lines of C++ code, and has been tested on a large number of case studies. It is available for Linux with libc6. A PASS executable and case studies can be downloaded from:

<code>http://depend.cs.uni-sb.de/pass</code>

References

1. Baier, C.: On Algorithmic Verification Methods for Probabilistic Systems, Habilitationsschrift, Universität Mannheim (1998)
2. Bianco, A., de Alfaro, L.: Model Checking of Probabilistic and Nondeterministic Systems. In: Thiagarajan, P.S. (ed.) FSTTCS 1995. LNCS, vol. 1026, pp. 499–513. Springer, Heidelberg (1995)
3. Hinton, A., Kwiatkowska, M., Norman, G., Parker, D.: PRISM: A Tool for Automatic Verification of Probabilistic Systems. In: Hermanns, H., Palsberg, J. (eds.) TACAS 2006. LNCS, vol. 3920, pp. 441–444. Springer, Heidelberg (2006)
4. Hermanns, H., Wachter, B., Zhang, L.: Probabilistic CEGAR. In: Gupta, A., Malik, S. (eds.) CAV 2008. LNCS, vol. 5123, pp. 162–175. Springer, Heidelberg (2008)
5. Wachter, B., Zhang, L.: Best Probabilistic Transformers. In: Barthe, G., Hermenegildo, M. (eds.) VMCAI 2010. LNCS, vol. 5944, pp. 362–379. Springer, Heidelberg (2010)
6. Wachter, B., Zhang, L., Hermanns, H.: Probabilistic Model Checking Modulo Theories. In: QEST (2007)
7. de Alfaro, L., Roy, P.: Magnifying-Lens Abstraction for Markov Decision Processes. In: Damm, W., Hermanns, H. (eds.) CAV 2007. LNCS, vol. 4590, pp. 325–338. Springer, Heidelberg (2007)
8. D'Argenio, P.R., Jeannet, B., Jensen, H.E., Larsen, K.G.: Reachability Analysis of Probabilistic Systems by Successive Refinements. In: de Luca, L., Gilmore, S. (eds.) PROBMIV 2001, PAPM-PROBMIV 2001, and PAPM 2001. LNCS, vol. 2165, pp. 39–56. Springer, Heidelberg (2001)
9. Kwiatkowska, M., Norman, G., Parker, D.: Game-based Abstraction for Markov Decision Processes. In: QEST, pp. 157–166 (2006)
10. Kattenbelt, M., Kwiatkowska, M., Norman, G., Parker, D.: Abstraction Refinement for Probabilistic Software. In: Jones, N.D., Müller-Olm, M. (eds.) VMCAI 2009. LNCS, vol. 5403, pp. 182–197. Springer, Heidelberg (2009)
11. Kattenbelt, M., Kwiatkowska, M., Norman, G., Parker, D.: Game-Based Probabilistic Predicate Abstraction in PRISM. In: QAPL (2008)
12. Condon, A.: The Complexity of Stochastic Games. Inf. Comput. 96, 203–224 (1992)
13. Han, T., Katoen, J.P.: Counterexamples in probabilistic model checking. In: Grumberg, O., Huth, M. (eds.) TACAS 2007. LNCS, vol. 4424, pp. 72–86. Springer, Heidelberg (2007)

14. Dai, P., Goldsmith, J.: Topological Value Iteration Algorithm for Markov Decision Processes. In: IJCAI, pp. 1860–1865 (2007)
15. Bruttomesso, R., Cimatti, A., Franzén, A., Griggio, A., Sebastiani, R.: The Math-SAT 4 SMT Solver. In: Gupta, A., Malik, S. (eds.) CAV 2008. LNCS, vol. 5123, pp. 299–303. Springer, Heidelberg (2008)
16. Beyer, D., Zufferey, D., Majumdar, R.: CSIsat: Interpolation for LA+EUF. In: Gupta, A., Malik, S. (eds.) CAV 2008. LNCS, vol. 5123, pp. 304–308. Springer, Heidelberg (2008)
17. McMillan, K.L.: An Interpolating Theorem Prover. Theor. Comput. Sci. 345, 101–121 (2005)

Arrival Curves for Real-Time Calculus: The Causality Problem and Its Solutions

Matthieu Moy and Karine Altisen

Verimag
Centre Équation - 2, avenue de Vignate 38610 Gières - France

Abstract. The Real-Time Calculus (RTC) [1] is a framework to analyze heterogeneous real-time systems that process event streams of data. The streams are characterized by pairs of curves, called arrival curves, that express upper and lower bounds on the number of events that may arrive over any specified time interval. System properties may then be computed using algebraic techniques in a compositional way. A well-known limitation of RTC is that it cannot model systems with states and recent works [2,3,4,5] studied how to interface RTC curves with state-based models. Doing so, while trying, for example to generate a stream of events that satisfies some given pair of curves, we faced a causality problem [6]: it can be the case that, once having generated a finite prefix of an event stream, the generator deadlocks, since no extension of the prefix can satisfy the curves anymore. When trying to express the property of the curves with state-based models, one may face the same problem. This paper formally defines the problem on arrival curves, and gives algebraic ways to characterize causal pairs of curves, i.e. curves for which the problem cannot occur. Then, we provide algorithms to compute a causal pair of curves equivalent to a given curve, in several models. These algorithms provide a canonical representation for a pair of curves, which is the best pair of curves among the curves equivalent to the ones they take as input.

1 Introduction

The increasing complexity of modern embedded systems makes their design more and more difficult. Modeling and analysis techniques have been developed that help taking or validating decisions on the conception of a system as early as possible in the design process.

There exists many methods among which we can distinguish two families. *Computational* approaches study fine-grain models of the system to represent its complete behavior. The validation of the system using such a model may involve simulation, testing and verification. As opposed, *analytical* techniques, such as Real Time Scheduling (founded with [7]) and Real Time Calculus [1], use purely analytical models, based on mathematical equations that can be solved efficiently. These models can represent in a simple way the amount of events to be processed and how fast they can be processed. Solving these equations can give, for example, the best and worst cases for performances.

J. Esparza and R. Majumdar (Eds.): TACAS 2010, LNCS 6015, pp. 358–372, 2010.

Both families of approaches have their advantages and drawbacks. Simulating precisely an embedded system gives very precise results, but only for one simulation, and one instance of a system. Analytical approaches, on the other hand, give strict worst case execution times, and usually give results very fast, but do so only for cases that the theory can take into account. For example, Real-Time Calculus cannot handle the notion of state in the modeling of a system. Recent studies try to combine the approaches to take the best of both [2,4,5,8,9]. The work we present in this paper fully takes its root and motivation in one of those studies, while trying to combine Real-Time Calculus, state-based models and abstract interpretation, using synchronous languages [3].

The *Real-Time Calculus (RTC)* [1] is a framework to model and analyze heterogeneous system in a compositional manner. It relies on the modeling of timing properties of event streams with curves called *arrival curves* (and service curves, which count available resources instead of events in a similar fashion). A component can be described with curves for its input stream and available resources and some other curves for the outputs. For already-modeled components, RTC gives exact bounds on the output stream of a component as a function of its input stream. This result can then be used as input for the next component. *Arrival curves* are function of relative time that constrains the number of events that can occur in an interval of time. For any sliding window of time of length Δ, the pair of arrival curves (α^u, α^l) gives *explicitly* the lower $\alpha^l(\Delta)$ and upper $\alpha^u(\Delta)$ bounds on the number of events (see examples in Figure 1). But, arrival curves may also contain *implicit constraints* indirectly deduced from explicit ones. This paper studies those implicit constraints and provides algorithms to make them explicit.

Motivation. Implicit constraints cause problems in several contexts. For simulation purpose [10], it is typical to produce a stream of events that satisfies some given arrival curves using a *generator of events*. Such generators are the computational representation of a pair of curves, they are built to generate any streams that satisfies the curves. There are multiple ways to write such generators [10,9,3,8] but many faced the problem. For the explanation, let us consider a straightforward one, in discrete time: it computes at each point in time the lower and upper bounds on the number of events allowed to be emitted, based on the events already emitted, and it emits a random number of events within these bounds. Now, it may happen, due to implicit constraints, that some upper bound is strictly lower than the lower bound, leading the generator to deadlock.

Another case where implicit constraints are problematic is the case of formal verification of a system, with inputs and outputs characterized by arrival curves. One may want to prove a property like "If the input complies with the arrival curve pairs α_I, then the output satisfies the arrival curve pairs α_O". But verification tools based on reachability analysis (see, e.g. [11]) usually allow only the expression of "If the input complies with α_I *up to time t*, then the output complies with the α_O *up to time t*". Then, the tool may find a counter-example violating α_O without violating α_I *up to time t*, but it can be the case that this finite counter-example cannot be extended into an infinite execution that satisfies α_I. This would therefore be a *spurious counter-example*. Getting rid of these counter-examples sometimes requires heavyweight state exploration techniques (for example, the `-causal` option of `lesar` [12] does this for Boolean programs) but not all tools are able to do it (`nbac` [11] cannot, for example, and the problem is known to be undecidable for integer programs). The technique that translates the constraints of arrival curves into a model to be analyzed by a verifier tool was used for, e.g., timed automata [2,8], event count automata [4] and synchronous programs [3]. For each tool, one can pose the questions: "what is the behavior of the tool when used on curves with forbidden regions?" and "do the tool output curves with forbidden regions?". Actually, except [3], the papers do not give answer to them. We will see that [2,8] do not create curves with forbidden regions while [4] could at least in theory, and we explain why. Each of the tools would badly behave in the presence of forbidden regions, and this paper gives a way to get rid of them before using any tool.

Implicit constraints on arrival curves. We distinguish two kinds of implicit constraints, that we call informally "unreachable regions" and "forbidden regions". The first one is a well-studied phenomenon within the Real-Time Calculus community [13] and the second, which may produce deadlocks in generators and spurious counter-examples in verification is the goal of this paper. Let us discover those using a pair of arrival curves (α^u, α^l) (see Figure 1 for an example).

Firstly, by splitting some interval into smaller ones, we can get additional constraints. As shown in Figure 1.(a), in an interval of size $\Delta = 6$, the curve says explicitly that the lower bound on the number of events is 1, but splitting this interval into three intervals of size 2, one can deduce a better bound, which is 3. Although the curve explicitly specified the bounds $\alpha^l(6)$ and $\alpha^u(6)$ to be 1 and 7, the number of events in a window of size 6 can actually never be equal to 1 ($\alpha^l(6)$). In other words, the actual implicit lower bound is greater than $\alpha^l(6)$: this means that the curve is equivalent to a tighter curve. A well-known result [13] is that the upper (resp. lower) curve does not have this kind of implicit constraints if it is sub-additive (resp. super-additive). The transformation of an arbitrary curve into an equivalent sub-additive (resp. super-additive) curve making those constraints explicit is called *sub-additive closure* (resp. super-additive closure). In this paper, we call the region between the curves and its sub-additive (resp. super-additive) closure *unreachable regions*. Unreachable regions are due to constraints of a single curve on itself, and can be computed at some point by looking only at the past, i.e. smaller Δ.

The second case of implicit constraints can be found by looking at both curves towards the future. Figure 1.(b) gives an example of such a case: since $\alpha^l(3) = 0$, the lower curve does not give a lower bound on the number of events that can occur in a window of time of size 3, but if an execution has no event during such a window, then the upper curve prevents it from emitting more than 3 events in the next 2 units of time, while the lower curve will force it to emit at least 4. It is therefore impossible to emit no events for 3 units of time. We call the regions that contain such points *forbidden regions*. No execution can cross a forbidden region unless it gets blocked some time latter, due to some contradiction between

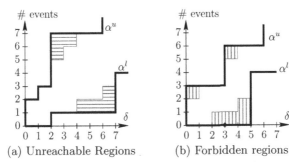

Fig. 1. Implicit and explicit constraints on arrival curves

lower and upper constraints. Borrowing the vocabulary used in [6], we call this kind of implicit constraints *causality constraints*. A pair of curves for which the beginning of an execution never prevents the execution from continuing is called *causal*. Intuitively, this is the same as having no forbidden region (but we will see that the relationship between absence of forbidden region and causality is only an implication).

Surprisingly, this question has received very little attention and to the best of our knowledge, no transformation has been published to make these implicit constraints explicit. One may wonder if this is a "true" problem, i.e. if such non causal curves can be encountered in practice. Indeed, a straightforward answer is that they cannot come from a real system, since curves derived from execution or simulation of real systems are always well-formed. The common practice is to use such curves for the inputs of RTC models. As RTC computations preserve the causality of the curves, non-causal curves were not considered as a problem so far. This may explain why no studies have been published yet on the subject. Things are different when instead of using RTC, one uses other tools for deriving output arrival curves, given some input arrival curves. Those tools, among them model-checking of timed automata [14] on abstracted models, abstract interpretation of Lustre programs [11], may compute non-causal arrival curves, even when the input is causal.

Additionally, non-causal curves contain implicit constraints that could be made explicit. If the output of a computation gives the curve in Figure 1, then making the implicit constraint explicit gives tighter bounds on the number of events (for example, a tighter bound on the number of events in a window of size 4). We encountered the case, when merging the output of several computations for the same set of flows of events [9] using different approximate methods. This provides several pairs of curves, each of them being a valid over-approximation of the expected result. The basic combination of these curves (point-wise minimum and maximum) can contain implicit constraints, and making them explicit gives more precise results from the same analysis.

Contributions. To solve these issues, this paper formally defines the causality problem and propose several solutions.

- We give a characterization of the notion of causal pairs of arrival curves.
- Combining this property with existing ones, we give a definition for a *canonical representation* of a pair of curves, which is causal and sub-additive/super-additive. We show that it is also the *tightest possible representation* of the original curve.
- We propose an algorithm that transforms a pair of arrival curves into its equivalent causal representation.

All results in the paper are proven (Due to place limitations, the proofs only appear in [15]) and may be applied to dense-time or discrete-time arrival curves on the one hand, to discrete-event or fluid-event models on the other hand. The implementation part has been developed for discrete-time discrete-event models, since this was our context of use, but we believe it could be adapted to other contexts. Furthermore, although all along the paper we talk about arrival curves, the reader should be convinced that every results also apply to service curves.

The outline of this paper is as follows: Section 2 defines *arrival curves* and some few algebraic operators; Section 3 defines *causality* and gives a *characterization* of it; Section 4 shows how to compute the *tightest causal representation* of arrival curves; and Section 5 gives an *algorithm* for computing it for discrete finite curves.

2   Arrival Curves

We now define the notion of arrival curves that characterize timing properties on a set of event streams. A pair of lower and upper arrival curves defines lower and upper bounds on the number of events allowed in a sliding window of size δ. Event streams that satisfy the pair of arrival curves are abstracted with cumulative curves that represent the number of events that occurs since the beginning $t = 0$. In this paper, we do not focus on a particular model and every results (except Section 5) apply to all of them. Namely, time can be either continuous or discrete, and we consider both the fluid and discrete event-model. Formally, functions we consider are from $\mathcal{T}$, the time, to $\overline{\mathcal{E}} = \mathcal{E} \cup \{\infty\}$, the event count; and $\mathcal{T}$ (resp. $\mathcal{E}$) can be either $\mathcal{R}^+$, the set of non-negative reals, or $\mathcal{N}$, the set of naturals. We note $\mathcal{F}$ the set of wide-sense increasing functions f from $\mathcal{T}$ to $\overline{\mathcal{E}}$ and such that $f(0) = 0$; $\mathcal{F}_{finite}$ is the set of such functions from $\mathcal{T}$ to $\mathcal{E}$.

Definition 1 (Arrival Curves and Cumulative Curves). *$R \in \mathcal{F}_{finite}$ can model a cumulative curve: $R(t)$ represents the (finite) amount of events that occurred in the interval of time $[0, t]$.*

A pair of arrival curves is a pair of functions (α^u, α^l) in $\mathcal{F} \times \mathcal{F}_{finite}$, such that $\alpha^l \leq \alpha^u$.

Let R be a cumulative curve and (α^u, α^l) be a pair of arrival curves. R is said to satisfy (α^u, α^l) noted $R \models (\alpha^u, \alpha^l)$ iff(def) $\forall x \in \mathcal{T}, \forall \delta \in \mathcal{T}, \quad R(x + \delta) - R(x) \in [\alpha^l(\delta), \alpha^u(\delta)]$

We say that a pair of arrival curves (α^u, α^l) is satisfiable *iff(def) there exists a cumulative curve R that satisfies (α^u, α^l).*

We note $R \models_{\leq T} (\alpha^u, \alpha^l)$, meaning that R satisfies (α^u, α^l) up to T iff(def)
$$\forall t \leq T, \forall \delta \leq t, \quad R(t) - R(t - \delta) \in [\alpha^l(\delta), \alpha^u(\delta)]$$

Next, comes the deconvolution operators that will be intensively used in the next sections. And then we briefly recall the notions of sub-additivity and super-additivity, that are used to erase the *unreachable regions* from the curves. Details on those notions can be find, e.g. in [13].

Definition 2 (Deconvolutions). *Let f, g be functions from $\mathcal{T}$ to $\overline{\mathcal{E}}$ and $x \in \mathcal{T}$,*

$$(f \oslash g)(x) \stackrel{def}{=} \sup_{t \geq 0} \{f(x + t) - g(t)\} \qquad ((min, +) \ deconvolution)$$

$$(f \,\overline{\oslash}\, g)(x) \stackrel{def}{=} \inf_{t \geq 0} \{f(x + t) - g(t)\} \qquad ((max, +) \ deconvolution)$$

Definition 3 (Sub/Super-Additivity and Closures). *Let $f \in \mathcal{F}$, f is said to be* sub-additive *(resp. super-additive) iff $\forall s, t \in \mathcal{T}$. $f(t + s) \leq f(t) + f(s)$ (resp $f(t + s) \geq f(t) + f(s)$).*

Let $f \in \mathcal{F}$. Among all the sub-additive (resp. super-additive) functions $g \in \mathcal{F}$ that are smaller (resp. greater) than f there exists an upper (resp. lower) bound called the sub-additive *(resp. super-additive) closure of f and denoted by $\overline{f}$ (resp. $\underline{f}$). A pair of arrival curves (α^u, α^l) is* Sub-Additive-Super-Additive *(denoted SA-SA for short) iff(def) α^u is sub-additive and α^l is super-additive. We call $(\overline{\alpha^u}, \underline{\alpha^l})$ the* SA-SA closure *of (α^u, α^l).*

SA-SA closure makes explicit some of the implicit constraints of an arrival curve. It makes explicit the *unreachable regions* (Figure 1.(a)), which are the regions between α^l and its super-additive closure $\underline{\alpha^l}$ in the one side, between α^u and its sub-additive closure $\overline{\alpha^u}$ on the other. Informally, they represents the points between α^u and α^l that are not reachable by any finite or infinite cumulative curves.

3   Causality: Definition and Characterization

We now define the notion of causality. The problem we are studying is the one of an event stream that is correct up to a certain time T, but "can not be continued" without violating the pair of curves. This can be seen as a deadlock of the flow, which could then neither let time elapse nor emit an additional event. A pair of arrival curves for which this problem can not happen is called *causal*. We first give a formal definition for causality, and then give a characterization with algebraic formulas.

Definition 4 (Causal Arrival Curves). *Let (α^u, α^l) be a pair of arrival curves. (α^u, α^l) is said to be* causal *iff any cumulative curve R that satisfies (α^u, α^l) up to T can be extended indefinitely into a cumulative curve R' that also satisfies (α^u, α^l). In other words, (α^u, α^l) is causal iff(def) $\forall T \geq 0$, $\forall R, (R \models_{\leq T} (\alpha^u, \alpha^l)) \implies (\exists R' \mid R' \models (\alpha^u, \alpha^l) \text{ and } \forall t \leq T, R(t) = R'(t))$*

Unlike the sub-additivity and super-additivity properties, the causality is really a property on a *pair* of curves; it does not make sense to say that α^u alone, or α^l alone, is causal since the impossibility to extend a cumulative curve can come only from a contradiction between an upper bound and a lower bound.

3.1   Characterization of Causality

Causality reveals new implicit constraints. Informally, we call *forbidden regions* the points between α^u and α^l that are reachable by finite cumulative curves, but for which the cumulative curves can trivially not be extended into infinite ones.

Let us consider the curve α^l, and try to define α^{l^*}, defined informally as "α^l without its forbidden regions". $\alpha^{l^*}(\delta)$ is the smallest value for which a cumulative curve R verifying $R(t+\delta) - R(t) \geq \alpha^{l^*}(\delta)$ is guaranteed to be extensible infinitely by emitting the maximum amount of events allowed by α^u, without violating α^l (this the same as saying that if $R(t + \delta) - R(t) < \alpha^{l^*}(\delta)$ for some t, then R cannot be extended without violating either α^u or α^l, which means that the region below α^{l^*} is forbidden). Computing the forbidden region of α^l at abscissa δ_0 means therefore computing the lowest N for which $\alpha^u(\delta) + N$ would not cross $\alpha^l(\delta_0 + \delta)$ for some $\delta \geq 0$. This is equivalent to finding the supremum of the N for which the curves would intersect. Formally, this can be written as $\alpha^{l^*} = \sup_{\delta \geq 0} \{\alpha^l(\delta_0 + \delta) - \alpha^u(\delta)\}$, which is the definition of the deconvolution: $\alpha^l \oslash \alpha^u$. A similar reasoning would lead to the curve $\alpha^u \overline{\oslash} \alpha^l$ for the forbidden regions of α^u.

We can therefore define more formally forbidden region as the area between a curve α^u (resp. α^l), and $\alpha^u \overline{\oslash} \alpha^l$ (resp. $\alpha^l \oslash \alpha^u$): intuitively, computing $\alpha^u \overline{\oslash} \alpha^l$ means "removing forbidden regions from α^u", and computing $\alpha^l \oslash \alpha^u$ means "removing forbidden regions from α^l". When $\alpha^u = \alpha^u \overline{\oslash} \alpha^l$ and $\alpha^l = \alpha^l \oslash \alpha^u$, we can say that the curves have no forbidden region. The contribution of this paper is the study of these forbidden regions, giving a formal characterization and algorithms to detect their presence and to eliminate them.

Theorem 1 (Characterization of Causality). *Let* (α^u, α^l) *be a pair of arrival curves. The following implications and equivalences hold:*

$$\begin{array}{c} \alpha^l = \alpha^l \oslash \alpha^u \\ and \\ \alpha^u = \alpha^u \overline{\oslash} \alpha^l \end{array} \quad \overset{(e)}{\Longrightarrow} \quad (\alpha^u, \alpha^l) \ is \ causal$$

$$\Big\Updownarrow (d) \qquad \nearrow (c) \qquad \Big\Updownarrow (b)$$

$$\begin{array}{c} \underline{\alpha^l} = \underline{\alpha^l} \oslash \overline{\alpha^u} \\ and \\ \overline{\alpha^u} = \overline{\alpha^u} \overline{\oslash} \underline{\alpha^l} \end{array} \quad \overset{(a)}{\Longleftrightarrow} \quad (\overline{\alpha^u}, \underline{\alpha^l}) \ is \ causal$$

The main result is equivalence **(c)** which gives an algebraic characterization of causality for any pair of arrival curves. Intuitively, it states that a pair of curves is causal if and only if its SA-SA closure has no forbidden region. A weaker version of this theorem is implication **(e)** which gives only a sufficient condition: a pair of arrival curves having no forbidden region is causal.

One could have expected for the converse to be true, i.e. that a pair of arrival curves is causal implies that it doesn't have forbidden regions. This result is indeed false in general: a pair of causal curves can have forbidden regions if they are included in their unreachable regions. This is shown in the counter-example of Figure 2. The vertically hatched region is a forbidden region, and we do not have $\alpha^l = \alpha^l \oslash \alpha^u$, but the curve is still causal. Actually, the forbidden region is below $\underline{\alpha^l}$, so it is not reachable.

The causality implies the absence of forbidden region for SA-SA curves though, since all unreachable regions have been erased from them: this is equivalence **(a)**. The remainders **(b)** and **(d)** are intermediate results.

Indication for the proofs: All the proofs are detailed in [15], most of them being relatively long and technical, using several intermediate lemmas. The following gives the overall structure and the chronology of the proofs.

(a) The proof is completely skipped here due to space limitations.
(b) The proof is relatively straightforward and based on the fact that $(\overline{\alpha^u}, \underline{\alpha^l})$ and (α^u, α^l) accept the same set of cumulative curves.
(c) This characterization is obtained by transitivity of **(a)** and **(b)**.
(d) The proof is omitted due to space limitations.
(e) The sufficient condition is obtained by transitivity of **(c)** and **(d)**.

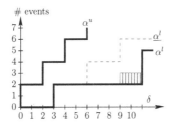

Fig. 2. Causal Curve with a Forbidden Region

4   Computing the Causality Closure

The goal of this section is to define the causality closure of a pair of curves (α^u, α^l): it is a pair of arrival curves which is causal and equivalent to (α^u, α^l). The first step is to define the $\mathbb{C}$ operator, which removes the forbidden regions from a pair of curves.

Notice that removing forbidden regions is done on the pair of curves, globally. As a result, while removing the forbidden regions on α^l, one may introduce new ones on α^u and vice-versa. One natural way to solve this issue is to iterate the forbidden region removal until one reaches the fix-point (assuming it is reached in a finite number of steps, which is not always the case).

To illustrate this, an example is given in Figure 3. The original curve (a) has both forbidden regions (vertically hatched) and an unreachable region (horizontally hatched).

One region of interest is the little square between $\delta = 4$ and $\delta = 5$, marked with a "?" in curve (a): if we consider the curves (α^u, α^l) before any transformation, it does not seem to be a forbidden region. An execution emitting only 1 event in 4 units of time seems to be able to continue by emitting 3 events right after. Actually, this is impossible, and there are at least two ways to show it. the first way to remove this "?"-region is to apply the forbidden regions removal twice: emitting 3 events as suggested above is not possible given the leftmost forbidden region of α^u. So, the "?"-region will have to be removed, as a consequence of the forbidden region on α^u. After the second iteration of the forbidden region removal, we reached the fix-point, and implication (e) guarantees the causality. This iterative approach will be detailed in Section 5.

However, an interesting property of the $\mathbb{C}$ operator is that it does not create new forbidden regions when applied on SA-SA curves: its application on $(\overline{\alpha^u}, \underline{\alpha^l})$ provides the causal canonical representative of (α^u, α^l) (this approach is further discussed in this section). Back to the example in Figure 3, a second way to show that the "?"-region should be removed from α^l is to work on $\underline{\alpha^l}$ instead of α^l: since $\underline{\alpha^l}(10) = 8$ and $\overline{\alpha^u}(6) = 6$, an execution has to emit at least two events in 4 units of time. This illustrates the approach followed in this section: we eliminate the forbidden regions with $\mathbb{C}$ (3.(c)) only after performing an SA-SA closure (3.(b)). The iterative approach will be kept for cases where the SA-SA closure cannot be applied due to algorithmic and coding limitations.

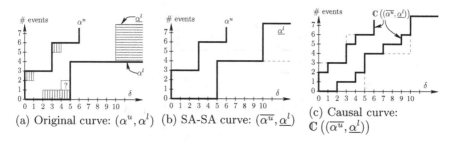

(a) Original curve: (α^u, α^l) (b) SA-SA curve: $(\overline{\alpha^u}, \underline{\alpha^l})$ (c) Causal curve: $\mathbb{C}\left((\overline{\alpha^u}, \underline{\alpha^l})\right)$

Fig. 3. Step-by-step causality closure

4.1   Removing Forbidden Regions: The $\mathbb{C}$ Operator

We defined pairs of arrival curves as pairs (α^u, α^l) of functions for which $\alpha^u \geq \alpha^l$. In addition, we write $\perp_{AC}$ the set of pairs of functions in $\mathcal{F}$ such that the former constraint is false. To simplify notations, $\perp_{AC}$ will be used as a single element even if it represents an infinite set of objects. We note AC the set of all pairs of arrival curves *plus* $\perp_{AC}$.

Definition 5. *We define the* $\mathbb{C}$ *operator from AC to AC as:*

$$\mathbb{C}\left(\perp_{AC}\right) = \perp_{AC} \quad and \quad \mathbb{C}\left(\alpha^l, \alpha^u\right) = \left(\begin{array}{l} let\ L = \alpha^l \oslash \alpha^u, U = \alpha^u \overline{\oslash} \alpha^l \\ if\ L \le U\ then\ (L, U) \\ else\ \perp_{AC} \end{array} \right.$$

When (α^u, α^l) is a pair of arrival curves then $L = \alpha^l \oslash \alpha^u$ and $U = \alpha^u \overline{\oslash} \alpha^l$ are functions in $\mathcal{F}$ (i.e. wide-sense increasing and equal to zero at zero). But they may cross each other (it may happen that $L \not\le U$): in these cases, the $\mathbb{C}$ operator computes the value $\perp_{AC}$. This means that the pair of arrival curves was not satisfiable (i.e. no cumulative curve satisfies it).

4.2 $\mathbb{C}(\overline{\alpha^u}, \underline{\alpha^l})$: The Canonical Representative and Its Properties

This section presents the main result of the paper. It basically states that $\mathbb{C}(\overline{\alpha^u}, \underline{\alpha^l})$ has all the desirable properties: SA-SA, causality, and it is indeed the best possible pair of curves equivalent to (α^u, α^l).

Theorem 2. *For any pair of arrival curves* (α^u, α^l),
- $\mathbb{C}(\overline{\alpha^u}, \underline{\alpha^l}) = \perp_{AC}$ *iff* (α^u, α^l) *is non-satisfiable;*
- $\mathbb{C}(\overline{\alpha^u}, \underline{\alpha^l})$ *is causal, SA-SA and equivalent to* (α^u, α^l), *otherwise.*
- *when* (α^u, α^l) *is satisfiable,* $\mathbb{C}(\overline{\alpha^u}, \underline{\alpha^l})$ *is the* tightest *pair of curves equivalent to* (α^u, α^l).

By *tightest*, we mean that $\mathbb{C}(\overline{\alpha^u}, \underline{\alpha^l})$ is made of the smallest (resp. the greatest) curve for the upper (resp. lower) part such that the properties are satisfied. The proofs are given in [15]. This gives an interesting result: given any pair of curves, one can compute $\mathbb{C}(\overline{\alpha^u}, \underline{\alpha^l})$, and get either the information that the curves are not satisfiable, or the best possible pair of curves equivalent to the original one. In addition to this optimality, one also gets the desirable properties: causality and SA-SA. This result is implementable on top of any algorithmic toolbox implementing the basic operators: convolution, deconvolution, sub-additive and super-additive closure.

Theorem 2 also provides the existence and uniqueness of a tightest pair of curves equivalent to a given one. As a result, the following theorem states that it is causal.

Theorem 3. *Let* (α^u, α^l) *be a pair of curves. If* (α^u, α^l) *is the tightest pair of curves representing a set of cumulative curves, then* (α^u, α^l) *is causal.*

Any computation giving the best possible pair of curves also gives a causal pair of curves. Theorem 3 *explains why*, in practice, most pairs of arrival curves usually manipulated in Real-Time Calculus are causal. Indeed, curves obtained for example by measurements on a real system are causal by construction; furthermore computations made in the RTC framework compute the optimal solution and thus preserve the causality property. It also probably explains why this problem received so little attention up to now.

On the other side, non-causal pairs of curves may arise whenever a computation is done in an *inexact manner*. This typically occurs using other tools than RTC algebraic solutions. Indeed, the recent works that interfaces RTC with state-based models face the problem. In [2], the authors get rid of it by constraining the class of curves they compute which are causal by definition (the extension to arbitrary curves which is part of their future works will have to deal with it though). But, in [9], the output curves are computed, one point at a time on an abstract model: this does result into non causal curves, which are refined after being computed. The CATS tool [8] relies on exact model-checking, so applied on a causal pair of curves, the tool would output causal curves. [4] also uses exact model-checking, but the long-term rate computation uses an approximation, which could generate non-causal curves (see [15] for an example).

Finally, in ac2lus [3] we use the abstract interpreter nbac [11], which also does some abstractions, and hence doesn't guarantee the causality of the curves computed.

5   Algorithms for Discrete Finite Curves

5.1   Definitions of Finite Arrival Curves

Up to this point, we dealt with infinite pairs of curves, but, as mentionned in the introduction, the original work that brought us to studying causality was to connect RTC curves to synchronous programming languages [3]. Our model uses a simple computer representation of arrival curves: we work in *discrete-time*, *discrete-event* model, and consider only *finite curves*, which makes them easy to represent and manipulate algorithmically speaking. We consider the infinite extension of the curves to remain in the theoretical framework presented in the previous sections and to be able to apply the same theorems. Therefore, instead of formalizing the notion of *finite* curves, we consider the *restriction* of infinite curves on a *finite* interval.

Working with discrete-time (resp. discrete-event) models doesn't change the above results, since we considered time (resp. event count) as the set T (resp. $\mathcal{E}$), being either $\mathcal{R}^+$ or $\mathcal{N}$. We now (in this chapter) set $T = \mathcal{E} = \mathcal{N}$. On the other hand, working with finite curves will change the results a bit: the notion of SA-SA-closure doesn't fit well in the finite model, since the SA-SA-closure of a finite curve could be infinite.

We first give some definitions for finite arrival curves and then an algorithm to efficiently compute the causality closure using the $\mathbb{C}$ operator.

Definition 6 (Finite restriction of an arrival curve). *We denote by* $(\alpha^u|_T, \alpha^l|_T)$ *the restriction of* (α^u, α^l) *to* $[0, T]$ *defined as:*

$$\forall t \leq T, \quad \alpha^u|_T(t) \stackrel{def}{=} \alpha^u(t) \text{ and } \alpha^l|_T(t) \stackrel{def}{=} \alpha^l(t)$$

$$\forall t > T, \quad \alpha^u|_T(t) \stackrel{def}{=} +\infty \text{ and } \alpha^l|_T(t) \stackrel{def}{=} \alpha^l(T)$$

$(\alpha^u|_{_T}, \alpha^l|_{_T})$ still applies to infinite event streams, but only gives constraints for finite windows of time. Intuitively, it could be a pair of curves defined over $[0, T]$. But defining them as functions over $\mathcal{N}$ has the advantage of remaining within the definition of arrival curves given above: $\alpha^l|_{_T}$ and $\alpha^u|_{_T}$ are still functions in $\mathcal{F}$, but they can be represented easily as finite arrays of naturals.

It should be noted that finite restrictions of arrival curves can not have the SA-SA property (as far as $\exists t > 0.\alpha^u(t) < +\infty$). However, one can define the property *SA-SA over* $[0, T]$ and the associated closure (see [15] for details). Additionally, [16], page 7, provides an efficient way to compute the sub-additive closure in discrete events. It can easily be adapted to compute the SA-SA closure over $[0, T]$ leading to a simple, quadratic algorithm.

5.2   Causality Closure for Finite Discrete Curves

Unfortunately, the valid result for infinite curves, stating that $\mathbb{C}(\overline{\alpha^u}, \underline{\alpha^l})$ was a causal curve equivalent to (α^u, α^l) is helpless from the algorithmic point of view with finite curves: computing it would require computing $(\overline{\alpha^u}, \underline{\alpha^l})$, which is an infinite curve.

But theorem 1(**e**) still holds (i.e. the fix-points of $\mathbb{C}$ are causal), and it can easily be shown that applying the $\mathbb{C}$ operator doesn't change the set of accepted cumulative curves. So, we can compute the fix-point by iterating $\mathbb{C}$.

We illustrate the process with an example in Figure 4. The original pair of curves is (a), and one can see that although the curves are SA-SA on $[0, 4]$ (but clearly not SA-SA because of the curve α^u with $+\infty$ values), one application of $\mathbb{C}$ is not sufficient: the curve (b) is not even SA-SA on interval $[0, 4]$, and still has forbidden regions. We iterate the $\mathbb{C}$ operator once more and get (c), which is causal, but not SA-SA.

Another option which may speed up the algorithm, is to apply a finite SA-SA closure before applying $\mathbb{C}$ again: this gives curves (d) and then (e) by applying $\mathbb{C}$ again. Then, neither the SA-SA closure nor $\mathbb{C}$ would change the curve anymore: we reached the fix-point. In this case, the final curve has both the causality and the SA-SA properties on interval $[0, 4]$.

Theorem 4. *For any $T > 0$ and any pair of arrival curves (α^u, α^l) with $\forall t \in [0, T], \alpha^u(t) \neq +\infty$, the sequence $\mathbb{C}^n(\alpha^u|_{T'}, \alpha^l|_{T})$ admits a fix-point (denoted $\mathbb{C}^\infty(\alpha^u|_{T'}, \alpha^l|_{T})$), which is either $\perp_{AC}$ or a causal pair of arrival curves equivalent to $(\alpha^u|_{T'}, \alpha^l|_{T})$.*

The above theorem states that, given an finite discrete pair of arrival curves, one may iteratively compute, by application of the $\mathbb{C}$ operator, a causal finite discrete pair of arrival curves which is equivalent to the original, if it is satisfiable; otherwise, the computation leads to $\perp_{AC}$. The convergence of the iterations can be accelerated by using, in addition to $\mathbb{C}$, other tightening operators that preserves the set of accepted cumulative curves like the SA-SA closure. This is expressed in the following theorem and applied in the example in Figure 4.(d) and 4.(e).

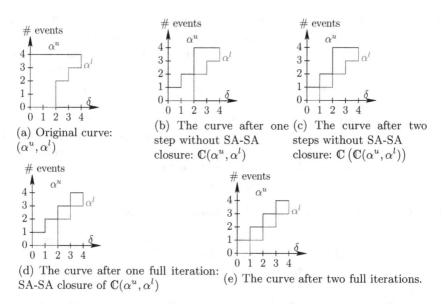

(a) Original curve: (α^u, α^l)

(b) The curve after one step without SA-SA closure: $\mathbb{C}(\alpha^u, \alpha^l)$

(c) The curve after two steps without SA-SA closure: $\mathbb{C}\left(\mathbb{C}(\alpha^u, \alpha^l)\right)$

(d) The curve after one full iteration: SA-SA closure of $\mathbb{C}(\alpha^u, \alpha^l)$

(e) The curve after two full iterations.

Fig. 4. Step-by-step causality closure for finite curves

Theorem 5. *For any $T > 0$ and any pair of arrival curves (α^u, α^l) with $\forall t \in [0, T]$, $\alpha^u(t) \neq +\infty$, the sequence defined by $(\alpha^u_0, \alpha^l_0) = (\alpha^u|_T, \alpha^l|_T)$ and $\forall n \geq 0$, $(\alpha^u_{n+1}, \alpha^l_{n+1}) = \mathbb{C}(\overline{\alpha^u_n}|_T, \overline{\alpha^l_n}|_T)$ admits a fix-point, which is either $\perp_{AC}$ or a causal and SA-SA pair of arrival curves equivalent to $(\alpha^u|_T, \alpha^l|_T)$.*

The detailed proof appears in [15]. It is made simple by the fact that we work in discrete time and events: this makes the set of possible curves finite. Since the sequence (α^u_n, α^l_n) becomes tighter and tighter, it has to reach a fix-point in a finite number of steps.

We still need a way to compute $\mathbb{C}$ efficiently: the definition of $\mathbb{C}$ contains the supremum of an infinite set, which as it is, would not be computable. Fortunately, the operator $\mathbb{C}$ applied to finite restrictions of curves is indeed much simpler. Since $\forall t > T$, $\alpha^u(t) = +\infty$ and $\alpha^l(t) = \alpha^l(T)$, the values of (α^u, α^l) beyond T do not have to be taken into account in the computation of the deconvolutions, so $\mathbb{C}$ can be easily computed quadratically.

5.3   Algorithm

The full algorithm for computing the causal and SA-SA pair of curves equivalent to the finite pair of arrival curves A_0 defined on $[0, T]$ is given in Figure 5.

The loop terminates but finding a bound on the number of iterations other than the brute-force (just knowing that the sequence is decreasing and that there is a finite number of possible curves tighter that the original one) is still an open question. In practice, however, the number of iterations required is low (one or two in the examples we tried).

$A \leftarrow A_0$
repeat
    $A \leftarrow$ SA-SA-closure(A)   /* Not mandatory, but speeds up convergence, and
    ensures SA-SA */
    $A' \leftarrow A$
    $A \leftarrow \mathbb{C}(A)$
until $A \neq \perp_{AC}$ or $A' = A$

Fig. 5. Computation of causality closure for finite, discrete curves

After the loop, A is either $\perp_{AC}$ or a causal pair of finite discrete curves; it is equivalent to A_0, the original pair of curves; and it is SA-SA on the interval $[0, T]$ if the SA-SA closure was applied (first line within the loop). In this case, it is the best pair of curves equivalent to the original A_0.

6   Conclusion

We formally defined the notion of causality for RTC curves, and set up a formal framework to study it. As already mentioned, and although all along the paper we talk about arrival curves, the results are applicable to arrival curves *as well as* to service curves. We started from the intuitive notion of forbidden region, and the definition of causality based on the possibility to extend a curve, and stated the equivalence (valid for SA-SA pairs of curves) between absence of forbidden regions and the definition.

To the best we know, the phenomenon has received little attention and no work has been yet on the subject. This is mainly due to the usual way arrival curves were used within the RTC framework on the one hand and to the restrictions of the studies to some already causal class of arrival curves in the other hand. We detailed in which conditions causality can appear and be problematic. Dealing with general causal pairs of curves in a simulator or a formal verification tool is very often mandatory (unless using, if at all possible, heavyweight roundabout computations). To avoid non-causal curves, we propose an algorithm that turns a non-causal pair of curves into a causal one. After application of this algorithm, event generators based on arrival curves cannot deadlock, and formal verifiers do no more produce spurious counter-examples linked to causality.

The additional benefit of the transformation is that it gives the tightest pair of curves equivalent to the original one, which is also a canonical representative of all arrival curve pairs defining the same set of event streams. Indeed, compared to the "mathematical refinement algorithm" proposed in [9], our algorithm is more general and potentially more precise. It would be an improvement to replace this refinement algorithm by the causality closure.

The theorems and algorithms work for discrete and fluid event model, discrete and continuous time for infinite curves. Given any subset of these models, one just has to implement the basic operators to be able to use them. They have also been adapted to discrete time and event model for the case of finite arrival curves, where the sub-additive and super-additive closure operators do not make sense. The later was implemented in the `ac2lus` [3] toolbox.

References

1. Thiele, L., Chakraborty, S., Naedele, M.: Real-time calculus for scheduling hard real-time systems. In: International Symposium on Circuits and Systems (ISCAS), Geneva, Switzerland, March 2000, vol. 4, pp. 101–104 (2000)
2. Lampka, K., Perathoner, S., Thiele, L.: Analytic real-time analysis and timed automata: A hybrid method for analyzing embedded real-time systems. In: 8th ACM & IEEE International conference on Embedded software (EMSOFT). ACM, New York (2009)
3. Altisen, K., Moy, M.: Connecting real-time calculus to the synchronous programming language lustre. Technical Report TR-2009-14, Verimag Research Report (2009)
4. Phan, L.T.X., Chakraborty, S., Thiagarajan, P.S., Thiele, L.: Composing functional and state-based performance models for analyzing heterogeneous real-time systems. In: Proceedings of the 28th IEEE International Real-Time Systems Symposium (RTSS), Washington, DC, USA, pp. 343–352. IEEE Computer Society, Los Alamitos (2007)
5. Mokrushin, L.: Compositional analysis of timed systems by abstraction. Power-Point Slides (2007)
6. Raymond, P.: Compilation efficace d'un langage declaratif synchrone: Le generateur de code Lustre-v3. PhD thesis, Institut National Polytechnique de Grenoble - INPG, Section 13.7, "Causalité", pp. 119–123 (November 1991)
7. Liu, C.L., Layland, J.W.: Scheduling algorithms for multiprogramming in a hard-real-time environment. J. ACM 20(1), 46–61 (1973)
8. DARTS, IT Dept., U.U.: Cats tool (2007), http://www.timestool.com/cats
9. Liu, Y., Altisen, K., Moy, M.: Granularity-based interfacing between RTC and timed automata performance models. Technical Report TR-2009-10, Verimag, Centre Équation, 38610 Gières (August 2009)
10. Künzli, S., Poletti, F., Benini, L., Thiele, L.: Combining simulation and formal methods for system-level performance analysis. In: DATE 2006: Proceedings of the conference on Design, automation and test in Europe, 3001 Leuven, Belgium, Belgium, European Design and Automation Association, pp. 236–241 (2006)
11. Jeannet, B.: Dynamic partitioning in linear relation analysis. application to the verification of reactive systems. Formal Methods in System Design 23(1), 5–37 (2003)
12. Raymond, P.: Lustre v4 Manual. Verimag (February 2000)
13. Le Boudec, J.Y., Thiran, P.: Network Calculus. LNCS, vol. 2050. Springer, Heidelberg (2001)
14. Henzinger, T.A., Nicollin, X., Sifakis, J., Yovine, S.: Symbolic model checking for real-time systems. Information and Computation 111, 394–406 (1992)
15. Moy, M., Altisen, K.: Arrival curves for real-time calculus: the causality problem and its solutions. Technical Report TR-2009-15, Verimag Research Report (2009)
16. Bouillard, A., Thierry, É.: An algorithmic toolbox for network calculus. Discrete Event Dynamic Systems 18(1), 3–49 (2008)

Computing the Leakage of Information-Hiding Systems

Miguel E. Andrés[1], Catuscia Palamidessi[2],
Peter van Rossum[1], and Geoffrey Smith[3]

[1] Institute for Computing and Information Sciences, The Netherlands.
[2] INRIA and LIX, École Polytechnique Palaiseau, France
[3] SCIS, Florida International University, USA

Abstract. We address the problem of computing the information leakage of a system in an efficient way. We propose two methods: one based on reducing the problem to reachability, and the other based on techniques from quantitative counterexample generation. The second approach can be used either for exact or approximate computation, and provides feedback for debugging. These methods can be applied also in the case in which the input distribution is unknown. We then consider the interactive case and we point out that the definition of associated channel proposed in literature is not sound. We show however that the leakage can still be defined consistently, and that our methods extend smoothly.

1 Introduction

By *information hiding*, we refer generally to the problem of constructing protocols or programs that protect sensitive information from being deduced by some adversary. In *anonymity protocols* [4], for example, the concern is to design mechanisms to prevent an observer of network traffic from deducing who is communicating. In *secure information flow* [17], the concern is to prevent programs from leaking their secret input to an observer of their public output. Such leakage could be accidental or malicious.

Recently, there has been particular interest in approaching these issues *quantitatively*, using concepts of information theory. See for example [13,5,10,6,4]. The secret input S and the observable output O of an information-hiding system are modeled as random variables related by a *channel matrix*, whose (s, o) entry specifies $P(o|s)$, the conditional probability of observing output o given input s. If we define the *vulnerability* of S as the probability that the adversary could correctly guess the value of S in one try, then it is natural to measure the information leakage by comparing the *a priori* vulnerability of S with the *a posteriori* vulnerability of S after observing O. We consider two measures of leakage: *additive*, which is the difference between the *a posteriori* and *a priori* vulnerabilities; and *multiplicative*, which is their quotient [19,3].

We thus view a protocol or program as a *noisy channel*, and we calculate the leakage from the channel matrix and the *a priori* distribution on S. But, given an operational specification of a protocol or program, how do we calculate the parameters of the noisy channel: the sets of inputs and outputs, the *a priori* distribution, the channel matrix, and the associated leakage? These are the main questions we address in this paper. We focus on *probabilistic automata*, whose transitions are labeled with probabilities and *actions*, each of which is classified as secret, observable, or internal.

J. Esparza and R. Majumdar (Eds.): TACAS 2010, LNCS 6015, pp. 373–389, 2010.

We first consider the simple case in which the secret inputs take place at the beginning of runs, and their probability is fixed. The interpretation in terms of noisy channel of this kind of systems is well understood in literature. The framework of probabilistic automata, however, allows to represent more general situations. Thanks to the nondeterministic choice, indeed, we can model the case in which the input distribution is unknown, or variable. We show that the definition of channel matrix extends smoothly also to this case. Finally, we turn our attention to the interactive scenario in which inputs can occur again after outputs. This case has also been considered in literature, and there has been an attempt to define the channel matrix in terms of the probabilities of traces [11]. However it turns out that the notion of channel is unsound. Fortunately the leakage is still well defined, and it can be obtained in the same way as the simple case.

We consider two different approaches to computing the channel matrix. One uses a system of linear equations as in reachability computations. With this system of equations one can compute the *joint matrix*, the matrix of probabilities of observing both s and o; the channel matrix is trivially derived from this joint matrix. The other approach starts with a 0 channel matrix, which we call a *partial matrix* at this point. We iteratively add the contributions in conditional probabilities of complete paths to this partial matrix, obtaining, in the limit, the channel matrix itself. We then group paths with the same secret and the same observable together using ideas from quantitative counterexample generation, namely by using regular expressions and strongly connected component analysis. In this way, we can add the contribution of (infinitely) many paths at the same time to the partial matrices. This second approach also makes it possible to identify which parts of a protocol contribute most to the leakage, which is useful for debugging.

Looking ahead, after reviewing some preliminaries (Section 2) we present restrictions on probabilistic automata to ensure that they have well-defined, finite channel matrices (Section 3). This is followed by the techniques to calculate the channel matrix efficiently (Section 4 and Section 5). We then turn our attention to extensions of our information-hiding system model. We use nondeterministic choice to model the situation where the *a priori* distribution on the secret is unknown (Section 6). Finally, we consider interactive systems, in which secret actions and observable actions can be interleaved arbitrarily (Section 7).

2 Preliminaries

2.1 Probabilistic Automata

This section recalls some basic notions on probabilistic automata. More details can be found in [18]. A function $\mu: Q \to [0, 1]$ is a *discrete probability distribution* on a set Q if the support of μ is countable and $\sum_{q \in Q} \mu(q) = 1$. The set of all discrete probability distributions on Q is denoted by $\mathcal{D}(Q)$.

A *probabilistic automaton* is a quadruple $M = (Q, \Sigma, \hat{q}, \alpha)$ where Q is a countable set of *states*, Σ a finite set of *actions*, $\hat{q}$ the *initial* state, and α a *transition function* $\alpha : Q \to \wp_f(\mathcal{D}(\Sigma \times Q))$. Here $\wp_f(X)$ is the set of all finite subsets of X. If $\alpha(q) = \emptyset$ then q is a *terminal* state. We write $q \to \mu$ for $\mu \in \alpha(q)$, $q \in Q$. Moreover, we write $q \xrightarrow{a} r$ for $q, r \in Q$ whenever $q \to \mu$ and $\mu(a, r) > 0$. A *fully probabilistic automaton* is a probabilistic automaton satisfying $|\alpha(q)| \leq 1$ for all states. In case $\alpha(q) \neq \emptyset$ we will overload notation and use $\alpha(q)$ to denote the distribution outgoing from q.

A *path* in a probabilistic automaton is a sequence $\sigma = q_0 \xrightarrow{a_1} q_1 \xrightarrow{a_2} \cdots$ where $q_i \in Q$, $a_i \in \Sigma$ and $q_i \xrightarrow{a_{i+1}} q_{i+1}$. A path can be *finite* in which case it ends with a state. A path is *complete* if it is either infinite or finite ending in a terminal state. Given a path σ, $\text{first}(\sigma)$ denotes its first state, and if σ is finite then $\text{last}(\sigma)$ denotes its last state. A *cycle* is a path σ such that $\text{last}(\sigma) = \text{first}(\sigma)$. We denote the set of actions occurring in a cycle as $\text{CyclesA}(M)$. Let $\text{Paths}_q(M)$ denote the set of all paths, $\text{Paths}^*_q(M)$ the set of all finite paths, and $\text{CPaths}_q(M)$ the set of all complete paths of an automaton M, starting from the state q. We will omit q if $q = \hat{q}$. Paths are ordered by the prefix relation, which we denote by $\leq$. The *trace* of a path is the sequence of actions in $\Sigma^* \cup \Sigma^\infty$ obtained by removing the states, hence for the above σ we have $\text{trace}(\sigma) = a_1 a_2 \ldots$. If $\Sigma' \subseteq \Sigma$, then $\text{trace}_{\Sigma'}(\sigma)$ is the projection of $\text{trace}(\sigma)$ on the elements of Σ'. The *length* of a finite path σ, denoted by $|\sigma|$, is the number of actions in its trace.

Let $M = (Q, \Sigma, \hat{q}, \alpha)$ be a (fully) probabilistic automaton, $q \in Q$ a state, and let $\sigma \in \text{Paths}^*_q(M)$ be a finite path starting in q. The *cone* generated by σ is the set of complete paths $\langle \sigma \rangle = \{\sigma' \in \text{CPaths}_q(M) \mid \sigma \leq \sigma'\}$. Given a fully probabilistic automaton $M = (Q, \Sigma, \hat{q}, \alpha)$ and a state q, we can calculate the *probability value*, denoted by $\mathbf{P}_q(\sigma)$, of any finite path σ starting in q as follows: $\mathbf{P}_q(q) = 1$ and $\mathbf{P}_q(\sigma \xrightarrow{a} q') = \mathbf{P}_q(\sigma) \, \mu(a, q')$, where $\text{last}(\sigma) \to \mu$.

Let $\Omega_q \triangleq \text{CPaths}_q(M)$ be the sample space, and let $\mathcal{F}_q$ be the smallest σ-algebra generated by the cones. Then $\mathbf{P}$ induces a unique *probability measure* on $\mathcal{F}_q$ (which we will also denote by $\mathbf{P}_q$) such that $\mathbf{P}_q(\langle \sigma \rangle) = \mathbf{P}_q(\sigma)$ for every finite path σ starting in q. For $q = \hat{q}$ we write $\mathbf{P}$ instead of $\mathbf{P}_{\hat{q}}$.

Given a probability space $(\Omega, \mathcal{F}, P)$ and two events $A, B \in F$ with $P(B) > 0$, the *conditional probability* of A given B, $P(A \mid B)$, is defined as $P(A \cap B)/P(B)$.

2.2 Noisy Channels

This section briefly recalls the notion of noisy channels from Information Theory [7].

A *noisy channel* is a tuple $\mathcal{C} \triangleq (\mathcal{X}, \mathcal{Y}, P(\cdot|\cdot))$ where $\mathcal{X} = \{x_1, x_2, \ldots, x_n\}$ is a finite set of *input values*, modeling the *secrets* of the channel, and $\mathcal{Y} = \{y_1, y_2, \ldots, y_m\}$ is a finite set of *output values*, the *observables* of the channel. For $x_i \in \mathcal{X}$ and $y_j \in \mathcal{Y}$, $P(y_j | x_i)$ is the conditional probability of obtaining the output y_j given that the input is x_i. These conditional probabilities constitute the so called *channel matrix*, where $P(y_j | x_i)$ is the element at the intersection of the i-th row and the j-th column. For any input distribution P_X on $\mathcal{X}$, P_X and the channel matrix determine a joint probability $P_\wedge$ on $\mathcal{X} \times \mathcal{Y}$, and the corresponding marginal probability P_Y on $\mathcal{Y}$ (and hence a random variable Y). P_X is also called *a priori distribution* and it is often denoted by π. The probability of the input given the output is called *a posteriori distribution*.

2.3 Information Leakage

We recall here the definitions of *multiplicative leakage* proposed in [19], and *additive leakage* proposed in [3][1]. We assume given a noisy channel $\mathcal{C} = (\mathcal{X}, \mathcal{Y}, P(\cdot|\cdot))$ and a

---

[1] The notion proposed by Smith in [19] was given in a (equivalent) logarithmic form, and called simply *leakage*. For uniformity's sake we use here the terminology and formulation of [3].

random variable X on $\mathcal{X}$. The *a priori vulnerability* of the secrets in $\mathcal{X}$ is the probability of guessing the right secret, defined as $V(X) \triangleq \max_{x \in \mathcal{X}} P_X(x)$. The rationale behind this definition is that the adversary's best bet is on the secret with highest probability.

The *a posteriori vulnerability* of the secrets in $\mathcal{X}$ is the probability of guessing the right secret, after the output has been observed, averaged over the probabilities of the observables. The formal definition is $V(X \mid Y) \triangleq \sum_{y \in \mathcal{Y}} P_Y(y) \max_{x \in \mathcal{X}} P(x \mid y)$. Again, this definition is based on the principle that the adversary will choose the secret with the highest a posteriori probability.

Note that, using Bayes theorem, we can write the a posteriori vulnerability in terms of the channel matrix and the a priori distribution, or in terms of the joint probability:

$$V(X \mid Y) = \sum_{y \in \mathcal{Y}} \max_{x \in \mathcal{X}} (P(y \mid x) P_X(x)) = \sum_{y \in \mathcal{Y}} \max_{x \in \mathcal{X}} P_\wedge(x, y). \tag{1}$$

The *multiplicative* leakage is defined as $\mathcal{L}_\times(\mathcal{C}, P_X) \triangleq \frac{V(X \mid Y)}{V(X)}$ and the *additive* leakage as $\mathcal{L}_+(\mathcal{C}, P_X) \triangleq V(X \mid Y) - V(X)$.

3   Information Hiding Systems

To formally analyze the information-hiding properties of protocols and programs, we propose to model them as a particular kind of probabilistic automata, which we call *Information-Hiding Systems* (IHS). Intuitively, an IHS is a probabilistic automaton in which the actions are divided in three (disjoint) categories: those which are supposed to remain secret (to an external observer), those which are visible, and those which are internal to the protocol.

First we consider only the case in which the choice of the secret takes place entirely at the beginning, and is based on a known distribution. Furthermore we focus on fully probabilistic automata. Later in the paper we will relax these constraints.

Definition 3.1 (Information-Hiding System). An information-hiding system (IHS) is a quadruple $\mathcal{I} = (M, \Sigma_\mathcal{S}, \Sigma_\mathcal{O}, \Sigma_\tau)$ where $M = (Q, \Sigma, \hat{q}, \alpha)$ is a fully probabilistic automaton, $\Sigma = \Sigma_\mathcal{S} \cup \Sigma_\mathcal{O} \cup \Sigma_\tau$ where $\Sigma_\mathcal{S}$, $\Sigma_\mathcal{O}$, and Σ_τ are pairwise disjoint sets of secret, observable, and internal actions, and α satisfies the following restrictions:

1. $\alpha(\hat{q}) \in \mathcal{D}(\Sigma_\mathcal{S} \times Q)$,
2. $\forall s \in \Sigma_\mathcal{S} \; \exists! q . \alpha(\hat{q})(s, q) \neq 0$,
3. $\alpha(q) \in \mathcal{D}(\Sigma_\mathcal{O} \cup \Sigma_\tau \times Q)$ for $q \neq \hat{q}$,
4. $\forall a \in (\Sigma_\mathcal{S} \cup \Sigma_\mathcal{O}) . a \notin \text{CyclesA}(M)$,
5. $\mathbf{P}(\text{CPaths}(M) \cap \text{Paths}^*(M)) = 1$.

The first two restrictions are on the initial state and mean that only secret actions can happen there (1) and each of those actions must have non null probability and occur only once (2), Restriction 3 forbids secret actions to happen in the rest of the automaton, and Restriction 4 ensures that the channel associated to the IHS has finitely many inputs and outputs. Finally, Restriction 5 means that infinite computations have probability 0 and therefore we can ignore them.

We now show how to interpret an IHS as a noisy channel. We call $trace_{\Sigma_S}(\sigma)$ and $trace_{\Sigma_O}(\sigma)$ the *secret* and *observable* traces of σ, respectively. For $s \in \Sigma_S^*$, we define $[s] \triangleq \{\sigma \in \text{CPaths}(M) \mid trace_{\Sigma_S}(\sigma) = s\}$; similarly for $o \in \Sigma_O^*$, we define $[o] \triangleq \{\sigma \in \text{CPaths}(M) \mid trace_{\Sigma_O}(\sigma) = o\}$.

Definition 3.2. Given an IHS $\mathcal{I} = (M, \Sigma_S, \Sigma_O, \Sigma_\tau)$, its noisy channel is $(\mathcal{S}, \mathcal{O}, P)$, where $\mathcal{S} \triangleq \Sigma_S$, $\mathcal{O} \triangleq trace_{\Sigma_O}(\text{CPaths}(M))$, and $P(o \mid s) \triangleq \mathbf{P}([o] \mid [s])$. The a priori distribution $\pi \in \mathcal{D}(\mathcal{S})$ of $\mathcal{I}$ is defined by $\pi(s) \triangleq \alpha(\hat{q})(s, \cdot)$. If $\mathcal{C}$ is the noisy channel of $\mathcal{I}$, the multiplicative and additive leakage of $\mathcal{I}$ are naturally defined as

$$\mathcal{L}_\times(\mathcal{I}) \triangleq \mathcal{L}_\times(\mathcal{C}, \pi) \quad \text{and} \quad \mathcal{L}_+(\mathcal{I}) \triangleq \mathcal{L}_+(\mathcal{C}, \pi).$$

Example 3.3. Crowds [16] is a well-known anonymity protocol, in which a user (called the *initiator*) wants to send a message to a web server without revealing his identity. To achieve this, he routes the message through a crowd of users participating in the protocol. Routing is as follows. In the beginning, the initiator randomly selects a user (called a *forwarder*), possibly himself, and forwards the request to him. A forwarder performs a probabilistic choice. With probability p (a parameter of the protocol) he selects a new user and again forwards the message. With probability $1-p$ he sends the message directly to the server. One or more users can be *corrupted* and collaborate with each other to try to find the identity of the initiator.

We now show how to model Crowds as an IHS for 2 honest and 1 corrupted user. We assume that the corrupted user immediately forwards messages to the server, as there is no further information to be gained for him by bouncing the message back.

Figure 1 shows the automaton[2]. Actions a and b are secret and represent who initiates the protocol; actions A, B, and U are observable; A and B represent who forwards the message to the corrupted user; U represents the fact that the message arrives at the server undetected by the corrupted user. We assume U to be observable to represent the possibility that the message is made publically available at the server's site.

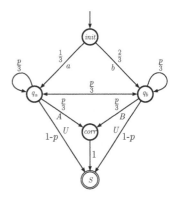

Fig. 1. Crowds Protocol

The channel associated to this IHS has $\mathcal{S} = \{a, b\}$, $\mathcal{O} = \{A, B, U\}$, and a priori distribution $\pi(a) = \frac{1}{3}$, $\pi(b) = \frac{2}{3}$. Its channel matrix is computed in the next section.

4   Reachability Analysis Approach

This section presents a method to compute the matrix of joint probabilities $P_\wedge$ associated to an IHS, defined as

$$P_\wedge(s, o) \triangleq \mathbf{P}([s] \cap [o]) \quad \text{for all } s \in \mathcal{S} \text{ and } o \in \mathcal{O}.$$

---

[2] For the sake of simplicity, we allow the initiator of the protocol to send the message to the server also in the first step of the protocol.

We omit the subscript $\wedge$ when no confusion arises. From $P_\wedge$ we can derive the channel matrix by dividing $P_\wedge(s, o)$ by $\pi(s)$. The leakage can be computed directly from $P_\wedge$, using the second form of the a posteriori vulnerability in (1).

We write x_q^λ for the probability of the set of paths with trace $\lambda \in (\Sigma_S \cup \Sigma_O)^*$ starting from the state q of M:

$$x_q^\lambda \triangleq \mathbf{P}_q([\lambda]_q),$$

where $[\lambda]_q \triangleq \{\sigma \in \mathrm{CPaths}_q(M) \mid trace_{\Sigma_S \cup \Sigma_O}(\sigma) = \lambda\}$. The following key lemma shows the linear relation between the x_q^λ's. We assume, w.l.o.g., that the IHS has a unique final state q_f.

Lemma 4.1. *Let* $\mathcal{I} = (M, \Sigma_S, \Sigma_O, \Sigma_\tau)$ *be an IHS. For all* $\lambda \in (\Sigma_S \cup \Sigma_O)^*$ *and* $q \in Q$ *we have*

$$
\begin{aligned}
x_{q_f}^\epsilon &= 1, \\
x_{q_f}^\lambda &= 0 \quad \text{for } \lambda \neq \epsilon, \\
x_q^\epsilon &= \textstyle\sum_{h \in \Sigma_\tau} \sum_{q' \in \mathrm{succ}(q)} \alpha(q)(h, q') \cdot x_{q'}^\epsilon \quad \text{for } q \neq q_f, \\
x_q^\lambda &= \textstyle\sum_{q' \in \mathrm{succ}(q)} \alpha(q)(\mathrm{first}(\lambda), q') \cdot x_{q'}^{\mathrm{tail}(\lambda)} \\
&\quad + \textstyle\sum_{h \in \Sigma_\tau} \alpha(q)(h, q') \cdot x_{q'}^\lambda \quad \text{for } \lambda \neq \epsilon \text{ and } q \neq q_f.
\end{aligned}
$$

Furthermore, for $s \in S$ *and* $o \in \mathcal{O}$ *we have* $\mathbf{P}([s] \cap [o]) = x_{\bar{q}}^{so}$.

Using this lemma, one can compute joint probabilities by solving the system of linear equations in the variables x_q^λ's. It is possible that the system has multiple solutions; in that case the required solution is the minimal one.

Example 4.2. Continuing with the Crowds example, we show how to compute joint probabilities. Note that $q_f = S$. The linear equations from Lemma 4.1 are

$$
\begin{array}{llll}
x_{init}^{aA} = \frac{1}{3} \cdot x_{q_a}^A, & x_{q_a}^A = \frac{p}{3} \cdot x_{q_a}^A + \frac{p}{3} \cdot x_{q_b}^A + \frac{p}{3} \cdot x_{corr}^\epsilon, & x_{corr}^A = x_S^A, \\
x_{init}^{bA} = \frac{2}{3} \cdot x_{q_b}^A, & x_{q_b}^A = \frac{p}{3} \cdot x_{q_a}^A + \frac{p}{3} \cdot x_{q_b}^A + \frac{p}{3} \cdot x_{corr}^A, & x_S^A = 0, \\
x_{init}^{aB} = \frac{1}{3} \cdot x_{q_a}^B, & x_{q_a}^B = \frac{p}{3} \cdot x_{q_a}^B + \frac{p}{3} \cdot x_{q_b}^B + \frac{p}{3} \cdot x_{corr}^\epsilon, & x_{corr}^B = x_S^B, \\
x_{init}^{bB} = \frac{2}{3} \cdot x_{q_b}^B, & x_{q_b}^B = \frac{p}{3} \cdot x_{q_a}^B + \frac{p}{3} \cdot x_{q_b}^B + \frac{p}{3} \cdot x_{corr}^\epsilon, & x_S^B = 0, \\
x_{init}^{aU} = \frac{1}{3} \cdot x_{q_a}^U, & x_{q_a}^U = \frac{p}{3} \cdot x_{q_a}^U + \frac{p}{3} \cdot x_{q_b}^U + (1-p) \cdot x_S^\epsilon, & x_{corr}^\epsilon = x_S^\epsilon, \\
x_{init}^{bU} = \frac{2}{3} \cdot x_{q_b}^U, & x_{q_b}^U = \frac{p}{3} \cdot x_{q_a}^U + \frac{p}{3} \cdot x_{q_b}^U + (1-p) \cdot x_S^\epsilon, & x_S^\epsilon = 1.
\end{array}
$$

4.1 Complexity Analysis

We now analyze the computational complexity for the computation of the channel matrix of a simple IHS. Note that the only variables (from the system of equations in Lemma 4.1) that are relevant for the computation of the channel matrix are those x_q^λ for which it is possible to get the trace λ starting from state q. As a rough overestimate, for each state q, there are at most $|\mathcal{S}| \cdot |\mathcal{O}|$ λ's possible: in the initial state one can have every secret and every observable, in the other states no secret is possible and only a suffix of an observable can occur. This gives at most $|Q| \cdot |\mathcal{S}| \cdot |\mathcal{O}|$ variables. Therefore, we can straightforwardly obtain the desired set of values in $O((|Q| \cdot |\mathcal{S}| \cdot |\mathcal{O}|)^3)$ time (using Gaussian Elimination). Note that using Strassen's methods the exponent reduces to 2.807, this consideration applies to similar results in the rest of the paper as well.

Because secret actions can happen only at the beginning, the system of equations has a special form. The variables of the form $x_{\hat{q}}^{so}$ only depend on variables of the form x_q^o (with varying o and $q \neq \hat{q}$) and not on each other. Hence, we can first solve for all variables of the form x_q^o and then compute the remaining few of the form $x_{\hat{q}}^{so}$. Required time for the first step is $O((|\mathcal{O}| \cdot |Q|)^3)$ and the time for the second step can be ignored.

Finally, in some cases not only do the secret actions happen only at the beginning of the protocol, but the observable actions happen only at the end of the protocol, i.e., after taking a transition with an observable action, the protocol only performs internal actions (this is, for instance, the case for our model of Crowds). In this case, one might as well enter a unique terminal state q_f after an observable action happens. Then the only relevant variables are of the form $x_{\hat{q}}^{so}$, x_q^o, and $x_{q_f}^\epsilon$; the $x_{\hat{q}}^{so}$ only depends on the x_q^o, the x_q^o only depend on $x_{q'}^o$ (with the same o, but varying q's) and on $x_{q_f}^\epsilon$ and $x_{q_f}^\epsilon = 1$. Again ignoring the variables $x_{\hat{q}}^{so}$ for complexity purposes, the system of equations has a block form with $|\mathcal{O}|$ blocks of (at most) $|Q|$ variables each. Hence the complexity in this case decreases to $O(|\mathcal{O}| \cdot |Q|^3)$.

5   The Iterative Approach

We now propose a different approach to compute channel matrices and leakage. The idea is to iteratively construct the channel matrix of a system by adding probabilities of sets of paths containing paths with the same observable trace o and secret trace s to the $(o|s)$ entry of the matrix.

One reason for this approach is that it allows us to borrow techniques from quantitative counterexample generation. This includes the possibility of using or extending counterexample generation tools to compute channel matrices or leakage. Another reason for this approach is the relationship with debugging. If a (specification of a) system has a high leakage, the iterative approach allows us to determine which parts of the system contribute most to the high leakage, possibly pointing out flaws of the protocol. Finally, if the system under consideration is very large, the iterative approach allows us to only approximate the leakage (by not considering all paths, but only the most relevant ones) under strict guarantees about the accuracy of the approximation. We will focus on the multiplicative leakage; similar results can be obtained for the additive case.

5.1   Partial Matrices

We start by defining a sequence of matrices converging to the channel matrix by adding the probability of complete paths one by one. We also define partial version of the a posteriori vulnerability and the leakage. Later, we show how to use techniques from quantitative counterexample generation to add probabilities of many (maybe infinitely many) complete paths all at once.

Definition 5.1. Let $\mathcal{I} = (M, \Sigma_S, \Sigma_O, \Sigma_\tau)$ be an IHS, π its a priori distribution, and $\sigma_1, \sigma_2, \ldots$ an enumeration of the set of complete paths of M. We define the *partial matrices* $P^k : \mathcal{S} \times \mathcal{O} \to [0, 1]$ as follows

$$P^0(o|s) \triangleq 0, \qquad P^{k+1}(o|s) \triangleq \begin{cases} P^k(o|s) + \frac{\mathbf{P}(\langle \sigma_{k+1} \rangle)}{\pi(s)} & \text{if } trace_{\Sigma_O}(\sigma_{k+1}) = o \\ & \text{and } trace_{\Sigma_S}(\sigma_{k+1}) = s, \\ P^k(o|s) & \text{otherwise.} \end{cases}$$

We define the *partial vulnerability* $V_{S,O}^k$ as $\sum_o \max_s P^k(o|s) \cdot \pi(s)$, and the *partial multiplicative leakage* $\mathcal{L}_\times^k(\mathcal{I})$ as $V_{S,O}^k / \max_s \pi(s)$.

The following lemma states that partial matrices, a posteriori vulnerability, and leakage converge to the correct values.

Lemma 5.2. Let $\mathcal{I} = (M, \Sigma_S, \Sigma_O, \Sigma_\tau)$ be an IHS. Then

1. $P^k(o|s) \leq P^{k+1}(o|s)$, and $\lim_{k \to \infty} P^k(o|s) = P(o|s)$,
2. $V_{S,O}^k \leq V_{S,O}^{k+1}$, and $\lim_{k \to \infty} V_{S,O}^k = \mathrm{V}(S|O)$,
3. $\mathcal{L}_\times^k(\mathcal{I}) \leq \mathcal{L}_\times^{k+1}(\mathcal{I})$, and $\lim_{k \to \infty} \mathcal{L}_\times^k(\mathcal{I}) = \mathcal{L}_\times(\mathcal{I})$.

Since rows must sum up to 1, this technique allow us to compute matrices up to given error ϵ. We now show how to estimate the error in the approximation of the multiplicative leakage.

Proposition 5.3. Let $(M, \Sigma_S, \Sigma_O, \Sigma_\tau)$ be an IHS. Then we have

$$\mathcal{L}_\times^k(\mathcal{I}) \leq \mathcal{L}_\times(\mathcal{I}) \leq \mathcal{L}_\times^k(\mathcal{I}) + \sum_{i=1}^{|\mathcal{S}|} (1 - p_i^k),$$

where p_i^k denotes the mass probability of the i-th row of P^k, i.e. $p_i^k \triangleq \sum_o P^k(o|s_i)$.

5.2 On the Computation of Partial Matrices

After showing how partial matrices can be used to approximate channel matrices and leakage we now turn our attention to accelerating the convergence. Adding most likely paths first is an obvious way to increase the convergence rate. However, since automata with cycles have infinitely many paths, this (still) gives an infinite amount of path to process. Processing many paths at once (all having the same observable and secret trace) tackles both issues at the same time: it increases the rate of convergence and can deal with infinitely many paths at the same time,

Interestingly enough, these issues also appear in *quantitative counterexample generation*. In that area, several techniques have already been provided to meet the challenges; we show how to apply those techniques in the current context. We consider two techniques: one is to group paths together using regular expression, the other is to group path together using strongly connected component analysis.

Regular expressions. In [9], regular expressions containing probability values are used to reason about traces in Markov Chains. This idea is used in [8] in the context of counterexample generation to group together paths with the same observable behaviour. The regular expression there are over pairs $\langle p, q \rangle$ with p a probability value and q a state, to be able to track both probabilities and observables. We now use the same idea to group together paths with the same secret action and the same observable actions.

We consider regular expressions over triples of the form $\langle a, p, q \rangle$ with $p \in [0, 1]$ a probability value, $a \in \Sigma$ an action label and $q \in Q$ a state. Regular expressions represent sets of paths as in [8]. We also take the probability value of such a regular expression from that paper.

Definition 5.4. The function $val : \mathcal{R}(\Sigma) \to \mathbb{R}$ evaluates regular expressions:

$$
\begin{aligned}
val(\epsilon) &\triangleq 1, & val(r \cdot r') &\triangleq val(r) \times val(r'), \\
val(\langle a, p, q \rangle) &\triangleq p, & val(r^*) &\triangleq 1 & \text{if } val(r) = 1, \\
val(r + r') &\triangleq val(r) + val(r'), & val(r^*) &\triangleq \frac{1}{1 - val(r)} & \text{if } val(r) \neq 1.
\end{aligned}
$$

The idea is to obtain regular expressions representing sets of paths of M, each regular expression will contribute in the approximation of the channel matrix and leakage. Several algorithms to translate automata into regular expressions have been proposed (see [14]). Finally, each term of the regular expression obtained can be processed separately by adding the corresponding probabilities [9] to the partial matrix.

As mentioned before, all paths represented by the regular expression should have the same observable and secret trace in order to be able to add its probability to a single element of the matrix. To ensure that condition we request the regular expression to be normal, i.e., of the form $r_1 + \cdots + r_n$ with the r_i containing no $+$'s.

For space reasons, instead of showing technical details we only show an example.

Example 5.5. We used JFLAP 7.0 [12] to obtain the regular expression $r \triangleq r_1 + r_2 + \cdots + r_{10}$ equivalent to the automaton in Figure 1.

$$
\begin{aligned}
r_1 &\triangleq \langle b, \tfrac{2}{3}, q_b \rangle \cdot \hat{r}^* \cdot \langle B, 0.3, corr \rangle \cdot \langle \tau, 1, S \rangle, \\
r_2 &\triangleq \langle b, \tfrac{2}{3}, q_b \rangle \cdot \hat{r}^* \cdot \langle \tau, 0.3, q_a \rangle \cdot \langle \tau, 0.3, q_a \rangle^* \cdot \langle A, 0.3, corr \rangle \cdot \langle \tau, 1, S \rangle, \\
r_3 &\triangleq \langle a, \tfrac{1}{3}, q_a \rangle \cdot \langle \tau, 0.3, q_a \rangle^* \cdot \langle A, 0.3, corr \rangle \cdot \langle \tau, 1, S \rangle, \\
r_4 &\triangleq \langle b, \tfrac{2}{3}, q_b \rangle \cdot \hat{r}^* \cdot \langle U, 0.1, S \rangle, \\
r_5 &\triangleq \langle a, \tfrac{1}{3}, q_a \rangle \cdot \langle \tau, 0.3, q_a \rangle^* \cdot \langle \tau, 0.3, q_b \rangle \cdot \hat{r}^* \cdot \langle B, 0.3, corr \rangle \cdot \langle \tau, 1, S \rangle, \\
r_6 &\triangleq \langle b, \tfrac{2}{3}, q_b \rangle \cdot \hat{r}^* \cdot \langle \tau, 0.3, q_a \rangle \cdot \langle \tau, 0.3, q_a \rangle^* \cdot \langle U, 0.1, S \rangle, \\
r_7 &\triangleq \langle a, \tfrac{1}{3}, q_a \rangle \cdot \langle \tau, 0.3, q_a \rangle^* \cdot \langle U, 0.1, S \rangle, \\
r_8 &\triangleq \langle a, \tfrac{1}{3}, q_a \rangle \cdot \langle \tau, 0.3, q_a \rangle^* \cdot \langle \tau, 0.3, q_b \rangle \cdot \hat{r}^* \cdot \langle \tau, 0.3, q_a \rangle \cdot \langle \tau, 0.3, q_a \rangle^* \cdot \\
&\quad \langle A, 0.3, corr \rangle \cdot \langle \tau, 1, S \rangle, \\
r_9 &\triangleq \langle a, \tfrac{1}{3}, q_a \rangle \cdot \langle \tau, 0.3, q_a \rangle^* \cdot \langle \tau, 0.3, q_b \rangle \cdot \hat{r}^* \cdot \langle U, 0.1, S \rangle, \\
r_{10} &\triangleq \langle a, \tfrac{1}{3}, q_a \rangle \cdot \langle \tau, 0.3, q_a \rangle^* \cdot \langle \tau, 0.3, q_b \rangle \cdot \hat{r}^* \cdot \langle \tau, 0.3, q_a \rangle \cdot \langle \tau, 0.3, q_a \rangle^* \cdot \langle U, 0.1, S \rangle,
\end{aligned}
$$

where $\hat{r} \triangleq (\langle \tau, 0.3, q_b \rangle^* \cdot (\langle \tau, 0.3, q_a \rangle \cdot \langle \tau, 0.3, q_a \rangle^* \cdot \langle \tau, 0.3, q_b \rangle)^*)$. We also note

$$
\begin{aligned}
&val(r_1) = \tfrac{7}{20}\,(b, B), \quad val(r_2) = \tfrac{3}{20}\,(b, A), \quad val(r_3) = \tfrac{1}{7}\,(a, A), \quad val(r_4) = \tfrac{7}{60}\,(b, U), \\
&val(r_5) = \tfrac{3}{40}\,(a, B), \quad val(r_6) = \tfrac{1}{20}\,(b, U), \quad val(r_7) = \tfrac{1}{21}\,(a, U), \quad val(r_8) = \tfrac{9}{280}\,(a, A), \\
&val(r_9) = \tfrac{1}{40}\,(a, U), \quad val(r_{10}) = \tfrac{3}{280}\,(a, U),
\end{aligned}
$$

where the symbols between brackets denote the secret and observable traces of each regular expression.

Now we have all the ingredients needed to define partial matrices using regular expressions.

Definition 5.6. Let $\mathcal{I} = (M, \Sigma_S, \Sigma_O, \Sigma_\tau)$ be an IHS, π its a priori distribution, and $r = r_1 + r_2 + \cdots + r_n$ a regular expression equivalent to M in normal form. We define for $k = 0, 1, \ldots, n$ the matrices $P^k : S \times O \to [0, 1]$ as follows

$$
P^k(o|s) = \begin{cases}
0 & \text{if } k = 0, \\
P^{k-1}(o|s) + \frac{val(r_k)}{\pi(s)} & \text{if } k \neq 0 \text{ and } trace_{\Sigma_O}(r_k) = o \\
& \text{and } trace_{\Sigma_S}(r_k) = s, \\
P^{k-1}(o|s) & \text{otherwise.}
\end{cases}
$$

Note that in the context of Definition 5.6, we have $P^n = P$.

SCC analysis approach. In [2], paths that only differ in the way they traverse strongly connected components (SCC's) are grouped together. Note that in our case, such paths have the same secret and observable trace since secret and observable actions cannot occur on cycles. Following [2], we first abstract away the SCC's, leaving only probabilistic transitions that go immediately from an entry point of the SCC to an exit point (called input and output states in [2]). This abstraction happens in such a way that the observable behaviour of the automaton does not change.

Again, instead of going into technical details (which also involves translating the work [2] from Markov chains to fully probabilistic automata), we show an example.

Example 5.7. Figure 2 shows the automaton obtained after abstracting SCC. In the following we show the set of complete paths of the automaton, together with their corresponding probabilities and traces

$$
\begin{aligned}
\sigma_1 &\triangleq init \xrightarrow{a} q_a \xrightarrow{A} corr \xrightarrow{\tau} S, \quad &\mathbf{P}(\sigma_1) = \tfrac{7}{40}, \quad &(a, A), \\
\sigma_2 &\triangleq init \xrightarrow{b} q_b \xrightarrow{B} corr \xrightarrow{\tau} S, \quad &\mathbf{P}(\sigma_2) = \tfrac{7}{20}, \quad &(b, B), \\
\sigma_3 &\triangleq init \xrightarrow{a} q_a \xrightarrow{U} S, \quad &\mathbf{P}(\sigma_3) = \tfrac{1}{12}, \quad &(a, U), \\
\sigma_4 &\triangleq init \xrightarrow{b} q_b \xrightarrow{U} S, \quad &\mathbf{P}(\sigma_4) = \tfrac{1}{6}, \quad &(b, U), \\
\sigma_5 &\triangleq init \xrightarrow{a} q_a \xrightarrow{B} corr \xrightarrow{\tau} S, \quad &\mathbf{P}(\sigma_5) = \tfrac{3}{40}, \quad &(a, B), \\
\sigma_6 &\triangleq init \xrightarrow{b} q_b \xrightarrow{A} corr \xrightarrow{\tau} S, \quad &\mathbf{P}(\sigma_6) = \tfrac{3}{20}, \quad &(b, A).
\end{aligned}
$$

Note that the SCC analysis approach groups more paths together (for instance σ_1 group together the same paths than the regular expressions r_3 and r_8 in the examples of this section), as a result channel matrix and leakage are obtained faster. On the other hand, regular expressions are more informative providing more precise feedback.

5.3   Identifying High-Leakage Sources

We now describe how to use the techniques presented in this section to identify sources of high leakage of the system. Remember that the a posteriori vulnerability can be expressed in terms of joint probabilities

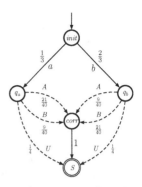

Fig. 2. Crowds after the SCC analysis

$$V(S \mid O) \;=\; \sum_o \max_s \mathbf{P}([s] \cap [o]).$$

This suggests that, in case we want to identify parts of the system generating high leakage, we should look at the sets of paths $[o_1] \cap [s_1], \ldots, [o_n] \cap [s_n]$ where $\{o_1, \ldots o_n\} = \mathcal{O}$ and $s_i \in \arg\left(\max_s \mathbf{P}([o_i] \cap [s])\right)$. In fact, the multiplicative leakage is given dividing $V(S \mid O)$ by $V(S)$, but since $V(S)$ is a constant value (i.e., it does not depend on the row) it does not play a role here. Similarly for the additive case.

The techniques presented in this section allow us to obtain such sets and, furthermore, to partition them in a convenient way with the purpose of identifying states/parts of the system that contribute the most to its high probability. Indeed, this is the aim of the counterexamples generation techniques previously presented. For further details on how to debug sets of paths and why these techniques meet that purpose we refer to [1,8,2].

Example 5.8. To illustrate these ideas, consider the path σ_1 of the previous example; this path has maximum probability for the observable A. By inspecting the path we find the transition with high probability $q_a \xrightarrow{A} corr$. This suggests to the debugger that the corrupted user has an excessively high probability of intercepting a message from user a in case he is the initiator.

In case the debugger requires further information on how corrupted users can intercept messages, the regular expression approach provides further/more-detailed information. For instance, we obtain further information by looking at regular expressions r_3 and r_8 instead of path σ_1 (in particular it is possible to visualize the different ways the corrupted user can intercept the message of user a when he is the generator of the message).

6   Information Hiding Systems with Variable a Priori

In Section 3 we introduced a notion of IHS in which the distribution over secrets is fixed. However, when reasoning about security protocols this is often not the case. In general we may assume that an adversary knows the distribution over secrets in each particular instance, but the protocol should not depend on it. In such scenario we want the protocol to be secure, i.e. ensuring low enough leakage, for every possible distribution over secrets. This leads to the definition of maximum leakage.

Definition 6.1 ([19,3]). Given a noisy channel $\mathcal{C} = (\mathcal{S}, \mathcal{O}, P)$, we define the maximum multiplicative and additive leakage (respectively) as

$$\mathcal{ML}_\times(\mathcal{C}) \triangleq \max_{\pi \in \mathcal{D}(\mathcal{S})} \mathcal{L}_\times(\mathcal{C}, \pi), \quad \text{and} \quad \mathcal{ML}_+(\mathcal{C}) \triangleq \max_{\pi \in \mathcal{D}(\mathcal{S})} \mathcal{L}_+(\mathcal{C}, \pi).$$

In order to model this new scenario where the distribution over secrets may change, the selection of the secret is modeled as *nondeterministic choice*. In this way such a distribution remains undefined in the protocol/automaton. We still assume that the choice of the secret happens at the beginning, and that we have only one secret per run. We call such automaton an IHS *with variable a priori*.

Definition 6.2. An IHS with variable a priori is a quadruple $\mathcal{I} = (M, \Sigma_\mathcal{S}, \Sigma_\mathcal{O}, \Sigma_\tau)$ where $M = (Q, \Sigma, \hat{q}, \alpha)$ is a probabilistic automaton, $\Sigma = \Sigma_\mathcal{S} \cup \Sigma_\mathcal{O} \cup \Sigma_\tau$ where $\Sigma_\mathcal{S}$, $\Sigma_\mathcal{O}$, and Σ_τ are pairwise disjoint sets of secret, observable, and internal actions, and α satisfies the following restrictions:

1. $\alpha(\hat{q}) \subseteq \mathcal{D}(\Sigma_\mathcal{S} \times Q)$,
2. $|\alpha(\hat{q})| = |\mathcal{S}| \wedge \forall s \in \Sigma_\mathcal{S} . \exists q . \pi(s,q) = 1$, for some $\pi \in \alpha(\hat{q})$,
3. $\alpha(q) \subseteq \mathcal{D}(\Sigma_\mathcal{O} \cup \Sigma_\tau \times Q)$ and $|\alpha(q)| \leq 1$, for all $q \neq \hat{q}$,
4. $\forall a \in (\Sigma_\mathcal{S} \cup \Sigma_\mathcal{O}) . a \notin \text{CyclesA}(M)$,
5. $\forall q, s \forall \pi \in \alpha(\hat{q}) . (\pi(s,q) = 1 \Rightarrow \mathbf{P}(\text{CPaths}_q(M) \cap \text{Paths}_q^*(M)) = 1)$.

Restrictions 1, 2 and 3 imply that the secret choice is non deterministic and happens only at the beginning. Additionally, 3 means that all the other choices are probabilistic. Restriction 4 ensures that the channel associated to the IHS has finitely many inputs and outputs. Finally, 5 implies that, after we have chosen a secret, every computation terminates except for a set with null probability.

Given an IHS with variable a priori, by fixing the a priori distribution we can obtain a standard IHS in the obvious way:

Definition 6.3. Let $\mathcal{I} = ((Q, \Sigma, \hat{q}, \alpha), \Sigma_\mathcal{S}, \Sigma_\mathcal{O}, \Sigma_\tau)$ be an IHS with variable a priori and π a distribution over $\mathcal{S}$. We define the IHS associated to $(\mathcal{I}, \pi)$ as $\mathcal{I}_\pi = ((Q, \Sigma, \hat{q}, \alpha'), \Sigma_\mathcal{S}, \Sigma_\mathcal{O}, \Sigma_\tau)$ with $\alpha'(q) = \alpha(q)$ for all $q \neq \hat{q}$ and $\alpha'(\hat{q})(s, \cdot) = \pi(s)$.

The following result says that the conditional probabilities associated to an IHS with variable a priori are *invariant* with respect to the a priori distribution. This is fundamental in order to interpret the IHS as a channel.

Proposition 6.4. *Let $\mathcal{I}$ be an IHS with variable a priori. Then for all $\pi, \pi' \in \mathcal{D}(\mathcal{S})$ such that $\pi(s) \neq 0$ and $\pi'(s) \neq 0$ for all $s \in \mathcal{S}$ we have that $P_{\mathcal{I}_\pi} = P_{\mathcal{I}_{\pi'}}$.*

Proof. The secret s appears only once in the tree and only at the beginning of paths, hence $\mathbf{P}([s] \cap [o]) = \alpha'(\hat{q})(s, \cdot) \mathbf{P}_{q_s}([o])$ and $\mathbf{P}([s]) = \alpha'(\hat{q})(s, \cdot)$. Therefore $\mathbf{P}([o] \mid [s]) = \mathbf{P}_{q_s}([o])$, where q_s is the state after performing s. While $\alpha'(\hat{q})(s, \cdot)$ is different in $\mathcal{I}_\pi$ and $\mathcal{I}_{\pi'}$, $\mathbf{P}_{q_s}([o])$ is the same, because it only depends on the parts of the paths after the choice of the secret. $\square$

Note that, although in the previous proposition we exclude input distributions with zeros, the concepts of vulnerability and leakage also make sense for these distributions[3].

This result implies that we can define the channel matrix of an IHS $\mathcal{I}$ with variable a priori as the channel matrix of $\mathcal{I}_\pi$ for any π, and we can compute it, or approximate it, using the same techniques of previous sectionsSimilarly we can compute or approximate the leakage for any given π.

We now turn the attention to the computation of the maximum leakage. The following result from the literature is crucial for our purposes.

Proposition 6.5 ([3]). *Given a channel $\mathcal{C}$, $\arg\max_{\pi \in \mathcal{D}(\mathcal{S})} \mathcal{L}_\times (\mathcal{C}, \pi)$ is the uniform distribution, and $\arg\max_{\pi \in \mathcal{D}(\mathcal{S})} \mathcal{L}_+(\mathcal{C}, \pi)$ is a corner point distribution, i.e. a distribution π such that $\pi(s) = \frac{1}{\kappa}$ on κ elements of $\mathcal{S}$, and $\pi(s) = 0$ on all the other elements.*

As an obvious consequence, we obtain:

Corollary 6.6. *Given an IHS $\mathcal{I}$ with variable a priori, we have $\mathcal{ML}_\times(\mathcal{I}) = \mathcal{L}_\times(\mathcal{I}_\pi)$, where π is the uniform distribution, and $\mathcal{ML}_+(\mathcal{I}) = \mathcal{L}_+(\mathcal{I}_{\pi'})$, where π' is a corner point distribution.*

Corollary 6.6 gives us a method to compute the maxima leakages of $\mathcal{I}$. In the multiplicative case the complexity is the same as for computing the leakage[4]. In the additive case we need to find the right corner point, which can be done by computing the leakages for all corner points and then comparing them. This method has exponential complexity (in $|\mathcal{S}|$) as the size of the set of corner points is $2^{|\mathcal{S}|} - 1$. We conjecture that this complexity is intrinsic, i.e. that the problem is NP-hard[5].

7   Interactive Information Hiding Systems

We now consider extending the framework to interactive systems, namely to IHS's in which the secrets and the observables can alternate in an arbitrary way. The secret part of a run is then an element of $\Sigma_\mathcal{S}^*$, like the observable part is an element of $\Sigma_\mathcal{O}^*$. The idea is that such system models an interactive play between a source of secret information, and a protocol or program that may produce, each time, some observable in response. Since each choice is associated to one player of this "game", it seems natural to impose that in a choice the actions are either secret or observable/hidden, but not both.

The main novelty and challenge of this extension is that part of the secrets come after observable events, and may depend on them.

Definition 7.1. Interactive IHS's are defined as IHS's (Definition 3.1), except that Restrictions 1 to 3 are replaced by $\alpha(q) \in \mathcal{D}(\Sigma_\mathcal{S} \times Q) \cup \mathcal{D}(\Sigma - \Sigma_\mathcal{S} \times Q)$.

---

[3] We assume that conditional probabilities are extended by continuity on such distributions.

[4] Actually we can compute it even faster using an observation from [19] which says that the leakage on the uniform distribution can be obtained simply by summing up the maximum elements of each column of the channel matrix.

[5] Since submitting this paper, we have proved that our conjecture is true.

Example 7.2. Consider an Ebay-like auction protocol with one seller and two possible buyers, one rich and one poor. The seller first publishes the item he wants to sell, which can be either cheap or expensive. Then the two buyers start bidding. At the end, the seller looks at the profile of the bid winner and decides whether to sell the item or cancel the transaction. Figure 4 illustrates the automaton representing the protocol, for certain given probability distributions.

We assume that the identities of the buyers are secret, while the price of the item and the seller's decision are observable. We ignore for simplicity the hidden actions which are performed during the bidding phase. Hence $\Sigma_{\mathcal{O}} = \{cheap, expensive, sell, cancel\}$, $\Sigma_{\tau} = \emptyset$, $\mathcal{S} = \Sigma_{\mathcal{S}} = \{poor, rich\}$, and $\mathcal{O} = \{cheap, expensive\} \times \{sell, cancel\}$. The distributions on $\mathcal{S}$ and $\mathcal{O}$ are defined as usual. For instance we have $\mathbf{P}([cheap\ sell]) =$

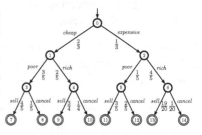

Fig. 3. Ebay Protocol

$\mathbf{P}(\{q_0 \xrightarrow{cheap} q_1 \xrightarrow{poor} q_3 \xrightarrow{sell} q_7, q_0 \xrightarrow{cheap} q_1 \xrightarrow{rich} q_3 \xrightarrow{sell} q_7\}) = \frac{2}{3} \cdot \frac{3}{5} \cdot \frac{4}{5} + \frac{2}{3} \cdot \frac{2}{5} \cdot \frac{3}{4} = \frac{13}{25}$.

Let us now consider how to model the protocol in terms of a noisy channel. It would seem natural to define the channel associated to the protocol as the triple $(\mathcal{S}, \mathcal{O}, P)$ where $P(o \mid s) = \mathbf{P}([o] \mid [s]) = \frac{\mathbf{P}([s] \cap [o])}{\mathbf{P}([s])}$. This is, indeed, the approach taken in [11]. For instance, with the protocol of Example 7.2, we would have:

$$\mathbf{P}([cheap\ sell] \mid [poor]) = \frac{\mathbf{P}([poor] \cap [cheap\ sell])}{\mathbf{P}([poor])} = \frac{\frac{2}{3} \cdot \frac{3}{5} \cdot \frac{4}{5}}{\frac{2}{3} \cdot \frac{3}{5} + \frac{1}{3} \cdot \frac{1}{5}} = \frac{24}{35}. \quad (2)$$

However, it turns out that in the interactive case (in particular when the secrets are not in the initial phase), it does not make sense to model the protocol in terms of a channel. At least, not a channel with input $\mathcal{S}$. In fact, the matrix of a channel is supposed to be *invariant* with respect to the input distribution (like in the case of the IHS's with variable a priori considered in previous section), and this is not the case here. The following is a counterexample.

Example 7.3. Consider the same protocol as in Example 7.2, but assume now that the distribution over the choice of the buyer is uniform, i.e. $\alpha(q_1)(poor, q_3) = \alpha(q_1)(rich, q_4) = \alpha(q_2)(poor, q_5) = \alpha(q_2)(rich, q_6) = \frac{1}{2}$. Then the conditional probabilities are different than those for Example 7.2. In particular, in contrast to (2), we have

$$\mathbf{P}([cheap\ sell] \mid [poor]) = \frac{\mathbf{P}([poor] \cap [cheap\ sell])}{\mathbf{P}([poor])} = \frac{\frac{2}{3} \cdot \frac{1}{2} \cdot \frac{4}{5}}{\frac{2}{3} \cdot \frac{1}{2} + \frac{1}{3} \cdot \frac{1}{2}} = \frac{8}{15}.$$

The above observation, i.e. the fact that the conditional probabilities depend on the input distribution, makes it unsound to reason about certain information-theoretic concepts in the standard way. For instance, the *capacity* is defined as the maximum mutual information over all possible input distributions, and the traditional algorithms to compute it are based on the assumption that the channel matrix remains the same while the input distribution variates. This does not make sense anymore in the interactive setting.

However, when the input distribution is fixed, the matrix of the joint probabilities is well defined as $P_\wedge(s, o) = \mathbf{P}([s] \cap [o])$, and can be computed or approximated using the same methods as for simple IHS's. The a priori probability and the channel matrix can then be derived in the standard way:

$$\pi(s) = \sum_o P_\wedge(s, o), \qquad P(o \mid s) = \frac{P_\wedge(s, o)}{\pi(s)}.$$

Thanks to the formulation (1) of the a posteriori vulnerability, the leakage can be computed directly using the joint probabilities.

Example 7.4. Consider the Ebay protocol $\mathcal{I}$ presented in Example 7.2. The matrix of the joint probabilities $P_\wedge(s, o)$ is:

	cheap sell	cheap cancel	expensive sell	expensive cancel
poor	$\frac{8}{25}$	$\frac{2}{25}$	$\frac{1}{25}$	$\frac{2}{75}$
rich	$\frac{1}{5}$	$\frac{1}{15}$	$\frac{19}{75}$	$\frac{1}{75}$

Furthermore $\pi(poor) = \frac{7}{15}$ and $\pi(rich) = \frac{8}{15}$. Hence we have $\mathcal{L}_\times(\mathcal{I}) = \frac{51}{40}$ and $\mathcal{L}_+(\mathcal{I}) = \frac{11}{75}$.

We note that our techniques to compute channel matrices and leakage extend smoothly to the case where secrets are not required to happen at the beginning. However, no assumptions can be made about the occurrences of secrets (they do not need to occur at the beginning anymore). This increases the complexity of the reachability technique to $O((|\mathcal{S}| \cdot |\mathcal{O}| \cdot |Q|)^3)$. On the other hand, complexity bounds for the iterative approach remain the same.

8 Related Work

To the best of our knowledge, this is the first work dealing with the efficient computation of channel matrices and leakage. However, for the simple scenario, channel matrices can be computed using standard model checking techniques. Chatzikokolakis et al. [4] have used Prism [15] to model Crowds as a Markov Chain and compute its channel matrix. Each conditional probability $P(o|s)$ is computed as the probability of reaching a state where o holds starting from *the* state where s holds. Since for the simple version of IHS's secrets occur only once and before observables (as in Crowds), such a reachability probability equals $P(o|s)$. This procedure leads to $O(|\mathcal{S}| \cdot |\mathcal{O}| \cdot |\overline{Q}|^3)$ time complexity to compute the channel matrix, where $\overline{Q}$ is the space state of the Markov Chain.

Note that the complexity is expressed in terms of the space state of a Markov Chain instead of automaton. Since Markov Chains do not carry information in transitions they have a larger state space than an equivalent automaton. Figure 4 illustrates this: to model the automaton (left hand side) we need to encode the information in its transitions into states of the Markov Chain (right hand side). Therefore, the probability of seeing observation a and then c in the automaton can be computed as the probability of reaching the state ac. The Markov Chain used for modeling Crowds (in our two honest and one corrupted user configuration) has 27 states.

For this reason we conjecture that our complexity $O(|\mathcal{O}| \cdot |Q|^3)$ is a considerable improvement over the one on Markov Chains $O(|\mathcal{S}| \cdot |\mathcal{O}| \cdot |\overline{Q}|^3)$.

With respect to the interactive scenario, standard model checking techniques do not extend because multiple occurrences of the same secret are allowed (for instance in our Ebay example, $P(cheap\ sell|rich)$ cannot be derived from reachability probabilities from the two different states of the automaton where $rich$ holds).

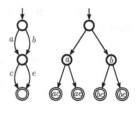

Fig. 4.   Automaton   vs   Markov Chain

9   Conclusion and Future Work

In this paper we have addressed the problem of computing the information leakage of a system in an efficient way. We have proposed two methods: one based on reachability techniques; the other based on quantitative counterexample generation.

We plan to use tools developed for counterexamples generation (in particular the Prism implementation of both techniques presented in Section 5) in order to compute/approximate leakage of large scale protocols. We also intend to investigate in more depth how the results obtained from those tools can be used to identify flaws of the protocol causing high leakage.

In Section 7 we have shown that when the automaton is interactive we cannot define its channel in the standard way. An intriguing problem is how to extend the notion of channel so to capture the dynamic nature of interaction. One idea is to use channels with history and/or feedback. Another idea is to lift the inputs from secrets to schedulers on secrets, i.e. to functions from paths to distributions over secrets.

References

1. Aljazzar, H., Leue, S.: Debugging of dependability models using interactive visualization of counterexamples. In: Proc. of the Int. Conf. on Quantitative Evaluation of SysTems 2008, pp. 189–198. IEEE Press, Los Alamitos (2008)
2. Andrés, M.E., D'Argenio, P., van Rossum, P.: Significant diagnostic counterexamples in probabilistic model checking. In: Chockler, H., Hu, A.J. (eds.) HVC 2008. LNCS, vol. 5394, pp. 129–148. Springer, Heidelberg (2009)
3. Braun, C., Chatzikokolakis, K., Palamidessi, C.: Quantitative notions of leakage for one-try attacks. In: Proc. of the 25th Conf. on Mathematical Foundations of Programming Semantics. ENTCS, vol. 249, pp. 75–91. Elsevier B.V., Amsterdam (2009)
4. Chatzikokolakis, K., Palamidessi, C., Panangaden, P.: Anonymity protocols as noisy channels. Inf. and Comp. 206(2-4), 378–401 (2008)
5. Clark, D., Hunt, S., Malacaria, P.: Quantitative information flow, relations and polymorphic types. J. of Logic and Computation 18(2), 181–199 (2005)
6. Clarkson, M.R., Myers, A.C., Schneider, F.B.: Belief in information flow. Journal of Computer Security (2008) (to appear)
7. Cover, T.M., Thomas, J.A.: Elements of Information Theory, 2nd edn. John Wiley & Sons, Inc., Chichester (2006)

8. Damman, B., Han, T., Katoen, J.-P.: Regular expressions for PCTL counterexamples. In: Proc. of the Int. Conf. on Quantitative Evaluation of SysTems 2008, pp. 179–188. IEEE Press, Los Alamitos (2008)

9. Daws, C.: Symbolic and parametric model checking of discrete-time markov chains. In: Liu, Z., Araki, K. (eds.) ICTAC 2004. LNCS, vol. 3407, pp. 280–294. Springer, Heidelberg (2005)

10. Deng, Y., Pang, J., Wu, P.: Measuring anonymity with relative entropy. In: Dimitrakos, T., Martinelli, F., Ryan, P.Y.A., Schneider, S. (eds.) FAST 2006. LNCS, vol. 4691, pp. 65–79. Springer, Heidelberg (2007)

11. Desharnais, J., Jagadeesan, R., Gupta, V., Panangaden, P.: The metric analogue of weak bisimulation for probabilistic processes. In: Proceedings of the 17th Annual IEEE Symposium on Logic in Computer Science, pp. 413–422. IEEE Computer Society, Los Alamitos (2002)

12. Jflap website, http://www.jflap.org/

13. Moskowitz, I.S., Newman, R.E., Crepeau, D.P., Miller, A.R.: Covert channels and anonymizing networks. In: Jajodia, S., Samarati, P., Syverson, P.F. (eds.) Workshop on Privacy in the Electronic Society 2003, pp. 79–88. ACM, New York (2003)

14. Neumann, C.: Converting deterministic finite automata to regular expressions (2005), http://neumannhaus.com/christoph/papers/
2005-03-16.DFA_to_RegEx.pdf

15. Prism website, http://www.prismmodelchecker.org

16. Reiter, M.K., Rubin, A.D.: Crowds: anonymity for Web transactions. ACM Transactions on Information and System Security 1(1), 66–92 (1998)

17. Sabelfeld, A., Myers, A.C.: Language-based information flow security. IEEE Journal on Selected Areas in Communications 21(1), 5–19 (2003)

18. Segala, R.: Modeling and Verification of Randomized Distributed Real-Time Systems. PhD thesis, Tech. Rep. MIT/LCS/TR-676 (June 1995)

19. Smith, G.: On the foundations of quantitative information flow. In: de Alfaro, L. (ed.) FOSSACS 2009. LNCS, vol. 5504, pp. 288–302. Springer, Heidelberg (2009)

Statistical Measurement of Information Leakage

Konstantinos Chatzikokolakis[1], Tom Chothia[2], and Apratim Guha[3]

[1] Department of Mathematics and Computer Science, Technische Universiteit Eindhoven
[2] School of Computer Science, University of Birmingham
[3] School of Mathimatics, University of Birmingham

Abstract. Information theory provides a range of useful methods to analyse probability distributions and these techniques have been successfully applied to measure information flow and the loss of anonymity in secure systems. However, previous work has tended to assume that the exact probabilities of every action are known, or that the system is non-deterministic. In this paper, we show that measures of information leakage based on mutual information and capacity can be calculated, automatically, from trial runs of a system alone. We find a confidence interval for this estimate based on the number of possible inputs, observations and samples. We have developed a tool to automatically perform this analysis and we demonstrate our method by analysing a Mixminon anonymous remailer node.

1 Introduction

Information theory provides powerful techniques to measure the relation between different probability distributions and so has proved useful for defining anonymity [26,15,24,29,9,11] and quantitative information flow [22,21,12,19,2]. Typically, secret user inputs or users identities are looked on as *inputs* to an information-theoretic *channel* and the publicly observable actions of the system are looked on as the *outputs* of the channel. The information theoretic notion of *mutual information* measures the amount of information that can be sent across this channel, under a particular usage pattern, and therefore measures the amount of information that leaks out about the secret inputs. *Capacity* is defined as the maximum possible mutual information for any input distribution and so equals the worst case leakage.

Previous work using capacity and mutual information to measure probabilistic information leakage has assumed that the exact behaviour of the system, that is the probability of each observation under any user, is known. Typically, one has to construct a model of the system and use a model checker to compute the actual probabilities. Even then, calculating the leakage is not straight forward, requiring specific assumptions about the system [9] or requiring the user to solve a set of equations [18,11]. In this paper we show that it is possible to quickly and accurately find these measures of information leakage from trial runs of an implemented system. Basing our method on sampled data, rather than say the output of a formal model, has the advantage of removing the need to create an accurate model of the system, which may be very difficult. It also helps to avoid the problem of the state space of the model becoming too big to be handled by model checking tools (a problem even harder for probabilistic model checking). Finally it is often the case that an information leakage attack exploits implementation faults and so only appears in the implementation itself.

J. Esparza and R. Majumdar (Eds.): TACAS 2010, LNCS 6015, pp. 390–404, 2010.

The user of our method defines the inputs of the system, which correspond to the values that we wish to keep secret, and the possible observations an attacker might make, which corresponds to defining the appropriate attacker model. The system under test is then run a number of times until an estimated probability transition matrix can be built up. For our results to hold, the outcome of each trial of the system must be independent of the previous runs. We apply the Blahut-Arimoto algorithm [1,5] to this matrix in order to estimate the capacity and hence the information leakage of the system.

Running a numerical process on sampled data does not necessarily produce meaningful results so we prove that our estimate converges to the true information leakage. To provide accurate bounds on the information leakage we find the distribution that our estimate comes from. This turns out to be a χ^2 distribution in the case that the capacity is zero and a normal distribution if the capacity is non-zero. In the latter case, the best estimate of capacity is the mean of the distribution minus a small correction. In finding this result we solve the more general problem of finding the distribution of mutual information between two random variables, when the probability distribution of one is known and the other is not. This result also makes it possible to estimate the mutual information of a system for uniform usage, or any other given prior.

The variance of the estimate is dominated by the number of inputs times the number of outputs, divided by the number of samples. Therefore a statistical estimate will be accurate if there are significantly more samples than the product of the number of inputs and all observable outputs. The ability to generate this many samples, in a reasonable amount of time, acts as a guide to which systems can and cannot be analysed statistically. This can be much more efficient than model-checking; complex systems can have many "internal" states, but generate few observations. In this case, generating samples is easier than constructing the state space of the system. If the number of observations is too big, concentrating on some of them may still lead to a useful analysis of the system.

Work outside the field of computer science has dealt with estimating mutual information (e.g. [25,6]). To the best of our knowledge ours is the first work to deal with estimating capacity. The contributions of this paper are: First, showing that information leakage, as defined by capacity and mutual information, can be automatically calculated from sampled data. Second, proving bounds on the error of the estimate, and so establishing what types of systems can and cannot be meaningfully analysed using a statistical approach. Third, defining a statistical test to detect when there is zero information leakage from a system. We demonstrate our method by analyzing a Mixminion remailer node. We collect data from a running node, using a packet sniffer, and we analyse this data to see if the timing and size of messages leaving a node leaks any information about their destination.

In the next section we motivate our approach and Sections 3 describes our system model. Section 4 describes how we can calculate an estimate of information leakage from sampled data. We find the distribution that our estimate is drawn from in Section 5 and in Section 6 we analyse a mix node. All the proofs and futher examples are given in a technical report [8]. Our toolset and futher examples are available at www.cs.bham.ac.uk/~tpc/AE.

Message orderings	out A,B,C	out A,C,B	out B,A,C	out B,C,A	out C,A,B	out C,B,A
in 1,2,3	0.1666	0.1666	0.1666	0.1666	0.1666	0.1666
in 1,3,2	0.1666	0.1666	0.1666	0.1666	0.1666	0.1666
in 2,1,3	0.1666	0.1666	0.1666	0.1666	0.1666	0.1666
in 2,3,1	0.1666	0.1666	0.1666	0.1666	0.1666	0.1666
in 3,1,2	0.1666	0.1666	0.1666	0.1666	0.1666	0.1666
in 3,2,1	0.1666	0.1666	0.1666	0.1666	0.1666	0.1666

(a) Probabilites of outputs for each input for a perfect mix node

Message orderings	out A,B,C	out A,C,B	out B,A,C	out B,C,A	out C,A,B	out C,B,A
in 1,2,3	0	0.3333	0.3333	0	0	0.3333
in 1,3,2	0.3333	0	0	0.3333	0.3333	0
in 2,1,3	0.3333	0	0	0.3333	0.3333	0
in 2,3,1	0	0.3333	0.3333	0	0	0.3333
in 3,1,2	0	0.3333	0.3333	0	0	0.3333
in 3,2,1	0.3333	0	0	0.3333	0.3333	0

(b) Probabilites of outputs for each input for a flawed mix node

Fig. 1. Probabilities of the Message Ordering for Theoretical Mix Nodes

2 Information-Theoretic Measures of Information Leakage

Information theory reasons about the uncertainty of random variables. Given two random variables X, Y we write $p(x) = P[X = x]$ and $p(y) = P[y = Y]$ for their probability distributions and $\mathcal{X}, \mathcal{Y}$ for their sets of values. The *entropy* of X is defined as: $H(X) = -\sum_{x \in \mathcal{X}} p(x) \log p(x)$ and, when the logs are base 2, measures the uncertainty about its outcome in bits. It takes the minimum value 0 when X is constant and the maximum value $\log |\mathcal{X}|$ when its distribution is uniform. The *conditional entropy* is defined as: $H(X|Y) = -\sum_{y \in \mathcal{Y}} p(y) \sum_{x \in \mathcal{X}} p(x|y) \log p(x|y)$ and measures the uncertainty about X that "remains" when we know Y. It takes its minimum value 0 when Y completely determines the value of X and its maximum value $H(X)$ when X, Y are independent.

The *mutual information* between X, Y, defined as $I(X; Y) = H(X) - H(X|Y)$ measures the information that we learn about X if we observe Y. It is symmetric ($I(X; Y) = I(Y; X)$) and ranges between 0 (when X, Y are independent) and $H(X)$ (when X, Y are totally dependent). Finally, the *relative entropy* between distributions p, q is defined as $D(p \parallel q) = \sum_x p(x) \log \frac{p(x)}{q(x)}$.

A *channel* consists of an input alphabet $\mathcal{X}$, an output alphabet $\mathcal{Y}$ and a probability matrix W where $W(y|x) = p(y|x)$ gives the probability of output y when x is the input. Given a channel and an input distribution on $\mathcal{X}$, we can define two random variables X, Y representing the input and output of the channel, and with a slight abuse of notation we write $I(X, W)$ for $I(X; Y)$. The *capacity* of the channel is defined as the mutual information between the input and the output, maximised over all input distributions: $C(W) = \max_{p(x)} I(X, W)$.

The analysis of information leakage aims to quantify the amount of information that an attacker can learn from observing a system. Many authors have pointed out the

Message orderings	out A,B,C	out A,C,B	out B,A,C	out B,C,A	out C,A,B	out C,B,A
in 1,2,3	0.0	0.0118	0.0473	0.0118	0.0059	0.9231
in 1,3,2	0.0117	0.0	0.0351	0.0292	0.0	0.924
in 2,1,3	0.005	0.0222	0.0278	0.0444	0.0056	0.8944
in 2,3,1	0.0060	0.012	0.0301	0.0361	0.0060	0.9096
in 3,1,2	0.0067	0.0133	0.04	0.02	0.0067	0.9133
in 3,2,1	0.0061	0.0122	0.0549	0.0244	0.0061	0.8963

Fig. 2. Probabilities of the Message Ordering from Mixminion Experiments

natural parallel between the amount of information an attacker can learn about secret inputs to a system from its public outputs and the amount of information that can be sent over a channel as measured by mutual information and capacity [22,24,29,12,9,11]. In such a framework, we have a set $\mathcal{X}$ of events that we wish to keep hidden and a set $\mathcal{Y}$ of observable events which model what the attacker can observe about the protocol. We assume that on each execution, exactly one $x \in \mathcal{X}$ and $y \in \mathcal{Y}$ will happen and that the output of the protocol is chosen probabilistically. The capacity of this system measures the most an attacker can learn about the secret inputs from observing the public outputs, that is the maximum possible information leakage of the system.

As an example we consider one of the basic building blocks of anonymous systems: a mix node [13]. These nodes will listen for encrypted messages and then reorder and forward all of the messages at the same time. The aim of such a node is to make it difficult for an observer to link a sender and a receiver. If we take the example in which 1 sends a message to A, 2 sends to B and 3 to C, then Figure 1(a) shows the behaviour of a perfect mix node. Here we consider if an attacker observing the order of the messages leave the mix could deduce anything about the order in which the messages entered (if an attacker could link these orders then they could work out who is communicating with whom). Each row shows the order in which the messages enter the mix, each column gives the order in which the messages are forwarded, and each cell gives the conditional probability of a particular output resulting from a particular input. The *capacity* of this matrix is zero, meaning that the idealised mix node leaks no information.

In Figure 1(b) we consider a flawed mix node that just reorders a pair of incoming messages. In this case an observer can deduce more about the order of the inputs from the observed outputs and this is reflected by a much higher capacity of 1 bit. For a full discussion of the use and merits of this metric for measuring information leakage we refer the reader to the papers cited above. The aim of this paper is to show how the leakage may be calculated for real systems. Other work in this area uses the entropy [26,15], conditional entropy [21] and relative entropy [14]. Our methods for calculating mutual information and capacity could also be adapted to compute these measures.

To apply this kind of analysis to a real system we ran a Mixminion remailer node and sent messages across it to three different e-mail addresses. We used a packet sniffer to detect the order in which messages left the node and the results are shown in Figure 2 (a full description of our tests are given in Section 6). In the general case, there is no analytical formula for capacity, we can find the capacity of the matrices in Figure 1 because they are so simple, matrixes such as Figure 2 pose more of a problem. Recently Malacaria et al. [18,11], showed that the capacity could be found by solving a series of equations, possibly in matlab. However, we wish to fully automate our analysis so instead we use the iterative Blahut-Arimoto algorithm [1,5], which can compute the capacity of an arbitrary channel to within a given precision. To explain this algorithm we first observe that mutual information can be written in terms of relative entropy D:

$$I(Q,W) = H(Q) - H(Q|Y) = \sum_x \sum_y Q(x)W(y|x) \log \left(\frac{W(y|x)}{\sum_{x'} Q(x')W(y|x')} \right)$$
$$= \sum_x Q(x)D(W(\cdot|x) \parallel \sum_{x'} Q(x')W(\cdot|x'))$$

We write $D_x(W \parallel QW)$ as short hand for $D(W(\cdot|x) \parallel \sum_{x'} Q(x')W(\cdot|x'))$. This leads to an upper bound for capacity; by observing that, for any set of numbers $\{n_1, \ldots, n_m\}$ and any probability distribution $\{p_1, \ldots, p_m\}$ it holds that $\sum_i p_i n_i \leq \max_i n_i$, we find that, for all probability distributions Q:

$$\sum_x Q(x)D_x(W \parallel QW) \leq C(W) \leq \max_x D_x(W \parallel QW) \tag{1}$$

It can be shown [5] that these inequalities become equalities when Q is the input distribution that achieves capacity.

The term $D_x(W \parallel QW)$ can be thought of as a measure of the effect that choosing the input x has on the output. Blahut and Arimoto showed that the maximising input distribution could be found by repeatingly increasing this measure. Given a channel W, the algorithm starts from an initial input distribution Q^0 (we start from a uniform one, if no better one is known) and in each step k we obtain a new distribution Q^{k+1} by updating the current Q^k for each input x as follows:

$$Q^{k+1}(x) = Q^k(x) \frac{\exp(D_x(W \parallel Q^k W))}{\sum_{x'} Q^k(x') \exp(D_{x'}(W \parallel Q^k W))}$$

The algorithm is guaranteed to converge to the capacity achieving distribution Q. Furthermore, (1) can be used as a stopping criterion, as for any $\epsilon \geq 0$, terminating the iterations when $\max_x D_x(W \parallel Q^k W) - I(Q^k, W) \leq \epsilon$ ensures that the estimate is within ϵ of the true capacity, with equality when the capacity has been found (i.e., $Q^k = Q$). Matz and Duhamel [20] propose an accelerated algorithm. They demonstrate super-linear convergence for this algorithm, and prove linear convergence in the general case.

Applying the Blahut-Arimoto algorithm to the matrix in Figure 2 finds the capacity to be 0.023, however it would be wrong to take this as evidence that there exists a small information leak from a Mixminion remailer node. As our data is from trial runs of the system, we must find a way to distinguish between true information leakage and noise in the results, which we do in the rest of this paper.

3   System Model and Assumptions

As in other work on information theoretic analysis of information leakage [22,24,29,12,9,11] a system in our framework consists of a set of secret inputs $\mathcal{X}$, a set of observable output actions $\mathcal{Y}$ and a probability transition matrix W that describes the behaviour of the system. We require that, given one particular secret input, the system behaves probabilistically. This means that if we run the system W with input x then there must be a fixed probability of seeing each observable output. In statistical terms, given a configuration of the system x the trial runs of the system must be independent and identically distributed: factors other than the input x, that are not accounted for by the probabilities of the outputs, must not have a statistically significant effect on the observed actions.

We consider a passive attacker that observes the outputs of the system and may try to make deductions from these outputs, but does not interact with the system directly. Capacity measures the most information that can be sent over a channel, no matter how it is used, so we do not require anything about the distribution of secret inputs. As long as the attacker does not have any prior knowledge about how the system is being used, there is no sequence of inputs, or clever processing of the observations, that can lead to a higher information leakage.

Given these assumptions, our analysis estimates the information leakage as the information-theoretic capacity of W. This is the maximum amount of information, in bits, that can be passed over W when it is regarded as a communication channel. In terms of anonymity, for instance, it is the maximum number of bits that the attacker can learn about which event took place, on average, from observing the system. An information leakage of $log_2(\#\mathcal{X})$ means that the system offers no anonymity at all, whereas an information leakage of 0 means that the system is perfectly anonymous. A capacity in between these values indicates a partial loss of information. As with any information theoretic measure of anonymity, we do not distinguish between a small chance of a total loss of anonymity and a high probability of a partial loss, rather our figure represents the average case for the average user. We also note that a statistical approach is ill suited to any measure that rates a tiny probability of a total loss of information as much worse than no loss of information because such a measure would not be continuous as the probability tended to zero and so would not allow for accurate confidence intervals to be found.

Our analysis method makes no assumptions about the distribution on secret inputs and assesses the whole system; this means that our results are valid no matter how the system is used but they cannot say anything about a particular observed run of the system. To do so would require one to make assumptions about the prior distribution as part of, for instance, a Bayesian analysis [3]. Such an analysis (e.g. [10,27]) gives the probability of identifying the culprit from given observations, but would not be valid if the assumptions are wrong or the users' behaviour changes.

4   Estimating Information Leakage

In this paper we focus on capacity as our measure of information leakage, we now describe how it can be calculated. There are two main obstacles to finding the capacity of a real system: firstly we must find a probability transition matrix that reflects the system under test and gives the conditional probabilities of any observable action (the outputs) given a particular usage of the system (the inputs). Secondly we must calculate capacity from this estimated matrix.

W	: the true probability transition matrix for the system
$\hat{W}_n$	: estimated probability transition matrix from n samples
Q	: the input distribution that maximises mutual information for W
$Q(\hat{W}_n)$	: the input distribution that maximises mutual information for a $\hat{W}_n$
$C(W) = I(Q, W)$	: the true capacity of W
$C(\hat{W}_n) = I(Q(\hat{W}_n), \hat{W}_n)$	: the true capacity of the matrix found by sampling
$\hat{Q}_m(\hat{W}_n)$	: the result of running the Blahut-Arimoto on $\hat{W}_n$ for m iterations
$\hat{C}(\hat{W}_n) = I(\hat{Q}_m(\hat{W}_n), \hat{W}_n)$	: our estimate of the capacity of W

Fig. 3. Key values for estimating capacity

To find the probability transition matrix we start by defining the inputs (the events that we wish to keep secret) and the outputs (the actions observable to an attacker). The latter corresponds to defining an attacker model. Some level of abstraction must be used; the user of our method, depending on the needs of the analysis, should make this choice. Our method requires many more samples than the number of observations so the more fine grained the attacker's observations are, the more samples we require; we quantify this in Section 5 where we calculate the variance of our results in terms of the number of inputs, outputs and samples. Defining the input and output of the channel is a challenging task and should be approached with some care, as it greatly influences the result of an information theoretic analysis. The data processing inequality states that for all functions F and G we have that $I(F(X); G(Y)) \leq I(X, Y)$ and picking a particular set of output actions can be looked on as picking the function G, therefore if we ignore some possible observations the attacker might make we obtain a lower bound for the true leakage. This paper primarily deals with the step after picking the inputs and outputs i.e., how to compute the leakage in a fully automated way.

Once the inputs and outputs are identified we may run trials of the system for each of the inputs and record the observable outcomes. We use these observations to construct an estimated matrix. Note that the approximate matrix can be generated using any probability distribution on the inputs, without having to making any assumptions about how the system is used. Calculating the capacity then finds the input distribution that leaks the most information. So we can collect our data for any usage of the system and then calculate the worst-case scenario.

There are two sources of error in the method we propose. The first comes from estimating the probability transition matrix for the system and the second from the approximation of capacity based on this matrix. Running a numerical approximation on inaccurate data does not necessarily lead to meaningful results, but we prove below that running the Blahut-Arimoto algorithm on an approximate matrix does return a result that tends to the true capacity as the sample size and the number of iterations increase.

The values and distributions used in our results are summarised in Figure 3. Our analysis of a system is based on the probability transition matrix W that gives conditional probabilities of each input given each output, $W(o|a) = p(o|a)$, i.e., the probability of the attacker seeing observation o given that the system is started in configuration a. We will estimate W by running the system n times with a uniform random input each time. This leads to an estimate $\hat{W}_n$, which is a matrix drawn from a normal distribution with mean W and a variance that decreases as n increases.

Next we have the input distribution that maximises the mutual information for W, which we label Q. The true capacity of the system C is given by the mutual information for input Q, denoted by $C(W) = I(Q, W)$. There is no direct formula to find Q exactly, so we estimate Q using the Blahut-Arimoto algorithm for m iterations; we write $\hat{Q}_m(W)$ for this distribution. We may also apply the Blahut-Arimoto algorithm to our estimated matrix to get $\hat{Q}_m(\hat{W}_n)$ which converges to the input distribution that maximises mutual information for the estimated matrix $\hat{W}_n$. This leads to our estimate of capacity for the system: $\hat{C}(\hat{W}_n) = I(\hat{Q}_m(\hat{W}_n), \hat{W}_n)$.

Our proposed method of analysing systems for information leakage is to use a value based on $\hat{C}(\hat{W}_n)$ in place of the true value $C(W)$. The estimated value can be automatically calculated from sampled alone, and the following theorem tells us that this estimate is good, i.e., with enough samples and iterations of the Blahut-Arimoto algorithm our estimate of capacity almost surely converges to the true value:

Theorem 1. *For any probability $p_e > 0$ and any real number $e > 0$ there exists integers n', m' such that for all $n > n'$ and $m > m'$ and for an estimated probability transition matrix found using n samples $\hat{W}_n$ it holds that*

$$p(|I(\hat{Q}_m(\hat{W}_n), \hat{W}_n) - I(Q, W)| > e) < p_e$$

Proof Sketch: Our proof is by contradiction. We assume that $\hat{C}$ does not almost surely converge to C. Mutual information is continuous and finite for a fixed number of inputs therefore our assumptions imply that there must also be a difference between $I(Q(\hat{W}_n), W)$ and $I(Q, W)$ or between $I(Q, \hat{W}_n)$ and $I(Q(\hat{W}_n), \hat{W}_n)$, however if these differences exist then either $Q(\hat{W}_n)$ does not maximise mutual information for $\hat{W}_n$ or Q does not maximise mutual information for W, leading to a contradiction.

5   Bounds on the Possible Error

To be sure of our results we need to know how close our estimate of capacity is to the real value. There are two ways in which we can find such a bound. We can estimate the error in each of the matrix entries and then calculate the maximum effect that all of these errors might cause on our final result. This method is relatively simple but leads to wide confidence intervals for the final results, we examine this method further in the technical report version of this paper [8]. A second method is to calculate the distribution that our results come from, in terms of the value we are trying to estimate. This method provides much tighter bounds but, due to the maximising nature of capacity, we must relate our results to a lower bound for capacity: $I(\hat{Q}_m(\hat{W}_n), W)$, rather than the true capacity $I(Q, W)$. While this is a lower bound, it is also zero if, and only if, the true capacity is zero:

Lemma 1. *Let $\hat{W}_n$ be a randomly sampled matrix from n samples and $\hat{Q}_m(\hat{W}_n)$ be the result of m iterations of the Blahut-Arimoto algorithm applied to this matrix, starting from a uniform distribution. Then $I(\hat{Q}_m(\hat{W}_n), W)$ is zero if and only if $C(W)$ is zero.*

The process of finding our estimation of capacity can be looked on as drawing a value from a distribution. In this section we show that the value comes from a χ^2 distribution if and only if the true capacity is zero and we also find the mean and variance of the distribution if the capacity is non-zero. This lets us calculate confidence intervals for a bound on the true capacity in terms of our estimated value.

The mean and variance of sampled mutual information has been found in the case that both distributions are unknown [17,23,25]. In our case we know the input distribution and only sample to find the outputs. Therefore we first solve the general problem of finding the mutual information when the input distribution is known and the matrix is sampled, then we describe how we use this result to calculate capacity.

5.1   The Distribution of Mutual Information

Let us denote the input distribution by X and the output distribution by Y. Suppose there are I inputs and J outputs. A slight abuse of notions lets us write the proofs in a more readable way, so we write $p_i = Q(i) = P(X = i), i = 0, \cdots, I-1, p_j = P(Y = j), j = 0, \cdots, J-1$, and $p_{ij} = P(X = i, Y = j)$, where the particular distribution (X or Y) is clear from the context. For the estimated values we write: $\hat{p}_{j|i} = \hat{W}_n(j|i)$=the estimated transition probability from input i to output j, $\hat{p}_{ij} = p_i \times \hat{p}_{j|i}$ =the estimated probability of seeing i and j, and $\hat{p}_j = \Sigma_i Q(i) W(j|i)$=the estimated probability of seeing j.

The mutual information can then be written:

$$I(X;Y) = \sum_{i=0}^{I-1} \sum_{j=0}^{J-1} p_{ij} \log \left(\frac{p_{ij}}{p_i p_j} \right),$$

and when both inputs and outputs are sampled the mutual information can be estimated as $\hat{I}'(X;Y) = \sum_{i=0}^{I-1} \sum_{j=0}^{J-1} \hat{p}_{ij} \log \left(\frac{\hat{p}_{ij}}{\hat{p}_i \hat{p}_j} \right)$, where the $\hat{p}$'s are the relative frequencies of the corresponding states, based on n samples. We also have that: $\hat{p}_i = \sum_{j=0}^{J-1} \hat{p}_{ij}$ and $\hat{p}_j = \sum_{i=0}^{I-1} \hat{p}_{ij}$.

It may be shown that when the inputs have no relation with the outputs, i.e. $I(X;Y) = 0$, then for large n $2n\hat{I}(X;Y)$ has an approximate χ^2 distribution with $(I-1)(J-1)$ degrees of freedom, see [6]. From that, one may say that $\hat{I}'(X;Y)$ has an approximate bias $(I-1)(J-1)/2n$ and approximate variance $(I-1)(J-1)/2n^2$. When $I(X;Y) > 0$, then it may be shown that $\hat{I}'(X;Y)$ has mean $I(X;Y)+(I-1)(J-1)/2n+O\left(\frac{1}{n^2}\right)$ and variance

$$\frac{1}{n} \left(\left(\sum_{i,j} p_{ij} \log^2 \left(\frac{p_{ij}}{p_i p_j} \right) - \left(\sum_{i,j} p_{ij} \log \left(\frac{p_{ij}}{p_i p_j} \right) \right)^2 \right) + O\left(\frac{1}{n^2} \right),$$

see Moddemejer [23]. Brillinger [6,7] states that this distribution is approximately normal.

In our case the situation is slightly different in that the input distribution is completely known. Hence, the estimate of $I(X;Y)$ is modified to

$$\hat{I}(X;Y) = \sum_{i=0}^{I-1}\sum_{j=0}^{J-1}\hat{p}_{ij}\log\left(\frac{\hat{p}_{ij}}{p_i\hat{p}_j}\right)$$

There exists no known result that deals with the asymptotic behaviour of the mutual information estimates in this situation. In this paper, we develop a distribution of the mutual information estimate for known input distribution when the output is independent of the input, i.e., the mutual information is zero, and then proceed to compute the asymptotic expectation and variance of the mutual information estimate when its actual value is non-zero.

Firstly, for $I(X;Y) = 0$, i.e. X and Y are independent, we have following;

Theorem 2. *When X and Y are independent with distribution of X known, for large n,* $2n\hat{I}(X;Y)$ *has an approximate* χ^2 *distribution with* $(I-1)(J-1)$ *degrees of freedom.*

We note that this theorem implies that if $I(X;Y) = 0$ then $\hat{I}(X;Y)$ is drawn from a distribution with mean $(I-1)(J-1)/2n$ and variance $(I-1)(J-1)/2n^2$.

When $I(X;Y) > 0$, the distribution is no longer χ^2. In this case, we have the following result:

Theorem 3. *When* $I(X;Y) > 0$, $\hat{I}(X;Y)$ *has mean* $I(X;Y) + (I-1)(J-1)/2n + O\left(\frac{1}{n^2}\right)$ *and variance*

$$\frac{1}{n}\sum_i p_i\left(\sum_j p_{j|i}\log^2\left(\frac{p_{ij}}{p_j}\right) - \left(\sum_j p_{j|i}\log\left(\frac{p_{ij}}{p_j}\right)\right)^2\right) + O\left(\frac{1}{n^2}\right)$$

To prove this we rewrite our estimate as: $\hat{I}(X,Y) = H(X) + \hat{H}(Y) - \hat{H}(X,Y)$, where $\hat{H}$ is the entropy calculated from the sampled data. As the distribution X is known we know $H(X)$ exactly. We proceed by taking the Taylor expansion of $\hat{H}(Y)$ and $\hat{H}(X,Y)$ to the order of $O(n^{-2})$. This gives us their expected values in terms of the powers of the expected difference between the entries of the probability transition matrix and their true values. As the rows of the matrix are multinomials we know these expectations (see e.g. [23]). Then, from the expected values of $\hat{H}(Y)$ and $\hat{H}(X,Y)$, we find the expected value of $\hat{I}(X,Y)$.

To find the variance we observe that:

$$V(\hat{I}_{XY}) = V(\hat{H}(X,Y)) + V(\hat{H}(Y)) - 2Cov(\hat{H}(X,Y),\hat{H}(Y))$$

As above we find the variance of $\hat{H}_{XY}$ and $\hat{H}_Y$, and their co-variance from the Taylor expansion and the expectations of the rows of the matrix. As suggested by Brillinger [6,7] we have verified experimentaly that this distribution is approximately normal.

It may be noted that the expression of the primary ($O(n^{-1})$) part of the variance above reduces to zero when X and Y are independent, which is consistent with variance of the estimate in the case that $I(X;Y) = 0$.

Comparing our result with that of Moddemejer [23], one point of interest is that the distribution of the estimate of the mutual information under independence of the input and the output (i.e. $C(W) = 0$) does not change whether we know the input distribution or not, and the expectation always remains the same, but the variance reduces when there is some information contained about the output in the input (i.e., C(W)¿0).

In both the zero and the non-zero cases we have a bound on the variance:

Lemma 2. *The variance of the estimates of mutual information in Theorem 2 and 3 are bound above by IJ/n where I and J are the sizes of the distributions domains and n is the number of samples used to find the estimate.*

This means that taking more samples than the product of the number of inputs and outputs ensures that the variance will be low and the results accurate. As running the Blahut-Arimoto algorithm on the data we collect can be done in linear time [20] the time taken to collect the sampled data will be the limiting factor of our method. The ability to generate more samples than the product of the inputs and outputs, in a reasonable amount of time, acts as a guide to which systems can and cannot be analysed statistically. We note, however that the variance can actually be much smaller than IJ/n therefore it may also be possible to get a low variance and accurate results with a smaller number of samples.

5.2   Using the Distributions for Information Leakage

Our results on the distribution of mutual information show that the mutual information is zero if, and only if, the distribution of the estimates has mean $(I-1)(J-1)/2n$ and variance $(I-1)(J-1)/2n^2$ (where I is the number of inputs and J the number of outputs). Whereas the mutual information is non-zero if, and only if, the mean is the true value plus $(I-1)(J-1)/2n$ and the variance is the value given in Theorem 3. Therefore our point estimate of information leakage is:

$$max(0, I(\hat{Q}_m(\hat{W}_n), \hat{W}_n) - (I-1)(J-1)/2n).$$

If a single test falls outside the confidence interval for zero mutual information then we may take it as evidence that the capacity is non-zero and calculate the confidence interval accordingly[1]. However a single test cannot distinguish between zero leakage and a very small amount. If the result is consistent with the χ^2 distribution then we may conclude that the result is between zero and the upper bound of the confidence interval for non-zero mutual information. This leads to the following testing procedure:

A Test to Estimate Information Leakage

1. Fix the secret inputs and observable outputs of the system under test. Ensure that each run of the system is independent.
2. Run n tests of the system with a random input and calculate an estimated matrix $\hat{W}_n$ (to be sure of good results pick $n \gg IJ$).

---

[1] Here we follow Brillinger and take the non-zero distribution to be normal.

3. Calculate $e = I(\hat{Q}_m(\hat{W}_n), \hat{W}_n)$ and the point estimate for anonymity $pe = max$ $(0, e - (I - 1)(J - 1)/2n)$, using enough iterations of the Blahut-Arimoto algorithm to make the error in capacity of the estimated matrix much smaller than the accuracy required by the user.

4. If $2n$ times e is inside the 95% confidence interval of the $\chi^2((I - 1)(J - 1))$ distribution then the confidence interval for the capacity is: 0 to $pe + 1.65\sqrt{v}$ where v is the variance as given in Theorem 3

5. If $2n$ times e is outside the 95% confidence interval of the $\chi^2((I - 1)(J - 1))$ distribution then the confidence interval for the capacity is: $pe - 1.96\sqrt{v}$ to $pe + 1.96\sqrt{v}$ where v is the variance as given in Theorem 3.

In many situations a very small leakage would be acceptable, however if we want to be sure of zero leakage then we have to run multiple tests and check the goodness of fit of the variance against the zero and non-zero predictions (tests based on the mean will not be able to distinguish zero and very small mutual information). To check compatibility of the variances we use the test that the observed variance divided by the true variance should be approximately χ^2 with mean one and variance two over the sample size minus one [4]. For very small values of mutual information the variance might be consistent with both predictions, however as the variance of the estimate of values that are truly zero is $O(n^{-2})$ and the variance of the estimate of values that are truly non-zero is $O(n^{-1})$ it will always be possible to distinguish these cases with a large enough n. Therefore, even though for large degrees of freedom a χ^2 distribution will start to resemble a normal distribution, a large enough sample size will always be able to tell the zero and non-zero distributions apart, due to the different orders of magnitude of the variances. This leads to the following test:

A Test for Zero Information Leakage

1. Fix the secret inputs and observable outputs of the system under test. Ensure that each run of the system is independent.

2. Run 40^2 analyses with sample size n (as described above), to find $\hat{W}1, \ldots, \hat{W}40$.

3. Calculate an estimate of the maximising input distribution $Q_e = Q_m(\hat{W}_1)$, then calculate $I(Q_e, \hat{W}1), \ldots, I(Q_e, \hat{W}40)$ and find the variance of these results: v.

4. Calculate the variance predicted by Theorem 2 v_{zero} and by Theorem 3 $v_{notZero}$.

5. If v/v_{zero} is inside the confidence interval for $\chi^2(2/n)$ and $v/v_{notZero}$ is outside the confidence interval then conclude that the information leakage is zero.

6. If v/v_{zero} is outside the confidence interval for $\chi^2(2/n)$ and $v/v_{notZero}$ is inside the confidence interval then conclude that the information leakage is non-zero.

7. If v is consistent with both predictions then repeat this process with a larger sample size n.

We note that, due to the differences in magnitude of the two variance predictions, this test is guaranteed to terminate.

---

[2] We use a sample size of 40 as this should be more than enough to accurately find the variance, see e.g. ([28], page 153).

6   Application to the Mixminion Remailer

Returning to the Mixminion remailer mix node from Section 2, we can now analyse the data properly. In this experiment we test whether an observer can learn anything about the order in which three short messages entered a mix node by observing messages coming out. Any link between the order of the inputs and outputs would help an attacker tell who was sending a message to whom, which is exactly what the mix is trying to hide. The messages we sent were of different lengths and sent to different e-mail addresses. In the different tests we alternated the order in which the messages entered the mix. So the secret inputs are the orders in which the three test messages arrive.

To find the observable outputs of the node we ran the WireShark packet sniffer on our test machine. This program recorded all incoming and outgoing packets sent to and from the mix node. To ensure that the observations of the packets leaving our mix were authentic we sent our messages to their destination via real nodes of the Mixminion network[3]. Once all the packets had been collected we recorded the size and number of packets sent to each of the destination mix nodes and the ordering of the packets to each node. These digests of the outgoing streams became the outputs of our channel.

In threshold mode the mix strategy is completely independent between firings. While background network traffic and other programs running on the computer may have an effect on the output, we avoid this affecting our results by randomising the order in which the different input messages orderings are tested. Therefore outside conditions will effect all the results equally, and so our experiments fit the requirement of independent and identically-distributed as described in Section 3. To gather our test data we ran our own Mixminion node. We set the mix time limit to be 2 minutes and in each interval sent three known test messages into the node, effectively running it as a threshold mix (we found that the mixes would occasionally take longer than the specified interval, so that if we set the interval for less than 2 minutes our test messages would occasionally straddle the boundary between mix firings and so invalidate our results).

We first ran 1000 tests looking only at the ordering of the packets entering and leaving the mix. The results are shown in Figure 2. Here message 1 was being sent to address A, 2 to B and 3 to C. It was clear that Mixminion usually sent the messages out in a fixed order (C then B then A), however occasionally a different order was observed. Was this unusual ordering, or anything else, leaking information on the order of the incoming messages? Or was it unrelated to the Mixminion software and due to the computer's network card, or network conditions? A quick run of our software finds that the capacity of this matrix is 0.023, which is well within the 95% upper confidence limit for zero leakage (0.0355), therefore there is no evidence of any loss of anonymity.

Next we ran 10000 tests, in batches of a few hundred, over the course of three weeks and, along with the ordering, also recorded the size and number of packets sent. We disregarded the results when there were large amounts of packet loss due to network disruption; we note that this may be a possible way to attack a mix network. We observed 436 different observable outputs in total. The most common observation by far was 33301 bytes in 32 to 34 packets send to each of the other nodes, with overlapping

---

[3] We only sent messages via nodes where we had received permission from the person running the node, as our test traffic could easily have looked like an attack on the network.

streams starting in a fixed order. Occasionally the streams would start in a different order and different numbers of packets, payload size and timings would be observed.

Our software calculated the point estimated of capacity as 0.0249, which is well within the 95% confidence intervals for the χ^2 distribution for the zero case. Leading to a 95% confidence interval for the information leakage as between 0 and 0.0414. Therefore our result is consistent with a capacity of zero and we may conclude that, in this instance, there is no evidence of any loss of anonymity due to the order that messages arrive and leave a Mixminion. There are known attacks that target more complicated aspects of networks of Mixminion nodes; we plan to investigate whether our method can scale up to detect such attacks in the future.

7 Conclusion

The capacity of a channel with discrete inputs and outputs has been proposed as a metric in a number of areas of computer security. We have shown that such measures of information leakage can be calculated from sampled data and so made it possible to apply this theory to real systems. Our calculation of the variance of the estimates can also be used to tell when systems are, or are not, too complex to successfully analyse statistically.

As further work plan to use our tool to look for information leaks from real systems. We also intend to find the distribution of estimates of conditional mutual information and an upper bound for capacity. For this, we can proceed in the same way as finding the lower bound; for conditional mutual information we can find the Taylor expansions of $H(X|Y)$ and $H(X|Y, Z)$ and for an upper bound on capacity we can find the expansion of $D_x(W \parallel XW)$. This would lead to the mean and variance in terms of the expected differences of the matrix entries, which are known. For conditional mutual information we can use the appropriate adaptation of the Blahut-Arimoto algorithm to find our approximation of the maximising input distributions [16].

References

1. Arimoto, S.: An algorithm for computing the capacity of arbitrary memoryless channels. IEEE Trans. on Inform. Theory IT-18(1), 14–20 (1972)
2. Backes, M., Köpf, B.: Formally bounding the side-channel leakage in unknown-message attacks. In: Jajodia, S., Lopez, J. (eds.) ESORICS 2008. LNCS, vol. 5283, pp. 517–532. Springer, Heidelberg (2008)
3. Bayes, T.: An essay towards solving a problem in the doctrine of chances. Philo. Trans. of the Royal Society of London 53, 370–418 (1774)
4. Bickel, P.J., Doksum, K.A.: Mathematical Statistics: Basic Ideas and Selected Topics. Prentice Hall, Englewood Cliffs (2006)
5. Blahut, R.E.: Computation of channel capacity and rate distortion functions. IEEE Trans. on Inform. Theory IT-18(4), 460–473 (1972)
6. Brillinger, D.R.: Some data analysis using mutual information. Brazilian Journal of Probability and Statistics 18(6), 163–183 (2004)
7. Brillinger, D.R.: Personal correspondence (April 2009)

8. Chatzikokolakis, K., Chothia, T., Guha, A.: Calculating probabilistic anonymity from sampled data. Technical report, University of Birmingham (2009)
9. Chatzikokolakis, K., Palamidessi, C., Panangaden, P.: Anonymity protocols as noisy channels. Information and Computation 206, 378–401 (2008)
10. Chatzikokolakis, K., Palamidessi, C., Panangaden, P.: On the bayes risk in information-hiding protocols. J. Comput. Secur. 16(5), 531–571 (2008)
11. Chen, H., Malacaria, P.: Quantifying maximal loss of anonymity in protocols. In: ASIACCS, pp. 206–217 (2009)
12. Clark, D., Hunt, S., Malacaria, P.: A static analysis for quantifying information flow in a simple imperative language. J. Comput. Secur. 15(3), 321–371 (2007)
13. Danezis, G., Dingledine, R., Mathewson, N.: Mixminion: Design of a type iii anonymous remailer protocol. In: Proceedings of the 2003 IEEE Symposium on Security and Privacy, pp. 2–15 (2003)
14. Deng, Y., Pang, J., Wu, P.: Measuring anonymity with relative entropy. In: Dimitrakos, T., Martinelli, F., Ryan, P.Y.A., Schneider, S. (eds.) FAST 2006. LNCS, vol. 4691, pp. 65–79. Springer, Heidelberg (2007)
15. Díaz, C., Seys, S., Claessens, J., Preneel, B.: Towards measuring anonymity. In: Dingledine, R., Syverson, P.F. (eds.) PET 2002. LNCS, vol. 2482, pp. 54–68. Springer, Heidelberg (2003)
16. Dupuis, F., Yu, W., Willems, F.M.J.: Blahut-arimoto algorithms for computing channel capacity and rate-distortion with side information. In: Proceedings of International Symposium on Information Theory. ISIT 2004, p. 179+ (2004)
17. Hutter, M.: Distribution of mutual information. In: Advances in Neural Information Processing Systems 14, pp. 399–406. MIT Press, Cambridge (2002)
18. Malacaria, P., Chen, H.: Lagrange multipliers and maximum information leakage in different observational models. In: PLAS 2008: Proceedings of the third ACM SIGPLAN workshop on Programming languages and analysis for security, pp. 135–146. ACM, New York (2008)
19. Mantel, H., Sudbrock, H.: Information-theoretic modeling and analysis of interrupt-related covert channels. In: Degano, P., Guttman, J., Martinelli, F. (eds.) FAST 2008. LNCS, vol. 5491, pp. 67–81. Springer, Heidelberg (2009)
20. Matz, G., Duhamel, P.: Information geometric formulation and interpretation of accelerated blahut-arimoto-type algorithms. In: Proceedings of the IEEE Information Theory Workshop (ITW), pp. 66–70 (2004)
21. McIver, A., Morgan, C.: A probabilistic approach to information hiding in Programming methodology, pp. 441–460. Springer, Heidelberg (2003)
22. Millen, J.K.: Covert channel capacity. In: IEEE Symposium on Security and Privacy, pp. 60–66 (1987)
23. Moddemejer, R.: On estimation of entropy and mutual information of continuous distributions. Signal Processing 16, 233–248 (1989)
24. Moskowitz, I.S., Newman, R.E., Syverson, P.F.: Quasi-anonymous channels. In: IASTED CNIS, pp. 126–131 (2003)
25. Paninski, L.: Estimation of entropy and mutual information. Neural Comp. 15(6), 1191–1253 (2003)
26. Serjantov, A., Danezis, G.: Towards an information theoretic metric for anonymity. In: Dingledine, R., Syverson, P.F. (eds.) PET 2002. LNCS, vol. 2482, pp. 41–53. Springer, Heidelberg (2003)
27. Troncoso, C., Danezis, G.: The bayesian traffic analysis of mix networks. In: Proceedings of the 16th ACM conference on Computer and communications security, pp. 369–379 (2009)
28. Wheeler, A.J., Ganji, A.R.: Introduction to Engineering Experimentation, 3rd edn. Prentice Hall, Englewood Cliffs (2009)
29. Zhu, Y., Bettati, R.: Anonymity vs. information leakage in anonymity systems. In: Proc. of ICDCS, pp. 514–524. IEEE Computer Society, Los Alamitos (2005)

SAT Based Bounded Model Checking with Partial Order Semantics for Timed Automata*

Janusz Malinowski and Peter Niebert

Laboratoire d'Informatique Fondamentale de Marseille
Université de Provence, 39 rue Joliot-Curie, Marseille, France
{peter.niebert,janusz.malinowski}@lif.univ-mrs.fr

Abstract. We study the model checking problem of timed automata based on SAT solving. Our work investigates alternative possibilities for coding the SAT reductions that are based on parallel executions of independent transitions.

While such an optimization has been studied for discrete systems, its transposition to timed automata poses the question of what it means for timed transitions to be executed "in parallel". The most obvious interpretation is that the transitions in parallel take place at the same time (synchronously). However, it is possible to relax this condition. On the whole, we define and analyse three different semantics of timed sequences with parallel transitions.

We prove the correctness of the proposed semantics and report experimental results with a prototype implementation.

1 Introduction

In this paper, we describe a SAT based model checking algorithm for timed concurrent systems that includes partial order concepts, as well as its implementation in the POEM model checker.

While symbolic state exploration with zones [10] as implemented in Uppaal [2] remains the most widely used algorithm for model checking timed automata, reductions to SAT solvers [15,13,1,17] have been studied with encouraging results. However, the situation is far from the dominance of SAT methods used to analyse synchronous circuits.

On the other hand, the zone based state exploration has seen several works investigating improvements based on partial order semantics [12,16,7,14]. In the development of timed automata, this investigation came late, maybe because the algorithms used defy the intuition of time as a total order. For instance, in [12] it is possible that the algorithm provides sequences where the time may go backwards between transitions (but these executions can nevertheless be reordered to represent real executions).

The basis of most so-called partial order approaches for model checking asynchronous systems is the structural observation that pairs of *independent transitions*, i.e. transitions that concern separate parts of a distributed system, may

---

* Partially supported by the ANR project ECSPER(ANR JC09_472677 ECSPER).

J. Esparza and R. Majumdar (Eds.): TACAS 2010, LNCS 6015, pp. 405–419, 2010.

be executed in any order with the same result. For timed automata, this was at first not obvious, since these transitions may reset clocks and the order of firing introduces a relation on the clock values. The cited works using partial order concepts for timed automata avoid in one way or another the introduction of this artificial relation and can therefore outperform the classical algorithms in many cases.

An obvious question occurs when combining two different methods (here SAT reductions and partial order semantics): will the performance improve on each method separately? For untimed asynchronous systems like safe Petri nets, a positive answer to this question was given in [9,11] and a few sequels. However, the answer given in those works was to improve the SAT reduction by allowing several independent transitions to actually occur in parallel, i.e. in one step. This concept was known before in Petri nets as *step semantics* [8], but it found an unexpected application. Intuitively, multisteps (transitions that are executed in parallel) allow to compress execution sequences leading to a state: while the overall number of executed transitions remains the same, the possibility of executing several of them in one parallel step means that there are less intermediate states to consider. Moreover, when coding reachability in SAT, differently from state exploration, the sub-formulae coding the possible execution of a transition are present for every step in the sequence anyway. From this perspective, requiring interleaving semantics can be perceived as nothing more than a restriction stating that in any multistep at most one transition takes place. In tight cases, the best SAT solver will have to try out every interleaving, i.e. every permutation of independent transitions. We cannot imagine a case where this interleaving requirement will have any benefit for the SAT approach, but relaxing it and allowing multisteps will very often give dramatic improvements.

The contribution of this work is to extend the reduction with *multisteps* to timed automata.

This being said, we invite the reader to consider what it means for several timed transitions to be executed "in parallel" or in the same multistep before reading on.

Indeed, the first idea that may come to ones mind is that these transitions should take place "at the same time", but this turns out to be just one of several options, which we call "synchronous". A more relaxed notion may require that each transition in a multistep has to be executed temporally before each transition of the following multistep, yet allowing the individual transitions to take place at different times, a notion we call "semi synchronous time progress". Based on notions from [12,14], the seemingly least restrictive sensible notion limits the time progress to transitions that are dependent, which we call "relaxed time progress". Based on previous work, we show that the three proposed notions of time progress are equivalent in the sense that the execution sequences of either semantics can be transformed into execution sequences of the other and into the classical notion of runs. However, they turn out not to be equivalent with respect to performance: the more relaxed notions are more complex to code in SAT but can in some cases yield superior results.

Plan. The paper is structured as follows: in Section 2, we introduce the basic notions of timed systems on a certain specification level: multithreaded programs with shared variables. It is essential to use such a model to understand the SAT coding. We also introduce notions from timed automata, notably "clocks", clock conditions and resets. For the sake of readability, we do not introduce state invariants at this point. In Section 3, we recall notions of independence in the context of timed automata and introduce semantics with multisteps. The main formal tools are developed here, different notions of time progress are formally defined and their equivalence is shown. In Section 4, we show how these concepts integrate into a SAT reduction for systems of the kind described in Section 2. This description, although held informal where possible, aims to give a self-contained description of how such a reduction is constructed and how the notions of Section 3 integrate in the construction of a SAT problem instance. In Section 5, we informally discuss how state invariants, an important modelling concept in timed automata can be integrated with each of the three notions of time progress. In Section 6, we illustrate the potential of the algorithms by a few benchmarks in our prototype implementation. We conclude and discuss related work in Section 7.

2 Preliminaries

Let T_i with $1 \leq i \leq N$ denote a thread with $trans_i$ its set of transitions. Let $trans = \bigcup trans_i$ the set of all transitions. Let V_i be the set of local variables of T_i and let V_g the set of global variables. Then we introduce $V = V_g \cup \bigcup V_i$ the set of all variables. Each variable $v \in V$ takes its values in the domain D_v. Control locations of a thread T_i are represented by a local variable $pc_i \in V_i$ (program counter).

A state of a program is a valuation of local and global variables, formally $s : V \longrightarrow \bigcup D_v$ with $s(v) \in D_v$. The set of all states is denoted by $S = \prod D_v$. We moreover assume an *initial state* s_0, i.e. an initial valuation of variables.

Expressions over the variables are defined as usual (e.g. arithmetic expressions). Atoms are comparisons over pairs of expressions and conditions are boolean combinations of atoms.

Syntactically, a transition t of T_i is enabled by a *condition* (boolean combination of atoms) ranging over $V_i \cup V_g$, and it has as effect an *action* defined as a set of assignments (of expressions to variables), i.e. values of variables are *written*. For both actions and conditions, the variables appearing in the expressions are *read*. If t is a transition from the control location loc_1 to control location loc_2 then the condition of t includes $pc_i = loc_1$ and the action includes $pc_i := loc_2$.

For two states $s, s' \in S$, $s \xrightarrow{t} s'$ denotes a state transition enabled at s and transforming s to s' when applying the action of t. Let $s \xrightarrow{t_1} s_1 \ldots \xrightarrow{t_n} s_n = s'$ denote a sequence of transition executions.

2.1   Adding Time

We introduce real valued variables called *clocks* which differ from other variables:

- Their values increase synchronously and proportionally with time: if x has value ρ at time τ then it has value $\rho + \delta$ at time $\tau + \delta$.
- The only assignments allowed are resets (to zero).
- We only allow comparisons of clocks with integer constants (e.g. $x \leq 3$).
- At the initial state s_0, all clocks are valued 0.

Now, each transition execution t_k has an execution time $\tau_k \in \mathbb{R}^+$ also called a *timestamp*. Then, we denote a timed transition t_k executed at time τ_k as $s \xrightarrow{(t_k, \tau_k)} s'$ and *timed sequence* as $s_0 \xrightarrow{(t_1, \tau_1)} s_1 \ldots \xrightarrow{(t_n, \tau_n)} s_n = s'$.

A timed sequence $s_0 \xrightarrow{(t_1, \tau_1)} s_1 \ldots \xrightarrow{(t_n, \tau_n)} s_n = s'$ satisfies *normal time progress* iff for every pair $k < l$, we have $\tau_k \leq \tau_l$.

The *reachability problem for timed automata* can be understood in this setting as the existence of a timed sequence with normal time progress leading from s_0 to a state s' satisfying a desired property.

3   Concurrency

In this section, we will review standard notions from classical partial order methods. Then we will introduce the notion of *multisteps*, i.e. the execution of several transitions *in parallel* and we will see how to analyse timed systems using multisteps.

3.1   Independence Relation

A classical definition underlying concurrency analysis is reader-writer dependency as first introduced in [6]: two transitions t_1 and t_2 are said to be *dependent* if a variable read in t_1 (in the guard or in the action) is written in t_2 (or vice versa), or if the same variable is written by t_1 and t_2. Otherwise, they are *independent*.

A timed sequence $s_0 \xrightarrow{(t_1, \tau_1)} s_1 \ldots \xrightarrow{(t_n, \tau_n)} s_n = s'$ satisfies *relaxed time progress* if for every pair $k < l$ with t_k, t_l dependent, we also have $\tau_k \leq \tau_l$. Note, that normal time progress as defined in the previous section trivially implies relaxed time progress.

We define the Mazurkiewicz equivalence of timed sequences as the least equivalence relation $\equiv$ such that any timed sequence $s_0 \ldots s_{k-1} \xrightarrow{(t_k, \tau_k)} s_k \xrightarrow{(t_{k+1}, \tau_{k+1})} s_{k+1} \ldots s'$ with t_k, t_{k+1} independent is equivalent to $s_0 \ldots s_{k-1} \xrightarrow{(t_{k+1}, \tau_{k+1})} s_k' \xrightarrow{(t_k, \tau_k)} s_{k+1} \ldots s'$ for some state s_k'. In other words, two timed sequences are equivalent if one can be transformed into the other by a finite number of exchanges of adjacent independent transitions together with their execution times.

Proposition 1. *If a timed sequence satisfies relaxed time progress, then so do its equivalent sequences. Each timed sequence satisfying relaxed time progress is equivalent to a timed sequence satisfying normal time progress*

Proof. This was originally shown in [12]. Indeed, the order of dependent transition executions is preserved by exchanges and hence so is relaxed time progress. For the second part, it is possible to transform a timed sequence with relaxed time progress by applying a "bubble sort" transformation: suppose that two adjacent transitions are in bad order with respect to their timestamps, then relaxed time progress implies that they are independent and it is possible to exchange them. The result follows by applying this reasoning in an induction. □

3.2 Concurrently Enabled Transitions

The notions proposed in the following have first come up in the context of (untimed) Petri nets under the name *step semantics* [8], generalized here for our purposes to timed automata. Let $MT = \{(t_1, \tau_1), \ldots, (t_n, \tau_n)\}$ a set of pairwise independent transitions with timestamps: it is *concurrently enabled* at global state s iff each transition is enabled at state s and at time τ_i. Note, that implicitly if $(t, \tau_a), (t, \tau_b) \in MT$ then $\tau_a = \tau_b$ because a transition is always dependent with itself. By definition of independence, all possible executions using all these transitions and beginning at s are equivalent, and lead to the same state s'. Then we say that they can be executed in parallel and we write $s \xrightarrow{MT} s'$.

A *multistep timed sequence* is a sequence $s_0 \xrightarrow{MT_1} s_1 \ldots \xrightarrow{MT_n} s_n = s'$. The interest here of multisteps is immediate: because several transitions are executed at each multistep, the execution can be shorter (i.e. a lower number of multisteps may be executed) to reach a certain state than with interleaving semantics.

3.3 Time Progress in Multistep Sequences

A *multistep timed sequence* $s_0 \xrightarrow{MT_1} s_1 \ldots \xrightarrow{MT_n} s_n = s'$ satisfies *relaxed time progress* if for every pair $k < l$ with $(t_1, \tau_1) \in MT_k, (t_2, \tau_2) \in MT_l, t_1, t_2$ dependent, we also have $\tau_1 \leq \tau_2$.

Lemma 1. *Let* $s_0 \xrightarrow{MT_1} s_1 \ldots \xrightarrow{MT_n} s_n = s'$ *be a multistep timed sequence that satisfies relaxed time progress, then there exists a timed sequence* $s_0 \xrightarrow{(t_1, \tau_1)} s_1 \ldots \xrightarrow{(t_m, \tau_m)} s_m = s'$ *with* $m = \sum |MT_i|$ *(the total number of single transition) that satisfies relaxed time progress.*

Proof. We build a timed sequence $s \xrightarrow{(t_1, \tau_1)} \ldots \xrightarrow{(t_m, \tau_m)} s_m = s'$ by extracting each (t_i, τ_i) from each MT_k respecting the order of the MT_k (the order of the (t_i, τ_i) extracted from the same MT_k is not important because they are independent). □

We now introduce alternative representations of time progress of a multistep timed sequence $s_0 \xrightarrow{MT_1} s_1 \ldots \xrightarrow{MT_n} s_n = s'$:

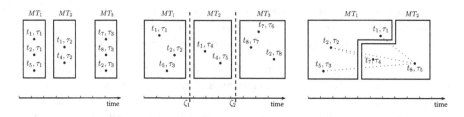

Fig. 1. Synchronous, semi synchronous and relaxed time progress in multisteps

- *synchronous time progress*: for all multisteps MT_k and for all pairs of transitions $(t_1, \tau_1), (t_2, \tau_2) \in MT_k$ it holds that $\tau_1 = \tau_2$ and for $k < l$ and any $(t_a, \tau_a) \in T_k$, $(t_b, \tau_b) \in MT_l$ it holds that $\tau_a \leq \tau_b$, i.e. all transitions in the same multistep are executed at the same time, and time progresses between multisteps.
- *semi synchronous time progress*: for all $k < l$ and any $(t_a, \tau_a) \in MT_k$, $(t_b, \tau_b) \in MT_l$ it holds that $\tau_a \leq \tau_b$, i.e. all transitions of a later multistep are executed at a later time than the transitions of an earlier multistep (but transitions of a same multistep may be executed at different times).

It is obvious that synchronous time progress implies semi synchronous time progress which in term implies relaxed time progress.

Theorem 1. *Let $s, s' \in S$, then the following elements can be transformed into each other:*

1) *A timed sequence $s \xrightarrow{(t_1,\tau_1)} \ldots \xrightarrow{(t_n,\tau_n)} s'$ with normal time progress.*
2) *A timed sequence $s \xrightarrow{(t_1,\tau_1)} \ldots \xrightarrow{(t_n,\tau_n)} s'$ with relaxed time progress.*
3) *A multistep timed sequence $s \xrightarrow{MT_1} \ldots \xrightarrow{MT_k} s'$ with synchronous time progress.*
4) *A multistep timed sequence $s \xrightarrow{MT_1} \ldots \xrightarrow{MT_l} s'$ with semi synchronous time progress.*
5) *A multistep timed sequence $s \xrightarrow{MT_1} \ldots \xrightarrow{MT_m} s'$ with relaxed time progress.*

Proof.   • 1 ⇒ 2: by definition
  • 2 ⇒ 1: see Proposition 1
  • 2 ⇒ 3: we build a multistep timed sequence $s \xrightarrow{MT_1} \ldots \xrightarrow{MT_n} s_n = s'$ where each MT_k is the singleton $\{(t_k, \tau_k)\}$; it is trivially a multistep timed sequence with synchronous time progress
  • 3 ⇒ 4: by definition
  • 4 ⇒ 5: by definition
  • 5 ⇒ 2: see Lemma 1   □

4   SAT Reduction

4.1   Context

We have implemented the SAT coding outlined below in the tool POEM (Partial Order Environment of Marseille).

Fig. 2. A diagram of POEM with a SAT BACKEND

POEM is a modular model checker written in OCAML. Its main executable is composed of three parts, a frontend (syntactic analysis), a core with static analysis and model transformation, and an analysis oriented backend. The frontend part reads the model written in a specification language (currently Uppaal [2], IF2 [5]) and transforms it into a common format (GDS) on which type verification, transformations and other aspects of static analysis (notably for dependency analysis) are applied.

The backends currently use as input the declaration of variables and processes and a list of transitions much like the one described in Section 2. In particular, for each transition the sets of written and read variables can be determined statically (an over approximation) or dynamically (context dependent) where the latter is close in practice to notions of dynamic dependency relations.

Previously, there was only a state exploration based backend with the underlying algorithms described in [12,14]. In this section, we will describe the way we coded the SAT backend, which is used to perform a Bounded Model Checking (BMC): given a multi-threaded program and a reachability property, we construct a SAT formula Φ that is satisfiable iff a state with the property can be reached by an execution of the program with up to K multisteps. This construction involves several aspects described below.

4.2 Coding Variables

Each *variable* $v \in V$ of the input model is transformed into a vector of boolean variables of size $\log_2 |D_v|$. As an example, let's examine the following declaration in an IF2 input model:

```
var x range 0..3;
```

This command declares a variable x taking its values over the domain $[0..3]$ or a total of 4 possible values. Then we need a boolean vector of size 2: $\{x_1, x_2\}$.

The *program counter* pc_i for each thread T_i is coded as a normal variable, i.e. as a boolean vector, its length depending on the number of states in the thread.

subsectionCoding expressions

Expressions are coded as digital circuits (like the simple adder below), where each port is coded as a small set of clauses concerning input and output variables and the auxiliary *cables* of the circuits (that are neither inputs or outputs, 3 for the adder circuit) are coded using additional boolean variables.

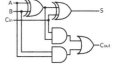

Boolean vectors are manipulated bit-wise, e.g. if x and y are two variables over the same domain $[0..3]$, then the equality test $x = y$ will be coded as $z = ((x_1 = y_1) \wedge (x_2 = y_2))$. Again, the boolean variable z is an implicit variable added to simplify the formula and to allow subformula sharing (when the expression $x = y$ appears in some context, it will be replaced by z).

4.3   Coding Time

Clock values increase with time, which is not easy to code in directly. Instead, we introduce new real valued variables $last_x$ to store the time of the last reset of clock x, e.g. if we have the following transition $s \xrightarrow[x:=0]{t,\tau} s'$, then the action $x := 0$ will be coded as $last_x := \tau$. A clock comparison in the transition $s \xrightarrow[x \bowtie c]{t,\tau} s'$ with $\bowtie \in \{\leq, <, =, >, \geq\}$ and c a constant will be coded as $\tau - last_x \bowtie c$. Hence, it is possible to substitute a clock x by the corresponding variable $last_x$ with assignments and conditions as above: in this practical coding, variables do not change *between* transition occurrences. The variables $last_x$ have the same expressive power as clocks.

As seen above, real valued variables are used to manipulate time such as $last_x$ and timestamps τ. However, as analysed in [15,18], it is possible to restrict time stamps to a bounded interval and fixed point numbers (a certain number of variables for the bits of the integer part and the bits of the fractional part), where both the size of the integer part and the precision of the fractional part depend on the length of the searched sequence (more precicely, the number of transition executions).

Alternatively, the coding could be applied for an SMT-solver as in [16,1], where all variables except the timestamps are coded with booleans but the timestamps are coded as real valued variables.

4.4   Duplication of Variables

Because the formula Φ must represent an execution of depth K, we need to add a copy of all variables for each step. We denote $v^i \in V^i$ with $1 \leq i \leq K$ the copy of $v \in V$ at step i. Then if $K = 5$ and $v \in [0..3]$, we have to allocate the following boolean vectors $\{v_1^1, v_2^1\}, \{v_1^2, v_2^2\}, \{v_1^3, v_2^3\}, \{v_1^4, v_2^4\}, \{v_1^5, v_2^5\}$.

The result is that the assignment $x := y + 3$ at step k will be coded as $x^{k+1} = y^k + 3$, i.e. an assignment becomes a relation between the value x^{k+1} of x after the current step and the value y^k of y before the current step. Note, that this transition reads y and writes x.

4.5   Transitions and Multisteps

Each execution of transition t in a multistep MT_k is coded with one boolean variable t^k indicating if the transition is executed or not.

If the transition $s_k \xrightarrow[cond,action]{t,\tau} s_{k+1}$ is executed, then its condition *cond* is true at s_k (at time τ) and the assignments of the action are performed (where *action* is coded as constraints between the variables at s_k and at s_{k+1} as indicated above. Formally it is coded as

$$t^{k+1} \rightarrow cond_t(s_k, \tau) \wedge action_t(s_k, s_{k+1})$$

At this point, if s_k is determined and the set of executed transitions includes a transition t that writes v, then $action_t(s_k, s_{k+1})$ also determines the value of v at s_{k+1}. If however, v is written by no executed transition, then its value must be maintained. Suppose that the set of transitions that writes v is $\{t_a, t_b, t_c\}$, then this requirement is coded by the clause

$$t_a^{k+1} \vee t_b^{k+1} \vee t_c^{k+1} \vee v_k = v_{k+1}$$

As for dependency, the condition of pairwise independence of transition executions in a multistep can be coded by a conjunction of constraints $(\neg t_a^k \vee \neg t_b^k)$ for dependent pairs t_a, t_b.

The combination of the action related clauses, dependency related clauses and the clauses for the keeping of values ensure the consistency of successor states. In practice, the constraints concerning writing and reading of variables and those for dependency are coded together, allowing for a more compact coding with sharing. Still, the conflict clauses constitute a significant part of the overall formula.

4.6 Coding Time Progress

- Synchronous: all transitions of a multistep MT_k are executed at the same moment τ_i, i.e. only one timestamp is needed for each step i. We get the following constraints :

$$\bigwedge_{i=1..K-1} \tau_i \leq \tau_{i+1}$$

- Semi synchronous: all transitions of multistep MT_k are executed before some moment ζ_k (additional variable) and all transitions of multistep MT_{k+1} are executed after ζ_k. Each transition t has its own timestamp τ_t, resulting to the following constraints

$$\bigwedge_{\substack{i=1..K-1 \\ t,t' \in trans}} (\tau_{t^i} \leq \zeta^i) \wedge (\zeta^i \leq \tau_{t'^{i+1}})$$

- Relaxed: it is not straight forward to code relaxed time progress since the condition given in Section 3.3 is not local to two adjacent multi steps. A trick can be used to make occurrence times of previous multisteps locally accessible: for transitions that are not executed, the timestamp τ_t^k has no meaning. We then use it to represent the *last execution time* of t before or including the current multi step. This leads to two cases : if the transition t, τ_t is not executed at step i then the value of τ_t must be maintained at step $i+1$ and if it is executed we add constraints $\leq$ with timestamps of the last executions of dependent transitions:

$$\bigwedge_{k=1..K-1} \bigwedge_{t \in trans} \neg t^k \rightarrow (\tau_t^k = \tau_t^{k-1}) \wedge$$

$$\bigwedge_{k=1..K-1} \bigwedge_{t_a \in trans} \bigwedge_{\substack{t_b \in trans \\ t_a D t_b}} t_a^k \rightarrow (\tau_{t_b}^{k-1} \leq \tau_{t_a}^k)$$

In this formula $t_a \, D \, t_b$ denotes that t_a and t_b are dependent transitions.

4.7 The Global Formula

We resume all the steps for the construction of the global formula Φ which states the existence of a timed multistep sequence:

- Allocate boolean vectors $v_1^k, \ldots, v_n^k$ for all $v \in V$ and for all $1 \le k \le K$
- Initialise Φ with initial assignments (constraints) for each variable v^0
- For each step $1 \le k \le K - 1$
  - $\Phi := \Phi \wedge$ transitions coding
  - $\Phi := \Phi \wedge$ dependency coding
  - $\Phi := \Phi \wedge$ value maintaining
  - $\Phi := \Phi \wedge$ time progress coding
- Add to Φ constraints to ensure the desired path property. For reachability, this can be achieved by stating that the last state satisfies the desired property.

5 Integrating State Invariants

The reader familiar with timed automata will have noticed that we have not dealt with "state invariants" in our reduction. In modelling frameworks like Uppaal, a state invariant is a condition on clocks that is attached to a state of a thread (a value of the local program counter in terms of Section 2) and which is intuitively a "residence permit": the condition $pc_3 = loc_1 \rightarrow x < 5$ states that the state 1 of thread 3 has to be left by a transition before clock x reaches 5. To avoid this violation, either a transition of this thread leaving the state could be executed or a transition of another thread could reset c, thus effectively extending the residence permit for this state.

More generally, state invariants are of the form $pc_i = loc_k \Rightarrow \bigwedge x_j \le c_j$, i.e. a state value implies a conjunction of upper bounds for clocks. For systems with just one thread, a state invariant has the same effect as adding the constraints to each outgoing transition of the state; they add nothing to the expressiveness of the formalism. For parallel systems, the invariants also imply additional constraints for the outgoing transitions (which must therefore be considered to be reading the corresponding clocks), however, they have a more global effect: the entire system is forced to execute some transition before the expiring of the invariants of each thread. This is very useful in modeling the coupling of subsystems by time, e.g. for modeling timeouts.

It is possible to extend the framework we have developed so far to include state invariants, but technically, this integration depends on the notion of time progress and it is quite complex for relaxed timed progress.

Interleaving Semantics and Synchronous Time Progress. Consider a timed sequence $s_0 \xrightarrow{(t_1, \tau_1)} s_1 \ldots \xrightarrow{(t_n, \tau_n)} s_n = s'$. For standard interleaving semantics, i.e. one transition at a time, the conjunction of all (thread local) state invariants at global state s_i must be satisfied at time τ_{i+1} (the execution time of the next transition after s_i). Obviously, since $\tau_{i+1} \leq \tau_{i+2}$ the invariant holding *after* the execution of the transition also (already) holds at τ_{i+1}.

For synchronous time progress, the same coding as for interleaving semantics is valid! Although we execute several transitions at time τ_{i+1} we do not execute any transition before that date and hence the state invariant must be satisfied at τ_{i+1}. Since intereavings of timed multisteps with synchronous time progress do not let time pass between the transitions of a multistep, it is easy to see that the condition is necessary and sufficient.

Semi Synchronous Time Progress. For semi synchronous time progress, a similar reasoning as for the synchronous case helps to understand why it is sufficient to require that for each execution time τ_{i+1}^k of some transition in the multistep the invariant must be satisfied.

This can be very efficiently coded by requiring the state invariant to hold at ζ_{i+1}, the separating variable introduced in Section 4.7 for coding semi synchronous time progres: if all τ_{i+1}^k satisfy the invariant then so does their maximum. ζ_{i+1}, by the time progress condition situated anywhere between the timestamps of MT_{i+1} and those of MT_{i+2} can be chosen minimal, i.e. the maximum timestamp of MT_{i+1}. Requiring ζ_{i+1} to respect the state invariant of s_i is thus equivalent to requiring this of every timestamp of MT_{i+1}.

One might argue that this condition, while sufficient, need not be necessary and that a more relaxed condition, while still sufficient, might allow shorter timed multi step sequences. However, then a technique as indicated below for relaxed time progress must be applied. We feel that the technique above is the natural way of dealing with state invariants in the semi synchronous setting.

Relaxed Time Progress. For relaxed time progress, a technique developed for handling invariants in the context of state exploration with zones and partial order semantics [14] can be used. We refer the reader to that paper for technical details and the somewhat involved development of the correctness proof. But we can give a hint on the constraints that actually need to be coded for that approach. One has to distinguish between a local and a global view of invariants: locally, transitions leaving a state must satisfy the invariant, as discussed at the beginning of this section. Globally, a transition resetting a clock must satisfy all variants of the current states of other threads that mention that clock. Finally, the final state must satisfy the global invariant. These three types of constraints are not very difficult to code (and are included in our prototype), the condition for relaxed time progress itself is more complex than this addition.

6   Examples and Experiments

In this section, we present results obtained with a working version of POEM as used in [14], but with a new SAT backend, implementing all multistep algorithms and using Picosat [4] as SAT solver.

The tests were performed on a Mac Pro quad-core 2.66 Ghz, with 16 GB of memory (but a single core is used only and no more than 1GB is required in these computations). The **time** function of the Unix systems was used to get the timings. By default, they all use seconds except when a 'm' appears for minutes. Uppaal [2] times are given for reference.

The numbers for interleaving (only one transition for each step) and multi-steps columns are in the order: the time for the SAT solver to find a solution, the number of clauses in the formula and the number of (multi) steps of the solution, e.g. $2.4/164K/10$ indicates a solving time of $2.4s$ for a formula with approximatively 164000 clauses and 10 multisteps. The symbol '−' is used when no solution has been found within 20 minutes.

Circuit Analysis

We introduce a simple circuit problem: several NOT gates are connected one to the other as in figure 3. Each gate has a delay to propagate its input signal to its output. Initially each value is equal to zero. We want to know if the circuit can stabilize, i.e. if there exists a time t where input values and output values are coherent (and thus will no longer change). Of course, the circuit can stabilize only if there is an even number of gates. It turns out that the desired state is reachable with one (synchronous) multi step. As can be seen, the more complex encodings yield no advantage here.

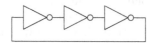

Fig. 3. A circuit with NOT gates

Table 1. Results for the circuit problem

nodes	UppAal	Interleaving	Multistep		
			synchronous	semi synchronous	relaxed
4	0	0/12K/2	0/8K/1	0/23K/1	0/53K/1
10	0.1	0.3/48K/5	0/22K/1	0.1/58K/1	0.9/139K/1
16	-	1.7/112K/8	0.5/38K/1	1.6/99K/1	1.2/242K/1
20	-	2.4/164K/10	0.8/48K/1	1.8/123K/1	1.3/301K/1
50	-	-	1.2/129K/1	2.3/327K/1	2.8/811K/1
100	-	-	3.1/279K/1	3.9/704K/1	5.6/1,7M/1
200	-	-	4.3/608K/1	6.1/1.5M/1	11.1/3,8M/1

Timed Network Protocols

We consider the following simplistic broadcast protocol: nodes arranged in a (non complete) binary tree can only send a signal to their children after receiving a signal from their parents. When a leaf receives a signal, it sends back an acknowledgement. When an interior node receives acknowledgements from its two children, it sends one to its own parent, and so on. To resume, a signal starts from the root, is asynchronously propagated to the leaves and back to the root. A random delay for each transmission between a parent and its children is added. The model checker is asked to find a completed broadcast within a tight interval of time. For this series of examples, the semi synchronous coding allows significantly shorter multi step runs than the synchronous coding and sometimes the relaxed coding allows even shorter sequences. It turns out that shorter here means (much) faster, whereas at the same length, the relaxed coding comes with an overhead over the semi synchronous coding and is slower.

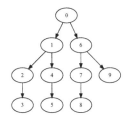

Table 2. Results for the network protocol problem

nodes	UppAal	Interleaving	Multistep		
			synchronous	semi synchronous	relaxed
5	0.0	0/11K/9	0.1/7K/6	0.2/19K/6	0.2/29K/6
10	0.1	2.9/49K/19	0.8/31K/12	0.3/59K/8	0.8/95K/8
15	20.0	19.0/110K/29	0.5/40K/10	0.5/90K/10	1.1/144K/8
20	-	4m46/196K/39	3.5/93K/18	3.5/175K/12	2.3/240K/10
50	-	-	18.2/292K/20	5.6/508K/12	8.2/846K/12
100	-	-	11m06/812K/28	19.2/1.2M/14	34.1/2M/14
200	-	-	-	3m09/2.7M/18	2m15/4.6M/16

7   Conclusions and Future Work

We have studied the problem of enhancing the SAT reductions of bounded model checking of timed automata with the help of multisteps. We have identified three different alternative semantics for coding and have given a few experiments to compare them.

Related work. While we are not aware of any work trying the combination we have considered here (SAT, partial order, timed automata), many aspects of this work find their origin in other works: The basic coding principles, including the variable transformation (using timestamps rather than clock values) are already present in previous works on BMC for timed automata, whether oriented towards pure boolean SAT or SMT (SAT modulo theories) [13,1,15,18]. "Relaxed semantics" with respect to time has been widely discussed in the context of symbolic state exploration of timed automata, e.g. in [3] whereas the idea of allowing timestamps to be commuted was first presented in [12]. When abstracting from time, the key idea of using step semantics in bounded model checking was stated in [9]. Beyond the context of bounded model checking, one work considers executing several transitions of timed automata in parallel in order to avoid zone splitting [19], but no indication towards SAT applications is found in that work.

Interpretation of experimental evidence. We have given two series of experiments that illustrate how the alternative semantics can dramatically improve the performance of the SAT approach to timed automata reachability. From these and non-documented experiments, our personal assessment is that "synchronous time progress" is always a good idea to start with (the smallest set of clauses at the same path length), and if it runs out of time with increasing path length to switch to semi synchronous time progress. We have not yet found examples where relaxed time progress yields an advantage in execution time (although sometimes shorter paths were found). Obviously, case studies on realistic examples are necessary for further evaluation.

Perspectives. We have not implemented a reduction to SMT, but, as outlined in Section 4, the coding would be the same except for the representation of time stamps by real valued variables and corresponding constraints. We believe that the improvement achieved for the current boolean only approach carry over seamlessly to the SMT case. We might explore an SMT variant of our implementation in the future.

References

1. Audemard, G., Cimatti, A., Kornilowicz, A., Sebastiani, R.: Sat-based bounded model checking for timed systems. In: Peled, D.A., Vardi, M.Y. (eds.) FORTE 2002. LNCS, vol. 2529. Springer, Heidelberg (2002)
2. Behrmann, G., David, A., Larsen, K.G., Hakansson, J., Petterson, P., Yi, W., Hendriks, M.: Uppaal 4.0. In: 3rd international conference on the Quantitative Evaluation of Systems QEST, Washington, DC, USA, pp. 125–126 (2006)
3. Bengtsson, J., Jonsson, B., Lilius, J., Yi, W.: Partial order reductions for timed systems. In: Sangiorgi, D., de Simone, R. (eds.) CONCUR 1998. LNCS, vol. 1466, pp. 485–500. Springer, Heidelberg (1998)
4. Biere, A.: PicoSAT essentials. Journal on Satisfiability, Boolean Modeling and Computation 4, 75–97 (2008)
5. Bozga, M., Graf, S., Mounier, L.: If-2.0: A validation environment for component-based real-time systems. In: Brinksma, E., Larsen, K.G. (eds.) CAV 2002. LNCS, vol. 2404, p. 343. Springer, Heidelberg (2002)
6. Courtois, P.J., Heymans, F., Parnas, D.L.: Concurrent control with "readers" and "writers". Commun. ACM 14(10), 667–668 (1971)
7. Dams, D., Gerth, R., Knaack, B., Kuiper, R.: Partial-order reduction techniques for real-time model checking. Formal Aspects of Computing 10, 469–482 (1998)
8. Genrich, H.J., Lautenbach, K., Thiagarajan, P.S.: Elements of general net theory. In: Proceedings of the Advanced Course on General Net Theory of Processes and Systems, London, UK, pp. 21–163 (1980)
9. Heljanko, K.: Bounded reachability checking with process semantics. In: Larsen, K.G., Nielsen, M. (eds.) CONCUR 2001. LNCS, vol. 2154, pp. 218–232. Springer, Heidelberg (2001)
10. Henzinger, T.A., Nicollin, X., Sifakis, J., Yovine, S.: Symbolic model checking for real-time systems. Information and Computation 111, 193–244 (1994)
11. Jussila, T., Niemelä, I.: Parallel program verification using BMC. In: ECAI 2002 Workshop on Model Checking and Artificial Intelligence, pp. 59–66 (2002)

12. Lugiez, D., Niebert, P., Zennou, S.: A partial order semantics approach to the clock explosion problem of timed automata. Theoretical Computer Science 345(1), 27–59 (2005)
13. Niebert, P., Mahfoudh, M., Asarin, E., Bozga, M., Jain, N., Maler, O.: Verification of timed automata via satisfiability checking. In: Damm, W., Olderog, E.-R. (eds.) FTRTFT 2002. LNCS, vol. 2469, pp. 225–244. Springer, Heidelberg (2002)
14. Niebert, P., Qu, H.: Adding invariants to event zone automata. In: Asarin, E., Bouyer, P. (eds.) FORMATS 2006. LNCS, vol. 4202, pp. 290–305. Springer, Heidelberg (2006)
15. Penczek, W., Wozna, B., Zbrzezny, A.: Towards bounded model checking for the universal fragment of TCTL. In: Damm, W., Olderog, E.-R. (eds.) FTRTFT 2002. LNCS, vol. 2469, pp. 265–290. Springer, Heidelberg (2002)
16. Ben Salah, R., Bozga, M., Maler, O.: On interleaving in timed automata. In: Baier, C., Hermanns, H. (eds.) CONCUR 2006. LNCS, vol. 4137, pp. 465–476. Springer, Heidelberg (2006)
17. Sorea, M.: Bounded model checking for timed automata. Electronic Notes in Theoretical Computer Science 68(5) (2002), http://www.elsevier.com/locate/entcs/volume68.html
18. Zbrzezny, A.: Sat-based reachability checking for timed automata with diagonal constraints. Fundam. Inf. 67(1-3), 303–322 (2005)
19. Zhao, J., Xu, H., Xuandong, L., Tao, Z., Guoliang, Z.: Partial order path technique for checking parallel timed automata. In: Damm, W., Olderog, E.-R. (eds.) FTRTFT 2002. LNCS, vol. 2469, pp. 417–431. Springer, Heidelberg (2002)

Preemption Sealing
for Efficient Concurrency Testing

Thomas Ball[1], Sebastian Burckhardt[1], Katherine E. Coons[2]
Madanlal Musuvathi[1], and Shaz Qadeer[1]

[1] Microsoft Research
[2] University of Texas at Austin

Abstract. The choice of where a thread scheduling algorithm preempts one thread in order to execute another is essential to reveal concurrency errors such as atomicity violations, livelocks, and deadlocks. We present a scheduling strategy called *preemption sealing* that controls where and when a scheduler is *disabled* from preempting threads during program execution. We demonstrate that this strategy is effective in addressing two key problems in testing industrial-scale concurrent programs: (1) tolerating existing errors in order to find more errors, and (2) compositional testing of layered, concurrent systems. We evaluate the effectiveness of preemption sealing, implemented in the CHESS tool, for these two scenarios on newly released concurrency libraries for Microsoft's .NET framework.

1 Introduction

Concurrent programs are difficult to design, implement, test, and debug. Furthermore, analysis and testing tools for concurrent programs lag behind similar tools for sequential programs. As a result, many concurrency bugs remain hidden in programs until the software ships and runs in environments that differ from the test environment.

Systematic concurrency testing offers a promising solution to the problem of identifying and resolving concurrency bugs. We focus on systematic concurrency testing as implemented in CHESS [16], a tool being used to test concurrent programs at Microsoft. A CHESS user provides a collection of tests, each exploring a different concurrency scenario for a program. A concurrency scenario might range from a simple harness that calls into a concurrent data structure, to a web browser starting up and rendering a web page. Given such a scenario, CHESS repeatedly executes the program so that each run of the program explores a different thread schedule, using novel stateless exploration algorithms [14,15].

Of course, selecting which thread schedules are most useful among the exponentially many possible schedules is a central problem for the effectiveness of a tool like CHESS. We faced the following two related problems when deploying CHESS at Microsoft, which helped motivate this work:

1. Users want the ability to find *multiple distinct bugs* so they can pipeline the testing process and not be blocked waiting for bug fixes.

J. Esparza and R. Majumdar (Eds.): TACAS 2010, LNCS 6015, pp. 420–434, 2010.

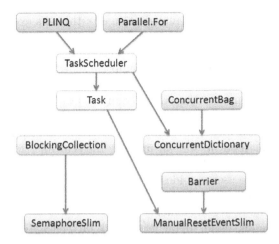

Fig. 1. Dependencies among .NET 4.0 concurrency classes. `SemaphoreSlim`, `Barrier`, and `ManualResetEventSlim` are synchronization primitives (SYN, purple). `Blocking Collection`, `ConcurrentDictionary`, and `ConcurrentBag` are concurrent data structures (CDS, orange). `Task` and `TaskScheduler` are part of a task parallel library (TPL, green). `PLINQ` and `Parallel.For` are parallel versions of LINQ and for-loops (blue).

2. Users want to perform *compositional testing* so they can focus the test on the components they are responsible for.

The first problem arises because many different thread schedules may manifest the same bug. Thus, even if the systematic search continues after finding a bug, that same bug may cause the system to crash repeatedly. This problem is important because large software systems often have a large number of bugs, some known and many unknown. Known bugs can be in various life stages: the tester/developer might be debugging, finding the root cause, designing a fix, or testing the fix. Depending on its severity, a bug may be fixed immediately or the fix may be deferred to a future release. As a result, it may be several weeks or even months before a bug is fixed. Thus, a tool such as CHESS will be most useful if it finds new bugs while avoiding schedules that trigger known bugs.

The second problem arises because a systematic search tests *all* possible schedules, even those that are irrelevant to the part of the system being tested. Well-engineered software consists of layered modules where upper layers depend on the services of lower layers, but not vice versa. Figure 1 shows an example of such a layered system from the .NET 4.0 libraries, which we will return to later in the paper. Usually, different teams are responsible for developing and testing different layers. A testing tool should allow users to "focus" the exploration on specific layers. If a particular layer, such as a low-level concurrency library, has been extensively tested or verified, then repeatedly testing its functionality when called from higher layers is a waste of valuable testing resources.

Preemption sealing is a simple but effective strategy to address these problems. A preemption is an unexpected interruption of a thread's execution caused, for example, by the thread's time slice expiring or a hardware interrupt occurring. A preemption-sealing scheduler disables preemptions in a particular scope of program execution, resorting to non-preemptive scheduling within that scope.

By resorting to non-preemptive scheduling, a preemption-sealing scheduler avoids exposing concurrency bugs that require at least one preemption within a given scope. To identify multiple errors, we seal preemptions in a scope related to the root cause of a bug. For example, if an error-inducing schedule contains a preemption in method m, we can instruct the scheduler to seal preemptions whenever control is within the scope of m in subsequent runs. To enable compositional testing, the user provides a set of methods or types that already have undergone thorough testing. By sealing preemptions in these scopes, the scheduler conserves valuable testing time.

Preemption sealing builds upon prior work on *preemption bounding* [14], a technique that first explores executions containing fewer preemptions. The hypothesis of preemption bounding is that most concurrency errors surface in executions that contain few preemptions. This hypothesis has been validated by various researchers [2,14,12]. Accordingly, a preemption-bounded scheduler explores executions with fewer preemptions first. Preemption bounding and preemption sealing are orthogonal scheduling strategies that combine naturally.

We implement preemption sealing in the CHESS concurrency testing tool and evaluate its effectiveness on a set of platform libraries for .NET that provide essential concurrency constructs to programmers. Testers for these libraries have been using CHESS over the past year to more thoroughly test these critical platform layers. We leverage 74 of their concurrency unit tests and use them to demonstrate preemption sealing's effectiveness in finding multiple errors and enabling compositional testing. Our experiments show that CHESS successfully finds multiple errors by sealing methods containing bug-inducing preemptions. Also, on average, compositional testing with preemption sealing cuts the number of executions explored during testing by more than half.

In the remainder of the paper, we formalize preemption-bounded scheduling (Section 2), define preemption sealing (Section 3), justify its use for finding multiple errors (Section 3.1) and compositional testing (Section 3.2), describe our implementation of preemption sealing and evaluate it on a set of .NET concurrency platform libraries (Section 4), discuss related work (Section 5), and conclude (Section 6).

2   Preemption-Bounded Scheduling

We model the execution of a concurrent program as a sequence of events, each corresponding to an operation performed by a thread. We represent an event with a five-tuple (tid, ctx, op, loc, blk), where tid is the thread id, ctx is the context of the thread including its program counter ($ctx.pc$) and its call stack ($ctx.stack$), op is the operation performed, loc is the (shared) memory location or object on which the operation is performed, and *blk* is a boolean flag that indicates whether the thread is blocked while performing the operation or not. We use $|E|$ to denote the length of execution E and $E[i]$ to denote the event at position i in execution E. We access the components of an event e with '.' notation:

$$(e.tid, e.ctx, e.op, e.loc, e.blk)$$

An event e is blocking if *e.blk* is true. A *completing event* for a blocking event e is the event $(e.tid, e.ctx, e.op, e.loc, false)$. A sequence is *well-formed* if for every blocking event e in an execution E, the next event performed by thread *e.tid* in E, if any, is the completing event for e. We only consider executions that are well-formed. Also, we use _ to denote the *op* and *loc* components of events that do not access shared state.

A *context switch* in an execution E is identified by an index c such that $0 \le c < |E| - 1$ and $E[c].tid \ne E[c+1].tid$. A context switch c is said to be *non-preemptive* if $E[c].blk$ is true or $E[c].op$ is the thread "exit" operation, signaling the end of the execution of thread $E[c].tid$. Otherwise the context switch is said to be *preemptive*. We call a preemptive context switch a *preemption*, for short.

The preemption bound of an execution E is the number of preemptions in E. Preemption-bounded scheduling ensures that each execution contains at most P preemptions, where P is a number chosen by the tester. Note that a preemption bound of zero simply means that the scheduler runs non-preemptively, executing the current thread until it blocks and then switching to a different (enabled) thread. If non-preemptive scheduling is unable make progress (because all threads are blocked), then the program contains a deadlock. Thus, when a preemption-bounded scheduler runs out of preemptions, it simply resorts to non-preemptive scheduling until the end of execution or a deadlock is encountered.

In addition to the choice of where to place preemptive context switches, the scheduler also has the choice of which enabled thread to execute after a context switch. This latter choice is typically constrained by a desire for fair scheduling, but fairness is beyond the scope of this paper (for more details about fair stateless model checking, see [15]). In this paper, we assume the scheduler is free to schedule any enabled thread after a context switch.

Figure 2(a) shows a buggy "bank account" class Acct and a test method TestAcct containing a test scenario. The test scenario creates three threads that test the class Acct. Thread t1 withdraws from the bank account, thread t2 reads the account balance, and thread t3 deposits to the account.

Figure 2(b) shows an execution of this program that exposes an assertion failure. For brevity, we represent the context by the program label and use the string "acc" to refer to the single instance of the Acct class. For example, the operation at label L2 is a lock operation on the object acc, while the operation at label L4 is a read operation on the field acc.bal. In this execution, the transition from (t1,L5,_,_,F) to (t3,L6,lock,acc,F) represents a preemption. Thread t1 is preempted at label L5 of the Read method after reading the account balance, but before acquiring the lock on acc at label L2 of the Withdraw method. Next, thread t3 executes the entire Deposit method. Then, because thread t3 has

(a)
```
      public class Acct {                  void TestAcct() {
        volatile int bal;                    var acc = new Acct(10);

        public Acct(int n) {                 var t1 = new Thread(o =>
          bal = n;                             { (o as Acct).Withdraw(2);
        }                               L9:    });
        public void Withdraw(int n) {
L1:       int tmp = Read();                  var t2 = new Thread(o =>
L2:       lock (this) {                        { var b = (o as Acct).Read();
            bal = tmp - n;              LA:      assert(b>=8);
L3:       }                             LB:    });
        }
        public int Read() {                  var t3 = new Thread(o =>
L4:       return bal;                          { (o as Acct).Deposit(1);
L5:     }                               LC:    });
        public void Deposit(int n) {
L6:       lock (this) {                      t1.Start(acc); t2.Start(acc);
            var tmp = bal;                   t3.Start(acc);
            bal = 0;                         t1.Join(); t2.Join(); t3.Join();
L7:         bal = tmp + n;
LU:       }                             LD: assert(account.Read() == 9);
L8:     }                               LE:
      }                                 }
```

(b)
(t2,L4,read,acc.bal,F) (t2,L5,_,_,F) (t2,LA,_,_,F) (t2,LB,_,_,F)
(t1,L1,_,_,F) (t1,L4,read,acc.bal,F) (t1,L5,_,_,F) (t3,L6,lock,acc,F)
(t3,L7,write,acc.bal,F) (t3,LU,unlock,acc,F) (t3,L8,_,_,F) (t3,LC,_,_,F)
(t1,L2,lock,acc,F) (t1,L3,unlock,acc,F) (t1,LA,_,_,F) (t0,LD,_,_,F)

(c)
(t3,L6,lock,acc,F) (t3,L7,write,acc.bal,F) (t3,LU,unlock,acc,F)
(t2,L4,read,acc.bal,F) (t2,L5,_,_,F) (t2,LA,_,_,F)

Fig. 2. (a) Simple bank account example with two bugs and (b)-(c) two executions
demonstrating the two bugs.

completed, a non-preemptive context switch returns control to thread t1, which
acquires the lock at label L2 and executes to completion. This execution violates
the assertion at label LD because thread t3's deposit is lost.

3   Preemption Sealing

Preemption sealing uses information associated with events to determine whether
an event meets certain criteria, which we call a "scope". If an event is within
scope, preemption sealing prevents the scheduler from performing a preemption
prior to that event.

A *scope* is a function F that takes an event as input and returns true if that
event is "in scope" and false otherwise. The function F may examine any data

associated with an event e, such as its thread id, $e.tid$, its operation, $e.op$, etc. In this paper, we assume a finite set of scopes, given by a finite set of functions. Thus, a scope F identifies a subsequence of an execution E containing those events $E[i]$ such that $F(E[i])$ is true. Operationally, for each event executed, we can apply the function F to determine if it is in the scope of F or outside it, though we use more efficient means in practice. Preemptions are disabled at events that are "in scope" and are enabled at events that are not in any scope.

By disabling preemptions in certain scopes, the scheduler effectively focuses its search on other parts of the search space. Disabling preemptions does not introduce new deadlocks. As noted in the previous section, when a scheduler has no preemptions to use, it simply resorts to non-preemptive scheduling. Thus, the only way the scheduler cannot make progress in the presence of preemption sealing is if the program deadlocks. Also, it is straightforward to see that disabling preemptions does not introduce additional behaviors in the program and thus does not introduce safety violations.

Preemption sealing can be seen as an extension of previous work that addresses the relationship between data races and the placement of preemptions [14]. In that work, Musuvathi and Qadeer partition the world of all objects into synchronization objects and data objects, as is typical when defining data races. They show that if a program is data-race free then it is possible to disable preemptions at operations on data objects without missing errors in the program.

Preemption sealing builds upon this work by disabling preemptions at operations on synchronization objects when those operations occur within a particular scope. We discuss circumstances under which preemption sealing can be done safely without missing errors. In the two scenarios we consider, finding multiple errors and compositional testing, we find that preemption sealing improves the efficiency and efficacy of systematic search by eliminating thread interleavings that fall within a well-defined scope.

3.1   Detecting Multiple Errors

Detecting multiple errors is a difficult problem because many different thread interleavings may expose the same bug. To alleviate this problem, preemption sealing capitalizes on the observation that during a preemption-bounded search, the preemptions involved in a failure-inducing schedule are good indicators of the *root cause* of the failure. This observation is a consequence of the following two reasons: (1) the scheduler always has a choice regarding whether or not to introduce a preemption prior to a given event and (2) the scheduler carefully exercises this choice to explore executions with fewer preemptions first. Thus, the preemptions in a failure-inducing schedule are crucial to expose the bug. Otherwise, the scheduler would have found the same bug with fewer preemptions.

We return to the bank account example in Figure 2(a) to illustrate the problem of finding multiple errors. Figure 2(b) shows an execution that ends in an assertion failure at label LD because the bank account balance is incorrect. This failure occurs because the Withdraw method does not contain proper synchronization, which makes its effect appear non-atomic. A preemption at label L2 in the `Withdraw` method, followed by complete execution of the `Deposit` method, will cause the assertion failure.

Figure 2(c) shows an execution that fails due to another defect in the class `Acct`. Because the `Read` method does not use synchronization, it may observe an intermediate value of the account balance (after it has been set to zero by the `Deposit` method). This execution leads to an assertion failure at label `LA`.

We wish to find both errors rather than first finding one, asking the programmer to fix it, waiting for the fix, and then running again to find the second error. We would like the search to avoid known errors once they have been identified by "tolerating" the error in a temporary way.

Our idea is inspired by the observation that programmers intend many, if not most, methods to appear atomic in their effect when executed concurrently [6]. Thus, once we find an error that requires a preemption in method m to surface, we wish to seal method m from being preempted in the rest of the search. Effectively, this means that once the scheduler starts executing method m, it executes it to completion (modulo the case where m blocks). Note that we could seal just at the specific program counter where the preemption took place, but there are likely many other preemption points in the same method that will expose the same error. The above observation implies that methods are a natural scope in which to seal preemptions.

We generalize this idea to multiple preemptions. Assume a preemption bounded search that explores all executions with P preemptions before exploring any executions with $P + 1$ preemptions. Thus, if no errors were found with P preemptions, then an error found with $P + 1$ preemptions could not be found with P or fewer preemptions. If an error surfaces in execution E with preemption set S of size $|S|$, then at most $|S|$ methods must be sealed. The *preemption methods* are the active methods (methods on top of the call stack) in which the preemptions occur: $\{m \mid s \in S, E[s].ctx.stack.top = m\}$. If two different tests fail with the same set of preemption methods, the failures are likely due to the same error.

Note that preemption sealing at the method level may not eliminate the failure. For example, suppose method m calls method n and a preemption in either method leads to the same failure. If the preemption in method n occurs first, then sealing only method n will not prevent the failure. If the preemption in method m occurs first, however, and we use dynamic scope when sealing the preemption in method m, then we will ensure that method n will not be preempted when called from m. Thus, we use dynamic scoping when sealing preemption methods.

3.2 Compositional Testing

Strict layering of software systems is a basic software engineering practice. Upper layers depend on the services of lower layers, but not vice versa. Different teams may develop and test the different layers. The efficiency of testing the entire system depends greatly on eliminating redundant tests. This observation implies that in a layered system, tests for the upper layers need not (indeed, *should not*) perform redundant tests on the functionality of the lower layers.

Complicating matters, each layer of a system may be "thread-aware", protecting its data from concurrent accesses by an upper layer's threads, while explicitly creating threads itself to perform its tasks more efficiently.

However, although one may imagine and craft arbitrarily complicated interactions between layers, in practice, function calls into lower layers are often meant to appear atomic to the upper layers. In fact, several dynamic analysis tools (such as SideTrack [18], Atomizer [6], and Velodrome [8]) rely on this programming practice, as they are designed to check the atomicity of such function calls. What this means for preemption sealing is that

> *if we can establish or trust the lower-level functions to be atomic, it is safe to disable preemptions in the lower layer while testing the upper layer.*

Although this claim may be simple to understand intuitively, it should be understood in the context of prior work on atomicity [6]. This work derives the definition of atomicity from the classic definition of conflict-serializability and treats all function calls into the lower layer as transactions.

The concept of layering means that we partition the code into an upper layer A and a lower layer B such that A calls into B, B never calls into A, and execution starts and ends in A. For an execution E, defined earlier as a sequence of events, we label all events as A-events or B-events. For simplicity, we assume that each thread executes at least one A-event or B-event in between any pair of calls/returns that transition between layers.

For a fixed execution E we define transactions as follows. Let E_t be the sequence of events by thread t. More formally, E_t is the maximal subsequence of E consisting of events by only t. We then define a *transaction* of thread t to be a maximal contiguous subsequence of E_t consisting of only B-events. Atomicity is now characterized as follows, in reverse order of logical dependency:

- The layer B is *atomic* if all executions E are serializable.
- An execution E is *serializable* if it is equivalent to a serial execution.
- Two executions are *equivalent* if one can be obtained from the other by repeatedly swapping adjacent independent events.
- Two events are *dependent* if either (1) they are executed by the same thread, (2) they are memory accesses that target the same location and at least one writes to the location, (3) they are operations on the same synchronization object, and are not both side-effect-free.[1]
- An execution E is called *serial* if there are no context switches within transactions. For any context switch at position c, the event $E[c]$ is either not part of any transaction, or is the last event of a transaction.

Thus, if B is atomic, then for any execution that reveals a bug, there exists an equivalent serial execution that also reveals the bug. Such a serial execution does not contain any preemptions inside B, so the search will still cover this serial execution even when sealing preemptions in B.

---

[1] An example of a side-effect-free operation is a failed (blocking) lock acquire operation.

4 Implementation and Evaluation

We implemented preemption sealing in CHESS, a tool for concurrency testing [14]. CHESS repeatedly executes a concurrency unit test and guarantees that each execution takes a different thread schedule. CHESS records the current thread schedule so that when it finds an error, it can reproduce the schedule that led to the error. CHESS detects errors such as assertion failures, deadlocks, and livelocks, as well as data races, which are often the cause of other failures. CHESS contains various search strategies, one of which is preemption bounding.

After finding an error, CHESS runs in "repro" mode to reproduce the error by replaying the last stored schedule. During this repro execution CHESS collects extensive context information, such as the current call stack, to produce an attributed execution trace for source-level browsing. During this execution, CHESS also outputs *preemption methods* from the stored schedule. The preemption methods consist of methods in which CHESS placed a preemption.

To implement preemption sealing, we extended CHESS's API with methods to enable and disable preemptions. We implemented a preemption sealing strategy via a CHESS monitor that tracks context information, such as which method is currently on the top of the call stack, and makes calls to the new API to enable/disable preemptions. Command-line parameters to CHESS enable preemption sealing based on assembly name, namespace, class name, or method name. For the purposes of this paper, we use two options: /dpm:M for "disable/seal preemptions in method M"; /dpt:T for "disable/seal preemptions in all methods in type T"[2]. As currently implemented, we disable preemptions in the dynamic scope of a method, which suits our two applications (as discussed previously). Other scoping strategies are possible within the framework we implemented.

We evaluated preemption sealing's ability to find multiple errors and enable compositional testing on new parallel framework libraries available for .NET. These libraries include:

- *Concurrency and Coordination Runtime* (CCR) provides a highly concurrent programming model based on message-passing with powerful orchestration primitives enabling coordination of data and work without the use of manual threading, locks, semaphores, etc. (http://www.microsoft.com/ccrdss/)
- *New synchronization primitives* (SYN), such as `Barrier`, `CountdownEvent`, `ManuelResetEventSlim`, `SemaphoreSlim`, `SpinLock`, and `SpinWait`;
- *Concurrent data structures* (CDS), such as `BlockingCollection`, `ConcurrentBag`, `ConcurrentDictionary`, etc.
- *Task Parallel Library* (TPL) supports imperative task parallelism.
- *Parallel LINQ* (PLINQ) supports declarative data parallelism.

In all of the experimental results below, we ran CHESS with its default settings: preemptions are possible at all synchronization operations, interlocked operations, and volatile memory accesses; the scheduler can use at most two preemptions per test execution.

---

[2] The sense for these switches could trivially be switched so that the user could disable preemptions everywhere *except* the specified scope.

Table 1. Evaluation of preemption sealing for detecting multiple errors (Rows 1-4), and for compositional testing (Row 5)

Sealed methods/types	Asserts	Timeouts	Livelocks	Deadlocks	Leaks	OK
∅	5	3	40	0	0	5
+ DQueue.TryDequeue	6	5	0	1	1	40
+ TEW.WaitForTask	5	5	0	2	1	40
+ Port.RegisterReceiver + Port.PostInternal	5	5	0	0	0	43
DQueue	5	5	0	2	0	41

4.1 Discovering Multiple Unique Errors

We first evaluate preemption sealing's ability to discover multiple unique errors on the CCR code base, which has an accompanying set of concurrency unit tests. Most of these tests ran without modification under CHESS. The only modification we made was to decrease the iteration count for certain loops. Some tests contained high-iteration count loops to increase the likelihood of new thread interleavings. Because CHESS systematically searches the space of possible thread interleavings, this repetition is unnecessary within a single test. We took all of the CCR unit tests from its *CoreSuite, CausalitySuite, SimpleExamples*, and *TaskTest* suites, which resulted in 53 independent concurrency unit tests.

Table 1 shows the results of running CHESS on each of the 53 tests. The first column shows the set of preemption-sealed methods/types (initially empty). The next five columns show the number of tests that failed: **Asserts** occur when a test assertion fails; **Timeouts** occur when a test execution takes longer than ten seconds (CHESS default); **Livelocks** occur when a test executes over 20,000 synchronization operations (CHESS default, most concurrency unit tests, including those in CCR, execute hundreds of synchronization operations); **Deadlocks** are self explanatory; **Leaks** means that the test terminates with child threads alive - CHESS requires that all child threads complete before the test terminates. The final column (**OK**) contains the number of tests for which CHESS successfully explored all schedules within the default preemption bound (of two) without finding an error.

During the first CHESS run (Row 1) we see five assertion failures. All of these failures occurred on the first test execution, which never contains a preemption. These five failures represent errors in the test harness code. The three timeouts also occur on the first execution. These timeouts have a single root cause, which is a loop in the CCR scheduler that contains no synchronization operations, and that does not yield the processor (a violation of the "Good Samaritan" principle [15]). Because these assertion failures and timeouts occurred on the initial execution, which contains no preemptions, they were not candidates for preemption sealing.

The 40 tests that failed with a livelock all failed well into CHESS testing. Each failure was found in a schedule containing a single preemption in the method DQueue.TryDequeue, as output by CHESS during the repro phase. To evaluate preemption sealing, we ran CHESS on the 53 tests again, sealing only the method `DQueue.TryDequeue` (Row 2). The effect of sealing is stark: all 40 of the tests that previously livelocked were able to avoid the livelock.[3] While sealing only one method, CHESS was able to avoid a livelock in 40 tests, verify 35 of those tests correct within the default preemption bound, and detect five new failures: one assertion failure, one deadlock, one thread leak, and two timeouts. The five new failures all have associated preemption methods, output by CHESS (`TEW` = `TaskExecutionWorker`):

- *Assertion failure*: `TEW.WaitForTask`, `TEW.Signal`;
- *Timeouts*: `TEW.WaitForTask`;
- *Deadlock*: `Port.RegisterReceiver`, `Port.PostInternal`;
- *Thread Leak*: `TEW.WaitForTask`, `Port.PostInternal`;

Based on these results, we performed two more runs of CHESS (Rows 3 and 4 of Table 1). In the third run, we sealed the additional method `TEW.WaitForTask`. This converted one test from an assertion failure into a deadlock. In the fourth run, we additionally sealed the methods that contained preemptions leading to the first deadlock: `Port.RegisterReceiver` and `Port.PostInternal`. As seen in Row 4, sealing these methods eliminated both deadlocks and the thread leak, converting both into passing tests.

The results of this experiment show the efficacy of preemption sealing at the method level for the CCR code base. Without any code modification, sealing the method that led to 40 livelocking tests resulted in five new bugs and 35 passing tests. Further sealing exposed an additional deadlock, and enabled more tests to run to completion.

4.2   Compositional Testing

When evaluating preemption sealing for compositional testing, we consider two metrics: (1) what is the bug yield relative to testing without preemption sealing?; (2) for tests that produce the same results with and without sealing, what is the run-time benefit of preemption sealing?

We take another look at CCR before moving to the other .NET libraries. CCR uses a queue (implemented by `DQueue`) containing tasks for the CCR scheduler to run. The scheduler removes tasks from this queue, while other CCR primitives create new tasks that are placed in the queue. Using the terminology from Section 3.2, the class `DQueue` is layer B, and the other components (the scheduler and the CCR primitives) are layer A, which make use of the services of B.

The last row in Table 1 shows the results of running CHESS with preemption sealing on all methods in the class `DQueue`. As expected, preemption sealing at this level will not find the livelock because the method `DQueue.TryDequeue` is sealed. However, CHESS discovers both deadlocks, which indicates that these

---

[3] An interesting twist to the livelock bug is that while the developer agreed that there was a potential performance problem, he thought it would not occur very often and decided not to address the issue. In this case, the ability to avoid the livelock without requiring a change to the code was crucial to make progress finding more bugs.

Table 2. Evaluation of preemption sealing for compositional testing. Columns labeled 'S' use preemption sealing and columns labeled 'N' do not. **Abbreviations**: Blk-Col (BlockingCollection), CBag (ConcurrentBag), SemSlim (SemaphoreSlim), MRES (ManualResetEventSlim), CDict (ConcurrentDictionary), TSchd (TaskScheduler), P (Pass), D (Deadlock), A (Assert), L (Livelock), T (Thread leak).

Test	Sealed scope	Result N	Result S	Executions N	Executions S	Seconds N	Seconds S	Execs/sec N	Execs/sec S	Speed-up
BlkCol1	SemSlim	D	D	59167	18733	527.0	206.0	112.3	91.0	2.6
BlkCol2	"	P	P	258447	106608	2128.0	1181.0	121.4	90.3	1.8
BlkCol3	"	D	D	265	265	1.8	2.2	147.2	120.5	0.8
BlkColRC1	"	P	P	1114	364	8.8	4.5	126.6	80.8	2.0
BlkColRC2	"	P	P	2406	510	22.8	7.2	105.5	70.8	3.2
BlkColRC3	"	P	P	6084	2391	49.0	33.9	124.1	70.5	1.4
BlkColRC4	"	P	P	5003	1012	36.9	13.7	135.6	73.9	2.7
BlkColRC5	"	D	D	1	1	0.2	0.3	5.0	3.3	0.7
BarrierRC1	MRES	P	P	776	109	5.5	1.5	141.1	72.7	3.7
BarrierRC2	"	P	P	166	92	1.7	1.0	97.6	92.0	1.7
BarrierRaw	"	A	A	96	33	0.7	0.7	137.1	47.1	1.0
CBagRC1	CDict	P	P	559	375	3.7	3.7	151.1	101.4	1.0
CBagRC2	"	P	P	559	375	3.8	3.9	147.1	96.2	1.0
CBagAPC	"	P	P	6639	4168	46.0	39.0	144.3	106.9	1.2
CBagACTA	"	P	P	8230	5727	58.0	57.0	142.9	100.5	1.0
CBagTTE	"	P	P	1212	793	7.6	7.5	159.5	105.7	1.0
CBagTTP	"	P	P	1529	775	12.9	5.6	118.5	138.4	2.3
NQueens1	TSchd	L	L	1145	1318	19.4	61.8	59.0	21.3	0.3
NQueens2	"	T	T	10146	1027	182.1	55.8	55.7	18.4	3.2
NQueens3	"	T	T	9887	1027	181.8	56.4	54.4	18.2	3.2
PLINQ	"	P	P	3668	1031	33.1	12.9	110.8	79.9	2.6

deadlocks are due to defects in layer A. The analysis in the previous section confirms this result. For the two deadlocks, CHESS with the DQueue class sealed found them in 4,662 schedules (59 seconds) and 142 scheules (2 seconds), respectively. The runs that found the deadlocks without sealing DQueue took 9,774 schedules (126 seconds) and 10,525 schedules (330 seconds), respectively.

The other concurrency libraries that we consider include the layers illustrated in Figure 1. This figure shows dependencies among a subset of the classes in these libraries. At the lowest level are the new synchronization primitives (SYN) and the concurrent data structures (CDS, mostly lock-free). On top of these two libraries sits a new task scheduler (TPL), with a set of primitives for task parallelism. Finally, on top of TPL sits the implementation of parallel LINQ (PLINQ) for querying LINQ data providers, and parallel for loops for data parallelism. The test team for these libraries explicitly developed CHESS tests for most of these classes. We used their tests, unmodified, for our experiments.

Table 2 shows the results of these experiments. The first column is the test name, which indicates the class being tested. **Sealed scope** lists the class that we told CHESS to seal based on the dependencies shown in Figure 1 (see caption for abbreviations). The next three columns, **Result, Executions**, and **Seconds**, present results for two CHESS runs, one without sealing (columns labeled 'N') and one with sealing (columns labeled 'S'). The column **Execs/sec** shows the executions per second for both runs. Finally, the last column is the speedup in total execution time attained via preemption sealing.

For example, the first row shows that CHESS found a deadlock in the test BlockColl both with and without preemption sealing. With class SemaphoreSlim sealed, however, CHESS found the deadlock after exploring one-third as many test executions, and 2.6 times faster.

The **Result** columns validate that preemption sealing at lower layers did not mask errors in higher layers. CHESS reported the same result for all tests both with and without preemption sealing. On average, preemption sealing reduced the number of executions explored by more than half. In all but three tests, preemption sealing reduced the time taken for CHESS to finish or left it the same, resulting in an average speedup of 1.83. We expect these numbers to improve if we optimize the instrumentation required to implement preemption sealing. In particular, our instrumentation results in a prohibitive overhead in the TPL tests, probably due to frequent calls to small methods.

5   Related Work

The main contribution of this paper is the concept of preemption sealing as a solution to two important problems in concurrency testing—finding multiple distinct bugs in a single test run, and compositional testing.

The idea of using preemption sealing to discover multiple distinct errors in concurrent programs can be viewed as a root cause analysis for concurrency errors. For sequential programs, using executions that pass to help localize the cause of failures has been popular [1,9]. For example, the SLAM software model checker [1] determines which parts of an error trace are unique from passing traces and places **halt** statements at these locations to guide the model checker away from the error trace and towards other errors. This idea is analagous to preemption sealing, but for the sequential rather than the concurrent case.

The idea of using preemption sealing for compositional testing is most closely related to the use of atomicity for simplifying correctness proofs of multithreaded programs (e.g., [7,4]). However, that work used atomicity only for the purpose of static verification; to the best of our knowledge, ours is the first effort to use this idea in the context of runtime verification. Our use of atomicity for compositional testing is orthogonal to the large body of work on runtime verification techniques for detecting atomicity violations (e.g., [13,8,5]). It is also worth noting that while most work on static compositional verification of concurrent programs requires manual specifications, our approach is fully automatic; we use the preemption-sealed version of a component as its specification.

Delta-debugging can be used to identify, from a failing execution, the context switch points that cause a multithreaded program to fail [3]. Our work exploits preemption bounding to make this problem simpler. Since preemptions are the likely causes of bugs and the erroneous execution discovered by CHESS has few preemptions, the problem of discovering the root cause is greatly simplified. Finally, our goal goes beyond root-cause analysis to find multiple qualitatively different bugs.

Apart from improving concurrency testing, preemption sealing can be used to make programs more resilient to concurrency errors in a spirit similar to recent work on tolerating locking-discipline violations [17] and deadlocks [20,11].

Recent work has investigated techniques for creating real data-races [19] and deadlocks [10] by using feedback from other conservative static or runtime analysis techniques. Our work is orthogonal and complementary to this work; while they focus on where to place preemptions we focus on where not to place preemptions, via preemption sealing.

6   Conclusions

Preemption sealing is a scheduling strategy that increases the efficiency and efficacy of run-time tools for detecting concurrency errors. Preemption sealing has many potential applications and we considered two of them in depth here: tolerating existing errors in order to find more errors; and compositional testing of layered systems. The power of preemption sealing is that it does not require code modifications to the program under test and can be easily implemented in existing schedulers, whether part of model checking, testing, or verification tools. Our evaluation shows that preemption sealing is effective at finding multiple bugs and testing layered concurrent systems more efficiently.

References

1. Ball, T., Naik, M., Rajamani, S.K.: From symptom to cause: localizing errors in counterexample traces. In: POPL, pp. 97–105 (2003)
2. Ben-Asher, Y., Eytani, Y., Farchi, E., Ur, S.: Producing scheduling that causes concurrent programs to fail. In: PADTAD 2006: Proceedings of the 2006 workshop on Parallel and distributed systems: testing and debugging, pp. 37–40. ACM, New York (2006)
3. Choi, J.-D., Zeller, A.: Isolating failure-inducing thread schedules. In: ISSTA 2002: International Symposium on Software Testing and Analysis, pp. 210–220 (2002)
4. Elmas, T., Qadeer, S., Tasiran, S.: A calculus of atomic actions. In: POPL 2009: Principles of Programming Languages, pp. 2–15 (2009)
5. Farzan, A., Madhusudan, P.: Monitoring atomicity in concurrent programs. In: Gupta, A., Malik, S. (eds.) CAV 2008. LNCS, vol. 5123, pp. 52–65. Springer, Heidelberg (2008)
6. Flanagan, C., Freund, S.N.: Atomizer: A dynamic atomicity checker for multithreaded programs. In: POPL 2004: Principles of Programming Languages, pp. 256–267. ACM Press, New York (2004)
7. Flanagan, C., Qadeer, S.: A type and effect system for atomicity. In: PLDI 2003: Programming Language Design and Implementation, pp. 338–349. ACM, New York (2003)

8. Flanagan, C., Freund, S.N., Yi, J.: Velodrome: a sound and complete dynamic atomicity checker for multithreaded programs. In: PLDI 2008, pp. 293–303. ACM, New York (2008)
9. Groce, A., Chaki, S., Kroening, D., Strichman, O.: Error explanation with distance metrics. STTT 8(3), 229–247 (2006)
10. Joshi, P., Park, C.-S., Sen, K., Naik, M.: A randomized dynamic program analysis technique for detecting real deadlocks. In: PLDI 2009, pp. 110–120. ACM, New York (2009)
11. Jula, H., Tralamazza, D.M., Zamfir, C., Candea, G.: Deadlock immunity: Enabling systems to defend against deadlocks. In: OSDI 2008: Operating System Design and Implementation, pp. 295–308 (2008)
12. Lu, S., Park, S., Seo, E., Zhou, Y.: Learning from mistakes: a comprehensive study on real world concurrency bug characteristics. In: ASPLOS 2008: Architectural Support for Programming Languages and Operating Systems (2008)
13. Lu, S., Tucek, J., Qin, F., Zhou, Y.: Avio: detecting atomicity violations via access interleaving invariants. In: ASPLOS 2006: Architectural Support for Programming Languages and Operating Systems, pp. 37–48 (2006)
14. Musuvathi, M., Qadeer, S.: Iterative context bounding for systematic testing of multithreaded programs. In: PLDI 2007: Programming Language Design and Implementation, pp. 446–455 (2007)
15. Musuvathi, M., Qadeer, S.: Fair stateless model checking. In: PLDI 2008: Programming Language Design and Implementation (2008)
16. Musuvathi, M., Qadeer, S., Ball, T., Basler, G., Nainar, P.A., Neamtiu, I.: Finding and reproducing heisenbugs in concurrent programs. In: OSDI, pp. 267–280 (2008)
17. Rajamani, S.K., Ramalingam, G., Ranganath, V.P., Vaswani, K.: Isolator: dynamically ensuring isolation in comcurrent programs. In: ASPLOS 2009: Architectural Support for Programming Languages and Operating Systems, pp. 181–192 (2009)
18. Sadowski, C., Freund, S.N., Flanagan, C.: Singletrack: A dynamic determinism checker for multithreaded programs. In: Castagna, G. (ed.) ESOP 2009. LNCS, vol. 5502, pp. 394–409. Springer, Heidelberg (2009)
19. Sen, K.: Race directed random testing of concurrent programs. In: PLDI 2008, pp. 11–21. ACM, New York (2008)
20. Wang, Y., Lafortune, S., Kelly, T., Kudlur, M., Mahlke, S.A.: The theory of deadlock avoidance via discrete control. In: POPL 2009: Principles of Programming Languages, pp. 252–263 (2009)

Code Mutation in Verification and Automatic Code Correction

Gal Katz and Doron Peled

Department of Computer Science, Bar Ilan University
Ramat Gan 52900, Israel

Abstract. Model checking can be applied to finite state systems in order to find counterexamples showing that they do not satisfy their specification. This was generalized to handle parametric systems under some given constraints, usually using some inductive argument. However, even in the restricted cases where these parametric methods apply, the assumption is usually of a simple fixed architecture, e.g., a ring. We consider the case of nontrivial architectures for communication protocols, for example, achieving a multiparty interaction between arbitrary subsets of processes. In this case, an error may manifest itself only under some particular architectures and interactions, and under some specific values of parameters. We apply here our model checking based genetic programming approach for achieving a dual task: finding an instance of a protocol which is suspicious of being bogus, and automatically correcting the error. The synthesis tool we constructed is capable of generating various mutations of the code. Moving between them is guided by model checking analysis. In the case of searching for errors, we mutate only the architecture and related parameters, and in the case of fixing the error, we mutate the code further in order to search for a corrected version. As a running example, we use a realistic nontrivial protocol for multiparty interaction. This protocol, published in a conference and a journal, is used as a building block for various systems. Our analysis shows this protocol to be, as we suspected, erroneous; specifically, the protocol can reach a livelock situation, where some processes do not progress towards achieving their interactions. As a side effect of our experiment, we provide a correction for this important protocol obtained through our genetic process.

1 Introduction

Model checking is a successful technique for comparing a model of a system with some formal specification. One of its limitations is that of state space explosion. This is combated by many techniques that avoid the simple enumeration of all the reachable states. Since model checking of concurrent systems is intractable, this is a very challengeable problem, with many interesting heuristics. Another limitation of model checking is that the method is mainly restricted to finite state systems, while the verification of infinite state systems is, in general, undecidable. The problem of synthesizing correct code or attempting to automatically correct errors is considered to be even harder than model checking. In some limited cases

J. Esparza and R. Majumdar (Eds.): TACAS 2010, LNCS 6015, pp. 435–450, 2010.

where this was shown to be decidable, the complexity was considerably higher than simple model checking.

In recent papers [8,9,10] we demonstrated the approach of combining model checking and genetic programming for the synthesis of correct-by-design programs. This is in particular effective for the automatic generation of code that is hard to program manually. Examples are mutual exclusion problems and various concurrent synchronization problems. In this paper we exploit a related technique, and extend the tool we developed, to assist the programming throughout the code development process. Specifically, we use the ability of mutating code, guided by ranking that is based on model checking, to find errors in some complicated parametric protocol, and, moreover, to correct the errors.

The first main challenge that we tackle here is to check communication protocols that are not limited to a particular number of processes or communication architecture. Although each instance of the protocol is a finite state system, this is a parametric problem, which means that in general, its verification is undecidable [1]. Furthermore, this protocol is not limited to a particular simple communication pattern or network topology (such as in [4]). We thus use code mutation to generate instances of the protocol that we want to check. Since there are several parameters that vary with the code (the number of processes, the communication network, etc.) it is not simple to detect an instance that would manifest the error, even if we suspect there exists one. We seek an alternative to a simple enumeration of the instances of such a protocol. Since the communication architecture is not fixed, the enumeration can easily progress in a direction that will not reveal the existence of an error (e.g., focusing on a particular architecture such as a ring and just extending the number of processes). We thus apply some ranking on the checked instances, based on the model checking results, in order to help direct the search in the space of syntactically constrained programs towards an instance with an error. Then, when the error is revealed, we apply similar techniques to help us correct the code.

In essence, we apply model checking techniques for finite state systems on instances of the code, using the genetic programming approach as a heuristic method to move between different variations of it, first to find the error, then to find a correction. The mutation at the search for errors is limited to the communication architecture and various related parameters. After finding an erroneous instance of the protocol in this way, we reverse the search and allow mutating the code in order to correct it. In this latter case, mutation is allowed on the protocol itself, rather than the architecture. Correcting the code of a parametric protocol is also challenging. When a new candidate (mutation) for the protocol is suggested, it is again impossible to apply a decision procedure to check its correctness. Thus, we have again to check each candidate against various architectures, a problem that is similar to the one we are faced with when trying to find the error in the original protocol. We thus alternate between using mutations for generating new candidate protocols, and using mutations for generating instances for model checking the suggested corrections. However, there is some learning process here, as architectures that were shown to create counterexamples for either the original algorithm or tested mutations can be used for the model checking of subsequent candidates. This alternation between the evolution of architectures and programs code is repeated, gradually adding new architectures against which the candidates for corrected code need to be checked. This process continues until a program that cannot be refuted by the tool is found.

Our running example in this paper is an actual protocol for coordinating multiprocess interaction in a distributed system, named α-core [13]. This is quite a nontrivial protocol, which extends the already difficult problem of achieving multiprocess communication in the presence of nondeterminism both on the sender and receiver side. The protocol we check appears both in a conference and in a followup journal paper and is of practical use. Reading the paper, we were suspicious of the correctness of the protocol, but due to its complexity and, in particular, its multiple architecture nature, could not pinpoint the problem with a manually constructed example. Except for the actual debugging of the protocol, we followed some remarks made by the authors of that protocol in the original paper [13] about subtle points in the design of the protocol, and have let our tool discover these problems automatically. Thus, we believe that a framework that performs a genetic model checking driven mutation, as we developed and used here, is very effective as an interactive tool in the process of protocol design.

2   Background

2.1   Model Checking Guided Genetic Programming

Genetic programming [11] is a program synthesis technique based on a search in the state space of syntactically constrained programs. The search is guided by providing fitness to the generated candidate programs, usually based on test cases, but recently also on model checking results [7,8,9].

The genetic search begins with the construction of some random candidate programs (typically, a few hundreds candidates). Then one iterates the following steps. Some candidates Γ are selected at random, then they are syntactically mutated by either erasing, adding or replacing program segments. The code is often represented using a tree, and the mutation operations may also involve adding some code, when the syntax requires it (e.g., just removing a test in a program may result in syntactically erroneous code, hence the missing construct is generated at random). A powerful operator that combines the code of several candidates, called crossover[1] may also be used, although there are also some arguments against its utilization. The mutation (and crossover) operations generate some set of candidates Δ. Fitness of the candidates $\Gamma \cup \Delta$ is calculated, trying to rank their potential to further evolve towards correct code. Traditionally, fitness is calculated in genetic programming by checking some test suite. In contrast, we use model checking for calculating this value. Then, instead of the old $|\Gamma|$ candidates selected, we return for the next iteration the $|\Gamma|$ candidates with highest fitness value among $\Gamma \cup \Delta$.

---

[1] In our work, we did not implement the crossover operation.

The iterative process stops either when a candidate that achieves a fitness value above some level is found, or some limit on the number of iterations expires. In the former case, provided that the fitness is well crafted, the candidate found has a good potential to be a solution of the synthesis problem. In the latter case, the search may restart with some new random candidates.

Model checking based fitness was introduced independently by Johnson [7] and by us [8]. In [7], fitness value reflected the number of temporal properties that were satisfied by the checked candidate. We [8] suggested a finer measure of fitness, with more levels per each property: (1) none of the executions satisfy the property, (2) some but not all the executions satisfy the property, (3) each prefix of an execution that does not satisfy the property can be continued into an execution that satisfies it (hence in order to not satisfy the property, infinitely many bad choices must be made) and (4) all the executions satisfy the property. This calls for a deeper model checking algorithm than the standard one [9,12].

In [10] we synthesized solutions for the leader election problem. Since this problem is parametric, properties were checked against all of the problem instances up to a predefined cutoff value, and the ranking depended on whether none, some or all of the instances satisfied the properties. We also used there aggressive partial order reduction to speed up the model checking.

In all cases, a secondary "parsimony" measure was added to the fitness function in order to encourage the generation of shorter and hopefully efficient programs. Correcting programs can follow a similar search as described above, by starting from the bogus version of the code rather than with randomly generated programs.

2.2 The α-Core Protocol

The α-core protocol is developed to schedule multiprocess interaction. It generalizes protocols for handshake communication between pairs of processes. For each multiprocess interaction, there is a dedicated coordinator on a separate process. To appreciate the difficulty of designing such a protocol, recall for example the fact that the language CSP of Hoare [5] included initially an asymmetric construct for synchronous communication; a process could choose between various incoming messages, but had to commit on a particular send. This was important to achieve a simple implementation. Otherwise, one needs to consider the situation in which after communication becomes possible between processes, one of them may already continue to perform an alternative choice. Later Hoare removed this constraint from CSP. The same constraint appears in the asymmetric communication construct of the programming language ADA. The Buckley and Silberschatz protocol [3] solves this problem for the symmetric case in synchronous communication between pairs of processes, where both sends and receives may have choices. Their protocol uses asynchronous message passing between the processes to implement the synchronous message passing construct. The α-core protocol, also based on asynchronous message passing, is more general, and uses coordinator processes to allow synchronization among any number of processes.

The α-core protocol includes the following messages sent from a participant to a coordinator:

PARTICIPATE. A participant is interested in a single particular interaction (hence it can commit on it), and notifies the related coordinator.

OFFER. A participant is interested in one out of several potentially available interactions (a nondeterministic choice).

OK. Sent as a response to a **LOCK** message from a coordinator (described below) to notify that the participant is willing to commit on the interaction.

REFUSE. A participant decides it does not want to commit on an interaction it has previously applied to, and notifies the coordinator. This message can also be sent as a respond to a **LOCK** message from the coordinator.

Messages from coordinators are as follows:

LOCK. A message sent from a coordinator to a participant that has sent an **OFFER.** requesting the participant to commit on the interaction.

UNLOCK. A message sent from a coordinator to a locked participant, indicating that the current interaction is canceled.

START. Notifying a participant that it can start the interaction.

ACKREF. Acknowledging a participant about the receipt of a **REFUSE** message.

Fig. 1(a) describes the extended state machine of a participant. Each participant process keeps some local variables and constants:

IS a set of coordinators for the interactions the participant is interested in.

$locks$ a set of coordinators that have sent a pending **LOCK** message.

$unlocks$ a set of coordinators from which a pending **UNLOCK** message was received.

$locker$ the coordinator that is currently considered.

n the number of **ACKREF** messages required to be received from coordinators until a new coordination can start.

α the coordinators that were asked for interactions but were subsequently refused.

The actions according to the transitions are written as a pair $en \rightarrow action$, where en is the condition to execute the transition, which may include a test of the local variables, a message that arrives, or both of them (then the test should hold *and* the message must arrive). The action is a sequence of statements, executed when the condition holds. in addition, each transition is enabled from some state, and upon execution changes the state according to the related extended finite state machine. The participant's transitions, according to the numbering of Fig. 1(a) are:

1. $|IS > 1| \rightarrow \{$ foreach $p \in IS$ do $p!$**OFFER** $\}$
2. $|IS = 1| \rightarrow \{$ $locker \Rightarrow p$, were $IS = \{p\}$; $locker!$**PARTICIPATE**; $locks, unlocks := \emptyset \}$
3. $p?$**LOCK** $\rightarrow \{locker := p$; $locks, unlocks := \emptyset$; $p!$**OK** $\}$
4. $p?$**LOCK** $\rightarrow \{locks := locks \cup \{sender\}\}$

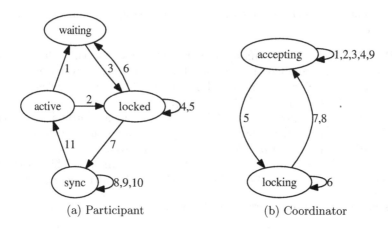

(a) Participant　　　　　　　(b) Coordinator

Fig. 1. State machines

5. $locks \neq \emptyset \wedge p?$**UNLOCK** $\rightarrow \{locker:=q$ for some $q \in locks$; $q!$**OK**; $locks:=locks \setminus \{q\}$; $unlocks:=unlocks \cup \{p\}\}$
6. $locks = \emptyset \wedge p?$**UNLOCK** $\rightarrow \{$ foreach $q \in unlocks \cup \{p\}$ do $q!$**OFFER**$\}$
7. $p?$**START** $\rightarrow \{\alpha:=IS \setminus unlocks \setminus \{locker\}$; foreach $q \in \alpha$ do $q!$**REFUSE**; $n := |\alpha|$; start participating in the joint action managed by $locker\}$
8. $p?$**LOCK** $\rightarrow \{\}$
9. $p?$**UNLOCK** $\rightarrow \{\}$
10. $p?$**ACKREF** $\rightarrow \{n:=n-1\}$
11. $n = 0 \rightarrow \{$ Let IS be the new set of interactions required from the current state. $\}$

For a coordinator, whose extended finite state machine appears in Fig. 1(b), we have the variables $waiting$, $locked$, $shared$ and α, holding each a set of processes, and n is a counter for the number of processes that indicated their wish to participate in the interaction. The constant C holds the number of processes that need to participate in the interaction (called, the *cardinality* of the interaction), and the variable $current$ is the participant the coordinator is trying to lock. The transitions, according to their numbering from Fig. 1(b) are as follows:

1. $n < C \wedge p?$**OFFER** $\rightarrow \{n:=n+1$; $shared:= shared \cup \{p\}$ $\}$
2. $n < C \wedge p?$**PARTICIPATE** $\rightarrow \{n:=n+1$; $locked:= locked \cup \{p\}$ $\}$
3. $p?$**REFUSE** $\rightarrow \{$ if $n > 0$ then $n:=n-1$; $p!$**ACKREF**; $shared:=shared \setminus \{p\}\}$
4. $n = C \wedge shared = \emptyset \rightarrow \{$ foreach $q \in locked$ do $q!$**START**; $locked, shared:=\emptyset$; $n:=0\}$
5. $n = C \wedge shared \neq \emptyset \rightarrow \{current:= \min(shared)$; $waiting:=shared \setminus \{current\}$; $current!$**LOCK**$\}$
6. $waiting \neq \emptyset \wedge p?$**OK** $\rightarrow \{locked:=locked \cup \{current\}$; $current:=\min(waiting)$; $waiting:=waiting \setminus \{current\}$; $current!$**LOCK**$\}$
7. $waiting = \emptyset \wedge p?$**OK** $\rightarrow \{locked:=locked \cup \{current\}$; foreach q in $locked$ do $q!$**START**; $locked, waiting, shared:=\emptyset$; $n:=0\}$
8. $p?$**REFUSE** $\rightarrow \{\alpha:=(locked \cap shared) \cup \{current, p\}$; foreach $q \in \alpha \setminus \{p\}$ do $q!$**UNLOCK**; $p!$**ACKREF**; $shared:=shared \setminus \alpha$; $locked:=locked \setminus \alpha$; $n:=n - |\alpha|\}$
9. $p?$**OK** $\rightarrow \{\}$

As with other concurrency coordination constructs, such as semaphores, the irresponsible use of the coordination achieved by the α-core protocol can result in deadlock situation (when processes attempt to get into conflicting coordinations in incompatible order). What the α-core protocol correctness is prescribed to guarantee is that if some processes are all interested in some coordination, then it, or some alternative coordination for at least one of the participant processes will eventually occur. As we will show later, this property does not really hold for this protocol.

3   Evolution of Architectures

The α-core algorithm is parametric, and should work for a family of architectures, where each architecture consists of a set of participants, a set of coordinators, and a particular connectivity between processes of the two kinds. Additional configuration parameters, such as buffer sizes, can be instantiated as well. When verifying the algorithm, we cannot simply perform model checking for all of the architectures up to some size. One reason for that is the large number of possible architectures. Another reason is the high model checking complexity for such a nontrivial protocol, which requires a considerable amount of time and memory, even after some reduction techniques (such as partial order reduction, and coarser atomicity) are used.

Instead, we introduce a new method for the evolution of architectures by genetic programming. The idea is to randomly generate portions of code representing various architectures, each being a basis for a distinct instance of the protocol. Then we gradually evolve these instances and improve them, until a good solution is found. A "good solution" in this context, is an instance of the protocol on which a counterexample for the given algorithm can be found. Thus, our goal at this point is the reverse of the conventional goal of genetic programming, where a good solution is a correct one.

3.1   Architecture Representation

A first step towards our goal is achieving the ability to represent architectures as portions of code. This is done by creating a dedicated initialization process (called *init*), and basing this process on code instructions and building blocks that can let it dynamically generate any relevant architecture. Depending on the problem we try to solve, these building blocks may allow the dynamic creation of processes of various types, and the instantiation of global and local parameters related to the created processes.

Considering our example, we observe that the α-core protocol involves an arbitrary number of processes of two types: participating processes, and coordinating processes. A coordinating process can be responsible for coordinating any given subset of the participating processes, and a participating process may, at each state, interact with any number of coordinators for coordinations it can be involved in. It is even possible that there are several coordinating processes that try to coordinate the same sets of processes. Fig. 2 presents an architecture

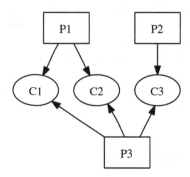

Fig. 2. An architecture with three participants and three coordinators

where there are three participating processes: $P1 - P3$, with three coordinators: $C1 - C3$. An edge appears between a participating process and a process that coordinates it. $P2$ is interested in a single interaction (handled by $C3$), while $P1$ and $P3$ are involved in multiple interactions.

To enable the generation of such architectures, the following building block are provided for the *init* process:

`CreateProc(proctype)` - Dynamically creates a new process of type `proctype`.
`Participant`, `Coordinator` - constants of type `proctype` representing participant and coordinator process types.
`Connect(part_proc_id, coord_proc_id)` - connects a particular participant and a coordinator whose process ids are given in the operands. The connection involves updating *IS* - the set of coordinators that the participant locally stores, and *C* - the cardinality of the coordinator.

A complete program representation includes the code for the *init* process, as well as skeleton code for each other type of process. At runtime, the *init* process is executed first, and according to its instructions, other processes are dynamically created and instantiated. This is similar to the way Promela code is written and executed in the Spin model checker [6], where the *init* process can dynamically create other processes. When searching for the goal architecture, a permanent code is given for each of the process types, where the genetic process is allowed to randomly generate and alter only the code of the *init* process. Using the above building blocks, the code for the architecture of Fig. 2 can look as follows.

```
CreateProc(Participant)        Connect(1, 4)
CreateProc(Participant)        Connect(1, 5)
CreateProc(Participant)        Connect(2, 6)
CreateProc(Coordinator)        Connect(3, 4)
CreateProc(Coordinator)        Connect(3, 5)
CreateProc(Coordinator)        Connect(3, 6)
```

The number of allowed processes, and accordingly, the range for the process ids are bounded. As usual, the fitness function is also based on a secondary parsimony measure which prefers shorter programs. This often leads to the removal of redundant lines from the code, and to the generation of simpler architectures and counterexamples.

3.2   The Fitness Function

The evolution of architectures is based on a fitness function which gives score to each program (consisting of architecture and other processes code). Like in our previous work, here too the fitness values are based on model checking of the given specification. However the function is different. Since the goal is to fail the given program, satisfying the negation of the specification increases the fitness rather than decreases it. This means that it is sufficient to find an architecture which violates *one* of the given properties, and since we are dealing with LTL properties, we only need to find a single execution path that violates a property. Thus (unlike in our previous work) there is no use in considering the amount of satisfied paths, or the need to make a distinction between the level of falsifying the specification (see Section 2.1) when ranking the candidate solutions. Instead, we apply a different method, and try to split properties into smaller building blocks (whenever possible) whose satisfaction may serve as an intermediate step in satisfying an entire property.

As an example, consider the LTL property $\varphi = \Box(P \rightarrow Q)$. We showed in [9] how programs satisfying φ can be evolved. However, we are now interested in progressing towards an architecture *violating* φ. We first negate it, obtaining $\neg\varphi = \Diamond(P \wedge \neg Q)$. Then, we can give intermediate ranking to solutions that contain a path satisfying $\Diamond P$, hoping that they finally evolve to solutions with a path satisfying the entire $\neg\varphi$. This method can be particularly useful in a common case where Q is an assertion about states, and P denotes the location in the code where Q must hold. That is, $P = at(\ell)$ for some label ℓ in the code. Then, when trying to violate the property φ, we can give higher fitness to programs that at least reach the location ℓ, and then give the highest fitness value if the state property Q is violated when reaching ℓ.

During the development of protocols, the developers often look at some intricate possible behaviors of the protocol. The kind of guided search suggested above, by mutating the architecture, can also be used, besides for finding errors in protocols, for finding such scenarios and documenting them. We first demonstrate this by two nontrivial transitions on the code of the α-core participant code, which due to its authors, stem from some intricacies (in Section 5.1 we will show how we used our method for finding a real error in the α-core protocol).

While being in the "sync" state, a participant usually receives **ACKREF** messages (transition 10 in Fig. 1(a)), but it can accidentally receive either a **LOCK** or **UNLOCK** messages (transitions 8 and 9 respectively), which it has to ignore. In order to verify that, we added assertions for the participant's code claiming that the received message under the "sync" state must be **ACKREF**, and then activated the tool in order to find architectures which refute this assertion. Within seconds, the two architectures depicted in Fig. 3 were generated. The architecture on the left is related to an example involving the **LOCK** message, and is simpler than the one presented in [13] (although coordinators with

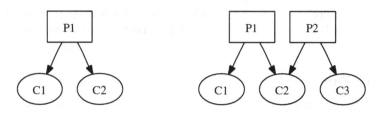

Fig. 3. Architectures found for intricacies with **LOCK** (left) and **UNLOCK** (right)

only one process are not so useful). For the case of the **UNLOCK** message, an identical architecture to the one described in [13] was found.

4   Co-evolution of Programs and Counterexamples

After finding a "wrong" architecture for a program, our next goal is to reverse the genetic programming direction, and try to automatically correct the program, where a "correct" program at this step, is one that has passed model checking against the architecture. Yet, correcting the program for the wrong architecture only, does not guarantee its correctness under different architectures. Therefore, we introduce a new algorithm (see Algorithm 1) which co-evolves both the candidate solution programs, and the architectures that might serve as counterexamples for those programs.

Algorithm 1: Model checking based co-evolution
MC-CoEvolution(initialProg, spec, maxArchs)
```
(1)          prog := initialProg
(2)          archList := ∅
(3)          while |archList| < maxArchs
(4)              arch := EvolveArch(prog, spec)
(5)              if arch = null
(6)                  return true // prog stores a "good" program
(7)              else
(8)                  add arch to archlist
(9)              prog := EvolveProg(archlist, spec)
(10)             if prog is null
(11)                 return false // no "good" program was found
(12)         return false // can't add more architectures
```

The algorithm starts with an initial program *initProg*. This can be the existing program that needs to be corrected, or, in case that we want to synthesize the code from scratch, an initial randomly generated program. It is also given a specification *spec* which the program to be corrected or generated should satisfy. The algorithm then proceeds in two steps. First (lines $(4) - (8)$), the *EvolveArch* function is called. The goal of this function is to generate an architecture on which the specification *spec* will not hold. If no such architecture is found, the *EvolveArch* procedure returns *null*, and we assume (though we cannot guarantee) that the program is correct, and the algorithm terminates. Otherwise, the found architecture *arch* is added to the architecture list *archList*, and the algorithm proceeds to the second step (lines $(9) - (11)$).

In this step, the architecture list and the specification are sent to the *Evolve-Prog* function which tries to generate programs which satisfy the specification under *all* of the architectures on the list. If the function fails, then the algorithm terminates without success. Since the above function runs a genetic programming process which is probabilistic, instead of terminating the algorithm, it is always possible to increase the number of iterations, or to re-run the function so a new search is initiated. If a correct program is found, the algorithm returns to the first step at line (4), on which the newly generated program is tested. At each iteration of the *while* loop, a new architecture is added to the list. This method' serves two purposes. First, once a program was suggested, and refuted by a new architecture, it will not be suggested again. Second, architectures which were complex enough to fail programs at previous iterations, are good candidates to do so on future iterations as well. The allowed size of the list is limited in order to bound the running time of the algorithm.

Both *EvolveProg* and *EvolveArch* functions use genetic programming and model checking for the evolution of candidate solutions (each of them is equipped with relevant building blocks and syntactic rules), while the fitness function varies. For the evolution of programs, a combination of the methods proposed in [9,10] is used: for each LTL property, an initial fitness level is obtained by performing a deep model checking analysis. This is repeated for all the architectures in *archList*, which determines the final fitness value. For the evolution of the architectures, the method explained in the previous section is used.

A related approach for automatic bug fixing was suggested in [2] where programs and unit tests were co-evolved. However, that work deals with functional programs, where no model checking is needed. In addition, that work started with a set of simple data structures, representing test cases, which can then be evolved by some search algorithm. In contrast, in our work architectures are represented as variable length programs which allow greater flexibility. Moreover, we start with a single architecture, and dynamically add new ones only when necessary during the evolutionary process. In a recent work [15], locating and repairing bugs on C programs were accomplished by manually defining positive and negative test cases, and using them in the fitness function.

5   Finding and Correcting Errors in α-Core

5.1   Generation of a Violating Architecture

One weakness of the α-core algorithm is that the **REFUSE** message is used both for canceling a previous offer to participate in an interaction, and as a possible response to a **LOCK** message. This may lead to some delicate scenarios, and the authors mention that ideally, it would have been better to add another message type. However, in order to keep the algorithm simple, they refrain from doing so, and instead try to deal with the intricate situations directly. This includes performing the following action when a coordinator receives a **REFUSE** message while being in the "accepting" state according to transition 3:

$$\text{if } n > 0 \text{ then } n := n - 1$$

The variable n serves as a counter for the number of active offers the coordinator currently has. If both the coordinator and one of its participants try to cancel the interaction concurrently, n may be wrongly decreased twice. The comparison to 0 is supposed to avoid the second decrease.

Reading that, we suspected that despite the above check, there may still be situations on which n is decreased twice due to a single participant refusal, thus causing n to no longer represent the correct number of active offers. In order to check that, we added the following assertion to the program of the coordinator just before receiving any message in the "accepting" state:

$$ASSERT(n = |shared| + |locked|)$$

We then applied our tool in order to dynamically search for an architecture that violates the assertion by the method described in section 3. After a short progress between various architectures, the tool found several architectures on which the assertion is indeed violated. The simplest of these architectures is shown at Fig. 4. It includes two participants denoted $P1$ and $P2$, which are both connected to two coordinators denoted $C1$ and $C2$. The message sequence chart at Fig. 5 shows the related counterexample, having the following messages (the comments on the right refer to the values of the counter n of $C2$): At messages (1)-(4) the two participants offers interactions to the two coordinators, which causes $C2$ to set its local counter n to 2. Coordinator $C1$ responses first, and successfully locks both participants (messages (5)-(8)). Coordinator $C2$ then tries too to lock $P1$ (message (9)), and its request remains pending. Then $C1$ asks the participants to start the interaction, which cause them to refuse the offers previously sent to $C2$ (messages (10)-(13)). $C2$ then cancels the interaction by sending messages (14) and (15) (and resetting n), and a new interaction is initiated by $P2$ (messages (16) and (17)), which sets n to 1.

Only then, message (11) with the refusal of $P1$ is received, and since $n > 0$ holds, n is wrongly decreased to 0, although there is an active offer by $P2$. After

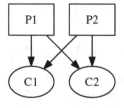

Fig. 4. An architecture violating the assertion

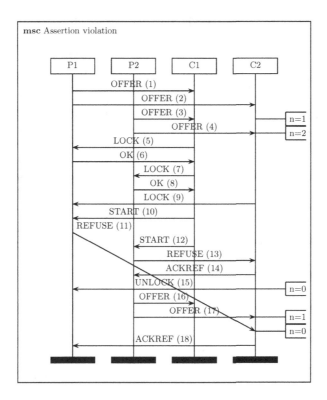

Fig. 5. A Message Sequence Chart showing the counterexample for the α-core protocol

that, if another process (such as $P1$) sends a new offer to $C2$ and no other coordinator tries to lock these participants, $C2$ will never execute the interaction (since n is smaller than its cardinality). This violate the property termed *Progress* in the α-core protocol paper [13], requiring that an enabled interaction (i.e., one in which the participating processes have requested **OFFER** or **PARTICIPATE** and did not subsequently sent a **REFUSE**) will eventually be executed. The result can be a livelock, as some of the processes are waiting for this subsequent coordination, which will not happen, or even deadlock, if this coordination is the only progress that the program is waiting for.

5.2   Generation of a Corrected Algorithm

After finding the error in the algorithm, we set our tool to automatically generate candidate programs correcting the error. The α-core code was divided into dynamic parts which the genetic process can change and evolve, and static parts which are permanent portions of the code, and remain unchanged. We set the code of the participant, and most of the code of the coordinator as static, and set as dynamic only the code that we manually identified as wrong by observing the counterexample we obtained during our search for an error phase. This is the code that deals with the **REFUSE** message. Although we could theoretically allow the dynamic evolution of the *entire* program code, the approach we took has two advantages. First, freely evolving the entire code could lead to a total change in the structure of the original algorithm, while our goal is to handle only some functional aspects of the code. Second, the search space for new code is much smaller, thus allowing a fast progress into correct solutions. Certainly, restricting the search space can make it impossible to reach a perfect solution, but in such cases, it is always possible to set more code portions as dynamic, keeping in mind the trade off between code expressibility and performance.

The tool first found a correction which holds for the architecture of Fig. 4. However, after reversing its search direction and goal, the tool discovered a new architecture on which that correction was not valid. This was followed by an alternating series of code corrections, and generation of new violating architectures (as described in Algorithm 1), until finally a simple correction was generated, without any architecture on which a violation could be found. The syntax tree that was generated for this simple correction, and its resultant code are depicted in Fig. 6.

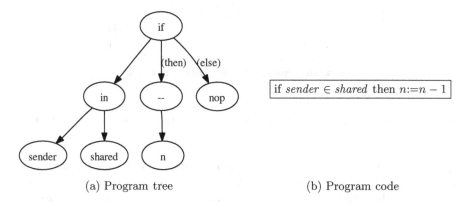

(a) Program tree   (b) Program code

Fig. 6. Final generated correction

This code replaces the original handling of the **REFUSE** message in transition 3 of the coordinator. Instead of the original code comparing n to 0, this code decreases n only if the sender participant belongs to the *shared* list. This indeed seems to solve the previous error, since after the first decrease of n, the sender is removed from the *shared* list, thus avoiding a second redundant decrease.

6   Conclusions

In this work we suggested the use of a methodology and a tool that perform a search among versions of a program by code mutation, guided by model checking results. Code mutation is basically the kernel of genetic programming. Here it is used both for finding an error in a rather complicated protocol, *and* for the correction of this same protocol. Although several methods were suggested for the verification of parametric systems, the problem is undecidable, and in the few methods that promise termination of the verification, quite severe restrictions are required. Although our method does not guarantee termination, neither for finding the error, nor for finding a correct version of the algorithm, it is quite general and can be fine tuned through provided heuristics in a convenient human-assisted process of code correction.

An important strength of the work that is presented here is that it was implemented and applied on a complicated published protocol to find and correct an actual error. The α-core protocol is useful for obtaining multiprocess interaction in a distributed system that permits also alternative (i.e., nondeterministic) choices. To the best of our knowledge, this error in the protocol is not documented. Such a method and tool can be used in an interactive code development process. It is, perhaps, unreasonable to expect in general the automatic generation of distributed code, as it is shown by Pnueli and Rosner [14] to be an undecidable problem. However, it is also quite hard to expect programmers to come up with optimized manual solutions to some existing coordination problems.

References

1. Apt, K.R., Kozen, D.: Limits for automatic verification of finite-state concurrent systems. Inf. Process. Lett. 22(6), 307–309 (1986)
2. Arcuri, A., Yao, X.: A novel co-evolutionary approach to automatic software bug fixing. In: IEEE Congress on Evolutionary Computation, pp. 162–168 (2008)
3. Buckley, G.N., Silberschatz, A.: An effective implementation for the generalized input-output construct of csp. ACM Trans. Program. Lang. Syst. 5(2), 223–235 (1983)
4. Emerson, E.A., Kahlon, V.: Parameterized model checking of ring-based message passing systems. In: Marcinkowski, J., Tarlecki, A. (eds.) CSL 2004. LNCS, vol. 3210, pp. 325–339. Springer, Heidelberg (2004)
5. Hoare, C.A.R.: Communicating sequential processes. Commun. ACM 21(8), 666–677 (1978)
6. Holzmann, G.J.: The SPIN Model Checker. Pearson Education, London (2003)
7. Johnson, C.G.: Genetic programming with fitness based on model checking. In: Ebner, M., O'Neill, M., Ekárt, A., Vanneschi, L., Esparcia-Alcázar, A.I. (eds.) EuroGP 2007. LNCS, vol. 4445, pp. 114–124. Springer, Heidelberg (2007)
8. Katz, G., Peled, D.: Genetic programming and model checking: Synthesizing new mutual exclusion algorithms. In: Cha, S(S.), Choi, J.-Y., Kim, M., Lee, I., Viswanathan, M. (eds.) ATVA 2008. LNCS, vol. 5311, pp. 33–47. Springer, Heidelberg (2008)
9. Katz, G., Peled, D.: Model checking-based genetic programming with an application to mutual exclusion. In: Ramakrishnan, C.R., Rehof, J. (eds.) TACAS 2008. LNCS, vol. 4963, pp. 141–156. Springer, Heidelberg (2008)
10. Katz, G., Peled, D.: Synthesizing solutions to the leader election problem using model checking and genetic programming. In: HVC (2009)
11. Koza, J.R.: Genetic Programming: On the Programming of Computers by Means of Natural Selection. MIT Press, Cambridge (1992)
12. Niebert, P., Peled, D., Pnueli, A.: Discriminative model checking. In: Gupta, A., Malik, S. (eds.) CAV 2008. LNCS, vol. 5123, pp. 504–516. Springer, Heidelberg (2008)

13. Pérez, J.A., Corchuelo, R., Toro, M.: An order-based algorithm for implementing multiparty synchronization. Concurrency - Practice and Experience 16(12), 1173–1206 (2004)
14. Pnueli, A., Rosner, R.: Distributed reactive systems are hard to synthesize. In: FOCS, pp. 746–757 (1990)
15. Weimer, W., Nguyen, T., Goues, C.L., Forrest, S.: Automatically finding patches using genetic programming. In: ICSE, pp. 364–374 (2009)

Efficient Detection of Errors in Java Components Using Random Environment and Restarts

Pavel Parizek and Tomas Kalibera

Distributed Systems Research Group, Department of Software Engineering,
Faculty of Mathematics and Physics, Charles University in Prague
Malostranske namesti 25, 118 00 Prague 1, Czech Republic
{parizek,kalibera}@dsrg.mff.cuni.cz

Abstract. Software model checkers are being used mostly to discover specific types of errors in the code, since exhaustive verification of complex programs is not possible due to state explosion. Moreover, typical model checkers cannot be directly applied to isolated components such as libraries or individual classes. A common solution is to create an abstract environment for a component to be checked. When no constraints on component's usage are defined by its developers, a natural choice is to use a universal environment that performs all possible sequences of calls of component's methods in several concurrently-running threads. However, model checking of components with a universal environment is prone to state explosion.

In this paper we present a method that allows to discover at least some concurrency errors in component's code in reasonable time. The key ideas of our method are (i) use of an abstract environment that performs a random sequence of method calls in each thread, and (ii) restarts of the error detection process according to a specific strategy. We have implemented the method in the context of Java components and the Java PathFinder model checker. We have performed experiments on non-trivial Java components to show that our approach is viable.

1 Introduction

The current practice in the application of model checking to real-world programs is that model checkers are used mostly as tools for detection of specific types of errors in the code (e.g. concurrency errors like deadlocks and race conditions), since exhaustive verification of complex programs is not possible due to state explosion. In this paper we focus on the detection of concurrency errors in Java components using the Java PathFinder model checker (JPF) [17]. We use the term *component* to denote an open Java program that has a well-defined interface — this includes, for example, Java libraries and individual Java classes.

One of the problems in the application of JPF to Java components is that it accepts only a runnable Java program with the `main` method on input, but a Java component typically does not contain `main`. Behavior of a Java component depends on the context (environment) in which it is used, e.g. on the order

J. Esparza and R. Majumdar (Eds.): TACAS 2010, LNCS 6015, pp. 451–465, 2010.

that component's methods are called by its actual environment. A common solution is to create an abstract environment (a model of an actual environment) for the component subject to checking and apply a model checker (JPF) to a runnable Java program composed of the component and its abstract environment. An abstract environment for a Java component typically has the form of a fragment of a Java program that contains the **main** method. The abstract environment performs various sequences of calls of component's methods with various combinations of method parameters' values — the goal is to cover as many control-flow paths in the component's code as possible, and, when the focus is on the detection of errors, to trigger as many errors in the component's code as possible.

When no constraints on the order of calls of component's methods are defined by the developers and no knowledge about the target environment (where the component will be deployed) is available, then a natural choice is to use an abstract environment that runs several threads concurrently and performs all possible sequences of calls of component's methods with many different input values in each thread — a *universal environment*. Such an environment exercises the component very thoroughly and therefore triggers a high percentage of errors in the component's implementation (if there are some). Nevertheless, model checking of a non-trivial component with a universal environment is typically infeasible due to state explosion, even if only a few threads (2-3) are run in parallel by the environment. JPF typically runs out of available memory quite soon (in the order of minutes).

We propose to address this problem by model checking a component with an abstract environment that (i) performs a randomly selected sequence of method calls in each thread and (ii) runs exactly two threads in parallel — we use the term *random-sequence environment* to denote such an abstract environment. We restrict the number of threads to two for the reason of feasibility of model checking, and also because a recent study [10] showed that a great majority of concurrency errors in real-world programs involve only two threads.

The motivation behind this approach is to discover at least some errors in the component in reasonable time, when model checking with a universal environment is not feasible. We show that although the use of a random-sequence environment helps to reduce the time and memory needed to find an error with JPF in most cases, still JPF can run for a very long time for some components and random-sequence environments due to state explosion. The cause is that time and memory requirements of checking with JPF depend very much on the specific random-sequence environment that is used. Moreover, a result of the random choice of a sequence environment determines whether an error in the component is found by JPF, since some random-sequence environments would not trigger any errors in the component. The whole state space of the program composed of the component and a particular random-sequence environment is traversed by JPF in the case of an environment that does not trigger any error, and therefore the running time of JPF can be very long.

In order to avoid very long running times of JPF and to ensure that errors are found (assuming there are some in the component), we also propose to apply restarts of the error detection process. The key idea is that if the running time of JPF for a particular random-sequence environment exceeds a predefined limit, then (1) JPF is stopped, (2) a new random-sequence environment is generated, and (3) JPF is started again on the Java program composed of the component and the new random-sequence environment. This is repeated until JPF finds an error in the component with some random-sequence environment. Our approach is greatly inspired by existing work on restart strategies for various long-running software processes in general [13] and for search tree traversal in SAT solvers specifically [5,8] — the goal of restarts is to improve performance (e.g., to decrease the response time). We show that the application of restarts to the error detection process significantly reduces the time and memory needed to find an error in a component, and, in particular, helps to avoid the long running times of JPF. Using our approach, errors in components' code are discovered by JPF in a reasonable time.

The rest of the paper is structured as follows. In Section 2 we describe Java components used for experiments and in Section 3 we provide information relevant to all experiments that we performed. We provide technical details of checking with universal environment and present the results of experiments in Section 4. Then we present the technical details and experimental results for checking with random-sequence environments and for application of restarts, respectively, in Sections 5 and 6. We evaluate our approach in Section 7, and then we discuss related work (Section 8) and conclude in Section 9.

2 Example Components

We have used three Java components of different complexity for the purpose of experiments: `AccountDatabase`, `ConcurrentHashMap`, and `GenericObjectPool`. All the three components contained known concurrency errors — either already present in the code or manually injected by us before the experiments. A short description of each component follows.

The `ConcurrentHashMap` component (2000 loc in Java) is a part of the `java.util.concurrent` package from the standard Java class library, as implemented in GNU Classpath (version 0.98) [20]. The component is an implementation of a map data structure that allows concurrent accesses and updates. We have manually injected a race condition into the Java code of the component.

The `GenericObjectPool` component (500 loc in Java) is a part of the Apache Commons Pool library (version 1.4) [19]. It represents a robust and configurable pool for arbitrary Java objects. Again, we have manually injected a race condition into the component's Java code.

The `AccountDatabase` component (170 loc in Java) is a part of the demo component application developed in the CRE project [1]. It works as a simple in-memory database for user accounts. The code of the component already contained a race condition.

3   General Notes on Experiments

Here we provide information that applies to all the experiments whose results are presented in Sections 4-7.

For each experiment, we provide total running time of the error detection process in seconds and, if it is relevant for the experiment, also the number of runs of the process and memory needed by the process in MBs. We have repeated each experiment several times to average out the effects of randomness. The values of numerical variables in the tables (except the number of runs) have the form $M +- CI$, where M stands for the mean of measured data and CI is the half-width of the 90% confidence interval.

All the experiments were performed on the following configuration (HW & SW): PC with 2xQuadCore CPU (Intel Xeon) at 2.3 GHz and 8 GB RAM, Gentoo Linux, Sun Java SE 6 Hotspot 64-bit Server VM. We have used the current version of Java PathFinder as of June 2009 and we limited the available memory for verification to 6 GB.

4   Checking Components with Universal Environment

In our approach, we have used a restricted form of a universal environment where only two threads run concurrently. Each thread performs a potentially infinite loop (termination of the loop depends on non-deterministic choice) and calls a non-deterministically selected method of the component in each iteration. The Java code of each thread corresponds to the template in Figure 1a. Since JPF explores the options of a non-deterministic choice in a fixed order from the lowest to the highest (from 1 to N in case of code on Figure 1a, where N is the number of component's methods), we eliminate the dependence of results of checking with JPF on a specific order of component's methods by randomization — the method to be called for a particular value of the non-deterministic choice (via `Verify.getInt(X)`) is determined randomly during generation of the environment's code.

```
while (Verify.getBoolean())        int len = Random.getInt(2*N);
{                                  for (int i = 1; i <= len; i++) {
  int idx = Verify.getInt(X);        int idx = Random.getInt(N);
  if (idx == 1) comp.method1(..);    if (idx == 1) comp.method1(..);
  if (idx == 2) comp.method2(..);    ...
  ...                                if (idx == N) comp.methodN(..);
  if (idx == N) comp.methodN(..);  }
}
                  a)                               b)
```

Fig. 1. Fragment of Java code of a single thread (a) in a universal environment and (b) in a random-sequence environment

Table 1. Results for checking components with a universal environment

Component	JPF running time
AccountDatabase	921 ± 121 s
ConcurrentHashMap	1426 ± 377 s
GenericObjectPool	1034 ± 308 s

Input data for the components (e.g., method parameters) are specified in a Java class that works as a container for the data values [15]. The environment then retrieves the parameter values from the Java class when it calls methods of the component. A user has to create the specification of data values manually such that for each method m of the component, all paths in the control-flow graph (CFG) of m are covered (explored by JPF) — for each path p in the CFG of m, at least one combination of values of m's parameters should be specified that triggers p when m is called by the environment.

The results of experiments for checking components with a universal environment of the restricted form, where only two threads run concurrently, are listed in Table 1. JPF run out of available memory (6 GB) in all experiments and therefore it found no errors — this clearly illustrates that JPF checking even with the restricted universal environment is not feasible for non-trivial Java components. We present only the running times of JPF in the table to show how fast it run out of memory.

5   Random-Sequence Environments

Similarly to a universal environment, a random-sequence environment calls methods of a component in two concurrently-running threads and retrieves method parameter values from the Java class provided by the user. The key difference is that, in the case of a random-sequence environment, each thread performs a randomly selected sequence of calls of the component's methods. The length of the sequence is a random number from the interval $[1, 2 \times |M|]$, where M stands for the set of component's methods — we set the maximal length of the sequence to $2 \times |M|$ to ensure that the sequence contains multiple calls of several methods with a high probability. The Java code of each thread corresponds to the template in Figure 1b, where N is the number of component's methods. The need for randomness in the selection of a sequence environment is motivated by the absence of any knowledge about the component's implementation and expected usage — in particular, it is not known in advance which sequence environments trigger an error and which do not, and therefore it is not possible to select only such sequence environments that trigger errors.

The results of experiments for checking components with random-sequence environments are listed in Table 2. Since some random-sequence environments do not trigger any errors, we distinguish between two groups of results based on whether JPF found an error in the component's code (value "yes" in the "Error found" column), or traversed the whole state space and found no error (value

Table 2. Results for checking components with random-sequence environments

Component	Error found	Runs	Time	Memory
AccountDatabase	yes	23	1040 ± 802 s	334 ± 134 MB
	no	17	12420 ± 8861 s	1784 ± 738 MB
ConcurrentHashMap	yes	37	173 ± 108 s	104 ± 19 MB
	no	3	14 ± 10 s	70 ± 12 MB
GenericObjectPool	yes	22	1934 ± 2208 s	186 ± 78 MB
	no	18	10230 ± 7979 s	1136 ± 789 MB

"no" in the "Error found" column). Note that JPF did not run out of available memory in any experiment with random-sequence environments.

The experimental results show that running times of JPF vary to a great degree independently of whether JPF found an error or not. Although the experimental results suggest that running times of JPF generally tend to be shorter when JPF finds an error and much longer when JPF is applied to a component in an environment that does not trigger any error (this is especially visible for AccountDatabase and GenericObjectPool), the results show that JPF can run very long even when it finds an error in the component. The Figures 2, 3 and 4 show graphs of the empirical cumulative distribution function for the experimental results for each component. A point $[t, p]$ in a graph means that the running time of JPF (regardless of whether JPF finds an error or not) will be shorter than t with the probability p. The time axis has a logarithmic scale in each graph. The graphs indicate that if JPF is running for a long time and has not found an error yet, then the chance that it will find an error (or terminate with no error found) in reasonable time is significantly decreasing. Solving this issue was our primary goal in the application of restarts to the error detection process.

6   Restart Strategies

Based on [13], we define a *restart strategy* as a sequence $(t_1, t_2, t_3, \ldots)$ of times at which the error detection process is restarted — i.e. as a sequence of *restart times*. The key idea is that if in the run n JPF either (a) does not finish in time t_n or (b) traverses the whole state space in a time shorter than t_n and does not find any error or (c) runs out of memory, then the whole error detection process is restarted with time limit t_{n+1} for the JPF run, and so on. We say that a run of the error detection process involves one or more runs of JPF (*iterations* of the run-stop-generate-restart loop) and terminates when a specific JPF run finds an error. For all iterations except the last one, it holds that either JPF traverses the whole state space before the restart time (and finds no error) or JPF runs out of the time limit (restart time). Restart of the error detection process involves three steps: (i) terminating the current run of JPF, (ii) generating a new random-sequence environment, and (iii) starting a new run of JPF on the Java program composed of the component and new environment.

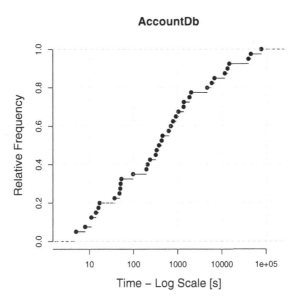

Fig. 2. Graph of the empirical cumulative distribution function for results of checking AccountDatabase with random-sequence environments

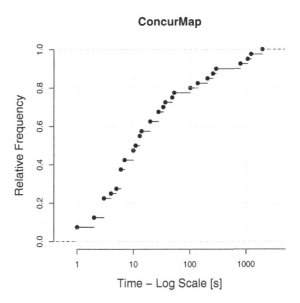

Fig. 3. Graph of the empirical cumulative distribution function for results of checking ConcurrentHashMap with random-sequence environments

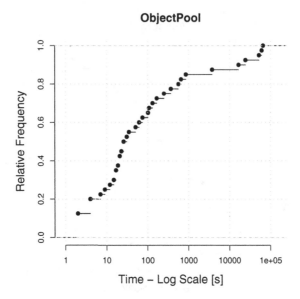

Fig. 4. Graph of the empirical cumulative distribution function for results of checking `GenericObjectPool` with random-sequence environments

The key challenge is to determine the best possible restart strategy. In this paper, we focus on the use of a predefined application-independent strategy, which is the typical approach of SAT solvers. Another possible approach would be to compute the strategy on the basis of a metric of component's code or state space traversal process, where the metric can be static, i.e. measured before a JPF run, or dynamic, i.e. measured on-the-fly during JPF checking — we discuss this approach in more detail in Section 9.

We have identified three restart strategies, which are widely and successfully used in state-of-the-art SAT solvers (e.g., [3,4]) and also in search problems of other kinds: fixed strategy, Luby strategy, and Walsh geometric strategy. We performed experiments for all the three strategies to find which gives the best results in the case of error detection with JPF.

Fixed strategy [5] is a constant sequence $S = t, t, t, \ldots$, where t represents the fixed restart time.

Luby strategy [12] is a sequence $S = k_1 u, k_2 u, k_3 u, \ldots$, where u is a restart time unit and k_i is computed using the following expression:

$$k_i = 2^{n-1}, \text{ if } i = 2^n - 1$$
$$k_i = k_{i-2^{n-1}+1} \text{ if } 2^{n-1} \leq i < 2^n - 1$$

The first few elements of the sequence k_i are $1, 1, 2, 1, 1, 2, 4, 1, 1, 2, 1, 1, 2, 4, 8$.

Walsh geometric strategy [18] is a sequence $S = u, ru, r^2u, r^3u, \ldots$, where u is a restart time unit and $r > 1$ is a ratio of the geometric sequence. In our case we used $r = \sqrt{2}$.

The Luby strategy was proposed in [12] for speedup of randomized algorithms of the Las Vegas type with unknown probability distribution of running time. However, the theoretical results presented in [12] (e.g., the bound on the running time with respect to optimal time) are not applicable in our case of model checking components with random-sequence environments, since our algorithm is not strictly of the Las Vegas type — in our case, an input of the algorithm is different for each run, since different sequence environments are randomly selected. Similarly, the model for restart strategies proposed in [13] cannot be used in our case, since the probability distribution of JPF running times for all random-sequence environments is not known in advance. Knowledge of the probability distribution is one of the requirements of the model.

We present results of experiments for all combinations of the three restart strategies — fixed, Luby and Walsh — and six different values of restart time unit — 1 second, 3 seconds, 10 seconds, 30 seconds, 60 seconds, and 600 seconds. We selected these values of restart time unit in order to cover a wide range of situations, including corner cases such as too early restarts and too late restarts. Restart time unit of 1 second is used only for the Luby and Walsh strategies, since it is too small for the fixed strategy which does not extend the restart time adaptively — initialization would form a significant part of JPF's running time in that case.

The results of experiments are listed in Table 3 for `AccountDatabase`, in Table 4 for `ConcurrentHashMap`, and in Table 5 for `GenericObjectPool`. Values in the "Time" column represent the total running time of the error detection process, i.e. the time needed to detect an error. Total running time of a single run of the error detection process equals to the sum of JPF running times in individual iterations. Similarly, values in the "Memory" column represent the

Table 3. Experimental results for error detection with restarts for `AccountDatabase`

Strategy	Unit time	Time	Memory
Fixed	3 s	197 ± 47 s	72 ± 1 MB
	10 s	153 ± 44 s	108 ± 4 MB
	30 s	152 ± 46 s	129 ± 11 MB
	60 s	287 ± 81 s	169 ± 14 MB
	600 s	1212 ± 488 s	430 ± 71 MB
Luby	1 s	215 ± 43 s	116 ± 8 MB
	3 s	240 ± 62 s	130 ± 11 MB
	10 s	158 ± 46 s	134 ± 14 MB
	30 s	244 ± 77 s	158 ± 14 MB
	60 s	323 ± 111 s	172 ± 20 MB
	600 s	609 ± 172 s	385 ± 78 MB
Walsh	1 s	216 ± 111 s	133 ± 19 MB
	3 s	663 ± 529 s	241 ± 90 MB
	10 s	284 ± 85 s	174 ± 23 MB
	30 s	270 ± 90 s	179 ± 27 MB
	60 s	387 ± 135 s	211 ± 37 MB
	600 s	1250 ± 545 s	486 ± 148 MB

Table 4. Experimental results for error detection with restarts for `ConcurrentHashMap`

Strategy	Unit time	Time	Memory
Fixed	3 s	19 ± 4 s	57 ± 1 MB
	10 s	13 ± 3 s	69 ± 6 MB
	30 s	29 ± 9 s	79 ± 7 MB
	60 s	26 ± 8 s	78 ± 8 MB
	600 s	136 ± 75 s	97 ± 15 MB
Luby	1 s	21 ± 4 s	57 ± 3 MB
	3 s	15 ± 3 s	61 ± 3 MB
	10 s	18 ± 5 s	71 ± 5 MB
	30 s	18 ± 6 s	70 ± 7 MB
	60 s	43 ± 12 s	89 ± 9 MB
	600 s	73 ± 37 s	82 ± 10 MB
Walsh	1 s	18 ± 7 s	59 ± 4 MB
	3 s	15 ± 4 s	64 ± 5 MB
	10 s	24 ± 5 s	75 ± 5 MB
	30 s	22 ± 7 s	72 ± 6 MB
	60 s	33 ± 9 s	87 ± 9 MB
	600 s	61 ± 36 s	83 ± 12 MB

Table 5. Experimental results for error detection with restarts for `GenericObjectPool`

Strategy	Unit time	Time	Memory
Fixed	3 s	28 ± 6 s	53 ± 1 MB
	10 s	29 ± 7 s	77 ± 3 MB
	30 s	79 ± 20 s	93 ± 6 MB
	60 s	120 ± 29 s	127 ± 14 MB
	600 s	549 ± 182 s	310 ± 66 MB
Luby	1 s	43 ± 9 s	64 ± 4 MB
	3 s	33 ± 12 s	65 ± 5 MB
	10 s	58 ± 16 s	83 ± 6 MB
	30 s	82 ± 24 s	103 ± 12 MB
	60 s	89 ± 37 s	117 ± 19 MB
	600 s	594 ± 278 s	300 ± 63 MB
Walsh	1 s	50 ± 21 s	74 ± 9 MB
	3 s	47 ± 12 s	80 ± 9 MB
	10 s	104 ± 73 s	102 ± 24 MB
	30 s	75 ± 26 s	105 ± 18 MB
	60 s	413 ± 398 s	173 ± 39 MB
	600 s	1197 ± 674 s	391 ± 100 MB

memory needed by the error detection processes. Memory needed by a single run of the error detection process equals to the maximal value over all iterations in the run. Note that JPF did not run out of memory in any experiment for restarts of the error detection process.

Experimental results show that extremely long running times of JPF can be avoided by restarts of the error detection process. On average, the time needed to detect an error is the lowest when the fixed strategy with a small restart time unit (1, 3, 10 or 30 seconds) is used. However, the results also show that use of too small a restart time unit (1 or 3 seconds) may actually increase the time needed to detect an error. The error detection process is restarted too early for JPF to find an error in such a case.

7   Evaluation

Results of all experiments that we performed show that the combination of checking with random-sequence environment and restarts of the error detection process has three main benefits: (1) errors are discovered in very short time in most cases and in reasonable time in the other cases, (2) extremely long running times of JPF are avoided, and (3) JPF does not run out of memory. Compared to checking with random-sequence environments only, the use of restarts always leads to discovery of an error (assuming there are some errors in the component) and an error is found in shorter time in most cases. Some random-sequence environments do not trigger any errors and thus none can be discovered by JPF, when such an environment is used. Nevertheless, when the checked component does not contain any errors, then the error detection process would be restarted again and again — it is up to the user to terminate the process after a reasonable time (when no error is found after several restarts). Compared to checking with a universal environment, an error is on average found in shorter time using random-sequence environments and restarts than it takes JPF to run out of memory when a universal environment is used.

As for the choice of a restart strategy and restart time unit, best results are achieved using the fixed strategy and short restart times. However, it is not true that the shortest restart time always provides the best result. Optimal restart time most probably depends on whether concurrency errors in the component are "shallow" or "deep". Shallow errors exhibit themselves in many thread interleavings (on many state space paths) and therefore can be found "early in the search" by JPF, while deep errors occur only in rare corner cases (for specific thread interleavings) and thus it takes JPF more time to find them. Use of short restart times would give better results in discovery of shallow errors than for deep errors.

Table 6 summarizes the results of experiments with different approaches described in this paper and also presents the results of application of a technique described in [14] on the same components. The technique described in [14] is our previous work in automated construction of abstract environment for Java

Table 6. Summary and results for a technique proposed in previous work

Component	Univ env	Random env	Restarts	Prev work
AccountDatabase	921 ± 121 s	1040 ± 802 s	152 ± 46 s	114 s
ConcurrentHashMap	1426 ± 377 s	173 ± 108 s	13 ± 3 s	64 s
GenericObjectPool	1034 ± 308 s	1934 ± 2208 s	28 ± 6 s	1590 s

components with the goal of efficient detection of concurrency errors. It is based on a combination of static analysis and a software metric — static analysis is used to identify method sets whose parallel execution may trigger a concurrency error, and the metric is used to order the sets by the likeliness that an error will really occur. Table 6 provides the following information for each component:

- the time it takes JPF to run out of memory when checking the component with a universal environment (the "Univ env" column),
- the time needed to find a concurrency error in the component when only a random-sequence environment is used (the "Random env" column),
- the time to find an error using a combination of checking with a random-sequence environment and restarts of the error detection process (in the "Restarts" column) — the lowest time over all restart strategies and restart time units is presented, and
- the time to detect an error using the technique described in [14] (the "Prev work" column) — the lowest time over all configurations of the metric is presented in the table.

Results in Table 6 show that the method proposed in this paper is an improvement over our previous work [14]. The proposed method gives significantly better results for the `ConcurrentHashMap` and `GenericObjectPool` components, while both methods give comparable results in case of the `AccountDatabase` component.

8   Related Work

Significant amount of work has been done in various optimizations aiming towards more efficient search for errors in program code via model checking. The existing approaches include heuristics for state space traversal, context-bounded model checking, and a combination of model checking with runtime analysis.

Heuristics for state space traversal are typically used to address state explosion with the goal of detection of specific errors in reasonable time and memory — for discovery of concurrency errors, a heuristic that prefers aggressive thread scheduling [6] can be used.

The idea behind context-bounded model checking [2,16] is to check only those executions of a given program that involve bounded number of thread context switches. The bound can apply to all threads together [16] or to each thread separately [2].

An example of a technique based on the combination of runtime analysis with model checking is [7]. The key idea of [7] is that runtime analysis is performed first with the goal of detecting potential concurrency errors in a program, and then a model checker (JPF) is run on the same program, using counterexamples provided by the runtime analysis as a guide during state space traversal.

A common characteristic of the approaches described above is that, like the method proposed in this paper, they sacrifice completeness of checking for the purpose of efficient detection of errors. Nevertheless, the existing approaches are complementary to the proposed method — they could be applied during model checking of a runnable program, i.e. during a single run of the error detection process, to reduce the time needed to find an error even further.

9 Summary and Future Work

We have proposed a method for efficient detection of concurrency errors in Java components with Java PathFinder, which is based on random-sequence environments and restarts of the error detection process according to a pre-defined application-independent strategy. Results of experiments that we performed show that the application of the proposed method significantly reduces the time and memory needed to find errors in components' code. In particular, JPF does not run out of memory as in the case of checking with a universal environment and extremely long running times of JPF, which occur in checking with random-sequence environments only, are also avoided by using restarts.

Although the proposed method is promising, there is a large space for improvements and optimizations that may further reduce time needed to find errors in the code. Moreover, we focused only on sequential and static restart strategies in this paper, but it is possible to use also other kinds of restart strategies. We will investigate some of the following approaches in the future:

- Use of dynamic restart strategies, e.g. such as proposed in [9], in which case the restart time could be determined dynamically during a JPF run using a heuristic. The heuristic could be based on the time JPF is already running or on the (estimated) size of the already traversed part of the state space (on the number of explored branches).
- Use of parallel restart strategies, e.g. based on the ideas and results published in [11]. The key idea would be to increase the chance that an error is found in shorter time by running several instances of the error detection process in parallel.
- Use of metrics of component's code to determine statically, i.e. before the start of the error detection process, the restart strategy and restart time.

Variants of the proposed method could be applied also to detection of other kinds of errors. For example, errors like null pointer exceptions or assertion violations often occur only for specific inputs (method parameters) — the idea would be to create an abstract environment that calls component's methods with randomly selected parameter values. We also plan to evaluate the proposed method on multiple larger case studies.

Acknowledgments. This work was partially supported by the Grant Agency of the Czech Republic project 201/08/0266 and by the Ministry of Education of the Czech Republic (grant MSM0021620838). We also thank Nicholas Kidd for his valuable comments and suggestions.

References

1. Adamek, J., Bures, T., Jezek, P., Kofron, J., Mencl, V., Parizek, P., Plasil, F.: Component Reliability Extensions for Fractal Component Model (2006), http://kraken.cs.cas.cz/ft/public/public_index.phtml

2. Atig, M.F., Bouajjani, A., Qadeer, S.: Context-Bounded Analysis for Concurrent Programs with Dynamic Creation of Threads. In: Kowalewski, S., Philippou, A. (eds.) TACAS 2009. LNCS, vol. 5505. Springer, Heidelberg (2009)

3. Biere, A.: PicoSAT Essentials. Journal on Satisfiability, Boolean Modeling and Computation (JSAT) 4 (2008)

4. Een, N., Sorensson, N.: An Extensible SAT-solver. In: Giunchiglia, E., Tacchella, A. (eds.) SAT 2003. LNCS, vol. 2919, pp. 502–518. Springer, Heidelberg (2004)

5. Gomes, C.P., Selman, B., Kautz, H.A.: Boosting Combinatorial Search Through Randomization. In: Proceedings of AAAI 1998 (1998)

6. Groce, A., Visser, W.: Heuristics for Model Checking Java Programs. International Journal on Software Tools for Technology Transfer 6(4) (2004)

7. Havelund, K.: Using Runtime Analysis to Guide Model Checking of Java Programs. In: Havelund, K., Penix, J., Visser, W. (eds.) SPIN 2000. LNCS, vol. 1885. Springer, Heidelberg (2000)

8. Huang, J.: The Effect of Restarts on the Efficiency of Clause Learning. In: Proceedings of the 20th International Joint Conference on Artificial Intelligence, IJCAI (2007)

9. Kautz, H., Horvitz, E., Ruan, Y., Gomes, C., Selman, B.: Dynamic Restart Policies. In: Proceedings of the 18th National Conference on Artificial Intelligence (AAAI 2002). AAAI Press, Menlo Park (2002)

10. Lu, S., Park, S., Seo, E., Zhou, Y.: Learning from Mistakes: A Comprehensive Study on Real World Concurrency Bug Characteristics. In: Proceedings of the 13th International Conference on Architectural Support for Programming Languages and Operating Systems (ASPLOS 2008). ACM, New York (2008)

11. Luby, M., Ertel, W.: Optimal Parallelization of Las Vegas Algorithms. In: Enjalbert, P., Mayr, E.W., Wagner, K.W. (eds.) STACS 1994. LNCS, vol. 775. Springer, Heidelberg (1994)

12. Luby, M., Sinclair, A., Zuckerman, D.: Optimal Speedup of Las Vegas Algorithms. Information Processing Letters 47(4) (1993)

13. van Moorsel, A.P.A., Wolter, K.: Analysis of Restart Mechanisms in Software Systems. IEEE Transactions on Software Engineering 32(8) (2006)

14. Parizek, P., Adamek, J., Kalibera, T.: Automated Construction of Reasonable Environment for Java Components. To appear in Proceedings of International Workshop on Formal Foundations of Embedded Software and Component-Based Software Architectures (FESCA 2009). ENTCS (2009)

15. Parizek, P., Plasil, F.: Specification and Generation of Environment for Model Checking of Software Components. In: Proceedings of International Workshop on Formal Foundations of Embedded Software and Component-Based Software Architectures (FESCA 2006). ENTCS, vol. 176(2) (2007)

16. Qadeer, S., Rehof, J.: Context-Bounded Model Checking of Concurrent Software. In: Halbwachs, N., Zuck, L.D. (eds.) TACAS 2005. LNCS, vol. 3440, pp. 93–107. Springer, Heidelberg (2005)

17. Visser, W., Havelund, K., Brat, G., Park, S., Lerda, F.: Model Checking Programs. Automated Software Engineering Journal 10(2) (2003)
18. Walsh, T.: Search in a Small World. In: Proceedings of the 16th International Joint Conference on Artificial Intelligence, IJCAI 1999 (1999)
19. Apache Commons Pool, http://commons.apache.org/pool/
20. GNU Classpath, http://www.gnu.org/software/classpath/

Author Index